OXFORD R

VERGIL'S *AENEID*

EDITED BY S. J. HARRISON

Oxford New York
OXFORD UNIVERSITY PRESS

This book has been printed digitally and produced in a standard specification
in order to ensure its continuing availability

OXFORD

UNIVERSITY PRESS

Great Clarendon Street, Oxford OX2 6DP

Oxford University Press is a department of the University of Oxford.
It furthers the University's objective of excellence in research, scholarship,
and education by publishing worldwide in

Oxford New York

Auckland   Cape Town Dar es Salaam Hong Kong Karachi
Kuala Lumpur Madrid Melbourne Mexico City Nairobi
New Delhi Shanghai Taipei Toronto
With offices in
Argentina Austria Brazil Chile Czech Republic France Greece
Guatemala Hungary Italy Japan South Korea Poland Portugal
Singapore Switzerland Thailand Turkey Ukraine Vietnam

Oxford is a registered trade mark of Oxford University Press
in the UK and in certain other countries

Published in the United States
by Oxford University Press Inc., New York

ISBN 978-0-19-814388-8

Preface

This collection of twenty-six essays on Vergil's *Aeneid* is intended to provide in convenient form a selection from the large mass of work on the poem published in classical periodicals and sources other than books on Vergil. It is hoped that it will be of use to undergraduates and sixth-formers as well as to their teachers. Particular attention has been paid to the topics most commonly covered in the study of the poem at school and university, and to reprinting essays of value which are rare, out of print, or otherwise difficult to obtain, though the editor's selection of pieces is no less subjective for that; care has also been taken not to reduplicate any item in Steele Commager's *Virgil: A Collection of Critical Essays* (1966), which reprints several classic pieces. After some thought it has been decided to confine the collection to essays published in English; by way of compensation, some of the main international trends in scholarship on the poem are indicated in the survey which forms the first essay.

The editor has a number of obligations to record. First, to the collection's contributors, who kindly gave their permission to reprint and (in some cases) made careful revisions; second, to a number of classical colleagues, whose support and advice was valuable—Robin Nisbet, David West, Oliver Lyne, Nicholas Horsfall, Ted Harrison, Tony Woodman, and Denis Feeney; last but not least, to Hilary Feldman and the Oxford University Press, *sine quibus non*. To all my considerable thanks.

Corpus Christi   S.J.H.
February 1989

Acknowledgements

All the essays in this collection except the first have been previously published elsewhere, as listed below. The editor and the Press are grateful to the publishers of the relevant journals and books for permission to reprint.

2 Reprinted from *Antichthon* 1 (1967), 29–41.

3 Reprinted from *Classical Quarterly*, NS 10 (1960), 145–51.

4 A substantially revised version of an article in *Phoenix* 24 (1970), 320–32.

5 Reprinted from *Harvard Studies in Classical Philology* 74 (1970), 101–68.

6 Reprinted from *Proceedings of the Virgil Society* 13 (1973–4), 1–13.

7 Reprinted from the author's *Lines of Enquiry* (Cambridge University Press, 1976), 32–53.

8 Reprinted from *Classical Quarterly*, NS 33 (1983), 204–19, with corrections.

9 Reprinted from *Greece and Rome*, NS 11 (1964), 48–63.

10 Reprinted from *Classical Philology* 67 (1972), 31–41.

11 Reprint of the author's *The Bough and the Gate*, 17th Jackson Knight Memorial Lecture (Exeter University Publications, 1987).

12 Reprinted from *Transactions of the American Philological Association* 88 (1957), 17–30.

13 Reprinted from *Journal of Roman Studies* 35 (1945), 1–14.

14 Reprinted from the author's *The Herakles Theme* (Oxford, Basil Blackwell, 1972), 131–49.

15 Reprinted from *Proceedings of the Virgil Society* 15 (1975–6), 1–7.

16 Reprinted from *Latomus* 30 (1971), 1108–16.

17 Reprinted from *Classical Quarterly*, NS 33 (1983), 188–203.

18 Reprinted from *Classical Quarterly*, NS 34 (1984), 179–94, with corrections.

19 Reprinted from *Greece and Rome* 3 (1933–4), 8–21.

20 Reprinted from *Proceedings of the Virgil Society* 18 (1978–80), 50–61.

21 Reprinted from *Greek, Roman and Byzantine Studies* 5 (1964), 61–84.

22 Reprinted from *Classical Quarterly*, NS 9 (1959), 181–92.

23 Reprinted from *Journal of Roman Studies* 59 (1969), 40–9.

24 Reprinted from *Classical Philology* 65 (1970), 241–3, with corrections.

25 Reprinted from *Proceedings of the Virgil Society* 5 (1965–6), 26–38, with corrections.

26 Reprinted from *Antichthon* 15 (1981), 141–50.

Contents

I

Some Views of the *Aeneid* in the Twentieth Century

S. J. HARRISON

The modern era in the criticism of the *Aeneid* can truly be said to begin with the twentieth century. In 1903 two highly influential books were published in Germany: Richard Heinze's *Vergils epische Technik*, and Eduard Norden's commentary on *Aeneid* 6.[1] As its title suggests, Heinze's book analysed Vergil's methods of working in the *Aeneid*, and especially the way in which he marshalled and dramatized his legendary and literary material with the intellectual tools of the Augustan age, revealing his sympathetic interest in the psychology of his characters and his grasp of Roman greatness; Aeneas was seen as developing through the poem into the ideal Roman hero of Vergil's age, a Stoic disciple learning to follow the will of destiny, and the poem was a sublime assertion of the might of Rome and Augustus. Norden's commentary, agreeing broadly with Heinze's approach,[2] followed its author's particular interests in ancient rhetoric, philosophy, and religion, and in stylistic and metrical effects in the Latin hexameter.[3] The fundamental importance of these two books is shown by the fact that both are still in print some eighty years later. Heinze's work led the way for many examinations of the treatment of material in the poem, and to the central issue of how Vergil 'Romanized' Homeric epic; Norden's was the first commentary of considerable length to devote itself to a single book of the *Aeneid*, and has been followed by a number of similar works, which share its concerns of detailed and scholarly analysis of the text of the *Aeneid* against an Augustan background.

[1] R. Heinze, *Vergils epische Technik* (Leipzig and Berlin, 1903, 1908, 1915; repr. most recently Stuttgart, 1976). E. Norden, *P. Vergili Maronis Aeneis Liber VI* (Leipzig and Berlin, 1903, 1916, 1927; repr. most recently Stuttgart, 1984).

[2] Heinze did not discuss Book 6 because he knew of Norden's forthcoming commentary (Heinze, preface to 1908 edn.).

[3] Norden also produced other important work on the *Aeneid*, especially *Ennius und Vergilius* (Leipzig and Berlin, 1915), and 'Vergils Aeneis im Lichte ihrer Zeit', *NJb* 7 (1901), 249–82, 313–34, repr. in E. Norden, *Kleine Schriften*, ed. B. Kytzler (Berlin, 1966), pp. 358–421.

Naturally, the work of Heinze and Norden did not spring from a vacuum. The *Aeneid* was taught in the schools of Rome from an early date, perhaps even during Vergil's own lifetime,[4] and had been at or near the centre of classical studies ever since; in the great growth of classical learning in the nineteenth century Homer had been more popular,[5] but several solid achievements in Vergilian studies stand out in this period. Most impressive is the crucial work on the text of Vergil in the edition of Otto Ribbeck, published between 1859 and 1862, with an important subsequent volume of *Prolegomena Critica*; this is the first truly critical examination and classification of Vergilian manuscripts, and has remained the foundation for all later work.[6] Several commentaries on the works of Vergil which are still significant had also been produced, the five-volume revision of Heyne's great work, itself already a classic for half a century, by Wagner (1830–41),[7] the three volumes of Conington (1858–71), and the edition with commentatry of Sabbadini (1884–8), which made important contributions to the text.[8] Comparetti's excellent work on Vergil's influence in late Antiquity and the Middle Ages had appeared in the 1870s;[9] the standard edition of Servius, the ancient commentator still invaluable for the interpretation of Vergil, was produced by Thilo and Hagen from 1878.[10] An admirable apparatus for the study of Vergil had thus been accumulated; however,

---

[4] Suetonius (*Gramm.* 16) mentions that Q. Caecilius Epirota, freedman of Cicero's friend Atticus, taught Vergil in his school at Rome.

[5] The continuing scholarly study of Vergil is indicated by the vast number of editions between the invention of printing and 1840, listed in Heyne–Wagner (n. 7), iv. 635–742. On the unpopularity of Vergil in some quarters in the 19th cent., cf. R. D. Williams, 'Changing Attitudes to Virgil' in D. R. Dudley, ed., *Virgil* (London, 1969), pp. 119–39.

[6] O. Ribbeck, *P. Vergili Maronis Opera*, 3 vols. (Leipzig, 1859–62); id., *Prolegomena Critica ad P. Vergili Maronis Opera Maiora* (Leipzig, 1866).

[7] C. G. Heyne, *P. Vergili Maronis Opera*, 4 vols. (Leipzig, 1767–75); C. G. Heyne and G. P. E. Wagner, *P. Vergili Maronis Opera*, 5 vols. (Leipzig 1830–41).

[8] J. Conington, *The Works of Virgil*, 3 vols. (London, 1858–71) (vol. iii was partly written by H. Nettleship, who also revised vol. ii (1884): vol. i was revised by Nettleship and subsequently by F. Haverfield (1898)); R. Sabbadini, *P. Vergili Maronis Aeneis*, 6 vols. (Turin, 1884–8; several times reprinted). Other commentaries of this period on the *Aeneid* which are still useful are the *Aeneidea* of James Henry, 4 vols. (London and Dublin, 1873–89; vol. v (Index), Meissen, 1892), and the 2-vol. school commentary by T. E. Page (London, 1894, 1900).

[9] D. Comparetti, *Virgilio nel Medio Evo* (Livorno, 1871, 1896), new edn. by G. Pasquali, 2 vols. (Florence, 1946); tr. as *Vergil in the Middle Ages* (London and New York, 1895).

[10] G. Thilo and H. Hagen, *Servii grammatici qui feruntur in Vergili carmina commentarii*, 3 vols. (Leipzig, 1878–1902). Valuable work on Servius was also done by E. Thomas, *Essai sur Servius* (Paris, 1879), and by H. Georgii, *Die antike Aeneiskritik* (Stuttgart, 1891).

the classical scholars of the nineteenth century had shown comparatively little interest in the evaluation of the *Aeneid* as literature,[11] and
this has been the main achievement of the twentieth.

The German Vergilian renaissance headed by Heinze and Norden
took some time to spread abroad, partly no doubt because of the
disruption of international scholarly communication by the First World
War. By the 1930s it had reached Britain, Italy, and the USA: R. S.
Conway's edition of *Aeneid* 1 and those of *Aeneid* 4 by C. Buscaroli and
A. S. Pease, the last particularly monumental in scale, followed
Norden's lead in providing substantial commentaries on single books of
the poem, while in 1927 the American scholar H. W. Prescott published
The Development of Virgil's Art, which in its account of the *Aeneid* was a
presentation of Heinze for the English reader, in which respect it is still
useful.[12] The general view of Vergil and of the *Aeneid* in the inter-war
period was especially clear in 1930–1, when (depending on one's
arithmetic) the celebration of the two-thousandth anniversary of the
poet's birth provided a particular pretext for stressing his cultural
centrality and contemporary relevance.[13] The *Aeneid* was seen by
scholars such as E. K. Rand as a classic, a foretaste of Christianity and a
fundamental document of Western civilization, and T. S. Eliot's well-
known assertion of this view in *What is a Classic?* (1945) and 'Virgil and
the Christian World' (1951) acknowledges a direct debt to the German
scholar Haecker, who had presented Vergil as 'Father of the West' in
1931.[14] J. W. Mackail's edition of the *Aeneid* (1930), likewise part of the
bimilleniary festivities, pursued a similar line.[15] This positive presentation of the *Aeneid* as a classic vindication of the European world-order,
happily consonant with Roman imperialism and the achievements and

[11] Some exceptions: F. H. Myers, *Essays Classical* (London, 1883), pp. 106–76; W. Y.
Sellar, *Virgil* (Oxford, 1877); H. Nettleship, *Vergil* (London, 1879). Still worth reading is
C. A. Sainte-Beuve, *Étude sur Virgile* (Paris, 1857), an influential work which gives the first
sympathetic account of Vergil's re-creation of Homer in the *Aeneid*.
[12] *P. Vergili Maronis Aeneidos Liber Primus*, ed. R. S. Conway (Cambridge, 1935); *P.
Vergili Maronis Aeneidos Liber Quartus*, ed. A. S. Pease (Cambridge, Mass., 1935); *Virgilio:
Il libro di Didone*, ed. C. Buscaroli (Milan, 1932); H. W. Prescott, *The development of Virgil's
Art* (Chicago, 1927).
[13] Much of this body of work is listed in Suerbaum (n. 55), pp. 37–8; particularly
interesting is Eduard Fraenkel's lecture *Gedanken zu einer deutschen Vergilfeier* (Berlin,
1930).
[14] E. K. Rand, *The Magical Art of Virgil* (Cambridge, Mass., 1931); T. S. Eliot, *What is a
Classic?* (London, 1945; often reprinted), 'Virgil and the Christian World' in *On Poets and
Poetry* (London, 1957), pp. 121–31); Th. Haecker, *Vergil, Vater des Abendlandes* (Leipzig,
1931), tr. as *Virgil, Father of the West* (London, 1934).
[15] J. W. Mackail, *The Aeneid of Virgil* (Oxford, 1930), pp. xii–xv.

political settlement of Augustus, found few dissenters between the two
World Wars.[16]

After 1945 it was perhaps to be expected that more complex views of
the *Aeneid* might emerge, not only because of developments in literary
criticism but also because of a more ambiguous appreciation of works
which appeared to celebrate military imperialism and absolute monarchical power. Two well-known examples of the application of contemporary literary ideas to the *Aeneid* appeared simultaneously on
opposite sides of the Atlantic in 1950: Viktor Pöschl's *Die Dichtkunst
Vergils*, later translated as *The Art of Vergil*, and Bernard Knox's article
'The Serpent and the Flame'.[17] Both explored Vergil's imagery in its
symbolic aspects: Knox showed how the use of snakes and fire in the
similes and metaphors of *Aeneid* 2 cohered with and supported the
poet's dark account of the fall of Troy, while Pöschl used the symbolic
interpretation of imagery to support Eliot's view of the *Aeneid* as an
assertion of the fundamental values of Western civilization, seen as
relevant to the post-war reconstruction of German society at the time he
wrote:[18] order and purpose overcome the forces of chaos and disintegration, but there is a humane pity for the victims in this battle—Dido and
Turnus are tragic figures.

Pöschl's book represents a watershed in Vergilian criticism, perhaps
the most significant since the appearance of Heinze and Norden almost
half a century earlier. His thoroughgoing treatment of imagery and
symbolism set the agenda for much future work on Vergil, particularly in
the USA; his positive view of the imperial ideology of the *Aeneid* has
been shared by most German critics;[19] his stress on Vergil's humane
treatment of both hero and victims has had much influence in Britain.
As always in the history of classical (and especially Vergilian) scholar-

---

[16] An interesting exception is F. Sforza, *CR* 49 (1935), 97–108, apparently written
against the background of Italian fascism.

[17] V. Pöschl, *Die Dichtkunst Vergils: Bild und Symbol in der Aeneis* (Innsbruck, 1950;
Berlin and New York, 1977), tr. as *The Art of Vergil* (Ann Arbor, 1962); B. M. W. Knox,
'The Serpent and the Flame: The Imagery of the Second Book of the *Aeneid*', *AJPh* 71
(1950), 379–400 (repr. in S. Commager, ed., *Virgil: A Collection of Critical Essays*
(Englewood Cliffs, NJ, 1966), pp. 124–42).

[18] Pöschl, op. cit. (Eng. tr.), p. 12: 'There is more at stake here than just the question of
Vergil; it concerns the foundations of western civilization. We are seeking ties of
communication to bind us together. We must therefore re-establish a firm place for the
Aeneid in our cultural consciousness as one of the bibles of the Western world.' For
Pöschl's sympathetic views of Dido and Turnus cf. ibid. 71, 93.

[19] For a useful survey of 20th-cent. German work on the *Aeneid* and its influences cf. A.
Wlosok, *Gymnasium* 80 (1973), 29–51.

ship, individual elements and details of Pöschl's point of view had been anticipated by others, but it was the impact of his synthesis which was so significant. The most interesting consequence of Pöschl's work was its use to promote a general view of the *Aeneid* which was in most respects the opposite of his own. The symbolic approach to the *Aeneid* was taken up by the so-called 'Harvard School' of Vergilian critics in the USA, emerging perhaps in the 1950s and coming into their own in the mid-1960s, amongst whose representatives may be classed Adam Parry, Wendell Clausen, and Michael Putnam.[20] In a reaction against the traditional view, promoted by Heinze, reiterated by Pöschl, and popularized in the Anglophone world by Eliot, that the *Aeneid* asserted the values of order and civilization by depicting their eventual victory, they tended to hold that the poem presented a pessimistic view alongside the surface glory of Aeneas and Rome, 'a public voice of triumph, and a private voice of regret'.[21] The dark side of political success and the cost of imperialism, a cost felt by victor as well as victim, was the essential message—the plot of the *Aeneid* is 'a long history of defeat and loss', matching its conception of Roman history as 'a long Pyrrhic victory of the human spirit', and Aeneas was an uncertain, sensitive, and quasi-existentialist hero, 'profoundly melancholy, half-paralysed by fate'.[22] For an outside observer it is difficult to separate such an interpretation from the characteristic concerns of US (and other) intellectuals in these years: the doubt of the traditional view of the *Aeneid* has at least some connection with the 1960s questioning of all institutions, political, religious, and intellectual, and in particular with attitudes towards America's own imperialism.[23] Pöschl's method of symbolical interpretation was used to support this position, especially by Putnam in *The Poetry of the Aeneid* (1965), which adds verbal repetition to Pöschl's imagistic armoury; any elements, iconographical or verbal, which seemed to indicate themes of doubt or hesitation on the part of Aeneas were taken as a kind of liberal self-examination rather than as human trials to be victoriously overcome, and details such as the initial non-compliance of the Golden Bough or the vague nature of the Gates of Sleep were taken

---

[20] A. Parry, 'The Two Voices of Virgil's *Aeneid*', *Arion* 2 (1963), 66–80; W. Clausen, 'An Interpretation of the *Aeneid*', *HSCPh* 68 (1964), 139–47 (both repr. in Commager— n. 17 above); M. C. J. Putnam, *The Poetry of the Aeneid* (Cambridge, Mass., 1965).

[21] Parry (n. 20) in Commager (n. 17), p. 121.

[22] Clausen (n. 20) in Commager (n. 17), pp. 81, 82, 86.

[23] W. R. Nethercut in *Vergil at 2000*, ed. J. D. Bernard (New York, 1986), p. 325.

to show that the poet had doubts about Aeneas' mission and the imperial future of Rome.[24]

This ambiguous and pessimistic view of the *Aeneid* has been highly influential in the last twenty years, especially (but certainly not exclusively) in its country of origin. As noted above, it was largely opposed to the general view of Pöschl, whose methodology it extensively appropriated. The positive view of the *Aeneid* taken by Pöschl, following Heinze and Norden, did not die out; it was understandably widespread in Germany, and is shared in essence (if not in emphasis) by two of the most extensive views of Vergil taken this century, those of Karl Büchner and Friedrich Klingner. Both wrote several important studies of the *Aeneid* over a number of years;[25] both summarized their approach in a monumental work, in Büchner's case in the book-length standard article on Vergil in Pauly–Wissowa, in Klingner's in a monograph of great size and importance.[26] Both held that the *Aeneid* was a mythical representation of the triumphant march of Roman history to the world-dominion of Vergil's own time; the success of Rome was guaranteed by the inexorable authority of fate, revealed by dignified and authoritative Jupiter; Aeneas was a hero who endured sufferings and overcame human weakness through the Roman virtue of *pietas*, a worthy parallel and laudatory comparison for the mighty Augustus, re-establishing the Roman nation in Vergil's time just as Aeneas had first established it long ago. The 'teleological' concept of the *Aeneid* as a representation of Roman history and its religious atmosphere were particularly stressed by Klingner, the primacy of Vergil's belief in fate and destiny by Büchner; both used a little of the symbolic method, though neither to the extent seen in the USA. The reassertion of the positive view of the *Aeneid* by means of the symbolic method was the achievement of an American, Brooks Otis, to whose work we shall shortly return.

In the 1950s and 1960s the middle ground between the positive German view and the pessimistic American view of the *Aeneid* can be

---

[24] Most of these characteristic elements are already in R. A. Brooks, *Discolor Aura: Reflections on the Golden Bough', AJPh* 74 (1953), 260–80, often considered as the first expression of the 'Harvard School' view.

[25] Klingner's essays on Vergil from 1931 are collected in his *Römische Geisteswelt* (Munich, 1961), pp. 239–311, 600–30; Büchner's views can be further exampled in his *Der Schicksalsgedanke bei Vergil* (Freiburg, 1946), and in his *Humanitas Romana* (Heidelberg, 1957), pp. 147–75.

[26] K. Büchner, *RE* 8A, 1021–486, pub. separately as *P. Vergilius Maro, der Dichter der Römer* (Stuttgart, 1955); F. Klingner, *Virgil: Bucolica, Georgica, Aeneis* (Zurich and Stuttgart, 1967).

said to have been held by the British, and (to a lesser degree) the French. The variety of the modest number of French contributions to Vergilian literature is remarkable. The much-read work of Sainte-Beuve in the nineteenth century (cf. n. 11 above) found few immediate followers, but a number of works of interest have emerged periodically from France: Cartault's provoking study (1926) should be read as a continuous commentary on the poem,[27] Guillemin, stressing with Heinze the originality of the *Aeneid* in the epic tradition,[28] took a moderately positive attitude to the poem, as did Brisson in his rather speculative historical and biographical view of Vergil's works.[29] More recently, the strong French interest in the technicalities of the Latin hexameter has been extended to a concept of 'rhythmical composition' in the *Aeneid* by Lesueur.[30] Perhaps the most stimulating French study of the *Aeneid* to date is Jacques Perret's *Virgile* (1952), a short book which contains an interesting analysis of the poem, which owes much to Pöschl, and particularly stresses the humanity of the hero and the poet; much more recently, Perret has also produced a useful Budé edition of the *Aeneid* with some interesting endnotes.[31]

The British moderation of these years was evident and characteristic. The chief scholarly interpreters of the *Aeneid* for a UK readership were the commentators R. G. Austin and R. D. Williams, who between them wrote commentaries on each book of the first half of the *Aeneid* from 1955,[32] Williams also producing much else, including a school commentary on the whole of the poem and a final book which summarized his views.[33] Williams's outlook on the *Aeneid* was influenced by the Harvard School (he talks of the tension between the 'public voice' and 'private voice' of the poem),[34] but sensibly avoided the views of some of its more extreme advocates on existential pessimism and the removal of

---

[27] A. Cartault, *L'Art de Virgile dans l'Énéide*, 2 vols. (Paris, 1926).

[28] A.-M. Guillemin, *L'Originalité de Virgile: Étude sur la méthode littéraire antique* (Paris, 1931); the same author produced a general study, *Virgile poète, artiste et penseur* (Paris, 1951).

[29] J.-P. Brisson, *Virgile: Son temps et le nôtre* (Paris, 1966).

[30] R. Lesueur, *L'Énéide de Virgile: Étude sur la composition rhythmique d'une épopée* (Toulouse, 1975).

[31] J. Perret, *Virgile: L'Homme et l'œuvre*, Paris, 1951 (1966); id., *Virgile: L'Énéide*, 3 vols. (Paris, 1977–80). For more recent French work cf. n. 103 (below).

[32] R. G. Austin: commentaries on Book 4 (1955), Book 2 (1964), Book 1 (1971), and Book 6 (1977), all Oxford.

[33] R. D. Williams: separate commentaries on Book 5 (1960) and Book 3 (1962), both Oxford; 2-vol. school commentary on the *Aeneid* (London and Basingstoke, 1972–3); and *The Aeneid* (London, 1987).

[34] e.g. pp. xx–xxii of the introduction to his school commentary (above).

the divine element from its essential role in the poem. Austin's outlook
was more characteristically English, and essentially followed influential
judgements by English men of letters in the previous century—Tennyson's address to Vergil, 'Thou majestic in they sadness / at the
doubtful doom of humankind', and Matthew Arnold's discovery of 'an
ineffable melancholy' and 'a sweet, a touching sadness' in the *Aeneid*;[35]
Vergil was primarily a poet of supreme *humanitas*, and though the *Aeneid*
did indeed celebrate as great the victories of Aeneas, Rome, and
Augustus, it also expressed a simultaneous sympathy with the sufferings
of both victor and victims—a sensitive Aeneas, a noble and tragic Dido,
a Turnus who is youthfully impetuous and unfortunate. Here we have
Vergil the musingly melancholic, a picture which has continued to
appeal to many British scholars.

As noted above, the most extensive recapitulation of the traditional/
German view of the *Aeneid* using the methodology of Pöschl was in fact
that of the American Brooks Otis. The second half of his major study of
Vergil, published in 1964,[36] is a book-by-book description of the *Aeneid*;
two earlier chapters encapsulate Otis's real contribution to the criticism
of the *Aeneid*, stressing Vergil's 're-invention' of epic through the
'subjective style', following up points made by Heinze and Klingner. A
particular feature of the work is its continual concern with episodic
structure within the poem, an expansion of the concerns of Heinze.
Dido and Turnus are treated as guilty parties, though not wholly
unsympathetically; echoes of Heinze and the German tradition are seen
in the characterization of the central concern of the *Aeneid* as 'the
formation and victory of the Augustan hero'.[37] Otis's powerful restatement of the traditional view for our time, though not always well
expressed, has become duly influential.

In the 1960s and early 1970s Germans continued to produce books
which supported the positive view of the *Aeneid*, exploring particular
angles: Buchheit, using the evidence of Naevius' *Bellum Poenicum*,
considered the presentation of Rome's mission to rule the world and the
parallel oppositions Venus/Juno and Rome/Carthage, while Binder
discussed the parallels between Aeneas and Augustus.[38] The most solid
achievement by a German scholar in this period, however, was not so

---

[35] Tennyson, *To Virgil* (1882); Matthew Arnold, 'The Modern Element in Literature',
inaugural lecture as Oxford Professor of Poetry, 1857.

[36] Brooks Otis, *Virgil: A Study in Civilized Poetry* (Oxford, 1964).

[37] Ibid. 313–19.

[38] V. Buchheit, *Vergil über die Sendung Roms* (Heidelberg, 1963); G. Binder, *Aeneas und
Augustus: Interpretationen zum 8. Buch der Aeneis* (Meisenheim, 1971).

important for its ideological position (a variation on the local orthodoxy) as for its sheer apparatus of scholarship—G. N. Knauer's *Die Aeneis und Homer*.[39] As its title suggests, the book treats afresh and with great learning the issue, central since Heinze, of the relation of the *Aeneid* to the Homeric epics. Though some of his larger ideas have been found unconvincing and the great lists of parallels may be augmented or questioned by close consideration of particular passages, Knauer's work is a remarkable achievement and liable to remain with Vergilians for generations.

Despite the firm and influential positive views still emanating from Germany, Anglophone scholarship on the *Aeneid* in the 1960s and 70s largely inclined towards the American pessimism of the 'Harvard School'. Kenneth Quinn's 'Critical Description' of the *Aeneid* (1968)[40] gave a fundamentally pessimistic account of the poem, using the kind of detailed practical analysis associated with the 'New Criticism' in English literature. Its first chapter gives an interesting view of the heroism of Aeneas, which (he holds) indicates that the traditional Homeric heroic code is shown up as inadequate in the world of the *Aeneid*; Quinn does not, like many others, believe that it is replaced by a new, Roman form of heroism centred about the various aspects of *pietas*, since for him the role of the gods has literary interest but does not contribute much to the ideology of the poem. Likewise, the note of Roman imperialism frequently struck by the poet is viewed by Quinn as usually undermined by a highly twentieth-century pacifism and irony. More overtly than the writers of the 'Harvard School', Quinn marries a pessimistic interpretation of the *Aeneid* to the political concerns and literary methods of his own time, not always with the greatest judiciousness. The pessimistic line on the poem was promoted more cautiously in an interesting and useful brief account by W. S. Anderson in 1969.[41]

In this same year there appeared in Britain the judicious and balanced introduction to the *Aeneid* by W. A. Camps.[42] Camps's cautiously positive appraisal of the poem and its ideology presented a tougher and more realistic view than that of Austin or Williams: stress was laid on the political realities of the historical background, the importance of the role of fate and of the gods, the promotion of Roman values, and the

---

[39] G. N. Knauer, *Die Aeneis und Homer* (Göttingen, 1964); Knauer's basic ideas were set out in an essay in English, 'Vergil's *Aeneid* and Homer', *GRBS* 5 (1964), 64–84 (repr. in this collection, Ch. 21).
[40] K. Quinn, *Virgil's Aeneid: A Critical Description* (London, 1968).
[41] W. S. Anderson, *The Art of the Aeneid* (Englewood Cliffs, NJ, 1967).
[42] W. A. Camps, *An Introduction to Virgil's Aeneid* (Oxford, 1969).

counterbalancing senses of cost and suffering, which did not (as the 'Harvard School' maintained) overshadow or question the achievements of Aeneas, Rome, and Augustus: the fates of individuals, though often tragic and always subordinate to the common objective, are dignified and elevated by the fact they are an integral part of the process which leads to greatness. This constitutes something of an answer for the anti-imperialists: as Camps argues, 'those who cannot enter with sympathy into Virgil's conception of Rome may find the meaning for themselves in its complementary theme, the impact of world forces and world movements on the lives of individuals and the human qualities displayed in their response'.[43] Lucidity, caution, and economy—qualities not always displayed in recent Vergilian criticism—have made this book a useful guide to the poem at all levels, and it has been deservedly popular in Anglophone schools and universities.

An interesting development of the pessimistic view of the *Aeneid* was seen in W. R. Johnson's *Darkness Visible*, published in 1976.[44] Reacting against both the 'Harvard School' and the traditional positivists, Johnson laid emphasis on the disturbing aspects of the divine dimension: the destructive and malevolent Juno is elevated into the central figure of the poem, and even Jupiter, so often claimed as the providential dispenser of destiny, is made to be darkly irrational. Gods of such a nature make the surface order and rationalism of the poem on the human level precarious and unreal. The heroism of Aeneas, though great, is simply insufficient to counterbalance destructive divinity, especially Juno, whose reconciliation in the last book of the poem Johnson views as unreal—Juno will after all emerge later as the champion of Carthage in the Punic Wars which so nearly destroyed Rome. Johnson agrees with many that the *Aeneid* is a microcosm of Roman and human history, but it shows the power of the dark and daemonic side of things to disturb and nullify human achievement, and can truly be said to be a 'terrifying poem'.[45] This sophisticated and powerful reading of the poem, reintroducing the cosmic and divine aspect of the poem emphasized by the Germans but comparatively neglected by the 'Harvard School' and using it to form a profoundly pessimistic interpretation, constitutes the most extreme opposition to the traditional positive view; it has found a number of admirers in recent years.[46]

---

[43] Ibid. 110.

[44] W. R. Johnson, *Darkness Visible* (Berkeley and London, 1976).   [45] Ibid. 15.

[46] e.g. D. C. Feeney, 'The Reconciliations of Juno', *CQ*, NS 34 (1984), 179–94 (repr. in this collection, Ch. 18).

The increasing specialization of classical scholarship in the twentieth century has led to a large number of studies of detailed aspects of the *Aeneid*. Many (though far from all) of these have become useful tools for the scholar, and the following selection gives some idea of work of lasting value on particular topics or sections within the poem. Amongst studies before 1945, the commentaries of Warde Fowler with their stress on Roman society and religion,[47] the commentary of Boas on the first part of *Aeneid* 7, particularly useful in its account of prodigies,[48] Rehm's work on Vergil's presentation of primitive Italy,[49] the books of Kvíčala and Cordier on the epic style and vocabulary,[50] Wickert's articles on arms and armour,[51] the work of Holland and Saunders on the names of minor characters,[52] that of Sparrow on half-lines and repetitions,[53] that of Bailey on the religion of the poem and of Drew on the allegory of the *Aeneid*[54] stand out particularly, though this is a small selection from a much greater body of work. Since 1945 scholarly interest in Vergil has greatly increased. Suerbaum's bibliography of material on the *Aeneid* for 1875–1975[55] is useful in navigating a course here through a *vastum aequor* of books, dissertations, and articles, varying immensely in character and quality; what follows is once more a subjective selection, pointing out some significant trends and approaches.

[47] W. Warde Fowler, *Virgil's 'Gathering of the Clans': Aeneid VII.* 601–817 (Oxford, 1918); *Aeneas at the Site of Rome: Observations on the Eighth Book of the Aeneid* (Oxford, 1918); *The Death of Turnus: Observations on the Twelfth Book of the Aeneid* (Oxford, 1919).

[48] H. Boas, *Aeneas' Arrival in Latium* (Amsterdam, 1938).

[49] B. Rehm, *Das geographische Bild des alten Italien in Vergils Aeneis* (*Philologus* Suppl. 34. 2 (Leipzig, 1932)).

[50] J. Kvíčala, *Vergilstudien* (Prague, 1878); *Neue Beiträge zur Erklärung der Aeneia* (Prague, 1881). A. Cordier, *Études sur le vocabulaire épique dans l'Énéide* (Paris, 1939); *L'Alliteration latine: Le procédé dans l'Énéide de Virgile* (Paris, 1939).

[51] L. Wickert, 'Homerisches und Römisches im Kriegswesen der Aeneis', *Philologus* 85 [NS 39] (1930), 285–302, 437–62.

[52] L. A. Holland, 'Place-names and Heroes in the *Aeneid*', *AJPh* 56 (1935), 202–15; C. Saunders, 'Sources of the Names of Trojans and Latins in Vergil's *Aeneid*', *TAPhA* 71 (1940), 537–55.

[53] J. Sparrow, *Half-lines and Repetitions in Virgil* (Oxford, 1931).

[54] C. Bailey, *Religion in Virgil* (Oxford, 1935); D. L. Drew, *The Allegory of the Aeneid* (Oxford, 1927).

[55] W. Suerbaum, 'Hundert Jahre Vergil-Forschung', *ANRW* II. 31. 1 (1980), 3–358. Useful discussions of the history of Vergilian criticism over this period are given by A. Wlosok, 'Vergil in der neueren Forschung', *Gymnasium* 80 (1973), 129–51, and F. Serpa, *Il punto su Virgilio* (Bari, 1987), pp. 3–93. Some useful connections of studies on the *Aeneid* are Commager, op. cit. (n. 17), Serpa (as above, pp. 94–188), *Wege zu Vergil*, ed. H. Oppermann (Darmstadt, 1966), and H. Bardon and R. Verdière, eds., *Vergiliana* (Leiden, 1971).

One trend of the German dissertation since 1945 is the study of a particular character in the *Aeneid*. Thus we have had accounts of Turnus by Schenk,[56] of Mezentius by Thome,[57] of Latinus by Balk,[58] and of Camilla by Brill,[59] all of which contribute at some level to our knowledge of the poem. Dido too has attracted separate treatment, largely in the Anglophone world,[60] as have Anchises[61] and Nisus and Euryalus,[62] and the nature of the character and heroism of Aeneas continues (of course) to be a matter of dispute.[63] Griffin has contributed a discussion of the creation of characters in general in the *Aeneid*, arguing against a typological conception.[64] The gods and the divine element have also proved popular: Thornton and Coleman have offered interpretations of the divine machinery of the poem,[65] Kühn of the scenes in which the gods appear in the poem,[66] Pötscher of Vergil's ideas about divine powers,[67] Grassman-Fischer and Steiner of the prodigies and dreams in the *Aeneid* respectively.[68] The concept of Fate and its relationship to the gods has never been allowed to rest for long.[69] Two elements of Vergil's

[56] P. Schenk, *Die Gestalt des Turnus in Vergils Aeneis* (Konigstein, 1984) (reviewed *CR*, NS 36 (1986), 40–3).

[57] G. Thome, *Gestalt und Funktion des Mezentius bei Vergil* (Diss. Frankfurt, 1979).

[58] C. Balk, *Die Gestalt des Latinus in Vergils Aeneis* (Diss. Heidelberg, 1968).

[59] A. Brill, *Die Gestalt der Camilla bei Vergil* (Diss. Heidelberg, 1972).

[60] e.g. K. Quinn, *Latin Explorations* (London, 1963), pp. 29–58; N. M. Horsfall, *PVS* 13 (1973–4), 1–13; Niall Rudd, *Lines of Enquiry* (Cambridge, 1976), pp. 32–53 (the last two repr. in this collection, Chs. 6 and 7). Recent treatments include R. C. Monti, *The Dido-Episode and the Aeneid* (*Mnemosyne* Suppl. 66), Leiden, 1981, an examination of the social values raised in this part of the poem, and several essays on Dido and tragedy (cf. n. 75, below).

[61] R. B. Lloyd, 'The Character of Anchises in the *Aeneid*', *TAPhA* 88 (1957), 44–55.

[62] G. E. Duckworth, 'The Significance of Nisus and Euryalus for *Aeneid* 9–12', *AJPh* 88 (1967), 129–50; P. G. Lennox, 'Virgil's Night-episode Re-examined (*Aeneid* 9. 176–449)', *Hermes* 105 (1977), 331–42.

[63] e.g. H.-P. Stahl, 'Aeneas—An "Unheroic" Hero?', *Arethusa* 14 (1981), 157–75; A. Wlosok, 'Der Held als Argernis: Vergils Aeneas', *WJA* 8 (1982), 9–21; G. K. Galinsky, 'The Anger of Aeneas', *AJPh* 109 (1988), 321–48.

[64] J. Griffin, *Latin Poets and Roman Life* (London, 1985), 183–97. The same author's short *Virgil* (Oxford, 1986), is an interesting brief introduction to the post.

[65] A. Thornton, *The Living Universe: Gods and Men in Virgil's Aeneid* (Dunedin, 1976); R. Coleman, 'The Gods in the *Aeneid*', *G & R* 29 (1982), 143–68.

[66] W. Kühn, *Götterszenen bei Vergil* (Heidelberg, 1971).

[67] W. Pötscher, *Vergil und die göttlichen Mächte* (Hildesheim, 1977).

[68] B. Grassman-Fischer, *Die Prodigien in Vergils Aeneis* (Munich, 1966); H. R. Steiner, *Der Traum in der Aeneis* (Berne, 1952). On the specific topic of foundation-prodigies there is a recent study by E. L. Harrison, 'Foundation Prodigies in the *Aeneid*', *PLLS* 5 (1985), 131–64.

[69] Cf. Suerbaum (n. 55), pp. 69–70, for publications up to 1975; since then cf. C. H. Wilson, 'Jupiter and the Fates in the *Aeneid*', *CQ*, NS 29 (1979), 361–71.

Underworld in Book 6 have received particular attention: the significance of the Golden Bough, and the meaning of the Gate of Dreams.[70] Another tendency, following Knauer and Norden's *Ennius und Vergilius* and a tradition which goes back to Macrobius and before, is the study of Vergil's poetical sources: Schlunk has followed up earlier suggestions that Vergil's reinterpretation of Homer was coloured by the comments of Hellenistic scholiasts,[71] Hügi and Mehmel,[72] and more recently Briggs, George, and Clausen,[73] have pursued Hellenistic models for particular scenes in the *Aeneid*, and Wigodsky has looked at Vergil's use of earlier Roman poetry.[74] Greek tragedy has also been considered as a source of and influence on Vergil's epic, following Heinze.[75] The technical prose sources of the *Aeneid* have also been discussed, following Rehm, particularly by Horsfall;[76] Vergil's treatment of the Aeneas-legend has also received important attention, from Perret, Galinsky, Lloyd, and Horsfall,[77] and the topography of the *Aeneid* has been discussed by Tilly, McKay, and Della Corte.[78]

[70] Cf. Suerbaum (n. 55), pp. 235–6, 241, and the recent consideration by D. A. West, 'The Bough and the Gate', 17th Jackson Knight Memorial Lecture (Exeter, 1987; repr. in this collection, Ch. 11).

[71] R. R. Schlunk, *The Homeric Scholia and the Aeneid* (Ann Arbor, 1974).

[72] M. Hügi, *Vergils Aeneis und die Hellenistische Dichtung* (Berne and Stuttgart, 1952); F. Mehmel, *Vergil und Apollonios Rhodios* (Hamburg, 1940).

[73] W. W. Briggs, 'Vergil and the Hellenistic Epic', *ANRW* II. 31. 2 (1981), 948–84; E. V. George, *Aeneid 8 and the Aetia of Callimachus* (Leiden, 1974); W. C. Clausen, *Virgil's Aeneid and the Tradition of Hellenistic Poetry* (Berkeley and London, 1987).

[74] M. Wigodsky, *Vergil and Early Latin Poetry* (Wiesbaden, 1972). Another work on Vergil's use of Republican poetry is S. Stabryla, *Latin Tragedy in Vergil's Poetry* (Wrocław, 1970).

[75] There has been much discussion of tragic features in the *Aeneid*, especially in the story of Dido: cf. Heinze (n. 1), pp. 466–70, Quinn (n. 40), pp. 324–49, Suerbaum (n. 55), pp. 134–5. Dido's tragedy has been a subject of much attention recently: cf. F. Muecke, *AJPh* 104 (1983), 134–55, J. L. Moles, *G & R* 31 (1984), 48–54, and in P. R. Hardie, L. M. Whitby, and M. Whitby, eds., *Homo Viator* (Bristol, 1987), pp. 153–61, and E. L. Harrison, 'The Tragedy of Dido', *Échos du Monde Classique* 33, NS 8 (1989), 1–21. The only general study of the relation of the *Aeneid* to Attic tragedy as a whole is A. König, *Die Aeneis und die griechische Tragödie* (Diss. Berlin 1970).

[76] N. M. Horsfall, 'Virgil and the Conquest of Chaos', *Antichthon* 15 (1981), 141–50 (repr. in this collection, Ch. 26); id., 'Varrone (e l'Eneide)' in *Enciclopedia Virgiliana* (cf. n. 107, forthcoming). On the relation of the *Aeneid* to Cato's *Origines* cf. N. Criniti in *Enciclopedia Virgiliana* (cf. n. 107) i. 708–10.

[77] J. Perret, *Les origines de la légende troyenne de Rome* (Paris, 1940); R. B. Lloyd, '*Aeneid* 3 and the Aeneas Legend', *AJPh* 78 (1957), 383–400; G. K. Galinsky, *Aeneas, Sicily, and Rome* (Princeton, 1969); N. M. Horsfall, 'Some Problems in the Aeneas Legend', *CQ*, NS 29 (1979), 372–90, and 'The Aeneas Legend' in J. Bremmer and N. M. Horsfall, *Roman Myth and Mythography* (London, 1987), pp. 12–24.

[78] B. Tilly, *Vergil's Latium* (Oxford, 1947); L. A. Mackay, *Vergil's Italy* (Greenwich, Conn., 1970); F. Della Corte, *La mappa dell'Eneide* (Florence, 1972). Perhaps more

Though Ribbeck had done much of the basic work in the nineteenth century, modern textual criticism of Vergil has made some advances. Important modern editions have been produced by Mynors and Geymonat:[79] the former has added considerably to our knowledge of the Carolingian manuscripts and to the plausibility of lost ancient sources behind their groupings, while the latter has painstakingly recollated all the major manuscripts and given us a very full *apparatus criticus*. On the *Aeneid* in particular, the 'Ille ego qui . . .' lines put by some at the head of the poem have now been authoritatively ejected by Austin;[80] the same scholar's defence of the authenticity of the 'Helen-Episode' of Book 2[81] has been weightily contradicted by Goold and Murgia,[82] and Courtney has interestingly challenged our habitual acceptance of oddities in the text of the *Aeneid*.[83] On the more technical side, working with the text of Vergil has been rendered easier by Warwick's computerized concordance to all the works,[84] and by the metrical analyses and reverse index compiled by Ott.[85] The eventual production of the remainder of the Harvard edition of Servius' commentary promises further aid for the elucidation of the text of the *Aeneid*,[86] as does the recent increase of interest in the ancient commentators on Vergil generally.[87]

appropriate to the *Aeneid* is the notion that Vergil wants to create a poetically convincing sense of place (τοποθεσία) rather than a strict and accurate topography (τοπογραφία)—cf. N. M. Horsfall, 'Illusion and Reality in Latin Topographical Writing', *G & R* 32 (1985), 197–208.

[79] R. A. B. Mynors, *P. Vergili Maronis Opera* (Oxford, 1969); M. Geymonat, *P. Vergili Maronis Opera* (Turin, 1973).

[80] R. G. Austin, '*Ille ego quondam . . .*', *CQ*, NS 18 (1968), 107–15, though supporters of the lines still arise (cf. S. Koster, *Ille ego qui: Dichter zwischen Wort und Macht* (Erlangen, 1988), pp. 31–47).

[81] R. G. Austin, *CQ*, NS 11 (1961), 185–98.

[82] G. P. Goold, 'Servius and the Helen Episode', *HSCPh* 74 (1970), 101–68 (repr. in this collection, Ch. 5), C. E. Murgia, 'More on the Helen Episode', *CSCA* 4 (1971), 203–17.

[83] E. Courtney, 'The Formation of the Text of Vergil', *BICS* 28 (1981), 13–29.

[84] H. H. Warwick, *A Vergil Concordance* (Minneapolis, 1975).

[85] W. Ott, *Metrische Analysen zu Vergils Aeneis*, 12 vols. (Tübingen, 1973–85); id., *Rucklaüfiger Wortindex zu Vergil* (Tübingen, 1974).

[86] Vol. ii (the commentary on *Aeneid* 1–2), published in 1946, received a notorious drubbing from Eduard Fraenkel (*JRS* 38 (1948), 131–43; 39 (1949), 145–54, repr. together in his *Kleine Beiträge* (Rome, 1964), ii. 339–90); vol. iii (the commentary in *Aeneid* 3–5) appeared in 1965, and the project continues—cf. C. E. Murgia, *Prolegomena to Servius 5: The Manuscripts* (Berkeley, 1975), pp. 12–13.

[87] Cf. J. E. G. Zetzel, *Latin Textual Criticism in Antiquity* (Salem, NH, 1981); H. D. Jocelyn, 'M. Valerius Probus', *CQ*, NS 34 (1984), 464–76; 35 (1985), 149–61, 466–74; S. Timpanaro, *Per la storia della filologia virgiliana antica* (Rome, 1986); M. L. Delvigo, *Testo virgiliano e tradizione indiretta* (Pisa, 1987).

The structure, language, and style of the *Aeneid* have been continual concerns. The structural organization of the poem, and especially its possible divisions (two halves, three thirds, four quarters), has been variously investigated, especially by Duckworth;[88] by contrast, comprehensive treatments of Vergilian style—a complex and extensive topic— are understandably still lacking. The symbolist approach of Pöschl has stimulated many particular interpretations of individual passages, as has the consideration of Homeric and other models. One attempt to construct a 'poetics' for the *Aeneid* has been that of Worstbrock,[89] whose study of interacting sense and word order is particularly interesting; the language of the *Aeneid* has also been involved in the most prominent general discussions about the nature of the Latin poetical vocabulary.[90] The artistic effect of repetitions, especially the imitation of Homeric formulaic diction, has been treated by Moskalew;[91] a stimulating return to earlier derivations of the stages of composition of the *Aeneid* from repetitions, 'half-lines', and other stylistic effects has been made by Berres,[92] while the 'half-lines' themselves have generated quite a discussion[93] (though their uniqueness in ancient hexameter poetry surely marks them out as signs of the poem's unrevised state). The technique of 'multi-correspondence' in the similes of the *Aeneid* has been valuably identified and discussed by West,[94] their subject-matter by Coffey,[95] and large-scale general treatments of similes have been attempted by Hornsby and Rieks.[96] The etymologies of the *Aeneid* have

---

[88] Cf. Suerbaum (n. 55), pp. 82–4, which refers to six works by Duckworth; various divisions are soberly discussed by Camps, op. cit. (n. 42 above), pp. 51–60. Particularly interesting is M. von Albrecht's work on the inversion of situations in the poem ('Die Kunst der Spiegelung in Vergils Aeneis', *Hermes* 93 (1965), 54–64); a recent addition to the bibliography is E. L. Harrison, 'The Structure of the *Aeneid*', *ANRW* II. 31. 1 (1980), 359–93.

[89] F. J. Worstbrock, *Elemente einer Poetik der Aeneis* (Munster, 1963).

[90] e.g. B. Axelson, *Unpoetischer Wörter* (Lund, 1945); Gordon Williams, *Tradition and Originality in Roman Poetry* (Oxford, 1968), pp. 722–43. A useful earlier study is that of L. P. Wilkinson, 'The Language of Virgil and Horace', *CQ*, NS 9 (1959), 181–92 (repr. in this collection, Ch. 22). R. O. A. M. Lyne is following up an interesting article, 'Diction and Poetry in Vergil's *Aeneid*', *Atti del Convegno mondiale scientifico di Studi su Virgilio* (Milan, 1984), ii. 64–88, in a forthcoming book.

[91] W. Moskalew, *Formular Language and Poetic Design in the Aeneid* (Leiden, 1982).

[92] T. Berres, *Die Entstehung der Aeneis* (Wiesbaden, 1982).

[93] Cf. F. W. Lenz, 'The Incomplete Verses in Vergil's *Aeneid*: A Critical Report' in *Vergiliana* (above, n. 55), pp. 158–74.

[94] D. A. West, 'Multiple-Correspondence Similes in the *Aeneid*', *JRS* 59 (1969), 40–9 (repr. in this collection, Ch. 23), 'Virgilian Multiple-Correspondence Similes and their Antecedents', *Philologus* 114 (1970), 262–75.

[95] M. Coffey, 'The Subject-Matter of Virgil's Similes', *BICS* 8 (1961), 63–76.

[96] R. A. Hornsby, *Patterns of Action in Vergil's Aeneid: An Interpretation of Vergil's Epic*

been treated by Bartelink,[97] its speeches by Highet,[98] and its narratives of battle and death by Raabe, Willcock, and Horsfall.[99]

This select list of more than fifty items on detailed topics gives some impression of the industry and diversity of scholarship on the *Aeneid* since 1945. In conclusion, consideration will now be given to the major trends in criticism of Vergil's epic in the present decade, which may indicate the relative effects of what preceded and the likely directions of future work. One recent approach to Vergil of note is that emanating from G. B. Conte and his followers in Italy, one in which advanced literary theory of a quasi-structuralist kind, complete with its (frequently opaque) idiolect, is combined with traditional classical learning to produce new perspectives on the *Aeneid*.[100] Here a semiotic interpretation of literary allusion has led to an interesting new angle on Vergil's use of Homer,[101] and the consideration of structural elements in the construction of a character or book of the *Aeneid*, or in the 'point of view' from which the events of the narrative are observed, can give some stimulating insights.[102] Another structuralist view of the *Aeneid* has been taken by J. Thomas, who attempts to extract 'structures of the imaginary' from selected elements in Vergil's imagery and descriptions, while further novel approaches can be seen in the work of P. Heuzé, who views the poem from the point of view of the human body, especially Vergil's presentation of violence and beauty, and in the Freudian analysis of D. Gillis, which, while few will wholly believe that Vergil is 'the greatest erotic poet that Rome ever produced' (p. 111), offers some provoking material.[103] These and other modern hermeneutic theories became

Similes (Iowa City, 1970); R. Rieks, 'Die Gleichnisse Vergils', *ANRW* II. 31. 2 (1981), 1011–110.

[97] G. J. M. Bartelink, *Etymologisering bij Vergilius* (Amsterdam, 1965).

[98] G. Highet, *The Speeches in Vergil's Aeneid* (Princeton, 1972).

[99] H. Raabe, *Plurima Mortis Imago* (Munich, 1974); M. M. Willcock, 'Battle Scenes in the *Aeneid*', *PCPhS*, NS 29 (1983), 87–99; N. M. Horsfall, 'Some Problems in Virgil's Battle-Scenes', *G & R* 34 (1987), 48–55.

[100] Now best sampled in G. B. Conte, *The Rhetoric of Imitation*, ed. and introduced by C. Segal (Ithaca, NY, 1986) (a condensed translation of Conte's two books *Memoria dei poeti e sistema letteraria* (Turin, 1974), and *Virgilio: il genere e il suo confini* (Milan, 1984)), and in the journal *Materiali e discussioni per l'analisi dei testi classici*, ed. by Conte from Pisa.

[101] A. Barchiesi, *La traccia del modello: Effetti omerici nella narrazione virgiliana* (Pisa, 1984) (reviewed *JRS* 76 (1986), 320).

[102] M. Bonfanti, *Punto di vista e modi della narrazione nell'Eneide* (Pisa, 1985) (reviewed *CR*, NS 37 (1987), 173–5).

[103] J. Thomas, *Structures de l'imaginaire dans l'Énéide* (Paris, 1981); P. Heuzé, *L'Image du corps dans l'œuvre de Virgile* (Paris, 1985); D. Gillis, *Eros and Death in the Aeneid* (Rome, 1983).

involved in the consideration of other literatures some years ago; their late arrival in Vergilian studies is a sign of the caution of Latinists—in many ways highly justified—and of the particular primary problems of interpreting such a dense and complex poem as the *Aeneid*.

Another evident trend in 1980s criticism of the *Aeneid* is a move towards the closer consideration of the second half of the poem, which had been comparatively neglected, perhaps because of the distaste of recent decades for the poetry of war. The late 1970s saw the publication of the first extensive commentaries on Books 7 and 8 (three on the latter) for over fifty years,[104] and scholarly commentaries on the remaining books 9, 10, 11, and 12 are now in preparation.[105] *Virgil's Iliad*, K. W. Gransden's literary study of Books 7–12, aimed at the general reader and the student of comparative literature as well as at the classicist, was published in 1984, and Vergil has recently received greater consideration as a Roman poet of war.[106]

The two-thousandth anniversary of Vergil's death in 1981–2 led to a large number of bimilleniary conferences and conference proceedings. This volume of work is still being digested by scholars; much of it consists of insubstantial productions liable to slip into early oblivion, though one clear exception is the celebratory *Enciclopedia Virgiliana*, three of whose five volumes have now appeared and which, despite the varying quality of contributions, gives promise of an important monument of Vergilian scholarship.[107] The occasion naturally led to a reassertion of the centrality of Vergil in European cultural life, and it may be that the lasting work from this bimilleniary crop will be that concerned with the poet's influence—this is certainly true of some volumes published in the Anglophone world,[108] and with increased interest generally in comparative literary studies and in the classical roots of vernacular literatures, this tendency in Vergilian criticism looks set to expand.

Finally, I come to a consideration of three current Anglophone

---

[104] Aeneid 7 & 8: ed. C. J. Fordyce (Oxford, 1977). *Aeneid* 8: ed. K. W. Gransden (Cambridge, 1975), ed. P. T. Eden (Leiden, 1975).

[105] By Philip Hardie (9), S. J. Harrison (10), K. W. Gransden (11) and R. J. Tarrant (12).

[106] R. G. M. Nisbet, '*Aeneas Imperator*: Roman Generalship in an Epic Context', *PVS* 18 (1978–80), 50–61 (repr. in this collection, Ch. 20); S. J. Harrison, 'Vergil as a Poet of War', *PVS* 19 (1988), 48–68.

[107] *Enciclopedia Virgiliana* (Rome, 1984–).

[108] e.g. R. A. Cardwell and J. Hamilton, eds., *Virgil in a Cultural Tradition* (Nottingham, 1986), J. D. Bernard, ed., *Vergil at 2000* (New York, 1986) (both reviewed in *CR*, NS 37 (1987), 175–7).

interpretations of the *Aeneid*, all published in the 1980s and all dealing
(inevitably) with familiar issues, though with some new insights and
emphases. The first of these is Gordon Williams's *Technique and Ideas in
the Aeneid*.[109] Here Williams applies to the *Aeneid* the theory of 'figures of
thought' which he had set out in an earlier book, by which 'the poet
would say one thing but expect this reader to understand also something
else, related to what was said by a process of association that was either
metaphoric or metonymic' (p. vii). Williams's most notable application
of this theory to the *Aeneid* concerns the central issues of the gods and
fate: the gods are seen as tropes for authorial intervention, human
motivation, and the reconciliation of free will and determinism, while
fate is 'a synecdoche for the historical process' (p. 5). This demytholo-
gizing of the *Aeneid* places its action and meaning entirely on the human
level; men are responsible for their own acts and their consequences,
and though the world-picture of the *Aeneid* provides some kind of
ultimate hope in the Augustan future, the poet's sense of moral
ambiguity, of the isolated fragility of the human condition, and of man's
consequent inability to achieve his ideals leads to a generally pessimistic
view of life and heroic achievement. Williams asserts that the *Aeneid*
expresses poetic ideas rather than a political ideology, and claims to
belong neither to the anti-Augustan pessimists nor to the pro-Augustan
imperialists; however, readers of this survey will see that his sympathies
lie with the 'Harvard School': by his removal of any meaningful
metaphysics and by his account of the human condition he clearly places
weight on the plight of the suffering individual, and undermines the
frequent assertions in the poem of the permanent and divinely spon-
sored reality of Rome's greatness.

A counterweight to the renewed pessimism expressed by Williams is
the work of Philip Hardie, whose *Virgil's Aeneid: Cosmos and Imperium*[110]
reasserts the positive view of the poem. Following Pöschl, Hardie points
to a correlation in the *Aeneid* between the natural world and the world of
heroic action and politics: the forces which assert order against chaos in
nature are analogous with those which do the same in the human sphere,
whether Aeneas' creation of the Roman state or Augustus' reconstruction of it. Thus the cosmological themes raised in the *Aeneid*, which
derive much from Lucretius, Vergil's great model for the poetry of the
cosmos, harmonize with its imperial programme: the victories of Aeneas

---

[109] Gordon Williams, *Technique and Ideas in the Aeneid* (New Haven, 1983).
[110] Philip Hardie, *Virgil's Aeneid: Cosmos and Imperium* (Oxford, 1986).

and Augustus are compared on a natural level with the quelling of unruly physical forces, and on a mythological level with the triumph of the gods over the giants in the Gigantomachy, culminating in the Shield of Aeneas, which becomes a 'cosmic icon' of both the world (*orbis*) and of the history of the city of Rome (*urbs*). This cosmological aspect of the poem, Hardie argues, is stressed by Vergil's use of universal polarities and hyperbole. All this is set against the background of cosmological allegorization of Homer, probably familiar (Hardie argues) to Vergil, and supported by a close comparison of the Gigantomachic iconography of the Attalids' Great Altar of Zeus at Pergamum with that of the *Aeneid* and of Augustus' own architectural propaganda. This is a weighty work of much learning, and a powerful restatement of the positive view of the *Aeneid* for our time.

Finally, an ideological contrast to Hardie is provided by R. O. A. M. Lyne's book *Further Voices in Vergil's Aeneid*.[111] As its title suggests, Lyne's work is essentially a reworking of the pessimistic 'Two Voices' theory propounded by Adam Parry and the Harvard School (see above): the primary voice in the narrative is that of the positive epic poet, but 'further voices add to, comment upon, question, and occasionally subvert the implications of the epic voice' (p. 2). Further voices are discovered in Vergil's text through a careful close reading in the manner of the New Criticism, often through Vergil's apparent reinterpretation of a literary source, a method which (along with some older techniques) produces many new insights to back up some familiar pessimistic notions. Aeneas is frigid, emotionally inadequate, and temperamentally unstable, the gods, even Jupiter, can lack dignity and moral authority, and the heroism which moves forward Roman history in the figures of both Aeneas and Augustus is made of the same stuff as the violence which opposes it. This is a challenging version of the dark view of the *Aeneid*, perpetually provoking thought in its ideas and individual interpretations.

Scholarship on the *Aeneid* has thus made many advances in the present century: numerous aspects of the poem, both detailed and general, have been extensively explored, while the technical tools for its analysis have never been better, and look set to improve. Yet, as the different interpretations of the poem in the 1980s show, there is no consensus about its meaning or fundamental ideology. In some areas of scholarly endeavour this might be regarded as undesirable; when

[111] R. O. A. M. Lyne, *Further Voices in Vergil's Aeneid* (Oxford, 1987).

dealing with great poetry, however, greater technical knowledge does not necessarily lead to unanimity or certainty on central issues, and the volume and variety of recent criticism is a tribute to the continuing literary interest and stature of the *Aeneid*.

2

The Purpose of the *Aeneid*

R. D. WILLIAMS

The ancient critics were not in doubt about the purpose of the *Aeneid*: it was to glorify Rome and Augustus. In the Donatus–Suetonius life we read (21) 'Last of all he began the *Aeneid*, a varied and complicated theme, a sort of equivalent of both Homer's poems; also it was concerned with characters and events which were both Latin and Greek, while in it (and this was his special interest) there would be contained the origin of the city of Rome and of Augustus' (... 'in quo, quod maxime studebat, Romanae simul urbis et Augusti origo contineretur'). Similarly Tiberius Claudius Donatus says (*Prooem. Aen.* i): 'he had to depict Aeneas as a worthy first ancestor of Augustus, in whose honour the poem was written' ('talem enim monstrare Aenean debuit, ut dignus Caesari, in cuius honorem haec scribebantur, parens et auctor generis praeberetur'). And again, Servius (in the introductory note to his commentary on the *Aeneid*): 'Virgil's intention is to imitate Homer and to praise Augustus by means of his ancestors' ('intentio Vergilii haec est, Homerum imitari et Augustum laudare a parentibus'); and he quotes *a magno demissum nomen Iulo* (1. 288).

There is good basis for these comments in the well-known passage[1] at the beginning of *Georgics* 3 when Virgil promises that after the *Georgics* he will sing of the fierce battles of Caesar (46); in the midst of this temple of song will be Caesar and his shrine (16), and on its doors pictures of defeated enemies, triumphant Romans, and Trojan ancestors of their race. There is also very much in the *Aeneid* itself to support the view that Rome and Augustus *were* Virgil's special interests, and this will be my first point. I do not want to suggest that the *Aeneid* is a panegyric of Rome, nor even a defence of Rome—but that the Roman way of life, the march of Roman history, the concept of Roman world-destiny form a

---

[1] For a discussion of this passage see U. Fleischer, *Hermes* 88 (1960), 280 f. The passage does not of course necessarily refer to the *Aeneid* as we have it, merely to an intention to write a poem of a Roman kind. It may well be that one of Virgil's original plans for his epic was more closely linked with contemporary history; another, according to Servius (on *Ecl.* 6. 3 *cum canerem reges et peoelia*...) was for a poem on the Alban kings.

central theme of the poem against which other aspects of human behaviour and aspiration can be explored.

Our interest in other aspects of Virgil's poetic achievement may lead us to minimize or ignore his sincere admiration for the aims of Augustan Rome.[2] In the late seventeenth and early eighteenth centuries (the Augustan Age in England) this element was frequently highlighted in comments on the *Aeneid*. Dryden speaks of the dilemma of Virgil with his 'republican principles' under a monarchical system, but lists the advantages of Augustus' rule and continues: 'these things, I say, being considered by the poet, he concluded it to be in the interest of his country to be so governed; to infuse an awful respect into the people towards such a prince: by that respect to confirm their obedience to him, and by that obedience to make them happy. This was the moral of his divine poem.' Or again Warton (Introduction to Pitt's translation, 1753) draws this lesson from the *Aeneid*: 'Piety to God, ... justice and benevolence to men, together with true valour both active and passive ... will engage Heaven on our side, and make both prince and people victorious, flourishing and happy.' The early nineteenth century on the other hand had little to say on this subject: they were much too busy reading and rereading Dido (and occasionally Turnus and the destruction of Troy) to have time to read any other parts of the poem; many felt, as Walter Savage Landor did, that the long desert of this 'most misshapen of epics' was worth traversing because of its occasional superb oases of romantic loveliness. But we should not now make the same mistake again. Interested as we are in structural and thematic appreciation, in the poet's buildup of colour and mood, we cannot really fail to be attuned to the contextual impact of Jupiter's promise to Venus in Book 1, the pageant of the heroes in 6, the shield of Aeneas in 8. For consider these passages for a moment. The opening episodes[3] of *Aeneid* 1 have been dark, threatening, laden with peril; Juno, the storm, the shipwreck, the despair of Aeneas. Then the scene shifts to Olympus, and Venus asks Jupiter what has become of his promises—*hic pietatis honos?* she cries (1. 253), and the leader echoes her protest. Jupiter's answer sheds a radiant and optimistic light over the whole of the gloom and uncertainty, and the long toil which will be necessary to found Rome is seen to be worth whatever it involves as he says:

---

[2] Some even deny it; see for instance the remarkable article of F. Sforza, *CR* 49 (1935), 97–108. But the book by Brooks Otis (*Virgil: A Study in Civilized Poetry* (1963)) presents the Roman ideals of the poem with power and conviction.

[3] See my analysis in *PVS* 5 (1965–6), 14 f.

his ego nec metas rerum nec tempora pono:
imperium sine fine dedi. (1. 278–9)

The imperial mission of Rome is presented in terms of proud certainty. And again:

aspera tum positis mitescent saecula bellis:
cana Fides et Vesta, Remo cum fratre Quirinus
iura dabunt; dirae ferro et compagibus artis
claudentur Belli portae; Furor impius intus
saeva sedens super arma et centum vinctus aenis
post tergum nodis fremet horridus ore cruento. (1. 291–6)

Wars will cease, civil strife exist no more (*Remo cum fratre Quirinus*), violence will disappear; and this not in an imagined Utopia, but in the real world of Roman civilization.

Here then in Book 1 we have Roman optimism dispelling the previous uncertainty. Similarly in Book 6 the pageant of heroes succeeds a series of events in which suffering and wretchedness have been depicted against a scenic background of the horror and gloom of the underworld. Aeneas meets the ghosts of his past, those for whose death he feels in some measure responsible, to whom he speaks in terms of guilt and remorse. First Palinurus (who he had wrongly thought would be safe because of his misinterpretation of Apollo's oracle)—Palinurus the faithful helmsman who had guided him safely through the long years of voyage and search for the ever-receding shores of Italy. Then Dido—again he tries to explain why he did what he had to do (*invitus regina . . . sed me iussa deum . . . nec credere quivi . . .* 6. 460 ff.). Finally Deiphobus: Aeneas explains that on that last night he searched for him, could not find him, and so paid the due rites at a cenotaph. Deiphobus tries to console him (*nihil o tibi amice relictum,* 509) as Palinurus had done, as Dido had not. Aeneas' journey through the underworld to Elysium has been a re-enactment of tragedies and disasters from which he had escaped but others had not, and the effect upon him has been to reopen the traumatic wounds of the past.[4]

Against this background of grey and black comes the golden radiant light of Elysium, the meeting with Anchises, and the revelation of the ghosts of Roman heroes waiting to be born. The significance of it is sharply pointed by Virgil: Anchises says to Aeneas (716 f.) that he has long been waiting to show him the figures of Rome's future so that he

---

[4] See Brooks Otis, op. cit. 290 f., and his article in *TAPhA* 90 (1959), 165 f.; R. D. Williams, 'The Sixth Book of the *Aeneid*', *G & R* 11 (1964), 48 f.

might rejoice the more at the discovery of Italy—'quo magis Italia mecum laetere reperta'. The initial experiences of Aeneas after his landing in Italy had given him little cause for joy. Then, as the pageant unfolds, and the shade of Augustus becomes visible next to Romulus ('hic vir hic est tibi quem promitti saepius audis / Augustus Caesar, divi genus'), Anchises tells of the restored golden age under his rule and interrupts his description to ask: 'et dubitamus adhuc virtutem extendere factis, / aut metus Ausonia prohibet consistere terra?' Do we still hesitate to press forward into the future, to fulfil the destiny of Rome? Aeneas does not reply, but we can reply for him. This destiny, which Anchises sums up as government, peace, and civilized life (*regere imperio . . . pacique imponere morem*),[5] must banish remorse and regrets: Aeneas' thoughts, which had been brooding sadly on the past, are now fired with love for future glory—'incenditque animum famae venientis amore' (889).

The last passage which I shall take for this Roman theme—though of course there are many more[6]—is at the end of Book 8, when the pictures on Aeneas' newly made shield are described.[7] Aeneas has no need for a new shield; he had not, like Achilles, lost his old one; but the need is thematic, connected with the mood of the poem. The passage comes at the end of two books (7 and 8) in which the first outbreak of hostilities has occurred and the war is inevitable, but in which there has been no large-scale fighting. It is in the ninth book that Virgil at last begins his battle-scenes, and just before he does so he shows us once more the nature of the destiny for which Aeneas fights. The choice of pictures on the shield is determined, in my view, by two primary considerations: the first is the visual impact of the scene, and the second the portrayal of Roman moral values. I will not elaborate this at length, but I pick an instance or two: the rape of the Sabines followed by the subsequent reconciliation of the two parties suggests the pacific and religious way of life which the Romans always associated with Numa, so that they came to be descendants of the courage of Romulus and the moral qualities of Numa; the punishment of Mettus is for breaking his word, for what

---

[5] The reading *pacisque* should now be finally abandoned; it has rested, as E. Fraenkel (*Mus. Helv.* 19 (1962), 133) has pointed out, on a misinterpretation of Servius.

[6] For example the visions and prophecies of Books 2 and 3 (2. 268 f., 679 f., 776 f.; 3. 90 f., 154 f., 374 f.), the words of Jupiter to Mercury in 4. 227 f., the prophecy to Latinus in 7. 96 f., the speech of the god Tiber in 8. 36 f., and especially the conversation of Jupiter and Juno in 12. 819–40.

[7] See W. Warde Fowler, *Aeneas at the Site of Rome* (Oxford, 1918), pp. 100 f.; J. R. Bacon, *CR* 53 (1939), 97 f.; C. Becker, *Wien. Stud.* 77 (1964), 111 f.

could be called *fides violata*; the battle against Porsenna and the Tarquins is fought *pro libertate*, and Cocles and Cloelia illustrate Roman *fortitudo* (of which they were often *exempla*, as in Valerius Maximus 3. 2). The sacred geese save the Capitol because the gods care for a religious people; Cato is shown in Elysium as lawgiver: *dantem iura Catonem*. These pictures are round the edge of the shield; in the middle are scenes connected with the battle of Actium and Augustus:

> hinc Augustus agens Italos in proelia Caesar
> cum patribus populoque, penatibus et magnis dis. (8. 678–9)

A united state, Italy as well as Rome, senate and people, and above all the gods. This is the image of his rule which Augustus aimed to project; far different from the Tarquins who had to be resisted *pro libertate*. Against the monstrous Egyptian gods and the yapping Anubis, Rome opposes Neptune, Venus, and Minerva, and especially Apollo. The final scene shows Caesar restoring the temples and receiving gifts from the conquered. It is the theme of Horace's sixth Roman ode (3. 6. 5): 'dis te minorem quod geris imperas' ('You rule because you bear yourself as inferior to the gods').

It is not surprising that Augustus pressed Virgil to send him something from the *Aeneid* as soon as anything was ready (Donatus— Suetonius 31): it is interesting, however, to reflect that the story continues that Virgil did not read any of the *Aeneid* to Augustus till much later, and then read him only Books 2, 4, and 6. Of these, 6 has a Roman ending, but 2 and 4 are the least Roman books in the poem. Did Virgil's interest in the Roman aspect diminish as time went on?

This brings me to my second point, which I have already partly anticipated, and it is this. While we must be agreed that the Roman vision was one theme of the poem, indeed the principal and dominant one (though not necessarily the most important), there are other themes against which the implications of the Roman theme are explored.[8] We might call the Roman element Virgil's public voice, if we may do so without implying that it was feigned in any way—for it was not; how shall we define the private voice of the poet? We associate it most strongly with Dido and the apparently senseless suffering of her tragedy; and with Turnus who does what he thinks right and loses his life; and with the old king Priam; with Pallas and Euryalus and Lausus and Camilla

---

[8] See A. Parry, 'The Two Voices of Virgil's *Aeneid*', *Arion* 2. 4 (1963), 66 f., and Wendell Clausen, *HSCPh* 68 (1964), 139 f.

and the countless warriors who fall in battle, like Aeolus the Trojan who died fighting in Latium:

> hic tibi mortis erant metae, domus alta sub Ida,
> Lyrnesi domus alta, solo Laurente sepulcrum. (12. 546–7)
>
> Here he came to the finish; he had a fine home at Lyrnesus
> Under Mount Ida, a fine home, but he sleeps in Laurentine soil.

(Day Lewis)

The sensitive pathos of Virgil and his personal involvement is easily felt by all readers: it is a world away from Horatius Cocles and Cloelia, from *pacique imponere morem*. It is the world of the individual not the state, a world of *lacrimae* not *imperium*: with Dido it is the individual *against* the state, against the public dictates of the national interests of Rome. But it is not put in political terms by Virgil: Dido does not profess, like Sophocles' Antigone, some higher principle which she invokes against Roman national demands. It is just that she is brushed aside by the march of public events, events in which she is not interested. With Turnus it is that he wishes to live his life in the way he intended before the invader came, and he sees no reason why he should not. Do we?

Let us move this tension between the glory of Rome and the sorrow of individuals into its literary setting. The stern national note in Virgil is in the tradition of Ennius:

> moribus antiquis res stat Romana virisque, (*Ann.* 500 V),
>
> The Roman state stands firm in its ancient ways and in its men.

and of Cicero and (in Virgil's time) of Livy and of Horace in his Roman odes; the sensitivity to the individual's feelings is in the Alexandrian tradition as presented in Rome by Catullus, Tibullus, Propertius. Virgil's debt to Catullus has recently been explored more fully than before by Westendorp Boerma:[9] what I want to draw attention to here is that there are relatively few major reminiscences of Catullus, but practically all of them are in well-known passages of Virgilian pathos— the flower simile at Euryalus' death (9. 435 f.), the flower simile at Pallas' funeral (11. 68 f.), and Aeneas' last sad words to him:

> nos alias hinc ad lacrimas eadem horrida belli
> fata vocant: salve aeternum mihi, maxime Palla,
> aeternumque vale. (11. 96–8)

We think of the last line of Catullus 101, 'atque in perpetuum frater ave

---

[9] R. E. H. Westendorp Boerma, *Acta Classica* 1 (1958), 55 f.

atque vale'. But most of all we hear Catullus in *Aeneid* 4, with reminiscences from Ariadne's speech to Theseus in poem 64: I give one or two examples.

Aen. 4. 316	per conubia nostra, per inceptos hymenaeos
Cat. 64. 141	sed conubia laeta, sed optatos hymenaeos
Aen. 4. 657–8	felix heu nimium felix si litora tantum
	numquam Dardaniae tetigissent nostra carinae.
Cat. 64. 171–2	Iuppiter omnipotens, utinam ne tempore primo
	Gnosia Cecropiae tetigissent litora puppes.

And finally the reminiscence in Dido's last pleas (4. 328 f.) 'si quis mihi parvulus aula / luderet Aeneas': compare Catullus:

> Torquatus volo parvulus
> matris e gremio suae
> porrigens teneras manus
> dulce rideat ad patrem
> semihiante labello. (61. 209 ff.)

Virgil's use of *parvulus* here is unique in the *Aeneid*: there is no other example in his epic of a diminutive adjective, and the use of a Catullan feature of style, the diminutive which belongs to family life, not to epic grandeur, brings the intimacy of emotion which is so marked a feature of Catullus' poetry. Dido's suffering is not distanced or muted: Virgil involves and deeply implicates the reader.

This then seems to me to be a major purpose of the *Aeneid*, to explore the relationship of the stern, strong, political, intellectual, organizational world of Roman life and the private, emotional, sensitive, vulnerable, frail world of the individual. For Rome, Dido was well out of the way— but not for Virgil. He explores the tension between two contrasting aspects of human experience, and more than any other Roman writer he understood both.

Now I want to consider another tension which seems to me basic in the poem: this is the relationship between the Homeric poems and the Roman world. Homer is just as vital a source of Virgil's poetic intentions as Augustan Rome or Catullan sensitivity. The legend of Aeneas suited Virgil's purposes most admirably because as well as being the founder of Rome Aeneas was a contemporary of Hector and Odysseus. The particular aspect of Virgil's use of Homer which I want to discuss here is concerned with the values of the heroic world compared and contrasted with those of Augustan Rome. In the first half of the poem Aeneas again

and again reminds us of Odysseus, not only in Book 3 when the account
of his journey automatically challenges comparison with the *Odyssey*, but
most especially in Book 1, where nearly all the subject-matter is based
on episodes and speeches from *Odyssey* 5–8, frequently with verbal
reminiscences of a striking kind.[10] The only parts, in fact, of *Aeneid* 1
which are without Odyssean sources are those concerned with the gods:
Juno at the beginning, Jupiter's prophecy, Venus, and Cupid. The storm
and Aeneas' despair, the meeting with a disguised goddess, the reception by Dido, the narrative of Ilioneus, the banquet and the speech of
welcome, the minstrel's song: all these are closely modelled on Homeric
incidents. And finally Dido asks for Aeneas' story and gets it in two
books, as Alcinous got Odysseus' story in four (*Od.* 9–12).

These are the similarities, but there is one vital difference: Odysseus
is trying to get home to resume his old life in Ithaca exactly as he left it,
but Aeneas has to find a new home and to build a new way of life.
Odysseus, that man of many devices, eventually returns, while his
comrades, lesser men, are all lost; Aeneas has to bring his lesser men
safely to Hesperia with him. Odysseus is the great individualist, but
Aeneas has to be the social man, *insignis pietate.* And this he has to learn
as he leaves the heroic world and leads his men into the complex
confusion of a more socially responsible way of life. Jupiter's prophecy
in Book 1 is the prolepsis of the *Aeneid*, the utterly non-Odyssean
element. Essentially the heroic world was a simple one, violent, pulsat-
ing, intense, exciting—a way of life was there to be lived, whether
happily or unhappily. But the Roman way of life was one involving
constant problems, and Aeneas had to try to develop the intellectual and
moral qualities appropriate to a leader in those different days. We see
him in Book 2 still the Homeric hero, rash, impulsive, brave, seeking
when all is lost the glorious death;[11] but in Book 3 he sails away from this
Trojan world and through the long tedium of journeying gradually
learns, with his father's help, more about the divine intention for
Rome.[12] After his father's death it needs Mercury in Book 4 to recall
him to his mission, and in 5 after the burning of the ships first Jupiter
and then Nautes and then the vision of his father's ghost intervene to

---

[10] See my discussion of this in *Phoenix* 17 (1963), 266 f.

[11] Cf. for example 2. 314–17 'arma amens capio; nec sat rationis in armis, / sed
glomerare manum bello at concurrere in arcem / cum sociis ardent animi; furor iraque
mentem / praecipitat, pulchrumque mori succurrit in armis'; 2. 353 f., 355 (the wolf
simile), 431 f., 575 (Helen) 'exarsere ignes animo; subit ira...', 588 'talia iactabam et
furiata mente ferebar', 668 f., 745 f.

[12] See my edition of *Aeneid* 3, Intro. pp. 3–7.

help his frail purpose. After the pageant in Book 6 he is at last ready for the wars he must fight. How does he fight them? We should expect him to show the idealized qualities of a Roman commander dealing with the task of conquering the proud—*debellare superbos*; qualities of high efficiency, high personal courage, responsibility for his men (*constantia, consilium, virtus, pietas*), and added to these[13] *clementia* (*parcere subiectis*), *humanitas, iustitia, moderatio, fides,* perhaps *mansuetudo*.[14] We expect him to be different from a Homeric hero, who fights because it is an essential and accepted element in his life, and to fight only because he must, in order to establish peace. He has a foil in Turnus, whose qualities are Homeric,[15] as Virgil often insists—*alius Latio iam partus Achilles* (6. 89). He has a foil on the other side in Latinus, the old king so wedded to peace that when trouble comes all he can do is abdicate his power and shut himself up in his palace. Somewhere between these two he must find his own standard of behaviour: he must modify his own Turnus-like attributes (which he showed in Book 2) in the direction of responsibility for the peace of the world. How does he succeed?

He succeeds very imperfectly. Sometimes indeed he shows revulsion from needless bloodshed: after he has killed Lausus he bitterly regrets it (10. 821 f.), and speaks in terms of deep sorrow to the lifeless body (a marked contrast to Turnus' behaviour over Pallas). After the funeral of Pallas, when the Latin envoys come for a truce to bury the dead, he grants it, saying: 'You ask me for peace for the dead? I would have wished to grant it to the living': 'pacem me exanimis et Martis sorte peremptis / oratis? equidem et vivis concedere vellem' (11. 110–11). And in Book 12 when the arrangements for single combat have been broken he seeks to restrain his followers:

> o cohibete iras: ictum iam foedus ... (12. 314)

But in most of the scenes of fighting Aeneas is ruthless, relentless,

---

[13] For Roman examples of these qualities see Valerius Maximus, *passim*; on the character of Aeneas in these terms see E. A. Hahn, *Class. Weekly* 25 (1931–2), 9 f., 17 f.; R. Heinze, *Virgils epische Technik*⁴ (Stuttgart, 1957), pp. 210 f., C. M. Bowra, *From Virgil to Milton* (London, 1945), pp. 56 f., Brooks Otis, op. cit. 313 f. The notional contrast between Aeneas and Turnus can be stated in Horace's terms, *vis temperata* against *vis consili expers*; but as the poem unrolls, it does not work out so simply.

[14] 'Mercy, humanity, justice, moderation, loyalty, gentleness.' Cf. Caes. *Gal.* 2. 14, Cic. *Ver.* 2. 5. 115.

[15] See W. S. Anderson, 'Vergil's Second *Iliad*', *TAPhA* 88 (1957), 17 f., J. W. Spaeth, 'Hector's Successor in the *Aeneid*', *CJ* 46 (1950–1), 277 f., G. E. Duckworth, 'Turnus and Duryodhana', *TAPhA* 92 (1961), 81–8.

Homeric; this is especially so in Book 10 where he spurns pleas for mercy, taunts the fallen, and rages in berserk anger for blood.[16] The resolution of this contrast in him might be expected in the final scenes—how will he deal with Turnus? As Turnus would have dealt with him? Or otherwise?

The two most recent books on the *Aeneid* give diametrically opposed interpretations of this scene. Brooks Otis (*Virgil: A Study in Civilized Poetry*, 1963) sees the death of Turnus as absolutely necessary; Aeneas could do no other than kill him. 'Virgil's *humanitas*', he tells us (p. 393), 'does not in any way negate his moral realism; he will not let Turnus or even Mezentius die without a tribute to their heroism, but he will not spare them.' For Otis, Turnus is a hero of false standards who must atone with his life for his sins.[17] M. C. J. Putnam, however, (*The Poetry of the Aeneid*, Cambridge, Mass., 1965), emphasizes the relation of Turnus' tragedy to Dido's, showing how our sympathy is aroused for him at every turn in these last scenes, and how Aeneas himself falls prey to violence and anger. 'The forces of violence and irrationality,' says Putnam, 'which swirl round Aeneas ... lead ultimately not to his triumph over them ... but rather to complete submission.' Certainly the words used of Aeneas here are very strong—*furiis accensus et ira terribilis*, and again *fervidus*. If Turnus has been our Achilles through the poem, Aeneas is Achilles now,[18] killing in anger over Pallas as Achilles had in anger over Patroclus. In this situation he does not control himself. Putnam is wrong in trying to persuade us that there is no justification at all, but it is certain that the poem ends with our thoughts concentrated on the tragedy[19] of Turnus, not the triumph of Rome. My point is this: how easy it would have been for the gentle Virgil to contrive different circumstances in which Aeneas could have acted otherwise. That he faced the issue and presented a situation so moving and so terrifying is the measure of his greatness as a poet.[20]

There is one other major tension against the principal theme which I should like to discuss. We have considered Rome against the individual,

---

[16] Cf. for example 10. 513 f., 545 f., 569–70, 575 f., 786 f.

[17] See Brooks Otis, op. cit. 380 f., 392 f.; cf. also S. G. P. Small, 'The Arms of Turnus: *Aeneid* 7. 783–92', *TAPhA* 90 (1959), 243 f., for an interesting discussion of the symbolism of Turnus' armour (the Chimaera as an emblem of archaic and barbaric energy); and Agathe H. F. Thornton, 'The Last Scene of the *Aeneid*', *G & R* 22 (1953), 82–4.

[18] See L. A. Mackay, 'Achilles as Model for Aeneas', *TAPhA* 88 (1957), 11 f., and the works cited in note 16.

[19] See V. Pöschl, *Die Dichtkunst Virgils* (Innsbruck, 1950), pp. 153 f.

[20] See L. A. Mackay, *TAPhA* 94 (1963), 157 f., especially 165.

and Rome against Homeric and heroic ideals; my last aspect is Rome against the poet's fancy, the real world against the mythological, the actual and mundane against the imaginary, this world against visions of some other world.

The divine machinery of the Olympian gods sets the human action in the poem in a relationship with non-human, preternatural forces. This could have been done without the mythology of gods, by using *fatum* (or *fortuna*) unpersonified (as Lucan did) or by abstract personifications like Pietas and Clementia in Statius; but Virgil has elected not only to use divinities, but to give them extremely vivid pictorial existence. We often comment upon how the Homeric gods in Virgil have lost their immediacy, have become distanced, and this is true; Virgil's Roman world could not accept the idea of a god in person helping on the battlefield in the same way as the Homeric world could. But although the gods can be said to be faded in a theological sense, they are tremendously real pictorially, as a part of the poet's visual imagination which has shaped his thought and given him his imagery.[21] We may by rationalizing see in Juno a personification of the forces of hostile circumstances which stand between a man and his goal, and in Venus the protective nurturing power which supports Rome, the great mother of men: we may go further and see in Allecto[22] a personification of man's own evil desires, so that when she arouses Turnus to fury we realize that this is the kind of man Turnus is and that in some sense he himself is responsible for what Allecto is said to do to him. She is his psychology, if you like. But above and beyond this use of the gods as symbolizing and rationalizing human and non-human forces there is the pure imagery and beauty and terror of this other world. The *Aeneid* does not move in it for most of the time, as the *Metamorphoses* of Ovid does: but in our search for Roman ideals, moral values, human emotions in the *Aeneid* we often greatly underrate the importance of these 'gleams of a remoter world'.

Think of Iris gliding down the rainbow, Mercury flying over Mount Atlas, Neptune riding the waves in his chariot with his retinue of sea-deities, Juno the majestic and terrifying Queen of Heaven, Jupiter smiling at Venus and kissing away her tears. I take just one passage in a little more detail. In *Aeneid* 2, when Aeneas is on the point of killing Helen, because she is responsible for the flames consuming his city, Venus appears to him and tells him that the gods are to blame, and she

[21] See R. D. Williams, *Vergilius* 11 (1965), 11 f.
[22] On this see Brooks Otis, op. cit. 323 f.

reveals to him what mortal vision cannot see: she says she will draw aside
the cloud which veils his mortal sight:

> aspice: namque omnem, quae nunc obducta tuenti
> mortales hebetat visus tibi et umida circum
> caligat, nubem eripiam ... (2. 604–6)

and she shows him the shapes of gods working Troy's downfall,
Neptune knocking down the walls, Juno at the Scaean gates, Pallas
Athene with her Gorgon, Jupiter himself helping the destruction. And
Aeneas sees them and knows resistance is useless now:

> apparent dirae facies, inimicaque Troiae
> numina magna deum. (2. 622–3)

Now this world is not only a world of Olympian or infernal deities: it
can also be an Odyssean world of people or creatures with supernatural
power. In *Aeneid* 3 the book of Aeneas' voyages, the Trojans come into
contact with the Harpies and with the Cyclops, and nearly into contact
with Scylla and Charybdis; in Book 5 they pass the islands of the Sirens,
at the beginning of Book 7 they sail past the land of Circe. What, we may
ask, are these Homeric fantasies doing in the well-charted Mediterranean with which the Romans were very familiar?

There is here a very remarkable tension in the poem, and what is
more remarkable still is its continuation into the non-Odyssean world of
the second half of the *Aeneid*. Here it is not so frequently met with: for
example the story of Hercules and Cacus in Book 8 is easily acceptable
because it is narrated by Evander as past history. I want to take the two
main examples. The first is Camilla. We meet her first in the catalogue[23]
of Turnus' forces at the end of Book 7. She is a warrior-maid of the
Volsci, in one sense real enough, a trained expert in war. But in another
sense she is a fairy princess, able to speed over growing corn without
bruising the shoots, or to skim above the sea. Her ambivalence is
splendidly portrayed in the last line of Book 7—she has a pastoral myrtle
tipped with iron: she belongs to both worlds, the pastoral dream-world
of idealized existence and the iron world of battle.

When we meet her in Book 11 she is at first entirely military, offering
Turnus assistance which is accepted in full military terms: 'tu Tyr-
rhenum equitem conlatis excipe signis' (11. 517). But immediately

---

[23] There are other mythological touches in the catalogue, such as the descriptions of
Aventinus and Virbius; see R. D. Williams, *CQ* 11 (1961), 146 f. Cf. also 10. 185 f.

afterwards the scene shifts to Olympus where Diana speaks to Opis about Camilla's impending fate and tells of her childhood and devotion to her cult; she plans vengeance upon Camilla's killer. Camilla performs great deeds of valour, without supernatural aid; she is killed by Arruns as she seeks the golden spoils of Chloreus. She dies in the full heroic tradition of the fallen warrior, and Arruns is killed by Opis' arrow. This is the only death in the war-scenes which is actually inflicted by a deity, and it closes a battle-story of strange ambiguity.

My other example is the most remarkable of all in the poem. At the beginning of Book 9, in the absence of Aeneas, Turnus and his Rutulians move against the Trojan camp: when he finds that the Trojans (in accordance with Aeneas' instructions) refuse to come out to battle, he leads his men to burn the Trojan ships. Virgil now halts the narrative to invoke the Muse, and inform us that Cybele had given Aeneas her sacred pines for building a fleet on the understanding from Jupiter that they should not ever be destroyed: he promised that they should be changed into sea-nymphs—'qualis Nereia Doto / et Galatea secant spumantem pectore pontum' (9. 102–3). We return to the narrative: the promised day is at hand, and Cybele intervenes. A supernatural light fills the sky, then a great cloud passes over the heavens with processions of Cybele's votaries; a might voice is heard telling the Trojans to have no fear, and ending: 'vos ite solutae, / ite deae pelagi: genetrix iubet'. And the ships like dolphins plunge downwards, and turn into sea-nymphs.

The Rutulians were amazed, *obstipuere animi Rutulis*: and so it must be confessed are we. We are not surprised when we find that this aspect of the Aeneas legend figures largely in Ovid's *Metamorphoses* (14. 530 f.), where it very properly belongs: but how does it fit in the hard world of Turnus going into battle against the proto-Romans? Servius (on 9. 82) reports uneasiness: he says that, although the passage may be partly excused as a *figmentum poeticum*, it nevertheless is blamed by the critics (*notatur a criticis*) because it lacks precedents—*quia exemplo caret*. The Renaissance commentators, Germanus and La Cerda, defend the passage by producing precedents for such a supernatural event; in Apollonius (4. 580 f.) the good ship *Argo* can talk, and in Homer (*Od.* 8. 557 f.) the Phaeacian ships steer themselves. True, we may say, but the *Argo* and the Phaeacians belong wholly to a heroic and Odyssean world, in contrast with Aeneas' fleet which is entering a proto-Roman world. Page regards the subject itself as 'somewhat ludicrous', but considers that Virgil's 'handling of it is marked by admirable tact'. Conington cryptically says that 'modern criticism will be more disposed to account for it than to justify it'.[24]

Nor is Virgil finished with the story: in Book 10 (219 f.), when Aeneas is returning with his Etruscan allies, he is met *en route* by the nymphs, and Cymodocea—who is the best of them at using human speech, *fandi doctissima*—tells him of how the camp is beleaguered, and gives his ship a push to help him get there more quickly.

Why then has Virgil done this? He himself was not unaware of the apparent incongruity: in his invocation to the Muse before the story he says: 'Tell me of it: the evidence is lost in the mists of time, but the story lives on—'dicite: prisca fides facto, sed fama perennis' (9. 79). This kind of apology for a supernatural story occurs also in *Aen*. 6. 173, whee Virgil tells how Misenus' death was caused because he dared to challenge the sea-god Triton to a trumpet contest—'aemulus exceptum Triton, si credere dignum est...'[25]

The best way of understanding the purpose of the passage is to consider its position in the poem. At the beginning of Book 9 Virgil describes the full-scale commencement of the war. The Rutulians march over the plain, the Trojans see the dark cloud and in accordance with Aeneas' instructions return within their camp. Turnus, terrible in full panoply, hurls his spear—'principium pugnae, et campo sese arduus infert' (9. 53). His men take up the battle-cry and follow him with terrifying shouts:

> clamorem excipiunt socii fremituque sequuntur
> horrisono. (9. 54–5)

Turnus is *turbidus*, like a wolf attacking lambs: *ignescunt irae*. It is a chilling and terrible picture of violence unleashed. Irresistibly (it seems) they fall in wild frenzy on the fleet—yet they *are* resisted, supernaturally.

---

[24] Heyne (ad loc.) says: 'Fabulam quae sequitur tamquam absurdam et epica gravitate indignam reprehendere in promptu est' ('The story which follows may readily be criticized as absurd and unworthy of epic seriousness'), and again, 'Nec nos infitiamur a nostris sensibus et phantasmatibus eam nimium quantum abhorrere' ('And I should not deny that it is extremely repulsive to my senses and imagination'). The story does not seem to have been in the general version of the Aeneas legend before Virgil: on the other hand, it is not at all likely that Virgil invented it, as Heinze implies. See K. Kuiper, *Mnemos.* 30 (1902), 277 f. In the legend its natural place would be immediately after Aeneas' arrival, as a symbol of the end of his voyage; in Virgil's version (which is influenced by the attack on the Greek fleet in *Iliad* 15) the emphasis is on salvation from destruction. There is some inconsistency with the earlier narrative, because one ship was lost in the storm off Carthage, and four were burned by the women in Sicily, without any intervention by Cybele to save them.

[25] Cf. *Geo.* 3. 391, and cf. Heinze, op. cit. 241–3.

Virgil snatches us away from the awful inevitability of unopposed military might into the pastoral world, where violence and destruction is avoided by supernatural power, where fire cannot burn nor brute force prevail, where at the moment of death there is intervention, escape, transformation from the mortal world. The ships are not confined within the mortal condition of extinction; for them there is another existence.

We do not stay long in this other world: there follows the story of Nisus and Euryalus, at once the bloodiest and most tragic episode in the *Aeneid*, and the rest of the book is filled with death. When the nymphs meet Aeneas and speak to him, it is again just before savage fighting, centering around the death of Pallas and Aeneas' fierce acts of revenge. And finally something of this contrast is given in Book 11, as we have seen, in the figure of Camilla, the devotee of Diana in the pastoral world of the woodland, who chose instead the real world of war and death at the hands of the Trojans.

This is the kind of function fulfilled by the episode of Misenus' death in Book 6 to which I have already referred. A world beyond ours is in our thoughts: Aeneas with the Sibyl and the talisman of the golden bough[26] is placed for the moment outside the normal condition of mortality. But in the real world, for Misenus, who has foolishly brought destruction upon himself, there is no escape from death. Aeneas may temporarily be allowed a moment in this other world, may because of his special qualities and responsibilities transcend mortality for a space; but not Misenus. Similarly the divine ships of Cybele can defy the mortal condition, can escape the burning fire-brands of the Rutulians; but not so the other victims of Turnus and his soldiers, not so Nisus and Euryalus. And yet they too survive in the minds of men—'nulla dies unquam memori vos eximet aevo' (9. 447); and perhaps too in the groves of the blessed beyond the grave. The nymphs symbolize for Virgil that the world extends beyond what is definable in terms of human realism. 'I can easily believe,' said Burnet, quoted by Coleridge at the beginning of *The Ancient Mariner*, 'that there are more invisible creatures in the world than visible ones.' Virgil was not enough of a Romantic to have moved easily in the world of *The Ancient Mariner*, and the world of the *Aeneid* is real much more often than it is visionary, but it seeks to embrace both these aspects of human experience.

*

[26] See R. A. Brooks, *AJPh* 74 (1953). 260 f. (for the bough as a dual symbol of life and death); and C. P. Segal, *Arion* 4 (1965), 617 f., and 5 (1966), 34 f.

The purpose of the *Aeneid* then, as I see it, was essentially an exploration of varying and sometimes contrasting aspects of human experience. The public aspect—Rome's mission to pacify and civilize the world—figured very largely in Virgil's thoughts, and it seems that his intention was to measure against this various other aspects of life which he felt intensely. His concept of Rome's mission was derived both from literature (Ennius especially, and perhaps contemporaries like Horace and Livy) and from life as he lived it and saw it lived by his friends in Rome, many of whom were in touch with the large-scale ordering of national policy. In this world he could see, at its best, organization and beneficial policy-making; at its worst, manipulation and cruelty in the interest of personal ambition. He wanted to present poetic situations in which these aspects could be explored, not from a fixed standpoint (like Lucan's Stoicism) but from varying standpoints. He has no dogmatic lesson to teach in this public world: he is not like Lucretius, trying to convert us to a powerfully held belief. He does not state the problems in political terms of left or right, senate or emperor; he does not hold that Augustus should be more despotic or less despotic; instead he presents situation after situation in his poem in which the public ideals of Rome seem excellent, or less excellent.

His private voice is generally in contrast with the public voice; sometimes based—like the public voice—on both literature and life, as when he portrays sensitive sympathy and pity in the tradition of Catullus and from his experiences in real life, or examines Homeric moral values against Roman ways of life as he knew them. But sometimes his private voice is divorced from real life, set in opposition to it, and comes from literature and art and dreams, and especially from Homer. Here in his other world of mythology, imagination, visions, of supernatural strangeness, a world transcending the mortal condition of the human scene, he is in a sense again the poet of the *Eclogues*, of Orpheus and Eurydice in the *Georgics*; and perhaps here, where the worlds of reality and fancy meet, he is most truly himself.

3

The Pictures on Dido's Temple
(*Aeneid* I. 450–93)

R. D. WILLIAMS

Shortly after his arrival at Carthage, while he is waiting for Dido to meet him, Aeneas finds that the walls of her temple are adorned with pictures of the Trojan War. 'Sunt hic etiam sua praemia laudi,' he cries to Achates, 'sunt lacrimae rerum et mentem mortalia tangunt' ('Here too glory has its reward; here there are tears for things done and mortal affairs touch the heart'). The description of the pictures which follows is a remarkable example of Virgil's ability to use a traditional device (ἔκφρασις, 'description') in such a way as to strengthen and illuminate the main themes of his poem. It is my object here first to reinterpret one of the scenes which has been misunderstood, and then to discuss how Virgil has chosen and arranged his episodes so that the description of a picture gallery becomes a part of an epic poem.

The pictures which Virgil describes are these: first a general scene of battle with the Greeks in flight, then a similar scene with the Trojans in flight and Achilles pursuing; next, four particular episodes ending at a climax, Rhesus, Troilus, the supplication to Pallas, the ransoming of Hector's body; finally a pendant concerned with pictures of Aeneas himself, of Memnon, of Penthesilea. In the central series the episode of Troilus, which is not Homeric, seems strangely inserted among three very prominent episodes of the *Iliad*, and it has also presented difficulties of interpretation. It is therefore with this scene that we must begin.

I. *The Troilus Episode*

Parte alia fugiens amissis Troilus armis,
infelix puer atque impar congressus Achilli,
fertur equis curruque haeret resupinus inani,
lora tenens tamen; huic, cervixque comaeque trahuntur
per terram, et versa pulvis inscribitur hasta. (*Aen.* I. 474–8)

It is generally thought that this picture represents the outcome of an armed combat deliberately sought by Troilus, in the course of which Troilus *amisit arma* (whatever that means), and having in flight fallen from his chariot is being dragged along with his spear trailing behind him. Servius evidently felt unhappy about this: on *hasta* his comment is 'hostili scilicet'. He presumably thought that Troilus, *amissis armis*, could not still have his spear. Modern critics have rightly refused to accept that the spear is Achilles' spear with which Troilus is transfixed.[1] For there is nothing in the passage to suggest that it is Achilles' spear; and, as Heyne gently says, if Virgil had meant Achilles' spear, he would have expressed himself otherwise. In any case Achilles' spear could not be *versa*. Servius recognized this objection to his interpretation, and was prepared to take *versa* from *verrere*; but this makes no sense, and in Conway's words 'Vergil never sets his readers such a trap'. The decisive argument against Servius is *Aen.* 9. 609 f., the use of the 'reversed spear' as a goad, 'versaque iuvencum / terga fatigamus hasta'. If then it is Troilus' spear which trails, how do we overcome Servius' difficulty? Modern critics mostly do it by referring *armis* to his shield only: Heyne says *clipeo ex manu dimisso*, Wagner *clipeo, nam hastam tenebat*, Forbiger *de solo clypeo intelligendum*, Lejay 'ses armes défensives, son bouclier', Mackail 'his armour flung away in flight', Conway 'perhaps only the shield is meant . . . in that case his spear may have been still in his hand, not merely entangled in his fall'. This would be odd Latin, and a strange and unsatisfactory picture of armed combat.

But what reason is there in the Virgil passage to think of armed combat? The phrase *amissis armis* refers to some event which occurred before the moment of the picture; in the picture Troilus is portrayed without his *arma*. One of the natural meanings of the phrase would refer to defensive[2] armour (ὅπλα—shield, helmet, and greaves), and this seems to me strongly supported by the words 'huic cervixque comaeque trahuntur / per terram'. Troilus is not wearing a helmet,[3] and obviously

---

[1] Achilles does in fact kill Troilus with a spear in some versions of the story (Stat. *Silv.* 2. 6. 32 f., Eustath. on *Il.* 24. 257); the imitations of the passage (applied to other warriors) in Stat. *Theb.* 10. 544 f., Sil. 4. 254 f. have nothing decisive.

[2] Varro, *LL* 5. 115 *arma ab arcendo, quod his arcemus hostem*; other Roman grammarians differentiate between *arma* and *tela* (see *TLL*, s.v. *arma*). Of course the word very often means fighting equipment of all sorts, but we can fairly say that it is at least as likely to mean 'armour' as to mean 'weapons'.

[3] I should not press this point far if we were concerned with rapidly changing and eventful narrative; a poet who describes many related scenes in quick succession may not remember, or be concerned to remember, whether a warrior when last mentioned was wearing a helmet, or had two spears or one, or was accompanied by a charioteer or alone.

he has not lost it during armed combat with Achilles in a chariot. It seems that he was unarmed when he met Achilles. If this is accepted, we still have not the evidence to explain the cirumstances in which Troilus has lost his armour; we may make conjectures in the light of the legend, to which I now turn.

In Homer (*Il.* 24. 257) the sole mention of Troilus is when Priam laments that Ares has left him not one of his sons alive, not Mestor, not Troilus, not Hector. From Proclus' abstract of the *Cypria* we hear that it was Achilles who killed Troilus. In the tiny extant fragments of Sophocles' *Troilus* there is not much added, but there is an important reference to this play by the scholiast on Hom. *Il.* 24. 257. He says that in it Sophocles told of Troilus ambushed and killed by Achilles while exercising his horses at the Thymbraeum:[4] Σοφοκλῆς ἐν Τρωίλῳ φησὶν αὐτὸν λοχηθῆναι (emended from ὀχευθῆναι) ὑπὸ 'Αχιλλέως ἵππους γυμνάζοντα παρὰ τὸ Θυμβραῖον καὶ ἀποθανεῖν. This scene of ambush is frequently portrayed in Greek art.[5] The most common representation is of Troilus on horseback, unarmed, ambushed by Achilles in full armour when he had come to a spring to water his horses. He is often accompanied by Polyxena with a pitcher.[6] There are also fairly frequent representations in art of the next scene, when Troilus is carried to the altar of Apollo and there killed (so Lycophron, *Alex.* 307 f.).

There was then a very strong Greek tradition that Troilus was ambushed when unarmed, and it is evident that this was current in Virgil's time.[7] On the other hand, there is no trace before Virgil of the chariot of Troilus; it seems that Virgil may have adopted the idea of

But I do stress it very strongly in this case where Virgil is describing one single scene only, one picture whose visual impact is not blurred by actions leading up to it or away from it.

[4] See A. S. Pearson's Intro. to the fragments of Sophocles' *Troilus*, and Roscher and Pauly–Wissowa, s.v. *Troilos*. M. Mayer in Roscher regards Virgil's version as confused, but rightly denies that Virgil altered the legend so as to portray an armed comabt. A. Lesky in P.–W. argues that Virgil followed an already existing legend involving armed combat, but the evidence for this is very faint indeed compared with the unarmed tradition.

[5] See, apart from Roscher and P.–W., P. N. Ure, *JHS* 71 (1951), 198 f. (on the Troilus vase in Reading University) and L. Banti, *Stud. Etr.* 24 (1955–6), 143 f. (on the Etruscan paintings on the Tomba dei Tori).

[6] It is noticeable that the literary evidence always tells of Troilus ambushed while exercising his horses; it knows nothing of Polyxena and the spring, so frequent in art.

[7] The evidence from Roman art suggests it (see P.–W., *ad fin.*), though it is much less clear than the Greek evidence. It occurs too in Greek writers of the Roman period, Apollodorus (*Epit.* 3. 32) and Dio Chrysostom (11. 77–8). The latter specifically links the death of Troilus with the early period of the war, when the Greeks were not in possession of much of the Troad; for otherwise 'Troilus would never have ventured outside the walls for exercise'.

being dragged behind a chariot from the story of Hector.[8] There are remarkably few references to Troilus in extant Latin literature,[9] and by the time of Dares (fifth century?) the legend has changed very considerably. The episode is now put later than the death of Hector,[10] and in it Troilus is a formidable warrior who has deliberately sought armed combat, has wounded Achilles, and only been killed by him after his own horse had been wounded (not by Achilles) and he had become entangled in the reins (Dares 30 f., esp. 33). Virgil has evidently had some influence on the later version (as would be expected), but except from a misunderstanding of the passage there is nothing in Virgil to suggest deliberate armed combat,[11] and the legend of the warrior Troilus is essentially associated with the placing of the episode after the death of Hector, which is patently not the case in Virgil.

There are additional reasons for believing that Virgil follows the traditional story of the ambush, some important, some less so. It might be said that the absence of a charioteer for Troilus (*lora tenens tamen*) suggests that he did not deliberately go out to fight, but rather that he was driving his chariot for some unwarlike purpose and unluckily came upon Achilles; it might be said that *infelix puer* suggests not the rash youth trusting too much in his self-confidence, but rather the hapless victim. But the two really important points, as we shall see, are firstly that the death of Troilus was one of the fated 'dooms' of Troy and it would be wholly out of place for Troilus himself deliberately to jeopardize his country's safety; and secondly that the Troilus episode, put next to the story of Rhesus, indicates increasingly the ruthlessness of the Greek enemy—the warrior Rhesus slain in his sleep, the boy Troilus caught defenceless by Achilles. 'Accipe nunc Danaum insidias et crimine ab uno / disce omnes.'

We can then interpret the Virgilian passage as follows: at a stage prior

---

[8] Conceivably the Greek pictures of Troilus riding one horse and leading another alongside may have given Virgil the idea of a chariot-team.

[9] From the first century we may note Sen. *Ag.* 747 f. (an echo of Virgil) 'nimium cito / congresse Achilli Troile', Stat. *Silv.* 2. 6. 32 f. 'circum saevi fugientem moenia Phoebi / Troilon Haemoniae deprendit lancea dextrae', *Silv.* 5. 2. 121 f. 'Troilus haud aliter gyro breviore minantes / eludebat equos' (evidently an echo of Virgil's chariot).

[10] So in Ausonius (*Epit.* 18), in a passage full of Virgilian reminiscence: 'Hectore prostrato, nec dis nec viribus aequis / congressus saevo Troilus Aeacidae, / reptatus bigis, fratris coniungor honori.' Dictys (4. 9) also puts the event after the death of Hector; Quintus of Smyrna (4. 430 f.) implies deliberate armed combat. Servius (on 1. 474) has a variant on the erotic element in the story as told by Lycophron.

[11] Lesky in P.–W. thinks that the word *congressus* is significant, but it need mean no more than 'coming up against', 'meeting'.

to the scene actually pictured Troilus has been caught by Achilles while he was occupied in some activity during which he was not wearing his armour. We do not know what this was. We might guess that he came out in his armour to exercise his horses; thinking himself safe he took off his armour and was then ambushed by Achilles. At all events in the picture on the wall Troilus is without his armour, and thus defenceless is trying to get away, *fugiens amissis Troilus armis*. His horses are running away with him, like those of the charioteer in *Geo.* 1. 514 'fertur equis auriga nec audit currus habenas'. He has fallen out backwards from his chariot, perhaps wounded, perhaps because one of his horses has been wounded and cannot be controlled. But he still grasps the reins, still tries to regain control. He is not yet dead, as Servius and others have suggested; his skill is in horsemanship (ἱππιοχάρμης, Hom. *Il.* 24. 257), and at the last, in spite of all (*tamen*), he still hangs on. In this piece of the description Virgil is thinking partly perhaps of Soph. *El.* 746 f. and Eur. *Hipp.* 1236 f. (where the drivers are dragged behind their chariots), but especially of *Il.* 22. 401–3 (Hector's corpse, stripped of the armour, dragged behind Achilles' chariot)

> τοῦ δ᾽ ἦν ἑλκομένοιο κονίσαλος, ἀμφὶ δὲ χαῖται
> κυάνεαι πίτναντο, κάρη δ᾽ ἅπαν ἐν κονίῃσι
> κεῖτο πάρος χαρίεν.

And there was a cloud of dust as he was dragged, and his dark locks streamed out about him, and his whole head, so fair before, lay in the dust.

This is the source of Virgil's 'huic cervixque comaeque trahuntur / per terram'.

The final touch in the picture, the dust scored by the reversed spear, adds an idea of motion to the static picture by giving a sort of 'wake' to the movement of the chariot. There is now no contradiction between *hasta* and *amissis armis*, whether we consider that Troilus had just time to seize his spear as he leapt into his chariot to escape, or whether (as seems much more likely) he was already in his chariot carrying a spear which he was using reversed as a goad (like the Rutulians in *Aen.* 9. 609 f. quoted above; in Greek art the otherwise unarmed Troilus is sometimes shown carrying a spear or a goad). As he fled he had the spear in one hand while he held the reins in the other (having no shield to occupy the use of one hand). When he fell backwards the spear, still held in his hand, trailed with the *point* on the ground. This is the only legitimate meaning here of *versa hasta*, which is sometimes wrongly taken to indicate that the dust was scored with the butt-end of the spear.

The normal position of a spear is pointing forwards, in the direction of motion; when it is *versa* it has the butt-end forward, and therefore when it trails it scores the dust with its point. The unwarlike intentions and utter helplessness of Troilus are thus symbolized in this final phrase.

II. *Virgil's Selection and Arrangement of the Episodes*

This series of pictures on Dido's temple is the first sustained account in the *Aeneid* of events in the Trojan War, the final stages of which are soon to be so powerfully described in *Aeneid* 2. The setting of the passage is made very emphatic by the stress laid on the profound effect which the pictures have on Aeneas (lines 450–65), and the description itself is integral with the main theme of the poem because of its subject-matter and because of the relationship of the pictures to one another. In this respect it is comparable with the description of Aeneas' shield at the end of Book 8, and quite different from a simple decorative *ἔκφρασις* like the pictures of Ganymede on the cloak in *Aen.* 5. 252 f.

It has often been noticed that the pictures are in pairs: (i) the Greeks flee, the Trojans flee; (ii) death of Rhesus, death of Troilus; (iii) supplication of the Trojan women, supplication of Priam; (iv) Memnon's Eastern armies, Penthesilea's Amazons. Again, we can observe contrasts, between war scenes and scenes of supplication, between general war scenes and particular war scenes. We can see that Homeric episodes are models for the Rhesus scene and the two supplication scenes, and that all the incidents selected for portrayal have a vivid pictorial impact. But all these aspects of choice and arrangement are subordinate to the main purpose, which is the relationship of the pictures to the motifs of the poem.

The passage begins (466) with general scenes of warfare, showing first the Trojans dominant and then the Greeks, with the threatening figure of Achilles prominent. Then follow the four scenes of the central block, leading to the climax expressed at 485 (*tum vero ingentem gemitum . . .*), and the description is concluded with three pictures of less intense emotional significance.[12]

The central block is conceived as a portrayal of the *fata Troiana*, the series of divine omens, portents, and prophecies associated with the doom of the city. Running alongside this theme is the theme of Greek ruthlessness, the *perfidia* and *crudelitas* of the enemy as seen by Aeneas

[12] The emotional structure and intensity of the passage has been well discussed by Th. Plüss, *JKPh* (1875), 639–42.

and described with such force in *Aeneid* 2. Let us look at the four episodes in the light of this double motif, *fata Troiana* and Greek cruelty. The death of Rhesus illustrates how Greek ruthlessness prevented the salvation of Troy. If the horses of Rhesus had cropped the grass of Troy and drunk from the river Xanthus (which they so nearly did but for the night ambush of Diomedes and Ulysses) then it was fated that Troy would not fall, and the sovereign city of Asia would still have been standing. This well-known aspect of the story of Rhesus is made explicit in lines 472–3 'prius quam / pabula gustassent Troiae Xanthumque bibissent'. Equally explicit is the cruelty of the slaughter of sleeping men (470–1) 'primo quae prodita somno / Tydides multa vastabat caede cruentus'.

The death of Troilus (not, as we have seen, an obvious subject to include) illustrates the same two themes. The story was that if Troilus lived to the age of twenty Troy could not be taken (*Myth. Vatic.* 1. 210 'Troilo dictum erat quod si ad annos xx pervenisset Troia everti non potuisset'). Virgil does not make the oracular connection of Troilus' fate explicit, but as he had done this with Rhesus he could expect the reader to be ready to do the same with Troilus. The story seems to have been well known, for in Plautus' *Bacchides* (in a passage probably based on Menander's Δὶς ἐξαπατῶν) it is mentioned as one of the three 'dooms' of Troy (953 f. 'Ilio tria fuisse audivi fata, quae illi forent exitio . . .'). The cruelty of Achilles' behaviour in killing his unarmed victim is reinforced by Virgil's comment 'infelix puer atque impar congressus Achilli', and by the sorrow in the lines which follow, so typical of Virgil's sorrow over youthful death; the incident therefore portrays a worse example of cruelty than the death of Rhesus.

After the two human illustrations of the doom of Troy there follows the divine embodiment of this doom, the hostile Pallas Athena, the champion of the Greeks.[13] The hopelessness of the Trojan supplication is made evident, and the cruelty of the goddess is shown in her epithet (*non aequae*) and in the unmoved enmity of the cold and terrifying line 'diva solo fixos oculos aversa tenebat'.

These three pictures then are the fates, the causes, the themes; and there follows the event, the death of Hector and the final certainty of the doom of Troy. It comes with an impact of inevitability; the actual death and ignominious treatment of the body have already occurred (the

[13] It is possible that a mental association can here be made with the loss of the *Palladium* (*Aen.* 2. 166), another of the three 'dooms' of Troy mentioned in the passage from Plautus cited above.

pluperfect tense is used), and the picture shows one aspect of the consequence, the sale of the body for gold. In two ways Virgil departs from the Homeric version, in order to emphasize the cruelty of Achilles: in Homer Hector was dragged around the tomb of Patroclus, but Virgil adopts the later and even more disgraceful version that he was dragged around the walls of his own now helpless town. Again, in *Iliad* 24 Achilles shows himself human before Priam; here he is coldly inhuman—*auro corpus vendebat.* This scene is the climax of Greek cruelty as well as of Trojan doom.

Virgil emphasizes this climax with the words *tum vero ingentem gemitum* . . ., and concludes it with the person of the old king Priam; it is a climax already foreshadowed for us by the mention of Priam in lines 458 and 461. The story of Troy's doom culminates here in the pictures, as it had in the *Iliad.*

As the central block had its introduction, both in the summary description of 456–8 and in Aeneas' few words in 459 f., so now it has its pendant telling of other pictures which illustrate events after the death of Hector. If we ask why the description does not end at its climax, we shall find much of the answer by relating the descriptive episode to the narrative technique of the poem. The tension has to be lessened for the transition to Dido's appearance. We must be brought away from the heart of Troy's tragedy, symbolized in Hector and Priam, by a diminuendo effect, still relevant but less intense. This is done by the three scenes of later events in the war. First is Aeneas himself, fighting in the forefront among the Greek leaders as had been prophesied (*Il.* 20. 332 f.), and as it was appropriate that he should when Hector was dead (*Il.* 5. 467 f.). This brief mention of Aeneas himself prepares us for Dido's *Tune ille Aeneas...?* (617), and also serves a psychological purpose, as we shall see. Then there come two heroes of the post-Iliad period of the war, who did not fight at Troy until after the death of Hector, with whom Quintus of Smyrna began his *Posthomerica.* They are both exotic and romantic figures, but neither of them causes the emotional reaction in Aeneas which had been caused by the four scenes of the central block. They bring the description to a close with a kind of half-unreal splendour, Memnon the strange king of distant lands, and Penthesilea, the semi-mythical Amazon warrior. We are reminded of how Virgil ends the catalogue in *Aeneid* 7 with the warrior-maid Camilla.

Finally, we should consider the relationship in this passage between art and literature, between the pictures and the poem in which they are described. Virgil does not give us a catalogue or a series of photographs of these mural paintings, but an impression of their effect on Aeneas; much of the unity of the themes which I have been discussing is a unity imposed by the observer (Aeneas) upon the series of the pictures. We are left with the feeling that Aeneas is recollecting it afterwards; that the pictures are coming to us through the mind of the beholder, coloured and interpreted by his own emotions. This effect is strengthened by the constant mention of Aeneas: he is very prominent in our minds before the beginning of the description, he is mentioned at the beginning (*namque videbat uti*...), then at 470 (*agnoscit lacrimans*), and then at the climax (*tum vero ingentem gemitum*...). This is immediately followed by the picture of Aeneas himself among these events—'quaeque ipse miserrima vidi / et quorum pars magna fui'; he himself is placed here in the series immediately after the climax to reinforce the subjective element in the interpretation of the tragic pictures, and to detach the diminuendo ending of Memnon and Penthesilea, who were not so closely connected with Aeneas personally. We notice too a subtle interrelationship of time and space: Aeneas is walking past the pictures—*ex ordine* (456), *nec procul hinc* (469), *parte alia* (474), yet the word *interea* (479) suddenly transforms the pictures into events, and three times we hear of aspects of events which are not portrayed in the pictures, indicated by different tense usage: *vastabat... avertit* (471–2), *amissis armis* (474), *raptaverat... vendebat* (483–4). The ἔκφρασις has been made real by the personal interpretation of the pictures; it is a story as well as an art gallery.

4

Divine Action in *Aeneid* Book Two

E. L. HARRISON

In his employment of divine intervention in the second book of the *Aeneid* Virgil is in general guided by the *Iliad* and by the battle-order which the Homeric poet, almost as if to make amends for its lateness, suddenly gives twice over in the twentieth book.[1] An Olympian theomachy of the Homeric type in the *Aeneid* is inconceivable,[2] and would in any case be pointless, since this is Troy's last hour and the pro-Trojan deities have naturally withdrawn. But the city's old Homeric enemies, Neptune, Juno, and Minerva, are in at the kill (608 ff.), and they are joined by Jupiter himself (617 f.), which accords with Zeus' promise in the *Iliad* that once Hector fell he would support the Greeks in their final onslaught (15. 69 ff.).[3] And Virgil's brilliant innovation whereby the flames of the blazing city provide a backcloth to the action from the very start of the Greek assault,[4] as against the usual tradition that the Greeks (much more practically) set fire to the city only as they withdrew,[5] may also derive ultimately from his employment of the Iliadic scheme: for the anti-Trojan fire-god who displayed such violence in the Homeric theomachy (*Il.* 21. 342–82) was surely not to be excluded at such a time as this. Thus the very first glimpse Aeneas gets of Troy's agony reveals Vulcan at work destroying the house of Deiphobus and Ucalegon (310 ff.). Now the placing of the god's name at such a

---

[1] *Il.* 20. 33 ff. and 67 ff. H. Fränkel, *Noten zu den Argonautika des Apollonius* (Munich, 1968), pp. 24 f., shows that such postponement of important information is characteristic of Apollonius' sophisticated style. But it is certainly not lacking in Homer: in addition to the above example, note how the general plan of the *Iliad* does not emerge clearly until Zeus' pronouncement at 13. 437 ff., and how the enmity of Poseidon towards Troy is not explained till 21. 434 f., that of Hera and Athene not till 24. 25 f.

[2] The theomachy on the shield of Aeneas (*Aen.* 8. 698 f.), where the Olympians unite to overthrow the monstrous deities of the oriental opposition, is of course very different.

[3] R. Allain, 'Le Merveilleux dans un épisode crucial de l'Énéide', *LEC* 17 (1949), misses this connection (326), and sees Jupiter's intervention in *Aen.* 2 as essentially Stoic in conception (328).

[4] R. Heinze, *Virgils epische Technik* (Leipzig, 1915), p. 28, took this to be a Hellenistic invention: but see R. G. Austin, *P. Vergili Maronis Liber Secundus* (Oxford, 1964), p. xiii, and commentary ad 2. 289 for its probable originality.

[5] Cf. e.g. Apollod. *Ep.* 5. 23; Eur. *Tr.* 1260.

significant point in the action, combined as it is with the verb *superante* (311), suggests that what we have here is something more than a mere dead usage: but a striking feature of what follows seems to have been overlooked. For subsequently, in spite of constant references to the holocaust,[6] Virgil avoids using the god's name again in this context, nor does he include Vulcan among 'the powers hostile to Troy' revealed later by Venus to Aeneas (608 ff.). The poet, I would suggest, was conscious of the dramatic inconsistency any emphasis of Vulcan's role in Troy's fall might expose: for although at this point in the poem he wished to employ the anti-Trojan fire-god of the *Iliad*, who was the husband of Charis, and had no association with the pro-Trojan Aphrodite (*Il.* 18. 382 ff.), he also wished to make a pro-Trojan deity of him elsewhere, drawing on the later tradition according to which the fire-god was Aphrodite's husband (*Aen.* 8. 370 ff., cf. *Od.* 8. 266 ff.). Here, then, it suited his purpose to make a single prominent reference to Vulcan's activity at the start, and leave it at that.

The high point of Virgil's use of the *Iliad* as guide in Book 2, however, is reached after Aeneas has witnessed from the palace-roof the death of Priam at the hands of Neoptolemus (550 ff.). Venus' sudden appearance in order to restrain his uncontrolled frenzy (cf. 594 f.) and prompt him to more rational action (596 ff.) recalls the celebrated passage in the *Iliad* where Athene intervenes in a similar fashion to check Achilles during his angry confrontation with Agamemnon (*Il.* 1. 193 ff.).[7] Moreover, the *Iliad* provides the poet with a device that proves crucial at this point. For Book 2 is, of course, spoken by Aeneas: and epic heroes, unlike epic poets,[8] normally lack the ability to recognize gods and their activities.[9] But just as Homer's Athene gives Diomede a special clarity of vision which enables him to identify individual deities as they intervene in the action on the battlefield (*Il.* 5. 129 f.), so now Venus, through Virgil's simple but brilliantly effective exploitation of the same device, provides

---

[6] 289, 311, 327, 329, 337, 353, 374, 431, 505, 566, 600, 632, 664, 705, 758, 764. Cf. Heinze, op. cit. 27 f.

[7] On the vexed question of the Helen episode (567–88) see the article of Goold, repr. in this collection (Ch. 5).

[8] *Aen.* 12. 318 ff., where Virgil confesses ignorance as to whether or not a god was responsible for the wounding of Aeneas, is an odd departure from the principle of the omniscient epic poet.

[9] Hence the sanctity of a stranger, who might prove to be a god in disguise (cf. *Od.* 17. 483 ff.). Hence also some of the discrepancies between what an epic hero says and what the poet tells us. Virgil, for example, reveals that a god is responsible for Palinurus' fall into the sea (*Aen.* 5. 854 ff.), but Palinurus himself in all innocence denies that this is the case (6. 347).

Aeneas and the reader with the great apocalypse which forms the
unforgettable climax of the book. For she removes the mist obscuring
Aeneas' mortal vision, and:

> apparent dirae facies inimicaque Troiae
> numina magna deum. (622–3)

Elsewhere, it should be added, the poet is able to supplement his
employment of this device by letting Aeneas refer to shrines and
temples: for the hero can, of course, readily identify these, and they can
be used to convey, in different ways, the notion of a god's activity. Thus,
when the two serpents which have devoured Laocoon and his sons
disappear into the shrine of Minerva (225 f.), the obvious implication is
that she is the deity responsible for Laocoon's punishment.[10] So, too,
the general hostility of Minerva and Juno is vividly symbolized in a
similar manner in the action which follows. For it is at Minerva's
temple[11] that disaster suddenly strikes when the Trojans actually seem,
for one fleeting moment, to have turned the tide (396 ff. and 402 ff.).
And it is highly appropriate that the very last vignette Virgil gives us of
Troia ruens (761 ff.) reveals Greek chieftains on guard over the booty and
prisoners they have assembled in the shrine of the city's most implacable
enemy, Juno.

If we bear in mind how the influence of the *Iliad* permeates this book,
and especially the Venus episode, it may help us with a textual problem.
Immediately after that episode, in obedience to the promptings of
Venus, Aeneas descends from the palace-roof and extricates himself
from the destruction and chaos all around him *ducente deo* (632). The
phrase we surely expect here, one which has naturally found its way into
the tradition, but is less well attested,[12] is *ducente dea*. After all, Venus has
just promised Aeneas her unfailing guidance (620), and the hero has
himself already told Dido he left Troy *matre dea monstrante uiam* (1.
382). Why, then, this sudden switch to the masculine form? The answer,
I take it, is that once Aeneas follows Venus' advice (597 ff.) and makes
the first move towards rescuing his family, he qualifies for a new kind of
divine guidance which will henceforward manifest itself with increasing
frequency. The use of *deus* to indicate its source, while appropriately
vague in the mouth of a hero who lacks the more precise knowledge of
the poet, is at the same time suitably ambiguous, since the term regularly

---

[10] Cf. K. Quinn, *Virgil's Aeneid* (London, 1968), p. 117.
[11] G. Lieberg, *A & R* 11 (1966), 153, overlooks Minerva's importance in this context.
[12] See Austin *ad* 632.

proves to be synonymous with Jupiter.[13] And as we shall see later, Jupiter's involvement in the rescue will soon become explicit when the Trojan withdrawal seems gravely threatened, and the guidance is transferred, in more drastic form, to Anchises.[14] Meanwhile, however, the sudden emergence of what proves to be Jupiter's guidance of Aeneas at this point brings us back to consideration of the *Iliad*, where we find that Zeus' position is entirely in harmony with the above arrangement. For although (as we saw) Zeus reveals his intention there of eventually switching his allegiance to the Greeks (15. 69 ff.), it is clear from another crucial episode that Aeneas is to be singled out from the rest of the Trojans for special treatment when that time comes. In the passage concerned (20. 300 ff.) Aeneas is about to succumb to Achilles when Poseidon (who is, of course, anti-Trojan) explains to Hera why he proposes to rescue a Trojan leader: it is Zeus' intention that Aeneas shall emerge unscathed from Troy in order to preserve the stock of his favourite son by a mortal, Dardanus.[15] And Aeneas will live on to establish a kingship over those Trojans who survive the fall.[16] At *Aen.* 2. 632 ff., then, the moment has arrived for that prophecy to begin finding its fulfilment: and Jupiter's guidance is at hand to ensure that it does.

In the introduction to his edition of Book 2 Austin found an unacceptable clash between the previous 'apocalypse of devils' and Aeneas blandly going forward in faithful obedience to divine guidance a few moments later:[17] and he concluded that the whole Venus scene must be regarded as an afterthought.[18] But we are surely *meant* to feel a jolt at this great turning-point: and far from being an afterthought, the Venus scene is so organic a part of the book, and plays so crucial a role in the action,[19] that it must have figured in Virgil's drafting at a very early stage. Elsewhere, indeed, Austin himself sees Venus' apocalypse not as an alien element superimposed on the rest, but as the climax of a mounting

[13] For the close association of *deus* (and *dei*) with Jupiter, see C. Bailey, *Religion in Virgil* (Oxford, 1955), p. 231; B. Grassmann-Fischer, *Die Prodigien in Vergils Aeneis* (Munich, 1966), p. 19 n. 66.

[14] Cf. 2. 679 f.

[15] For the historical background to this prophecy, see F. Jacoby, *Hermes* 68 (1933), 42–4; G. L. Huxley, *Greek Epic Poetry* (London, 1969), p. 131.

[16] That Virgil had this prophecy in mind when he composed the *Aeneid* is clear from 3. 97 ff., where he produces his own version of it, suitably expanded in scope, and transferred, as we might have expected, from Poseidon to Apollo.

[17] Op. cit., p. xxi.

[18] Ibid. Elsewhere (p. xii) Austin cites the presence of two half-lines in the Venus-scene as an indication of its lateness: but there is no necessary connection between incompleteness and order of composition.

[19] Allain, op. cit. 334, describes the scene as 'un véritable pivot spirituel de l'Énéide'.

indictment (p. xx). And if we refer to Brooks Otis's general analysis,[20] in which he stresses the presence of so many corresponding elements in the book's two antiphonal sections (13–267 and 634–729), it seems reasonable to conclude that the Venus scene as a whole acts as a counterpoise to the sinister influence of Minerva in the opening section. Nor does Austin's view that the apocalypse is the product of a sudden outburst of pessimism towards the end of the poet's life seem acceptable.[21] All we have here, surely, is that vacillation between despair and hope which is a constantly recurring feature of the *Aeneid*.[22] For Virgil's readers, no less than for Aeneas, it is a question of striking a balance: the fall of Troy, and all the misery that brings, must be weighed against the emergence from its ashes of a new and greater Troy.[23] Venus knows this already:[24] Aeneas will gradually come to know it. At this point in the action the goddess confronts her son with the naked cruelty of the *fata Troiana*: but one day she will present him with a very different picture. She will hand over to him the magic shield forged by Vulcan, and Aeneas will rejoice at the glorious *fata Romana* depicted on it (8. 615 ff., 729 ff.).

In the meantime, however, the Venus passage marks the beginning of Aeneas' progress to a new kind of heroism.[25] Previously in the action at Troy he has been at the mercy of a series of impulses—an irrational turmoil of anger, courage, recklessness, and sheer frenzy. The call to a more responsible code, in accordance with which he should put the preservation of the Trojan stock and Troy's gods before all else, has failed to find any response, even though it was made at two levels—on the divine[26] by Hector's ghost (2. 289 ff.), and on the human level by Apollo's priest, Panthus (318 ff.).[27] But now Venus comes to make a fresh appeal: and, as gods in ancient epic so often do, she supplements spontaneous feelings which have already begun to stir (559 ff.). Indeed,

[20] Brooks Otis, *Virgil: A Study in Civilized Poetry* (Oxford, 1964), pp. 246 f. H. L. Tracy makes a similar antithetical analysis on the basis of the conduct and moods of the opposing sides in 'The Pattern of Vergil's *Aeneid* 1–6', *Phoenix* 4 (1950), 2.

[21] Op. cit., p. xxi.

[22] Cf. J. Perret, 'Optimisme et tragédie dans l'*Énéide*', *REL* 45 (1967), 342–62.

[23] Cf. Quinn, op. cit. 120; V. Buchheit, *Vergil über die Sendung Roms* (Heidelberg, 1963), p. 107 n. 437.

[24] 1. 239: *fatis contraria fata rependens*.

[25] Otis, op. cit. 243 f.

[26] On the supernatural status of the Roman, as opposed to the Greek, ghost, see H. R. Steiner, *Der Traum in der Aeneis* (Berne, 1952), pp. 98 f.

[27] The significance of Panthus in this context rests not so much on his words (234 ff.), which are so full of despair, as on the fact that he bears the *sacra*, just commended to Aeneas' protection by Hector's ghost (293).

her removal of the mist which has hitherto obscured Aeneas' vision of the gods (604 ff.) itself symbolizes the disappearance of the frenzy which up to now has stifled his more rational impulses.[28] Venus' appeal, it is true, unlike Hector's, is narrowly based: she begs her son simply to be mindful of his family (596 ff.).[29] But that is precisely why she succeeds where Hector failed. For Aeneas, who does not yet grasp the significance of his mission, will achieve a new kind of heroic stature only gradually and through experience. Through his *pietas* towards his family, and towards Anchises in particular, he will come to understand what *pietas* means for him as the guarantor of the future Roman world.[30]

If the *Iliad* supplies the key for an understanding of Book 2's divine action in general, to understand the important role in the opening section of Minerva in particular we need to consider briefly Virgil's handling of material drawn from later sources. In the tradition there were four principal themes, which originally were distinct from each other: and although there may have been some interplay between them before Virgil,[31] it seems clear that he was the first to bring them together so that they formed a composite whole. These themes were: (1) the stealing of the Palladium by Odysseus and Diomede (Servius *ad* 166); (2) Apollo's punishment of his priest, Laocoon, for unpriestly conduct (Servius *ad* 201); (3) the entry into Troy of the Wooden Horse, made by Epeius with the help of Athene (*Od.* 8. 492 ff.; *Ilias parua*, OCT Homer vol. v, p. 107); (4) the entry into Troy of the disguised Sinon and his raising of the fire-signal (*Iliu persis*, OCT Homer vol. v, p. 107). Virgil's method of bringing unity to these various elements was to make the theme of the Wooden Horse central, and to impart a direct bearing on this main theme to each of the rest. Thus Sinon's role now is no longer to give a warning signal to the Greeks (Helen does that: cf. 6. 518 f.) but to ensure the entry of the Horse into Troy, and to open it up when he

---

[28] Cf. Allain, op. cit. 332; B. Fenik, *AJPh* 80 (1959), 7 f.; M. C. J. Putnam, *The Poetry of the Aeneid* (Cambridge, Mass., 1965), p. 29.

[29] There is a tendency to extend Venus' immediate contribution further than it goes: cf. G. K. Galinsky, *Aeneas, Sicily, and Rome* (Princeton, 1969), pp. 20 f., where she is said to remind Aeneas of 'the greater responsibility to his family and the survival of the Trojan race'. Cf. also Allain, art. cit. 331 f.; J. B. Garstang, *CJ* 57 (1962), 343. But all Venus does for Aeneas is 'emphasize his absolute impotence, his inability to do anything but go home' (Brooks Otis, *Gnomon* 41 (1969), 599). As far as divine action is concerned, the rest lies with Jupiter.

[30] Cf. Otis, *Virgil*, p. 250.

[31] Cf. F. Klingner, *Virgil* (Zurich, 1967), p. 412. In this context Heinze, op. cit. 7 f., influenced by his views on Quintus Smyrnaeus and Tryphiodorus, tends to underestimate the probable extent of Virgil's originality.

himself receives the signal to do so from the Greeks as they return
unexpectedly by sea (2. 57 ff., 250 ff.) Similarly, the theft of the
Palladium does service now in Sinon's argument to get the Horse
accepted, forming a crucial element in the rigmarole which so successfully hoodwinks the Trojans (162 ff.). But it is to the Laocoon story that
this process of fusion imparts the most significant changes: for since the
Horse is now the focus of interest, Laocoon's sin and punishment, like
everything else in this section, have to be given direct reference to it.
Laocoon therefore is no longer a priest of Apollo, committing a sin
against his patron deity and paying the penalty in isolation. Instead he is
now a prominent Trojan who not only opposes the entry of the Horse,
but also desecrates its sanctity with his spear (40 ff.). And his resultant
death speeds the entry of the Horse into the city (199 ff.).

Virgil's handling of Laocoon is worth further consideration, both for
the different levels at which his death can be interpreted, and for the
typical inventiveness behind the development of his role.

Laocoon's death can be considered at three different levels. (1) For
the reader following the story it is a simple enough matter. Minerva has
clearly punished Laocoon for desecrating the Horse with whose creation she was closely associated (*Aen.* 2. 15 f., cf. *Od.* 8. 493), her
concern for its welfare matching that of Apollonius' Athene for the
welfare of the *Argo*. The destination of the serpents after they have
fulfilled their grisly mission confirms this obvious inference (225 ff.). (2)
For the Trojan bystanders the issue is not so simple. They also rightly[32]
conclude that Laocoon has been punished for desecrating the Horse,
but do so on a quite different and erroneous basis. For Virgil lets Sinon
radically alter the nature of Minerva's association with the Horse in his
lying account, so that now it becomes a gift to the goddess, offered by the
Greeks in order to atone for the desecration of the Palladium by
Odysseus and Diomede (183 f.).[33] Thus when Laocoon is punished,
and Minerva's association with the Horse is thus clearly confirmed, the
Trojans naturally interpret that association in the sense given to it by

---

[32] K. Büchner, *RE* 8A (1958), 1349, and Austin, op. cit. 94, both imply that there is no
real connection between Laocoon's spear-throwing and his death, and that the notion of
his punishment by Minerva is simply an erroneous inference on the part of the Trojan
bystanders. But the latter are surely correct about the source of the punishment: where
they go astray is simply in interpreting the punishment in Sinon's terms.

[33] Virgil dissociates his Trojans from this failed talisman in the *Aeneid*: but the reverse-
type of a *denarius* of Julius Caesar on which Aeneas is shown carrying his father and the
Palladium out of Troy indicates that the poet's version was by no means canonical. (For a
fine reproduction, cf. Galinsky, op. cit., Fig. 2a.)

Sinon: and equally naturally they go on to accept the rest of his story, too—including the promise that if they take the Horse into Troy ultimate victory over the Greeks will thereby be assured (192 ff.). (3) Finally, for the reader taking a broader view of the events at Troy, and for Aeneas himself as he now looks back on them, the destruction of Laocoon and his sons by the serpents assumes all the marks of a familiar phenomenon: a neglected prodigy foreshadowing a great catastrophe, as they so often do in the pages of Roman history.[34]

With regard to the development of Laocoon's role, it was inevitable from the start, no doubt, that he should lose his connection with Apollo. This deity, whose prophetic activity is to be so closely associated with the Roman future in the rest of the epic, and especially in the following book, and who will emerge later as champion of the *gens Iulia* and the Augustan regime,[35] was surely not to be associated in any way with Troy's fall, or with the grim tale of the death of one of his priests. At the same time, however, Virgil saw an opportunity to fill the gap thus created with an Apolline priest of his own, and introduced Panthus, whose association with Apollo, if not his actual priesthood, derives from the *Iliad*.[36] And Panthus plays the kind of role we would expect a priest of Apollo to play in the *Aeneid*, passing on to Aeneas the *sacra* that are to become in due course the central symbol of Troy's renewal (318 ff.).

In Virgil's working out of the story, then, Laocoon is no longer a priest of Apollo, but makes his first appearance simply as a prominent Trojan (cf. 40: *magna comitante caterua*) whose sudden arrival and vigorous intervention in the discussion about the Horse break in on the scene with powerful dramatic effect. The climax of this phase of the action comes when Laocoon hurls his spear at the Horse (50 ff.): and for this violation of an object whose construction was under the sponsorship of Minerva he will in due course be punished. But only in due course: for Virgil at this point introduces a second and more surprising intervention, this time by Sinon (57 ff.), and holds up the actual destruction of

---

[34] Cf. H. Kleinknecht, 'Laokoon', *Hermes* 79 (1944), 66–111; Quinn, op. cit. 118; Büchner, op. cit. 1350. Büchner stresses the prodigy aspect to the exclusion of the punishment motif, but the complexity of the event's significance is typical of Virgil, and such a position is too rigid. Klinger (op. cit. 413 f.) suggests that in this retrospective role as prodigy we see part of the earlier tradition breaking through. (Cf. *Iliupersis*, OCT Homer vol. v, p. 107: τῷ τέρατι δυσφορησάντες ('being vexed at the portent'). According to the rest of that tradition Aeneas and his followers withdrew to Mt Ida immediately after Laocoon's death.)   [35] Cf. *Aen.* 9. 638 f., 8. 704 f.

[36] At *Il.* 5. 9 ff. Hephaestus rescues a son of Dares because Dares is his priest. Thus when Apollo rescues one son of Panthus (15. 524 f.), and ensures the protection of the corpse of another (17. 70 ff.), the inference that Panthus is his priest seems clear enough.

Laocoon and his two sons until this Greek agent has reached the end of his protracted and deceitful tale (199 ff.). Thus when Minerva's snakes arrive at last to exact her revenge on Laocoon, this third and most dramatic intervention of all seems finally to confirm Sinon's story, and imparts to the action an impetus which culminates in the admission of the Horse into Troy (234 ff.).

Such an arrangement, however, presented Virgil with a problem: what was he to do with Laocoon during Sinon's drawn-out story? He could not let him stand his ground and challenge the Greek's account, for although Sinon's tissue of lies is splendid rhetoric, it prevails as such only because it is never exposed to the slightest sceptical probing. Nor, on the other hand, could he expect the reader to accept that a man of Laocoon's strong and impetuous character would stand silently by while Sinon proceeded to beguile his fellow-countrymen without a challenge. Virgil's solution was in fact simple, and no doubt Laocoon's original role as Apollo's priest pointed the way. For at the end of Sinon's account, when the information becomes relevant, the reader is told that Laocoon has in the meantime been busy elsewhere, sacrificing to Neptune, having been previously selected by lot to be his priest (201 ff.). Such sacrifice at this juncture is entirely appropriate, since the assumption is that the enemy fleet is now at the mercy of the sea-god: and Laocoon's new appointment is also reasonable, since the altar of the god by the sea-shore, together with the priesthood associated with it, would naturally have been abandoned during the presence near by of the Greeks.[37] Moreover, with such an arrangement Virgil is able to produce an effectively ironical reversal, whereby the sacrificing priest suddenly finds himself to be a victim.[38]

Since *Aeneid* 2 is concerned above all with Troy's fall, so far this account has naturally concentrated on aspects of the divine activity behind that fall. But even before Aeneas wakes during Troy's last night, Jupiter's promotion of a plan for a future to be centred on him is already implicit in the appearance of Hector's ghost to the sleeping hero, warning him that Troy is doomed, and commissioning him to establish a

---

[37] Cf. Heinze, op. cit. 17 ff.

[38] It is striking how often in Book 2 death seems to have sacrificial undertones. Not only does Laocoon die at an altar in the act of sacrificing, but even the simile introduced to illustrate his cries (223 f.) keeps within the same framework of reference. The very first Trojan casualty we hear of, Coroebus, *diuae armipotentis ad aram procumbit* (424–5); and the last, king Priam himself, is slaughtered by Neoptolemus at the palace's central altar, which is already drenched with the blood of his son, Polites (550–3). And before all this the motif of human sacrifice forms the ominous basis of Sinon's lying tale (108 ff.).

new home for its gods in a great city he is to found overseas (289 ff.). Hector's is the first in a series of ghosts which will appear to Aeneas in the first half of the epic: and in view of the dire urgency of the situation it is not surprising that this opening message concentrates on essentials and lacks any reference to the authority behind it. But later in Book 2 (776 ff.), when the dead Creusa makes her appearance, she quickly cites the authority of *superi regnator Olympi* (779) before clarifying Hector's message with both geographical and personal detail (780 ff.). And finally, although other ghosts communicate with Aeneas later, it is that of Anchises which puts it beyond doubt that any prophetic guidance such ghostly visitations provide comes from Jupiter himself. For in Sicily, when Aeneas is actually thinking of abandoning his mission after the women in the party have burnt four of the ships, Anchises' ghost appears to him in his sleep (like Hector's) and summons him to the Underworld to learn of his destiny: and the ghost's message opens with the words 'imperio Iouis huc uenio' (5. 726). Hence, indeed, the complaint made to Jupiter by Venus in the divine assembly held later in the epic, that on the one hand the Trojans have obeyed a series of oracles conveyed to them by deities and ghosts, yet on the other Jupiter has in effect made a mockery of such obedience by allowing his order to be subverted by Juno (10. 33 ff.). As for the plan behind those orders, we should remember here Venus' vital contribution to its formation. Although, as we saw earlier, her perspective in Book 2 seems narrow in its scope, we gather from what she says to Jupiter in Book 1 (234 ff.), and from Jupiter's words to Mercury in Book 4 (227 ff.), that before Troy fell she secured from her father the consoling promise that there would spring from Aeneas and his band of survivors the future Roman race, destined one day to rule the world: while for her part Venus assured Jupiter that her son would prove equal to the task of laying the foundation for this great destiny. The dialogue implied in these two passages would perhaps have provided a suitable divine prologue to Book 2, but, as we noted earlier, Olympian activity of this kind was, of course, beyond the ken of the narrating Aeneas.

Since Jupiter's plan involved the mixing of Trojan and Italian blood in order to establish a new race (7. 98 ff., 12. 835 ff.), with Aeneas marrying the king's daughter after reaching Latium (2. 783 ff.), Virgil naturally followed the tradition according to which Creusa did not quit Troy with the other survivors, but vanished during the turmoil of the sack.[39] But

---

[39] Naevius, on the other hand, depicts the wives of both Anchises and Aeneas as tearfully withdrawing from Troy in the night (*Bellum Punicum* fr. 4, Morel).

instead of leaving it at that, he saw here an opportunity to introduce into
the action of the *Aeneid* (and, indeed, it would appear, for the first time
into the Aeneas legend) the Asiatic mountain goddess, Cybele, known
more familiarly by her title Magna Mater: for now Creusa is not simply
lost in the débâcle, but is detained in a mysterious afterlife of service to
this *magna deum genetrix* (788). Unlike Aeneas and his followers, this
goddess had played a real part in Rome's earlier history, when her image
was solemnly escorted from Asia to Rome towards the end of the
Hannibalic War (204 BC), in a move which no doubt stemmed both from
a desire to boost morale after fourteen years of Hannibal's unwelcome
presence in Italy, and from Rome's developing interest in Asia: and in
191 BC a temple was finally dedicated to her on the Palatine. By Virgil's
day the festival called after her Greek name, the Megalesia, was one of
the most important in the Roman calendar, but the goddess's orgiastic
cult, and the effeminate Asiatic priests to whom responsibility for its
maintenance was rigidly confined, remained embarrassingly alien to
their Roman environment. Even so, Cybele was closely associated with
the Troad, and therefore, by implication, with Aeneas and his supposed
descendants, the *gens Iulia*. Hence Augustus included her temple
(which was close to his own house) in his restoration programme,[40] and
had himself depicted on the celebrated *gemma Augustea* being crowned
by her with a laurel wreath:[41] and Virgil, for his part, ensured that this
Asiatic goddess played a significant role in Rome's national epic.[42]

I mentioned earlier Jupiter's drastic intervention, centred on
Anchises, when the Trojan withdrawal is suddenly threatened. In fact
there are two occasions towards the end of Book 2 when the fate of the
future Roman world seems to hang in the balance. When Aeneas
reaches the prearranged assembly point and finds that Creusa is
missing, he loses all self-control as he rushes back into the fray, and puts
the whole enterprise into jeopardy by charging about the blazing city,
repeatedly shouting her name (752 ff.). It is at this point that Creusa's
ghost appears and, by explaining her own position and clarifying
Aeneas' future, brings the crisis to an end (775–95). But just prior to this
a similar crisis arises which is ended only by a complex pattern of
intervention by Jupiter himself (634 ff.). For when Venus proves the
futility of further resistance by revealing the gods hostile to Troy busily

---

[40] *Res gestae* 19.
[41] Cf. T. P. Wiseman, in Tony Woodman and David West, eds., *Poetry and Politics in the Age of Augustus* (Cambridge, 1984), p. 127.
[42] Cf. M. Grant, *PVS* 3 (1963–4), 7–8; R. J. Littlewood, *CQ* 31 (1981), 381 and n. 4.

pursuing in their different ways the destruction of the city (604 ff.), and Aeneas returns to his father's house in order to rescue his family, the aged Anchises, unwilling to outlive Troy in exile, is determined to stay put (634 ff.). Aeneas, equally determined not to leave Troy without his father, in his despair seems on the point of a suicidal charge back into the fray when Creusa intervenes, filling the house with her pathetic cries as she pleads with Aeneas not to desert his family at such a time (673 ff.). It would be difficult to imagine a scene more fraught with such conflicting and powerful emotions: nor could Virgil have set the stage more successfully for a display of the instantaneous efficacy of that most striking feature of Roman religion, the prodigy. Ascanius (or Iulus) has just become the centre of attention, as Creusa holds him towards Aeneas and names him first in her pleas to his father (674, 677). Whereupon:

> ecce leuis summo de uertice uisus Iuli
> fundere lumen apex, tactuque innoxia mollis
> lambere flamma comas et circum tempora pasci. (683 ff.)[43]

While Aeneas and Creusa, like the servants in Livy's account of the similar Servius Tullius story,[44] react in a purely secular fashion, and are concerned simply with Iulus' personal safety, the whole situation is at once transformed by the reaction of Anchises, and the change is vividly signalled by the sudden and surprising appearance of the emphatically placed *laetus* to qualify him:

> at pater Anchises oculos ad sidera laetus
> extulit et caelo palmas cum uoce tetendit. (687–8)

A little earlier, when rejecting Aeneas' attempt to rescue him, Anchises had recalled how Jupiter once crippled him with his thunderbolt (648 ff.),[45] a recollection which was scarcely encouraging as far as his relationship with the god was concerned. But now the way is opened up for a new and more fruitful relationship with his divine ancestor,[46] when

---

[43] For the imagery involved here, and how it fits into a complex pattern which recurs throughout the book, see B. M. W. Knox, *AJPh* 71 (1950), 396 ff. [44] 1. 39. 2.

[45] This was the punishment for his failure to keep silent about the liaison with Aphrodite which produced Aeneas (*Homeric hymn* 6. 286 ff.). The introduction of this motive paves the way for the celebrated vignette of *pius Aeneas* bearing his feeble and crippled father from the sacked city in the last line of the book (804). But before long Anchises seems to have put all that behind him, and by the end of Book 3 his death comes as a surprise to both Aeneas and the reader (709 f.).

[46] This will be fully established after his death, when Anchises' ghost will become Jupiter's emissary (5. 724 f.), and, as commentator on the parade of future Romans in the Underworld, will in effect summarize what *Fatum* has in store.

Anchises identifies the flame as a sign sent by Jupiter, and calls on him to confirm the omen:

> 'Iuppiter omnipotens, precibus si flecteris ullis,
> aspice nos, hoc tantum, et si pietate meremur,
> da deinde augurium, pater, atque haec omina firma.' (689 ff.)

The so-called *augurium oblatiuum* (or unsolicited sign) is then followed by one specifically requested (*impetratiuum*):[47] and it proves in fact to be that most powerful sign of Jupiter's approval, thunder on the left, on this occasion accompanied by a shooting star which points the way to safety as its trail ends in the woods on Mount Ida. For there the Trojans will find a safe temporary refuge and the timber they need for the ships that will take them eventually to Italy.

Here it is perhaps worth while to add a few further comments on this crucial episode. In the first place we should not make too much of Anchises' reaction to the flame-prodigy, nor should we accept the view that there is an echo here of the earlier tradition that he had special prophetic powers. Anchises operates simply as *paterfamilias*, though no doubt he has more experience of the divine than most, and many more than his immediate family are involved in his decisions. On this crucial occasion, of course, his judgement is sound: but before long this same *paterfamilias* will go disastrously wrong in his interpretation of Apollo's instructions at Delos (3. 102 ff.), and the Trojans will suffer most cruelly as a result (3. 135 ff.). It is worth noting, too, that the central figures in this critical divine episode are Ascanius and Anchises, with Aeneas reduced to the role of a mere spectator. But the episode is only the first half of a frame which encloses the whole voyage from Troy to Latium. Here the divine signal is given for the enterprise to begin: and in the corresponding episode which signals its end in Latium (7. 107 ff.), a prodigy is once more centred on young Ascanius, as he innocently jests about the Trojans eating their tables. But now Aeneas has inherited his father's sacral role, and it is he who, as *paterfamilias*, recognizes the prodigious nature of his son's cry as marking the fulfilment, in a totally unexpected way, of two prophecies from the past.[48] Moreover, the frame is then completed when Aeneas' prayer to Jupiter and other deities is in turn answered by its own supporting claps of thunder (7. 141 ff.). Finally, since two critical stages in the story of Rome's emergence from the ashes of Troy are thus marked by Jupiter's supreme sign, we should

---

[47] Cf. Bailey, op. cit. 19.
[48] Cf. 3. 251 ff., 7. 122 ff.

perhaps note how the sequence is completed in the third generation.[49] In Book 9, when everything in the besieged Trojan camp seems to be going wrong in the absence of Aeneas, and Ascanius himself has contributed to the deterioration in no small measure, he suddenly emerges from the general gloom to vindicate Trojan honour in the face of taunting vilification at the hands of Turnus' truculent brother-in-law, Numanus. The other detail of this much-discussed scene need not concern us here: suffice it to say that before disposing of the Rutulian with an arrowshot, Ascanius offers to Jupiter a prayer which Aeneas himself could not have bettered (9. 625 ff.), and the response is immediate:

> audiit et caeli genitor de parte serena
> intonuit laeuum ... (9. 630 ff.)[50]

---

[49] According to Dionysius (2. 5. 5) Ascanius was the first recipient of the honour, after the deaths of Anchises and Aeneas.

[50] For the propitious left side, cf. Cicero, *Div.* 2. 74: 'sinistrum auspicium optimum habemus ad omnis res praeterquam ad comitia'. The brightness of the sky, which naturally figures in imaginative writing to increase the impact, is for Lucretius a scientific impossibility (6. 400 ff.), for Horace a light-hearted pretext for abandoning Epicureanism (*Odes* 1. 34).

5

Servius and the Helen Episode

G. P. GOOLD

The principal issue discussed in this article[1] permits of a simple formulation, 'Is the Helen Episode authentic?' and of a simple answer, 'No'. But the road which leads from the enunciation of the thesis to the final QED of the proof is long and winding, typical less of the unswerving advance of a Euclidean theorem than of the anfractuousness of a drunkard's homeward path. To judge from current opinions, however, it is a road which badly needs mapping. It is certainly significant that not until the last few years has the external evidence for the passage been accorded a full-scale discussion. As Rowell justly complains, 'it has usually been thought sufficient to refer to "Servius" or the "Servian Commentary" as its place of preservation and, unfortunately, this vague procedure has continued to prevail down to the present time'.[2] In his article Rowell sought to remedy the insufficiency of judgements based only on an appraisal of the contents of the disputed verses, and concluded that we owe the verses to Donatus' commentary, that Donatus clearly believed the testimony of his sources, and that the verses are Virgil's own. Touching the matter of authenticity he thus pronounces a benediction upon the verdict of Austin, Büchner, Duckworth, Otis, and Quinn, to mention some only of the living Virgilians who have expressed an opinion. This, then, is the moment for the voice of dissent. The problem is one of source-criticism and involves a study of Virgil's ancient commentators; and besides advancing a particular thesis this article will serve to indicate work being done on volume i of the Harvard Servius, which, if far from completion, is nevertheless well under way.

The case will be presented in the following sequence of propositions. *First, that the only authority for the Helen Episode is Servius.* One must

---

[1] I acknowledge with grateful thanks my indebtedness to Professor Charles E. Murgia of Berkeley both for considerable light he has shed on problems in Servian studies and for long discussions with me over the first draft of this article; and also to Professor C. P. Jones of Toronto for many valuable criticisms.

[2] Henry T. Rowell, 'The Ancient Evidence of the Helen Episode in *Aeneid* II', in Luitpold Wallach, ed., *The Classical Tradition* (Ithaca, 1966), p. 211.

discriminate between the two commentaries (1) Servius and Servius Auctus and realize (2) how Servius Auctus was put together by the Compiler. The latter (3), already in possession of Donatus' Life of Virgil, found it unnecessary to preserve all of the inferior Servian Life, and consequently transcribed from it only (4) the allusion to the ninth *Eclogue*, and—here it is convenient to discuss (5) the posthumous editing of the *Aeneid*—(6) the *ille ego* verses, and (7) the Helen Episode. *Second, (8) that Servius' unsupported testimony is insufficient to establish a matter of fact.* Third, that the contents of the Helen Episode cannot be reconciled with Virgilian authorship. This section begins with (9) an examination of the text and the manuscripts offering it; then we proceed (10) to the studied way in which the Helen Episode has been put together, even to the contrivance of a Golden Section (11). Genuineness is excluded by a consideration of (12) the linguistic data and (13) Virgil's dramatic design for the second book of the *Aeneid*. *Finally, that the available evidence about the Virgilian tradition supports the contention that the Helen Episode is not authentic.* It is argued (14) that Varius cannot have seen it; that some Virgilian commentators issued false statements about the Virgilian autographs; and (15) that the canonical text never included the Helen Episode. Possibly (16) composed as an exercise in the Neronian Age, it was taken from some older commentary by Servius, who carelessly applied to it the explanation he customarily attaches to spurious passages, namely that it was athetized by Virgil's editors.

PART ONE: SERVIUS

I. *Servius and Servius Auctus*

The Helen Episode, that is *Aen* 2. 567–88, is not found in any primary manuscript of Virgil. In fact, the text is preserved by two sources only, (a) Servius' Life of Virgil (which introduces his commentary on the *Aeneid*) and (b) the anonymous commentary often referred to as Servius Auctus, at *Aen.* 2. 566. Similarities in the wording of Servius and Servius Auctus make plain that the two sources are imtimately connected. Thilo believed that Servius Auctus took the passage from Servius, whilst Rowell, who walks in the footprints of Eduard Fraenkel,[3] believes that the Servian testimony is interpolated from Servius Auctus. One or the other proposition must be true in view of the relationship between the two commentaries, and to this relationship we now must turn.

---

[3] Eduard Fraenkel, *JRS* 38 (1948), 132 (*Kleine Beiträge*, II 340).

The commentary of Servius (S) reaches us in a well-articulated text, the oldest manuscripts showing for a work of this kind remarkably little deviation from each other. Servius set out, it seems, to write a commentary on the *Aeneid*, but upon the successful completion of that task decided to go ahead and annotate the whole of the poet's work. At any rate, his commentary is prefaced by a Life of Virgil and is followed by notes on the *Aeneid*, notes on the *Eclogues*, and notes on the *Georgics*. The whole may be schematized as Sp-Sa-Se-Sg. And that this is the order of composition Servius' cross-references make quite plain. For example, on *Geo.* 1. 488 he says *ut docuimus in Aeneide*, and the relevant annotation is found at *Aen.* 10. 272, which must therefore have been written earlier. Similarly, the words *sicut in Bucolicis diximus* at *Geo.* 4. 101, referring to *Buc.* 9. 30, prove that Servius wrote on the *Eclogues* before he wrote on the *Georgics*.

Complications, however, are caused by a small number of manuscripts which present an expanded text of Servius. These exhibit, in addition to the complete text of Servius (which, however, is frequently adapted to accommodate the new material), alternative explanations, further quotations, and extra comments; and it was first assumed that here was the full text of Servius, the vulgate manuscripts furnishing merely an abridgement. After the name of Pierre Daniel, who in 1600 first edited these manuscripts, this expanded text is most commonly known as Servius Danielis, though occasionally it is referred to as Servius Auctus. This latter designation is here preferred, as being non-committal, for Daniel often deviates by addition or omission from the strict testimony of his manuscripts. Nevertheless, the abbreviation DS, which enjoys universal acceptance, will be retained.

The nineteenth century brought the important realization that DS represented an amalgamation of Servius' commentary (S) with a large mass of non-Servian scholia (which let us call D): the inclusion in the latter of otherwise unknown but evidently genuine fragments from such authors as Naevius and Accius and Cato proved that much at least of D possessed a unique authority. Though he did not pursue his line of reasoning further, Lion deduced that such references as the following could not derive from the Servian commentary for the simple reason that no annotation of *Eclogues* and *Georgics* occurred until the commentary on the *Aeneid* was completed:

D *Aen.* 2. 172 … *quod in Bucolicis scriptum est* (cf. D *Buc.* 7. 31);
D *Aen.* 4. 462 … *quod plenius in primo Georgicorum dictum est* (cf. D *Geo.* 1. 39).[4]

---

[4] H. Albertus Lion, *Commentarii in Virgilium Serviani* (Göttingen, 1826), pp. vii f.

Émile Thomas, whose *Essai sur Servius* still provides the most helpful introduction to these studies, recognized the 'variorum' nature of the DS commentary, a conception which Thilo clarified considerably by adducing scores of striking connections between D scholia and ancient commentators from Aemilius Asper to Macrobius and demonstrating that D draws upon authorities behind Servius himself. The most important advance was achieved by Barwick, who, by carefully analysing the way in which the D scholia had been, often all too clumsily, fused on to Servius, revealed their homogeneous nature as annotations lifted from a single pre-Servian commentary on Virgil; and he concurred in the opinion, already hazarded by Thilo, that the amalgamation of D and S into the DS commentary took place in Ireland in the seventh century.[5] For Thilo, DS was something of a stew, with the D element representing ingredients drawn from several sources. But what Irish cook of the seventh century commanded a larder which contained, for example, texts of Fabius Pictor, Cincius, Postumius Albinus, Cassius Hemina, and a dozen other republican historians to sprinkle over his confection?

Barwick refrained from identifying the D commentary, which he supposed to have survived into the Dark Age and to have been at the Irishman's disposal, but Thilo had observed that DS must, like Donatus, have begun with the *Eclogues*, and that, where Servius refers to Donatus, DS sometimes omits the name (which, of course, would have been absent from the body of Donatus' commentary). Barwick himself stressed that DS is normally punctilious in furnishing exact information where Servius is content with a vague attribution, e.g., DS *Aen.* 2. 225 *alii, ut Cincius, dicunt*, where Servius has merely *alii dicunt* and DS *Aen.* 7. 543 *quidam commentarius, Firmianus*, where Servius fails to give the name (D most likely had *Cincius dicit* and *Firmianus* respectively). Not surprisingly three scholars in the next few years, Lammert, Wessner, and Rand, each came forward—and independently—with the suggestion that the author of the D commentary was none other than Aelius Donatus, whose work indeed Servius on his own admission used.[6] Rand went a good deal farther than the others. If, he argued, Servius took his material from Donatus, as most people believe, and if someone in the Middle Ages has added to a text of Servius a substantial amount of scholia from Donatus, do we not then possess in DS essentially the commentary of Donatus himself? This speculation provided much of the energy and enthusiasm which went towards the planning of the Harvard Servius, and in the very year the first instalment of the project appeared—happy omen—two Italian scholars, Santoro and Marinone, published independent studies which seemed to confirm that the valuable D scholia are in fact derived from Donatus.[7]

What needs now to be recognized is that the equations DS = S(ervius) + D(onatus), though fundamentally true, greatly oversimplifies the situation. It leaves out of account the medieval compiler who expanded Servius, the seventh-century Irishman of Thilo and Barwick. A warning was sounded by the dissertation of Travis, who, comparing the stylistic features of the D scholia and those of Donatus' commentary on Terence in the confident expectation of being able to prove identity of authorship, acknowledged his disappointment at the negative results he obtained.[8] The Compiler is the man whose style Travis was vainly comparing with Donatus', and a closer look at the Compiler forms the next step in our disquisition.

II. *The Compiler of Servius Auctus*

Whether or not he lived in Ireland, we must envisage a man who possessed a copy of Servius. Into his hands has come the D commentary—the commentary of Donatus. The result requires us to believe that into his Servius he copied large amounts of those scholia in D which he found wanting in Servius. Why, one will ask, did he not simply use or transcribe the D commentary? No certain answer is possible. Perhaps the D commentary lacked the text of Virgil which his Servian commentary contained—certainly, the Lemovicensis (the manuscript which preserves the DS commentary for part of the *Georgics*) by giving such readings as *Geo.* 1. 19 *trip GEORG tolemum* and 1. 39 *elysio LIB I grana* seems to point to the headings of a Virgil text in its exemplar. Perhaps the Compiler, as Murgia suggests, had already invested time and trouble in adding notes of his own to his copy of Servius, for we shall soon prove the existence of non-Donatian matter among the D scholia.

[7] A. Santoro, 'Il *Servio Danielino* è Donato', *SIFC* 20 (1946), 79–104, also *Esegeti virgiliani antichi* (Bari, 1946); N. Marinone, *Elio Donato, Macrobio, e Servio* (Vercelli, 1946).

[8] Albert H. Travis, *De Servii carminum Vergilianorum interpretis dicendi rationibus* (diss. Harvard, 1940), summarized in 'Donatus and the Scholia Danielis: A Stylistic Comparison', *HSCPh* 53 (1942), 157–69; see also *CP* 45 (1950), 38 f.

But his motives hardly count. What matters is the fact that he stitched D scholia on to the fabric of Servius. Stocker cites a telling example from *Aen.* 1. 448,[9] where Servius had attempted to explain why the portals of Dido's temple were constructed of bronze:

(S) AEREA uel quod aes magis ueteres in usu habebant, uel quod religioni apta est haec materies; denique flamen Dialis aereis cultris tondebatur.

In his D commentary the Compiler finds more than this, so from it he writes:

(D) *aut quia uocalius ceteris metallis, aut quia medici quaedam uulnera aere curant,*

but then goes on to add

(D) *aut dicit quia ueteres magis aere usi sunt.*

Now this is precisely what Servius had said to begin with: it is clear that the Compiler has carelessly copied out from D what was already in his own text. We catch here a glimpse of Servius at work: Donatus gave alternative explanations, from which Servius, a man of judgement whatever his faults, has selected what he thought worth preserving. The Compiler, however, fails to notice the item which Servius has specially singled out for mention at the head of his scholium and has copied it out all over again. The Compiler is no critic, and is heedless of inconsistencies and contradictions. Moreover, he is a meddler, and his meddlings with the language of Servius run like a fugal theme through the DS commentary. At *Aen.* 2. 686 Servius had somehow got hold of a faulty reading *sacros*, and in commenting on it said:

(S) SACROS RESTINGVERE FONTIBVS IGNES non quos tunc sacros sciebant, sed quos mox probarunt.

Here Donatus gives the correct reading, which together with a lengthy explanation the Compiler has copied out. But he has modified the Servian note, which cannot have been in Donatus' commentary at all (especially since D explains *sanctos* as *sacros* without alluding to textual trouble). Possibly from some glossed text of Virgil, the source of such a note as *Gl. Ansil.* SA 106, the Compiler has glossed SACROS with *religiosos*, and, his taste offended by *mox* in conjunction with a preterite, has altered *probarunt* to *probaturi sunt* (anyone with a sense of style would have written *erant*). Here Murgia considers the possibility that the gloss on SACROS was inherited with the Virgil text and that tinkering with

---

[9] Arthur F. Stocker, 'Servius Servus Magistrorum', *Vergilius* 9 (1963), 12.

probarunt antedated transcription of D material. In any event *Ed. Harv.* II gives a wrong impression by printing these alterations to Servius as the common S and DS text. Thilo's editorial method shows to advantage here, and for *Ed. Harv.* I (on *Eclogues* and *Georgics*, where, to be sure, the problems are different from those in the *Aeneid*) a modification of Thilo's method is being adopted, whereby roman type indicates the text of Servius, italic the additions of the DS text, deletions made by the Compiler being indicated by square brackets;[10] the useful device of splitting the page so as to present S on one side and DS on the other will be employed wherever this secures a gain in clarity. According to this scheme the above scholium would be printed thus:

(S/DS) SACROS RESTINGVERE FONTIBVS IGNES *religiosos*, non quos tunc sacros sciebant, sed quos mox [probarunt] *probaturi sunt*.

Earlier in this article mention was made of Servius' practice of referring back to previous notes, doubtless to avoid unnecessary repetition; and the different arrangement of the D commentary was alluded to. But who is it that is making cross-references in the D scholia? Are Donatus' cross-references being faithfully transcribed? Or is the Compiler modifying these, as we shall see later on he modified those of Servius? At *Buc* 7. 26 a wholly Servian scholium contains the words *sicut etiam in Aeneide diximus* (the reference is to 7. 499): the D scholia could not have contained this reference, since their order was e-g-a. Consequently, when we find the DS version of the scholium reading *sicut etiam in Aeneide dictum est*, we may confidently ascribe the change to the Compiler, and not to the D commentary he was excerpting.

Let us examine the Compiler's references. He seems to have gone through the text systematically altering occurrences of *ut supra diximus* to *ut supra dictum est*. So we find:

S/DS *Aen.* 1. 37   ut superius [diximus] *dictum est*
S/DS *Aen.* 1. 76   ut supra [notauimus] *notatum est*
S/DS *Aen.* 1. 175 ut [diximus] supra *dictum est*
S/DS *Aen.* 1. 292 ut superius [diximus] *dictum est*
S/DS *Aen.* 1. 294 ut superius [diximus] *dictum est*
S/DS *Aen.* 1. 301 ut supra [diximus] *dictum est*
S/DS *Aen.* 1. 382 quod autem [diximus] *dictum est*
S/DS *Aen.* 1. 451 ut supra [diximus] *dictum est*
S/DS *Aen.* 1. 461 ut supra [diximus] *dictum est*

---

[10] This proposal was made by Professor Philippa Forder of Mount Holyoke College, who is collaborating with me on Harv. Serv., vol. i.

And so on, at 1. 488, 506, 626, 630, 666, 683, 726, and 729. Of course, in none of these places should *Ed. Harv.* II have fathered on Servius the impersonal form written by the Compiler. Note that at 76 and 301 the DS reading survives only as an interpolation in the Γ tradition of the Servian manuscripts (a phenomenon more clearly discernible at 37 and 175). Likewise in *Aen.* 2 Servius' references to previous annotations are altered at 61, 69, 158 (here the DS reading survives only in one manuscipt of the Γ tradition), 199, 296, 431, 471, 557, and 592. From the beginning of the *Aeneid* up to this point not a single instance has been left unaltered (at 2. 19 and 142 and 250 and 513 the references have been suppressed, and at 2. 215 the testimony of the Cassellanus, our only trustworthy guide to the DS text in this book, is missing). Hereafter, however, we encounter hardly an instance of *diximus* being altered to *dictum est*. Did the Compiler become tired and give up? We must not make too much of Servius' references at *Aen.* 2. 668 and 755, where the Cassellanus is missing. However, in *Aen.* 3 (where the Floriacensis takes over as our authority for DS) the Servian references are unaltered: see 70, 103, 125, 159, 163a, 246, 279, 280, 284, 302, 333, 363, 395, 407, 433, 491, 566, 615, 678, and 710 (at 163b *ut supra dictum est* is another DS reading attested only by interpolated Servian manuscripts and corresponding to nothing in Servius).

A few sporadic examples do occur: at *Aen.* 6. 6, 7. 764, 8. 43, 9. 410, 10. 89; *Buc.* 4. 31, 6. 47, 6. 61, 10. 23; and *Geo.* 1. 278. One of these deserves a notice:

S/DS *Aen.* 9. 410 ... quos *supra insolubiles* [diximus supra] *dictum est.*

Here the retention of the accusative *quos*, against all grammar and quite impossible for Donatus, reveals the careless and mechanical nature of the adjustment.

Possibly these alterations to the impersonal form are to be imputed to fitful activity on the Compiler's part. Possibly, as Murgia is inclined to believe, the DS impersonals have been changed to personals through interpolation with the Servian practice. This we have to assume at

S/DS *Aen.* 8. 43 ut *supra dictum est* [diximus supra].

Here the DS manuscript (F) and M (i.e., **DS**, Γ) attest the Servian reading, the impersonal verb (i.e., the genuine DS text) being preserved by the Δ tradition of the Servian manuscripts.

We must remember that the DS text has not survived intact for the whole of Virgil's works. It is altogether missing for the first three *Eclogues* and virtually missing for most of the *Georgics* (the Vatican Scholia being a drastic abridgement and reworking of DS) and *Aeneid* 6 and 7. Even so, for the portion covered by the primary DS manuscript Lemovicensis the Compiler seems to have left untouched the Servian formula at *Buc.* 4. 34, 5. 45, 7. 1, 7. 20, 8. 92, 9. 38, 10. 1, 10. 9; *Geo.* 1. 21 and 1. 27.

Nevertheless, when the Compiler is inserting notes into his Servian text, he adheres to the impersonal formula *(sic)ut (supra) dictum est*: see, for example, D *Aen.* 3. 7, 24, 60, 68, 124, 131, 164, 178, 212, 213, 311, 407, 420, 437, 545, and 550.

Now consider the adjustments made at *Buc.* 6. 61:

S/DS ... quod plenius in Aeneidos tertio libro [memorauimus] *memoratum est, ubi etiam de ipsis malis fabula relata est.*

The last eight words cannot have been found in the D commentary: when the notes on the *Eclogues* were written, comment on the *Aeneid* still lay in the future. So here we detect the Compiler penning an extra note of his own. Similar reasoning tells us that at *Geo.* 1. 8

S/DS CHAONIAM PINGVI GLANDEM MVTAVIT ARISTA Epiroti-cam, *quae cur Chaonia dicta sit, in tertio Aeneidis* (334) *plenius habes, et hic ideo Epiroticam* a loco ...

all the italicized words, and not merely the reference, are the Compiler's.

Look carefully at the Compiler's cross-references to fables. Where he refers back, we read (e.g., at *Buc.* 6. 27) *quod in septimo Aeneidis plene habes.* Where he refers forward, we see that he uses a different verb and tense:

D *Aen.* 1. 651 ... *quod in secundo plenius inuenies* (→ *Aen.* 2. 601)
D *Aen.* 3. 211 ... *quod in septimo ... plenius inuenies* (→ *Aen.* 7. 790)
D *Aen.* 3. 399 ... *quod ibi inuenies ubi ait ...* (→ *Aen.* 11. 265)
D *Aen.* 5. 105 ... *de Phaethonte in decimo plenius inuenies* (→ *Aen.* 10. 189)

He must therefore be referring forward in the following places:

D *Aen.* 3. 274 *hoc ... plenius in Bucolicis ... inuenies* (→ *Buc.* 8. 59)
D *Aen.* 9. 213 *de inferiis ... plenius in quarto Georgicorum inuenies* (→ *Geo.* 4. 545)

It seems then that the order of the DS Commentary is DSa-DSe-DSg. Murgia questions this by adducing one instance of *inuenies* unarguably referring back:

S/DS *Aen.* 7. 764 quam historiam plene in secundo [diximus] *inuenies.*

This must be deemed an inconsistency on the Compiler's part: in any case his own practice would have led us to expect *dictum est*. Thus it follows that the Compiler's Servius displayed the order Sa-Se-Sg. True, all extant copies of Servius point to an archetypal Se-Sg-Sa. But in the original order of Servius the *Aeneid*, immediately preceded by the Life, certainly came first, and this sequence may well have survived to the Compiler's time.

The Compiler also reveals his hand in his dealings with the names Donatus and Urbanus in Servius. Naturally Donatus never mentioned himself by name in his commentary; nor did he refer to Urbanus, whose activity must be dated after Donatus and before Servius. And naturally neither of these names ever occurs in the additional D notes. Now, when the Compiler saw that scholia occurring in his D commentary were, when referred to by Servius, labelled with the names Donatus or Urbanus, he decided to suppress the names: possibly, whilst willing to retain the names of older authorities like Probus and Asper, he declined to reveal his dependence on the later commentators. Hence:

S/DS *Geo.* 1. 198 sic enim [Donatus sensit] *in omnibus commentatoribus legitur...*

S/DS *Aen.* 3. 242 quod [Donatus dicit] *alii dicunt.*

S/DS *Aen.* 4. 624 [Vrbanus dicit] *alii dicunt.*

Likewise at *Aen.* 7. 556, 8. 333, 9. 389 and 544. However, in many other places the Compiler has seemingly made no alteration. Of course, we must remember to exclude from consideration such sections of the text for which the DS Commentary is not extant: thus we can infer nothing about the attitude of the Compiler towards the names of Donatus and Urbanus at *Buc. praef.* 9, 20; 2. 17; 3. 38; *Geo.* 1. 425; 2. 4, 324, 412, 424, 514; 4. 150, 345.

At *Aen.* 6. 177 we are faced with a conundrum: 'Probus tamen et [Donatus] *ceteri commentatores*'. The merest glance at Thilo's edition will disclose that contact with the D commentary has been lost in this area of the text: it looks as if the Compiler has suppressed Donatus' name without any reference to the D commentary at all.

Did the Compiler tire of making these changes and fail to complete his design? Or, where no change is indicated by our DS manuscripts, is it possible that the Compiler's autograph has not been accurately reproduced? Apart from *Aen.* 2. 557 all cases involve the Floriacensis (see above, page 000): *Aen.* 3. 535, 636; 4. 384, 469; 5. 493, 517; 6. 230, 339, 535, 609, 623; 7. 1, 543, 563; 8. 373, 642; 9. 30, 361, 672, 760; 10.

331, 463, 497, 661; 11. 31, 124, 316, 318, 762; 12. 365, 366, 507, 514, 529, 585. Here and there we come across clues that the Compiler's intentions have not always been carried out.

S/DS *Geo.* 1. 120 [ut etiam] Donatus dicit. Rather all four words were meant to be expunged.

S/DS *Aen.* 2. 798 EXILIO ad exilium. *alii* Donatus contra metrum sensit, dicens ... Rather, as Thilo suggests, *alii* [Donatus] contra metrum [sensit, dicens] *senserunt, dicentes* ... was meant.[11]

S/DS *Aen.* 4. 548 [Vrbanus hoc diuidit] *alii hoc diuidunt*, licet alii iungant, et [uult] *uolunt* hunc esse sensum: *Vrbanus hoc diuidit*. The whole purpose of the Compiler's intervention was to suppress the last three words: he certainly never added them at the end.

Several passages demonstrate that from time to time the Compiler transferred scholia (both S and D) to other lemmata than those under which he found them. We consider three.[12]

(1) On *Aen.* 1. 119 *arma uirum* 'weapons of men' Servius remarked that the poet did well to add *uirum* (gen. plur.), thus leaving no doubt as to the sense of *arma*.

S *Aen.* 1. 119 ARMA VIRVM bene addidit 'uirum', arma enim dicuntur cunctarum artium instrumenta, ut (177) 'Cerealiaque arma'.

The Compiler—we can hardly impute this to Donatus—mechanically copied out the note at 1. 1 *arma uirumque cano*, where it becomes quite absurd—as if *uirum* in the first line of the *Aeneid* were a genitive plural, a mere afterthought of the poet's, added for the purpose of clarifying the first word. True to himself, the Compiler has stuck in an *autem* and played about with the wording, though not enough to conceal the source of his remark.

S/DS *Aen.* 1. 1 VIRVM *autem* quem non dicit, sed circumstantiis ostendit Aenean. *et bene addidit post arma 'uirum', quia arma possunt et aliarum artium instrumenta dici, ut* (177) 'Cerealiaque arma'.

(2) At *Aen.* 1. 171 Servius explains that *telluris amore* does not signify love of Carthage, but merely denotes the desire of the shipwrecked to reach any dry land, and he refers to two other passages to support his contention. This prompted the Compiler to write similar notes on these two passages, neither of which called for comment: in the first *quod-cumque*, and in the second *post* (*mare*) give him away.

[11] Georg Thilo, *Servii Grammatici ... Commentarii*, vol. i (Leipzig, 1881), *praef.* p. xv.
[12] Cf. Heinrich Georgii, *Die antike Aneiskritik* (Stuttgart, 1891), pp. 14 f.

S *Aen.* 1.171 TELLVRIS AMORE cuiuscumque terrae post pericula. unde et superius (157) 'quae proxima litora cursu contendunt', et paulo post (172) 'optata potiuntur Troes harena'.

D *Aen.* 1. 157 PROXIMA LITORA ideo, quia post periculum non eligitur litus, sed quodcumque occurrit occupatur.

D *Aen.* 1. 172 et HARENA aut pro terra posita est, aut et harena grata potuit esse post mare.

(3) When used in the temporal sense, says Servius farther on, the preposition *sub* takes an accusative.

S *Aen.* 1. 662 ET SVB NOCTEM CVRA RECVRSAT circa noctem. et sciendum quia, cum tempus significatur, 'sub' praepositio accusatiuo cohaeret.

Later he has occasion to remark on *super* with the ablative, and he quotes 1. 662, thus:

S *Aen.* 1. 750 SVPER PRIAMO de Priamo. nam eius praepositionis officio fungitur pro qua ponitur, ut supra (662) 'et sub noctem cura recursat'.

The Compiler, looking back at 662, saw the note and decided to repeat it here, where it is absolutely redundant. Hence:

S/DS *Aen.* 1. 750 ... ut supra (662) 'et sub noctem cura recursat', *id est circa noctem. et sciendum quod, cum tempus significatur, 'sub' praepositio accusatiuo haeret semper.*

Note his pettiness: he alters *quia* to *quod*, *cohaeret* to *haeret*, and throws in *semper* for good measure.

To these instances of the Compiler's activity one can add more, and one can add many more where it is probable, though not certain, that he has repeated notes (or parts of notes) at passages cited in the original scholium. At D *Geo.* 1. 12 is discussed the locution *aqua fremit*, with quotation of two Ennian passages and *Aen.* 11. 299: at the latter we find in D an abridged note quoting only one of the Ennian passages. After S *Aen.* 4. 409, the Compiler's note at *Aen.* 4. 567 repeating a small part of it can hardly be ascribed with certainty to the D commentary, which probably treated the matter fully and finally at *Geo.* 3. 221 (now unfortunately lost in its complete form: see the D note at *Aen.* 8. 677).

Having established the propensity of the Compiler to add cross-references and notes of his own, and even to repeat whole notes elsewhere, let us look at a much-discussed scholium, where it is possible to get a rough idea of what Donatus wrote and how first Servius and then the Compiler adapted it to their own ends. This we are enabled to do by

G. P. Goold

a passage in Macrobius, who himself has made abundant use of the Donatian commentary in writing or rather compiling his *Saturnalia*.

DONATUS (conjectural)	MACROBIUS (*Sat.* 3. 8. 2)	SERVIUS (= S and DS)
Aen. 2. 632		
⟨AC DVCENTE DEO		AC DVCENTE DEO
(1) doctissime 'deo' non 'dea',	(1) cum … doctissime dixerit 'ducente deo' non 'dea'.	
(2) secundum eos qui dicunt utriusque sexus participationem habere numina.		(2) secundum eos qui dicunt utriusque sexus participationem habere numina.
(3) nam et apud Caluum Haterianus affirmat legendum 'pollentemque deum Venerem', non 'deam':	(3) am et apud Caluum Haterianus affirmat legendum 'pollentemque deum Venerem', non 'deam'.	(3) nam Caluus in libro suo ait 'pollentemque deum Venerem'.
(4) item Vergilius 'nec dextrae erranti deus afuit', cum aut Iuno fuerit aut Allecto.		(4) item Vergilius 'nec dextrae erranti deus afuit', cum aut Iuno fuerit aut Allecto.
(5) signum etiam eius est Cypri barbatum,	(5) signum etiam eius est Cypri barbatum,	(5) est etiam in Cypro simulacrum barbatae Veneris.
		SERVIUS AUCTUS (DS only)
(6) corpore et ueste muliebri, cum sceptro ac statura uirili,	(6) corpore et ueste muliebri, cum sceptro ac statura uirili,	(6) *corpore et ueste muliebri, cum sceptro et statura uirili,*
(7) et putant eandem marem et feminam esse.	(7) et putant eandem marem et feminam esse.	
(8) Aristophanes eam 'Αφρόδιτον appellat.	(8) Aristophanes eam 'Αφρόδιτον appellat.	(8) *quod* 'Αφρόδιτον *uocant,*
(9) Laeuius etiam sic ait 'Venerem igitur almum adorans, siue femina siue mas est, ita uti alma noctiluca est'.	(9) Laeuius etiam sic ait 'Venerem igitur almum adorans, siue femina siue mas est, ita uti alma noctiluca est'.	
(10) Philochorus quoque in Atthide	(10) Philochorus quoque in Atthide	

eandem affirmat esse
lunam,
(11) et ei sacrificium
facere uiros cum ueste
muliebri, mulieres cum
uirili, quod eadem et
mas aestimatur et
femina.
(12) ueteres interpretes
deum ut unum ex
magnis numinibus
accipiebant, quae supra
(623) poeta meminerat.

(13) alii fatum uolunt
dictum,

pleraque enim
repentinis
impulsionibus nata
mirisque prouentibus
deo ascribi solent ut
'hinc me digressum
uestris deus appulit oris'
et Sallustius 'ut tanta
repente mutatio non sine
deo uideretur'.)

eandem affirmat esse
lunam,
(11) et ei sacrificium
facere uiros cum ueste
muliebri, mulieres cum
uirili, quod eadem et
mas aestimatur et
femina.

VERONA SCHOLIA
(ad loc.)

(13) qui legunt DEO
fatum uolunt dictum.

DONATUS
(Ter. Eun. 875)

pleraque repentinis
impulsionibus nata
mirisque prouentibus
deo ascribi solent ut ...
'hinc me digressum
uestris deus appulit oris'
et Sallustius 'ut tanta
repente mutatio non sine
deo uideretur'.

(11) *cui uiri in ueste
muliebri, mulieres in uirili
ueste sacrificant.*

(12) *quamquam ueteres
deum pro magno numine
dicebant.*

(13) *Sallustius 'ut tanta
mutatio non sine deo
uideretur'.*

Beneath this bewildering consarcination lies a real and crucial issue, which, as we shall see later, has a direct bearing on the Helen Episode. Troy is falling and Aeneas, too, would fall, did not Venus appear and promise that she will escort him to safety (*Aen.* 2. 620). She then vanishes (621). The mighty deities come on to destroy the city (623). Aeneas hastens to his home *ducente deo* (632). The problem is this: to whom does *deo* refer?

The most convenient answer (A: scholium sections 1–11) would be Venus. But, to say nothing of her departure at 621, Virgil never uses *deus* of a goddess. In this dilemma most of the ancient critics resorted to the fantastic explanation that Venus partook of the male sex, or—a more intelligent if drastic alternative—emended the text (in fact our oldest manuscripts all read *dea*, not *deo*). Some in desperation suggested (B: 12) that Aeneas' guide was one of the *numina magna* mentioned in line 623 as entering the scene after Venus' departure: but this will not do, because they have come only to bring destruction to Troy. The most judicious critics, however—among them we must include the Verona Scholiast and Donatus on Terence *Eun.* 875 (who must therefore have written something similar here)—abandoned any attempt at a precise identification and simply interpreted the phrase (C: 13) as 'with heaven's guidance', 'with a god's guidance'.

Naturally, one cannot assume—except where they exactly agree—that either Macrobius or Servius (or Servius Auctus) has kept the precise words of Donatus, who probably introduced his comment with a different phrasing in 1 and 2, furnished fuller detail and perhaps an authority for 5, and understood the point of 12. We may at least be sure that he quoted Sallust (*Hist.* 4. 60) in the same form he gave in his commentary on Terence, being confirmed in this by the Verona Scholia.

Servius distinguishes himself by the clear simplicity which characterizes the great and successful teacher, and conformably with the ideals of lucidity and directness he sweeps aside without obvious reluctance the dusty memorials of Roman scholarship. But if he demonstrates his sense of the commentator's proper business in preferring to explain Virgil from Virgil himself and discarding the abstruse, irrelevant, and dreary knowledge which dazzled Macrobius, he forfeits, as an Orbilius must and as a Macrobius cannot, the title of scholar. An elementary teacher, to reach in due season the end of his curriculum, must every hour turn a Nelson eye to serious problems and refrain from pursuing truth beyond the charted boundaries of the textbook. Servius accepts the reading of Haterianus in Calvus without so much as indicating the existence of a variant: he states as a fact what on the evidence before him is pure conjecture. May Venus be styled *deus*? 'Yes,' says Servius, 'for besides the testimony of a verse in Calvus there is the statue of a bearded Venus in Cyprus.' Kindly elucidate, we ask. But no, time will not allow; much more remains of our prescribed text, and we must move on: we may not stay even to hear the alternative explanations. Clearly, if we wish to get to the bottom of an intricate problem, we dare not rely on Servius to conduct us to it.

The Compiler, no doubt, had long savoured the learning of Servius. But we can hardly wonder that, when he fell upon the commentary of Donatus, he determined to enrich his copy of Servius from its contents.

However, in embarking on the task of repairing the shortcomings of his old cicerone, he bit off a good deal more than he could chew. We must not blame him for abbreviating; circumstances of which we know nothing may have confined him to a narrow compass of time and space. Nevertheless, he is revealed as a hack, without taste or learning or brains. Within the confines of this single note he unbares his appalling limitations: he passes over, if he ever noticed, Servius' misrepresentation of the textual evidence of 3, content merely to start where Servius had left off; he omits all the authorities meticulously indicated by Donatus (who may have named more in 12 and 13); where the latter cites Aristophanes as referring to a bisexual Aphroditos, he misapplies the citation to the Cyprian statue, suppressing Aristophanes' name and mendaciously attributing the remark to a plurality of sources (as at *Geo.* 3. 89 he wrote *poetae Graeculi* where Donatus, as we know from the Bern Scholia, had specified *Alcman lyricus*); and out of the mutually exclusive 12 and 13 he has produced a single piece of nonsense. Yet he is never tired of tampering with Donatus' Latin and frustrating a Travis's endeavour to identify it: in 6 he has changed an *ac* to an *et*, in 8 he substitutes the verb *uocare* for *appellare*, 11 is recast, with the preposition *cum* twice changed to *in*, and in 13 he omits a stylishly placed adverb from the fragment of Sallust. Possibly this is an error of the source *f*, as *natura* (*f*) is here assumed to be an error for the correct *statura* in 6. But in 11 the uncouth Latin is his: Clausen would delete the second *ueste* and rightly, in the sense that it derives from an original without it;[13] but in the DS text it is genuine, that is to say, it is a word deliberately written by the author of the sentence in which it occurs; this naive repetition is a characteristic of the man's dreadful Latin style (as Clausen's parallels show), and in this case, at least, we can see that we shall not restore Donatus' *ipsissima verba* by adjusting this feature alone. Thus does a single scholium disclose what a pale shadow of Donatus we possess in Servius Auctus. Yet without Macrobius to inform us we should hardly have known of the ruthless omissions and petty trifling of the Compiler.

For an editor of these commentaries the lesson is plain: he cannot pretend to be able to restore Donatus; he must take as his principal goal the establishment of the Servian text and clearly indicate the differences (whether addition, omission, or amendment) of the DS text. How far the extra material, D, represents the words or even the thought of Donatus rather than the Compiler cannot be formulated in a general proposition:

---

[13] Wendell Clausen, 'Adnotatiunculae in Servium', *HSCPh* 71 (1967), 58.

each case must be examined separately, and with distressing frequency an editor will find himself devoid of a basis for reaching precise conclusions.

III. *The Preface to Donatus' Commentary*

In his review of *Ed. Harv.* II Fraenkel complained that no attempt had been made to break up scholia into their separate parts, a valid criticism, but one applying to all editions of Servius, and in some measure to Servius himself, in whose work, as in much late Latin exegesis, comment frequently rambles on in a continuous and even confused sequence. The criticism applies also to the Lives of Virgil, no edition of which presents the material in a way permitting easy comparison and analysis. Anyone whose avocations take him to the *Vita Donati* in the Oxford text may be pardoned for wondering, as he takes a first glance round, whether he has strayed into a slum area, crying out for someone to clean up the confusing litter of posters and give the place a fresh coat of paint.

To drop the metaphor, let us discard every system of reference for Donatus save Hagen's section numbers; and let us supply a like set for Servius, as follows:

1 in ... explanatio	12 et ... oculis
2 Vergilii ... est	13 titulus ... Codri
3 patre ... Venetiae	14 qualitas ... loquentes
4 diuersis ... studuit	15 est ... compositum
5 adeo ... fuit	16 est ... grandiloquum
6 primum ... Diras	17 intentio ... Iulo
7 postea ... emendasse	18 de ... C
8 item ... annis	19 ordo ... Vergilium
9 postea ... incendi	20 sola ... sufficiat
10 Augustus ... tamen	21 nam ... obseruatio
11 unde ... cano	22 sciendum ... profanis

This will enable us to see the texts as they were originally designed.

DONATUS, *Praef. Buc.*		SERVIUS, *Praef. Aen.*	
		1	Schema
1–5	VITA (a) Origo	2–3	VITA (a) Origo
6–7	(b) Domicilium	4	(b) Domicilium
8–12	(c) Habitus	5	(c) Habitus
13–14	(d) Fortuna		
15–34	(e) Res gestae	6–12	(d) Res gestae [...

35–36	(f) Obitus		
37–42	(g) Testamentum		
43–46	(h) Testimonia		...]
47–49	TITULUS	13	TITULUS
50	CAUSA	14–16	QUALITAS
51—57			
58—63	(a) ab origine		
(b)	a uoluntate		
64–66	INTENTIO	17	INTENTIO
67–68	NUMERUS	18	NUMERUS
69	ORDO	19	ORDO
70–72	EXPLANATIO	20–22	EXPLANATIO

In like fashion Servius' introduction to the *Eclogues* will appear in *Ed. Harv.* I divided up into sections, with headings added in italics to aid the eye.

Servius' general dependence on Donatus is obvious. Thilo's conjecture of a lacuna after Serv. *Vit.* 12 adequately accounts for the failure to mention Virgil's death and the matter said by Servius at *Praef. Buc.* 20 to have been included in his *Vita*. One cannot gainsay Fraenkel that the section *periit ... duces*, accepted in *Ed. Harv.* II (p. 3) as genuine, is an interpolation: indeed, it is difficult to believe that VWN, the s group of Servian manuscripts, really do preserve a genuine tradition independent of all the others; they belong to the Γ tradition, which they represent less reliably than B and M; when they come up with some striking reading, those that are not transparent conjectures all seem to derive from the DS tradition, whence they are interpolated.

Some have held that the Servian Life does not survive in its original state, that its exiguous form and manifest inferiority to Donatus' point to its being a mere excerpt. The argument lacks cogency, for the lacuna posited by Thilo will have contained all we have reason to believe is lost; and the statement at *Aen.* 7. 1 *ut in principio diximus* refers to *Aen.* 1. 1 *prius de erroribus Aeneae dicit, post de bello*. Moreover, it fails to appreciate the peculiar interests of Servius, who was a literary man and evinced no aptitude or enthusiasm for historical research. Quintilian (1. 8. 18) had advised the teacher of literature to comment on the historical background, modifying his precept, however, with the injunction *non tamen usque ad superuacuum laborem*. This was a warning which Servius took to heart. He makes no independent attempt to deal with historical matters, and will suddenly reveal the most appalling ignorance, thinking, for example, that Julius Caesar was murdered in May (*Praef. Buc.* 13; *Geo.* 1.

466), confusing Varus the poet with Varus the general (*Buc.* 6. 6), and
evidently believing that the campaign of Actium took place during the
composition of the *Eclogues* (*Buc.* 9. 67).

The great disparity between Donatus' detailed Life and Servius'
threadbare one (which even before the lacuna we see degenerating into
literary charivari) comes therefore as no shock. Nor shall we be
surprised that the Compiler, on comparing with the Life in his Servius
the ampler and much more satisfactory one he found at the beginning of
the D Commentary, seems to have decided—as all scholars confronted
with the choice have done—to abandon Servius and embrace Donatus.
Imagine his situation: before him he has his new-found Donatus (Dp-
De-Dg-Da) and his own manuscript (Sp-Sa-Se-Sg), destined after he
has entered all his notes and additions to become the DS commentary;
he seems to have marked the Servian Life for deletion, and substituted
in its place the preface to Donatus. Thus the final result was Dp-DSa-
DSe-DSg.

The facts seem to admit no other explanation. The DS manuscript
containing *Aen.* 1–2 lacks the Servian Life and quite obviously by
design, for in the scholium on 1. 1, where Servius wrote *sicut in praemissa
eiusdem uita monstratum est*, the Compiler has deleted *eiusdem uita* and
substituted *narratione*, referring to the preface to the *Aeneid* proper. The
curios preservation of the beginning of Donatus' commentary is thus
explained: to be quite accurate, it consists of the dedicatory letter, the
Life, and the special preface to the *Eclogues* (all preserved in Par. Lat.
11308, a manuscript connected with the DS tradition). It would be
otherwise very difficult to explain why this much, and no more, of
Donatus' commentary was transcribed verbatim. This consideration
puts a coping stone on the theory that Donatus is the author of the D
commentary: all the other evidence has won for that theory a high
degree of probability, but here we can connect the actual name and text
of Donatus with the compilation of the DS commentary. This final
proof receives a yet further reinforcement.

Scholars have always felt somewhat perplexed at the anonymous
character of the DS manuscripts, and a little uneasy that none of the
primary manuscripts for the *Vita Donati* actually ascribes it to Donatus.
These circumstances turn out to be a necessary consequence of what
has been sketched above. In enlarging his Servius with copious additions from Donatus and extra exegesis from himself, the Compiler was
planning a large variorum edition of his own—very much as
Adamnanus, abbot of Iona from 679 to 704, had fused together scholia

of Servius and other commentators in the margins of a text of Virgil to produce that tohubohu which Funaioli in his *Esegesi Virgiliana antica*, the bible of these studies, calls the Filagrian Sylloge and which survives in the Bern Scholia, the two sets of *Explanationes* of the so-called Philargyrius, and the *Breuis expositio*. The Compiler had of necessity to expunge all indications of authorship. Where he transcribed a scholium from Donatus including the words *ut supra diximus*, he altered them to *ut supra dictum est*; where Servius said *ut supra diximus*, he altered that, too. Where in his manuscript had been written COMMENTARII SERVII GRAMMATICI (or the like) out came his pen to delete it; and the same treatment befell the title COMMENTARII DONATI GRAM-MATICI at the head of the Life of Virgil. That he preserved the text of Donatus' dedicatory letter is surprising. But this may be the Compiler's whimsy; and otherwise to account for its survival would be very difficult.

It was Rand's belief that the DS Commentary was originally divided into several volumes. Whether or not this be true, the manuscript traditions of the Compilation Dp-DSa-DSe-DSg descends to us in separate streams. Dp may be deferred for a moment. DSa is principally represented by the codex Cassellanus (following Thilo and dissenting from *Ed. Harv.* II we identify this as Daniel's Fuldensis),[14] which contains the full DS commentary for *Aen.* 1 and 2 only, and by the Floriacensis (= Bern. 172 + Par. Lat. 7929), which, though containing the whole poem, has DS comment only for Book 3 and onwards. For DSe-DSg we have only the extant portion of the Lemovicensis (Leid. Voss. O.80), which begins at *Buc.* 4. 1 and ends at *Geo.* 1. 278. Savage observes that the missing initial quires, known to be three in number, could not have contained the DS commentary (i.e., S + the Compiler's additions from D) for the whole of *Buc.* 1–3.[15] By our calculations, based on a ratio of S 58 to D 42, they would just have held DS *Buc.* 2. 11–4. 1. Now *Buc.* 2. 11 is a significant place. All our manuscripts of Servius lack *Buc.* 1. 37–2. 10, and probably the Compiler's lacked it, too. But except by the tallest coincidence Donatus will have supplied this great lacuna. We are tempted to wonder if the Compiler took a short cut in building up his DS edition by simply transferring Dp + De (1. 1–2. 10) to his own manuscript. This would explain the otherwise remarkable

---

[14] Thilo (above, n. 11), pp. xlviii–lvii. On this matter a sharp dissent from the opinions of the Harvard editors was included in his review by Rodney P. Robinson, *CW* 43 (1950), 232 f.

[15] John J. H. Savage, 'The Manuscripts of the Commentary of Servius Danielis on Virgil', *HSCPh* 43 (1932), 81 and n. 1.

preservation of Dpe; and it may explain why *diximus* and other personal verbs have not been altered in Don. *Praef. Buc.* 47, 58, 66, 69, 70. But if so, like other sections of DS, that containing *Buc.* 1. 1–2. 10 is now lost.

In the DS Commentary, as we envisage it, none of the sections, Dp, DSa1–2, DSa3–12, DSe–DSg bore any indication of authorship, though in the case of the preface the dedicatory letter (Dd) would furnish a pretty strong hint that the Life (Dv) and the preface to the *Eclogues* (Dpe) were the work of Donatus. If, however, a scribe were to copy out Dv and Dpe only, the transcript would not show Donatus' name at all. This explains why the primary manuscripts MERABG (Dv–Dpe) are without ascription; only P (Dd–Dv–Dpe) contains the name of Donatus (EL DONATVS in the salutation), and not until the twelfth century has this clue been spread abroad and brought about the correct ascription in later copies of the Life.

Critics inimical to the above theory will suggest that the Donatian Life and preface to the *Eclogues* survived only as a convenient introduction to the text of Virgil and have nothing to do with DS. However, to say nothing of the manuscript affiliations involved, this will mean postulating that *two* copies of Donatus survived into the Middle Ages. Most improbable.

We seize this moment to advert on a marginal reference in Bern. 363 (fo. 41b), the significance of which was detected by Savage:[16] *Donatus alter qui in totum Virgilium exposuit in Leotica*, rendered by Lindsay as: 'The Donatus alluded to here as a Virgil-commentator is not the well-known Donatus [i.e. Tiberius Claudius Donatus], but a second Donatus, who wrote a commentary on the *Eclogues* and *Georgics*, as well as on the *Aeneid*. There is a manuscript of his commentary at Liége.' Perhaps this was—not Donatus—but the DS Commentary itself.

IV. *A Cross-Reference in the Servian Life*

The Compiler, we have seen, was in the habit of transferring portions of Servian scholia to other parts of Servius indicated by cross-references. The decision to discard the Servian Life in favour of that by Donatus gave him a special reason to indulge his practice here, for no collector likes to throw away that for which a suitable receptacle exists. The Servian Life contains more than one reference to passages in Virgil's text, and the first of these prompted the Compiler to action.

---

[16] Ibid. 191.

SERVIUS (*Praef. Aen.* =) *Vita* 7

postea ortis bellis ciuilibus inter
Antonium et Augustum, Augustus
uictor Cremonensium agros, quia pro
Antonio senserant, dedit militibus
suis. qui cum non sufficerent, his
addidit agros Mantuanos, sublatos
non propter ciuium culpam, sed
propter uicinitatem Cremonensium;
unde ipse in Bucolicis (9. 28):
'Mantua uae miserae nimium uicina
Cremonae.'

SERVIUS AUCTUS *Buc.* 9. 28b

NIMIVM *autem* VICINA id est usque
ad periculum,
*nam ortis bellis ciuilibus inter Antonium
et Augustum, Augustus uictor
Cremonensium agros, quia pro Antonio
senserant, dedit militibus suis. qui cum
non sufficerent, his addidit agros
Mantuanos, sublatos non propter ciuium
culpam, sed propter uicinitatem.*

As Murgia pointed out to the writer some years ago, the D addition here
comes straight from Servius: its egregious error, that Anthony had
suffered defeat at the hands of Augustus before the composition of the
ninth *Eclogue*, has already been noted as a delusion of Servius; Donatus,
on the other hand, gives in *Vit.* 19 a version which, besides its fuller
detail, accords with historical fact. Notice the Compiler's fussy *autem*.
We must not overlook a puzzling textual variation: in Servius all
manuscripts give *sufficerent* (except V, which has *suffecissent*); Servius
Auctus has *sufficissent*, an obvious error, altered by a later hand to
suffecissent. Servius repeats in slightly different language the same
account at *Praef. Buc.* 13, where all manuscripts (V is illegible) attest
sufficerent: because of the syllable -*fic*- in L one is inclined to assume that
the DS version gave *sufficerent*, too. It seems that V, remarkably, has at
Serv. *Vit.* 7 suffered interpolation from DS *Buc.* 9. 28, a strange but not
impossible state of affairs, since for the *Georgics* V gives a Servian text
with DS excerpts loosely inserted into it.

V. *The* Editio Princeps *of the* Aeneid

Since the two other references to Virgil's text in the Servian Life involve
discussion of the posthumous editing of the *Aeneid*, let us begin with our
fullest and most trustworthy source, Donatus' Life 37–41. The remaining Lives all derive from Donatus', being contracted from it and
augmented with material, mostly transparent fabrications, drawn from
other sources: one examines them only in case they have secured
something of value from Jerome, who used Suetonius as a source. As we

shall see later, Jerome's testimony does not much affect the present point of discussion. Now, the thesis that Donatus substantially reproduces Suetonius' Life of Virgil, though long no more than an article of faith, received in 1938 a brilliant proof from Heinrich Naumann.[17] Defending the high authority of the Life against the attacks of Valmaggi, Klotz, and Wieser, he built on Donatus' use of Suetonius' *Vita Terenti* by pointing out small but recognizable differences of view between Donatus' Life and Donatus' preface to the *Eclogues* and meticulously demonstrating the Suetonian grammar and style of the Life. His conclusions, closely scrutinized by Geer, Paratore, and Bayer in the last thirty years,[18] will require some adjustments but in the passage now to be cited he has secured the full approbation of his challengers. This being so, we anticipate the reader's permission to dispense with a formal proof that, excepting only the bracketed section, we are here perusing Suetonius.

37 heredes fecit ex dimidia parte Valerium Proculum, fratrem alio patre, ex quarta Augustum, ex duodecima Maecenatem, ex reliqua L. Varium et Plotium Tuccam. [qui eius Aeneida post obitum iussu Caesaris emendauerunt.

38 de qua re Sulpicii Carthaginiensis extant huiusmodi uersus:

> iusserat haec rapidis adoleri carmina flammis
> Vergilius, Phrygium quae cecinere ducem.
> Tucca uetat Variusque; simul tu, maxime Caesar,
> non sinis et Latiae consulis historiae.
> infelix gemino cecidit prope Pergamon igni,
> et paene est alio Troia cremata rogo.]

39 egerat cum Vario, priusquam Italia decederet, ut si quid sibi accidisset, Aeneida combureret; at is facturum se pernegarat; igitur in extreme ualetudine assidue scrinia desiderauit, crematurus ipse; uerum nemine offerente nihil quidem nominatim de ea cauit.

40 ceterum eidem Vario ac simul Tuccae scripta sua sub ea condicione legauit, ne quid ederent, quod non a se editum esset.

41 edidit autum auctore Augusto Varius, sed summatim emendata, ut qui uersus etiam imperfectos ... reliquerit...

38 adoleri *Rostagni ex Gell.* 17. 10. 7: aboleri *codd.*

Suetonius gives a clear and consistent account. Virgil had willed his

[17] Heinrich Naumann, 'Suetons Vergilvita', *RhM* 87 (1938), 334–76.
[18] R. M. Geer, 'Non-Suetonian Passages in the Life of Virgil Formerly Ascribed to Donatus', *TAPhA* 57 (1926), 107–15; E. Paratore, *Una nuova ricostruzione del 'De Poetis' di Suetonio* (Rome, 1946), pp. 117 f.; K. Bayer, *Der Suetonische Kern und die späteren Zusätze der Vergilvita* (diss. Munich, 1952).

papers jointly to his friends Varius and Tucca, forbidding them to publish anything not already published by himself. Before embarking on his journey to Greece, he had unsuccessfully attempted to secure from Varius—who is thus revealed as Virgil's chief confidant—a promise that in case of his death the manuscript of the *Aeneid* would be consigned to the flames. In the event, Augustus commanded Varius—again indicated as the principal executor—to edit the poem, which he did, says Suetonius, in such a way as to leave half-lines; and the singular verb confirms that Varius discharged the task.

Corroboration is supplied in the only other passage in the Life to refer to the matter, (42) *Nisus ... aiebat Varium ... commutasse et ... transtulisse, etiam correxisse...* The evidence permits no doubt: Varius, and only Varius, edited the *Aeneid*.

Of course, Tucca, as a close friend of Varius' and with him a co-inheritor of Virgil's papers, will have been consulted by Varius. But editing a manuscript is a one-man job, and Tucca probably did no more than endorse Augustus' charge to Varius and leave him to get on with it. The association of Varius and Tucca as co-inheritors caused many to assume that Tucca was invested with joint responsibility for publishing the *Aeneid* and to refer to the two of them loosely as the editors. Donatus is perhaps beguiled into this loose talk out of a desire to effect a connection between Suetonius and the verses of Sulpicius which he cannot bear to part with: thus we read (37): *L. Varium et Plotium Tuccam, qui eius Aeneida post obitum iussu Caesaris emendauerunt.* And it looks very much as if this sentence is the source of Jerome (*Chron.* 166e14): *Varius et Tucca ... qui eius Aeneidum postea libros emendarunt.*

The poem of Sulpicius does not actually make Varius and Tucca co-editors, but merely unites them as opposed to Virgil's wishes. Why has Varius here surrendered his place of primacy to Tucca? That is easily answered. Varius will not scan as the first word of a verse in the elegiac metre: the poet was obliged to reverse the proper order. Any sources, therefore, which speak of Tucca and Varius in that sequence we may suspect of being influenced by these verses.

The principal one is Servius. We may dismiss the Life of the so-called Probus, a corrupt and garbled account which is universally acknowledged to depend on Servius. Four times Servius refers to the editorship of 'Tucca and Varius'.

(1) S *Aen.* 4. 436 ... DEDERIS CVMVLATAM ... quam lectionem Tucca et Varius probant. nam male quidam legunt ... DEDERIT ... CVMVLATA ...

This verse, says Conington, is 'well known as the most difficult in Virgil'. Variant readings, as Servius' note reveals, existed in his own day; and the reference to 'Tucca and Varius'—as if the *editio princeps* of the *Aeneid* boasted an apparatus criticus!—shows only, what we have come to expect from Servius, that he is inventing an authority for his statement. Even on the most favourable interpretation he can only mean that *dederis cumulatam* was the reading of the first edition. But *extremam hanc ... dederit* certainly seems confirmed by the parallelism with 429 *extremum hoc miserae det munus amanti*. DEDERIS is no more than an incorrect conjecture based on the parenthesis *miserere sororis* ('pardon your sister's weakness').

(2) S *Aen.* 5.871 ... sciendum sane Tuccam et Varium hunc finem quinti esse uoluisse: nam a Vergilio duo uersus sequentes huic iuncti fuerunt: unde in nonnullis antiquis codicibus sexti initium est 'obuertunt pelago proras, tum dente tenaci'.

If Virgil had ended Book 5 with (6. 2) ... *adlabitur oris*, no problem would have arisen. It is difficult to visualize an editor transferring the two lines forward to the next book, if in fact Virgil placed them at the end of this one. On the other hand, it is easy to conceive of Virgil copying Homer's book-enjambment (cf. *Od.* 12–13; *Aen.* 1–2) and placing them at the head of Book 6, and dissatisfied or puzzled critics transferring them back to the end of the previous book. Indeed, Ribbeck has done so. And so did Probus in antiquity, causing texts so corrupted to appear in circulation (Serv. *Aen.* 6. 1). Servius knew what the canonical text gave, but at the same time he felt sympathy with Probus' opinion. His own invented 'Tucca and Varius' enabled him to confer authority on both views.

(3) S *Aen.* 7. 464 FVRIT INTVS AQVAI / FVMIDVS ... hanc autem diaeresin Tucca et Varius fecerunt: nam Vergilius sic reliquerat 'furit intus aquae amnis' et '... exuberat amnis': quod satis asperum fuit.

The statement passes belief and must be rejected out of hand. Again Servius is attempting to settle a textual crux by imputing to Virgil what is plainly a corruption and to 'Tucca and Varius' what is plainly the original reading. The actual sequence was surely that *aquai* (*ed princ.*) was in some texts corrupted, to *aquae*, then miscorrected to *aquae uis* or the ghastly *aquae amnis*. With F and R the manuscripts of Macrobius (*Sat.* 5. 11. 23) proffer *aquae uis*, but, as Bentley acutely remarks, Macrobius' paraphrase of the crux, *amnem fumidum exuberantem spumis atque intus furentem*, suggests that he read *aquai*.[19]

Such editorial misconceptions constitute no unique phenomenon, for in the text of Euripides we encounter the same situation, with Apollodorus of Tarsus and Didymus playing the role of Servius to the 'Tucca and Varius' of 'the actors'.[20] In these three passages, then, we hope to have established that Servius has not the slightest authority for referring to 'Tucca and Varius'. Irrefutable evidence will be forthcoming in a fourth passage, discussion of which will suitably fit in with discussion of the next cross-reference in the Servian Life.

VI. Ille Ego Qui Quondam...

First let us set the passage beside the relevant portion of Donatus, square brackets again being employed to indicate non-Suetonian material.

DONATUS (*Praef. Buc.* =)	SERVIUS (*Praef. Aen.* =)
Vita 41	*Vita* 10
41 edidit autem auctore Augusto Varius, sed summatim emendata, ut qui uersus etiam imperfectos [sicut erant] reliquerit; quos multi mox supplere conati non perinde ualuerunt [ob difficultatem quod omnia fere apud eum hemistichia absoluto perfectoque sunt sensu, praeter illud (Aen. 3. 340): 'quem tibi iam Troia'.]	10 Augustus uero, ne tantum opus periret, Tuccam et Varium hac lege iussit emendare, ut superflua demerent, nihil adderent tamen.
42 Nisus grammaticus audisse se a senioribus aiebat, Varium duorum librorum ordinem commutasse, et qui nunc secundus sit in tertium locum transtulisse, etiam primi libri correxisse principium, his uersibus demptis:	11 unde et semiplenos eius inuenimus uersiculos, ut (Aen. 1. 534) 'hic cursus fuit', et aliquos detractos, ut in principio, nam ab armis non coepit, sed sic:

ille ego, qui quondam gracili modulatus auena
carmen, et egressus siluis uicina coegi

---

[19] Cf. A. Stachelscheid, 'Bentleys Emendationen von Macrobius', *RhM* 36 (1881), 324–26.
[20] Cf. G. Zuntz, *An Inquiry into the Transmission of the Plays of Euripides* (Cambridge, 1965), pp. 253 f. and n. 1, p. 254.

ut quamuis auido parerent arua colono,
gratum opus agricolis; at nunc horrentia Martis—
arma uirumque cano.

41 sicut *Gronouius*: si qui *codd.*
42 *uix sanum* duorum *del. Reifferscheid, idem post* sit *add.* in primum, tertium in secundum, et primum *coll. Seru. Praef. Aen.* 19

We are unable to dogmatize about this part of the Donatian Life. Bayer hesitatingly denies to Suetonius (41) *sicut erant* but confidently repudiates *ob difficultatem ... iam Troia.* For Paratore it is section 42 which Donatus has added. Actually it does not matter, for the crucial report goes back to one Nisus, 'who used to say that he had heard the following account from older men', presumably contemporaries of Varius. This suggests that the writer lived himself not much later than Nisus, namely is Suetonius rather than Donatus. But it does not matter. The author of the Life shows here a proper sense of handling evidence. He undertakes no responsibility for the truth of the account, he merely repeats it: a professor *used to say* (so that there is no suggestion that his statement was a written one, though we know he did write: a work of his is cited by Priscian, *GL* 2. 503. 16), and used to say that *he had heard from older men* (so that the account is gossip: no documents are mentioned, no informant named). In short, the account has by external criteria very little evidential value.

Nor does it acquire from its internal merits the slightest hold upon our credence. Varius cannot possibly have arranged the books of the *Aeneid* as we have it, for the unassailable reason that the contents of the poem demand the order we have and permit no other. What Nisus heard is false. But it is not meaningless. Sabbadini and others have shown that Book 3, though in its present form a part of Aeneas' narration to Dido, bears many indications of having at an earlier stage of composition occupied a different place in the sequence and been written as proceeding from the poet's own lips. Detected soon after publication, the difficulty was explained—as we have just seen others explained by Servius—as arising from editorial manipulation.

We can never know precisely what Varius allowed himself in editing Virgil's manuscripts. Who has ever doubted his fitness for the charge? He was of that select little company for whom Horace (*Serm.* 1. 5. 41 f.), not a man given to extravagant affection, has issued an incontestable voucher: 'animae qualis neque candidiores / terra tulit, neque quis me sit deuinctior alter'. To his own work time has denied immortality, but the Romans esteemed it as deserving that reward. He, if anyone, was qualified to smooth over with his own composition such marks of incompleteness as a sensitive artist might deem unsightly in a poem so close to perfection. Significant that no carping critic ever rose to accuse him of a less than satisfactory performance; and if no devotee of Virgil has ever said 'well done', why, that in itself is the consummation of praise. It is all too plain that the *Aeneid* was in fact *summatim emendata*, 'minimally touched', so that even half-lines were published as the poet left them: with such respect the editor treated the poet's creation.

Nisus' hearsay evidence about the alleged prooemium *ille ego* is equally worthless. Of course the lines (which, let us confess, are superb) were never written by Virgil. Like the four verses of *Catalepton* 15 and the quatrain introducing our texts of Ovid's *Amores*, they belong to that small genre of verse which may be styled editorial. Their *raison d'être* has nothing to do with epic poetry but springs from an editor's desire to produce an attractive volume. Brandt has placed beyond doubt their epigrammatic nature (cf. *CIL* III. 3676; VI. 1372, 1692, 11407; XI. 1122), convincingly deducing from Mart. 12. 186. 2 that they were designed for a frontispiece of Virgil in an edition de luxe of the *Aeneid*.[21] The author of the verses had no intention to deceive. What happened was that some readers of this handsome edition were beguiled by the word *ego* into a firm conviction that the lines were authentic, just as others on reading *Mantua me genuit* saw in the pronoun proof that the poet himself had composed the couplet. Even more than the *ille ego* Virgil's epitaph merits the highest praise: its economical but elegant precision coupled with its restraint in suppressing the poet's name and fame places it among the most successful examples of lapidary verse. Naturally, even the gullible realized that Virgil could not have written it without knowing of his death in Brundisium, hence Jerome (*Chron.* 165h21) refers to the inscription as *quem moriens ipse dictauerat*.

On turning to Servius (*Praef. Aen.* 10 f.) we learn more or less the same story, but with a shocking difference. It is not so much that Servius swallows with shut eyes and open mouth what Donatus had without obvious sign of acceptance or rejection reported dispassionately. The distressing thing is that Servius alters, nay he fabricates, the evidence to suit his beliefs. The alleged deletion of the *ille ego*, which, as we have seen, rested upon the vaguest of oral reports, has been elevated by him

---

[21] Edward Brandt, 'Zum Aeneisprooemium', *Philol.* 83 (1927), 331–5.

to fact as solid and self-evident as the half-lines we observe in our texts. From the report, moreover, he has guessed and, having guessed, proclaimed as fact the principles under which the editor (or rather 'Tucca and Varius') worked: they were commanded to remove *superflua* (as if there were reason to believe that needless passages would be found in the draft *Aeneid*), as they were forbidden to complete half-lines (as if Augustus knew that any would be found). Servius is not alone to blame. When Jerome writes (*Chron.* 166e14): *Varius et Tucca ... emendarunt sub ea lege ut nihil adderent*, he is reporting observed fact as though it were designed; as Leo remarks, 'that nothing was added could clearly be seen by anyone who saw the half-lines'.[22] Nor can a critical judgement heed Bill's plea that Servius knows of many passages removed by Tucca and Varius when he says *ut in principio*, 'as *for example* at the beginning'.[23] This sounds like the man not sure of his facts. We find no 'for example' in Donatus, who retails a much more careful version of the matter, and must wonder if Servius is not letting his tongue run away with him. Interestingly, he perceives that 'Tucca and Varius' could not have altered the order of the books of the *Aeneid*; as a result, this item is suppressed and only mentioned for ridicule in *Praef. Aen.* 19: *licet quidam superflue dicant...* 'though there are those who needlessly assert...' We detect again the attitude of the elementary teacher, who must concentrate on essentials and pass over all needless detail.

The Compiler was not much concerned about the Servian Life. Donatus' version gave him much more. As we have concluded above, he seems to have marked the Servian Life for deletion but salvaged part of section 7 by transferring it to *Buc.* 9. 28, to which it contained a reference. Thus at the beginning of the DS *Aeneid* commentary we should expect no Life, but merely the special preface (13): *titulus est Aeneis*, etc.

Actually we find the abbreviated and evidently headless remains of Serv. *Praef. Aen.* 11 and 12. The scribe of the Cassellanus has mistaken the initial words as the beginning of the DS commentary, as is shown by the majuscules he uses. Apparently the Compiler deleted everything down to *nam ab armis*, which he will have slightly modified, somewhat as is here suggested.

---

[22] Friedrich Leo, *Plautinische Forschungen*[2] (Berlin, 1912), p. 41.
[23] Clarence P. Bill, 'Vergiliana', *CP* 27 (1932), 168–71.

SERVIUS (*Praef. Aen.* =)	SERVIUS AUCTUS
Vita 11	*Praef. Aen. ad init.*

11 ... et aliquos detractos, ut in principio, nam ab armis non coepit, sed sic: ille ego ... at nunc horrentia Martis—arma uirumque cano.	⟨ *Vergilium constat in principio ab armis non coepisse, sed sic: ill ego ... at nunc horrentia Martis* ⟩
12 et in secundo hos uersus constat esse detractos:...	*ARMA VIRVMQVE CANO ET IN SECVNDO LIBRO ALIQVOS VERSVS POSVERAT quos constat esse detractos ...*
13 titulus est Aeneis...	*titulus est Aeneis...*

It is to this passage so constituted that the Compiler's reference at D *Aen.* 1. 1 (*in praemissa narratione*) will then allude. Elder, followed by Rowell, argues that, when the scribe of C (or of its exemplar) addressed himself to the task of transcribing the DS Commentary, the first page was missing, and so he began at the first words preserved: *arma uirumque cano.*[24] Strange that such famous words should by chance come at the top of page 3. This is stretching coincidence too far. Moreover, the scribe's use of majuscules (such as one uses in titles) shows that he believed that he really was beginning the commentary.

It is more likely that the marks of the deletion postulated above obscured the actual place where the beginning was intended. The scribe was none too bright, but he knew the opening words of the *Aeneid*, and consequently began his apograph two or three lines lower than he should have done.

PART TWO: THE HELEN EPISODE

VII. *The External Evidence*

Possibly the Compiler was induced to retain a note about *ille ego* (which, after all, he had in the Donatian Life) by the scholium on *Aen.* 1. 1. He had no compelling reason to keep mention of it—and out of place, too—before the *Titulus* section of the *Aeneid* preface. But he may have been encouraged by a greater difficulty he faced in connection with the Helen verses. These are referred to three times: in the Preface (S/DS); at 2. 566 (DS); and at 2. 592 (S/DS). Consider the last passage first.

S/DS *Aen.* 2. 592a DEXTRAQVE PREHENSVM ea corporis parte qua ictum Helenae minabatur, quae in templo Vestae stabat ornata. ut enim

[24] J. P. Elder, *De Servii Commentarii Danielinis, ut aiunt, in Aeneidos libros primum et secundum confectis* (diss. Harvard, 1940), p. 148; Rowell (above, n. 2), pp. 216 f.

| in primo diximus, aliquos | *dictum est, uersus illos qui* |
| hinc uersus | *superius* (566) *notati sunt, hinc* |

constat esse sublatos, nec immerito. nam et ... Lacaenae.

The note, embedded in Servius' commentary, elucidates 592 *dextraque prehensum* in the light of the Helen Episode (for the text of which Servius refers his reader back to the Preface) and approves of the assumed decision of the editors to remove them. For the moment we merely observe that Servius' solution of a difficulty in the canonical text—here a break in Virgil's composition rather like the half-lines (*quos multi mox supplere conati*, we may remember)—follows a pattern noticed earlier. He imputes to Virgil a seemingly unacceptable text (location of Helen in a place contradicted by *Aen.* 6. 523 ff.) and imputes to 'Tucca and Varius' correction to the initial difficulty. The version of Servius Auctus is identical, except for deviations characteristic of the Compiler's activity. That is to say, we are to infer that the Compiler found nothing in the D commentary, the commentary of Donatus, to add to or subtract from or with which to modify the Servian text: the changes he made, he made purely on his own account. They are (a) his customary substitution of *dictum est* for *diximus*, and (b) alteration of the reference from *in primo* to *superius*, i.e., from *Praef. Aen.* to *Aen.* 2. 566. The second change was forced upon him by his earlier decision to suppress the Servian Life and move suitable material in that Life to relevant places in the body of the Servian commentary. Let us now look at the passage to which Servius referred back.

| SERVIUS (*Praef. Aen.* =) | SERVIUS AUCTUS |
| *Vita* 12 | *Praef. Aen. ad init.* |

12 et in secundo hos uersus constat esse detractos: 'aut ignibus aegra dedere—iamque adeo ... mente ferebar—cum mihi se non ante oculis'.

et in secundo libro aliquos uersus posuerat quos constat esse detractos, quos inueniemus cum peruenerimus ad locum de quo detracti sunt.

Besides the Compiler's characteristic cross-reference ahead, *inueniemus* (probably the correction of Modius: *-imus* the Cassellanus), we note his clumsy and overexpressed Latin: *libro* added to *secundo*; *aliquos* for *aliquot* (which we should refrain from conjecturing with Ribbeck); relative piled upon relative, *quos ... quos...*; and the repetitiousness of *esse detractos ... de quo detracti sunt*. A further consideration yields decisive proof. If the text of the verses were original to the D commentary (Fraenkel, Rowell) and given at the appropriate place in that commentary, that is, at D *Aen.* 2. 566, the question of their deletion by the editors would have been discussed at the same time. In other words, instead of two notes, one at 2. 566 and another at 2. 592, we should have encountered only one. On this point Servius makes sense: the Helen Episode is given in the preface as non-canonical and not qualifying for annotation, and in his commentary he only alludes to the passage when confronted with words of Virgil's text which provide a suitable opening for the subject—not 566, but 592. An original D scholium (= Donatus) at 2. 566 would have dispensed with the need for comment at *Aen.* 2. 592, just as the D scholium at *Aen.* 1. 689 dispensed with the need for comment at *Aen.* 1. 695, where in fact the Compiler has excised the Servian note. We proceed to the third reference.

D *Aen.* 2. 566 *IGNIBVS AEGRA DEDERE post hunc uersum hi uersus fuerunt, qui a Tucca et Vario sublati sunt: 'iamque adeo … mente ferebar'.*

qui a Tucca et Vario sublati *Bergk* quia tucca et uarius obliti *C* quos Tucca et Var(r)us obliti *Modius copying C, vulg.* qui a Tucca et Vario obliti *Thilo, Ed. Harv.* ferebar *Daniel ex Serv.*: loquebatur *C*: loquebar *Modius*

To establish the text first: *loquebatur* (sc. *Aeneas*) has probably crept in from a gloss explaining that Aeneas has been reporting his own words in direct speech from 577; and no one seems to doubt that the Servian *ferebar* is the original reading. No one, however, seems to understand that Bergk's *sublati* is mandatory. Aided perhaps by *qui a* becoming *quia*, transposition of vowels produced *uariusoblati*, misdivided as *uarius oblati*. Whoever made the correction to *obliti* (probably the scribe of C) must have intended the verb *obliuiscor*. By chance *obliti* is a legitimate form from *oblino*, and everybody these days so construes it. The resulting sense, however, 'blotted over', is not quite appropriate to the context: this requires a word meaning 'removed', and *sublati* is guaranteed by being the verb used in the scholium to 2. 592.

The combination 'Tucca and Varius' points to the Servian origin of the scholium. The Compiler has followed up his plan of transferring the passage from Serv. *Praef. Aen.* 12, being sent to this particular spot—rather than 592 a few lines lower—by the catchwords (566) *aut ignibus aegra dedere* given by Servius (and hence the precise gloss). Notice the naïve style of *post hunc uersum hi uersus*, a footprint of the Compiler's Latin.

We have demonstrated that the authority for the Helen Episode, both for its text and for the statement that it was removed from the poet's manuscript by Tucca and Varius, is Servius. Every word of every

mention of it in Servius Auctus derives from Servius and thus possesses
no evidential value whatever.

What source supplied Servius with his information? The temptation
is to answer: Donatus. Certainly it looks as if Donatus had in two places,
at least, quoted non-canonical verses.

(1) D *Aen.* 3. 204 *ERRAMVS PELAGO et reliqua.*

> *hinc Pelopis gentes Maleaeque sonantia saxa*
> *circumstant pariterque undae terraeque minantur.*
> *pulsamur saeuis et circumsistimur undis.*

hi uersus circumducti inuenti dicuntur et extra paginam in mundo.

The Compiler did not invent this note: he must have taken it from
Donatus. As to its substance, we are compelled by its sharp contradiction of the context (the Trojans could not see) to regard it as a fake.
Moreover, the faker, whoever he was, has been at some pains to deceive:
notice the elaborate embroidery of 'circled around . . . and in the margin
outside the written page'. Worse still, though whether by art or lack of
art it is hard to tell, he has fabricated not a continuous passage such as
Varius would never have omitted but such an inchoate morsel as might
lend an air of verisimilitude to his deception. Mackail's note admirably
illustrates the effect he intended. But for us the important point lies in
the word *dicuntur.* Donatus did not represent the story as a fact, but
merely quoted it as alleged by some Nisus.

(2) D *Aen.* 6. 289 GORGONES . . . *sane quidam dicunt uerus alios hos a poeta hoc
loco relictos, qui ab eius emendatoribus sublati sint:*

> *Gorgonis in medio portentum immane Medusae,*
> *uipereae circum ora comae, cui sibila torquent*
> *infamesque rigent oculi, mentoque sub imo*
> *serpentum extremis nodantur uincula candis.*

Here likewise we infer from the words *quidam dicunt* that Donatus did
not commit himself to an acceptance of the report (*quidam* is probably
the Compiler's: Donatus' practice is to give us the actual name). The
verses seem to have been composed as an alternative to 289 by someone
who was offended at the plural *Gorgones* and wished to replace it with a
description of Medusa.

We conclude then that, if Donatus had quoted the Helen Episode, he
would have named or at least indicated his source of information. In any
case, his reference in the Life to Varius' editorial procedure rules out
the possibility of his believing the passage authentic. The editor effected

minimal changes; he left half-lines: he hardly removed a connected passage of twenty-two finished verses. Donatus writes (*Praef. Buc.* = *Vit.* 41) of many attempts to complete the half-lines (Servius quotes one at *Aen.* 8. 41, and Seneca *Ep. Mor.* 94. 28 gives *Aen.* 10. 284 in a supplemented form), so that we may without rashness infer that some attempts were made to complete other (real or imaginary) unfinished particulars of the poem. Nisus knew of a story that four lines had been removed by Varius. Why should Donatus mention a mere report of the lesser, if he possessed proof of the greater? Clearly, if Donatus knew of the Helen Episode, he regarded it as spurious. Further, if he mentioned it in his commentary, it seems very strange that the Compiler (who had dealings with it in three separate places) added not a single word of Donatus' comment to Servius'. The most reasonable conclusion is that Donatus never mentioned the passage at all.

Whence, then, did Servius get it? Probably from some commentary little used and of no great authority and influence. If the Helen Episode had really been found in Virgil's manuscript and then been excluded by Varius and been later published, then we should have known of this from a source other than Servius. And that not a solitary mention should anywhere occur to confirm or even modify Servius' account of this passage naturally casts more than a penumbra of doubt upon his trustworthiness.

VIII. *Servius' Treatment of his Sources*

Questioning Servius' trustworthiness does not imply impeachment of his honesty. Austin's defence of the Helen Episode includes the words 'Servius' good faith'.[25] This suggests that Servius has uttered his evidence under oath. By no means. Much more appropriate and much closer to the truth are the words Austin penned in the first lines of his article: 'Few critics [*rather* "commentators"] can ever have shown more lighthearted thoughtlessness towards an anxious posterity than Servius in his casual preservation of the "Helen-Episode".' But Servius had no reason to feel that after ages would regard his work as a unique source of information. 'I believe', says Thomas, 'that the commentary was *destined for schools*, and that it summarized the instruction given by its author *to his most advanced pupils*.'[26] This view derives from a just and accurate appreciation, except that we can now put the name of Donatus, rather

[25] R. G. Austin, 'Virgil, *Aeneid* 2. 567–88', *CQ* 55 (1961), 197.
[26] Émile Thomas, *Essai sur Servius et son commentaire sur Virgile* (Paris, 1880), p. 182.

than that of Servius, to the one who taught the advanced classes. Rowell
has shown that Servius simply passed over Donatus' quotations from
Naevius: this was an author not on his list of prescribed books.[27] In
following up Rowell's research Lloyd has established the general nature
of this phenomenon, namely that Servius consistently reduces the older
commentator's copious quotations to suit the smaller size and scope of
his own work, quotations from some authors (like Cato and Sisenna)
being retained and others being passed over altogether, whilst in the
case of those who qualify for retention the title and book-number of the
work are suppressed.[28] In this we must recognize that, so far from
disputing the superiority of Donatus as a source of knowledge, Servius
is confessing it.

Closer study of Servius makes ever clearer the nature of the complete
canvas which we, with so much republican literature lost to us, see in
detail only here and there, where the DS commentary permits us a peep
at Donatus. Could we cross-examine Servius over his quotation at *Geo.*
3. 363, he would cheerfully admit, after consulting his Donatus and
other texts, that he really meant the other Flaccus: not Persius, but
Horace. If we pointed out to him that at *Aen.* 1. 435 and *Geo.* 4. 286 he
has cited the same passage of Pliny differently, he would obligingly
harmonize them; and as we confronted him with scores of such
inexactitudes he might—no doubt expressing himself less politely—give
us the opinion of Thomas: 'We must therefore first of all put aside the
notion ... that Servius can be used to correct the texts of authors. His
quotations are merely items of evidence which require confirmation.'[29]
He would question the purpose to which we were putting him. As for
our concern over his habit of presenting half-truths, rumours, and even
fables as definitive knowledge by suppressing his source of information,
he would sarcastically ask if we expected him to document every single
fact. He would ridicule us if we were to fault him for stating on his own
authority at *Aen.* 8. 176 what we later found was lifted from Book 18 of
the *Exegetics* of Cornelius Balbus. 'If you wish this degree of exactitude
and this kind of needless detail,' he would say, 'you must go to Donatus.'

While that commentary still survived, there was no danger that
Servius' cavalier treatment of his sources would deceive. But now that

[27] Henry T. Rowell, 'Aelius Donatus and the D Scholia on the *Bellum Punicum* of
Naevius', *YCS* 15 (1957), 113–19; also 'The Scholium on Naevius in *Parisimus Latinus*
7930', *AJPh* 78 (1957), 1–22.
[28] Robert B. Lloyd, 'Republican Authors in Servius and the Scholia Danielis', *HSCPh*
65 (1961), 291–341.
[29] Thomas (above, n. 26), p. 193.

Donatus has perished, we run the risk of being misled by Servius wherever we must rely on him alone. No teacher who habitually censors and even doctors the information he purveys can be set up as a tribunal to whom a final appeal can be made. We cannot take his words at face value. When Servius in referring to the removal by Tucca and Varius of the Helen lines employs the word *constat*, we cannot be sure that it possesses any significant meaning at all. He says, for example, of the child of the fourth *Eclogue* (according to him the son of Asinius Pollio) *quem constat natum risisse statim.* This sort of stuff is all very well at the kindergarten level, but it has no place in the world of scholarship. We might even extend the words of Thomas and claim that all Servius' statements 'ont besoin d'etre confirmes'. Consider his references to Catullus.

(1) S *Geo.* 2. 95. The opinion here ascribed to Catullus lacks confirmation in the extant poems. Servius seems to be reporting prose, and '*Catullus*' may be an error.

(2) S *Aen.* 4. 409 (after a note on verbs like *ferueo / feruo* and after quotations from Virgil and Horace): ... ut 'cauo, cauis'. hinc etiam Catullus 'cauere' dixit.

Servius' source referred to 50. 18 f.; 61. 145 *cauĕ*, but he himself seems to think that the form *cauĕre* occurs in the poet's works. It is a fair inference that he had no first-hand knowledge of them.

(3) S *Aen.* 5. 591 a FRANGERET deciperet, falleret.
                   b est autem uersus Catulli.

The two parts of the scholium should be kept distinct. In the second, Servius (who, let it be known, refrains from comment at *Aen.* 6. 460) implies that Virgil copied the whole verse from Catullus. Virgil's indebtedness, however, falls somewhat short of being total.

Virg. *Aen.* 5. 591   frangeret indeprensus et irremeabilis error.
Cat. 64. 115   tecti frustraretur inobseruabilis error.

Acceptance of Servius' words would have led to considerable misunderstanding. Servius enormously overstates the closeness of Virgil and Theocritus at *Buc.* 7. 1: *ecloga haec paene tota Theocriti est*; and the closeness of Virgil and Apollonius at *Aen.* 4. 1: *Apollonius Argonautica scripsit et in tertio inducit amantem Medeam: inde totus hic liber translatus est.* Similar wild exaggeration doubtless colours the scholium at *Buc.* 10. 46: *hi autem omnes uersus Galli sunt, de ipsius translati carminibus.*

    Mention of Gallus makes this a suitable place for a brief digression on yet another error in Servius, highly relevant to our study as showing both the gross and careless misunderstanding of which Servius is capable and the astounding credulity which scholars have accorded to his uncorroborated statements.

We may suppose that some ancient, like some modern, commentators wondered whether the Aristaeus section of *Geo.* 4 did not fill a disproportionate space and perform an alien function in that work, and speculated that the poet's didactic treatment up to that point encouraged one to expect a different conclusion; some commentators—in unrelated criticism—hinted at the impropriety of the praise of Gallus in the tenth *Eclogue*, murmuring that in consequence of that man's disgrace the poet would have done better to excise the final portion of the *Eclogues* and substitute something else.

Whether Servius or another, someone misread *in postrema Bucolicorum parte* as *in postrema Georgicorum parte*, and connected the two criticisms. In an endeavour to reconcile the irreconcilable he has come up with what we read at S *Buc.* 10. 1:

Gallus ... primo in amicitiis Augusti Caesaris fuit: postea cum uenisset in suspicionem, quod contra eum coniuraret, occisus est. fuit autem amicus Vergilii adeo, ut quartus Georgicorum a medio usque ad finem eius laudes teneret: quas postea iubente Augusto in Aristaei fabulam commutauit.

The story is moonshine from start to finish and was satisfactorily shown to be impossible historically and untenable in view of the internal evidence by Anderson, who by way of supporting his contention that *Buc.* 10 rather than *Geo.* 4 contained the *laudes Galli* referred to Ammianus (17. 4. 5): ... *Gallus poeta, quem flens quodam modo in postrema Bucolicorum parte Vergilius carmine leni decantat.*[30] But for all that the pages of scholarship, including *RE* and the latest edition of the *Georgics*, are littered with quixotic attempts to save Servius' credit.

(4) S *Aen.* 5. 610 ... notandum sane etiam de Iride arcum genere masculino dicere Vergilium: Catullus et alii genere feminino ponunt, referentes ad originem, sicut 'haec Attis' et 'haec gallus' legimus.

One would imagine that Catullus had used *arcus* 'rainbow' as a feminine noun. But Servius has with culpable inattention abridged his source. Under *alii* must come Ennius, who did treat *arcus* as feminine (*Ann.* 409 = Priscian, *GL* 2. 259 ff.), whilst only *haec Attis* justifies mention of Catullus (cf. Cat. 63. 27, etc.). Even *haec gallus* is incorrect of Catullus, who employs the feminine form *galla* (63. 12, 34).

[30] W. B. Anderson, 'Gallus and the Fourth *Georgic*', *CQ* 27 (1933), 36–45; also *addendum*, ibid. 73.

(5) S *Aen.* 7. 378 TVRBO Catullus hoc turben dicit, ut hoc carmen.

Not in our texts of Catullus. At 64. 107, the only occurrence of the nominative, the word is *turbo* and is masculine. Most likely Servius has confused Catullus and Tibullus, who at 1. 5. 3. did write (so Charisius, *GL* 1. 145. 8) *turben*. Still, even this does not quite fit: Tibullus, like everyone else, regards the word as masculine. Servius has gratuitously, and erroneously, superimposed mention of gender upon the mere specification of stem-formation: *Turbo, Turbonis, si proprium hominis nomen* (Charisius, *GL* 1. 144. 30); *turbo, turbinis, ut uirgo, uirginis* (cf. Probus, *GL* 4. 210. 35); *turben, turbinis, ut carmen, carminis.*

(6) S *Aen.* 12. 587 ... 'in pumice' autem iste masculino genere posuit, et hunc sequimur, licet Catullus dixerit feminino.

The relevant verse is Cat. 1.2 *arido modo pumice expolitum.* The archetype of Catullus attests the masculine, as do the manuscripts of the ancient writers who quote the verse: Isidore, Marius Victorinus, Caesius Bassus, and Terentianus. The Verona Scholia (*Buc.* 6. 1) also quote the verse, and also with *arido.* How after our acquaintance with Servius can we approve of altering the text to *arida* (Teubner and Oxford texts) against all the evidence? 'There is no reason to distrust Servius', says Fordyce innocently.

Actually, there is. No grammarian lends his authority to the statement that *pumex* was ever feminine. It is true that Caper in his short tract on words liable to error gives (*GL* 7. 111. 3): *PVMEX HIC recte* (that is, the masculine is correct), but this need not imply that the use of the word as a feminine enjoyed any literary warrant. Indeed, Probus rather suggests the opposite (*GL* 4. 209. 16): *PVMEX masculini generis est, ut Vergilius (Aen.* 5. 214) '*latebroso in pumice uidi'. SILEX CORTEX masculino genere dicuntur; apud antiquos feminina erant, ut* (Verg. *Aen.* 8. 233) '*stabat acuta silex'.*

Possibly Servius (or his source) has carelessly given the wrong entry from some lexicon he consulted. Possibly he looked up *pumex* but copied out part of the entry for the preceding word *puluis* by mistake. We may imagine the following:

PVLVIS masculini generis est, licet Propertius dixerit 'qui nunc iacet horrida puluis'. masculini item CINIS, licet Catullus dixerit feminino, ut 'acerba cinis'.

PVMEX masculini generis est, ut Vergilius ...

See Charisius, *GL* 1. 89. 22 and 1. 101. 10. If there is anything to this speculation we cannot impute this kind of error to Servius' scribes. A very similar one occurs at S *Buc.* 9. 35: *Varius poeta fuit: de hoc Horatius 'Varius ducit molle atque facetum.'* Obviously, the quotation (*Serm.* 1. 10. 44. f.) should read: *'forte epos acer, / ut nemo, Varius ducit.'* The words which follow in Horace, *molle atque facetum*, refer to Virgil. Someone has written down the wrong portion of the reference; but that someone can hardly have been a scribe copying out *forte . . . ducit*.

Thus we see that in referring to the text of Catullus, where, as in the case of the Helen Episode, Servius is dealing with information he has received at second hand, he is in error practically the whole time.

Bearing in mind Servius' flagrant inaccuracies in reporting the words of others, let us turn to an overlooked portion of his scholium on the disputed passage.

S *Aen.* 2. 592d hinc autem uersus fuisse sublatos Veneris uerba declarant dicentis (601): 'non tibi Tyndaridis facies inuisa Lacaenae'.

'That verses were removed from this place is proved by Venus' words in 601.' Is this not a strange remark under the circumstances? Servius has just sold us, neatly tagged with instructions for their proper insertion, a full packet of verses duly branded with the validating label *Tucca et Varius sustulerunt.* Why this sudden offer of a proof that such verses really existed? Has our vendor reason to believe that once they did not? Already we have seen that this kind of label is peculiar to Servius. If we strip it off, we shall find something like this beneath: *hinc autem aliquid deesse Veneris uerba declarant,* 'Venus' words show that there is a lacuna here.' Servius' scholium contains an inference from verse 601 about the nature of the manuscript tradition at 566 f. (that is, 566 followed immediately by 589). It makes sense only if an original statement of a lacuna has been converted into a certification of what has repaired that lacuna. Furthermore, that original statement argued that the lacuna contained a mention of Helen. Consequently we may not argue that the conception of the Helen Episode lay beyond the power of an interpolator. When Virgil makes Venus ask 'Will you not rather see where you have left Anchises?' using the verb *aspicio*, and makes her turn Aeneas' anger from the hated (*inuisa*) beauty of Helen (*Tyndaris*), he is leaving the way open for a would-be interpolator to manufacture *Tyndarida aspicio* and bring *inuisa* into the context.

Summing up our inquiry so far, we are driven to even further doubts about the credibility of the witness Servius by his admission—in fact, we have to remark on his reluctance to answer counsel's questions—that, although he first jauntily said that everyone accepted as genuine the missing jewels in his possession, he knew all the time that other investigators had written them off as lost and even insinuated that they may never have been cut.

IX. *The Text of the Helen Episode*

In establishing the text of Servius—for by this tradition the Helen Episode has descended to us—we must be careful to cite not only the manuscripts of Servius but also those of Servius Auctus. This naturally follows from a recognition that Servius Auctus is made up of Servius and additions and modifications. Except where the Servian text has been affected by the activities of the Compiler, we have in Servius Auctus a most valuable check on the ordinary Servian tradition. Table 1 will make this plain.

The reader should note that the relationships of the pure Servian manuscripts (S) are exceedingly complicated. Fortunately, we are able, thanks to Murgia's skilful analysis, to sort out the ramifications into the two main traditions, which he calls Δ and Γ respectively.[31] Very briefly, Δ is the better tradition, but is missing for considerable portions of Servius. The manuscript A, for example, generally bears witness to Δ, but where Δ has perished goes over to the Γ text. We may dispense with further detail here,[32] since the Helen Episode occurs in a section not attested by the Δ tradition, and all extant manuscripts represent Γ.

From a textual point of view, the readings of DS and S are remarkably close, and the archetype must lie not far behind the extant sources. In orthography DS generally inspires more confidence than S:

DS/S *Buc.* 9. 1d   zeugma *DS*: zeuma *S*
DS/S *Buc.* 9.11b   miloniana *DS*: meloniana *S*

Shared errors are surprisingly few:

DS/S *Buc.* 5. 1a   laudant se **Seru. R ex coniect.**: laudantes *DS*: laudant *S*

---

[31] Charles E. Murgia, 'Critical notes on the Text of Servius' Commentary on *Aeneid* III-V', *HSCPh* 72 (1968), 31 ff.

[32] A crucial issue, left unresolved in the accompanying stemma, concerns the relationships of **DS**, **Γ**, and **ΔΔ**. Do **DS** and **ΓΓ** share a hyparchetype, as Murgia is inclined to think, or did the Compiler's Servius descend from a source independent of the source of **ΓΓ** and **ΔΔ**? Because of the large amount of horizontal transmission and editorial activity in the tradition it is not easy to decide between these alternatives. That **DS** and **ΔΔ** are connected (to the exclusion of **ΓΓ**) may, however, be regarded as out of the question.

TABLE I. The Tradition of Servius and Servius Auctus

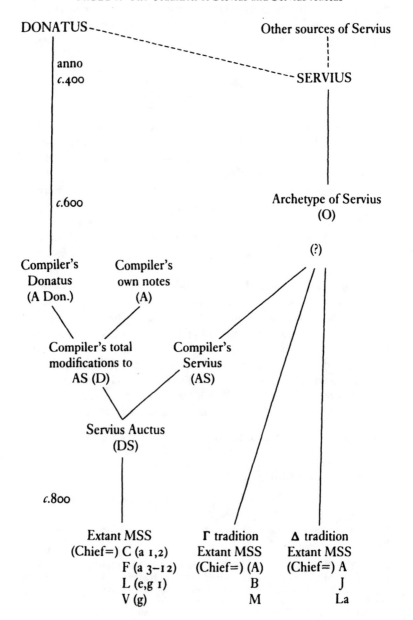

DS/S *Aen.* 1. 499 cardo dictus ⟨ἀπὸ τῆς καρδίας⟩ quasi cor ianuae, quo
   mouetur.

   graeca om. O, suppl. Fraenkel ex Isid. Orig. 15. 7. 7

Once or twice DS permits the filling of a lacuna in S.

DS/S *Buc.* 6. 35a ... canebat etiam quemadmodum ⟨se duarare coeperit
   solum et mixtam sibi ante aquam sua contractione
   discludere ...
   36 ET RERVM PAVLATIM SVMERE FORMAS canebat
   etiam quemadmodum⟩ terra rerum sumpserit formam.

   se ... quemadmodum *DS: om. S per parablepsin*

Of course DS is not without corruptions of its own:

DS/S *Buc.* 9. 7a   SVBDVCERE C(OLLES) / I(NCIPIVNT) ...

   C.I. S: cicero *DS (male ci pro abbreuiatione interpretatus)*

The closeness of *DS* and *S* in the *Eclogues* and *Georgics* has led to the
decision to plan a single apparatus for *Ed. Harv.* I; the manuscript
tradition is much simpler in these works than it is in the *Aeneid*, where
the number of manuscripts testifying to the DS text sometimes varies
from scholium to scholium.

The text of the Helen Episode, then, whilst not as solidly attested as
the canonical text of Virgil, can thus be taken back to an archetype of a
date hardly later than the seventh century and quite possibly earlier. The
following discussion will make clear that doubt as to the original reading
is confined to but two or three places.

567   iamque adeo super unus eram, cum limina Vestae
      seruantem et tacitam secreta in sede latentem
      Tyndarida aspicio; dant clara incendia lucem
570   erranti passimque oculos per cuncta ferenti.
      illa sibi infestos euersa ob Pergama Teucros
      et *Danaum poenam* et deserti coniugis iras
      praemetuens, Troiae et patriae communis erinys,
      abdiderat sese atque aris inuisa sedebat.

Danaum poenam *S*: Danaum poenas *DS*: poenas Danaum *ed. Mant., edd.*

Murgia, who is to be followed here, contends that *poenas* of DS is an
error, possibly a mere slip induced by *iras* at the end of the verse,
possibly a deliberate alteration of the unusual singular (in a particulariz-
ing sense). Emendation seems unjustified, since it is difficult to imagine
how the vulgate *poenas Danaum* ever became transposed to the unmetrical *Danaum poenas*. Furthermore, there are strong indications that the

author of this passage varied his inflections, *poenam* being varied in *poenas* (576) and *iras* in *ira* (575).

> 575 exarsere *ignes* animo; subit ira candentem
>   ulcisci patriam et sceleratas sumere poenas.

ignes *DS* (= *O*): *ignis* (-i *B*) *S*

Study of the finer points of classical Latin orthography encounters a formidable obstacle in the wholesale introduction of standardized spellings into Latin manuscripts at a period (eighth century and earlier) antedating that to which we owe our oldest texts of most classical authors. A scribe, armed with the knowledge that third-declension *i*-stems once made accusative plurals in -*is*, would without a moment's thought alter into -*is* any accusative plural in -*es* which happened to catch his attention. Sometimes, as here, he gives himself away by picking on a nominative. B (a manuscript not far removed from the archetype) seems here, as at 585 below, to have been copied from an exemplar which gave *ignes* with *i* written above the ending (the interpolator intending -*is*), and the copyist falsely inferred that *igni* was the corrected reading.

> 577 'scilicet haec Spartam incolumis patriasque Mycenas
>   aspiciet, partoque ibit regina triumpho,
>   coniugiumque domumque, *patres* natosque uidebit,
> 580 Iliadum turba et Phrygiis comitata ministris?
>   occiderit ferro Priamus? Troia arserit igni?
>   Dardanium totiens sudarit sanguine litus?

patres *O*: patris *Menag. alt.*

'Is she to see husband and home, parents and children?' Austin adopts the conjecture ('father's house')—though all his alleged parallels give *domus* without epithet and so support the tradition—because literary Latin furnishes no warrant for *patres* in the sense of 'parents'.[33] But the hymenaeal rhythm seems perfectly in order, and the collocation *A et B, C et D* is certainly unobjectionable: *Aen* 8. 679 *cum patribus populoque, penatibus et magnis dis.*

> 583 non ita: namque etsi nullum memorabile nomen
>   feminea in poena est *nec habet* uictoria laudem,
> 585 extinxisse nefas tamen et sumpsisse *merentes*
>   laudabor poenas, ...

nec habet *Seru. V*: habet haec *O*   merentes *DS, Seru. AQVN* (= *DS interpol.*): merentis (-i *B*) *Seru. HPTZBEM* (= *S*)

[33] Austin (above, n. 25), p. 191.

To dispose of the simpler problem first: the transmission of *merentes* exactly parallels that of *ignes* in 575; the word is clearly accusative plural. Austin's painful attempts to defend *habet haec* (which have naturally led him to despair over *tamen*) should by now have dispelled any doubt as to the correct reading of 584;[34] and perhaps the traditional text and interpretation would have remained unshaken, had not Fraenkel branded *nec habet* as an interpolation. It is that. But, in a sense, so is every true conjecture. The words *nec habet* became by the slightest of changes *hec habet*, of which *habet haec* is a further corruption, representing a metrical adjustment. Watt, supporting Austin, explains the palaeography back to front;[35] but in the sequence *habet hec uictoria* a corruption to *nec* would be extremely unlikely. 'For though there is no lasting renown in taking vengeance on a woman, and the triumph wins no praise, I shall even so be praised for having destroyed the evil and having exacted the due penalty.' The meaning is crystal clear, even if the Latinity falls short of correctness.

> 586   ... animumque explesse iuuabit
> †ultricis *famam* et cineres satiasse meorum.'
> talia iactabam et furiata mente *ferebar*...
>
> famam *S*: famae *DS*: flammae *Seru. N*   ferebar *S*: loquebatur *DS* (explained above, p. 91)

'... and I shall rejoice to have fulfilled my desires and ... to have satisfied the shades of my people.'

Verse 587 presents undeniable difficulties. Critics have embarked on a hopeless course in explaining *ultricis famae* or *flammae* as a genitive after the verb *explesse*. Since the composer could have written *ultrici fama* (or *flamma*), the regular construction, without affecting the metre, it is virtually certain that he intended something else. To Austin must be conceded that the sense is complete at *iuuabit*.[36] But in that case *et* may be corrupt, since the author of this passage does not elsewhere postpone the conjunction; and corrupt the preceding word *famam* certainly is (*famae* and *flammae* seem like attempts at correction). If it be granted that a ligatured *-que* (qe) might be misread as *sf* and *nu* misread as *m*, then some probability would accrue to Friedrich Schoell's *ultricique manu*, for the step from *ultricisfmam* to the Servian reading is slight and predictable.

---

[34] Austin, ibid.; also ed., *P. Vergili Maronis Aeneidos Liber Secundus* (Oxford, 1964), p. 226.

[35] W. S. Watt in Austin's edn. (above, n. 34), p. 292.

[36] Austin (above, n. 25), p. 193.

X. *Internal Analysis*

The verses contain much which echoes the language of Virgil. But then, this is precisely what an imitator of Virgil would strive to attain. Moreover, these echoes are not evenly and randomly spread over the poet's work, but cluster in a rather suspicious fashion about well-known parts of the *Aeneid*, as though these had provided conscious inspiration. Consider the following:

(1) *Aen.* 2

321	limina	331	Mycenis
324	-abile	337	erinys
325	Dardaniae	344	Phrygibus
327	incensa	345	furentis

(2) *Aen.* 2

407	furiata mente	425	ad aram
413	-tu atque ereptae	431	cineres ... meorum
	uirginis ira	434	meruisse

(3) *Aen.* 2

501	per aras	514	arae ...
502	sanguine ... ignes	515	... sedebant

(4) *Aen.* 4

91	furori	96	adeo
93	laudem	101	ardet
94	memorabile numen	102	communem
95	femina uicta	103	Phrygio

(5) *Aen.* 4

363	oculos ... pererrat	376	furiis incensa feror
364	accensa	379	scilicet

(6) *Aen.* 4

605	implessem	626	Dardanios
606	extinxem ... dedisse	656	ulta ... poenas inimico
610	ultrices	658	Dardaniae
623	cineres	660	iuuat
625	ultor	667	femineo

(7) *Aen.* 5

785	Phrygum exedisse nefandis	788	furoris
786	poenam traxe	864	iamque adeo ...
787	cineres	867	... cum ... errare

(8) *Aen.* 6

555	sedens	556	uestibulum ... seruat

560 scelerum facies	565 poenas
561 poenis	570 ultrix
563 sceleratum limen	575 facies quae limina seruat

(9) *Aen.* 11

258 scelerum poenas	269 patriis ... aris
260 ultorque	270 coniugium ... uiderem
264 uersosque penatis	275 haec adeo ... cum
267 coniugis infandae	289 uictoria

(10) *Aen.* 12

939 uoluens oculos	946 furiis accensus et ira
940 fiamque ... cum ...	949 poenam scelerato ... sumit

Collectively these passages, none of which contains the difficulties of Latinity which characterize the Helen Episode, suggest a deliberate and careful imitation of Virgilian vocabulary. Could this suggestion be hardened into proof, non-Virgilian authorship would necessarily be proved also.

Now consider the word *praemetuens* in 592. The rareness of the verb ('to pre-fear' is logically tautologous, all fear being an anticipation) has caused some to doubt whether Virgil would have employed it, a doubt which has drawn from defenders of Virgilian authorship the rejoinder that the word occurs in Lucretius and thus no basis for scepticism exists. Ah, but let it be observed that the Lucretian passage is one of that poet's best-known and provides just such another cluster. Virgil, when borrowing striking words from his predecessors, does not so echo the whole context.[37]

(11) *Lucr.* 3 (the underworld a fable)

1004 explere ... satiare	1015 sceleris
10011 Furiae	1019 praemetuens
1014 poenarum	1028 occiderunt

Turn to the matter of metre. Norden condemned the passage for the excessive occurrence of certain types of elision.[38] Now, although Austin has no difficulty in showing that they can all be paralleled in Virgil, we may wonder whether Norden's point has met with a satisfactory explanation. The elisions at the caesura (e.g., *et Danaum poen[am] et*) almost seem to labour this aspect of Virgil's technique, as though the

[37] This is difficult to prove positively but seems to follow from the parallels amassed by Macrobius in the sixth book of the *Saturnalia*: these show Virgil to have been a discriminating borrower.
[38] Eduard Norden, ed., *P. Vergilis Maro Aeneis Buch VI*[4] (repr. Darmstadt, 1957), p. 454.

writer were more at home in the smoother hexameters of Ovid or Lucan. Certainly, if an imitator of Virgil manufactured these verses, it would seem to follow that in respect of metre he made a great effort to reproduce his model's style.

That the whole passage has indeed been carefully composed emerges from an inspection of its structure. In this regard a simple tabulation is worth several paragraphs of exegesis, and Table 2 gives in self-explanatory fashion the analysis embodied in the more detailed '*tabula ad explicandam loci compositionem effecta*' appended to Gerloff's dissertation.[39] Although analysing the passage as two parts balanced in Golden Mean ratio, Gerloff himself did not notice the proportion, unaware of the significance that would later be attached to it.

TABLE 2. Structure of the Helen Episode (after Gerloff)

A	Aeneas	567			
		568	(b1) seruantem	(b2) latentem	
SCENE:		569			
		570	(a1) erranti	(a2) ferenti	
B	Helen	571			
		572		*poenam ... iras* (links with 575 f.)	
		573			
		574	(b2) abdiderat	(b1) sedebat	

──────────────── Golden Section ────────────────

X	Anger	575	(x1) ignes animo	(x2) *ira*	
Y	Desire	576	(y1) ulcisci	(y2) sumere *poenas*	
Z	Question	577			
	Greek	578	(1) auspiciet	(2) ibit	
ACTION:		579	(3) uidebit		
		580			
	Trojan	581	(1) occiderit	(2) arserit	
		582	(3) sudabit		
Z	Answer	583			
		584			
Y	Desire	585	(y2a) extinxisse	(y2b) sumpsisse poenas	
		586			
		587	(y1a) ultricis	(y1b) satiasse	

──

X	Anger	588	(x2) iactabam	(x1) furiata mente	

[39] Iohannes Gerloff, *Vindiciae Vergilianae: Quaestiones criticae de Aeneidis Libri II 567–588* (diss. Jena, 1911).

XI. *The Golden Section in the* Aeneid

What now of Duckworth's claim that Virgil constructed the *Aeneid* out of passages balanced in Golden Mean ratio?[40] Will not the existence of this ratio in the Helen Episode confirm Virgilian authorship? Not confirm. That word we must deny. Cannot an imitator have known this device of the poet's composition? Duckworth must needs assent to this, for according to him Ennius, Lucretius, Catullus, Horace, and the authors of the *Appendix* were all not only familiar with Golden Mean ratio but employed it themselves. Getty adds Lucan. Well then, if many knew, many could have imitated this feature. Nevertheless, evidence for the theory outside Virgil is distressingly scanty. Rather we assume, on general grounds of probability, that Virgil's practice would have been known to his literary friends and through them to others. True or false, the theory of the Golden Section in the *Aeneid* constitutes no decisive criterion for the authenticity of the Helen Episode.

Tempting to leave the matter there and evade the question. Let us therefore assent that Virgil did consciously and deliberately employ Golden Mean ratios. Too many paragraph limits from which Duckworth derives his numerical data were established before the announcement of the theory to permit us to dismiss it as a mirage. If the evidence suggests that the divine Mantuan composed with a stilus in one hand and an abacus in the other, we should brave Dalzell's ridicule and follow the evidence.[41] But this is an extravagant inference, for the most convincing ratios are all connected with the Fibonacci series (1, 2, 3, 5, 8, 13, 21, 34, 55 . . .), which could thus have been used as the basis of calculation. To take two simple examples (the *Duckworthverzeichnis* being given in parentheses):

$$\begin{array}{lll} \text{(D 2)} \; Aen. & \text{1. 34--75} & 42 \; (21 \times 2) \\ & 76\text{--}101 & 26 \; (13 \times 2) \\ \text{(D 113)} \; Aen. & 4 \; .672\text{--}692 & 21 \\ & 693\text{--}705 & 13 \end{array}$$

Relax the qualification for editorial paragraphing, and more passages of Fibonacci lengths appear, for instance:

$$\begin{array}{lll} \text{(D 255)} \; Aen. & \text{9. 638--658} & 21 \\ & 659\text{--}671 & 13 \end{array}$$

---

[40] George E. Duckworth, 'Mathematical Symmetry in Vergil's *Aeneid*', *TAPhA* 91 (1960), 184–220; *Structural Patterns and Proportions in Vergil's Aeneid* (Ann Arbor, 1962).

[41] A. Dalzell, review of Duckworth's *Structural Patterns* (above, n. 40) in *Phoenix* 17 (1963), 314–16.

$$
\begin{array}{lll}
\text{(D 351)} \ \textit{Aen.} \ 12. & 919\text{–}939 & 21 \\
& 940\text{–}952 & 13
\end{array}
$$

Relax the requirement for exact Fibonacci numbers, but reinstate the strict condition of prior editorial paragraphing, and we meet with such a sequence as the following:

$$
\begin{array}{lll}
\text{(D 327)} \ \textit{Aen.} \ 12. & 238\text{–}256 & 19 \ (21 - 2) \\
& 257\text{–}288 & 32 \ (34 - 2) \\
\text{(D 330)} & 289\text{–}323 & 35 \ (34 + 1) \\
& 324\text{–}345 & 22 \ (21 + 1) \\
\text{(D 331)} & 346\text{–}382 & 37 \ (34 + 3) \\
& 383\text{–}440 & 58 \ (55 + 3)
\end{array}
$$

Virgil's modification of the series warns us to be prepared for some flexibility on his part: he is not rigidly tied to a particular set of numbers. Here the mathematical pattern is still clear enough, but it is obvious that he is on the point of moving away from ratios which permit us, given one component, to predict the other. Once the poet takes this step, we cannot be quite sure of detecting his ratios, assuming they exist, and—what is worse—we run the risk of deluding ourselves with ones that he never intended.

If the passages making up the *Aeneid* gave only ratios conforming to the principles which determined the previous examples, we should be compelled to regard the Golden Mean as an integral formal element, not equalling the precision of metre, but still sufficiently capable of identifaction to be used as a critical tool. This, unfortunately for those who would like it so, is far from being the case. Ratios arrived at by a selection of component parts (a + c/b; or a + c/b + d; or a + c + e / b + d), unsupported by impartial editorial analysis, necessarily carry less and less weight in proportion to their intricacy, for the simple reason that it becomes more and more easy to rig the results. This is a charge Duckworth invites upon himself at *Aen.* 12. 505–47, where the ratio (D 932) has been secured by throwing out the simile (521–8) and cutting the rest up into six (a + c + e / b + d + f). The larger the numbers involved, the more likely it is that a break will occur within the area assumed to give a significant ratio (.600–.636). Verses 105–7 are omitted from Duckworth's continuous analysis of *Aen.* 2 (D 29–D 60), but are duly worked into the large calculations (cf. D 367). Whilst all books are represented as completely made up of Golden Mean ratios, the total lines of some books (1, 3, 9, 11, 12) defy division by the Golden

Section, a phenomenon which casts some doubt on the reality of the other total ratios.

The sectioning of a passage of eight (and a fortiori fewer) lines carries little weight. Even bridge players not in the Goren class know that, when eight cards of a suit are held by the two unseen hands, the odds favour a 5–3 as against a 4–4 or a 6–2 split. How can we be sure that *Aen.* 4. 1–8 is designed as a unit composed of 1–5 and 6–8 (D 1009)? The break at 8 is much less obvious than the break after 5; and the analysis of 9–29 (D 1011) as a b + c / a + d proportion looks contrived.

The half-lines in Virgil bring the argument on to firmer ground. About three-quarters of them, asserts Duckworth, were intentional, giving a closer approximation to the Golden Section than whole lines would have done. With this assertion he reveals how far beyond the possible he has pushed his theory. That Virgil meant to complete his half-lines may be settled without reference to mathematics.

Stichic verse, and hexameter verse in particular, provides a rhythmical continuum serving as a base to the reciter or listener in much the same way as a road serves a motorist or as the pages of a book serve a reader; and a half-line causes much the same breakdown as a ten-foot gap in a road or the physical loss of half a page. We are not to suppose that the metrical breakdown after a half-line renders a pause or a caesura more effective in any way. Just as a car may come to a halt without the road being blown up; just as a typographer may leave half a page blank without tearing it out; so the poet may contrive an arresting pause—an interminable pause, even—without interrupting the rhythmical continuum. It happens frequently in drama, for example, as when one character takes over from another in the middle of a verse. *Aen.* 2. 13 provides a good instance of an effective pause: 'magnificent', raves Austin in his commentary. And one can readily think of many another, where a reciter attuning his utterance to the demands of the context is forced to a halt. How else except by coming to a complete stop after the caesura can one recite *Aen.* 6. 883 (*tu Marcellus eris. manibus date lilia plenis*)?

Secondly, the context of the half-lines provides evidence that the poet had not quite finished the process of composition. Virgil's 58 half-lines fall, for the most part, into three separate groups, which let us designate by the letters *a*, *b*, and *c*.

1.534 c	2.720 a	4.44 b	5.792 b	8.41 b	10.284 a
1.560 c	2.767 c	4.361 a	5.815 a	8.469 a	10.490 a
1.636 c	2.787 b	4.400 c	6.94 b	8.536 b	10.580 a

2.66 b	3.218	4.503 c	6.835 b	9.167 c	10.728
2.233 c	3.316 b	4.516 c	7.129 b	9.295 a	10.876 a
2.346 b	3.340 b	5.294 c	7.248 a	9.467	11.375 a
2.468	3.470 c	5.322 c	7.439 c	9.520 c	11.391 b
2.614 c	3.527 a	5.574 c	7.455 a	9.721 c	12.631 a
2.623 c	3.640 b	5.595 c	7.702 c	9.761 c	
2.640 b	3.661	5.653 a	7.760 c	10.17 a	

The first group (*a*) shows the poet at pains to avoid Homeric formularity in introducing, beginning, ending, or proceeding from direct speech: at 4. 361, for example, *Italiam non sponte sequor*, he has achieved a splendid ending to the speech, and obviously no more was to be added; but it remains for him to adjust the beginning of 362 (probably composed earlier), so that he may proceed directly from the word *sequor* (for the sake of illustration let us suggest that he might have filled up the line with *dum talia dicit*).

In the second group (*b*) the poet has achieved in the middle of a verse, a satisfactory beginning or ending to an emotional passage consisting usually of a question, imperative, or exclamation; and sooner than part with the half-line he has created, prefers to wait for further inspiration. Thus at 6. 835, *proice tela manu, sanguis meus*, Virgil is anxious to end the appeal at the bucolic caesura, the double-short cadence intensifying its poignancy; but this means that he must continue with *ille* . . . and recast the following verse or verses.

The third group (*c*) consists of half-lines from passages plainly unfinished (this evaluation is given for most by Sparrow).[42] Here, if anywhere, we encounter *tibicines*, stopgap phrases destined for expansion, for example:

Aen. 1. 559	talibus Ilioneus; cuncti simul ore fremebant Dardanidae.
Aen. 2. 622	apparent dirae facies inimicaque Troiae numina magna deum.
Aen. 4. 503	ergo iussa parat.
Aen. 5. 573	cetera Trinacriis pubes senioris Acestae fertur equis.
Aen. 9. 166	conlucent ignes, noctem custodia ducit insomnem ludo.

Of the five hemistichs unaccounted for, one 2. 468 *telorum interea cessat genus*, will not scan properly unless the verse is continued by a word

---

[42] John Sparrow, *Half-Lines and Repetitions in Virgil* (Oxford, 1931), pp. 30 ff.

beginning with an open vowel; otherwise *-sat genus* must be reckoned a cretic. Three others, 3. 218 *ora fame*, 3. 661 *solamenque mali*, 10. 728 *ora cruor*, exert no special metrical or emotional force, so that there is no reason why the poet should not have wished to complete them. The last, 9. 467 *Euryali et Nisi*, replete indeed with pathos, is nevertheless unlikely in view of 5. 294 to have been intended as final.

The conclusion is inescapable: Virgil had no intention of leaving half-lines in the *Aeneid*. Any argument for a contrary hypothesis must therefore be faulty. Let us direct our attention, then, to Duckworth's table X, 'Ratios more accurate with half-lines as fractions'. Most of these ratios are arrived at by calculations too subjective to be acceptable. For example:

Aen. 9 (half-line 167)
(D 845)   159–163 / 168–171a / 174–175   a + c + e   10.2
          164–167 / 171b–173   b + d   6.2

In some an obvious adjustment will avoid difficulty. For example:

Aen. 12 (half-line 631)
(D 337)   631–642   11.2
          643–649   7

There was no need to count the half-line, *Turnus ad haec*, at all: the relevant passage need not involve more than Turnus' speech; the ratio 11:7 is abundantly attested.

Some ratios would be perfectly acceptable with the half-line completed. For example:

Aen. 1 (half-line 636)
(D 25)   613–630   18   (18 = 9 × 2)
          631–642   11.6   (12 = 6 × 2)

Compare in the same book D 16 (387–392 / 393–401) with a 6:9 ratio.

In several instances it looks as if Virgil may have intended to eliminate (not complete) the half-line. For example:

Aen. 2 (half-line 720)
(D 57)   699–706   8
          707–720   13.2
(D 58)   707–711   5
          712–720   8.2

The text is as follows:

719 ... attrectare nefas, donec me flumine uiuo

720   abluero.'
721   haec fatus latos umeros subiectaque colla...

It would be easy to write *abluero.' sic fatus eram, subiectaque colla...*, eliminating the half-line and preserving the Fibonacci numbers, though we can hardly claim that Virgil must have done so.

It is true that on rare occasions he places a Golden Section within the line. If we may speak of Virgil arranging his poem in paragraphs, we have in *Aen.* 2. 13 proof that he was capable of beginning a paragraph in the middle of a verse. The ratio involved (D 30) seems perfectly acceptable as a signficant one, the poet modifying slightly the Fibonacci integers, not with any idea of going into decimal or fractional calculations, but solely because he wishes to secure an arresting pause after *incipiam* (similarly at 7. 45).

(D 30)   *Aen.* 2.   1–13a   13–
                          13b–20   8–

We are therefore not entitled to draw from significant ratios involving half-lines the inference that Virgil was prepared to leave half-lines uncompleted. The natural expectation that he would either have expanded the sentence or contracted it (or even have entirely reworked the passage) stands unaffected.

Nevertheless, even after we have subtracted as illusory or undesigned several hundreds of Duckworth's ratios, enough remain to enforce the general proposition that here and there in the *Aeneid* Virgil consciously contrived ratios approximating to the Golden Section. But beyond this simple assertion we cannot safely proceed. The eye can appreciate the Golden Section in space; the ear cannot in time. This naturally follows from those principles which Lessing expounds in his famous treatise *Laokoon* by way of defining the different spheres of the plastic arts and poetry. In Virgil we are to regard mathematical ratios as an idiosyncratic and certainly flexible means of ensuring an artistic asymmetry and of diversifying the lengths of component passages without losing control of measurement. Alas! The very nature of such a purpose should be enough to warn us that to try to specify definitively Virgil's calculations is an enterprise fraught with hazard, if not doomed to failure.

XII. *Latin Style in the Helen Episode*

From the preceding discussions we have gained an important clue. The Helen Episode is a finished product. Whoever composed it meant it to stand as it is. It is a fair copy, as good as its maker could achieve. If Virgil's, there can be no question of its being 'ringed or only marginally inserted in the autograph' (Mackail)[43] or otherwise marked out for deletion in the event of posthumous publication. But were it Virgil's, we should expect it to betray Virgil's Latin style; and it does not. Hitherto, defenders of Virgilian authorship have pleaded in mitigation that the verses are 'too obviously unrevised' (Mackail), are only temporary props (Büchner), are 'a collection of drafts forming a series of approaches to ideas that were never worked up' (Austin).[44] These pleas are false: we have now seen that the verses form a finished whole.

The non-Virgilian Latinity of the Helen Episode has with commendable discrimination already been listed by Austin, who, as the chief champion of authenticity, gallantly exonerates us from a possible accusation of prejudice. His article contains this indictment:

There are, however, other problems, notably the repetitive vocabulary and expression: *aspicio* (569), *aspiciet* (578, used differently); *poenas Danaum* (572), *sceleratas sumere poenas* (576), *feminea in poena* (584), *sumpsisse merentis* ... *poenas* (585–6); *deserti coniugis iras* (572), *subit ira* (575), *furiata mente* (588); *exarsere ignes animo* (575), *Troia arserit igni* (581, differently); *ulcisci* (576), *ultricis* (587); *patriae* (573, of Greece), *patriam* (576, of Troy), *patrias Mycenas* (577); *laudem* (584), *laudabor* (586), *famam* (?) (587), with *nomen* (583). There are contradictions: Aeneas sees Helen *limina Vestae servantem* (576), in 574 Helen *aris invisa sedebat*; in 572 she is afraid of Menelaus, in 579 she is imagined in happy reunion with him. The last line (588) looks like a stopgap: *furiata mente* is rather obvious, and if the passage had been fully integrated with what follows, one would not have expected *talia iactabam et*... but *talia iactanti*, dependent on a following verb.[45]

These nails in the coffin of Virgilian authorship he hammers firmly home in his commentary:

569   aspicio: 'I catch sight of' ... no other clear example in the *Aeneid*.

575   exarsere ignes: Virgil does not use *ignis* elsewhere of anger, and *exardescere* is not found elsewhere in classical Latin with *ignis* as subject.

576   sceleratas sumere poenas: this very remarkable phrase has no parallel in any other author.

577   patrias: ... here could obviously not have stood in a single, finished passage after *patriam* in 576.

581   arserit igni: this could scarcely have stood in a finished passage with *exarsere ignes* (575).

[43]   J. W. Mackail, ed., *The Aeneid* (Oxford, 1930), p. 77.
[44]   Austin, ed. (above, n. 34), p. 218.   [45] Austin (above, n. 25), p. 194.

585 **nefas:** ... no Virgilian parallel.
     merentis: ... if ... accusative plural, it is an experiment like *sceleratus sumere poenas* (576), but even bolder, and plainly both phrases could not have stood in a finished version.
587 **satiasse:** ... not used elsewhere by Virgil.
588 This looks like a stopgap.
     furiata mente: ... in this context it has all the look of a patch.

Austin's candid observations clearly disclose the non-Virgilian style of the passage. We have already seen that the Helen Episode cannot be regarded as a preliminary draft.

But grant that it could: did Virgil's versification in its early stages ever take such an imperfect shape? All the evidence points to the contrary. In the manuscript or manuscripts which Varius edited the poet had written down only elegant verse. This we may confidently affirm from those sections which end in half-lines, and from those passages, such as the Wanderings of Aeneas, which analysis shows were not fully assimilated to a final structure. When we speak of the imperfect state of the *Aeneid*, we mean unfinished, not inartistic. Little was left for an editor to do. Unlike the executors of Lucan, Varius was able to publish an epic essentially complete. No book is wanting; no book is unbearably defective. Nothing entitles us to imagine that Virgil composed in such a way that his verses needed polishing up. Completion of unfinished passages; addition to give finality to scene or action; and, above all, smooth connection of portions separately composed: these the poem lacks. But perfection of language the *Aeneid* already possesses, like every foot of verse that Virgil ever fashioned.

XIII. *Aeneas on the Palace Roof*

Book 2 of the *Aeneid*, though one of the most magnificent, is by no means among the most finished. Indeed, for this very reason Ribbeck has questioned the text of Donatus (*Vit.* 32), which states that the poet recited Books 2, 4, and 6 to the imperial family, and plausibly proposed to emend the text (*i* for *ii*) to read Books 1, 4, and 6; and Murgia has now considerably strengthened this proposal with a persuasive discussion of Serv. *Aen.* 4. 323.[46] However this may be, the Laocoon episode (40–56; 199–233) is undeniably an insertion not organically welded to the context, and the book contains a larger number of half-lines than any

---

[46] Murgia (above, n. 31), pp. 332–5.

other. Moreover, the poet had not yet elaborated his conception of Aeneas on the palace roof.

Virgil faced a formidable difficulty in getting Aeneas to describe in satisfactory detail the fall of Troy without loss of plausibility and without detriment to his hero. This difficulty he overcame admirably by contriving that Aeneas should mount the palace roof whence he might witness the entire disaster. The passage is brilliant. The action moves rapidly and so thoroughly engages our emotions that we never stop to wonder why Aeneas is so helpless, so motionless, and so far from the foe. The horror of Priam's death arouses him to an awareness of his own father's plight, and he hastily descends from the roof and hurries home. This summary, however, omits (besides the Helen Episode) lines 589–623, and to Peerlkamp goes the credit of first having realized that these verses constitute a later addition. Never one for half measures, he scratched them out of the text. In 1878, however, was published Henry's superior suggestion (made independently, it would seem) that in his first draft Virgil passed at once from 567 to 624 and the ensuing lines but was subsequently moved by afterthoughts to expand the passage.[47] So, too, again independently, Körte, who in 1916 convincingly argued that the poet, uneasy over Aeneas' passive role, had begun though not completed an additional scene to furnish its motivation.[48] Virgil's unfinished addition is to be recognized in the Venus scene; and the Helen Episode is nothing else but an attempt to finish it.

We must iron out a slight discrepancy between Henry and Körte. The question concerns the verses 624–31, which probably belong to the first composition (Henry) rather than to the incomplete addition (Körte). The simile of the husbandmen felling a mountain ash, as Henry points out, does not quite suit the image of the *numina magna deum*; the juxtaposition of 625 *Neptunia Troia* with 610 *Neptunus*, by putting Neptune on both sides, emphasizes that awkwardness; and the half-line 623 is more explicable at the end of a passage than in the middle (we already have one at 614).

The argument, and further discussion of it, will be easier to follow from a tabulation; and Table 3 schematizes this entire section of Book 2, half-lines being indicated by numbers and dots. Virgil's decision to insert an additional scene obligated him to much alteration, little of which has been accomplished. At 664–7 Aeneas refers to his mother's intervention on his behalf, that is, to the new scene: we may infer that the

[47] James Henry, *Aeneidea*, vol. 2 (Dublin, 1878), p. 302.
[48] Alfred Körte, 'Zum zweiten Buch von Vergilis Aeneis', *Hermes* 51 (1916), 145–50.

TABLE 3. Aeneas on the Palace Roof

First Composition	Incomplete Addition	Helen Episode
(458–558) I mount the palace roof and behold (468) ... the death of Priam. (559) Then I am gripped by horror. (560–63) I think of my father and family. (564–66) I look about me: all my companions have gone.		
		(567–88) *Now I see Helen hiding at the altar. 'Is she to go free? No, I shall be happy to have taken vengeance on her.' So was I saying—*
	(589–623) —when my mother appeared. 'Why this fury?' said she. 'Will you not succour your family? It is not Helen or Paris who is to blame for this disaster. The gods are responsible. I will draw the veil from your eyes and show you them: Neptune, Juno (614) ... Minerva, Jupiter. Now hurry. I will protect you.' She vanishes, and the dread deities come to view (623) ...	
(624–31) Then all Ilium seemed to come crashing down. (632 ff.) I descend and, guided by a god, make my way to my father's house. (640) ...		

context of these verses harmonizes with the intended expansion. On the other hand, 632 *ducente deo* becomes something of a conundrum: most likely 632 f. were to be rewritten. Furthermore, Venus in 596 ff. provided a new motivation for Aeneas' return home: accordingly the old one in 560–4 was to be deleted. Virgil's intention is clear. After 558 Aeneas was to have embarked on a course of action from which he is restrained by the sudden intervention of his mother in 589.

A few clues point to Virgil's conception. In the first place, the poet still envisaged Aeneas on the palace roof. Aeneas must occupy a postion of wide survey for his mother to show him the gods at their battle stations (604 ff.). Thus 570 *erranti*, which conceives of Aeneas at ground level, is alien to the scene in Virgil's imagination; and it is also difficult to understand how from the rooftops Aeneas could see anyone lurking in the penetralia of Vesta. In the second place, as Heinze and Körte stress, Venus bases her admonition to Aeneas to withdraw, not on the impropriety of his meditated action, but on its impossibility: the gods stand in the way. To Aeneas, as he appears in the Helen Episode, Venus' line of argument is irrelevant: he has conceded that Troy is fallen; his thoughts are bent on the spiteful killing of Helen, never mind what happens to himself; he rushes forward and in a moment would have accomplished the deed. Why tell him in this situation that the gods are destroying Troy? How could Venus expect to deter him from striking the blow by announcing a communiqué that Neptune was shaking the city walls, that Juno was holding the Scaean gates, and that Minerva had occupied the citadel on high? Venus' report constitutes an unanswerable case against any attempt to stem the Greek incursion: as a deterrent against murdering Helen it is a waste of breath. In the third place, Venus seems to criticize Aeneas' logic when she declares: 'it is not the hated beauty of Helen that is destroying Troy, nor is it the reviled Paris'. The words *facies inuisa* imply some allusion on Aeneas' part to Helen's beauty, and *culpatusue Paris* implies some revilement by Aeneas of Paris. The Helen Episode provides neither.

The case is clear: the Helen Episode does not represent Virgil's conception. The author, as was argued above, has been led by the mention of Helen to create and interpolate the passage preserved by Servius. His words *Tyndarida aspicio . . . inuisa* reveal the starting-point of his composition. That this scene, though spurious, has by its vividness and dramatic power captured the imagination of readers throughout the centuries—indeed, has been preferred to what Virgil intended—it would be foolish to deny. But the schools from Tiberius to Nero, as one gathers from the writings of the Senecas and Petronius, often occupied themselves with *tours de force* and academic displays, and it would come as no surprise if it turned out that some gifted schoolman composed the Helen Episode, marked as it is by its theatrical *uariationes* and dramatic bloodthirstiness.

What Virgil intended we can only speculate. We cannot even be sure of the dimensions of the new scene he has partially inserted. That Aeneas' helplessness brought on a rage in which he ranted against Helen and Paris, and that, impassioned beyond endurance at the injustice of the suffering which the innocent must experience, he resolved to launch one last demonic attack upon the foe—this would satisfy the clues. In 655, a passage we have established as harmonized to the new scene, he says *rursus in arma feror mortemque miserrimus opto* and again at 668, *arma, uiri, ferte arma.* Brilliantly conceived and vigorously executed though the Helen Episode may be, dare one suggest that Virgil possessed the genius to produce something finer and more relevant?

Entbehren sollst Du, sollst entbehren. This is the lesson—it is the hardest of all—which Aeneas must learn before he can set his unhappy followers on the shores of their future greatness. Just as at the court of Dido he will have to relinquish personal happiness, so in the war at Troy he must decline his opportunity for heroic glory. Noble and brave, mighty as one heaven-born, he, like Augustus, must yield to the realization that the tempting laurels of the splendid warrior are not for him. Virgil does not mean that Aeneas is in any way prevented from rushing to a foolish fate, but rather that he comprehends in his greatness of soul—his emotions are externalized as his mother's intervention—that the forces of the universe are marshalled to encompass not only his but all his people's extinction, should he elect to continue the fight. He clearly sees that a heroic stand will involve the sacrifice of those whose salvation it is his duty and lies within his power to assure; success in extricating his band against overwhelming odds will earn him only the unglamorous and uninspiring title *pius.* In this tense interlude the Roman poet intended to raise to a loud crescendo his theme that Aeneas no more willingly turns his back on Troy than he later sets out for Italy. And what he found strength to renounce was certainly a more intrepid, puissant, and terrible feat of arms than dealing a furtive quietus to a timid woman in the dark. *Reddite me Danais; sinite instaurata reuisam / proelia* (669 f.): these are the sort of words which linger on his lips after he has taken his decision but while his resolve is still unsteady, and from them we learn the alternative he had, but in bitterness, rejected.

XIV. *The Autographs of Virgil*

If we conclude, as a just appreciation of the evidence requires, that Virgil did not compose the Helen Episode, we still have to face a difficult technical problem. When Varius alighted on the manuscript sheets of the *Aeneid*, he cannot have found precisely what he edited:

RESPICIO ET QVAE SIT ME CIRCVM COPIA LVSTRO
DESERVERE OMNES DEFESSI ET CORPORA SALTV
AD TERRAM MISERE AVT IGNIBVS AEGRA DEDERE
CVM MIHI SE NON ANTE OCVLIS TAM CLARA VIDENDAM
OBTVLIT ET PVRA PER NOCTEM IN LVCE REFVLSIT
ALMA PARENS ...

The construction *respicio et lustro—deseruere ... dedere—cum mihi se uidendam obtulit parens* is quite grammatical, but obviously not what the poet intended. At his death the passage had not been completed. The autograph had reached the form 564, 565, 566, 624, 625, etc., with—perhaps in the margin, perhaps separately—verses 589–614 (half-line) and 615–23 (half-line) of the unfinished new scene. But is it likely that the poet (or his amanuensis) wrote down a sentence (... *cum obtulit) with no beginning?*[49] We must frankly acknowledge that the introduction to the *cum*-clause was in all probability composed and later deleted. We must also own to some puzzlement why Varius chose to effect a juncture between 566 and 589: if he had found a headless inverted *cum*-clause, he could simply have altered *cum* to *hic*. Perhaps Virgil did compose a line specifying the moment when Venus appeared, and Varius felt forced to delete it as too harsh an indication that the preceding verses were never composed.

The thesis that these preceding verses were none other than the Helen Episode is, apart from argument given above, still untenable. If Varius judged that this section of the poem had not attained a satisfactory coherence, what possessed him to include the incomplete speech of Venus (half-line at 614) and the incomplete conclusion (half-line at 623) and to exclude the completed Helen scene—and, furthermore, cut

---

[49] It is just possible. At *Aen.* 1. 535 we come upon an invested *cum*-clause not actually headless, but introduced by the merest stopgap:

hic cursus fuit,
cum subito adsurgens fluctu nimbosus Orion
in uada caeca tulit ...

Clearly, the *cum*-clause was composed before Virgil had conceived the main clause in any detail.

it off in the middle of a sentence? If he decided that he had to excise a whole passage, the perfect solution stared him in the face: omit all the marginal verses and retain the earlier sequence ... 565, 566, 624, 625, etc. But the evidence, namely the retention of half a sentence at 589 and half-lines at 614 and 623, supports the view that in exercising his editorial prerogative he did not willingly part with a single word.

Now some scholars, admitting that Varius would never have deleted the Helen Episode, yet strong in their faith of its authenticity, have altogether abandoned the Servian position and retreated to more shadowy ground. 'Virgil's workshop must have been littered with rough drafts' (Shipley).[50] Thus it is hinted that the Helen Episode may be one of these alleged rough drafts and later found its way into the hands of a publisher.

Two passages from Aulus Gellius have been cited to support this hypothesis. The first is patently a fraud. At 1. 21 Gellius refers to the text of *Geo.* 2. 246 f.:

> at sapor indicium faciet manifestus, et ora
> tristia temptantum sensu torquebit amaro.

The meaning is clear, the majuscules unanimously attest this text, and Macrobius adds his confirmation at *Sat* 6. 1. 47. According to Gellius, however, Julius Hyginus claimed in his commentary on Virgil, and claimed with some insistence, that he had found *in libro qui fuerit ex domo atque familia Vergilii* the reading:

> et ora
> tristia temptantum *sensus* torquebit *amaror.*

Several of the learned at once agreed that logic demanded *sensus ... amaror,* whilst Gellius' friend, the philosopher Favorinus, no sooner heard Hyginus' comment than he became mightily displeased with *sensu ... amaro,* and pointed out Lucretius' use of *amaror* as *amaritudo* at 4. 224. Servius repeats the assertion that *amaror* is the correct reading and adds the Lucretian reference but typically forgets to mention the necessary alteration to *sensus.* Virgil's practice and customary elegance forbid the uncouth *amaror,* and governing a genitive, too. Pleonasms of the type *sapor ... sensu torquebit* are a feature of Latin verse style. Housman has collected a large list at Man. 1. 539; 3. 496; 4. 472; 4. 644; and Luc. 1. 102, of which a Virgilian example may be given here: *Aen.* 1.

---

[50] F. W. Shipley, 'Virgilian Authorship of the Helen Episode, *Aeneid* II 567–588', *TAPhA* 56 (1925), 184.

246, *it mare proruptum et pelago premit arua sonanti,* where *pelago* ...
sonanti after *mare* exactly corresponds to *sensu* ... *amaro* after *sapor*.
Clearly Hyginus is either trying to fool us or was fooled himself by an
incorrect conjecture.

In the second passage, at 13. 21, Gellius' testimony rests on the
hearsay of an unnamed acquaintance. Valerius Probus, discussing *i*-
stem accusative plurals, remarked on the fine discrimination which
prompted Virgil to write *urbis* at *Geo*. 1. 25 (PRg: *-es* M) but *urbes* (FMP)
at *Aen*. 3. 106. By way of emphasizing his point he added that his *Georgics*
manuscript was corrected by the poet's own hand. We cannot build
much on this. In the two readings Probus' manuscripts agree with ours,
and they were doubtless excellent. But whether ancient booksellers
adhered scrupulously to the truth in advertising copies of the *Georgics* as
'corrected by the author's own hand' and whether Virgil is likely to have
devoted much of his day to such drudgery are questions that Probus
might not, could we challenge him, be too confident about answering in
the affirmative.

In section 33 of the Life, Donatus records that Virgil held private
recitations, chiefly to poll the opinions of others over passages of his
work concerning which he felt some doubt. Assume that at some such
soirée a shorthand writer took down the Helen Episode, and we shall be
able to argue that some ancient Pitman published it when it failed to turn
up in the Varian edition. This and other such speculations must fail on
the score of probability. The preceding paragraphs have given some
idea of the minutiae which occupied the first Virgilians. If Aulus Gellius
had come upon such treasure as twenty-two lines of genuine but
uncanonical Virgil, we may be sure that he would have told us all about
it. Or if not he, then someone else; for many voices, as we now shall see,
inform us by their testimony of what Virgil wrote.

XV. *The Academic Tradition of Virgil*

Virgil had become a classic before his death. According to Suetonius,
Quintus Caecilius Epirota, who founded his school at Rome about
26 BC, first added the author to the curriculum. That on publication the
Aeneid was immediately used as a textbook, we can hardly doubt. The
tracts and treatises which it at once evoked betray as much an academic
as a literary interest. However, adoption straightaway by the schools had
one excellent effect: the canon of the poet's work was established before
any question of authenticity or spuriousness could arise. Not half a line

could be lost; not half a line could be added. No one could hope to deceive such associates as Varius and Horace with verse falsely alleged to be the creation of Rome's greatest poet. These knew the facts and would have spoken out. Of course, this protective period could not last long, though it hardly ended before the death of Augustus. But it lasted long enough for the commentators to establish what may be called the academic tradition of Virgil. This tradition, which is attested in our oldest manuscripts of the poet, was handed on to, and in turn by, the ancient scholars who studied and taught and annotated Virgil—Hyginus and Modestus and Cornutus and Asper and Probus and so on; to all who drew upon them—Seneca, Pliny, Quintilian, Suetonius, Gellius, Macrobius; to the scholiasts on other authors—on Terence, Horace, Persius, Lucan, Juvenal; to the grammarians—Charisius, Diomedes, Priscian; to the lexicographers Festus and Nonius; to the fathers—Jerome, Augustine, Isidore. Naturally, their evidence is in general vague and cannot match the sharp focus on detail presented by our manuscripts; but in one respect, namely what verses of text they quote, their collective testimony has much greater authority. What needs to be recognized is that the witnesses here named are merely our oldest sources: in all probability the whole of these quotations existed as quotations, that is as an academic tradition, within fifty years of Virgil's death.

Table 4 lists this testimony for *Aen.* 2. 525–624, that is for a 100-verse section including the Helen Episode. Each line quoted or partially quoted is followed by a reference to the quoting source; only one source is given, but where two or more are to be found, a plus sign is appended; in the case of the Virgilian commentators care has been taken to use as evidence, not the text they are annotating, but only their quotations. Further research with Ribbeck's testimonia will disclose that similar results obtain for the whole of *Aeneid* 2. For the portion under scrutiny it emerges that rarely does any authority quote more than two lines at a time (for any sizeable portion, therefore, we possess a wide coverage of support); that half the text enjoys support from two or more witnesses; and that the largest unattested portion is of three lines (607–9), the largest doubly unattested portion of six (604–9). Except, of course, the Helen Episode. The total absence of 567–88 proves pretty conclusively that the Helen Episode never formed part of the academic tradition.

The same is true of the *Culex*, for Nonius' quotation of 53 (211. 24) and Donatus' of 413 f. (*Vit.* 18) are all the testimonia that can be found. Fraenkel has demonstrated, for the benefit of any who might still doubt,

TABLE 4. Ancient Testimony to *Aeneid* 2. 525–624

525	Nonius 384. 7	563	Audax *GL* 7. 328 +
526	Arusianus *GL* 7. 472	564	Schol. Hor. *Serm.* 1. 1. 57 +
528	Servius *Aen.* 12. 476 +		
529	Servius *Aen.* 7. 533 +	589	Servius *Aen.* 1. 407
530	Servius *Aen.* 7. 533	590	Servius *Aen.* 1. 407
531	Nonius 294. 12	591	Servius *Buc.* 8. 102 +
533	Servius *Aen.* 2. 377	593	Acron Hor. *Carm.* 3. 3. 12
534	Arusianus *GL* 7. 501	595	Charisius *GL* 1. 269
535	Macrobius *Sat.* 4. 2. 2 +	596	Priscianus *GL* 3. 254
536	Priscianus *GL* 3. 97 +	597	Priscianus *GL* 3. 254 +
537	Servius *Aen.* 11. 856 +	598	Priscianus *GL* 3. 254 +
538	Servius *Aen.* 1. 114 +	599	Priscianus *GL* 3. 254 +
539	Servius *Aen.* 1. 114	600	Priscianus *GL* 3. 254
540	Quintilianus 5. 11. 14 +	601	Macrobius *Sat.* 5. 17. 16 +
541	Quintilianus 5. 11. 14 +	602	Priscianus *GL* 3. 62 +
544	Nonius 267. 25 +	603	Donatus Ter. *Andr.* 883 +
545	Nonius 267. 25 +	604	Macrobius *Somn. Scip.* 1. 3. 19
546	Porphyrion Hor. *Epist.* 1. 3. 32 +	605	Macrobius *Somn. Scip.* 1. 3. 19
547	Nonius 381. 22 +	606	Macrobius *Somn. Scip.* 1. 3. 19
548	Donatus Ter. *Adelph.* 116 +	610	Priscianus *GL* 2. 343 +
549	Charisius *GL* 1. 268 +	611	Priscianus *GL* 2. 343 +
550	Macrobius *Sat.* 4. 4. 14 +	612	Schol. Hor. *Carm.* 3. 3. 23
551	Macrobius *Sat.* 4. 4. 14 +	613	Schol. Hor. *Carm.* 3. 3. 23
553	Seneca *Suas.* 4. 5 +	614	Servius *Aen.* 1. 16
554	Acron Hor. *AP* 35 +	615	Schol. Hor. *Carm.* 1. 15. 11 +
555	Acron Hor. *AP* 35	616	Schol. Hor. *Carm.* 1. 15. 11 +
556	Macrobius *Sat.* 4. 3. 6	617	Nonius 386. 5 +
557	Macrobius *Sat.* 4. 3. 6 +	618	Diomedes *GL* 1. 411 +
558	Schol. Veron. *Aen.* 7. 337 +	619	Servius *Aen.* 1. 382
559	Diomedes *GL* 1. 408	620	Schol. Veron. *Aen.* 2. 633 +
560	Macrobius *Sat.* 4. 6. 9 +	622	Servius *Aen.* 1. 407
561	Schol. Iuven. 4. 94 +	623	Servius *Aen.* 1. 407
562	Nonius 403. 27	624	Probus *GL* 4. 223 +

why the *Culex* cannot have been written by Virgil.[51] More than that, he explains the motives which prompted the fake and adopts W. R. Hardie's reasoning that it was executed in the reign of Tiberius. The really significant thing, however, is that whilst the *Culex* 'was at an early stage accepted as Virgilian by men of good judgement and high rank in

[51] Eduard Fraenkel, *JRS* 42 (1952), 1–9 (*Kleine Beiträge*, II 181–97).

literature, Lucan, Statius, Martial, and Suetonius', the canon had
already been definitively established by the academic tradition. The
Culex could never become a text for the commentator. It was too late.
Texts of Virgil had spread to schools and libraries all over Italy and the
Empire. However skilful a faker might be, he lacked the means to
impose his fraud on the world at large. The man responsible for the
deception had to rest content with his limited success in tainting the
biographical tradition. Notice again the terms of Virgil's will in Donatus
Vit. 40: 'he bequeathed his writings jointly to Varius and Tucca,
stipulating that they should publish nothing not already published by
himself'. The stipulation is absurd: Virgil had published the *Eclogues*
and *Georgics*: therefore they were not to publish the *Aeneid*. Then why
not say so? The clause only makes sense when we realize that it is a
fabrication to account for the absence of the spurious minor works from
the academic tradition.

XVI. *The Author of the Helen Episode*

To conclude, let us attempt a composite description of the author of the
Helen Episode. We have seen that he was thoroughly conversant with
Virgil's *Aeneid*; that he was aware of Virgil's employment of the Golden
Section; that he has overdone Virgil's metrical technique, giving one the
impression that he himself wrote in smoother hexameters; that his
theatrical sense and skilful use of verbal variation mark him out as an
effective rhetorician and student of the drama. He was evidently familiar
with Ennius' *Hectoris Lytra* (cf. Sc. 181 and *Aen.* 2. 582) and Euripides'
Orestes (cf. 1137 ff.). To this we may now add that he composed the
verses before AD 65, which seems assured by Lucan's dependence on
them at 10. 53 ff. (tentatively suggested by Haskins, accepted by
Francken, more cautiously by Austin, and finally established by
Bruère[52]):

> 53   *iam* ...
> 56   ... *cum* ... Cleopatra ...
> 59   dedecus Aegypti, Latii furialis *erinys*,
> 60   Romano non casta malo. quantum impulit *Argos*
>   *Iliacasque domos facie Spartana nocenti*,
>   Hesperios auxit tantum Cleopatra *furores*.
>   terruit illa suo, si *fas*, Capitolia sistro
>   et Romana petit imbelli signa Canopo
> 65   Caesare captiuo Pharios ductura *triumphos*.

[52] Richard T. Bruère, 'The Helen Episode in *Aeneid* 2 and Lucan', *CP* 59 (1964), 267.

Unfortunately, Bruère tries to prove too much: that 'Virgil's Helen episode remained in Lucan's memory as he continued his tenth book'. He sees traces of *limina Vestae/ seruantem et tacitam secreta in sede latentem/ Tyndarida* in:

> 458   ceu puer imbellis uel captis femina muris,
>   quaerit tuta domus; spem uitae in limine clauso
> 460   ponit, et incerto lustrat uagus atria cursu.

These verses, however, draw their inspiration from *Aen.* 2. 515 ff. (516 *ceu* ... 528 *uacua atria lustrat*): the unwarlike youth and the roaming through the rooms recall Polites (not Aeneas), and the word *femina* recalls Hecuba (not Helen). As for *sumpturus poenas* a little later, at 10. 462, that need have no particular source (cf. *Aen.* 2. 103, 6. 501, 11. 720, 12. 949). Naturally, it would be helpful to know that Lucan found the Helen Episode in the text of an edition of *Aen.* 2, but the evidence falls short of this. Lucan was steeped in Virgil: Heitland's incomplete list of parallels fills no less than sixteen pages.[53] Moreover, Lucan was, like Persius, a pupil of the eminent rhetorician Lucius Annaeus Cornutus, who wrote a commentary on Virgil. We cannot be sure that Lucan's echoes of the Helen Episode derive from a text of Virgil rather than from sources into which a study of the *Aeneid* had taken him. Besides his obvious interest in that epic, he was sufficiently fascinated by the fall of Troy to write a poem so titled. Lucan attributed the *Culex* to Virgil, and it is quite possible that he similarly erred in attributing the Helen Episode to him, too. But it does not necessarily follow that he found either in an edition of the poet.

Indeed, since persons to whom fakes are traced draw upon themselves the eye of suspicion, we might spare a thought for the possibility that Lucan composed the Helen Episode himself. He certainly fits the composite description we have sketched above. It is futile to expect much evidence from the *Civil War*, for, as we have seen in respect of metre, the author of the Helen Episode is attempting to disguise his own person by putting on the mantle of another. One consideration deserves attention, for it is this which has led so many to place absolute trust in their intuition with sublime disregard of the case against authenticity: Lucan above all others possesses the requisite genius.

The author of the disputed verses is no poetaster, like the authors of the *Culex* and the *Ciris*. 'The happiest imitation of Virgil's manner',

---

[53] W. E. Heitland in C. E. Haskins, ed., *M. Annaei Lucani Pharsalia* (London, 1887), pp. cx–cxxvi.

wrote Charles James Fox, 'that I ever saw. I am indeed so unwilling to
believe them any other than genuine, that rather than I would consent to
such an opinion, I should be inclined to think that Virgil himself had
written and afterwards erased them on account of their inconsistency
with the account he gives of Helen in the Sixth Book.' Herein finds voice
the common feeling of all Virgilians; or, at least, of all modern editors of
Virgil, not one of whom has brought himself to leave these verses where
Servius left them. But, though such admiration decreases by not a grain
the mass of evidence against their genuineness, it correspondingly raises
the stature of the composer, whoever he was. 'None but a Virgil ever
wrote them,' pronounced Henry, 'and there never was but one Virgil.'[54]
Our era of scholarship may not care to dispute these frabjous syllo-
gistics, but former times brought forth impressive judges who lent a
sympathetic ear to Lucan's defiant challenge: *et quantum mihi restat / ad
Culicem?* Not without cause did Shelley prefer him to Virgil, and
Macaulay place some of his speeches above Cicero's best. Experience of
life he lacks, but what do you ask? He died at an age when neither Virgil
nor Horace had published a word.

The shroud of time now covers up the evidence which alone could
identify the author of the Helen Episode. We must leave him nameless.
The notion that he is the poet Lucan, in all probability false, will
nevertheless restrain us, when we ponder the facts of the case, from too
ready a confidence in some vaguer but incompatible hypothesis; and it
may suggest the time and milieu in which composition took place.
Furthermore, with the words of Fox ringing in our ears and the fantastic
thought that the composer might just conceivably have been the greatest
of Roman literary prodigies—*heu, miserande puer, si qua fata aspera
rumpas!*—we shall be able to reconstruct the drift of that scholium,
perhaps from the very commentary of Cornutus, which Servius with his
breezy disregard for accuracy has rewritten to the perplexity and
deception of after ages:

Schol. ad *Aen.* 2. 592: ⟨ ... hinc autem aliquid deesse Veneris uerba declarant
dicentis (601) 'non ... Lacaenae.' unde ingeniosus quidam poeta, ut locum
expleret, uersus composuit sequentes. qui tamen mirumquantum Vergilium
sapiunt, adeo ut dixerit quispiam potius ab ipso scriptos esse et postea ab eius
emendatoribus sublatos: 'aut ignibus aegra dedere—iamque adeo ...'⟩

[54] Henry (above, n. 47), p. 277.

6

Dido in the Light of History

N. M. HORSFALL

'Inhumana crudelitas, perfidia plus quam Punica, nihil veri, nihil sancti, nullus deum metus, nullum ius iurandum, nulla religio' (Liv. 21. 4. 9). That, of course, is Livy on Hannibal, and though Romans *did* admire Hannibal for his generalship and achievements (K. H. E. de Jong, *Mnemos.* (1928), 186 ff.), Livy's charges are repeated by his contemporaries both against Hannibal himself and against the Carthaginians in general.[1] Three wars had left an ineradicable legacy of fear and hate; Seneca writes of the 'timor qui Hannibale post Cannas moenia circumsidente lectoris percurrit animos' (*Ira* 2. 5. 2), and Horace of Hannibal as *parentibus abominatus* (*Epodes* 16. 8): his very name was a bogey to be averted by Roman parents (Horsfall, *Philol.* (1973), 138). Twice, no, probably three times (Hor. *Od.* 3. 6. 36, 4. 4. 42, and ? 2. 12. 2) Horace calls Hannibal *dirus*, and the adjective is noted by Quintilian as a peculiarly appropriate epithet (8. 2. 9). There are two main charges: Carthaginian cruelty—from the *barbarus tortor* awaiting Regulus (Hor. *Od.* 3. 5. 49 f.; cf. Cic. *Off.* 1. 39, Sen. 75) to Hannibal himself, whom 'propter crudelitatem semper haec civitas oderit' (Cic. *Amic.* 28; cf. *Off.* 1. 38, Sen. 75, V.M. 9. 2. 2.); and Carthaginian perfidy—the ironic and proverbial *fides Punica* (A. Otto, *Die Sprichwörter und sprichwörtlichen Redensarten der Römer* (Leipzig, 1890), 291), familiar from Plautus' *Poenulus* (113, 1125; cf. fr. 33W) on, exemplified again by Hannibal, whom Cicero calls *callidus* (*Off.* 1. 108; cf. 1. 38 *Poeni foedifragi*) and Horace *perfidus* (*Od.* 4. 4. 49; cf. 3. 5. 33). The *incendia Karthaginis impiae* (*Od.* 4. 8. 17) were her just deserts, and the behaviour of Regulus a *documentum fidei* developed in deliberate ideological contrast (Sen. *Dial.* 1. 3. 9, Gell. 6. 18). And one might add Carthaginian wealth, luxury, and arrogance—Horace writes of the *superbas invidae Karthaginis arces* (*Epod.* 7. 5 f.; cf. *Od.* 2. 2. 10 f.) and the theme may be illustrated from the historians and Virgil alike. Time and again Horace

---

[1] Cf. E. Burck in J. Vogt, *Rom und Karthago* (Berlin, 1943), pp. 336 ff.; J.-P. Brisson, *Hommages à Marcel Renard*, ed. J. Bibauw (Brussels, 1969), i. 101–3.

returns to Carthage's threat to Rome—the climax of his list of Rome's perils in *Epode* 16 (3 ff.)—and to Rome's slow bloody elimination of that threat: her victories symbolized the martial virtues of earlier generations: 'non his iuventus orta parentibus infecit aequor sanguine Punico' (*Od.* 3. 6. 33 ff.; cf. *Epod.* 7. 5 f.); they were a worthy theme for epic commemoration (*Od.* 2. 12. 2. f., 4. 8. 16. f.); the Metaurus could still be claimed as a turning-point in the defeat of Hannibal to the undying glory of the Claudii Nerones (*Od.* 4. 4. 37 ff.) and only Octavian's own victory at Actium could rival the younger Scipio's achievement in destroying Carthage in 146 (*Epod.* 9. 25). Yet Horace's obsession with the Punic peril is surpassed by Virgil's.

It has been noticed (e.g. by Brisson, loc. cit.) that neither in Jupiter's great prophecy, nor on Aeneas' shield is there any allusion to Rome's conflict with Carthage. But these are not significant silences: Jupiter predicts universal rule for Rome: 'imperium sine fine dedi' (1. 279); that assumes the defeat of all Rome's enemies, and the selection of Greece—rather than Carthage—for mention is aimed at consoling Venus for the defeat of Troy by the Greeks; to describe the naval victories of the Aegates Islands or Ecnomus, Zama, or the burning of Carthage on the Shield would have been to duplicate the historical allusions of the Parade of Heroes—something which Virgil is at pains to avoid doing (cf. J. G. Griffith, *PVS* (1967–8), 54 ff.): Anchises points out to Aeneas Regulus—that is Serranus (844), the *duo fulmina belli Scipiadas cladem Libyae* (842 f.), Quintus Fabius Maximus *unus qui nobis cunctando restituis rem* (846), and the victories (858) of M. Claudius Marcellus, five times consul during the second Punic war. Nor is that by any means all: for Virgil, Carthage is *studiis asperrima belli* (1. 14), and the omen of a horse's head discovered at her foundation portended that she would be *bello egregiam et victu facilem per saecula gentem* (1. 444; cf. V. Buchheit, *Gymnasium* (1964), 429 ff.). To Dido's curse, invoking the vengeance of Hannibal upon Rome I shall return (4. 622 ff.). In its solemn declaration of hostilities a Roman reader could well have seen prefigured Hannibal's famous vow, made at the age of nine, that 'cum primum posset, hostem fore populo Romano' (Liv. 21. 1. 4; cf. A. S. Pease on 4. 425 ff.). Jupiter predicts that there will come a proper time (10. 11 ff.) for battle, hatred, strife, and rapine 'cum fera Karthago Romanis arcibus olim exitium magnum atque Alpes immittet apertas', to which Venus' response in ironic submission is that Jupiter may as well bid Carthage crush Ausonia *magna dicione*; from that quarter there will be no opposition to the Tyrian cities (53 ff.): a wish which Virgil's readers knew came all too near fulfilment. There is also an elaborate typological anticipation of Hannibal's descent on Rome to be found in Virgil's narrative of Turnus' attack on the Trojan camp in Book 9. Rather more clearly, Juno's acquiescence in the plan of destiny (12. 816 ff.) is meant to convey an allusion to the ritual of placating Juno practised in 207, during the second Punic war, as Servius on 12. 841 observes. This was an occasion of great *literary* moment too: Livius Andronicus composed a *carmen* for it, and Ennius apparently commemorated the ritual in the *Annales*: 'placata Iuno coepit favere Romanis'.[2] Virgil, finally, looks forward to the defeat of Carthage in 146: as Eduard Fraenkel pointed out (*Glotta* (1954), 157 f.), Dido's offer to Ilioneus at 1. 573 is ambiguous: *urbem quam statuo vestra est* can mean not only the obvious 'is at your service' but also, quite legitimately, 'is yours'—i.e. in your hands or possession—the inevitable and familiar outcome of generations of hostility induced by Dido's curse. The effect of Dido's suicide brings Carthage's fall more sharply to our notice, for the lamentation throughout the city as Fama spreads the news is 'non aliter quam si immissis ruat hostibus omnis Karthago aut antiqua Tyros flammaeque furentes culmina perque hominum volvantur perque deorum' (4. 669 ff.)—a passage which we perhaps recall when Aeneas, bound for Sicily, looks back at Carthage and sees the walls aglow with flames (5. 3 f.).

But the place in the *Aeneid* assigned to relations between Rome and Carthage is far more important than this rapid survey of historical allusions might suggest: when Virgil asks the Muse *quo numine laeso quidve dolens* Juno has driven Aeneas, for all his piety, to suffer so (1. 8 ff.), the answer is twofold; in historical terms and mythological the link is ingeniously wrought at 1. 23 f. 'id metuens'—summarizing the historical explanation which stands first and prominent—'veterisque memor Saturnia belli prima quod ad Troiam pro caris gesserat Argis'— but I shall be only incidentally concerned with Juno's mythological *gravamina*, however legitimate. Argive Hera's hostility to Troy was a truth handed down from Homer; Juno's connections with Rome's great enemies, Veii, Falerii, and Carthage—where she was identified with Tanit (Pease on 4. 91)—were matters of history. There was in ancient times a city—of Tyrian foundation, rich and warlike—explains Virgil, *Karthago, Italiam contra Tiberinaque longe ostia* (1. 13 f.): the sharp juxtaposition of *Karthago* and *Italiam*, and the ambiguity of *contra*—

---

[2] Enn. *Ann.* 291 V; cf. Liv. 27. 37. 7; V. Buchheit, *Vergil über die Sendung Roms* (Heidelberg, 1963), pp. 144 f.; G. Lieberg, *AR* (1966), 162 ff.

geographically 'facing', and historically 'against' underline the importance *for the epic* of Rome's *actual* hostility towards Carthage. This city
Juno loved even more than Argos, second only, indeed, to Samos: 'hoc
regnum dea gentibus esse, si qua fata sinant, iam tum tenditque
fovetque'. But against this love expressed in expansionist political
ambitions, and military success, for this was where (1. 16 f.) Juno kept
her chariot and arms, and against Carthage's intended sway over the
nations, Juno had heard that a race of Trojan descent was arising 'Tyrias
olim quae verteret arces': from this stock 'populum late regem belloque
superbum venturum excidio Libyae; sic volvere Parcas'. Unmistakably,
in the prooemium, we are confronted with the Punic wars: Romans *bello
superbi* face Carthage *studiis asperrima belli*; a Roman empire *late regem*
confronts Juno's ambitions for Carthage, *regnum ... gentibus esse*. Her
plans are qualified by *si qua fata sinant*; Rome's eventual destruction of
Carthage is confirmed by *sic volvere Parcas*. Juno's struggle to ensure that
tantae molis erat Romanam condere gentem is from the very first characterized as a struggle against the fated order of things, against the
destinies of Aeneas and Rome. She knows she cannot keep Aeneas from
Italy—*quippe vetor fatis* (1. 39), but her attempts to do so, notwithstanding, are massively symbolic of Rome's historic struggles towards empire.

Juno's anger against Troy and fear for Carthage drive her to unleash
Aeolus against Aeneas, revealing her as the enemy of all order—of the
order through which Aeolus rules the madly raging winds (1. 51 ff.), and
Neptune controls the mad, swirling Ocean (107, 127, 141 f.), of the
ordered calm with which Aeneas comforts his people and reminds them
of their glorious future (205 ff.), of the order which Jupiter imposes on
the universe (255), and of the order which Augustus will impose upon a
world long harried by *furor impius* (291 ff.). The political implications of
the storm which Juno raises are confirmed by the famous simile of 1.
148 ff., where Neptune's calming of the waves is compared to a riotous
mob, inspired by *furor*, falling silent at the sight of a statesman *pietate
gravem ac meritis*. Virgil has in mind both internal and external aspects of
Rome's struggles towards greatness and stability: the simile and the
conventional symbolic correspondence of the storm with internal strife
point one way, the explanation of Juno's hostility in terms of the historic
opposition of Rome and Carthage the other. But the essentially immoral
and disorderly character of Juno's support for Carthage, fundamentally
opposed to Troy, Aeneas, Jupiter, Italy, Rome, and Fate is left unambiguous and clearly drawn at the moment of Aeneas' arrival on Carthaginian territory: Venus reiterates to Jupiter that Juno's opposition is

keeping the Trojans not merely from Italy (1. 250 f.), but also from their historical destiny, for Jupiter had already promised that the Trojans would have descendants 'qui mare, qui terras omnis dicione tenerent' (236). Jupiter's response, anticipating the reconciliation scene in Book 12 which I have already mentioned is that 'aspera Iuno ... consilia in melius referet mecumque fovebit Romanos rerum dominos gentemque togatam' (279 ff.): national pride balances international dominion. This promise stands between the undertaking *imperium sine fine dedi* and the assurance that a time will come when Trojan stock will reconquer Greece: that is to say, as Servius on 1. 281 suggests, that Juno's reconciliation in 207 BC is a necessary prelude to the defeat of Carthage, the first great obstacle to *imperium sine fine* encountered by Rome overseas and to the great wave of foreign conquests she undertook in the sixty years after the Punic war—including, of course, *Pthiam clarasque Mycenas*.

But that is all in the future. Here and now, the second great threat to his mission that Aeneas faces—Dido—closely recalls the first—the storm—in respect of Juno's intervention, of the role of *furor*, and of the anticipation of Rome's historical struggles. Upon the first two elements of parallelism I shall only touch: it is fear of what Juno may intend in the circumstances of Aeneas remaining at Carthage that drives Venus to fire Dido with love for Aeneas (1. 661 ff.; cf. 4. 96 f.); it is Juno, goddess of marriage, to whom, above all, the love-struck Dido prays (4. 59); it is Juno who proposes to Venus a joint Trojan–Carthaginian people— which will have the effect of keeping the Trojans from Italy (102 ff., 105 f.); it is Juno who pretends that she will get Jupiter to approve this proposal (115); it is Juno who watches over the scene in the cave (166). And under this patronage Dido is struck with *furor*, with an explicitly and violently irrational passion for Aeneas (4. 65; cf. 101, 298 ff., 465 ff., etc.). This combination of Juno and madness recurs again in the burning of the ships in Book 5, in the Allecto-scenes in Book 7, and in the burning of the ships in Book 9: each time it stands opposed to Aeneas and Rome. Thus in terms of theology and psychology, as well as historically, the reader is alerted to Dido's function as a dark and terrible threat to Rome's future greatness.

When we read at 1. 297 ff. that Jupiter sends Mercury to ensure 'ut terrae utque novae pateant Karthaginis arces hospitio Teucris, ne fati nescia Dido finibus arceret', we cannot but recall Virgil's powerful initial development of the historical theme of hostility between Rome and Carthage. Is there not something badly wrong, unnatural, and out of character here? Is a relationship of *hospitium* between Rome's ancestors and the Carthaginians really credible or tolerable in the long run? And that scepticism and hesitation are the correct reaction is confirmed by the effect of Mercury's arrival: 'ponuntque ferocia Poeni corda volente deo; in primis regina quietum accipit in Teucros animum mentemque benignam' (303 ff.)—that is to say, *ferocia* would be their natural reaction to the Trojans, and *benignitas* is what Mercury's presence secures. Ilioneus' experience is illuminating: he complains (525) that the natives have tried to fire his ships and as he gains in confidence bursts out: 'quod genus hoc hominum, quaeve hunc tam barbara morem permittit patria? hospitio prohibemur harenae; bella cient primaque vetant consistere terra' (539 ff.). That would appear typically brutish Punic behaviour;—but when Ilioneus protests that he has not come to plunder the penates of Libya or to carry off stolen booty to the shore (526 f.) we know that his descendants in 204 and 146 will do just that. Dido protests that circumstances force her to a hostile reaction (563–4); she offers her help—or 'voltis et his mecum pariter considere regnis? urbem quam statuo vestra est; subducite navis; Tros Tyriusque mihi nullo discrimine agetur' (572 ff.). Juno makes a similar proposal to Venus at the beginning of Book 4 to which I shall come shortly. Dido's offer has political advantages for her in terms of protection against Tyre and the Nomades (4. 320 f., 535 f.) and is normally described as kind and generous. But I wonder whether that would have been quite a Roman's reaction: it is, after all, in direct conflict with what has already been said in the poem of relations between Carthage and Rome and with the Roman historical experience. We should remember that only Mercury's intervention prevented the premature outbreak of the first Punic war. And looking ahead, we recognize that the final outcome of Dido's proffered *hospitium* is her curse: 'litora litoribus contraria, fluctibus undas imprecor, arma armis; pugnent ipsique nepotesque' (4. 628 f.). But there, in *nullus amor populis nec foedera sunto* (624) and in Jupiter's description of the Carthaginians as a *gens inimica* (4. 235), we recognize a ring of historical truth, which is more than can be said of Dido's offer in Book 1. The same goes for Aeneas' ingenuous response to Dido's offer to Ilioneus (which he had heard from within his cloud): 'semper honos nomenque tuum laudesque manebunt, quae me cumque vocant terrae' (609 f.): how could Roman feelings stay favourable towards the foundress of Carthage? In the Underworld, Aeneas' feelings of love for Dido remain unaltered (6. 455), but she goes off to rejoin Sychaeus, her first husband, returning decisively to her Phoenician origins, and rejecting any link between Carthage and Rome. In passing, I would observe that in the Underworld we are strongly reminded once again of the national, political, if you prefer, character of the threat which Dido presented to Aeneas by the phrasing of Anchises' remark to Aeneas: 'quam metui ne quid Libyae tibi regna nocerent'. Not 'Dido' or 'the queen' or 'Libya', but the *Libyae regna*, the *regna* which Juno intended should hold sway over the nations (1. 18).

To return to Book 1: Venus at least is not deceived by Dido's friendliness and plans to send Cupid to fire Dido with love for Aeneas: 'quippe domum timet ambiguam Tyriosque bilinguis; urit atrox Iuno et sub noctem cura recursat' (661 f.); she makes her fears even more explicit when addressing Cupid (671 f.): 'nunc Phoenissa tenet Dido blandisque moratur vocibus; et vereor quo se Iunonia vertant hospitia; haud tanto cessabit cardine rerum'. In just what sense, we must ask, are Dido's *hospitia* to be described as *Iunonia* here? This hospitality rests, of course, upon Jupiter's instructions to Mercury but it is 'inspired by Juno' inasmuch as it is hospitality from Juno's city, hospitality which must be seen in terms of Juno's plans for Carthage against Rome, hospitality which must turn out to reflect its true origins and character. Venus must use tricks—*doli* (673)—to ensure that Dido *ne quo se numine mutet* (674). *Ambiguam, bilinguis, mutet* all hint at the characteristic conception of *Punica fides*, and the importance of this conception becomes clearer if we look on to Book 4: there Juno says to Venus 'nec me adeo fallit veritam te moenia nostra suspectas habuisse domos Karthaginis altae' (96 f.). Juno is quite right: Venus' attitude of wary concern has not changed since 1. 670 ff. and her anticipation of Junonian or Punic treachery is immediately justified: for Juno suggests that since Dido is now in love with Aeneas thanks to Venus, they may as well—recalling Dido's offer to Ilioneus—bring about *pacem aeternam pactosque hymenaeos*—a joint people with a Trojan ruler. We recall Virgil's emphasis on the fundamental opposition of Rome and Carthage and share in Venus' tepid response: would Jupiter want there to be a joint people? 'sensit enim simulata mente locutam quo regnum Italiae Libycas averteret oras' (4. 105 f.). Such an alliance would mean an end to conflict, but an end to Rome too. Contrast the alliance between Trojans and Italians agreed by Jupiter and Juno in Book 12: that is in accordance with destiny, a true fusion of compatible peoples with a glorious future; just as we may also contrast the Trojans' dark and lowering anchorage on the African coast (1. 162 ff.) with their sunny, bright, and pleasant arrival at the Tiber mouth in 7 (25 ff.). No reader aware from the first of Aeneas'

Italian destiny and the opposition of Carthage to that destiny can anticipate anything but tragedy as the outcome of Dido's love and *hospitium*. A formal, though perhaps unnatural relationship of *hospitium* has—as we have seen—been established between Trojans and Carthaginians (cf. 1. 299, 540, 731, 753; 4.10, 51, 323), and Dido's reaction against this solemn pledge, however justifiably outraged we may feel her to have been by Aeneas' actions, is no better than a Roman would expect of a *Punica* and her *fides*: Mercury warns Aeneas (560 ff.) that Dido will set fire to his fleet if dawn finds him still at Carthage and this warning is confirmed by Dido's waking reactions (592 ff.): 'non arma expedient totaque ex urbe sequentur diripientque rates navalibus? ite, ferte citi flammas'. Her charges of *dissimulatio* and *perfidia* against Aeneas (4. 305 f.) do not carry great weight. Her own *perfidia* intended against an *hospes* aside, she lapses from *fides* in deceiving old Barce to get away from the pyre (632 ff.), and in deceiving Anna when planning her suicide (476–7; cf. 500, 675, 679). But these are minor peccadilloes in comparison with *non servata fides promissa Sychaeo* (552), as she says herself. Her vows to remain *univira*, loyal to Sychaeus' memory, were unambiguous (1. 720, 4. 15 ff.) and her breach of them shocking to herself and to a Roman, more familiar than us with the moral and religious status of the *univira*.[3] Virgil mixes sympathy for her moral lapse with censure; that a breach of *fides* is involved is ironically fitting for the first queen of Carthage.

It is a commonplace to say that Dido and Aeneas would have fallen in love anyway, even without divine intervention: they are portrayed as resembling each other, but the apparent similarities between them are rich in historical ambiguities and ironic undertones, Dido claims (1. 630) that 'non ignara mali miseris succurrere disco' because 'me quoque per multos similis fortuna labores iactatam hac demum voluit consistere terra' (1. 628 ff.). But has their fortune been really and essentially *similis*? Granted that they are both leaders of a group of involuntary exiles, trying to found a new city, that both have recenly lost a well-loved spouse, that the death of Sychaeus *ante aras* (1. 349) is reminiscent of that of Priam, and that the vision of Sychaeus warning Dido to leave Tyre is reminiscent of Hector warning Aeneas to leave Troy, the differences are every bit as striking as the similarities: Dido has to leave Tyre because of the characteristically Punic impiety and treachery of Pygmalion (1. 350 f.), whereas the Trojans are forced to

---

[3] G. Williams. *JRS* (1958), 23; id., *Tradition and Originality in Roman Poetry* (Oxford, 1968), pp. 378 ff.; cf. Phinney, *CJ* (1964–5), 356 f.

leave by eventual military defeat. There is a tremendous emphasis on the role of *money* in Dido's story: Sychaeus was *ditissimus auri* if Huet's emendation for *agri* at 1. 343 is right (I am not convinced), he was killed by the *avarus* Pygmalion *auri caecus amore*; Sychaeus tells Dido of an *ignotum argenti pondus et auri* for her travels, whereas Hector tells Aeneas of the Penates; the Tyrian exiles load their ships with gold, whereas the Trojans are *omnium egeni* (599); Dido's people buy land to settle, as much as an oxhide will cover—an oxhide which, as the story goes, they craftily cut into strips, whereas Latinus offers the Trojans land (7. 260 f., 11. 316 ff.). Dido's story suits the origins of a great merchant people, with an unpleasant reputation for sharp dealing which goes back to the kidnapping of Eumaeus and the kidnapping of Io in Herodotus 1. 1. By contrast with the Trojans' sufferings, the story told by the disguised Venus can hardly be intended to evoke unqualified sympathy.

There is effective dramatic irony in Aeneas' arrival at Carthage, aware of, but not disturbed by Carthage's murky origins, but quite unaware—for there is no word of it in the oracles and visions he had encountered—of Carthage's threat to the Aeneadae, which Virgil has impressed upon his readers from the very beginning of the poem. This irony is increased by Aeneas' first reactions to Carthage (421 f.): 'miratur molem Aeneas, magalia quondam, miratur portas strepitumque et strata viarum'. This splendid, glowing description of the city's construction reaches its climax in 'o fortunati quorum iam moenia surgunt' (437): but we should still be astonished at the ancestor of Rome casting blessings upon the foundation of Carthage. Aeneas is far from founding his own city and discouraged by repeated failures *en route*; his first sight of Dido is as a great beauty—and a great leader, legislator, and works supervisor: 'iura dabat legesque viris operumque laborem partibus aequabat iustis aut sorte trahebat' (1. 507 f.). Aeneas is captivated by Punic luxury (1. 637 ff., 699 ff., 4. 193, 215 ff., 261 ff.), and after a winter of idleness—'non coeptae adsurgunt turres' (4. 86)— actually participates in the building of Carthage (4. 260, 265 f.), forgetful of his own *regnum* and that due to Ascanius (4. 194, 275, 355, 432), with its glorious future (4. 299 ff.). His actions threaten Rome's destinies and help Rome's enemies. However much we (and Aeneas) admire Dido's activity as foundress—and we are clearly expected to do so (cf. 4. 347 f., 591, and particularly 655 ff.)—we must react differently to its historical outcome. History is prefigured by Dido's threat to pursue Aeneas *atris ignibus* (4. 384) as Juno symbolically does in Books 5, 7, and 9 (5. 604 ff., 641, 7. 445 ff., etc., 9. 1 ff. 69 ff.), and by her curse bringing down upon Aeneas suffering and delay in the fulfilment of his destiny, again exactly in Juno's manner (1. 12 ff., etc., 4. 612 ff.); history is brought vividly before the reader when her curse reaches its climax, invoking the horrors of war awaiting Rome at the hands of the city which Dido founded and built. Our view of Dido should therefore, as we read, be open to continuous adjustment and correction.

There remain two further passages towards which the possible reaction of a Roman reader must be evaluated with care. First, Dido's exercise of magic: this does occupy a lot of space—478–519—more, really, than the magic's importance *for the plot* requires (R. Pichon, *RPh.* (1909), 247 ff.) and enough to have suggested an element of poetic self-indulgence, following the lavish descriptions of Apollonius and Theocritus. The only actual *function* of Dido's magic—regardless of its pretended *intention* to bind Aeneas to Dido or to loose Dido from him— is to blind Anna to her sister's intended suicide while securing the provision of a pyre. Eitrem's detailed analysis of Dido's magic (summarized by Austin in his commentary, p. 149) shows convincingly that the ritual as described could not have worked within the terms of ancient magic, and his inference that it was not meant to work is legitimate. The importance of Dido's resort to magic for our reaction to her cannot rest simply upon (492 f.) 'testor, cara, deos, et te, germana, tuumque dulce caput magicas invitam accingier artis'. Granted that she is innocent of serious belief in magic—both Anna and the old nurse Barce are clearly more committed than she is—the fact remains that her appeals to orthodox divinities (56 ff.) for their blessing on her liaison have failed, and that despite her protestation of non-involvement, she is prepared to make use of these murky rituals for her convenience. Her use of magic hardly 'estranges' the reader (cf. Pease, p. 407), but though the description may rouse 'pity and terror' (Austin, p. 150) at Dido's plight, may it not also be meant to lower her in our esteem? Servius sensibly comments 'quia multa sacra Romani susciperent semper magica damnarunt: ideo excusat'—referring to 493, and it is unnecessary to reinforce his statement by reference to (for instance) Horace and Roman Law. Medea keeps a fine store of magic charms in a box in her bedroom (*A.R.* 3. 812, 844) whereas Dido is informed secretly by a priestess from the westernmost ends of the earth: the action in her case must be strange, abnormal, and therefore discreditable.

Secondly, the pictures in the temple in Book 1: Aeneas sees in them sympathy for his plight and an earnest for the future: 'hoc primum in luco novas res oblata timorem leniit, hic primum Aeneas sperare

salutem ausus et afflictis melius confidere rebus' (450 ff.; cf. 463). But
the reader will question whether any true *salus* can come from Carthage,
whether the cruel and grasping Carthaginians are really the people to
express lasting sympathy for the exile and the vanquished, and whether,
above all, in a temple dedicated to Juno (and Aeneas can hardly be aware
of its dedication, or after his experiences of Junonian persecution he
could hardly be so ready to seek consolation from such a quarter) there
could be any valid testimony to pro-Trojan sympathy·and humanity.
The irony of Aeneas' warm reactions, when Carthage is to bring him
and his people nothing but suffering and disaster has often been
recognized.[4] Dido, of course, knows all about the war from Salaminian
Teucer (1. 619 ff.)—and, we may feel, Troy can have had few bitterer
enemies, if we recall just who this Teucer was—a son of Priam's sister
Hesione; Hesione was given to Teucer's father Telamon as a reward for
Telamon's help to Heracles when Heracles captured Troy, having been
cheated of *his* reward for saving Troy from a monster to whom Hesione
was about to be sacrificed; this monster had been sent by Neptune who
had himself been cheated of *his* reward for helping to build Troy: thus
Telamon had not merely his ten years of siege, but a rich family
experience of Trojan misconduct. This may help us to answer the
question of why these pictures occur in a temple dedicated to Juno, who
had supported the Argives, and of why Dido should be interested in just
these scenes. I doubt whether it will do to dismiss the problem of why
Virgil selects the scenes he does for so prominent an ecphrasis by
reference simply to variety, or pictorial quality, or the desire for balance
and contrast. Rhesus is shown exhausted on arrival in his tent, betrayed
by Dolon, and slaughtered by a bloodthirsty Diomedes: 'primo quae
prodita somno Tydides multa vastabat caede cruentus' (470 f.). Troilus'
death is described next: the brutality of this event is stressed—the boy is
ambushed by Achilles when unarmed—'infelix puer atque impar congressus Achilli'; he is dragged dangling backwards by his chariot. The
women of Troy are shown going in supplication *ad templum non aequae
Palladis*; like Juno, Pallas fought steadily *against* the Trojans: 'omnis
spes Danaum et coepti fiducia belli Palladis auxiliis semper stetit' (2.
162 f.). Achilles is shown towing Hector's body not merely round the
tomb of Patroclus, as in the *Iliad*, but three times right round the city,
before the pathetic figure of Priam begs for its return, again not as
in Homer, but against reward: 'exanimumque auro corpus vendebat

---

[4] Brooks Otis, *Virgil: A Study in Civilized Poetry* (Oxford, 1964), p. 238; K. Stanley,
AJPh (1965), 273 f., etc.

Achilles' (484). Only in Aeneas' sighting of himself and in the finale of
Memnon and Penthesilea is there no explicit brutality, though we may
recall that both these allies of Troy were, like Troilus and Hector, killed
by Achilles. There is minimal evidence of Trojan victory and heroism;
not one of their great feats of arms is specifically mentioned. Just as one
would expect in a temple of Juno, the choice of pictures illustrates the
success of her favourites; while Aeneas is delighted to see that Troy is
not forgotten, he quite fails to observe, as we must do, that the attitude to
Troy shown in these pictures is neither friendly nor sympathetic. They
illustrate just those qualities which Carthaginians might admire in the
victorious Greeks—greed and brutality, for which they themselves had
such a fine reputation.

    Now if it is indeed the case that in the creation of Virgil's Dido we can
see at work a tradition which has nothing to do with the heroines of
Greek literature, or with Catullus' Ariadne, but which has its roots in
Roman history and Roman prejudice, then we may be able to advance a
step further and see if this tradition can be identified. In investigating
the legend of Dido before Virgil, there is one fundamental point of
which we must never lose sight: that is the ancient tradition about
Virgil's originality, one so strong that it cannot legitimately be questioned.[5] Macrobius refers to the *fabula lascivientis Didonis* (5. 17. 5),
quam falsam novit universitas—but which through so many ages has
acquired the *specimen veritatis* so as to become a favourite theme for
painters and sculptors. What does Macrobius mean by *falsam*? An
epigram of the Planudean appendix, of which there is a Latin translation
attributed to Ausonius, explains further (*AP* 16. 151; Aus. *Epigr.*. 118;
early Empire—P. Maas, *Hermes* (1914), 517 n. 1): 'Neither did I ever set
eyes on Aeneas nor did I reach Libya at the time of the sack of Troy, but
to escape a forced marriage with Iarbas I plunged the two-edged sword
into my heart. Ye Muses, why did ye arm chaste Virgil against me to
slander thus falsely my virtue?' Christian writers—Tertullian, Minucius
Felix, Jerome—come hotly to Dido's defence (Pease, p. 66 n. 498) as an
exemplar of chastity and praise her courage in preferring death to a
second marriage. Augustine's point is different (*Conf.* 1. 13. 21): on the
question 'utrum verum sit quod Aenean aliquando Karthaginem
venisse poeta ·dicit', he differentiates: 'indoctiores nescire se
respondebunt' while 'doctiores autem etiam negabunt verum esse'.
Here the dispute must turn on chronology: we note the *aliquando* and

---

[5] Cf. H. Dessau, *Hermes* (1914), 517; J. Perret, *Les Origines de la légende troyenne de Rome*
(Paris, 1940), p. 91.

recall that the Planudean epigram suggested that this was a problem; Carthage was not yet founded at the time of the Trojan War, being assigned by most authorities to the ninth century.[6] But it is clear from Augustine too that it is Virgil's version of the story of Dido that is peculiar and open to criticism because it conflicts with the established tradition: in the case of Dido, the tradition—that in exile in Africa she committed suicide to avoid remarriage to a local prince—goes back clearly and firmly to Timaeus (Pease, pp. 16 f., etc.). But the only point of which we can be *quite* certain is that no author before Virgil had Dido commit suicide for love of *Aeneas*: that in some earlier account they *met* cannot yet be ruled out. The argument from chronology is not decisive against such a meeting: Virgil may be casual in his synchronizing of minor legends, but the foundations of Rome and Carthage are *not* minor events, and the gap of three hundred years and more which he ignores would be a great deal less disquieting to the critic if we could suppose that he had some substantial literary precedent for ignoring the conventional chronology. Have we, therefore, any account which places the foundation of Carthage about the time of Troy's fall, or which places Aeneas' exile around the time of the conventional date of the foundation of Carthage? The answer to the former question is, simply, no; to the latter, yes: the earliest Greek historians to recount the foundation of Rome—with the exception of Antiochus of Syracuse—placed it at most three, and often two generations after the fall of Troy;[7] that implies either an early date for the foundation of Rome, or a late date for the fall of Troy, which would involve Aeneas' journey to the West taking place at the precise date of the foundation of Carthage. Both Ennius and Naevius made Romulus a grandson of Aeneas (Servius Danielis, *Aen.* 1. 273) and the possibility that Naevius could have synchronized Dido and Aeneas is therefore a very real one. So we come face to face with the question of whether Naevius, in the *Bellum Punicum*, related an encounter between Dido and Aeneas. What we have established so far is first, that there is no chronological obstacle to his having done so, and secondly, that if he did so, the meeting cannot have been of the same character as Virgil's: to this second point we shall have shortly to return.

In the *Bellum Punicum*, Naevius referred to the fall of Troy and the departure of Aeneas, Anchises, and their wives (fr. 4, 5 Morel) in his first book 'Venus Troianis tempestate laborantibus cum Iove queritur et

---

[6] Pease, p. 58 n. 468; Th. B. de Graff, *Naevian Studies* (New York, 1931), 23 ff., etc.

[7] De Graff, pp. 26 ff.; Pease, p. 17; H. A. Sanders, *CP* 3 (1908), 317 ff.; Jacoby Comm. *FGH* 566 F 59–61.

secuntur verba Iovis filiam consolantis spe futurorum' (fr. 13): the influence of these scenes on *Aeneid* 1 is stressed by Macrobius (6. 2. 31). We cannot be quite certain (cf. Buchheit, p. 39) that the storm occurred in the same place—i.e. off north Africa—as it does in the *Aeneid*, but when Servius Danielis observes on 1. 198 that 'totus hic locus de Naevio Belli Punici libro translatus est', the case in favour of its having done so, despite the vagueness and conventionality of the scholiast's form of expression (cf. Serv. 4. 1, Macr. 5. 2. 4, 17. 4), becomes somewhat stronger. That Naevius mentioned Dido is certain: Servius Danielis on 4. 9 comments 'cuius filiae fuerint Anna et Dido Naevius dicit'; it is also inevitable that sailing from Troy to the west coast of Italy Aeneas had to pass fairly near Carthage. But this is, of course, not proof that they met, and we shall not find watertight proof, for all that is left is a reference to *Bellum Punicum* 2: 'blande et docte percontat (asks) Aenea quo pacto Troiam urbem liquisset' (fr. 23). Who was the subject of *percontat*? The bibliography on this topic is huge (most recently, E. Paratore, *Forschungen zur römischen Literatur: Festschrift Karl Büchner*, ed. W. Wimmel (Wiesbaden, 1970), ii. 224–43), and scholars are divided (unevenly) between Dido and an *hospes Italicus*, probably Latinus, possibly Evander. In favour of Dido are the following: first, the question reminds us strikingly of the situation at the end of *Aeneid* 1, as shown in 'nunc Phoenissa tenet Dido blandisque moratur vocibus' (670 f.) and also in ' "immo age et a prima dic, hospes, origine nobis insidias" inquit "Danaum casusque tuorum erroresque tuos" ' (753 ff.). Secondly, the adjective *docte* would suit Dido's interrogation as presented in the *Aeneid* (1. 750 ff.), where she is repeatedly shown as knowing a great deal about Troy (1. 459 ff., 561 ff., 613 f.), and though it would not be true to claim that *blande* could only be used of a female questioner,[8] it is equally not easy—on the basis of our many accounts of Aeneas' landing in Italy—to conceive of a situation in which an Italian ruler could put questions 'in an ingratiating and well-informed manner' (Paratore, pp. 236 ff.). Thirdly, the attribution of this question is, in *BP* 2, more appropriate to Dido than to an *hospes Italicus*: the episode containing the question will not have taken up much space (Mariotti, p. 38); the fragments (4, 5) actually recounting Aeneas' departure from Troy belong to Book 1, and are in the third person, so we must infer either (intolerably) that Aeneas' adventures were related twice, or (inescapably) that in some way the

---

[8] Buchheit, p. 34; K. Büchner, *Humanitas Romana* (Heidelberg, 1957), pp. 332 f., n. 18, 19; H. Haffter, *DLZ* (1937), 660; S. Mariotti, *Il Bellum Poenicum e Carte di Naevio* (Rome, 1955), pp. 30 f.; Serrao, *Helikon* (1965), 526 ff.

request went unanswered (W. Richter, *NGG* (1960), 45, Paratore, pp. 233 f.). But even a short dialogue between Aeneas and an *hospes Italicus* in *BP* 2 would mean—so far as we can tell, for we have no other relevant information about *BP* 2—that at least part of Book 2, as well as part of Book 3—when Anchises is still alive on Italian soil (L. Strzelecki, *RF* (1963), 451, fr. 3)—would be concerned with Aeneas' arrival in Italy, and that very great weight of emphasis would be extraordinarily hard to explain in a mythological excursus inserted into an epic about the first war between Rome and Carthage.[9] The only obstacle to the attribution of our question to Dido which actually rests on a numbered fragment of the *BP* is that Prochyta, an island in the Bay of Naples, named after a relative of Aeneas, was mentioned in *BP* 1 (fr. 17), from which the strong—though not conclusive—inference[10] is that Aeneas reached Italy at some point in Book 1. But there is no evidence that he reached *Latium*, and it is quite permissible to suppose—for instance—that he was blown back to Dido from Campania just as Aeneas was blown back from Sicily.[11]

If then the balance of argument is somewhat in favour—and at least this much I hope to have shown—of Naevius having brought Aeneas and Dido together in *BP* 2, then some scraps of information probably all belonging to the period between Naevius and Virgil assume great significance (cf. F. Klingner, *Virgil*, p. 382, Perret, pp. 92 ff.). We are informed that Ateius Philologus 'librum suum sic edidit inscriptum' an amaverit Didun Aeneas' (Charisius, *Gramm.* 1. 127. 17 f.); this Ateius was born in 100 BC at the latest (Perret loc. cit.) and would therefore have been a very old man by the time the *Aeneid* appeared; we cannot rule out the possibility that he wrote about the story of Dido as recounted by Virgil, but the issue in the *Aeneid* is utterly unrewarding—Aeneas explicitly did love Dido, 4. 395—and undeserving of enquiry by an elderly and distinguished scholar. If, however, Ateius approached the topic before Virgil, then the problem of chronology, as presented by Naevius, and the role of Anna as portrayed by Varro—to which I shall now turn—could form the basis for a valid and interesting investigation. Varro is attested as saying that Aeneas was loved by Anna (Serv. *ad Aen.* 5. 4), and that 'not Dido but Anna was driven by love of Aeneas to kill

---

[9] H. T. Rowell, *AJPh* (1966), 214; E. V. Marmorale, *Naevius Poeta* (Florence, 1950), pp. 242 ff.; Richter, p. 65; L. Strzelecki, *RF* (1960), 441 ff., etc.; Buchheit, pp. 34 ff.

[10] Büchner, p. 332 n. 15; Marmorale ad loc.; Serrao, pp. 517 f.; M. Barchiesi, *Nevio Epico* (Padua, 1962), p. 521.

[11] L. Ferrero, *RF* (1948), 117; *BP* ed. L. Strzelecki (Wrocław, 1959), p. 67.

herself on the pyre' (Servius Danielis 4. 682). Does this mean that in Varro Anna was in love with Aeneas behind Dido's back, as Virgil's Dido once seems to imply (4. 420 ff.)? Or that Varro refused to link Dido and Aeneas either because of chronological difficulties or because such a story conflicted with the version in Timaeus, but nevertheless accepted Aeneas' sojourn at Carthage with one Anna, his contemporary? Or even, hypercritically (H. Dessau, *Hermes* (1914), 520 f.), that Varro made Anna the foundress of Carthage, and had her commit suicide on a pyre, but never connected her with Aeneas, whatever the scholiasts in their muddled way may have thought? Ovid (*Fast.* 3. 543 ff.) tells an aetiological story about the goddess Anna Perenna which has Anna flee from Iarbas after Dido's death and fall in love with Aeneas in Italy: this version seems to combine Virgil (love of Dido and Aeneas), Timaeus (lecherous Tunisian), and Varro (love of Aeneas and Anna).[12] But what matters is Varro: why should he have troubled to set up Anna as a paramour of Aeneas if there were not already a version in existence which linked him with Dido? There would have been no need to introduce Anna into the story if all he had before him was Timaeus' version of Dido and the African prince, with no Aeneas. Varro's Anna looks as if she may have been intended as a criticism of Naevius' Dido!

But are we in a position to say anything about the function and character of Dido in the *BP*? Or about the influence of Naevius' Dido on Virgil's? Any reconstruction is a mere house of cards: fr. 20—'it came into his (or her) mind (that) the fortunes of men . . .'; 'ei venit in mentem hominum fortunas—has been compared to Dido's 'compassionate' remarks to the Trojans in *Aeneid* 1:[13] 'non ignara mali miseris succurrere disco' (630; cf. 562 f., 615 ff.). Fr. 10—'clothing of gold clean and lovely and citrus-scented'—*puram pulchramque ex auro vestem citrosam*—could describe presents given by Aeneas to Dido, like those in 1. 647 ff.[14] Fr. 7—'they carry beautiful bowls and golden goblets'; *ferunt pulcras creterras aureas lepistas*—might refer to a banquet given by Dido for Aeneas, as in *Aeneid* 1. 723 ff.[15] There is only one fragment actually attributed to *BP* 2 that might help—no. 22: 'and by now fortune had rendered his (or her) mind quiet'—*iamque eius mentem Fortuna fecerat quietam*, which has recently—and perhaps with some plausibility—been compared with

---

[12] Cf. Paratore, p. 225; Dessau, *Hermes* (1917), 470 ff.; Strzelecki, *RF* (1963), 449 f., *De Naeviano BP carmine* (1935), pp. 21 f.

[13] Büchner, pp. 27 f.; Richter, p. 46; Barchiesi, p. 471.

[14] Strzelecki (1959), p. 69; Barchiesi, p. 515.

[15] Richter, pp. 45 ff.; Klussmann ad loc.; Barchiesi, p. 365.

Aeneas' complacent behaviour when comfortably established at Carthage (4. 232 ff., Richter, p. 50 f.). Now of one thing we may be certain: since Naevius wrote the *BP* as an old man (Cic. *Sen.* 49) during the closing years of the second Punic war, about the first Punic war, in which he had himself served (Gell. 17. 21. 45), a favourable or sympathetic portrait of the foundress of Carthage will have been unthinkable (Paratore, p. 228, cf. Pichon, pp. 252 f., Perret, p. 97). What then was she? Evil, treacherous, insidious, a magician, having the worst qualities of Circe and Calypso, who had recently been presented to Roman readers in Livius Andronicus' *Odissia*? That is not unlikely—and that characterization is not incompatible with her having welcomed Aeneas in the first place: after all, a welcome followed by a rupture—as we have in Virgil—is allegorical of the centuries of peace between Rome and Carthage which preceded the first Punic war (L. Strzelecki, *RF* (1963), 442, W. Richter, *Das Epos des Gn. Naevius* (Göttingen, 1960), p. 47, Buchheit, pp. 49 f., arguing from the strength of the *hospitium*-motif in Virgil). Given such a Dido, another Naevian problem may be removed (Paratore, pp. 228 f.): it is, as I have said, pretty well certain that in the *BP* Anchises survived till the Trojans reached Italy (Strzelecki (1963), 450 ff.); in Virgil, this elderly, pious, and austere figure dies before Aeneas reaches Carthage—'ne parum decoro amori intersit' (Serv. *ad Aen.* 3. 711, Buchheit, p. 37), and in the Virgilian morality it is necessary that he should do so. But in Naevius, with quite conceivably a very differently characterized Anchises—he had, after all been Venus' lover (cf. fr. 13a, Paratore, p. 229)—the paternal presence may simply not have constituted an embarrassment, not least if Dido was portrayed either as asexual or not as attractive and romantic in her role as seductress but as vicious and untrustworthy. But we should also recall that in Naevius both Anchises and Aeneas left Troy with their wives (fr. 4; cf. Buchheit, p. 38), and unless they both died *en route* for Carthage, *their* presence will certainly have affected the action, possibly involving Dido as a would-be adulteress. But I conclude that a full-scale romantic entanglement, portrayed with rich Hellenistic sensibility—as in *Aeneid* 4—cannot have occurred in Naevius. The function of Dido in the *BP* cannot, however, have been merely incidental: she did found the city opposed to Rome, she did, most probably, meet Aeneas, the grandfather of Rome's founder. The hypothesis, first made by Niebuhr,[16] that in some way the relations of Aeneas and Dido served as

[16] Niebuhr, *History of Rome* (trans., London, 1844), iv. 25; cf. H. Oppermann, *RhM* (1939), 213 f.; Strzelecki (1959), pp. 70 f.; id. (1963), p. 442.

an *aition* for the first Punic war is highly persuasive. Whereas Herodotus used the myths at the beginning of Book 1 as an example of the trivializing of historical causation, Naevius introduced *his* myth to elevate the subject-matter of his historical poem (Richter, pp. 48 f.). Exactly how Naevius linked myth and history is not clear, but Dido's great curse upon Aeneas and his descendants in *Aeneid* 4 suggests a way (4. 622 ff., cf. 384 ff., Brisson, p. 162, Richter, p. 53). In the *BP* the *libros futura continentes* (fr. 13a) which Venus gave Anchises, and better, the *verba Iovis filiam* (i.e. Venus) *consolantis spe futurorum* (fr. 13) during the storm in Book 1 of the *BP*—which may have brought the Trojans to Carthage—could have pointed towards the ultimate Roman victory, reaching out from the mythical excursus into the main narrative, as Virgil's Dido, introducing Hannibal into her curse, reaches out from myth into history.

   The violence, greed, duplicity, and hatred which Dido displays in the *Aeneid* are, I hope to have shown, characteristics linked by Virgil and his contemporaries with the old hatreds of the Punic wars: this unromantic historical element in the *Aeneid*, so alien to what Virgil derives from Apollonius in particular, is precisely appropriate to the Dido of the *BP*; the influence of Naevius' Dido on Virgil's in character and function was, I suspect, vastly greater than can now be plausibly guessed, let alone proved.

APPENDIX

Postscript 1988

On the relationship of Virgil to Naevius I should have cited M. Wigodsky, *Vergil and Early Latin Poetry*, *Hermes* Einzelschr. 24 (1972), 29–34. A. La Penna's survey, *Enciclopedia Virgiliana* 2, s.v. *Didone*, is excellent. My exploration of the historical ironies in *Aen.* 1 and 4 seems not to have been received with much enthusiasm. See, however, F. Muecke, *AJPh* 104 (1983), 134–55, and D. Feeney, *CQ* 34 (1984), 179–84. The remarks of J. Moles in *Homo Viator: Classical Essays for John Bramble*, ed. L. M. Whitby, P. R. Hardie, and M. Whitby (Bristol, 1987), 153–61 are notably well balanced.

7

Dido's *Culpa*

NIALL RUDD

It has long been acknowledged that the story of Dido in Books 1 and 4 of the *Aeneid* has some of the elements associated with tragedy. These elements have been listed by A. S. Pease on pp. 8–11 of his massive commentary and discussed at greater length by De Witt, Maguinness, Quinn, and others.[1] We therefore enquire from time to time what tragic view the episode embodies. In a lecture to the Virgil Society in 1951 Professor R. G. Austin described the death of Dido with his usual blend of sympathy and scholarship, adding as a comment: 'The Queen of the Gods ... had ended her sport at last. You will remember Hardy's words at the end of *Tess*: they have their place here.' Hardy's words come, of course, in the last paragraph of the book, just after Tess has been executed for murder: ' "Justice" was done, and the President of the Immortals (in Aeschylean phrase) had ended his sport with Tess.' In his introduction to the same novel Hardy cites as a precedent for this remark Gloucester's well-known words in the fourth act of *King Lear*:

> As flies to wanton boys are we to the gods;
> They kill us for their sport. (IV. i. 37–8)

The two quotations are connected by the idea of divine sport. Men and women suffer and die to provide amusement for the gods. On the plainest interpretation both Gloucester and Hardy are claiming that the gods take a malevolent pleasure in destroying human lives. Even if we modify the idea of deliberate cruelty implied in this conception, we are still left with the notion of caprice. The gods' behaviour does not indicate any rational purpose.

Stated in these terms the idea can hardly be applied to the action of the *Aeneid*; for there, we are told, Jupiter does have a rational purpose. He is shaping the events of history so as to bring about the foundation

[1] N. W. De Witt, *CJ* 2 (1907), 283–8; W. S. Maguinness in his presidential address to the Virgil Society, 1955; K. Quinn, *Virgil's Aeneid: A Critical Description* (London, 1968), pp. 323–39.

and development of Rome's imperial power. Austin, to be sure, was talking about Juno, not Jupiter. Yet Juno too had her purpose:

> hoc regnum dea gentibus esse,
> si qua fata sinant, iam tum tenditque fouetque. (1. 17–18)

That this city [i.e. Carthage] should rule the world, if in any way the fates allowed it—this was even then the goddess's aim and cherished plan.

And so it would hardly be fair to see Dido as Juno's plaything. This difficulty was, one imagines, observed by Austin himself when he came to write the introduction to his commentary on Book 4. For although he incorporated a certain amount from the earlier lecture and again called attention to Hardy's tragic insight, he did not reproduce the reference to *Tess of the D'Urbervilles*. I shall come back later to Gloucester's comment in *Lear*, because in spite of what has just been said it seems to embody an important truth about the *Aeneid*. For the moment, however, I would suggest that another well-known quotation from the same play is a more accurate reflection of what Virgilian critics have tended to feel. I mean the words of Edgar in Act v, when he addresses the dying Edmund:

> The gods are just, and of our pleasant vices
> Make instruments to plague us. (v. iii. 170–1)

This notion has been more attractive than the other for two reasons: first, because in the civilized periods of European history men have been reluctant to believe in a god that used his power in a wholly arbitrary way, bringing ruin and misery without just cause; and secondly, because this theory makes it seem possible to reconcile divine providence with the freedom of human will. Although many factors in Dido's life, such as race, rank, and sex, have been assigned to her by fate, she remains responsible for her own decisions and acts. That, as I say, is an attractive idea, and I used to think it might be true. I now suspect that it is a misleading oversimplification.

> The gods are just, and of our pleasant vices
> Make instruments to plague us.

What, then, was Dido's vice? Or, to use the more polite term, what was her 'moral flaw'? Before we try to answer this it is well to be sure about what kind of thing we are looking for. A moral flaw is a disposition or tendency to act reprehensibly in a certain way in response to certain conditions. Hence it is a flaw in a man's character if he is prone to anger, avarice, gluttony, jealousy, lechery, pride, and sloth—to name only the more familiar vices. So what was Dido's moral flaw? I must admit I am quite unable to say. Was she, perhaps, inordinately susceptible to men? This can hardly be so. Since her husband's death she had had no dealings with any men, and this (we are assured) was not from a lack of opportunity. In Anna's words:

> aegram nulli quondam flexere mariti,
> non Libyae, non ante Tyro; despectus Iarbas
> ductoresque alii, quos Africa terra triumphis
> diues alit. (4. 35–8)

Sick at heart as you were, no suitors in the past prevailed upon you, not in Libya, not earlier in Tyre; Iarbas was scornfully rejected and also other chieftains reared in Africa, that land rich in triumphs.

Nor, again, is there anything in the text of Book 1 to suggest that she was given to acts of wild impetuosity. On the contrary, we are given an impression of steadiness and dignity. So although it makes sense, if very incomplete sense, to say that Macbeth's ambition or Othello's jealousy was a flaw which led to disaster, Dido's tragedy cannot, it seems, be discussed in these terms.

If we look more closely at Pease's introduction we may possibly see how the mistake arose. On p. 9 he says 'Hero and heroine have each a distinct blemish in character, Dido's being her unfaithfulness to her vows to Sychaeus, that of Aeneas his temporary neglect of his divine mission . . .' But surely this is rather a confused way of thinking. Dido broke her vows to Sychaeus, yes. But that was an act—an act entailed by entering into a relationship with Aeneas. But an act can never be a blemish of character. The two things belong to different logical categories. It is interesting to find a similar mistake in C. M. Bowra's *From Virgil to Milton* (London, 1945). After speaking of 'great women whose character is their doom', Bowra goes on to say (p. 49) that 'Dido, like Turnus, has a tragic fault. She has taken a vow to be faithful to the spirit of her dead husband Sychaeus, but she breaks it when she unites herself to Aeneas.' The word 'fault' tends to conceal the confusion of categories, but it is there none the less.

If we go further and enquire what led Pease to look for a blemish in Dido's character, we shall probably find the answer on p. 39 of his introduction: 'Yet admirable as Dido's character in many respects is, it illustrates—and was surely intended to illustrate—that flaw or error which Aristotle recognized as necessary for a tragic hero or heroine.' This raises the old question about the meaning of *hamartia* in Aristotle's

Poetics (13. 1453 a 10). Pease says 'flaw or error', but these are two different things, and there is only one word in Aristotle. 'Flaw' has been the more popular interpretation since the appearance of Butcher's essay on Aristotle's theory of poetry and fine art,[2] but 'error', 'mistake', or 'misapprehension' is more probably what Aristotle meant. The matter is discussed in some detail by D. W. Lucas in the fourth appendix of his commentary on the *Poetics*,[3] and that is his conclusion. Even if we are tempted to compromise and to look for some intermediate concept which will include both an ethical and an intellectual element,[4] we must still (I believe) reject the simple notion of a moral flaw.

Nevertheless, it may yet be possible to hold that Dido's suffering was a punishment for her sinful relationship with Aeneas. This view would enable us to retain the idea of divine justice, emending Shakespeare to read:

> The gods are just, and of our pleasant sins
> Make instruments to plague us.

Someone better versed than I am in the history of Virgilian scholarship could no doubt show that this opinion has been held for centuries. It can be found in its most extreme form in Servius (though we cannot be sure that he is giving his own view). On the first line of Book 4 he comments 'uidetur et post amissam castitatem etiam iustus interitus'—'After the loss of her chastity even her death appears to be just.' In the 1920s H. W. Prescott put the same point in a slightly different way: 'Dido deserved her death; she broke her solemn oath to Sychaeus.'[5] It may be apposite here to quote an observation by A. C. Bradley: 'We might not object to the statement that Lear deserved to suffer for his folly, selfishness, and tyranny; but to assert that he deserved to suffer what he *did* suffer is to do violence not merely to language but to any healthy moral sense.'[6]

I doubt if many readers of Virgil share Prescott's opinion, but it does raise a question of methodology which is sometimes overlooked, namely 'Is Virgil's judgement of Dido invariably identical with Dido's judgement of herself?' Brooks Otis believes it is. On p. 78 of his *Virgil* he writes: 'Dido ... reflects Virgil's own morality. In fact Dido's speeches ... convey ... a generalized analysis of the total moral-historical

---

[2] S. H. Butcher, *Aristotle's Theory of Poetry and Fine Art*, 4th edn. (London, 1911).

[3] D. W. Lucas, *Aristotle, Poetics* (Oxford, 1968).

[4] See, e.g., G. M. A. Grube, *Aristotle on Poetry and Style* (New York, 1958), pp. xxiv–xxv, and G. M. Kirkwood, *AJPh* 92 (1971), 711–15.

[5] H. W. Prescott, *The Development of Virgil's Art* (Chicago, 1927, repr. 1963), p. 290.

[6] A. C. Bradley, *Shakespearian Tragedy* (London, repr. 1949), p. 32.

situation as both she and Virgil see it.' Well, that may often be true, but consider the following case. Towards the end of Book 4, after pondering and rejecting various courses of action, the heroine cries:

> quin morere ut merita es, ferroque auerte dolorem. (547)

No! Die, as you deserve, and with steel put an end to your pain.

Are we therefore to conclude that Virgil also thought she deserved to die? Luckily one does not have to argue from probability; the poet has been quite explicit. In vv. 693 ff. Iris is sent down to release Dido from her agony because she has not yet been formally assigned to death. And why has she not be en assigned to death?

> quia nec fato merita nec morte peribat. (696)

Because it was not by fate's decree nor by a deserved death that she was dying.

So the queen did not deserve to die, and Virgil's verdict is not the same as Dido's own.

But did she deserve to suffer? And if so, why? Let us take first the contention that, in Otis's words, '[Dido] violates her duty to Carthage.'[7] What effect does the liaison have on Carthage as a whole? We are not told very much about this. In the period just before the 'marriage', work in the city comes to a halt, military exercises cease, and people are (one assumes) beginning to talk (86–9, 91, 170). After the 'marriage' has been consummated Fama (Rumour) redoubles its activities, putting about the report that Dido and Aeneas are spending the entire winter in sensual pleasure:

> regnorum immemores turpique cupidine captos. (194)

Forgetful of their kingdoms, prisoners of foul lust.

But Fama, as Virgil says, tells lies and half-truths as well as facts (190). It is not clear that Dido *is* forgetful of her kingdom, though it could certainly be argued that Aeneas is forgetful of the kingdom which he is supposed to found in the future.[8] At any rate some caution is advisable in view of the line which sums up Fama's reports:

> haec passim dea foeda uirum diffundit in ora. (195)

These were the tales which the filthy goddess spread abroad on men's lips.

---

[7] Brooks Otis in *Virgil*, ed. D. R. Dudley (London, 1969), p. 57.

[8] See v. 267. When Rumour, reinforced by the prayers of Iarbas, reaches Jupiter, he turns his eyes towards the lovers. They are now said to be *oblitos famae melioris* (221), which is not the same thing as *regnorum immemores*.

If we give weight to such evidence, we must also bear in mind that when Mercury comes to remind Aeneas of his mission he finds him, not in the queen's boudoir, but on the building sites of Carthage *fundantem arces et tecta nouantem* (260)—'laying the foundations of towers and building new dwellings'. This busy activity is further emphasized in Mercury's reprimand:

> tu nunc Karthaginis altae
> fundamenta locas pulchramque uxorius urbem
> exstruis? (265–7)

Are you now laying the foundations of lofty Carthage and building a fine city in devotion to your wife?

Some scholars are reluctant to admit this as evidence of Dido's renewed activity, because Dido herself is not immediately present. But dramatically Dido cannot be present, because Mercury's words are for the ears of Aeneas alone. In any case it is clear that work has been resumed, and so the stoppage mentioned earlier must be regarded as temporary.

Caution is again required when we come to assess certain things said by Dido and her sister. In v. 321 Dido claims that because of her liaison with Aeneas the Tyrians are now hostile to her (*infensi Tyrii*). But this is part of a tremendous rhetorical appeal to Aeneas, and allowance must be made for exaggeration.[9] So too, when Dido in v. 468 sees herself looking for the Tyrians in a desolate land, we must remember that this is the dream of a desperately unhappy woman overwhelmed by grief and shame. The balance has to be corrected the other way when Anna cries:

> extinxti te meque, soror, populumque patresque
> Sidonios urbemque tuam. (682–3)

You have destroyed yourself and me, my sister, and the senate and people of Sidon, and your own city.

That too is the rhetoric of distraught affection. It implies that the survival of the state was utterly dependent on the queen. In literal fact, of course, it wasn't. Carthage was still to enjoy centuries of prosperity. What we can say for sure is that the city was at first stunned by the news of Dido's suicide and then broke into wild lamentation (666–71). From

---

[9] From Jupiter's words in v. 235 it might seem that the Carthaginians were bitterly hostile to Aeneas: 'qua spe inimica in gente moratur?' But Jupiter may be speaking in his full knowledge of destiny. It is perhaps significant that when Mercury conveys the message to Aeneas the point is not mentioned. Instead the question is changed to: 'qua spe Libycis teris otia terris?' (271).

this it is fairly clear that at the deepest level Dido had not lost the hearts of her people.

Taking all these points together it is fair to conclude that at some point the Carthaginians began to disapprove of Dido's union with Aeneas, and that this weighed heavily on her conscience after she had been deserted. Nevertheless, we also have to remember that at an earlier stage of the relationship Dido had good reason to believe that an alliance with the Trojans would help rather than harm her city. Although she had other, different, scruples about falling in love with Aeneas, it never for a moment occurred to her that she was failing in her duty to Carthage. The political arguments advanced by Anna in vv. 39–49 were not questioned at the time: Carthage was surrounded by hostile peoples, there was danger of pursuit from Tyre itself; but with a Trojan alliance the state of Carthage had immense prospects of power and glory. Professor Otis says in his *Virgil*: 'It is made quite plain that Anna is wrong to undermine Dido's ... resolve' (78). Well, it may be plain to someone who knows the outcome, but it certainly wasn't plain to Anna, or to her sister. One sometimes forgets that as early as 1. 572 ff. Dido offered the Trojans an equal share in her kingdom. In other words, without any prompting from Anna and before she even *saw* Aeneas, Dido thought it desirable for the Trojans to stay. So did Juno, who certainly had Carthage's interests at heart.

So although we may grant that there was some political failure on Dido's part—even if only a failure of tact—this ought not to be judged too harshly. More important, that failure was in no way a *cause* of her desertion and humiliation. It was rather a consequence of her passionate attachment to Aeneas. Hence her political failure cannot be regarded as part of her initial guilt.

When scholars speak of Dido's guilt they are, of course, referring primarily to her breach of faith with her dead husband Sychaeus. T. R. Glover, whose treatment of this episode is still among the best, chides the queen very gently for 'sacrificing her sense of right to her inclination'.[10] Earlier he says: 'To resolve to win the love of Aeneas is no wrong thought or action, but to attempt it against her conscience is the first step towards shame.'[11] The point is put more forcefully by K. Quinn: 'She could have resisted passion more successfully: she could have known, or learnt, to put duty or *pudor* before infatuation; and after yielding to infatuation she could have been honest enough with herself not to

---

[10] T. R. Glover, *Virgil* (London, 1912), p. 203.
[11] Ibid. 190.

pretend she had marriage within her grasp.'[12] Brooks Otis is even more severe: 'Dido now realises her plight and her guilt (*En quid ago?* 534 f.), her helplessness and the criminal folly of her deed.'[13] This represents an impressive body of testimony, but before we reach a final conclusion (if indeed finality is ever possible in such a matter) let us look once more at the relevant passages.

At the end of Book 1 Venus instructs Cupid to assume the form of Ascanius and inflame Dido's heart with love. Cupid must therefore gradually efface [her feelings of obligation to] Sychaeus—*paulatim abolere Sychaeum* (720), and occupy her long inactive affections with a living love. No censure so far—simply a statement of fact. At the banquet the queen drinks deep draughts of love (749), and by the time Aeneas has finished his tale she is wholly infatuated. Speaking to Anna at the beginning of Book 4, she says in effect: 'Had I not resolved to have done with marriage after Sychaeus' death I could perhaps have yielded to this one *culpa*' (15–19). The logic of this deserves comment. Strictly speaking, if Dido had not resolved to remain single then presumably she could have contemplated marrying Aeneas without any misgivings and there would have been no question of *culpa*. In fact she *has* made such a resolution and so marriage with Aeneas *would* involve *culpa*. These two ideas are compressed into one. The phrase *succumbere culpae* is hard to translate. One cannot properly be said to surrender to a 'frailty', 'weakness', or 'lapse', and yet in this particular line 'sin' is too heavily condemnatory. Perhaps 'surrender to this one temptation' would come nearest to the meaning, though *culpa* normally does not mean 'temptation'.

At any rate it is clear from what follows that at this point Dido is claiming that her modesty and her sense of loyalty to Sychaeus prevent her from forming an attachment to Aeneas. She reaffirms her oath, saying in effect 'May I die before I do violence to *pudor* (shame, modesty, self-respect), and may Sychaeus keep my love with him in the grave' (24–30). So the first suggestion that a new marriage would be in some way reprehensible comes from Dido herself. Then follows the speech of Anna, who, we are told, 'fanned into flame the queen's heart already kindled with love, gave hope to her wavering mind, and undid her *pudor*'—*soluitque pudorem* (54–5). The repeated image of fire in v. 54 may well imply destructiveness, and here I would agree with Brooks Otis

[12] K. Quinn, *Virgil's Aeneid*, p. 325.
[13] Brooks Otis, *Virgil: A Study in Civilized Poetry* (Oxford, 1964), p. 84. Cf. 'Dido's moral lapse is deliberate' etc., p. 77.

(78). But that doesn't prove that Virgil is censuring Anna for giving such advice or Dido for taking it. Virgil can imply that the passion is destructive because he knows the outcome. This knowledge (which we share with the poet after our first reading of the book) lends a sad irony to the next phrase, because giving hope to someone in doubt is normally a kind thing to do; Anna was not to know that such hope was doomed. Finally, the undoing or unfastening of *pudor* (a quasi-sexual phrase) is in itself a neutral idea. It is a task which may be faced not only by a seducer but also by a first or even a second husband. Suppose that Aeneas had been free to settle in Carthage, would there have been anything wrong on Dido's part in allowing herself to have hopes of marrying him? That is a question we shall have to discuss.

With the symbolic marriage in the cave a further stage is reached.

> Ille dies primus leti primusque malorum
> causa fuit; neque enim specie famaue mouetur
> nec iam furtiuum Dido meditatur amorem:
> coniugium uocat, hoc praetexit nomine culpam. (169–72)

That day first was the cause of death and woe. For Dido ceases to be moved by appearances or by what people say. Nor does she engage any longer in a clandestine love-affair. She calls it marriage; with this name she provides a respectable covering for her wrong behaviour.

Virgil does not think it necessary to tell us how many Carthaginians were against the union in principle (and how strong their feelings were) and how many were simply indignant that there had been no official celebration. All we know is that people disapproved of what Dido was doing. So too, we aren't told whether Dido hopes they will accept the position in time, or whether she is defiant or merely indifferent. All we know is that she goes ahead. She calls the union marriage (and, with whatever justification, she has convinced herself that it *is* marriage[14]), but the wording of v. 172 cautions the reader against accepting this view, and we find later that Aeneas explicitly rejects it (338–9). The important word for us is *culpam*. In view of the case developed so far one wonders whether it might mean simply 'what she regarded as her guilt', but this won't do. For here *culpa* is distinguished from *coniugium*, and the word *nomen* implies that the relationship isn't really a *coniugium* at all. The phrase therefore cannot represent Dido's view of what is happening. When Dido was still in two minds, she believed that *coniugium* with

---

[14] The passages which establish this are conveniently listed by Gordon Williams in *Tradition and Originality in Roman Poetry* (Oxford, 1968), p. 381.

Aeneas would *be* a *culpa*. Now that she has, as she believes, married him, an appropriate comment would be 'She marries him and suppresses her feelings of guilt at having done so.' But that is not what Virgil says. We must therefore assume that he is not describing her feelings but condemning her conduct. Nevertheless, it is worth noting that this is the only line in which Virgil makes such a definite judgement. And even here he does not decide for us how serious in moral terms her guilt is. The *results*, of course, are disastrous, but how wicked is the queen herself? We are not yet in a position to say.

It is natural—and significant—that we hear no more of Dido's own sense of guilt until she realizes that Aeneas is about to leave her. Then it all comes flooding back. 'It was on your account', she cries to Anna, 'that my *pudor* was destroyed and my previous good name, which was my only path to immortal glory' (321–3). Later, after all her pleas have failed, we learn for the first time that Dido has kept in her palace a marble shrine in memory of Sychaeus (457–9). She is now so overwrought that at night-time she hears her dead husband's voice calling to her from the shrine; other sounds and visions also terrify her. She resolves to die and begins to make preparations. We then have a splendid soliloquy, ending with the lines:

> Non licuit thalami expertem sine crimine uitam
> degere more ferae, talis nec tangere curas;
> non seruata fides cineri promissa Sychaeo. (550–2)

I was not allowed to remain unmarried, passing my life without blame like a creature of the wilds, immune from such unhappy love. The promise made to the ashes of Sychaeus has not been kept.

Here again the assertion that Dido is to blame for being unfaithful comes from the queen herself. Finally, when she sees the Trojans actually departing she launches into another powerful speech in which she says:

> infelix Dido, nunc te facta impia tangunt? (596)

Luckless Dido, is it now that your godless deeds are coming home to you?

Facta impia—that is the last and most bitter of all her reproaches against herself. Once more we must ask whether Virgil means us to judge the queen as harshly as she judges herself.

At this point we should consider the ideal of what Tertullian calls *uniuiratus*.[15] How important was it that a woman should have only one

---

[15] The status of the *uniuira* is mentioned in Pease's long note on v. 29. The relevance of

husband in her lifetime? In very early days certain religious ceremonies could only be conducted by *uniuirae*. Servius on 4. 19 mentions the crowning of Fortuna Muliebris, Livy speaks of sacrifices to Pudicitia, Varro says that in marriage ceremonies the *pronuba*, or matron of honour, had to be a woman who had married only once,[16] and Valerius Maximus (2. 1. 3) refers to special honours reserved for *uniuirae*. Let us look more closely at two of these passages. The first is Livy, 10. 23. 5. In the year 296 BC, the senate decreed two days of supplications to avert numerous portents which had occurred. During the celebrations a quarrel broke out among the matrons in the shrine of Pudicitia Patricia. It seems that a patrician woman called Verginia had been excluded from the rite on the grounds that she had married a commoner. Verginia retaliated by setting up a shrine in her own house. Calling the plebeian matrons in she said 'I dedicate this altar to Pudicitia Plebeia.' The plebeian altar, like the other, was tended by matrons of proven modesty who had been married to one man alone. Then, perhaps a little sadly, Livy adds: 'Afterwards the cult was degraded by ritually disqualified women, not matrons only but women of every station, and it finally passed into oblivion' (10).

The context of the passage of Valerius Maximus is also interesting. It occurs in Book 2 in the third section of the chapter headed *De Institutis Antiquis*. One such custom was that whereby women sat at meals while the men reclined. This custom was extended to religious observances, in which Jupiter lay on a couch while Juno and Minerva sat on chairs. Valerius adds: 'In our age this kind of austerity is retained on the Capitol more assiduously than in our homes, no doubt because it is more vital that goddesses should be kept in order than women.' Then comes the section beginning 'quae uno contentae matrimonio fuerant corona pudicitiae honorabantur' ('those women who had been content with a single marriage were honoured with the garland of virtue')—notice the tenses. Section four tells us that the first divorce took place five hundred years after the foundation of Rome, i.e. about 250 BC, if the text is emended on the basis of Aulus Gellius.[17] Finally, section five says that the use of wine was once unknown to Roman women—'uini usus olim Romanis feminis ignotus fuit'. The sober Valerius explains: 'No doubt it

this to *Aen.* 4 is explored by Gordon Williams in *JRS* 48 (1958), 23–5. I am much indebted to Williams's discussion, though I reach rather different conclusions.

[16] Servius on *Aen.* 4. 166.

[17] There is a penetrating discussion of this divorce by A. Watson in *Revue d'Histoire du droit* 33 (1965), 38–50—a reference which I owe to Mr R. Seager.

was for fear that they might lapse into some kind of disgraceful conduct, because after Liber, the father of intemperance, the first step is usually to illicit sex.' These passages indicate that the *religious* importance of *uniuiratus* was by 25 BC very much a thing of the past.

No doubt it still survived as a social ideal, though how widespread and how deeply cherished it was is hard to assess. Some of the evidence that has been used in discussing the problem is less helpful than it seems. In Plautus, *Mostellaria* 190, a courtesan is listening to her maid, who says 'matronae non meretricium est unum inseruire uirum'—'It's for a married lady not for a courtesan to devote herself to one man.' In Terence's *Eunuchus* 122 Parmeno says to the courtesan Thais: 'neque tu uno eras contenta neque solus dedit'—'You weren't content with one man nor did just one of them reward you.' Here marriage to one man is opposed to the life of a prostitute.

In Plautus' *Mercator*, the old slave-woman Syra complains about the double standard whereby wives are divorced for infidelity though husbands aren't:

> nam uxor contenta est, quae bona est, uno uiro:
> qui minus uir una uxore contentus siet? (*Mer.* 824–5)

A wife, if she's good, is content with one man. Why shouldn't a man be content with one wife?

In poem 68. 135 Catullus complains, as if he were an aggrieved husband, that his mistress is not content with him alone: 'uno non est contenta Catullo'. In these two passages a permanent relationship with one man is contrasted with infidelity.

Horace provides yet another type of contrast:

> felices ter et amplius
> quos irrupta tenet copula nec malis
> diuulsus querimoniis
> suprema citius soluet amor die (*Odes* 1. 13. 17–20)

Thrice happy and more are those who are held together by an unbroken bond, whose love is not wrenched apart by bitter quarrelling, and who stay united until the final day.

Here a permanent relationship with one man means a marriage not broken by divorce. Turia's husband makes a similar point when he writes in her epitaph: 'rara sunt tam diuturna matrimonia finita morte non diuertio interrupta'—'Rare are marriages that last so long, terminated by death not dissolved by divorce.'[18] None of these cases, therefore, provides the type of contrast which would be relevant to Dido—viz., that between a widow who marries again and one who does not.

The same point must be borne in mind when we consider the numerous epitaphs containing phrases like *solo contenta marito, uno contenta marito, uni deuota marito,* etc.[19] Granted such phrases include the idea that the dead woman was never previously married to anyone else, but surely the important assertion is that she was never divorced. This is sometimes brought out elsewhere in the epitaph. In *Carm. Epigr.* 652, for example, we have the words:

> contemptisque aliis me dicto iure secuta es

and rejecting others you loyally followed me.

When Cornelia pronounces her own encomium in Propertius 4. 11, the poet makes her say: 'in lapide hoc uni nupta fuisse legar' (36)—'on this stone you will read that I was married to one husband'. Perhaps she *is* claiming that she wasn't married to anyone else before she married Paulus, but her primary purpose is surely to state that she was never divorced. This is supported by the sentence immediately following, which says (in paraphrase) 'I call my dead ancestors to witness that I never caused the Censor's rule to be relaxed and that my hearth never blushed for any sin of mine.' Similarly, when she says to her daughter 'see to it that, like me, you remain attached to a single husband'—*teneas unum uirum*—the intention uppermost in her mind is to warn the girl against divorce.[20]

Some further information can be gathered from Seneca's remarks on marriage in his *De Matrimonio,* bits of which are embodied by St Jerome in his work *Aduersus Iouinianum* (Migne, vol. 23. 222 ff.).[21] On p. 286 Jerome begins a section on wives who refused to survive after their husbands' deaths. This includes a summary of Timaeus' account of Dido's suicide (see below) and an approving reference to the Indian custom of suttee. On p. 287 he goes on to mention certain Roman widows who resolved not to remarry. This he finds admirable, but the reasons given by the ladies themselves range from 'For me my husband is always alive' to 'I don't see any man who wants me more than my

---

[18] *Laudatio Turiae CIL* vi. 1527, 27. See M. Durry, *Éloge Funèbre* (Paris, 1950), p. 9.

[19] See *Carm. Epigr.* 455, 643. 5, 736. 4.

[20] See D. R. Shackleton Bailey's note on Propertius 4. 11. 68 in *Propertiana* (Cambridge, 1956), p. 265.

[21] Printed in Seneca, *Supplementum,* ed. F. Haase (Leipzig, 1902), pp. 26–32.

money.' One notices, too, that the words were spoken in reply to someone who thought the decision either odd or ill-advised. Annia, for instance, was urged by a kinsman to marry again, because she was still young and attractive. The younger Porcia is supposed to have asserted 'felix et pudica matrona nunquam praeterquam semel nubit' ('a happy and respectable wife marries only once'), but she said it when she heard someone praising a woman of good character (*quaedam bene morata*) who had married again. This would suggest that the women mentioned by Seneca were rather exceptional. Seneca himself clearly thought that for a woman second marriages were wrong, but one wonders how typical this censorious outlook was. For later sections of Jerome (pp. 291 ff.) show that Seneca also took a rather jaundiced view of *first* marriages. The marital troubles of Cicero, Socrates, Sulla, Pompey, and Cato the Censor are all referred to, and we are reminded of notorious women like Pasiphaë, Clytemnestra, Eriphyla, and Helen. The fact is that to the Stoic sage women were a nuisance; they interfered with his autonomy. So inasmuch as Seneca aspired to that ideal he felt at liberty to take an anti-feminist line. In another essay, entitled *How to cope with misfortune*, he addresses a man who is mourning the death of a good wife: 'How do you know she'd have *remained* good? Nothing is so fickle and unreliable as the female disposition. We all know of marriages that have broken up and of quarrels even more ugly than divorce between incompatible partners.'[22] These words of comfort indicate that like St Paul, his fictitious correspondent, Seneca considered marriage only marginally preferable to combustion. The fact that he himself married twice and was apparently very happy (at least with his second wife) merely illustrates that here, as in other areas, there was an enormous gap between the great man's preaching and his practice.

Let us concede, then, that a certain amount of old-fashioned, rather sentimental, respect was still paid to women who had never been divorced and who, when widowed, chose not to remarry. Nevertheless, in the last century of the republic both divorce and remarriage were extremely common. This was especially true among the families of the aristocracy, in which marriage had an important political function. Augustus himself was Scribonia's third husband, and the Empress Livia, the most respected lady of the age, was not an *uniuira*, in spite of the polite fiction entertained by Horace in *Odes* 3. 14. 5. When Augustus drafted his social legislation remarriage took on a new importance. We

---

[22] *De Remediis Fortuitorum*, in the *Supplementum*, ed. cit. 54.

don't know how prominently it figured in the abandoned programme of 28 BC, but certainly the Lex Iulia of 18 BC penalized widows if they *didn't* remarry. If, then, we put the question in the form most relevant to our enquiry, viz. 'Was it regarded as a disgrace for a widow to remarry?' the answer must surely be No. In Book 3 of the *Aeneid* the character of Andromache, who has been married to Hector, Pyrrhus, and Helenus, is treated with tenderness and respect. In Lucan's epic the same is true of Cornelia. Although she reproaches herself for bringing trouble to two husbands (Crassus and Pompey), no one else thinks her in any way blameworthy. As she leaves Lesbos the people grieve openly:

> tanto deuinxit amore
> hos pudor, hos probitas castique modestia uultus. (8. 115–16)

So great was the affection with which she held them by her decency and goodness and by her pure and model looks.

We have been discussing how deeply the Romans of the period from, say, 70 to 20 BC disapproved of widows' remarrying. It may, of course, be argued that the character of Dido is constructed on a much older model; that she holds before her the ideal of the early Roman *matrona*; and that the values of Virgil's day are not strictly relevant. It is quite true that Dido does prize the ideal of *uniuiratus*, but that is only part of a complex situation; for she is not in fact in the same position as an early Roman *matrona*. She is the queen of a young, forward-looking community; and so, over and above her latent maternal feelings, she has a duty to produce an heir for the royal family. The citizens of republican Rome had no immediate parallel in their own experience. But a somewhat analogous situation arose when the Emperor Augustus planned to continue his dynasty through the marriage of his daughter Julia. These plans were, as we know, tragically frustrated. Her first husband, Marcellus, died in 23 BC at the age of nineteen. She was then married to Agrippa and finally to Tiberius. If Augustus had any respect for the ideal of *uniuiratus*, such feelings were set aside without compunction when the interests of the state so demanded.

Dido also had reasons of state, which, as Virgil well knew, were inseparable from her own longings. With characteristic subtlety he arranges for the love of the childless queen to be awakened in the first place by Cupid in the form of Aeneas' son Ascanius. This is one of the many points in which Virgil departs from the story of Jason and Medea as told by Apollonius; more will be said about it below. Anna then adds fuel to the fire: 'You are dearer to your sister than the light of life. Are

you going to pine away through the whole of your youth in loneliness and
sorrow, and not know the sweetness of children and the joys of love'—
'nec dulcis natos Veneris nec praemia noris?' (33). In his note on this
line Servius Danielis carefully points out that intercourse precedes
birth, and he supplies a technical term for Virgil's change of order.
Buscaroli remarks that the second expression is coloured by the purity
of the first.[23] Pease understands Anna to mean 'neither parental nor
(even) conjugal joys'. But could it not be that Anna's discreet nuance
reflects Dido's emotional priorities? Soon after, we are told that when
Aeneas is not with her Dido takes Ascanius on her knee (84–5). Later,
when Aeneas decides to leave she appeals to him to pity her dying
house—*miserere domus labentis* (318). It is not certain (though quite
probable) that this includes the notion that without an heir the royal
family will become extinct. But the thought of an heir emerges
unmistakably:

> saltem si qua mihi de te suscepta fuisset
> ante fugam suboles, si quis mihi paruulus aula
> luderet Aeneas, qui te tamen ore referret,
> non equidem omnino capta ac deserta uiderer. (4. 327–30)

At least, if before you hurried away I had borne a child of yours, if I had a little
Aeneas playing in the palace whose face would remind me of you in spite of
everything, I would not feel so utterly ruined and desolate.

Consider a leader from an old royal house, whose marriage has been
broken by death; one who, when warned by a dream, escaped the
enemy's sword and led a band of followers to found a new city in exile;
one who through many vicissitudes on land and sea has been distinguished for piety. Such a leader is Dido. It has, indeed, often been
pointed out that in many respects she is Aeneas' *alter ego*. But there is
one parallel which does not seem to be commonly mentioned. As Troy is
burning Aeneas feels again and again the pull of the old heroic ideal—to
die gloriously for one's country.[24] In the end he is persuaded to make his
escape from Troy and to survive for the sake of his people's future, but
he is more than once assailed by feelings of guilt and regret:

> o terque quaterque beati,
> quis ante ora patrum Troiae sub moenibus altis
> contigit oppetere! (1. 94–6)

[23] C. Buscaroli, *Il libro di Didone* (Milan–Rome, 1932), p. 65.
[24] See, e.g., Homer, *Il.* 22. 73; Horace, *Odes* 3. 2. 13; Virgil, *Aen.* 2. 431–4.

Thrice and four times blessed are you who had the good fortune to die before your father's eyes under the high walls of Troy!

So too, one might reasonably say that Dido reveres the old ideal of *uniuiratus* and cannot abandon it without remorse. Granted the balance of emotions is different in the two cases, but the dilemma is surely analogous. If, therefore, we are determined to judge the morality of Dido's behaviour, it seems unfair to present it simply as a conflict between love and duty. On one side was her love for Sychaeus, her duty to his memory, and the force of the oath which she had sworn. On the other her love of Aeneas, her desire for children, and her hopes for the future of her people.

Before leaving the question of Dido's loyalty to her dead husband let us consider for a moment what function Sychaeus performs within the epic. In the account preserved by the third-century Sicilian historian Timaeus the Libyan king was determined to marry Dido. She was unwilling, but was pressed by her people to agree. Finally, pretending she was going to conduct a ritual which would release her from her oath to her husband, she built a pyre by the palace wall, lit it, and leaped into the blaze. Substantially the same version is given by Justin, writing in the third century AD. According to him, Dido built the pyre on the pretext of appeasing the spirit of her dead husband. Aeneas is not mentioned in either account. This may serve to remind us that the story of Dido and Sychaeus has no necessary connection with the story of Dido and Aeneas. Dido could, after all, have been captivated and then deserted by Aeneas even if she had not sworn to remain a widow or even if she had never previously been married.

Virgil, of course, uses the Sychaeus story with masterly skill. Thanks to Sychaeus, Dido's character is given an extra dimension in time. We are told how as a girl in Tyre she loved him and grieved at his death—perhaps with an added bitterness in that he was murdered by her own brother.[25] It is Sychaeus who constitutes the cause of her inner struggle—a struggle which gives her moral stature even though she has no chance of winning it. A psychological critic might further argue that Dido's feelings as a woman were the more powerful because they had been so long suppressed, and that the morbid and excessive nature of her passion was directly related to the torments of her guilty conscience.

Yet even if all these points are conceded it remains true that what brings disaster is not Dido's guilt but her love of Aeneas. Everything

---

[25] *Aen.* 4. 21.

comes back to that. Thus if we set aside the notion of a moral flaw and choose the other, more Aristotelian, idea of an error or mistake, we may find the error, as Quinn does, in her failure to realize that the relationship did not mean the same to Aeneas as it did to her; or we may point to the fact that Dido has heard and overlooked all the prophecies given to Aeneas by the Penates and Celaeno and Helenus about his Italian destiny; in either case the mistake was an immediate consequence of her love.

When we look more closely at the nature of this love we face a final question which is bound to affect our total view of the tragedy. As a way of leading into the point let us think for a moment about Dido's death. Her motives for killing herself may be stated in various forms, but most readers would probably agree that she does so because she has been betrayed and humiliated. The only way she can retrieve her dignity is by taking her own life. But while the act of suicide reflects her proud heroic temper, it is still the result of a rational decision. Venus did not compel her to die, nor did Juno. As Virgil says, she died not as a result of fate's decree but before her time (*ante diem*). She could have chosen otherwise.[26]

The same, however, is not true of her falling in love with Aeneas. This is a point of central importance. Antigone buries her brother in the full knowledge of the consequences. Agamemnon, in agony of mind, chooses to kill his daughter so that the Greek fleet may sail for Troy. But Dido never chooses to fall in love with Aeneas. It may, of course, be objected that no one ever chooses to fall in love; but normally a romantic relationship, however ardent, can be fostered or discouraged. People do consider whether or not to become more deeply involved. But Virgil makes it quite clear, I think, that this privilege was never given to Dido. When her conversation with Anna takes place at the beginning of Book 4, it is already too late. 'The queen has long been injured with a deep love; she nourishes the wound with her life-blood, and is consumed by the fire which she keeps concealed.' To state the argument in a determinist form one might refer to the intervention of Venus, later abetted by Juno, and maintain that the goddesses' combined will was too strong for any mortal to withstand. A more libertarian reader might prefer to say that the divine action in the *Aeneid* should not be understood as a *cause* of human behaviour but rather as a parallel

[26] See the note of R. D. Williams on *Aen.* 4. 696–7. The phrase *subitoque accensa furore*, however, is rather difficult. How far it is consistent with our interpretation depends on what phase of Dido's *furor* is referred to.

phenomenon lending weight and universality to the drama below. Yet it doesn't really matter which view one takes, because wherever Dido's passion originates (from without or within) it is portrayed as a force which by its very nature overpowers resistance.

Let us recall how it began. Venus substitutes Cupid for Ascanius with the deliberate intention of making Dido fall madly in love:

> At Cytherea nouas artis, noua pectore uersat
> consilia, ut faciem mutatus et ora Cupido
> pro dulci Ascanio ueniat, donisque furentem
> incendat reginam atque ossibus implicet ignem (1. 657–60)

But the Cytherean devises new wiles and new schemes within her heart: Cupid, with his appearance and face altered, is to come instead of Ascanius, by his gifts he is to inflame the queen to madness and wind fire around her bones.

She explains the plan to her son:

> quocirca capere ante dolis et cingere flamma
> reginam meditor (1. 673–4)

And so I intend to forestall [Juno], taking the queen by a trick and encircling her with flame.

She will steal Ascanius away to prevent him from discovering her trick (*dolos*). Cupid is to assume his appearance:

> tu faciem illius noctem non amplius unam
> falle dolo. (1. 683–4)

You by a trick are to counterfeit his appearance for just one night.

[When Dido takes you on her lap and kisses you]

> occultum inspires ignem fallasque ueneno (1. 688)

You are to breathe into her an invisible fire and secretly administer poison.

These lines all emphasize Venus' trickery. The essence of a trick is, of course, its unexpectedness. The victim must be unaware of what is happening until it is too late. In due course Dido takes Cupid on her knee and fondles him, 'little knowing how mighty a god is sitting there and what misery he brings her'—

> inscia Dido
> insidat quantus miserae deus. (1. 718–19)

In other words, the fatal passion comes on Dido unawares. Her resistance is undermined before she can collect herself.

Another important word in vv. 657–60 (quoted above) is *furentem*. Cupid is to inflame the queen to *madness*. In Book 4 there are many variations on the theme of madness, but the only madness that concerns us here is that which afflicts Dido before Aeneas decides to leave; for this is the madness of Eros. Later, other emotions become mingled with it. We first hear of Dido's *furor* in Book 4 when she and Anna are conducting sacrifices to the deities of marriage with the intention of obtaining their good will and in particular of releasing the queen from her oath of loyalty to Sychaeus. It looks as if the priests of Carthage tried to give an encouraging interpretation of the ritual, but whatever they said was utterly irrelevant:

> heu uatum ignarae mentes! quid uota furentem,
> quid delubra iuuant? est mollis flamma medullas
> interea et tacitum uiuit sub pectore uulnus.
> uritur infelix Dido totaque uagatur
> urbe furens, qualis coniecta cerua sagitta,
> quam procul incautam nemora inter Cresia fixit
> pastor agens telis liquitque uolatile ferrum
> nescius. (65–72)

Alas for the ignorance of the priests' minds! What use are prayers, what use are shrines to one who is in a frenzy? All the time the flame devours her soft marrow, and the wound remains silently alive beneath her breast. The wretched Dido is on fire and paces through every part of the city in a frenzy, like a deer after the shooting of an arrow, a deer which, all unwary, amid the woods of Crete has been pierced from afar by a shepherd's hunting-weapon; he has left the flying steel behind him, unaware of what has happened.

This is a very significant passage. The word *incautam* reminds us once again that Dido was caught unawares; the repetition *furentem . . . furens* emphasizes the irrational nature of her love; and its raging intensity is brought out by the images of the fire and wounding.

The motif of fire is introduced by Venus as early as 1. 660, where she instructs Cupid to inflame the queen and wind fire round her bones. It reappears in 1. 673 and 688 (also quoted above). We are told of Cupid's burning face—*flagrantis uultus* (710), and of Dido's love which grows more intense as she gazes at him—*ardescit tuendo* (713). The fire is still raging in the second line of Book 4—*caeco carpitur igni*. The motif recurs again and again throughout the book, eventually finding its consummation in the flames of Dido's funeral pyre, which are visible to the departing Trojans from far out at sea (5. 1–7). The motifs of hunting, wounding, poison, and illness are slightly less prominent, yet each has its own significance. The hunt, for instance, is prefigured by the epiphany of Venus in Book 1, where she is dressed as a huntress (318 ff.); Dido goes forth to hunt in 4. 136 ff.; but all the time she herself is the stricken quarry. The motif of the wound follows a similar course to that of fire; for Dido's wound of love becomes eventually the wound inflicted on her own body.

All these images reinforce one another. The violence of madness, fire, and wounding conveys the overwhelming power of Dido's passion, which sweeps aside all scruples, however honourable. One of the few scholars to stress this point is W. A. Camps, who says: 'the obsessive love that seizes her is a demonic force, not an impulse which her will could have overcome'.[27] The pity we feel as we see her in the grip of this terrible power turns to horror as we watch her total disintegration. But even when she is screaming for vengeance and calling down a curse of eternal enmity, it hardly occurs to us to condemn her. For whatever her deserts may have been (and I have argued that it is not easy to make a clear case against her) she did not deserve to suffer so cruelly.

And so we return to the quotation from *Lear* which we discussed at the beginning:

> As flies to wanton boys are we to the gods;
> They kill us for their sport.

We thought it unwise to accept this as a motto for the *Aeneid* because it implied that the gods acted merely from caprice. We have to believe, I take it, that in Virgil's view there *was* a divine purpose discernible in history. He did not hold such a view in his early days as an Epicurean, and to the end of his life he may well have had serious doubts, but it is hard to see how he could have brought his great epic to the verge of completion if this faith had not on the whole remained dominant in his mind. Nevertheless, he was too honest not to acknowledge that the process of history, whether divinely controlled or not, had always worked and continued to work without any regard for the merits of individual people, or even for the merits of nations. One recalls the feelings of Aeneas when he saw Dido for the last time:

> nec minus Aeneas, casu percussus iniquo,
> prosequitur lacrimis longe et miseratur euntem. (6. 475–6)

Yet none the less, Aeneas, stunned by the unfairness of her fate, follows her with tears from afar and pities her as she departs.

---

[27] W. A. Camps, *An Introduction to Virgil's Aeneid* (Oxford, 1969), p. 34.

Casu percussus iniquo. That is a feeling which thinking men have experienced in every age. Their response may be said to constitute the history of theology—and of atheism.

8

The Taciturnity of Aeneas

D. C. FEENEY

AENEAS: Good, good, my lord; the secrets of nature have not more
gift in taciturnity.

(Shakespeare, *Troilus and Cressida*, Act IV scene iii)

I

Aeneas' speech of defence before Dido (*Aen.* 4. 333–61) is the longest
and most controversial he delivers. Although by no means typical, it can
open up some revealing perspectives over the rest of the poem.

The exchange between the two, having as its kernel a dispute over
obligations and responsibilities, requires some words of context. The
early part of the book describes the establishment of a liaison between
the refugee leaders, while revealing amongst the poem's characters a
wide discrepancy of opinion over the nature of that liaison. Juno
announces that she will arrange the marriage of the couple (125–7);
after the ensuing marriage-parody of the cave-scene (165–8), Dido also
calls what now exists a 'marriage': 'coniugium uocat, hoc praetexit
nomine culpam' (172). Fama too, moving around Libya, speaks as if
Dido has taken Aeneas for husband (192). But the local King Iarbas
regards Aeneas as a pirate who has carried off a successful job of
plunder (217), while Jupiter looks down from heaven and sees 'lovers',
amantis (221). Mercury is able to address Aeneas as *uxorius* (266).

Some scholars would have it that there is a genuine ambiguity of fact
here.[1] As they point out, Roman marriage was a matter of cohabitation

I refer to the following books by author's name only: G. Highet, *The Speeches in Vergil's
Aeneid* (Princeton, 1972); R. Heinze, *Virgils epische Technik*[3] (Leipzig, 1915); A. S. Pease,
P. Vergili Maronis Aeneidos Liber Quartus (Harvard, 1935); R. G. Austin, *P. Vergili Maronis
Aeneidos Liber Quartus* (Oxford, 1955).

[1] G. Williams may fairly be taken as representative, *Tradition and Originality in Roman
Poetry* (Oxford, 1968), pp. 378–83. Cf. J. Beaujeu, 'Le Mariage d'Énée et de Didon',
Revue du Nord 36 (1954), 115–19. R. C. Monti goes even further, arguing that there is no
ambiguity, and that Aeneas is indubitably married, *The Dido Episode and the Aeneid: Roman
Social and Political Values in the Epic* (*Mnemosyne* Suppl. 66, Leiden: Brill, 1981), pp. 45–8.

and intent: any accompanying ceremonies had no legal status and were, strictly, irrelevant to the inception of the marriage.[2] Dido, by this view, is quite justified in regarding their liaison as a real marriage: Aeneas is living with her and co-operating with her as consort, in building the new city of Carthage.

There are serious obstacles, however, to believing that Vergil can have intended his audience to regard it as a possibility that this 'marriage' might be an established fact.[3] Elaborate ceremonies may not have been a legal necessity, but individuals of status and importance lived a public life in which such connections were formally marked and openly advertised. The ancient commentators have it right, when they elaborate upon Aeneas' later denial that a marriage exists between them, showing that for persons of this rank there is more to a marriage than mere cohabitation. Donatus paraphrases Aeneas' words thus: 'iunctus sum, inquit, tibi, sed illud non potest coniugium uocari; non enim semper mulieris ac uiri conuentio matrimonium facit. aliud uocatur quod gessimus. Quale enim matrimonium est ubi nullus testis interfuit, nulla ex more sollemnitas, nulla pactio, faces nullae, nulla ipsius foederis consecratio?'[4]

The ambiguity here is not one of fact—are they really married or not?—because in real terms it is plain enough that they are not married. The ambiguity resides in the characters' own interpretation. Aeneas is, by the Roman view, behaving in such a way as to give Dido (and various other characters) some justification for imagining that his intention involves marriage. By directing his focus away from Aeneas until the intervention of Mercury (259 ff.), Vergil is able to maintain a silence over his hero's own beliefs on this score.[5]

Mercury's message reduces Aeneas to panic. He tells his men to conceal their preparations for departure: he will wait for the right opportunity to inform the Queen (287–94). Dido senses the deception and seeks Aeneas out. The speech which she then delivers (305–30) is conventionally described as being in the 'high tragic-rhetorical tradi-

---

[2] Cf., e.g., J. P. V. D. Balsdon, *Roman Women* (London, 1962), pp. 181 f.

[3] Objections of various kinds given by F. Klingner, *Virgil* (Zurich, 1967), pp. 443 f.; J. Sparrow, *Dido v Aeneas: The Case for the Defence, The Sixth Jackson Knight Memorial Lecture* (Abbey Press, 1973), pp. 5 ff.

[4] On 339; Servius Auctus has similar comments. On the scale and cost of marriage ceremonies in the upper classes, see L. Friedlaender, *Drastellungen aus der Sittengeschichte Roms*[9] (Leipzig, 1919), I. 274 f.

[5] For the direction of the narrative away from Aeneas here, see Klingner, op. cit. (n. 4), pp. 444–6; R. E. Grimm, 'Point of View in Virgil's Fourth Aeneid', *CW* 63 (1969), 81–5.

tion',[6] the most important paradigms being the speeches of Euripides' and Apollonius' Medea.[7] Austin feels obliged to assert that 'the strength of Dido's personality towers above all the rhetoric',[8] but we do not drain her speech of its emotion or individuality if we recognize its rhetorical organization and impetus. Vergil has given her an ideal rhetorical animus. She has a good case and she argues it all the way and from every side, with rage (305 f.), close logic (311–13), and appeals to pity (320–30).[9] Above all, two crucial points that admit of some doubt are transformed by her words into plain fact: the nature of his leaving, and the nature of their relation to each other. To Dido, there is no question about these matters, he is simply in the wrong: Servius Auctus has the tone of it, 'hic quasi reus Aeneas a Didone accusatur'.[10]

Aeneas' opening words in reply give the first sign of the distinction between the two in their use of speech, and of Aeneas' recognition of that difference. To begin with 'pro re pauca loquar' (337). *pauca*, of course, is odd, since this is his longest speech in the poem; but the word betrays Aeneas' intuition that anything he might say will be inadequate after a speech such as Dido's. Conington's comment on the earlier use of *pauca* (*tandem pauca refert*, 333) is equally applicable to this one: ' "pauca" . . . seems to express Virg.'s feeling that the words come slowly and with effort, and bear no comparison to what the lover would have said had he given way to his emotion'.[11]

The meaning of *pro re* is a matter of dispute: 'the urgency of the case

---

[6] Austin, p. 98.

[7] Eur. *Med.* 465–519, A.R. 4. 335–90. For detailed comparisons see, besides the commentators, Heinze, p. 134 n. 1, and Highet, pp. 220 ff.

[8] p. 98.

[9] Cf. the brief remarks of M. Clarke, 'Rhetorical influences in the Aeneid', *G & R* 18 (1949), 21: 'the rhetorical system of eliciting all the arguments inherent in a situation lies behind Dido's speech in Virgil as it lies behind Ovid's letter [*Her.* 7]'; also p. 26.

[10] On 305. If my discussion of Dido's speeches, here and below, appears harsh, let me say that I do not consider we are ever intended to lose our sympathy for the Queen (here I cannot agree with Quinn's idea of a 'shift' in attitude as the book goes on, 'Vergil's Tragic Queen', *Latin Explorations* (London, 1963), pp. 48 ff.). It is not a matter of 'judging', still less of deciding which 'side' we favour: cf. the sensible remarks of A. E. Douglas, in his excellent address to the Vergilian Society ('The Realism of Vergil', *PVS* 1 (1962–2), 15–24; 'What Vergil has done is to present an unpartisan view of all the issues. He has told the truth' (p. 17).

[11] George Eliot catches the sensation in a passage extensively modelled on this scene, when Daniel Deronda attempts to address the shattered Gwendolyn Harleth: 'he paused a little between his sentences, feeling a weight of anxiety on all his words', *Daniel Deronda* (Harmondsworth, 1967), p. 839. Deronda's attempts at self-control remind one irresistibly of Aeneas: 'Deronda, too, felt a crushing pain; but imminent consequences were visible to him, and urged him to the utmost exertion of conscience' (ibid.).

admits only a brief reply' (Conington ad loc.); 'I shall speak only briefly, in view of the situation' (Highet, p. 76); 'I will now briefly deal with the charge' (Page);[12] 'let me speak a few words to meet the case' (Austin ad loc.). Austin and Page come closet to the mark. Servius understood *res* thus, in the meaning 'a matter at issue (in a dispute, esp. in a court of law)':[13] 'remoto ingrati crimine descendit ad causam'.[14] Seneca took the phrase the same way, if we may judge by his imitation (which provides a parallel for the use of *pro*): 'pauca pro causa loquar / nostra' (*Her. F.* 401 f.).

There is also present a very important subsidiary connotation of 'fact as opposed to words': cf. Matius to Cicero, 'te rogo ut rem potiorem oratione ducas' ('I ask you to place the fact above its expression', Cic. *Fam.* 11. 28. 5, 'the facts of Matius' present situation and past record', as Shackleton Bailey paraphrases in his commentary); Cic. *Tusc.* 5. 32, 'rem opinor spectari oportere, non uerba' ('I think the fact should be considered, not words'); Quint. 3. 8. 32, 'quod nos honestum, illi uanum ... uerbis quam re probabilius uocant' ('what we call honourable, they call empty ... with greater probability of word than fact').[15] Euripides exploits a similar two-sidedness in πρᾶγμα, when Hippolytus begins to answer the charges of his father: τὸ μέντοι πρᾶγμ' ἔχον καλοὺς λόγους, / εἴ τις διαπτύξειεν, οὐ καλὸν τόδε (984 f.): 'your *case*, your *charge*[16] affords the opportunity for fine words, but if one should open it up, the *facts of the matter* are not at all fine'. In Hippolytus' speech, the λόγος / ἔργον antithesis is explicit in the collocation of πρᾶγμα and λόγους; in Aeneas', the antithesis is more diffuse, looking forward to *ne finge* (338), and referring back to *quae plurima* fando / *enumerare uales* (333 f.).

It has been argued[17] that Aeneas is insulting Dido with these words, 'quae plurima fando / enumerare uales'. But since Dido has in fact referred to her kindness to Aeneas only very briefly in her first speech (si bene quid de te merui', 317), it is more sensible to follow the interpretation of Servius Auctus, which refers the meaning to the future.[18] If the words refer to the future, we look to the future, and we find there, in

---

[12] *CR* 7 (1893), 417.   [13] *OLD* s.v. 'res' 11a.   [14] On 337.

[15] Vergil has capitalized upon the antithesis twice in the preceding section: 'heu quid *agat?* quo nunc reginam ambire furentem / audeat *adfatu?*' (283 f.); 'temptaturum aditus et quae mollissima fandi / tempora, quis *rebus* dexter modus' (293 f.).

[16] Barrett ad loc. compares Arist. *Rhet.* 1415 b 22, οἱ πονηρὸν τὸ πρᾶγμα ἔχοντες, 'those speakers with a bad case to argue': see LSJ s.v. III 4 for this meaning.

[17] See Pease on 333.

[18] 'quantacumque enumerare potueris in me tuo beneficio conlata, eorum tibi debere gratiam non repugno' (on 335): 'however many benefits you could list as conferred on me by your kindness, I do not refuse to owe you gratitude for them'.

Dido's second speech, a list of precisely the sort which Aeneas here tells her is superfluous: 'eiectum litore, egentem / excepi et regni demens in parte locaui. / amissam classem, socios a morte reduxi' (373 ff.). What is the force of Aeneas' language in this clause? *enumerare* has aroused no comment, but it is an odd word to find in an epic. Vergil uses it once elsewhere, in its basic sense of 'numbering off', when Anchises in the Underworld announces that he will 'count off' his future progeny: 'hanc prolem cupio enumerare meorum' (6. 717). What Vergil intends here is quite different. He uses the word in its technical rhetorical sense of making an *enumeratio*, συναθροισμός, a list of conclusions, complaints, etc., which could be used in various parts of the speech.[19] Apart from Vergil, the only poets who exhibit the verb in this specialized rhetorical sense are those two most 'rhetorical' poets, Ovid[20] and Statius.[21] Aeneas' words are, more specifically, part of the 'long enumeration' motif, which stresses the undesirability or impossibility of making a long or complete list.[22]

Aeneas here is at once conceding the value of all that she has done for him and defensively anticipating that she can make up a fine list if she wants to. But it will do no good. *pro re pauca loquar* is a plea for both of them to eschew a parade of words, to face the facts, to stick to the point. Of course, to Dido (and to many readers), the services she has done for him *are* the point, and she returns to them in her next speech (373 ff.), listing them over until she is mad with pain (*heu furiis incensa feror!* 376), unable to believe that to Aeneas they are not everything as well.

Aeneas moves on to the two matters at issue, his 'flight' and their 'marriage': 'neque ego hanc abscondere furto / speraui (ne finge) fugam, nec coniugis umquam / praetendi taedas aut haec in foedera ueni' (337–9). These two and a half lines are all he has to say on the two counts. The two items are linked; moreover, it is important to realize that the linking is not a matter of economy: they are viewed under the same aspect. The problem of the marriage was discussed above: I turn to that of the departure.

When, after Mercury's visitation, Aeneas orders his men to prepare to

---

[19] See J. Martin, *Antike Rhetorik: Technik und Methode* (Munich, 1974), p. 307; for many examples of the technical use of the verb, see *TLL* s.v. 618. 44 ff., 'sensu technico rhet . . .'.

[20] Twice: *Met.* 1. 215; *Ars* 1. 254 ff., 'quid tibi femineos coetus uenatibus aptos / enumerem . . . ? / quid referam Baias . . . ?'

[21] Seven times: e.g. *Ach.* 1, 140, 'sed longum cuncta enumerare'; *Silv.* 3. 1. 102, 'uix opera enumerem'.

[22] Cf. Nep. *Lys.* 2.1, 'ne de eodem plura enumerando defatigemus lectores'; Cic. *Planc.* 74, 'omnes (gratias) enumerare nullo modo possent'.

leave, he tells them 'classem aptent *taciti* sociosque ad litora cogant, / arma parent et quae rebus sit causa nouandis / *dissimulent*' (289–91). When Dido's first sentence of attack only fourteen lines later picks up these very words ('*dissimulare* etiam sperasti, perfide, tantum / posse nefas *tacitusque* mea decedere terra?' 305 f.), the correspondence is seized upon by Highet as a sure means of exposing the shabbiness which Aeneas displays when he denies that he was attempting to run away without telling her: 'to his hearer, and to nearly all readers, this must appear to be a bare-faced lie'.[23] Vergil, however, takes four lines (291–4) to tell us that Aeneas fully intends to speak to the Queen before going; so that when Aeneas replies that he had not planned to run away without speaking to her, we have no option but to believe him.

The correspondence between Aeneas' words and Dido's serves to establish in the question of the departure the same ambiguity and the same atmosphere of partial justification which Vergil had set up in the question of the marriage. Dido has feared all along that Aeneas would run away from her,[24] and she is now entitled to believe that it is happening, because Vergil has created a ready illusion that this is what Aeneas is in fact doing. Aeneas *is* deceiving her, but she does not know that he is deceiving her only for a time.[25] She pounces on his actions and treats them as plain in fact and motive, with the (partial) justification for her interpretation made plain to Aeneas and the audience by her use of his very words. This is the quagmire which the poet, by a sleight of hand, reveals before his hero, as Aeneas hears his own words being, as it were, quoted back to him. .

Aeneas digs his heels in and doggedly insists that she is mistaken. Faced with a tangle of right and wrong, of motive and justification, with an opponent, not an interlocutor, so single-mindedly insistent on her interpretation alone, he is blunt in disillusioning her.[26] The terse defensiveness of his speech, so notoriously chastised by Page and others,[27] corresponds to the familiar silence or strained taciturnity of more modern heroes, when faced with an uncompromising attack from

---

[23] p. 75; cf. p. 289. It is surprising that, so far as I discover, Highet is the only writer on the problem to attempt to explain this striking and significant correspondence.

[24] Cf. 298, 'omnia tuta timens'; 419 f., 'hunc ego si potui tantum sperare dolorem, / et perferre, soror, potero'.

[25] Nor, of course, does she know why he is going.

[26] Though it does not seem to be recognized that when Aeneas says 'nec coniugis umquam / praetendi taedas' he is in fact admitting a grave moral failing. If a man of Aeneas' (even compromised) integrity says that he did not use promises of marriage as a pretext, he is not simply telling the woman she has nothing to complain about.

[27] See, conveniently, Pease, pp. 45 f., Austin, p. 105.

wife or lover.[28] Thus Vronsky before Anna, towards the end: 'And standing before her he brought out slowly: "Why do you try my patience?" He looked as if he could have said a good deal more but was holding himself in.'[29] Governing all these reactions is the same sense of incapacity before an insistent pressure of words.

Dido's determinedly one-sided view both of his departure and of their 'marriage' is rejected as if in one breath, for the same irresolvable problems of appearance and half-truth apply to both questions. *hanc fugam* and *haec foedera* are parallel, and some of the force of *ne finge* carries over into the second clause: 'this running away you speak of, those relations you speak of, they do not in reality exist: do not mould things so that it looks as if they do'.

With *ne finge* Aeneas' criticism of her speech comes into the open. The words are perhaps weary, or even plaintive, rather than brutal, but the force of the rebuke becomes apparent in the context of Vergil's use of *fingere* elsewhere. The verb occurs in relation to speech in four other places. When Fama moves about Libya, she is described as 'tam ficti prauique tenax quam nuntia ueri' (4. 188). Turnus tells off the disguised Allecto for trying to alarm him about the Trojans: 'ne tantos mihi finge metus' (7. 438), 'don't invent such fears and foist them upon me'. Finally, in the great clash of words between Drances and Turnus in Book 11, each man throws the word at the other. First Drances, 'inuisum quem tu tibi fingis (et esse / nil moror)' (11. 364 f.), 'I whom you misrepresent as being hostile to you.' Then Turnus, 'uel cum se pauidum contra mea iurgia fingit, / artificis scelus' (11. 406 f.). Aeneas' use of the word is not as savage as in the Turnus–Drances exchange— nor is it as indulgent as Turnus' reproach to Allecto. What Aeneas tells her is that she should not 'mould' the facts into her own view; English perhaps says 'twist'. Vergil puts into his mouth, to convey the criticism, a word that pinpoints with some precision the moulding and misrepresentation which is part of the orator's stock-in-trade: cf., e.g., Cic. *Flacc.* 51, 'tota enim conuertet atque alia finget'.[30] Hence the mutual charges of

---

[28] Such is the preconception behind R. Speaight's bluff appraisal of Aeneas' predicament: 'There are situations in which there is practically nothing a man can say', *The Vergilian Res* (London, King's College, 1958), p. 8.

[29] L. Tolstoy, *Anna Karenina* (Harmondsworth, 1954), p. 776. Simone de Beauvoir catches the predicament acutely, with a mother facing her daughter: 'She had a talent for jumbling the true and the false with such skill that I was overwhelmed by the effort I'd have to make to contradict her. Weakly, I said "You've got everything all twisted"' (*The Mandarins* (London, 1960), ch. 6, p. 464).

[30] 'He will turn everything around and make it different.' Further examples in *TLL* s.v. IIb of *fingere* as the hallmark of oratorical or impassioned speech.

distortion and pretence that pass betwen Turnus and Drances; hence Aeneas' protest against Dido's use of apparent 'fact' in her presentation of her charge on the matters of the departure and the marriage.[31]

Aeneas now attempts to make Dido understand the pressures upon him. The comment of R. D. Williams upon this central section is extreme, but not unrepresentative of modern views: 'His effort to minimise the pain of the situation by avoiding emotion makes his speech seem hard and unfeeling.'[32] This desiccation of Aeneas' words is a result of the false point of view from which his conflict is normally regarded: love for Dido on the one hand, dry duty on the other. Monti[33] has sympathetically demonstrated that the issue is a clash between two 'loves':[34] his obligations to his son, his men, his father's memory, his gods, these are emotional commitments, the force of which he expounds with urgency to Dido, trying to enable her to see why he must act as he does.

At the end of his exposition of the human and divine pressures upon him, Aeneas once more addresses Dido personally, saying 'desine meque tuis incendere teque querelis' (360). *querelis* has been described as 'one of the few words in the episode that are characteristic of the erotic elegy',[35] but such is not the tone here. Only once elsewhere does Vergil use the word of an articulate creature, when he puts it in the mouth of Juno, who rounds off her speech against Venus in Book 10 by pouring scorn on the other goddess' remonstrations: 'nunc sera querelis / haud iustis adsurgis et inrita iurgia iactas' (10. 94 f.). In Juno's mouth the word carries its technical rhetorical meaning of 'expostulation' or 'protest'. Cicero gives as an example of the 'communes' of earlier orators 'uitiorum et peccatorum acrem quamdam cum amplificatione incusationem aut querelam' (*De Orat.* 3. 106); and in the *Topica* he lists *querelae* in the subheading 'practical questions relating to emotion': 'quo

---

[31] For the antithesis present here between *res* and *fingere*, cf. Cic. Brut. 149, 'uereor ne fingi uideantur haec, ut dicantur a me quodam modo: res se tamen sic habet'.

[32] In 'Dido's Reply to Aeneas (*Aen.* 4. 362–387)', in H. Bardon and R. Verdière, eds., *Vergiliana* (Leiden, 1971), p. 423.

[33] A convenient collection of the views of the consensus in Monti, op. cit. (n. 1), note 11 to ch. 4 (p. 104). Austin is aware of the emotional force of Aeneas' words at some points in this central portion: see his remarks on 351 ff. Similarly Lefévre, 'Aeneas' Antwort an Dido', *WS* NS 8 (1974), 111 f.

[34] Op. cit. (n. 1), pp. 42 f. Cf. note 10 to ch. 4 (p. 104): '. . . Aeneas tells Dido not only that his obligations prevent him from remaining with her, but also that he faces the choice between love for her and love for her own people and that he does not decide in her favor. This is not to deny that Aeneas loves Dido; it is a question of choices.'

[35] N. W. De Witt, 'The Dido Episode in the Aeneid of Virgil' (diss. Chicago, 1907), p.78.

ex genere sunt querelae, incitationes, miserationesque flebiles' (86).[36]

The rhetorical reference of *querelis* is brought out by the rhetorical reference of *meque ... incendere teque. incendere* is commonly used to describe the inflammatory effect of speech, whether on a crowd or an individual,[37] and Vergil has this usage often: 'incenditque animum dictis' (*Aen.* 4. 197); 'talibus incensa est iuuenum sententia dictis' (12. 238).[38] More specifically, *incendere* attains the status of a semi-technical term in Cicero's oratorical writings, to describe the effect of the emotional weapons of which he was so fond—*hae dicendi faces*, as he calls them (*De Orat.* 2. 205). The orator will use his words to set his audience ablaze with emotion. Thus Demosthenes in the *De Corona*, though beginning calmly, 'post sensim incendens iudices, ut uidit ardentis, in reliquis exultauit audacius' (*De Orat.* 26).[39]

Aeneas' words, however, are more pointed than this: *both* of them are being set on fire by her remonstrations (*meque ... teque*). Such is the power of her words that the more she tries to set Aeneas on fire the more inflamed she herself becomes, and the more inflamed she becomes the more she tries to set him on fire. This mutual conflagration is the effect which Cicero, and after him Quintilian,[40] describe as the aim of the orator who wishes to achieve most effective 'pathos'. No orator, says Antonius (*De Orat* 2. 189 ff.), can set his listeners alight unless he himself is on fire: 'ut enim nulla materies tam facilis ad exardescendum est, quae nisi admoto igni ignem concipere possit, sic nulla mens est tam ad comprehendendam uim oratoris parata, quae possit incendi, nisi ipse inflammatus ad eam et ardens accesserit' (ibid. 190). Antonius singles out Crassus as supreme here: so powerful, he says, is Crassus' repertory, 'ut mihi non solum tu incendere iudicem, sed ipse ardere uidearis' (ibid. 188).[41]

What Aeneas is telling Dido here is that her words are a reckless

---

[36] Cf. *Part.* 121, 13, *Brut.* 88; in speeches, *Lig.* 23, *Scaur.* 39, *Flacc.* 55, 87.

[37] Plaut. *Pseud.* 201, 'sermone huius ira incendor'; Liv. 1. 59. 11, 'his ... memoratis incensam multitudinem perpulit ut...' etc.

[38] Cf. 1. 50, 'talia *flammato* secum dea corde uolutans'; 11. 376, 'talibus exarsit dictis uiolentia Turni'.

[39] Cf. *De Orat.* 3. 23; Quint. 4. 2. 75, 'peroratio incendit et plenos irae [iudices] reliquit'; ibid. 114.

[40] 6. 2. 26 ff., esp. 28.

[41] 'That to me you seem not only to set the judge on fire, but even to be alight yourself.' Speaking of his own prowess in the *Orator*, Cicero claims 'nulla me ingeni sed magna uis animi inflammat, ut me ipse non teneam; nec umquam is qui audiret incenderetur, nisi ardens ad eum perueniret oratio', 'no force of intelligence inflames me, but rather that of spirit, to the extent that I can't restrain myself; nor would the listener be inflamed, unless the speech came to him burning' (132).

incitement of passion, by which both of them are being made to suffer for no purpose: with remonstration and passionate protest alone nothing can be achieved but torture. She is, by a different metaphor, 'intoxicated' by her language. The effect he fears continues in her next speech. She uses her words to stoke her passion, until she feels herself ablaze with indignation and hurt—'heu furiis incensa feror!' (376).

Aeneas' criticism here is of a piece with his criticism at the beginning of his speech. No solution or reconciliation is possible if her words are only vehicles of a one-sided offensive which, by its very nature, precludes compromise or understanding. We note, too, that his criticism is couched in specific, even technical language, which relates precisely to the use (or misuse) of language as employed by the orators: I return later to the significance of this fact.

It is impossible to tell how Vergil would have finished the speech had he lived to complete the poem. All we have is a truncated reference—the only one—to Aeneas' emotions: 'Italiam non sponte sequor' (361). But Aeneas is interrupted ('bene "dicentem" non postquam dixit', Servius Auctus on 362)[42] by a Dido who expresses only contempt for his explanations: 'scilicet is superis labor est . . .' etc. (379). Of his father, his son, his people, she makes no mention. Her second speech (362–87) abandons any attempt at persuasion, and develops passionately the attack which had formed only part of her first speech.[43]

She interrupts herself by fleeing his presence (388 ff.). And he is left, 'multa metu cunctantem et multa uolentem / dicere' (390 f.). After the gulf that has opened between them, the enjambment and isolation of *dicere* harshly expose the inadequacy of mere speech. Thus was Orpheus left standing by his wife, 'prensantem nequiquam umbras et multa uolentem / dicere' (*G.* 4. 500 f.); thus, more appositely, was Aeneas left by the shade of his wife Creusa in Book 2, 'lacrimantem et multa uolentem / dicere deseruit' (790 f.). The comfort he wishes to give Dido he cannot provide (393–6): any hope of solace or reconciliation is denied.

II

If we look at this block of speeches with our attention centred on the character Aeneas, two points stand out. First, the distinction, patent in

---

[42] Whenever Vergil has *dicens* (2. 550; 10. 744, 856; 12. 950) or *dicente* (10. 101), he means 'even as X spoke'.

[43] My description of this second speech is only a précis of the article by Williams (op. cit., n. 32).

the speeches themselves and picked out by Aeneas, between Dido's use of speech and Aeneas'. Second, the ineffective and unnaturally truncated nature of the dialogue, with the denial to Aeneas of the opportunity to speak the words he wishes to speak.

We saw that Vergil marks the breaking-off of the dialogue with words that recall Aeneas' enforced silence in Book 2, when the shade of his wife vanishes before he can reply to the speech it has delivered. With his mother Venus the same frustration of speech is to be observed. Near the beginning of Book 1 Aeneas has a long and important conversation containing much information and instruction (321–401); but he does not know he is speaking with his mother, for she is in disguise. As she turns away he recognizes her; he follows while she flees from him (*fugientem*, 406), calling out, 'cur dextrae iungere dextram / non datur ac ueras audire et reddere uoces?' (408 f.). Their conversation has not in fact been genuine, and contact between them is deliberately broken off by the mother before the son may speak and hear *ueras uoces*. 'The distance between god and man remains irremovable, even between mother and son', remarks A. Wlosok on the passage, with a degree of truth;[44] but it is not simply because Venus is divine that Vergil has represented her as inaccessible to her son's speech.[45] Aeneas also suffers one such broken exchange with his father, at the end of Book 5 (722 ff.), when Anchises' shade flees at the approach of dawn. *iamque uale*, says Anchises (738); the same phrase in the same position is spoken to Aeneas by Creusa's ghost (2. 789).[46] Aeneas speaks as the shade vanishes, 'quo deinde ruis? quo proripis? .../ quem fugis? aut quis te nostris complexibus arcet?' (741 f.). As the silent shade of Dido turns away from him, Aeneas likewise calls out, *quem fugis?* (6. 466); he follows his mother as she runs away from him, *fugientem* (1. 406).

These episodes are examples of a feature of the *Aeneid* which has often been commented upon, namely, the poem's small share of dialogue or conversation. Heinze chose this observation as the starting-point for his discussion of the speeches, taking Homer as the standard of comparison;[47] Highet provides statistics, with some further discussion.[48] Some picture of the Homeric model is necessary in order to

---

[44] *Die Göttin Venus in Vergils Aeneis* (Heidelberg, 1967), p. 87.
[45] Further discussion of the lack of intimacy between Aeneas and Venus in Highet, pp. 37 f.
[46] And to Orpheus by Eurydice's ghost (*Geo.* 4, 497).
[47] p. 404.
[48] pp. 22 ff.

establish the background.[49] The aspect I wish to concentrate on is the efficacy, the potency of Homeric speech and dialogue, the way in which speech is used by Homer's men and women to approach each other, to attain an end, to achieve a solution.

The councils of the Achaean chiefs in the *Iliad* reveal progress and development as the words spoken work their way upon the minds of the hearers. Book 9 has two fine examples. At the beginning of the book there is a lengthy debate, in which we hear speeches from Agamemnon, Diomedes, Nestor, Agamemnon, and finally Nestor again. Agamemnon had at first been in despair, suggesting that they all go home to Greece (13–28); as one speech follows another, the men move away from this disastrous proposal and eventually arrive at a solution: ambassadors will go and plead with Achilles to abandon his wrath and be reconciled. The ambassadors do not succeed in their aim, but the various effects of their various styles of oratory work progressively upon Achilles, turning him to modify his stand.[50] At first he is threatening to sail home the next day (356–63). After Phoenix's long speech (434–605) he relents so far as to say that he will decide on the next day whether to sail home or not (618 f.). But it is the blunt rebuke of Ajax which crowns the weakening process (624–42), for his words prompt instinctive agreement from Achilles: πάντα τί μοι κατὰ θυμὸν ἐείσαο μυθήσασθαι, 'You appear to speak entirely in accordance with my mind' (645). All thought of leaving is now gone, and Achilles will fight if Hector comes to the ships of the Myrmidons (650–5).

The most accomplished exponent of speech in the Homeric poems is, of course, Odysseus, who is kept alive by his wits and tongue in his wanderings,[51] talking his way home through a world which is 'menacing ... with the mysteriousness of undeclared motives, inscrutable people, liars and cheats',[52] and, once he is arrived, talking his way into a position where he can kill his enemies and regain his standing. The use of words between Odysseus and Penelope in their reunion scene (23. 85 ff.) has

[49] I might dispense with this section if there were an appropriate discussion to which I could refer; but I do not know of one. Indeed, there is surprisingly little written on the subject altogether, as J. Latacz remarks in the introduction to his useful survey, 'Zur Forschungsarbeit an den direkten Reden bei Homer (1850–1970): ein kritischer Literatur-Überblick', *Grazer Beiträge* 3 (1975), 395.

[50] The modification of Achilles' position is well traced by C. Whitman, *Homer and the Heroic Tradition* (Cambridge, Mass., 1958), p. 190; cf. A. Lesky, 'Homeros', *RE* Suppl. 11, pp. 790 f.

[51] Cf. P. Walcot, 'Odysseus and the Art of Lying', *Anc. Soc.* 8 (1977), 1–19; W. B. Stanford, *The Ulysses Theme*² (Oxford, 1963), pp. 13 ff.

[52] J. Griffin, *Homer on Life and Death* (Oxford, 1980), p. 80.

been well described by Stanford, who traces the modulation of their reactions as they speak to each other, feeling their way until recognition and reconciliation are achieved.[53] Twenty years of separation still divide them, and Athene gives them a double night (241 ff.). τὼ δ᾽ἐπεὶ οὖν φιλότητος ἐταρπήτην ἐρατεινῆς, / τερπέσθην μύθοιδι, πρὸς ἀλλήλους ἐνέποντε, 'and when the pair had taken their pleasure in delightful love, they had pleasant talk, conversing with each other' (300 f.); as they speak to each other, sharing what each has suffered alone, their reunion is made complete: husband and wife re-establish their intimacy and heal their private hurt.

The healing and unifying power of dialogue is a constant feature of the Homeric poems. In *Odyssey* 4, for example, we see Menelaus greeting Telemachus and Peisistratus, the son of Nestor. In speaking of his lost friends, Menelaus mentions Odysseus, so that Telemachus is moved to tears (113 ff.). Helen enters and guesses his identity (141–4), so that first Peisistratus may openly speak of Telemachus' troubles (156–67), and then Menelaus may speak again of his own grief for his old friend (169–82). Their words bring the purging tears to all four (183–7); Peisistratus is moved to commemorate his brother Antilochus (190–202), and Menelaus graciously puts the seal on their weeping (212). Their open talk of their pain, and the resulting tears which they shed together, provide some measure of solace.

The Odyssean scene is a more humble statement of the theme which dominates the last book of the *Iliad*.[54] The gods have ordered Achilles to surrender Hector's body, and he has said that he will give it to any Trojan who may come (134–40). The arrival of Priam himself is completely unexpected, and stuns Achilles and his friends (480–4). Achilles' reaction is left in suspense, and the factor that determines his response is, quite simply, Priam's speech. Priam establishes between them the strongest link there can be, by reminding Achilles of his own father (486–506). They weep together, Priam for Hector, Achilles for Patroclus and for his father Peleus (509–12). Griffin's comment on this scene is characteristically just: 'as the great enemies ... meet and weep together, we see the community of suffering which links all men'.[55] So from the audience's point of view. For the two men, the 'community of suffering' is not an awareness that comes spontaneously upon them; it is a truth established by the words of Priam, a truth recognized and

[53] Op. cit. (n. 51), pp. 56 ff.
[54] Cf. Griffin, op. cit. (n. 52), p. 69.
[55] Ibid.

acknowledged by Achilles when he too compares the lot of his father
with that of Priam (534–48), thus putting into new perspective the pity
for his father which has been a cloud on his mind ever since he accepted
the inevitability of his own early death.[56]

The link established is still fragile. Priam overplays his hand when he
asks for the exchange to be made immediately, and provokes an angry
outburst from Achilles (560–70); but it is Achilles who makes the next
overture, by inviting Priam to eat and drink (599–620). After the meal,
in a famous scene, they look at and admire each other (628–32). Priam
marvels at Achilles, ὅσσος ἔην οἷός τε, 'so large and such was he' (630);
it passes oddly unremarked that the marvelling on Achilles' side is not
simply parallel: εἰσορόων ὄψίν τ' ἀγαθὴν καὶ μῦθον ἀκούων, 'seeing his
goodly appearance and listening to his words' (632). Achilles marvels at
Priam's power of speech: this is his ἀρετή (excellence).[57]

In this way does Homer portray the palliation of a grief apparently
beyond resource. The shared tears and the shared meal represent to us
the stages in their reconciliation; but the reconciliation is made possible
by the power of speech to draw men together and establish connections
between them.[58]

It is a shock to return to the *Aeneid* after the world of Homer.[59] 'In the
Homeric poems it is unusual for one character to address another
without receiving a spoken reply, and conversations in which three or
four people join are common. In Vergil, the reverse ... of the 333
speeches in the *Aeneid*, 135 are single utterances which receive no reply
in words.'[60] Heinze's discussion of Vergil's restrictions is still very

---

[56] Cf. 18. 330 f.; 19. 334 f.; 23. 144 ff.

[57] The allusion to Priam's speech must, as Colin Macleod puts it in his commentary,
refer to things said while they ate; it cannot refer to the moment, because as they look at
each other they are silent. This is plain from the lines immediately following: 'when they
had had their fill of *looking at each other*, then god-like Priam was the first one to speak'
(632–4).

[58] Griffin's observation is too bleak: 'No Egyptian drug can obliterate the sufferings of
the *Iliad*, for which there is no alleviation and the gods can only recommend endurance ...'
(op. cit. (n. 52), p. 69 n. 36). Men *can* do better than this in the *Iliad*, even if their sufferings
are not 'obliterated'. Contrast Priam's mad grief before the reconciliation scene (24.
162 ff.) with his self-possession afterwards (713 ff., 777 ff.), a self-possession which is
itself in strong contrast with the unrestrained passion of the mourning women.

[59] In attempting to put Vergil's speeches in perspective, I am afraid I may have put
Homer's speeches out of perspective. There is certainly unsuccessful speech in Homer;
the first exchanges of words in the *Iliad* are disasters. But it is Homer's norm which is
important (if I may borrow the terminology of W. R. Johnson, *Darkness Visible: A Study of
Vergil's Aeneid* (Berkeley and Los Angeles, 1976). ch. 2).

[60] Highet, pp. 23 f. Of these 135, as Highet notes, eight are soliloquies, and there are a
few more deductions to be made: see p. 24.

valuable, especially on the subjects of Vergil's concern for compression and narrative pace;[61] but a more thorough-going curtailment is at work. The world of the *Aeneid* is lacking in the Homeric style of open, co-operative, and sustaining speech. Vergil consistently excludes from his poem the intimacy, companionship, and shared suffering which Homer's men and women hold out to each other through speech.

In Book 3, for example, Aeneas arrives at Buthrotum in Epirus, where he finds Andromache mourning Hector on the shore. We think of such scenes as that from *Odyssey* 4 where shared memory and tears brought some relief to the bereaved and isolated. Such a solution is not to be looked for in Vergil. Andromache's tears are in vain (*incassum*, 345). Aeneas makes no reply to her long speech, nor to all the questions she asks him (337–43), since Helenus arrives and leads him off (345–8). We are not told what happens to Andromache, whether she follows, or whether she stays, weeping by the *tumulus* of Hector where Aeneas found her. When the Trojans leave, her obsessive misery is precisely the same as when they arrived (486–91).[62]

The *Aeneid* is rigidly undomestic. We hear no human conversation between husband and wife,[63] father and son,[64] mother and child.[65] Viewed as a tableau, the single 'homely' scene in the poem is the sinister moment when Ascanius/Cupid hangs in an embrace from his 'father's' neck, and then goes to sit in Dido's lap and infect her with love (1. 715–22). The gods, to whom everything is easy, are a foil. The delightful scene between Venus and Vulcan in Book 8 (370 ff.), with the homely simile following (407 ff.), is unimaginable in the human action. Jupiter and Juno reach a reconciliation in Book 12 (791–842) in a way that no human characters do. Vergil has pruned back Homer's gods, but there remains a freeness and domesticity in the scenes in heaven (e.g., 1. 227 ff., 4. 90–128) which is never seen on earth. W. R. Johnson is right to stress the importance in the poem of 'the rarity of the conversations

---

[61] pp. 405 ff.

[62] Cf. R. E. Grimm, 'Aeneas and Andromache in *Aeneid* 3', *AJPh* 88 (1967), 151–62. Grimm analyses well the lack of contact between the two, although I cannot accept his conclusions.

[63] No speech between Helenus and Andromache in Book 3. Amata speaks once to Latinus (7. 359–72), but he does not answer; at 12. 10 ff. Latinus and Amata are both present, with Turnus and Lavinia, but do not address each other.

[64] Aeneas and Anchises only *converse* in the Underworld. Evander speaks once to his son alive ('...dum te, care puer, mea sola et sera uoluptas, / complexu teneo ...' etc., 8. 581 ff.), and once to his corpse (11. 152 ff.). Pallas never speaks to his father.

[65] Apart from the 'unreal' conversation between Aeneas and the disguised goddess in Book 1 (321 ff.). At 8. 612 ff. she speaks briefly to Aeneas, but he makes no reply.

and debates between the actors (which ease the sense of isolated anxiety, bad solitude, which is a Vergilian hallmark)'.[66] The most intense expression of this anxious solitude is Dido's dream: 'agit ipse furentem / in somnis ferus Aeneas, semperque relinqui / sola sibi, semper longam incomitata uidetur / ire uiam et Tyrios deserta quaerere terra' (4. 465–8).

From the beginning to the end of the poem Vergil keeps the character of Aeneas before our eyes as the principal exemplar of this un-Homeric isolation. His lack of contact with mother and wife[67] has already been noted. Of his affair with Dido only the formal beginning and the wretched ending are represented.[68] We hear no conversation between Aeneas and his father Anchises, at least while Anchises is alive and upon the earth. In Book 2 there are four unconnected utterances between father and son:[69] from Aeneas, an outburst of angry grief when his father refuses to be carried from home (657 ff.), and an instruction to pick up the household gods and mount on his back (707 ff.); from Anchises, a line of acquiescence (704), and a line and a half of panic as the pair make their way out of the city (753 ff.). More remarkably, during the course of Book 3, when father and son co-operate in steering the Trojans' fortunes, Vergil does not once show us Aeneas addressing his father,[70] while Anchises speaks to his son on one occasion only, seven lines acknowledging the Penates' instructions to Aeneas to make for Italy (182–8). In the Underworld there is the form of a conversation, but there is something more than disquieting about the fact that Vergil allows his hero such indulgence only in this unreal place. Even here, although Anchises has held forth the hope 'notas audire et reddere uoces' (6. 689), the conversation between them is strangely formal and unintimate; Aeneas' questions are a naturalistic way of directing and organizing Anchises' exposition.[71]

---

[66] Op. cit. (n. 59), p. 179. See also G. Lieberg, 'Vergils Aeneis als Dichtung der Einsamkeit', in Bardon and Verdière, eds., *Vergiliana*, pp. 175–91.

[67] Earlier in Book 2, when Aeneas and Creusa are together in Anchises' house, she speaks once to him, without receiving a reply (657 f.).

[68] '[Aeneas] is never heard saying any special words of love to Dido, as Paris does to Helen (*Il.* 3. 438–46); nor is he ever seen embracing her, like Odysseus with Penelope (*Od.* 23. 231–40)', Highet, p. 35.

[69] 'Nicht Rede und Gegenrede', says Heinze (p. 410) of the bursts of speech in Anchises' house.

[70] One line of reported speech, pared and bald: 'Anchisen facio certum remque ordine pando' (179).

[71] Cf. Austin's introductory remarks on 679–702 (ed. *Aen.* 6); Highet, p. 34. Lieberg, art. cit. (n. 66), p. 189, has some good comments on the emptiness of contact between Aeneas and Anchises at this point.

To his son Ascanius, heir of all his hopes[72] and companion throughout his travels,[73] Aeneas speaks once only: 'disce, puer, uirtutem ex me uerumque laborem, / fortunam ex aliis ...' etc. (12. 435–40). This single address is a farewell, and it has the adumbrations of being a final farewell. Its models are Hector's prayer for Astyanax,[74] and Ajax' words to his son.[75] In each of these models the father never sees his son again, although Hector only suspects this fact (cf. 6. 448 ff.), while Ajax is determined upon it.[76] Ascanius, in his turn, never speaks to his father in the course of the poem.

If Aeneas' only words to his son are in the guise of a final farewell, his only words to Pallas, his 'Patroclus', are such in fact. As the Trojans arrive at Pallanteum, Pallas rushes to interrogate them (8. 110–14). Aeneas does not know him when he replies, 'Troiugenas ac tela uides inimica Latinis' (117); he goes on to speak in the plural, 'ferte haec et dicite ...' etc. (119). Pallas welcomes him, and takes his right hand (122–4), but Aeneas makes no reply. From that moment until Pallas is killed, Aeneas does not address him; it is only to his corpse that Vergil represents him speaking, in a lament (11. 42–58), and a short farewell (11. 96–8: ' "salue aeternum mihi, maxime Palla / aeternumque uale". *nec plura effatus* ad altos / tendebat muros'). His terseness at such crises is most poignant, as are his appalled and resourceless silences before scenes of great pity or terror (3. 47 f., at Polydorus' *tumulus*; 6. 331 ff., seeing the souls of the unburied), or his strange reticence when we expect speech from him (8. 617 ff., 729 ff., looking at his shield).

Aeneas is distant from his men also.[77] He moves in solitude through a world which yields him no intimacy or comfort, which progressively severs his ties with those who are close to him, and to whom he wishes to be close.[78] His conversations are stifled, unconsummated. Here he is at his most un-Homeric, particularly in Book 3, when he is following in the footsteps of his voluble Greek predecessor, Odysseus, conspicuously failing to engage in the whole range of discourse of which the more

[72] See esp. 1. 646; 4. 234, 274–6, 354 f.; 12. 436 f.
[73] Except for Books 8 and 9, when Aeneas is at Pallanteum without Ascanius.
[74] *Il.* 6. 476–81.
[75] Soph. *Aj.* 550 f., or Accius, *Armorum Iudicium* fr. 10 Ribbeck.
[76] This is so even if we accept the relocation of Ajax's speech in Accius, as suggested by H. D. Jocelyn, *CQ* NS 15 (1965), 128.
[77] Highet, pp. 41 f.
[78] On Aeneas' solitude, see Lieberg, op. cit. (n. 66), pp. 176 ff.; G. Elftmann, 'Aeneas in his Prime: Distinctions in Age and the Loneliness of Adulthood in Vergil's *Aeneid*', *Arethusa* 12 (1979), 175–202; especially H. Liebing, *Die Aeneasgestalt bei Vergil* (diss. Kiel, 1953), pp. 22, 95, 110, 152.

versatile hero is master. But even if Aeneas is cut off from the converse
which enriches and supports the human life of the Homeric poems,
much of his speech is effective, although not reciprocal or personal. He
offers prayer to win the goodwill of the gods for the common enterprise,[79] and confidently interprets the signs they send (e.g. 7. 120–34, 8.
532–40). He encourages his men after disaster (1. 198–207), and orders
them to decisive action. He is shown at the moment of decision ordering
Anchises to get on his back and to pick up the household goods, telling
his *famuli* to follow on (2. 707–20). We hear him inaugurate the funeral
games of his father, in a long[80] and formal oration which is the first stage
in re-establishing the group's confidence and trust, weakened by the
sojourn in Carthage (5. 45–71).[81] He orders his army to the crucial step
of marching on the city of Latinus, speaking in the harsh and authentic
tone of the Roman commander (12. 565–73). He speaks as the
representative of his people in diplomacy, most notably when he seals
the vital alliance with Evander (8. 127–51).[82] He does not make the
initial alliance with Latinus in Book 7; one of the many reasons for this is
that the alliance is broken, and whenever Aeneas makes a diplomatic
arrangement it sticks (with the disastrous exception of his pact with
Dido in Book 1): note his promise of friendship with the descendants of
Helenus (3. 500–5), and the ties he establishes as he founds the city for
Acestes (5. 749–61).

The effectiveness of Aeneas' public speech, either civil or military, is
put into perspective when seen beside the speech of the other characters
in the poem. We look in vain in the *Aeneid* for examples of the Homeric
type of many-sided debates leading to a worthwhile result. On the few
occasions in the *Aeneid* when more than four speeches from three or
more speakers come together in a cluster, the atmosphere is panic-
ridden and hysterical. The 'Homeric' consultation scene in Book 9, with
speeches from Nisus, Aletes, Ascanius, Euryalus, and Ascanius again
(234–302), is an undisciplined and excited shambles, which issues in
disaster: Aeneas, of course, is absent from his army. The set-piece
debate in the Latin Senate in Book 11 is a mere shouting match;
Latinus' proposals for peace are buried in the exchange of words
between Drances and Turnus (225–461). The bedlam is shown for
what it is by an interruption: 'illi haec inter se dubiis de rebus agebant /

---

[79] Highet, p. 39.   [80] The second longest he makes.

[81] Cf. Quinn, op. cit. (n. 10), p. 48: 'One of the functions of Book V is to heal this
alienation of commander from his men.'

[82] His third longest speech in the poem.

certantes: castra Aeneas aciemque mouebat' (445 f.). As they tussle away Aeneas acts.[83] Perhaps here lies some part of the explanation for the avoidance of conversation between Aeneas and Anchises in Book 3. Vergil may have been afraid that, by representing constant consultation instead of implying it, he would produce an impression, not of harmony, but of dither. Such an impression would undermine the image he wanted of an effective leadership, as opposed to the disorder of unstructured debate.

A more profound distinction is that which we saw at work in the private sphere, in the opposed speeches of Aeneas and Dido. Speech is not available as a palliative or a private bond in the *Aeneid*: worse, men and women use speech against each other and against their own interests, deceiving or bludgeoning with words to produce disastrous results. The most spectacular example is Sinon's speech in Book 2,[84] but virtually all the major emotional speeches of persuasion or coercion contain falsehood and misrepresentation, generate and are generated by passion, and lead to calamity: so the speeches of Amata in Book 7 (359–72), Turnus and Drances in Book 11 (343–444), Tolumnius in Book 12 (259–65).[85] Highet's conclusion is substantially correct: 'Vergil, it seems, held that powerful oratory was incompatible with pure truth, and that every speaker presented his or her own case by misrepresenting the facts.'[86]

It is as well to be precise about this, for there is little profit in bandying about the word 'rhetorical' as an indiscriminate term of abuse. Much of Highet's discussion is vitiated by the stance he adopts on the 'Vergilius poeta an orator' question,[87] a stance which is little more than 'poetry good, rhetoric bad'. Rhetorical elements in the organization of the speeches in the *Aeneid* are simply an observable fact,[88] and if we describe any particular speech as 'rhetorical' we do not commit ourselves to a

---

[83] A similar perfervid atmosphere prevails at the beginning of Book 12 (10–80), when we hear speeches from Turnus, Latinus, Turnus, Amata, Turnus. The appeals of Latinus and Amata, so far from inducing Turnus to give up the war, drive him into an even greater frenzy.

[84] 'talibus insidiis periurique arte Sinonis / credita res, captique dolis lacrimisque coactis / quos neque Tydides nec Larisaeus Achilles, / non anni domuere decem, non mille carinae' (195–98).

[85] See Heinze, pp. 421–4; Highet, pp. 285–90. On Anna's speech in Book 4 (31–55), see G. S. West, 'Virgil's Helpful Sisters: Anna and Juturna in the *Aeneid*', *Vergilius* 25 (1979), 10–19.

[86] p. 289.

[87] pp. 277–90.

[88] See G. Kennedy, *The Art of Rhetoric in the Roman World* (Princeton, 1972), pp. 390 ff.; D. A. Russell, *Criticism in Antiquity* (London, 1981), pp. 126–8.

necessary value judgement. What does emerge from the *Aeneid* is a
mistrust of powerful language that divides into two aspects, corresponding to the two heads under which Aeneas criticizes Dido's speech:
powerful language distorts reality, or the truth, in its single-minded
pursuit of its particular aim; and it exploits ungovernably the emotions of
speaker and audience. The power of words in a private and a public
context is thus suspect in analogous ways.

The rhetoricians themselves were fully alive to the force of such
criticisms: 'quidam uehementer in eam (rhetoricam) inuehi solent ...
eloquentiam esse quae poenis eripiat scelestos, cuius fraude damnentur
interim boni, consilia ducantur in peius, nec seditiones modo turbaeque
populares sed bella etiam inexpiabilia excitentur, cuius denique tum
maximus sit usus cum pro falsis contra ueritatem ualet', 'Some habitually make strong attacks against rhetoric, saying that it is speech which
saves the wicked from punishment, and that by its deception good men
are sometimes condemned, plans come out the worse, and not only
popular seditions and riots but also irremediable wars are roused, and
finally that its use is greatest when it prevails for falsehood against truth',
Quint. 2. 16. 1 f.[89] But when they are praising high-powered oratory,
and giving advice on its use, the oratorical writers are almost disarmingly
candid about their aims and methods: 'ubi uero animis iudicum uis
adferenda est et ab ipsa *ueri* contemplatione abducenda mens, ibi
proprium oratoris opus est ... sicut amantes de forma iudicare non
possunt quia sensum oculorum praecipit animus, ita omnem *ueritatis*
inquirendae rationem iudex omittit occupatus adfectibus', 'But when
force is to be applied to the minds of the jury, and when their attention
must be distracted from the bare contemplation of the truth, that is the
proper task of the orator ... just as lovers are no judges of beauty
because excitement removes their power of sight, so a juryman leaves
behind every mode of inquiring into the truth when seized with
emotion', Quint. 6. 2. 5 f.; 'nihil est enim in dicendo ... maius, quam ut
faueat oratori is, qui audiet, utque ipse sic moueatur, ut impetu quodam
animi et perturbatione, magis quam iudicio aut consilio regatur. plura
enim multo homines iudicant odio aut amore aut cupiditate aut iracundia aut dolore aut laetitia aut spe aut timore aut errore aut aliqua
permotione mentis, quam *ueritate* aut praescripto aut iuris norma aliqua
aut iudicii formula aut legibus', 'Nothing is more important in oratory
than that the listener should sympathize with the speaker, and be moved

---

[89] These words should be read with *Aeneid* 7, 11, and 12 in mind.

himself in such a way that he is ruled by mental excitement and disturbance rather than by prudence and judgement. For men make more judgements through hate, love, desire, anger, joy, hope, fear, error, or some excitement of the mind, than through truth or prescription or any rule of the court, or formula of judgement, or laws', Cic. *De Orat.* 2. 178; 'illud autem genus orationis (*sc.* uehemens) non cognitionem iudicis, sed magis perturbationem requirit', 'That [powerful] type of oratory requires not the judging capacity of a juryman, but rather his disturbance', ibid. 2. 214. High rhetoric does not admit of dubiety: it is concerned in the first and last resort, not with any objective establishment of a truth, but with getting its way; and it gets its way by whirling speaker and audience up in a grip of passion in which judgement and discrimination are deliberately expunged, in which partial justification, half-truth, uncertainty are nothing but irrelevancies. Criticisms of such language as an evil have a long history, of which the *Aeneid* is a part.[90]

Aeneas stands out prominently against this background. He does not lie when he speaks:[91] often he speaks with great emotion, but he does not use words to win his way by overpowering one emotion with another. The lassitude which so many readers sense in Aeneas' speeches[92] is in fact a restrained disavowal of the fervour which animates the language of the other characters when they seek to influence their listeners. The restraint tightens progressively into terseness as the tension of the last third of the poem increases, as Aeneas' role is restricted to the business of leading armies and killing Latins.[93]

We are left with a discrepancy, blunt but not distorting, between Aeneas' private and public speech. In the private realm, he is the poem's most consistent and prominent paradigm of the weak and insubstantial

---

[90] See G. Kennedy, *The Art of Persuasion in Greece* (Princeton, 1963), pp. 14 ff.; H. von Arnim, *Leben und Werke des Dio von Prusa* (Berlin, 1898), ch. 1, pp. 4–114, 'Sophistik, Rhetorik, Philosphie in ihrem Kampf um die Jugendbildung'; P. Vicaire, *Platon: Critique Littéraire* (Paris, 1960), pp. 276 ff.; A. Hellwig, *Untersuchungen zur Theorie der Rhetorik bei Platon und Aristoteles* (*Hypomnemata* 38, Göttingen, 1973), pp. 304 ff.

[91] Despite Highet's claims (pp. 287 ff.) that Aeneas distorts the truth like other speakers. His examples are ill founded. At, e.g., 1. 200 f., Aeneas tells his men, 'uos et Scyllaeam rabiem penitusque sonantis / accestis scopulos'. 'Aeneas speaks as though he and his men had actually braved the dangers of Scylla and Charybdis, whereas the narrative shows that they avoided them by sailing southward along the Sicilian coast . . .' (Highet, p. 288). Aeneas in fact tells his men that they *went close to* Scylla and Charybdis (*accestis*, 1. 201), and this is precisely what happened: 'laeuam cuncta cohors remis uentisque petiuit. / tollimur in caelum curuato gurgite, et idem / subducta ad Manis imos desedimus unda . . .' etc. (3. 563 ff.).

[92] e.g. 5. 45–71, 8. 127–51, 11. 108–19.

[93] See Highet, pp. 39 f.

nature of human interchange; in the public realm, he is increasingly successful through the course of the poem as the leader of the Trojan enterprise, whether as diplomat or general, with exhortation, encouragement, and direction, free from the manipulation and distortion which controls the words of the other outstanding orators of the poem. Highet sketched out the right area for an understanding of the problem when he attempted to refer it to Vergil's observation of Augustus, but his analysis is rather confused.[94] A more satisfying discussion is that of D. J. Stewart,[95] who writes with the assumption that 'one of the tasks ... Virgil set for himself in the *Aeneid* was to write literature about institutions and the political vocation'.[96] He catches well, though one might quarrel with some of his expression, the truth about Aeneas' position: 'All those flat, dull speeches of encouragement, all that weariness, that general hangover quality which Aeneas both experiences and communicates when he looks out over the world, are the politician's special burden. He must pretend to enthusiasms he does not feel, repress emotions he does feel, and generally behave not as a free individual but as the incorporation of a society's needs, a trust-officer for other people's future.'[97] Again, on Dido, 'the Dido story is a metaphor for what any politician must be prepared to do: to sacrifice every last personal tie, if necessary, to help keep the political enterprise going'.[98] The same design guides the denial to Aeneas of free interchange with all those closest to him.

It is not a matter of Vergil looking at Augustus and writing down what he saw. Here is Highet's baulk, for as Highet says, 'Augustus was far more sociable and less lonely than Aeneas.'[99] When we consider Aeneas, aloof, repressed in speech, devoid of close friends, the public

[94] He concludes, 'For Vergil both Augustus and his prototype Aeneas were more godlike than human; and a god, as we know from Aristotle, cannot have human friends' (p. 43). But his consequent remarks are more valuable: 'Did he not also wish to show him as one who, after almost unendurable losses and sufferings, had grown into the melancholy of middle age and the grave contemplation of approaching death?' (ibid.).

[95] 'Mortality, Morality and the Public Life: Aeneas the Politician', *Ant. R.* 32 (1972–3), 649–64.

[96] p. 650.

[97] pp. 659 f. A fine example is the worthy but flat oration with which Aeneas inaugurates the funeral games (5. 45–71); this is the ancient equivalent of the Cabinet Minister's speech at the opening of the bridge or factory.

[98] p. 660.

[99] p. 42. One suspects that it was the early part of Augustus' principate, when Vergil knew him, that provided the material for the conventional assessment of his *comitas* (Suet. *Aug.* 53. 2 f., 66. 1–3, 74). Vergil did not see the Augustus who lived through the deaths of all his early friends, and of Gaius and Lucius, who saw the disgrace of daughter and granddaughter, and survived into 'the atmosphere of gloom and repression that clouded the last decade of the reign' (R. Syme, *History in Ovid* (Oxford, 1978), p. 205).

servant without control over his own destiny and attachments, it is not Augustus who comes to mind: it is Tiberius. What other Julio-Claudian could have spoken with more feeling the words of Aeneas, 'me si fata meis paterentur ducere uitam / auspiciis et sponte mea componere curas...' (4. 340 f.)? Douglas was not being facetious when he compared Aeneas' last sight of Dido ('prosequitur lacrimis longe et miseratur euntem', 6. 476) with Suetonius' melancholy description of Tiberius' last encounter with the wife Augustus had forced him to divorce:[100] 'sed Agrippinam et abegisse post diuortium doluit, et semel omnino ex occursu uisam adeo contentis et [t]umentibus oculis prosecutus est, ut custoditum sit ne umquam in conspectum ei posthac ueniret', 'But he grieved that he had driven away Agrippina after their divorce, and when he once saw her quite by chance he followed her with such strained and swollen eyes, that care had to be taken that she should never thereafter come into his sight' (*Tib.* 7. 3).[101]

I am not suggesting that Vergil was attempting to foresee events;[102] nor was he looking back, as C. A. McKay argues when he proposes Julius Caesar as the model for Aeneas.[103] Aeneas is not a *portrait* of Augustus or of any other individual. He represents generally the extreme case of the pressures and cruelties inflicted upon the individual who embodies in his own person the aspirations and future of a whole nation.[104] Augustus was the only man Vergil knew who was such a 'man of destiny'; while it is impossible to believe that Augustus was not a major influence on Vergil's conception of his hero, it is likewise impossible to make any precise suggestions as to the nature of that influence.[105] The character of Aeneas stands essentially in its own right, the representative of a predicament which his creator did not see as unique.

As Stewart observes, in the passage quoted above, 'the Dido story is a

---

[100] Op. cit. (n. 10), p. 21.

[101] Following Ihm's Teubner text for [t]umentibus.

[102] Cf. Douglas, loc. cit. (n. 100), 'Vergil was dead before these events, but he knew all about dynastic marriages of convenience'.

[103] 'Hero and theme in the *Aeneid*', *TAPhA* 94 (1963), 157–66.

[104] Cf. Stewart, op. cit. (n. 95), p. 651: 'The *Aeneid* is a study of the preternatural strains and anxieties a political vocation brings to mere natural man.'

[105] But I cannot resist quoting the following passage from Suetonius, to which Prof. Nisbet referred me as being illustrative of Augustus' constrained and inhibited use of speech: 'sermones quoque cum singulis atque etiam cum Liuia sua grauiores non nisi scriptos et e libello habebat, ne plus minusue loqueretur ex tempore', 'His more important conversations with individuals and even with Livia were wholly written down and taken from a note-book, in case he said too much or too little off the cuff', *Aug.* 84. 2.

metaphor for what every politician must be prepared to do'.[106] It is in his confrontation with Dido that the tensions inherent in Aeneas' role become most acute. In Dido he faces the most impassioned and eloquent speaker in the poem. He feels the justice and the injustice of her speech, but he does not answer her in the same tenor. With hard-won self-control he tells her that the way she uses words is profitless and cruel, and he attempts to give an explanation, to reach some understanding. His words do not achieve their aim: but there is nothing in the poem to give us reason to believe that any other words would have been more effective.

[106] Loc. cit. (n. 98).

Poetry, folklore, philosophy, religion → Vergil does not sell out in his Marcellus

9

The Sixth Book of the *Aeneid*

R. D. WILLIAMS

The sixth book is the focal point of the *Aeneid*; it completes and concludes what has gone before, and it provides a new impetus for the second half of the poem. It is not an isolated piece of theology; it has its work to do within the design of the poem. It is of vital importance in the development of the main themes of the *Aeneid*, and it is on three of these that I want to concentrate as we accompany Aeneas on his journey from the cave at Avernus to the Gates of Ivory. We shall be concerned firstly with how a memorable picture—or perhaps two memorable pictures—of the world after death is built up from the rich and tangled heritage of poetry, folklore, philosophy, and religion. In the words of T. R. Glover—to whose warm and sensitive appreciation of the poet Virgilian studies are deeply indebted—'we find here as elsewhere that Virgil tries to sum up all that is of value in the traditions, the philosophies, and the fancies of the past'.[1] It is in the later part of Book 6 that Virgil comes nearest to a solution of the problem of human suffering with which the whole poem is so preoccupied, as he gropes towards a conception of the life after death in which sin is purified away and virtue rewarded. Secondly, the golden hopes for the future of Rome and the Roman world are in this book expressed with a patriotic pride more complete than anywhere else; the vision of the temporal destiny of the world follows upon the vision of the spiritual afterlife. Thirdly, and this is the aspect which I shall stress most because it is not generally stressed enough, this book (like the rest of the *Aeneid*) is above all about Aeneas himself, his character and resolution, his experiences, past, present, and future. We must always remember that the aim of the book is not primarily philosophical or theological—and in this it differs from the myths of Plato to which it owes so much; the aim is to present a poetic vision which has special reference to Aeneas and Rome within the design and framework of the total epic poem.

[1] T. R. Glover, *Virgil* (7th edn., London, 1942), p. 258.

The source material[2] from which the sixth book is built may be traced very far back, beginning in Greek literature with the eleventh book of the *Odyssey*. Virgil's debt to Homer, as we shall see, is considerable and significant in the part of the book concerned with the journey to Elysium, but practically non-existent in the last part. In Homer death was not seen as a welcome deliverance from life, but as a wretched and cheerless existence in every way inferior to life on earth. The notion of the afterlife as a release from toil which we find in the last part of Book 6 of the *Aeneid* probably springs from popular belief and folklore crystallized and organized by Orphic mystery religions[3] and Pythagorean philosophy; many Orphic ideas were developed by Plato, and many were assimilated in Stoicism. Orphic poems describing a descent into the Underworld (a *katabasis*) began to be written, perhaps from the sixth century onwards. The two most famous heroes who performed this exploit were Hercules and Orpheus himself (whose story is told in the second half of the fourth *Georgic*). Orpheus was also connected with the elaborate and exclusive ritual of the Eleusinian mysteries, but the relationship of the sixth book of the *Aeneid* to these secret initiation ceremonies is not nearly as close as is sometimes stated. It is only in the most non-technical sense of the word that we can speak of the 'initiation' ritual[4] of Aeneas.

One of the best-known journeys to the Underworld is the *katabasis* of Dionysus in Aristophanes' *Frogs*, where we see the background of Orphic mysticism dominated, as one would expect in comedy, by meetings with the figures of popular folklore (Charon, Cerberus, Aeacus, Pluto). Exactly the opposite is the case in the myths of Plato. These have a background of popular topography (Styx, Acheron, Cocytus, Lethe), but the whole emphasis is on the judgement and purification of the souls. Beyond doubt the myths of the *Phaedo*, *Gorgias*, *Phaedrus*, and perhaps especially the story of Er in the *Republic*, Book 10, played a great part both in shaping Virgil's deepest thought and in awakening his poetic imagination.

In Latin literature the first book of Ennius' *Annals* had a famous passage connected with Pythagorean beliefs,[5] and Cicero's *Somnium*

[2] For a short and clear account of the sources see H. Butler's *Aeneid VI*, Introduction. F. Fletcher (*Aeneid VI*, Intro.) gives translations of the passages from Plato.

[3] On Orphism see W. K. C. Guthrie, *Orpheus and Greek Religion* (London, 1952), esp. ch. 5.

[4] See Guthrie, op. cit. 154 f., on the Eleusinian mysteries; see also L.-A. Constans, *L'Énéide de Virgile* (Paris, 1938), pp. 208 f.

[5] Ennius *Ann.* 15 V, a reference to transmigration of souls and Ennius' dream that he

Scipionis gives a romanized version of a Platonic myth about the souls in the Underworld. We have fragments of evidence about other writings which may have been Virgil's more immediate models, and Norden argues strongly[6] that a lost work of Posidonius was the immediate source from which Virgil drew much. But the essential thing about Book 6 of the *Aeneid* is that Virgil here aims at a synthesis of a long literary traditon which will fulfil his poetic purposes at this stage in the *Aeneid*, and his creative imagination is more likely to have been fired by Homer and Plato than by Posidonius.

Book 6 may naturally be divided into three sections—the preparations for the descent (to l. 263), the journey through the Underworld (to l. 675), and the explanation of the rebirth and the vision of Roman heroes. I shall not deal here with the first section, save only to say that one of its main functions is to build up an aura of solemnity and mystery. Symbols of magic and folklore, such as the labyrinth[7] and the golden bough,[8] and the detailed description of ritual sacrifice combine to produce a supernatural atmosphere of awe and dread appropriate for the descent to the Underworld at the lake where no birds fly.

The events in the Underworld are presented in two parts: first a journey, a *katabasis*, through the various territories of the land of ghosts; and secondly a philosophical or theological account by Anchises of the notions of purification and rebirth, which introduces the pageant of Roman heroes by the stream of Lethe. Now in a way these parts are independent of one another, they perform different functions in the poem, and they certainly have not been combined by Virgil into a single consistent doctrine. That is what I meant at the beginning by speaking of Virgil's two pictures of the Underworld. The static presentation of Limbo, for example, where we are led to think that Dido and Deiphobus will always stay, does not cohere with the doctrine of rebirth expounded by Anchises. Attempts to minimize the inconsistency by suggesting that

was a reincarnation of Homer. Cf. Hor. *Ep.* 2. 1. 52 (of Ennius), *somnia Pythagorea*, and *Odes* 1. 28. 9 f.

[6] E. Norden, *Aeneid VI* (3rd edn., Leipzig, 1926, repr. 1957).

[7] Some references are given in my note on *Aen.* 5. 588, where the simile of a labyrinth is applied to the *lusus Troiae*.

[8] Virgil's sources for the talisman of the golden bough are not known. We do not find it in earlier classical literature and its significance in Roman folklore cannot be defined with precision. Frazer, in the great work on comparative anthropology and folklore to which he gave the title of *The Golden Bough*, associates it with various kinds of tree magic and particularly with the mistletoe (with which Virgil compares it in a simile, 205 ff.). Servius links it with the worship of Diana at Aricia and the *rex nemorensis*. See also R. A. Brooks, *AJPh* 74 (1953), 260 f., where the bough is discussed as a dual symbol of life and death.

the βιαιοθάνατοι, the untimely dead, stay in Limbo only for the term of the rest of their natural life (as Norden originally argued) do not correspond with the text: some of them would already have completed their stay before Aeneas came. It is much more to the point to look for the poetic reasons for the discrepancies; an admirable example of this approach, to which I am much indebted in parts of this paper, is the stimulating short article recently published by Brooks Otis.[9] Briefly, what we may say is this: that the mythology of the *katabasis* gives a setting for events of the tragic past, and the theology a setting for hopes of the future. Within the framework of the *katabasis* come the ghosts of Aeneas' past—Palinurus, Dido, Deiphobus; in the theology is Virgil's message of hope beyond the grave, leading to his patriotic presentation of the character and ideals of Rome, for which Aeneas must continue to strive onwards. These are points which I shall elaborate further on. Let us first consider the events and intention of the *katabasis*.

For the framework of Aeneas' journey through the Underworld Virgil has selected and organized from the rich material available in past literature, popular folklore, and probably pictorial art.[10] But within this traditional setting of the well-known rivers, of the monsters and mythology of the past, he has included the individual ghosts special to the story of Aeneas, those of Palinurus, Dido, Deiphobus. In this book he reiterates (in reverse order) tragic events from the earlier part of the poem, and brings us again in another context face to face with the same reality of death, the death of those already known to us. The setting is dark and melancholy; little or no consolation is suggested; no hint is given here of the hope of expiation. In this part of the book Aeneas journeys amidst the sorrows of the past.

There is in the *katabasis* a quite marked similarity in incident and episode to the *Odyssey*, Book 11, affording a sharp contrast with the wholly un-Homeric note of hope after death which Virgil presents in the last section of the book. The topography is, of course, un-Homeric, for in Homer there is no journey: the ghosts come up to the pit which Odysseus has dug. But the motivation of the visit is similar: the instructions given to Aeneas by Helenus (to consult the Sibyl) and by Anchises (to meet him in Elysium) both recall *Od.* 10. 490 ff., where Circe tells Odysseus that he must go to Hades in order to consult

---

[9] *TAPhA* 90 (1959), 165 ff.

[10] See Pausanias 10. 28 f. for a full description of Polygnotus' picture of the Underworld.

Teiresias about his future voyage. In Virgil as in Homer the hero meets ghosts of his past, with the difference that in Virgil there is far more emphasis on the previous events of the poem. The women with Dido in the *lugentes campi* recall Homer's heroines (especially in *Od.* 11. 321 ff.); the judge Minos is mentioned by both poets; Virgil's Tartarus includes the traditional sinners described by Homer.

There are similarities of incident too. Elpenor is clearly a model for Palinurus; each comes first in the description, each had died recently and begs for burial. The silence of Dido (6. 469 ff.) recalls the silence of the angry Ajax (*Od.* 11. 563 f.). The dialogue between Aeneas and Deiphobus has some points of similarity with that between Odysseus and Agamemnon. Finally Virgil has some verbal reminiscences of the *Odyssey* (e.g. *Aen.* 6. 305 ff., *Od.* 11. 36 ff., the ghosts come flocking; *Aen.* 6. 700 ff., *Od.* 11. 206 ff., the ghost eludes embrace).

To these Homeric reminiscences Virgil has added ideas from many other sources (as we have seen), especially from Orphic 'Descents to the Underworld', and has used this traditional material to present an experience which is essentially personal to Aeneas himself, and above everything an integral part of the development of Aeneas' character and resolution. In his journey Aeneas is in a sense travelling again through his past life; he must come to terms with the past in order to face the future. As Brooks Otis puts it,[11] he cannot alter the past; 'he can only leave it, but in recalling it and leaving it he achieves also freedom from its "traumatic" hold on him'.

The journey is prefaced with a new invocation (264 ff.), asking the gods to allow the poet to reveal things deep hidden in darkness. It begins in slow and sonorous lines:

> ibant obscuri sola sub nocte per umbram
> perque domos Ditis uacuas et inania regna,
> quale per incertam lunam sub luce maligna
> est iter in siluis, ubi caelum condidit umbra
> Iuppiter et rebus nox abstulit atra colorem. (6. 268–72)

Thus the scene is set; immediately round the porch of Hades throngs a crowd of horrid shapes, personifications of evil things, of earthly experiences or ideas concerned with suffering or sin: Grief, Avenging Cares, War, Furies, Discord. Past the entrance are monsters, Scyllas, Chimaeras, Gorgons, and many more, the supernatural enemies of mankind against whom the greatest of heroes (such as Hercules) were

[11] Op cit. 168.

often matched in myth. The opening scene has been like a medieval iconography of Hell, full of the terrors of popular folklore which Lucretius had tried so passionately to dispel from men's minds.

The route leads to Acheron, or Styx, the river which the unburied may not cross. Virgil lingers on his description of the ferryman Charon, perhaps the best known of all Pluto's people. He is a 'demon' of folk-story, often portrayed (as Charun) on Etruscan tombs, but in literature he had become less terrifying: he is a grumpy but not unattractive character in Aristophanes' *Frogs*, and Virgil's presentation of him is to some degree mock-heroic, affording a contrast with the pathos of other elements in this part of the story. To Charon come flocking the shades of the newly dead, thick as leaves in autumn or birds migrating when summer is over:

> stabant orantes primi transmittere cursum
> tendebantque manus ripae ulterioris amore. (6. 313–14)

Aeneas asks why some are taken across the river and others not, and the Sibyl tells him that only those who have been buried may cross; the others must wait for a hundred years. Here Aeneas sees Leucaspis and Orontes, who were shipwrecked off Carthage (1. 113 ff.), and then his trusted and beloved helmsman Palinurus, lost overboard on the last stages of the voyage.[12] This is Aeneas' first personal experience in the Underworld, and their meeting and conversation is described at some length. It is the first of the events of the past which Aeneas must live through again as he journeys in the Underworld.

The tone now changes abruptly as Charon sees Aeneas and the Sibyl and hails them brusquely. We cannot quite call the scene comic, but it is handled with a certain irony and detachment. Palinurus has been very real, Charon we need not believe in. He shouts at his visitors from a long way off (*iam inde*, 385; *iam istinc*, 389), and his words are peremptory, blustering, and a little naïve as he tells of previous occasions when he wrongly stretched a point in favour of Hercules and Theseus. The Sibyl first appeals to him by the *pietas* of Aeneas, but it is the production of the golden bough which Charon can better understand, and he gives in at once. He brings his boat in, shifts the other passengers up, and takes the weighty figure of Aeneas aboard. The boat creaks and the water comes in at the seams—but they get across.

The irony continues in the description of Cerberus.[13] The monsters

---

[12] On this see M. C. J. Putnam, *HSCPh* 66 (1962), 205 ff.

[13] Cerberus the watchdog occurs in Hom. *Il.* 8. 366 ff. and *Od.* 11. 623 ff., but not yet

of Orcus present no real terrors. As the golden bough had convinced Charon, so the sop suffices for Cerberus, and as he lies extended and unconscious on the ground. Aeneas and the Sibyl make their way onwards. In this part of the journey the 'machinery' of Hell, the horrid shapes at the entrance, the ferryman, the dog, have acted as background; in the foreground, because of the personal involvement of Aeneas, has been the shade of the unburied Palinurus.

Immediately across the Styx is Virgil's Limbo, the region of the ἄωροι, the βιαιοθάνατοι, the untimely dead. Here are those who died in infancy, those who were falsely condemned (with Minos rejudging their cases), those who committed suicide; then in the Fields of Mourning those who died of love, and at the end of the region warriors who died gloriously in battle. The first three divisions are briefly described; then Virgil introduces the Fields of Mourning with a rapid list of seven mythological heroines making little claim on our personal sympathy. The impact is sudden and violent when he continues:

> inter quas Phoenissa recens a uulnere Dido
> errabat silua in magna. (6. 450–1)

Aeneas speaks to the dim phantom in terms which take us back in the most compelling way to the fourth book with reminiscences of thought and diction: *infelix Dido* (6. 456, 4. 596), *inuitus regina* (6. 460. 4. 361), *sed me iussa deum* (6. 461, 4. 396), and finally (with powerful irony) Aeneas' words *quem fugis?* (6. 466) recall Dido's *mene fugis?* (4. 314). Dido makes no reply, as the ghost of Ajax in Homer had made none to Odysseus, and turning from Aeneas in hatred goes to join Sychaeus. Aeneas tries to follow her—

> prosequitur lacrimis longe et miseratur euntem. (6. 476)

At this moment he is looking back to the sorrows and tragedy of the past, not forward to the glory of Rome.

In the region of the famous warriors Virgil again gives a long list of well-known names before concentrating our attention upon one. Three heroes of the Theban saga are mentioned, then eight Trojans, none of them strongly particularized; then a host of Greeks, turning to flight with feeble cries, like the faint phantoms of the Homeric Underworld. And now again after the crowd scenes the light turns on to one single figure—Deiphobus. He has not himself played the large part in the story

named. He is first named in Hes. *Theog.* 311. By Virgil's time he was very much a figure of literary convention; cf. Hor. *Odes* 2. 13. 33 ff., 3. 11. 15 ff.

of the *Aeneid* which Palinurus and Dido had played: the only previous mention of him was in connection with the burning of his house in Troy (2. 310). But here he stands for the whole of the second book of the *Aeneid*; as Palinurus represents the voyage and Dido the stay in Africa, so Deiphobus represents the events of Troy's last night. He, like Palinurus and Dido, belongs to the past; but his last words as he says farewell to Aeneas take us forward to the future:

i decus, i, nostrum; melioribus utere fatis. (6. 546)

Between Limbo with its ghosts of Aeneas' past and the vision of the unborn future with which the book ends stand the descriptions of Tartarus and Elysium. Virgil's Tartarus is firmly based on the literary tradition: the torments of Tityos, Tantalus, and Sisyphus are described in Homer,[14] and Tartarus as the place of punishment for the great sinners is an essential part of the Underworld in Platonic myth.[15] A fine passage in Lucretius[16] gives the Epicurean rationalization of the myths of Tityos, Tantalus, and Sisyphus, and there are frequent references in Horace's *Odes* to these familiar figures of literature and folklore. Virgil's description is set in the form of a speech by the Sibyl, a method which increases the rhetorical possibilities of a subject naturally suited to the grandiose style. As well as the named sinners the Sibyl tells of groups of people defined by their particular sin. This again is traditional,[17] but here is specially pointed by particular relevance to the Roman world in references to family and civil strife ('hic quibus inuisi fratres ... quique arma secuti impia ... uendidit hic auro patriam ... fixit leges pretio ...'), or to moral turpitude ('fraus innexa clienti ... ob adulterium caesi ... uetitosque hymenaeos').

But the Sibyl hastens Aeneas' steps, the golden bough is presented, and we come into the full light of Elysium. Again there is a Homeric prototype for this passage (the description of the Elysian plain which is the home of those born of gods),[18] but there are Orphic elements too, as is indicated at the beginning by the mention of the Thracian priest (Orpheus, 645) and at the end by the meeting with Musaeus, his disciple; and there are quite marked similarities with Orphic elements in Pindar.[19] Virgil has woven a picture of haunting beauty, using all his metrical skill to make a tone-poem of serenity and peace:

[14] *Od.* 11. 576 ff.
[15] *Phaedo* 113 e, *Gorg.* 526 b.   [16] 3. 978 ff.
[17] Plato, *Phaedo* 113 e, Aristoph. *Frogs* 146 ff.
[18] *Od.* 4. 561 ff.
[19] e.g. *Ol.* 2. 61 ff., *Fragg.* 114, 127 (Bowra).

his demum exactis, perfecto munere diuae,
deuenere locos laetos et amoena uirecta
fortunatorum nemorum sedesque beatas.
largior hic campos aether et lumine uestit
purpureo, solemque suum, sua sidera norunt. (6. 637–41)

Interwoven with the description of Elysium are two lists of its inhabitants. First come the names of the greatest Trojan heroes of the past, those who have made possible the national achievement of Rome soon to be prophesied by Anchises. Secondly there are the unnamed people whose place is won by their special qualities. These lines deliberately recall by contrast the list of sinners in Tartarus (608 ff.). The emphasis here is not on initiation or ritual, but on moral qualities. There are those who were wounded fighting for their country, pure priests, poets devoted to their art, those who enriched human life by discoveries, and (a very wide category indeed, in no way exclusive) those who made people remember them by their service—'quique sui memores aliquos fecere merendo'. Here is the note of hope, the prospect for the good of a life of bliss in the hereafter. Homer's Elysian plain was exclusively for those of divine birth; Virgil's groves of the blessed are open to all human beings who by their virtue have deserved to be in paradise.

When Musaeus leads Aeneas to Anchises the journey through the Underworld is concluded, and we come to the final section of the book, the revelation in search of which the journey has been made. Aeneas is still at this moment a person involved in his past, somewhat bewildered and uncertain. Anchises' first words to him reveal the anxiety which he had felt as he watched his son's groping efforts to fulfil his mission. 'Venisti tandem', he says, 'you are here at last, and the dangers of the journey (*iter durum*) have been overcome by your sense of mission (*pietas*).' 'Quantis iactatum nate periclis', he continues, and 'quam metui ne quid Libyae tibi regna nocerent.' Here is the end of the story of Dido; it is now in the past where it must belong, and the memory of those tragic events is to be muted, though by no means erased, by the prospects and hopes of a new destiny for Troy.

For a little longer the emphasis stays on the human frailty of Aeneas. Anchises' work is done, and his paradise achieved; for Aeneas much remains to be done. The solitude of Aeneas is poignantly presented in the lines from Homer:

ter conatus ibi collo dare bracchia circum;
ter frustra comprensa manus effugit imago,
par leuibus uentis uolucrique simillima somno. (6. 700–2)

We see him still bewildered, asking his father about the ghosts at the
river of Lethe, quite unaware of the mysteries about to be revealed to
him.

Anchises' explanation of the doctrine of purification and rebirth is
very short (twenty-eight lines altogether), and written in a style most
reminiscent of Lucretius, who had expounded his ideas of the world at
much greater length and to a very different effect. The Orphic and
Pythagorean ideas of this passage had to a large extent (though not
wholly) been assimilated in Stoicism, and in several places Anchises'
words are very close to orthodox Stoic belief.[20] The body is thought of as
a tomb in which the soul is temporarily buried; here we have the essence
of the Orphic doctrine made famous by Plato. The body stains and
defiles the soul with its mortal passions and behaviour, and at death
much of this defilement still remains. It is therefore necessary for the
soul to be purified of its taints, by wind or water or fire. During this
process all endure their own selves—*quisque suos patimur manes*—that is,
are conscious of their guilt and sins and have to live with them until they
are purged away. Then all pass through Elysium; a few remain there
while purification is completed (before moving on to the ultimate heaven
of the good), and the rest go to the river of forgetfulness to prepare for
rebirth.

We must dwell for a moment on this passage about Elysium. It has
given rise to great difficulty, and to all sorts of ingenious and unconvincing transpositions and punctuations, and the perusal of Conington's
long and complicated note engenders a feeling of bewilderment, and
makes the faint-hearted ready to accept his conclusion that 'here we
have one of the passages in the *Aeneid* which Virgil left unfinished'. But
the difficulty arises entirely from the false assumption that Elysium here
is the ultimate home of the blessed. The correct interpretation has been
given quite often before and after Conington, but it still has by no means
won the total assent which it deserves. It consists of accepting that Virgil
means what he says in the order in which he has said it: that after
purification by wind, water, or fire all go through Elysium and a few stay
there until the long passage of time (i.e. 10,000 years) completes their

---

[20] Specially Stoic are the *spiritus intus*, the *igneus uigor*; see C. Bailey, *Religion in Virgil*
(Oxford, 1935), pp. 275 ff.

purification and makes them fit to go on from Elysium to their ultimate paradise. The remainder wait 1,000 years in a separate part for rebirth.

> ergo exercentur poenis ueterumque malorum
> supplicia expendunt; aliae panduntur inanes
> suspensae ad uentos, aliis sub gurgite uasto
> infectum eluitur scelus aut exuritur igni.
> quisque suos patimur manes. exinde per amplum
> mittimur Elysium et pauci laeta arua tenemus
> donec longa dies perfecto temporis orbe
> concretam exemit labem, purumque relinquit
> aetherium sensum atque aurai simplicis ignem.
> has omnes, ubi mille rotam uoluere per annos,
> Lethaeum ad fluuium deus euocat agmine magno,
> scilicet immemores supera ut conuexa reuisant
> rursus, et incipiant in corpora uelle reuerti. (6. 739–51)

The idea that Elysium is not the final paradise but the place from which the blessed move on to their ultimate communion with God is suggested in Plato (e.g. *Phaedo* 114 c) and seems to have been frequent in Neo-Platonic and Orphic eschatology. In cosmological terms the soul moved from the air above the earth where it underwent its purification to Elysium the moon, before finally proceeding to the sun, or the pure ether of God.

Why then has so much difficulty been felt about this passage? Because at the end of the *katabasis* Virgil has given the impression that Elysium *is* the ultimate home of the blessed. But this is because Elysium is and must be the end of the journey of the *katabasis*. There is no question of Aeneas and the Sibyl going any farther. The ultimate ether of God cannot be in the Underworld, and in any case Anchises is waiting in Elysium. The requirement of Virgil's art ends at Elysium in the journey, but in the theology it extends further, to the future and final home of the spirit. The viewpoint is different. Just as the static presentation of Limbo (needed for Dido and Deiphobus) does not come into the theology, so Elysium suffices as the ultimate home in the journey, but not in the theology. We often say vaguely that the sixth book of the *Aeneid* is the creation of a poet not the consistent doctrine of a theologian; if the statement is to have any meaning, it is this: that the poetic requirement of the journey (for Aeneas to live again through his past) and the poetic requirement of the doctrine of rebirth (to reveal the future) are each more important to Virgil than the consistency of a single standpoint. We must accept Aeneas' arrival in Elysium after his journey as the end of what has gone before, and Anchises' speech as the beginning of what comes after.

In this speech of Anchises we have the fullest exposition which the *Aeneid* affords of Virgil's religious attitude. The general picture is one of hope after death, one in which virtue is rewarded, one in which the unexplained suffering of this life may find its explanation. The emphasis on mortal life which we see in Homer and early Greek lyric poetry had been challenged from the sixth century onwards by the Orphic idea of an afterlife more real and rewarding than mortal life, and at this point in Book 6 Virgil has brought Aeneas right away from the ideas of the Homeric world of Troy to the spiritual climate of his own Rome.

The doctrine of rebirth thus expounded by Anchises gives a most natural setting for the final section of the book, the patriotic description of the pageant of Roman heroes yet unborn, awaiting their turn by the banks of Lethe. In a certain sense they already exist and as it were pass before us as persons. The impact is therefore more immediate and actual than in either of the other two great patriotic foreshadowings of Roman achievement, the words of Jupiter in *Aen.* 1. 257 f., and the pictures on Aeneas' shield in *Aen.* 8. 626 f. Between the spoken prophecy of Jupiter and the pictorial prophecy of Vulcan comes the cavalcade of the ghosts of the heroes themselves.

Virgil's purpose is to portray, to Aeneas as he reaches his promised land and to his readers at the turning-point in the centre of his poem, the qualities and values of the Roman way of life as exemplified in the heroes of her long history. We can trace the influence of the *exempla*[21] of the philosophical and rhetorical schools; we can observe how Virgil's picture is affected by the carved processions to be seen everywhere in Rome on friezes and monuments of all kinds (for example, Silvius leaning on his spear gives a statuesque impression[22]); but, above all, the method he uses is that of the poet, employing the movement of the verse to explain and emphasize the subject-matter, at one time building up an impression with a rapid grouping of names, at another dwelling for a time in more heightened diction on an individual's achievement, making a unity from a wide variety of emotional and intellectual presentations of the character of Rome.

The pageant begins chronologically with Silvius of Alba, the successor of Ascanius who was born in the forest and gave his name to the

---

[21] As Cicero proudly said (*Off.* 3. 47), 'plena exemplorum est nostra res publica'; cf. also ibid. 1. 61, and the work of Valerius Maximus, which is arranged as a series of *exempla*.

[22] Other pictorial touches are at 722, 779–80, 784 ff., 808, 824–5.

dynasty that ruled in Alba Longa. Next follow in rapid succession Procas, Capys, Numitor, Silvius Aeneas; and the tension begins to rise as we hear of the famous little towns of the Alban confederacy which they were destined to found. Then the movement rises to a crescendo as we come to Romulus, first founder of the city itself, of Rome the great mother-city, *felix prole uirum.* In a strikingly pictorial simile the turret-crowned hills of Rome are compared with the mural crown of Cybele, great mother of the gods, a Trojan deity destined—like Aeneas and his men—to come to Italy. At this point the chronological arrangement is broken, and the crescendo swells to its loudest for Rome's second founder,[23] the Emperor Augustus, who will restore the Golden Age and spread Rome's sway over all the world, over vaster tracts even than Hercules or Bacchus had traversed.[24] And it is here, at this moment of highest emotion, that Anchises breaks off to ask his son whether he still feels any hesitation about continuing his task:

> et dubitamus adhuc uirtute extendere uires
> aut metus Ausonia prohibet consistere terra? (6. 806–7)

Now there will be no more hesitation (as there had been, for instance, in Sicily when the ships were set on fire and Aeneas wondered whether to stay there, forgetting the fates, *oblitus fatorum*). Now Aeneas is strengthened by this vision for the fulfilment of his task, however difficult.

This supreme moment of the pageant passes, and we turn to its continuation. In quick succession follow other kings of early Rome: Numa, Tullus, Ancus, the Tarquins; then the founder of the republic, the proud-hearted[25] Brutus with his inflexible devotion to discipline. Again comes a throng of famous names—Decii, Drusi, Torquatus, Camillus—and then the two great leaders Caesar and Pompey—leaders of civil war.

The theme of Roman guilt is left on an unfinished line—

---

[23] There had been a proposal that Augustus should receive the title Romulus (Suet. *Aug.* 7).

[24] Augustus is thus compared with two of the most famous of deified mortals; cf. Hor. *Odes* 3. 3. 9 f., where Augustus is associated as a god with Pollux, Hercules, Bacchus, Romulus.

[25] The suggested punctuation after *superbam*, so as to give the epithet to Tarquin, is wholly unacceptable. It results in a misplacement of -*que* in the next line which is totally un-Virgilian. In Virgil's presentation of the tradition about Brutus' sons we are not asked to approve or disapprove, but to sympathize. Necessarily some thought of Brutus the conspirator (another *Brutus ultor*) occurs to the reader, but Virgil does not here take up any political position. On the attitude of the early empire to the conspirators see the fine passage in Tac. *Ann.* 4. 34–5.

proice tela manu, sanguis meus... (6. 835)

and we pass again to triumph, this time the triumph of the Trojan-Romans over the Greek world which had so recently destroyed Troy. The victory is stated in terms appropriate to Aeneas' own times: Rome will overcome Argos and Agamemnon's Mycenae and the Macedonian kings descended from Achilles, thus avenging the city of their ancestors. Last of all in the cavalcade comes a torrent of famous names: Cato, Cossus, the Gracchi, the Scipios, Fabricius, Regulus, and finally Fabius Maximus Cunctator. Fabius has the position of honour at the end because he symbolizes Rome's survival against Hannibal, the greatest of all her enemies, and he exorcizes the memory of Dido's 'exoriare aliquis nostris ex ossibus ultor'. His achievement is described in the well-known phrases of Ennius,[26] a quotation which deepens and completes the sense of antiquity and tradition which characterizes the whole passage.

Now Anchises sums up Rome's mission in seven famous lines:

> excudent alii spirantia mollius aera
> (credo equidem), uiuos ducent de marmore uultus,
> orabunt causas melius, caelique meatus
> describent radio et surgentia sidera dicent:
> tu regere imperio populos, Romane, memento
> (hae tibi erunt artes), pacique imponere morem,
> parcere subiectis et debellare superbos. (847–53)

The Greeks are not named, so obvious is it that they are the people whose intellectual and artistic achievements are described in the first four lines; their contribution to the Greco-Roman culture of the time of Augustus is admitted to be supreme in sculpture, oratory, and astronomy. It is interesting to set this passage against the words of Cicero at the beginning of the *Tusculan Disputations* Looking back, he says 'the Greeks surpassed the Romans intellectually and in all branches of literature' ('doctrina Graecia nos et omni litterarum genere superabant'; he adds that this was because 'we weren't trying', 'in quo erat facile uincere non repugnantes'), 'and in music, painting, geometry, and mathematics. The Romans have been superior in practical and ethical qualities' (*mores, instituta uitae, leges, res militaris, grauitas, constantia, magnitudo animi, probitas, fides*, 'ethical character, institutions of life, laws, military achievements, dignity, fortitude, greatness of spirit,

---

[26] Quoted by Cicero (*Off.* 1. 84 and *Sen.* 10) and by Livy (30. 26. 9). Servius wisely says 'sciens quasi pro exemplo hunc uersum posuit'.

integrity, loyalty'). But of oratory (which Virgil has singled out to concede to the Greeks) Cicero makes an exception—'we have had such great orators that we yielded hardly at all, if at all, to the Greeks' ('ut non multum aut nihil omnino Graecis cederetur'). Whether Cicero was including himself or not—he does not actually mention himself, the words are 'inde ita magnos nostram ad aetatem'—there is some truth in his claim, and oratory is the branch of literature which comes closest to the arts of government and law at which the Romans claimed to be outstanding. Nevertheless, Virgil concedes literature, along with the fine arts, symbolized by sculpture, and the theoretical sciences, symbolized by astronomy; and against these arts he sets the Roman achievements, using the word *artes* of his own countrymen to denote a different contribution to civilized life which may balance, or indeed outweigh, the others. The Roman 'arts' will be those of government and empire, of conquest and just rule, of settled organization (*morem*) and peace. *Pacique imponere morem*: 'to add to peace a settled way of life'. The old reading here, *pacisque imponere morem*, 'to impose the habit of peace', must now be finally discarded, partly because there are parallels for this moral meaning of the singular of *mos*,[27] and partly because the last prop of the reading *pacis*, the alleged support of Servius, has been knocked away by Professor E. Fraenkel, who has shown that Servius' comment does not after all imply that he read *pacis*.[28] *Pax* then and *mos*; the nature of the mission both of Aeneas and of the Roman people is here presented very clearly in its bipartite form. The first task is to conquer in war, and the second to establish a peace in which the people are ruled with mercy and given the benefits of Roman civilization and settled ways of life. Here is the concept—no doubt imperfectly realized, but very real always in Roman thought—which could lead Claudian four centuries later to write of Rome: 'This is the only nation which has received conquered people in her embrace, and protected the human race under a common name like a mother not a tyrant, has called those whom she defeated her citizens, and has united the distant parts of the world in a bond of affection for her':

> haec est in gremium uictos quae sola recepit,
> humanumque genus communi nomine fouit
> matris non dominae ritu, ciuesque uocauit
> quos domuit nexuque pio longinqua reuinxit
>
> (*De Consolatu Stilichonis*, 3. 150–3)

[27] e.g. *Aen.* 8. 316, 'quis neque mos neque cultus erat'.
[28] *Museum Helveticum* 19 (1962), 133.

Anchises' description of the aims and ideals of Augustan Rome summarizes and seemingly concludes the pageant, but there follows, as a sort of pendant (*haec mirantibus addit*), a passage of tribute, a sort of funeral panegyric, for the young Marcellus, a possible successor to Augustus, who died at the age of eighteen in 23 BC. The note of sorrow is introduced at a most triumphant part of the poem, just as at the end of Book 11 at the moment when Aeneas completes his mission we are made to think not of the mission but of the death of his courageous adversary:

> ast illi soluuntur frigore membra
> uitaque cum gemitu fugit indignata sub umbras. (12. 951–2)

Success and failure, life and death, triumph and defeat, joy and sorrow; this is the equipoise of the *Aeneid*.

The book now ends quickly, without further detail and with no scenes of farewell. Anchises tells Aeneas what he must do in Italy, fires his mind with a passion for the glory which awaits him, and sends him back to earth by the ivory gate. There is a long literary tradition of the twin gates of sleep, horn for true shades and ivory for false, and their significance in Virgil has been much discussed.[29] At the simplest we may say that Virgil uses the traditional imagery solely to construct a closing scene, to provide a method of exit as the cave at Avernus was the method of entry; and that Aeneas goes out by the ivory gate because he is not a true shade. But most readers will feel that more is meant, perhaps that Aeneas leaves the Underworld having learned much but not all, perhaps that the religious revelation is dim and groping, based on hope not faith, far indeed from the gloom and tenuous ghosts of Homer, but far too from the certainty of religious conviction upon which Milton's *Paradise Lost* is built; perhaps above all that it has been in a sense the dream of Aeneas, personal to himself. He has journeyed again through his past, and learned to look forwards not backwards, and has seen something of the future. In his journey towards Elysium he moved in the gloom of a Homeric afterlife; with his father in Elysium he saw dimly a new kind of world-order, both spiritual and temporal. That is why the two parts of his experience in the Underworld are different and even in some ways contradictory: he moves from one to the other.

Let us begin with Homer, Quintilian said, and most certainly the *Aeneid* takes its origin from the vivid pictures of human life and activity

[29] For a first-rate brief summary of views and an excellent conclusion see Brooks Otis, op. cit. 173 ff.

which Virgil loved to read about in the *Iliad* and the *Odyssey*, with which his narrative is chronologically contemporary. But this is the life which Aeneas must leave behind in order to be the pioneer of a new kind of civilization. At the beginning of the *Aeneid* we see him again and again in the situation of Odysseus, but with a different task before him. Odysseus returns to the old life, but Aeneas must journey out into the new; he must learn to move from the Homeric world into a complex Roman world of new values and social responsibilities, in accordance with a still imperfectly understood divine destiny. And so here in Book 6, at the centre of the poem, he takes his final leave of the Trojan and Homeric past and turns towards the Roman future.

Aeneas & Odysseus ✓ Ultimately are more similar than different because as Odysseus leaves the underworld to return to his old life Aeneas must find his new one.

⟶ Aeneas leaves the Trojan & Homeric past

The World of the Dead in Book 6 of the *Aeneid*

FRIEDRICH SOLMSEN

When Eduard Norden's famous commentary on the Sixth Book of the *Aeneid* was published in 1903,[1] it was customary to posit two main sources for Virgil's 'Underworld' and, in correspondence with the postulated sources, to divide the description itself into two main parts. The first half of the account was called 'popular' or 'mythological'; the second, 'philosophical'. Disagreement was confined to the question whether the sinners in Tartarus and the pious in Elysium (548–665) should be included in the former or in the latter part. Norden himself, after some wavering, sided with Albrecht Dieterich and decided in favour of the philosophical (or 'theological') source as Virgil's authority for the categories of the sinners and the blessed, mentioning the eschatological myths of Plato and Plutarch as the kind of source he had in mind.[2]

More recently, a different view has gained ground. Instead of dividing Virgil's account into two main parts, the new theory distinguishes three phases: a mythological or Homeric, a moral, and a philosophical Underworld. The idea of these three distinct 'Underworlds' may be traced to A. Cartault's book on the *Aeneid*.[3] Lately it has found its most strenuous champions in Frances Norwood and Brooks Otis.[4] Unlike

---

[1] *P. Vergilius Maro, Aeneis Buch VI*[3] (Leipzig and Berlin, 1926).

[2] Ibid. 10 ff. (see also p. 10 for references to earlier studies); A. Dieterich, *Nekyia* (Leipzig, 1893), pp. 150 ff. H. E. Butler in the Intro. (pp. 19–36) to his *Sixth Book of the Aeneid* (London, 1920) seems today closer to Norden than he himself thought at the time of publication. He is equally generous in tracing much of Virgil's material to 'Orphic' sources although more restrained on the question of Posidonius' influence (p. 33 and n. 3).

[3] *L'Art de Virgile dans l'Énéide* (Paris, 1926), pp. 461 and n. 1, 474 f., 490 f. C. Bailey, *Religion in Virgil* (Oxford, 1935), approximates the scheme in his analysis, see esp. pp. 270 ff., 273 ff.

[4] F. Norwood, 'The Tripartite Eschatology of *Aeneid* VI', *CP* 49 (1954), 15 ff.; B. Otis, *Virgil: A Study in Civilized Poetry* (Oxford, 1963), pp. 289 ff. P. Boyancé, *La Religion de Virgile* (Paris, 1963), p. 156, distinguishes 'trois grandes parties' without identifying them clearly.

earlier scholars, the proponents of this theory do not worry about inconsistencies among the different phases; still less do they censure Virgil for his failure to remove them. To Mrs Norwood, the discrepancies are evidence that it is a mistake to 'integrate' the phases; Virgil's intention was not to present an extrinsically unified picture but rather three pictures, each somehow complete in itself and existing in its own right. The three phases correspond to the distinction made by the pontifex Scaevola between the religion of the citizen, the poet, and the philosopher; they satisfy in turn the primitive, the moral, and the rational or philosophical facet of man's nature.[5] For Otis, what matters most is the significance of the three divisions in Virgil's overall artistic and philosophic scheme. He regards the mythological Hades as oriented toward Aeneas' past; the philosophical, in which he, unlike Mrs Norwood, includes the great vision of Rome's history, toward the future. Tartarus and Elysium, though for him too the second main division, are 'summarily treated and constitute an obviously secondary part of the narrative'; still, they illustrate the rule of Justice, an idea by which Virgil must have set great store.[6]

Undeniably, this tripartite division has its attractions. Some impressions and observations advanced in its support are not open to dispute. It may seem obvious, for example, that in 540 ff., before the description of Tartarus, something new is announced, and that the meeting with Anchises leads up to revelations of great significance. In fact, the tripartite structure may acquire additional support from the historical development of Greek conceptions regarding man's fate after death that underlie this scheme.

Mrs Norwood labels the first division (295?–547) as 'Homeric', and it doubtless corresponds to the Underworld of the Homeric *nekyia* in *Odyssey* 11. For—if we except *Od.* 11. 568–600 (on which presently)— there is no mention in it of punishment or reward; the characters are ἀμενηνὰ κάρηνα, neither acting nor suffering; in the absence of new experiences, they dwell on what happened to them while they were alive. All this is in accord with the 'Homeric' section of *Aeneid* 6. For us, Book 11 of the *Odyssey* is the only literary document to embody

[5] Norwood, op. cit., 18. *Religio civilis* (as defined after Varro in Aug. *Civ. Dei* 6. 5, 254. 14 Dombart-Kalb) cannot be equated with Tartarus and Elysium, nor should I consider the Homeric section 'a world which a savage could understand perfectly'. These, however, are minor infelicities. On the inconsistencies and contradictions in the Virgilian Underworld, I find myself in complete agreement with Mrs Norwood's approach.

[6] See esp. pp. 297 ff.

this stage of Greek beliefs regarding the hereafter. We need not here discuss the probability that there were other *katabaseis* of the same type.

Odyssey 11. 568–600, however, which includes the ordeals of Tityus, Tantalus, and Sisyphus, is conceived in a different spirit;[7] and even though the motif of punishment is here confined to a few mythical figures of exceptional hubris, we have a right to look upon it as heralding a new outlook, the second of the three stages that we distinguish. The idea of punishment and reward after death used to be associated in particular with the Orphic movement.[8] In the present stage of research, it is difficult—and perhaps unnecessary—to trace it to a specific group, although mysteries and itinerant prophets doubtless played a role in propagating these beliefs. Everybody is familiar with the reflections of this view in Pindar, in Aristophanes' *Frogs*, and in Platonic myths.[9] Conceivably, the bliss in Elysium or the Islands of the Blessed was originally promised only to those who had earned it by participating in certain strictly defined rituals; the extension to the ἐσθλοί (good) or the εὐσεβεῖς (pious) may be a secondary development.[10] We do not know at what time groups or categories began to be set up both for those who merited Elysium and for the wicked whose conduct consigned them to Tartarus. The poetic *katabasis* recently discovered on a papyrus,[11] which includes an extensive listing of categories on both sides, seems to have originated in the Hellenistic centuries; yet, while the categories are likely to have fluctuated from one account to the next, the idea of classifying the sinners and the elect must go back to an earlier period, at least to the fifth century. The newly found poem has one category in common with Virgil (besides others that are close to his); for, as Max Treu has pointed out, the words αἴ (sc. ψυχαί) δὲ βίον σοφίῃσιν

---

[7] The section has in ancient as well as modern times been considered foreign to the original conception of the *nekyia*; see the excellent discussion in D. Page, *The Homeric Odyssey* (Oxford, 1955), pp. 25 ff. and 50; see also G. S. Kirk, *The Songs of Homer* (Cambridge, 1962), pp. 236 f.

[8] Wilamowitz at one time went so far as to declare the sufferers in *Od.* 11 an 'Orphic interpolation' (*Homerische Untersuchungen* (Berlin, 1884), pp. 149 ff., 199 ff.).

[9] Passages of importance are *Hymn. Hom. Cer.* 480 ff.; Aesch. *Suppl.* 230 ff.; Pind. *O.* 2. 61 ff.; Aristoph. *Ran.* 145 ff., 355 ff.; Plato *Phaed.* 69 C, *Rep.* 363 C f., 364 E; and the 'reflections' in Plato's own myths at the end of *Gorg.*, *Phaed.*, and *Rep.*

[10] Compare from this point of view *Hymn. Hom. Cer.* 480–2 with Pind. *O.* 2. 61 ff. and Frag. 129 Snell as introduced by Plut. *De lat. viv.* 1130 C. On *O.* 2. 61 ff., see my note in *Hermes* 96 (1968), 503 ff.

[11] For all purposes the *editio princeps* of the poem is R. Merkelbach's in *Mus. Helv.* 8 (1951), 2 ff.; see esp. cols. II^r., III^r. Cf. also the illuminating discussion of M. Treu in *Hermes* 82 (1954), 24 ff.

ἐκόσμεον ('[the souls] who enhanced life with skills') parallel Virgil's 'inventas aut qui vitam excoluere per artes' (663).[12]

Finally, what we may call the third historical stage is characterized by its focusing on the soul as the surviving and eternal part of man, by its concomitant insistence on a fundamental difference between the soul and the body, and—in its early phases at least—by its belief in reincarnations. There are good reasons for agreeing with the current opinion which considers Pythagoras as the thinker who established these beliefs.[13] It is unnecessary to discuss the influence of this outlook on Plato's thought, or the appeal which the doctrine of the soul as a separate entity and its immortality exerted in later centuries; still less need we rehearse the varying definitions and conceptions of the soul in the philosophical schools. Whether or not they accepted the idea of successive incorporations, it was the fate of the soul that was of primary concern for the intellectuals and perhaps even for wider circles.[14]

No effort is required to correlate these three stages in the development of Greek thought with the tripartite division of Greek thought with the tripartite division of Virgil's account. Each of the three historical stages is somehow more 'mature' than the preceding one, offering a fuller and more meaningful answer to the question of man's destiny. By embodying the answers in a sequence which corresponds to their successive emergence in the course of Greek speculation, Virgil seems to lead us to ever higher degrees of clarity and understanding; Aeneas and the reader are given a progressive initiation (the τέλεια and ἐποπτικά, 'the final and full mysteries', materializing in Anchises' revelation). This impression cannot be entirely wrong;[15] yet the support

[12] Treu, op. cit., 25, equates col. III[r]. 7 with *Aen.* 6. 663; for other similarities see Merkelbach's annotations on I[r]., II[r]., and III[r]. I should take the view that Virgil knew specimens of this literature but not necessarily this particular poem. See, however, Boyancé, op. cit. (n. 4), pp. 158 f., 163 f.

[13] Cf. esp. W. Burkert, *Weisheit und Wissenschaft: Studien zu Pythagoras* (Nuremberg, 1962), pp. 98 ff.; K. von Fritz, *s.v. Pythagoras, RE* 47 (1963), 187 ff.; J. A. Philip, *Pythagoras and early Pythagoreanism* (Toronto, 1966), pp. 153 ff.; H. S. Long, *A Study of the Doctrine of Metempsychosis in Greece* (Princeton, 1948), pp. 13 ff.

[14] The developments as such are familiar, and we cannot here attempt a listing of the countless studies dealing with the conception of the soul in Plato, Stoicism (Posidonius?), later Platonism, etc. There seems to be no synoptic treatment comparable to the final chapter in E. Rohde's *Psyche*[2] (Freiburg, 1897), pp. 263 ff.

[15] Cf. my study, 'Greek Ideas of the Hereafter in Virgil's Roman Epic', *PAPhS* 112 (1968), 8 ff. P. Boyancé, in a fine paper (*REL* 32 (1954), 248) takes a somewhat different line, speaking of 'corrections' which the speech of Anchises makes to the earlier Homeric picture of the Underworld. I am sceptical regarding Treu's attempt (op. cit., 37 ff.) to find in the newly discovered poem a section (III[r].) comparable to Anchises' revelation. Even if souls arrive without the 'garment of the body' (III[r]. 8; cf. Emped. B 126), it remains

which the three stages of Greek thought lend to the tripartite scheme is deceptive. The three stages have a bearing on the question of Virgil's sources rather than on his own organization of what these sources presented. To be sure, both Mrs Norwood and Otis deprecate an excessive interest in Virgil's sources and try to keep their path clear of its disturbing interference.[16] Should they nevertheless have done more for the reconstruction of Virgil's sources than for the understanding of his own work? Or does the condition of the sources, and thereby the stages of Greek thought which these sources represent, shine through his own design? Should one structural scheme be superimposed upon another? Attractive and fashionable as this hypothesis may be, if put to the test, it does for some hundreds of lines neither harm nor good and in the end breaks down at the same point where the tripartite scheme itself comes to grief. When at 540 ff., the Sybil speaks of the places 'partis ubi se via findit in ambas', one road leading to Tartarus, the other to Elysium, the reader may think of these two regions as complementary. So they ought to be, with or without tripartite scheme. Still, the fact remains that at 637–8 ('his demum exactis ... devenere locos laetos') we pass abruptly from the world of sadness and horror into a totally different one of bliss and joy.

The situation is deceptive also in the case of a specific motif which appears on all three levels and is invoked by Mrs Norwood to strengthen her thesis.[17] Each of the three divisions includes a judgment or something akin to a judgment. Using some of her observations, we may put the matter briefly as follows: in the mythological or Homeric Hades, Minos acts as judge. He does so also in the *Odyssey*, yet in Virgil his functions are somewhat different: he assigns to the shades their 'places'.[18] For there is somewhat better and clearer order than in Homer; each of the groups that Aeneas meets has its *loca*. In the 'second phase', Rhadamanthys has his *durissima regna*, administering justice in Tartarus; he forces the sinners to confess and hands them over to their

doubtful whether rain and hail (III'. 9–11) have a purifying function, and there is nothing of a broader cosmological vision (see Treu himself, p. 39).

[16] Norwood, op. cit., 16; Otis, op. cit., 290 n. 1. Otis's critique of Norden (ibid.) strikes me as rather 'anachronistic'. A book of 1903 cannot be expected to apply critical methods in vogue sixty years later. Moreover, Norden's very sensitive stylistic observations do much to enhance our perception of the poetic qualities.

[17] Op. cit., 17. The pertinent passages are 431–5, 566–9, and 739–51.

[18] I infer this from 431, 'nec vero hae ... datae sine iudice sedes', although I understand Bailey's doubts (op. cit., 254 f.); for *crimina discit* (433) suggests a different function. Probably Virgil was familiar with divergent traditions, which he did not reconcile; yet the explanations offered by Butler, op. cit., *ad* v. 431, seem extravagant.

torturers. Finally, in the 'philosophical Hades', there seems to be no individual or personal judge (except for the *deus* of 749 who calls souls to the river Lethe). It is made abundantly clear, however, that each soul expiates its *mala* and is after death treated in accordance with its record: everybody has his individual *manes* (this much we understand from 743). Again, however, what looks like an argument in support of the tripartite division is delusive and will on closer examination reveal the fatal flaw of this theory.

The crucial question may be whether we are entitled to place a major break at (or near) 679, where Aeneas finds his father somewhat apart from the other inhabitants of Elysium. But before we come to this point, it will be well to consider briefly the preceding sections, going some of the way with the sponsors of the tripartite scheme. On the first of the three divisions, they offer somewhat divertent opinions. Otis speaks of the 'Mythological Hades'; Mrs Norwood, of the 'Homeric Under-world'. Otis places the beginning of this section at 264; Cartault, at 426, after the crossing of the Styx; Mrs Norwood appears to waver. The divergences are not fatal to their theory; still, no matter which version we favour, we cannot close our eyes to the fact that the population of the regions traversed by Aeneas is far from homogeneous. The Palinurus episode (337–83) has so much in common with the Elpenor episode of the *Odyssey* (11. 51–80) that we can hardly exclude it from the 'Homeric Hades'. Yet Charon and Cerberus,[19] who do not appear in the *nekyia*, introduce something new and strange into the Homeric atmosphere. Moreover, Aeneas, before finding himself securely on Homeric ground, meets some other most unattractive denizens of the Underworld. At the very entrance (*vestibulum ante ipsum*), there are *Luctus, Curae, Morbi, Senectus, Metus, Fames, Discordia*, and other utterly un-Homeric entities (273–84). We can understand how they came to be here. For ghosts, the Underworld is the natural habitat. Even in the *nekyia*, Odysseus fears that he might encounter the Γοργείη κεφαλή, 'Gordon's head' (634); in the *Frogs* (285 ff.), Dionysus does meet the Empusa. Moreover, the Hesiodic *Theogony* places Night and two of her children, Sleep and Death, in the Underworld. With this precedent it would be natural for the poets of *katabaseis* to transfer more of Night's unpleasant offspring, as listed in the *Theogony*, to these dark abodes.[20] To sum up, Aeneas has

---

[19] Charon, 385 ff. (298 ff.); Cerberus, 417 ff. Charon is attested for the *Minyas* (Frag. 1 Kinkel), a somewhat mysterious epic; hence, according to Pausanias (10. 28. 7), his presence on the famous picture of Polygnotus.
[20] Cf. Norden, op. cit., 213; Butler, op. cit., ad loc. See Hes. *Theog.* 746–66, and for the catalogue of Night's children, which has many items in common with Virgil, *Theog.* 211–

to face an assortment of frightening, ghost-like sights before he enters the Homeric Hades with its human population.

As for this Hades, it is well known that just as the Palinurus episode is inspired by the Elpenor episode of the *nekyia*, so the Dido episode is modelled on Odysseus' meeting with Ajax and the horrifying tale of Deiphobus on Agamemnon's similar report about the treachery of his wife.[21] What differs in these scenes is the result partly of intervening developments in Greek poetry, partly of Virgil's own creativity. Thus, while in the meeting with Dido attitudes and gestures parallel those of the *nekyia*, the feelings are far more delicate and the effect is far more disturbing. This is Virgil's own poetic achievement; yet that Dido and other heroines known for unhappy love find themselves in a myrtle grove is probably a motif of Hellenistic poetry, which, being deeply interested in erotic subjects, would have treated the sorrow (*curae*) of these heroines with more sympathy than did the author of the *nekyia*.[22] There is one notable departure from the Homeric paradigm: unlike Odysseus, who converses at length with Achilles, Ajax, and Agamemnon, Aeneas does not meet any of the outstanding Trojan warriors. There is no Hector, no Polydamas, not even a Paris or a Sarpedon. The *multum fleti* (481) Trojans to whom Aeneas gives much time (yet Virgil remarkably little, 481–8) are rather undistinguished individuals. However, instead of speculating about Virgil's motives for this innovation, let us rather note with Mrs Norwood[23] that all characters in this part of the Underworld are preoccupied with the experiences in their life on Earth; recollection of these determines their mood and actions. (This is true even of 489–93, where the Greek warriors, instinctively obeying the impulse of fear, take to flight, an episode which the ancient reader need not have considered an interlude of comic relief.)

What matters next, in Tartarus and Elysium, is not life as lived and experienced by the individuals but as judged by a higher power. Crime is punished and merit rewarded. But is there in this respect no difference

---

32. δείματα, 'objects of fear?' (whatever this word may mean) in Hades are attested for the *Nostoi* and the *Minyas* (Paus. 10. 28. 7).

[21] Cf., after many other scholars, Otis, op. cit., 292. Boyancé, op. cit. (n. 4), p. 151, who deals interestingly with philosophical interpretations of the Homeric Hades, considers Virgil as influenced by these interpretations and feels entitled to speak of an 'accord' between the mythical and the philosophical life after death.

[22] Cf. Otis's perceptive observations, op. cit., 292, on differences between Virgil's treatment and his models; for the myrtle grove, see Norden, op. cit., 250, and Butler, op. cit., *ad* vv. 440–76.

[23] Op. cit., 18 (see also p. 19 on the different conception of Tartarus).

between Tartarus and Elysium? We should, at this point, be in the second division of the tripartite scheme. Like Pindar, like the Greek *katabaseis*, including the newly found poem, and like Plato in his myths, Virgil too brings out the contrast between the population of these two regions, chiefly by means of the classes or categories of which we have spoken. On the one side are '... quibus invisi fratres dum vita manebat ... aut qui divitiis soli incubuere repertis ... quique ob adulterium caesi', *et al.*; on the other, 'quique sacerdotes casti dum vita manebat, / quique pii vates et Phoebo digna locuti, ... quique sui memores alios fecere merendo'.[24] Since the discovery of the papyrus, we know even more definitely that this technique is a traditional form. The contrast is bound to be felt by the reader, but what is its function in Virgil's own design? Does it serve to pull Tartarus and Elysium together or to set them far apart?

Before we reach the five lines (660–4) which enumerate the classes of the elect, we have been transported into surroundings far more beautiful than anything on Earth—and the complete opposite of all that we have seen or heard before. Surely at 637 f., 'his demum exactis ... devenere locos laetos et amoena virecta', we are passing from one world and one atmosphere into another, diametrically different one. We leave behind the realm of sadness and horror and enter the realm of bliss; from 'loca lenta situ, nox profunda, tristes sine sole domus, loca turbida',[25] and the even more appalling places of punishment and torture, we move on to *loci laeti* resplendent with the light of sun and stars. There is a definite break at 637; a sharp dividing line cuts across the section 548–678, which the current theory happily treats as a unit, making it the second main division in its tripartite scheme.

We must beware of putting one hard and fast scheme in the place of another. Yet Elysium is, after all, the goal of Aeneas' wanderings through Hades. It is here that he was bidden to find his father (5. 734 ff.). The verses 'largior hic campos aether et lumine vestit / purpureo; solemque suum, sua sidera norunt' (640–1), give our emotions and our imagination a radically new orientation. The *strepitus Acherontis avari* is *sub pedibus*; we are no longer in the Underworld. The opposition of past and future, on which Otis lays much stress, is less conspicuous than the opposition of darkness and light.[26]

[24] 608–14, 621–4, 660–4.
[25] 462, 534; cf. 268 ff.
[26] Otis, op. cit., 293 ff., 296, and 297. The importance of the opposition between darkness and light is recognized by Mrs Norwood, op. cit., 20. Cf. also K. Büchner, *s.v.*

The horrors of Tartarus are in no way lessened—in fact they become more concentrated and intense—by being reported in the speech of the Sibyl. (If Aeneas had gone from one sufferer to the next, learning about the crime and fate of each, the effect would not be the same.)[27] The gruesome story of Deiphobus' maltreatment may have been deliberately placed last in the Homeric Hades, to form a kind of prelude to greater terrors. But now at 637, a happy and relaxed atmosphere envelops us. The style is sublime, conveying the assurance of undisturbed enjoyment. All that is pleasant in life is here preserved; all imperfections are absent.

After once entering Elysium we never in Book 6 leave it. The revelation about the fate of the souls as well as the vision of Rome's greatness are presented in Elysium. It is true that Anchises has his place somewhat apart from the other heroes and groups whom Aeneas sees on arriving in this region. Still, the Sibyl has every right to expect Anchises in the *amoena piorum concilia*.[28] With the exception of Orpheus and Musaeus—figures most appropriate to Elysium—the only individuals mentioned as present (650) are 'Ilusque Assaracusque et Troiae Dardanus auctor', Trojans of earlier generations and by this token the obvious company in which to look for Anchises. In fact, since Anchises calls the heroes of Roman history to whom he introduces his son 'Dardania proles' and 'animae nostrum(que) in nomen iturae' (756, 758),[29] continuity extending from *Ilus(que) Assaracusque . . .* to Anchises and beyond him to the future leaders of Rome would seem to be more important than the opposition between past and future.

For the separate place in Elysium which Virgil has assigned to Anchises various reasons may be suggested, but it suffices that we have not passed outside the confines of Elysium. As Musaeus helping Aeneas and the Sibyl to find Anchises says (673), there is in Elysium *nulli certa domus* (whereas in the 'Homeric' Hades specific *sedes* were assigned,

Vergilius, *RE*, ser. 2, 16 (1958), 1388; and J. Perret, *Virgile* (Paris, 1965), pp. 114 f., who combines the two oppositions and seems to recognize the change of atmosphere after Tartarus.

[27] I am unable to agree with Otis's judgement (see above, p. 209) regarding the 'secondary importance' or 'summary' treatment of Tartarus and Elysium. The unparalleled ὕψος attained in 577 ff., 585–94, 617–20, and 625–7 makes it impossible to take this view. See also Boyancé, op. cit. (n. 4), pp. 158 f. Cf. A. Ruegg, *Die Jenseitsvorstellungen vor Dante* (Einsiedeln, 1945), i. 149.

[28] See again 5. 734 ff. Not only the appearance of Anchises at 5. 721 ff., but the whole of Book 5, has, if possible, heightened even more the authority which he possesses throughout the first half of the *Aeneid*.

[29] Cf. also 681 ff., 716 ff.

431 ff.). For the rest, we gladly recognize that the 'animae superum(que) ad lumen iturae', which Anchises is found contemplating at 680, introduce a new topic and that their mention here is intended to lead up to another and final revelation about man's life and death. We shall presently study the devices by which we gradually reach this final knowledge. First, however, we may note that Anchises' revelation about the fate of the souls includes the sojourn in Elysium[30] but knows nothing of Tartarus. For if the souls too receive 'punishments' (*exercentur poenis,* 739), they are utterly different from those in Tartarus. As described in 739–42, they are actually purifications, and they are temporary, not— like those in Tartarus—eternal. Conversely, as Mrs Norwood has quite correctly observed, 'The judgment of Rhadamanthys (566–7) is confined to the guilty who are destined for Tartarus';[31] it does not at all extend to Elysium. Unlike the judges in the myth of Plato's *Gorgias* (523 B, 523 E f.),[32] Rhadamanthys does not send some souls to the one, others to the other place. If the tripartite scheme has so many holes, it cannot be the last word on Virgil's own composition. He knows the three conceptions of the hereafter but he uses, modifies, and interconnects them for his own purposes. What is preserved of the contrast between Tartarus and Elysium conveys a more fundamental dualism; and, where this contrast is not preserved, we may find our clues for Virgil's own design and original creativity.

In the relevation itself, Platonic and Stoic motifs are combined with others of a different, less philosophical cast, e.g. that souls 'panduntur inanes (!) suspensae ad ventos'.[33] Still, the substance is definitely Platonic; the idea that *noxia corpora tardant* (*sc.* the souls) and the lines in which Anchises, speaking of the temporary association of souls with bodies, explains 'hinc metuunt cupiuntque dolent gaudentque' (733 ff.), inevitably remind us of the *Phaedo*.[34] However, in this instance, it does

[30] See below, p. 218.
[31] Op. cit., 20. Cf. also Bailey, op. cit., 272, 274; Boyancé, op. cit. (n. 4), pp. 165 f.; see above, pp. 212–13.
[32] Cf. also *Rep.* 614 C, *Phaed.* 113 D ff. (although this passage provides for additional differentiations).
[33] 740–1; the closest parallel I know is Plut. *De gen.* 590 B, where the soul is 'spread out' (ἐκπετανvυμένη) like a sail.
[34] *Phaed.* 65 B ff.; cf. also 81 A, 82 B, 82 C, 83 B ff. Cf. Servius *ad* v. 703; Butler, op. cit., *ad* v. 733 (see also P. Boyancé, *Études sur le songe de Scipion* (Paris, 1936), pp. 126 ff.). Otis, op. cit., 300, says correctly that Virgil could find most of the thoughts in Plato's own myths or in others written in imitation of them. However, the idea of the *spiritus* (725 ff.), the *igneus vigor* in the σπέρματα, 'seeds' (730 f.), and the words used in 747 suggest a concept of ψυχή, 'soul', quite different from Plato's immaterial soul. For a Stoic component, cf. Bailey, op. cit., 265, 275 ff., who rightly refers to *Geo.* 4. 219 ff.; and

not suffice to name Virgil's (proximate or ultimate) source. For such thoughts are bound to acquire a new meaning when from a philosophical work written to deprecate man's emotional nature they are transferred to an epic in which almost every episode shows human beings in the grip of desire or hope, fear or grief. Here for once we rise above this view of life, so natural for a poem in the Homeric tradition and so deepened by Virgil's συμπάσχειν (sympathy) with his characters, and are taught to regard all experiences of the kind as part of man's mortal nature, not of his true being.

After expounding how the souls are in water, air, and fire cleansed of the evils contracted in the body—the stage which corresponds to the Christian purgatory[35]—Anchises continues, 'exinde per amplum / mittimur Elysium et pauci laeta arva tenemus' (743–4; only here, where he mentions Elysium, does Anchises speak in the first person).[36] However, the sojourn in Elysium is not the final condition of the souls. As becomes clear in the next lines ('donec longa dies perfecto temporis orbe / concretam exemit labem purumque relinquit / aetherium sensum atque aurai simplicis ignem', 745 ff.), for the *pauci* the purification continues in Elysium until their souls have regained their pristine nature and are again identical with the aether spirit, i.e. the (Stoic) *pneuma* which, as we have learned, keeps the world and all its parts in being.[37] All other souls

Boyancé, op. cit. (n. 4), pp. 167 f., who reckons with Antiochus of Ascalon and Varro (cf. Servius *ad* v. 703) as intermediaries.

[35] See St Augustine's comments (*Civ. Dei* 21. 13, in a discussion of this Virgilian passage) on the difference between the *purgatoriae poenae* of the Platonists and of the Christians. The most illuminating study of Platonic influences in the formation of the Christian purgatory seems still to be G. Anrich's in *Theologische Abhandlungen: Festgabe für H. J. Holtzmann* (Tübingen and Leipzig, 1902), pp. 97 ff. F. Cumont, *Les Religions orientales dans le paganisme romain*[4] (Paris, 1929), p. 202, explains a picture as showing 'purification by air, water, and fire'. Boyancé's view of Virgil's purgatory (see n. 37) is problematic.

[36] We hardly need this additional piece of evidence for Anchises' finding himself in Elysium. The difficulties which Mrs Norwood detects in Anchises' role (op. cit., 21) are of her own making. She decides that Anchises must be in the 'Moral Underworld' and that the 'philosophic introduction to the (historical) review is spoken by him but does not apply to him'. This is at variance with Virgil's own words (743 ff.).

[37] Cf. Norden's discussion and his translation of the doctrine into Greek terms, op. cit., 16 f. The different designations of this divine element—*spiritus, aura, aether, ignis*—were clearly a matter of indifference to Virgil. They need not disturb us either; for the Stoic background of all of them, cf. G. Verbeke, *L'Évolution de la doctrine du pneuma* (Paris and Louvain, 1945), as well as M. Pohlenz, *Die Stoa* (Göttingen, 1948), i. 73 f., 83, and *passim*. Curiously, even the first passage which introduces the (originally medical) πνεῦμα (breath) concept into philosophical psychology (Arist. *Gen. an.* 2. 3, 736^{b}30–737^a) also refers to the θερμόν (warm element) and treats 'the element of the stars' (= αἰθήρ, 'heaven') as part of the σπέρμα (seed); cf. my paper in *JHS* 77 (1957), 119 ff. For some other observations, cf.

must, after a period of a thousand years, drink of the river of Forgetting and enter new bodies. Virgil does not tell us by what criterion the *pauci* are separated out from 'all' others (*has omnis*, 748), but there can be no doubt that in the doctrine which he adapts the souls that need not re-enter bodies are the best which are thus rewarded for a blameless record.[38] Aeneas himself, after all, expresses astonishment (719–21) that any souls should 'desire' a return to *tarda corpora* (he is soon disabused of the idea that it is a matter of their own choice). However, Virgil has the best of reasons for being discreet about qualitative differences between souls. Since those about to begin a new life on Earth are to be the noble figures of Rome's history, any intimation that they are second-class souls would have been the height of tactlessness.

As we have seen, while Elysium has its place in the soul's itinerary, and therefore also in Anchises' initiation of his son into the cosmic secrets, Tartarus does not figure in it at all. Tartarus is a place of no return; 'sedet aeternumque sedebit / infelix Theseus' (617 f.) completely disregards the story which told of his liberation by Heracles. The moral motifs, such as the message, 'discite iustitiam moniti et non temnere divos' (620), the judgment of Rhadamanthys, the punishment inflicted by Zeus for provocation or hubris (582 ff., 592 ff.) have no analogues in the description of Elysium. Although we are free to imagine that some groups, e.g. the *pii vates* (622) or *qui(que) sui memores alios fecere merendo* (664), are in Elysium as reward for their life on Earth, the moral point of view does not at all predominate, and it is only by stretching the concept of morality that we could include *genus antiquum Teucri* or the *magnanimi heroes*, who, to be sure, are *nati melioribus annis* (648 f.),[39] in the conception of a just world order. If Orpheus and Musaeus (as is likely enough) originally acquired their place in these Fields of Bliss because they had shown mankind the way to a better life

---

Boyancé in *Hommages à Georges Dumézil* (= *Collection Latomus* 55 (1960)), pp. 60 ff., esp. 62 ff., 70 f.

[38] See, e.g., Plato *Phaed.* 114 B (οἳ ἂν δόξωσι διαφερόντως πρὸς τὸ ὅσιον βιῶναι). See also 114 C, *Rep.* 619 D–E, *Phaedr.* 248 E ff., *Laws* 10; Plut. *De def. or.* 415 B f., *De fac.* 943 A f., 945 A.

[39] In Greek literature, the first group of whose translation to the μακάρων νῆσοι (Islands of the Blest) we read is, after all, the generation of heroes (Hes. *Op.* 167 ff.). Treu (op. cit., 28 f.) distinguishes, perhaps somewhat too rigidly, both in the newly found poem and in *Aen.* 6, between moral and cultural merits. Boyancé, op. cit. (n. 4), pp. 163 f., distinguishes the warrior heroes from the other *élus*. Unlike Virgil, the papyrus introduces no individual (mythical) figures in Tartarus or Elysium. Does Virgil reflect an earlier scheme? See my comments, op. cit. (n. 15).

and to salvation,[40] Virgil completely ignores this aspect, using Orpheus instead to create with his lyre and music the atmosphere of happiness and enjoyment (645 ff.). In short, while the report about Tartarus combines description and explanation, ordeals and the meaning of these ordeals in a divine scheme, the account of Elysium is by comparison one dimensional; in 637–65, we only learn what sights present themselves. This time the reason and rationale—the λόγον διδόναι—are reserved for later, and it becomes once more clear that it is not possible to sever the links between Elysium and the revelation which defines its place in a comprehensive cosmological or theological order.

The language used to describe Elysium has created an aura of festive solemnity, which, even if an episode of more personal character intervenes (679–702), is the appropriate atmosphere for the sublime revelation of Anchises. V. Pöschl and others[41] have compared this revelation with the initiation into the secrets of the cosmos which Scipio Aemilianus receives in Cicero's *Somnium*. The setting of that initiation is an *illustris et clarus locus* (*Somn.* 11). These words would be equally applicable to the environment in which Aeneas is introduced to the divine power operative in the world and the divine quality of the souls. What is essential for both conceptions is that the recipient of the initiation and, with him, the reader have been transported into a realm far superior in beauty and dignity to ordinary life, into a world from which everything *mortale et caducum* is absent (*Somn.* 17). Whether we consider the environment, the political-historical motif, the philosophy of soul, or finally the poetic atmosphere, the continuity remains unbroken from the arrival in the *loci laeti* (638).

It may be a slight exaggeration if we describe all encounters with old friends in the 'Homeric Underworld' as distressing, for Aeneas and his Trojan fellow warriors enjoy (*iuvat*, 487) their meeting. Still, sadness certainly is the mood which predominates in these encounters, whereas the reunion in Elysium with Anchises is a joyful experience for both. If the Dido episode reminds us of Ajax' reactions in the *nekyia*, and if there are meaningful parallels between the fate of Palinurus and Elpenor (as well as between that of Agamemnon and Deiphobus), the meeting of

---

[40] Cf. Bailey, op. cit., 272. It is impossible to be sure, for Orpheus with his lyre appears on vase pictures of the Underworld; see J. E. Harrison, *Prolegomena to the Study of Greek Religion*[3] (Cambridge, 1922), pp. 600 ff. Still, in the *Aeneid* he is associated not with Eurydice (as in the *Georgics*) but with Musaeus, and the latter too is prominent (645 ff., 667 ff.); cf. Plato *Rep.* 363 C, 364 E f.

[41] Norden, op. cit., 47 f.; Butler, op. cit., 35 and *passim*; V. Pöschl, *Die Dichtkunst Virgils* (Innsbruck and Vienna, 1960), p. 45; Boyancé, op. cit. (n. 34), pp. 38 ff.

Aeneas with his father is comparable both to Odysseus' reunion with his mother (152–224) and to his consultation of Teiresias (90–150).[42] With the former it shares the intimate, personal quality; with the latter, the imparting of authoritative knowledge. Moreover, it was for the purpose of seeing his father and learning about the future that Aeneas had ventured into Hades. It is the only meeting for which we are prepared, all others being unexpected. In this respect, as well as in the joy and satisfaction experienced by father and son, it forms a contrast to the meetings in the former half, and it is certainly significant enough to balance them. Once more, the tripartite scheme proves irrelevant or inadequate. Weighty elements of Virgil's own composition suggest the overriding importance of a dichotomous pattern.

On finally meeting his father, Aeneas finds him engaged in contemplating 'animas superum(que) ad lumen ituras' and learning in the same act about the future of his progeny and of Rome ('omnemque suorum / forte recensebat numerum carosque nepotes', etc., 679 ff.). Thus Virgil at once combines with the personal motif of the reunion between father and son indications pointing ahead to the philosophical and to the historical subjects soon to be treated. Very naturally, Anchises and Aeneas first surrender themselves to the full enjoyment of the desired reunion; yet intense as the feelings of joy on both sides are, Virgil has concentrated their expression into relatively few lines. After twenty lines (at 703), we are called back to the souls ready for a new life on Earth. Aeneas, astonished at the gathering he sees in the valley of Lethe, asks for an explanation (710–12). Anchises' answer once more combines the religious and the historical aspects of the reincorporation (713–15, 716–18). Since it was Virgil's plan to conclude Book 6 with the panorama of Rome's future, the religious (or philosophical) topic must be taken up first, and we understand why Aeneas' next question, indifferent to the progeny motif and to the happy prospects of his landing in Italy, focuses on the return into bodies, thereby leading up to the philosophical revelation. Still 'quae lucis miseris tam dira cupido?' (721) is not only from the compositional point of view the right question for him to ask. The astonishment is amply justified as long as we still consider ourselves in the beautiful surroundings of Elysium (this point need probably no longer be laboured). Yet the question also expresses the ethos of the

---

[42] Cf. (also for what follows) Norden's 'Schlussbetrachtung', op. cit., 357 ff., 360; and the very detailed investigation of G. N. Knauer, *Die Aeneis und Homer* (Göttingen, 1964), pp. 107 ff., although not all of Knauer's observations are equally to the point. Whether *Od.* 24. 320–55 (Odysseus and Laertes) also served as a model for the reunion of father and son in *Aen.* 6 remains uncertain; like Knauer, p. 127 n. 1, I fail to find close similarities.

man for whom life and the task which destiny has imposed upon him are a burden rather than a joy.[43] The motif of the *proles meorum* (717), in abeyance while Anchises speaks as hierophant of the cosmic laws, becomes dominant at 752 or 756 (*Dardaniam prolem*) and remains so for the rest of the Book.

Anchises' first answer (713–18) has reaffirmed the identity, known to us ever since 679 ff., of the souls to be reincarnated with the great figures of Rome's history. There was no need for Virgil in the metaphysical section or in the subsequent display of Rome's glory to emphasize this identity. He may well have considered it an advantage to treat each of these subjects without reference to the other. How little he has done to integrate them[44] and how such integration might have been achieved becomes clear if we once more turn to the *Somnium Scipionis*, which in the midst of the cosmic vision (*Somn.* 13) provides the assurance: 'nihil est enim illi principi deo, qui omnem mundum regit, quod quidem in terris fiat, acceptius quam concilia coetusque hominum iure sociati, quae civitates appellantur; harum rectores et conservatores hinc profecti huc revertuntur.' ('Nothing that happens on earth is more acceptable to that chief of gods who rules the whole universe than the councils and gatherings of men associated by law, which are called states; their directors and preservers come from this place and return here.') It is probably characteristic of Virgil that he kept the world of politics apart from the religious and philosophical.

In the *Aeneid*, Virgil is the poet of Rome's greatness—Book 6 includes the message, 'tu regere imperio populos, Romane, memento', etc. (851 ff.)—but he is more than this. He also is the poet whose feelings respond with a warmth unknown before his days to the sorrows and struggles of individuals, who would wonder whether such trials were all that the divine world order had allotted to man, and who would be receptive to the Platonic and Stoic teachings about release from the world and the return of soul to its sublime origin. Even in his national epic, his sympathy with the individual in his physical or emotional sufferings manifests itself everywhere. In Book 6 it demands a separate place. Only after we have learned the truth about the meaning of life in a divine world scheme may the galaxy of Roman warriors and statesmen display itself before our eyes.

[43] Cf. Otis, op. cit., 300.

[44] *Pace* Otis, op. cit., 301. See also R. Lamacchia, *RhM* 107 (1964), 268 ff., for an excellent statement and a not-so-convincing solution of the problem. Pöschl, op. cit., 39 f., is important.

In the presentation of Rome's glorious future the perspective from beyond is maintained; yet the merits and virtues of this life come more and more to predominate. When, in the passage which concludes the historical vision, the premature death of Marcellus is lamented in moving verses of superlative beauty, the emphasis is on what his life would have meant for Rome. No thought is given to the greater bliss which awaits noble minds of such distinction in the hereafter.[45]

[45] See 860–86.

II

The Bough and the Gate

D. A. WEST

I. *The Problems*

This lecture will tackle two problems:

(i) Why does Aeneas take a golden bough with him when he goes down into the Underworld in the sixth book of the *Aeneid*?

(ii) Why does he emerge from the Underworld by the gate of ivory, the gate of false dreams, and not by the gate of horn, the gate of true shades? (6. 893–6)

These are ancient problems and modern scholars are still at a loss. W. F. Jackson Knight in *Cumaean Gates* (1936) writes of the labyrinth on the temple gate and the golden bough as two of the most important unexplained details in Virgil, and proceeds to a profound exploration of the labyrinth.[1] 'The bough remains an enigma', concludes R. G. Austin (1977) on 6. 138 f., 'even if Virgil did have some source in folk lore, the imagination and beauty of its use is wholly Virgilian, a wonder of ancient poetry.'[2] And R. D. Williams, making all things clear for sixth-formers in 1984 in the brilliant new magazine *Omnibus*, speaks of 'the mysterious talisman of the Golden Bough, a kind of symbol of light in darkness'.[3] Austin and Williams sound impressive but are not helpful. 'A force de vouloir être grand, il devient un peu vague' in the words of M. de la Rue (1784).[4]

As for the ivory gate, the embarrassment of scholars is best represented by Servius, writing at the end of the fourth century AD. After the stupendous revelation of the future of Rome which Aeneas receives in the Underworld, when he emerges by the gate of false dreams, Servius says that poetically the sense is clear. Virgil wants it to be understood

---

[1] W. F. Jackson Knight, *Cumaean Gates: A Reference of the Sixth Aeneid to the Initiation Pattern* (Oxford, 1936), p. 21.

[2] R. G. Austin, *P. Vergili Maronis Aeneidos liber sextus* (Oxford, 1977), p. 83.

[3] R. D. Williams, 'Virgil's Underworld', *Omnibus* 7 (1984), 5–7.

[4] M. de la Rue, cited in K. Woodbridge, *Landscape and Antiquity: Aspects of English Culture at Stourhead 1718–1838* (Oxford, 1970), p. 97.

that everything he has said is false. 'Poetice apertus est sensus: uult enim intellegi falsa esse omnia quae dixit.'

II. *The Problem of the Golden Bough*

accipe quae peragenda prius. latet arbore opaca
aureus et foliis et lento uimine ramus,
Iunoni infernae dictus sacer; hunc tegit omnis
lucus et obscuris claudunt conuallibus umbrae.
sed non ante datur telluris operta subire
auricomos quam quis decerpserit arbore fetus.
hoc sibi pulchra suum ferri Proserpina munus
instituit. primo auulso non deficit alter
aureus, et simili frondescit uirga metallo.
ergo alte uestiga oculis et rite repertum
carpe manu; namque ipse uolens facilisque sequetur,
si te fata uocant; aliter non uiribus ullis
uincere nec duro poteris conuellere ferro. (6. 136–48)

... listen to what must first be done.
Hidden in a dark tree there is a golden branch.
Golden too are its leaves and pliant stem
and it is sacred to Proserpina, the Juno of the underworld.
A whole grove conceals it and the shades
of a dark encircling valley close it in,
but no man may enter the hidden places of the earth
before plucking the golden foliage and fruit of this tree.
The beautiful Proserpina has ordained
that this is the gift that must be brought to her.
When one golden branch has been torn from the tree,
another comes to take its place
and the stem puts forth leaves of the same metal.
So then lift up your eyes and look for it
and when in due time you find it, take it in your hand
and pluck it. If you are the man called by the Fates,
it will come easily of its own accord. But if not,
no strength will prevail against it,
and you will not be able to hack it off with hard steel.

Let us start with J. G. Frazer, *The Golden Bough* (1890),[5] in the grove of the temple of Diana at Nemi in Aricia with 'the priest who slew the slayer and shall himself be slain'. To be allowed to challenge the priest,

[5] J. Frazer, *The Golden Bough: A Study in Comparative Religion* (London, 1890; 3rd edn. London, 1907–15).

his would-be assailant had first to pluck a branch from a tree in the
temple grove. 'Tradition averred', wrote Frazer, 'that the fateful branch
was that golden bough which Aeneas plucked before he essayed his
perilous journey', and this is where Frazer began his great journey
round all the societies in which he could find tree spirits, vegetable gods,
and priest kings.

The tradition on which Frazer builds his great edifice is Servius'
commentary on 6. 136, and Servius does *not* say that the branch picked
by the challenger was the golden bough:

LATET ARBORE OPACA AVREVS licet de hoc ramo hi qui de sacris
Proserpinae scripsisse dicuntur, quiddam esse mysticum adfirment,
publica tamen opinio hoc habet. Orestes post occisum regem Thoantem
in regione Taurica cum sorore Iphigenia, ut supra
diximus, fugit et Dianae simulacrum inde sublatum haud longe ab
Aricia collocavit. in huius templo post mutatum ritum sacrificiorum
fuit arbor quaedam, de qua infringi ramum non licebat.
dabatur autem fugitivis potestas, ut si quis exinde ramum potuisset
auferre, monomachia cum fugitivo templi sacerdote dimicaret: nam
fugitivus illic erat sacerdos ad priscae imaginem fugae. dimicandi
autem dabatur facultas quasi ad pristini sacrificii reparationem.
nunc ergo istum inde sumpsit colorem, ramus enim necesse erat
ut et unius causa esset interitus: unde et statim mortem subiungit
Miseni: et ad sacra Proserpinae accedere nisi sublato ramo non poterat.
inferos autem subire hoc dicit, sacra celebrare Proserpinae.

(Servius on *Aen.* 6. 136)

What Servius says is that after Orestes had killed King Thoas, he fled to
Italy and founded a temple near Aricia with a sacred tree; if any runaway
could cut off a branch of the tree, he was entitled to single combat with
the priest of the temple who was himself a runaway, thereby reproducing
ritually the murder of Thoas by Orestes. This, according to Servius, is
where Virgil got the idea of the golden bough; *inde sumpsit colorem*. For it
was necessary that the bough should be the cause of one death, and
therefore Virgil goes on immediately after this passage to describe the
death of Misenus.

This will not do. A runaway plucks a branch off a sacred tree and
fights a priest to the death. But the branch that Aeneas picks is a metal
branch, a branch of gold, and it is Aeneas' comrade that dies. Aeneas
goes down into the Underworld, but the runaway's branch has nothing
to do with the Underworld. Tradition therefore does not aver that the
fateful branch of the runaway was 'that golden bough which Aeneas

plucked before he essayed his perilous journey'. Frazer was heavily attacked on this point, notably by O. Gruppe (1914: see the account of this historic controversy in Conway, 1928),[6] and himself gave up the theory by the time of his third edition (1913).

But the damage was done. Anthropology had entered the *Aeneid*. In his great commentary on *Aeneid* 6, E. Norden starts with Frazer's second thoughts, with the simile in which Virgil compares the golden bough to the mistletoe. 'This gives us the sphere in which our researches must move', he says, and following Frazer's third edition he reflects upon the magic powers of the mistletoe: its connection with winter, its connection with death.[7] (In Norse mythology Balder is the god of summer sun, beloved by all but threatened with death. Loki is an evil spirit who persuades the blind god Hödur to throw a branch of mistletoe at Balder and so kill him.) The mistletoe is connected also with the Underworld (no doubt because its growth in winter suggests life in death). So the mistletoe is a complex symbol denoting an amalgam of magic, winter, the Underworld, death, and life in death.

This Scandinavian explanation depends upon the identification of the Golden Bough and the mistletoe. This identification is firmly made by Norden. Of this two demonstrations. First he says (on p. 167) that we read in Virgil that Charon, the ferryman of the dead, is subject to the will of him who bears the mistletoe. This is not so. What we read (in 406–7) is that the objections of Charon ended when he recognized the branch. 'At ramum hunc ... adgnoscas'. No word of mistletoe. The second demonstration that Norden identifies the two is his comment on 211. The Sibyl at 146 said the branch would come easily *uolens facilisque*. Why did it hesitate at 211 (*cunctantem*)? The obvious solution to this conundrum is that at 146 Virgil is employing the Excalibur motif to demonstrate that his hero is the chosen one of Fate whereas at 211 he is demonstrating Aeneas' boldness and strength. Tycho rules (see Dawe, 1963).[8] But scholars have preferred and do prefer other answers. Norden's answer was that the branch was mistletoe. From mistletoe we make birdlime. Birdlime is a sticky paste. So stickiness or cunctation is a permanent characteristic of mistletoe. Hence *cunctantem*, the hesitation of the golden bough.

    [6] O. Gruppe, review of Frazer, *BPhW* 49 (1949), 1534–60, pp. 1555–9; R. S. Conway, *Harvard Lectures on the Virgilian Age* (Cambridge, Mass., 1928), pp. 41–5.
    [7] E. Norden, *P. Vergilius Maro Aeneis Buch VI* (Leipzig, 1903; 6th edn. Stuttgart, 1976).
    [8] R. D. Dawe, 'Inconsistency of Plot and Character in Aeschylus', *PCPhS* 189 (1963), 21–62.

Against this identification we must insist that whatever the golden
bough is, it is not mistletoe, and that this parade of Scandinavian deities
(I call it Balderdash) has no place in Graeco-Roman epic. The golden
bough is not mistletoe or any other plant. It is metal. This is explicit in
the text at 144 *simili metallo*, and at 209 where *brattea* is metal foil.
Besides, whatever the golden bough is, it cannot be mistletoe for the
simple reason that it is compared to mistletoe in the simile starting at 6.
205. It would be a strange simile that compared a thing to itself. It might
be argued that the effect of the simile is to confer upon the golden bough
the mystic and symbolical connotations of the mistletoe. But an
examination of the Latin is enough to refute this theory:

> uix ea fatus erat, geminae cum forte columbae
> ipsa sub ora uiri caelo uenere uolantes,
> et uiridi sedere solo. tum maximus heros
> maternas agnouit auis laetusque precatur:
> 'este duces, o, si qua uia est, cursumque per auras
> derigite in lucos ubi pinguem diues opacat
> ramus humum. tuque, o, dubiis ne defice rebus,
> diua parens.' sic effatus uestigia pressit
> obseruans quae signa ferant, quo tendere pergant.
> pascentes illae tantum prodire uolando
> quantum acie possent oculi seruare sequentum.
> inde ubi uenere ad fauces graue olentis Auerni,
> tollunt se celeres liquidumque per aera lapsae
> sedibus optatis gemina super arbore sidunt,
> discolor unde auri per ramos aura refulsit.
> quale solet siluis brumali frigore uiscum
> fronde uirere noua, quod non sua seminat arbos,
> et croceo fetu teretis circumdare truncos,
> talis erat species auri frondentis opaca
> ilice, sic leni crepitabat brattea uento.
> corripit Aeneas extemplo auidusque refringit
> cunctantem, et uatis portat sub tecta Sibyllae. (6. 190–211)

No sooner had he spoken
than there chanced to come two doves out of the sky
and settle there in the grass in front of him.
Then the great Aeneas knew
they were his mother's birds and he was glad.
'Be my guides,' he prayed, 'and if there is a way,
direct your swift flight through the air into the grove
where the rich branch shades the fertile soil.
And you, goddess, my mother,

do not fail me in my time of uncertainty.'
So he spoke and waited
to see what signs they would give
in what direction they would move.
They flew and fed and flew again
always keeping within sight of those who followed.
Then when they came to the foul-smelling throat of Avernus,
first they soared and then they swooped
down through the clear air and settled
where Aeneas had prayed they would settle
on the top of the tree that was two trees
from whose green there gleamed the breath of gold
along the branch. Just as the mistletoe,
not sown by the tree on which it grows
puts out fresh foliage in the woods in the dead of winter
and twines its yellow fruit around the slender tree trunks,
so shone the golden foliage on the dark holm-oak,
so rustled the golden foil in the gentle breeze.
Aeneas seized the branch instantly.
It resisted but he broke it off impatiently
and carried it into the home of the priestess, the Sibyl.

The Golden Bough is compared to the mistletoe in four respects, and none of these explicit correspondences is symbolical or mystical. The bough is gold (*auri* 204, 208); the mistletoe is yellow (*croceo* 207). (Incidentally, J. Sergeaunt (1920) tells us that there are two varieties of mistletoe and that the variety with the yellow oval berry was held to give a better product for birdlime than the common type of which the berries are round and white.[9]) The second explicit correspondence is in 204 where the gold gleams along the branches of the holm-oak (*per ramos*), while in 207 the mistletoe goes round the trunks of its parent tree (*circumdare truncos*). Third, the gold foliage of 208 (*auri frondentis*) corresponds with the new foliage of 206 (*nova . . . fronde*). Fourth, the gold foliage in the dark holm-oak, 208–9, corresponds to the mistletoe growing on a tree that did not seed it (*quod non sua seminat arbos* 206). Note also in the narrative that the breath of gold, *auri aura* 204, a strange susurration heard also by Horace in the third stanza of the Pyrrha *Ode* I. 5 (*aurea . . . aurae*), is caught by the reprise in 209, *brattea uento*, metal foil in the wind; and incidentally Sergeaunt tells us *en passant* that a harsh rustling can be heard when the wind blows in the leaves of the holm-oak. This detail apart, the emphasis is visual. The mistletoe simile is about

[9] J. Sergeaunt, *The Trees, Shrubs, and Plants of Virgil* (Oxford, 1920), pp. 62, 137–8.

the appearance of gold shown up against the dark evergreen leaves of the ilex. Not a whisper of Balder or Loki or Hödur. No hint of magic, of the Underworld or winter, of life or death.

But anthropological theory dies hard. R. A. Brooks's 1953 article[10] is frequently cited as though it were of some use, but nobody has been able to summarize it. I have tried several times and have found little more than a rehash of Norden's 'life and death and the Underworld' material diluted by fashionable obscurantism. Try this: 'Aeneas never fully possesses the light or the kingdom ... or that divine order of which he is the ... carrier.' Or again:

Aeneas looks for a sign, and finds it to be but a mirror-image of himself, life-in-death confronting death-in-life. The *amor* which impels him to pass living into death receives no answer. This deeper antithesis of success in action/frustration in knowledge is the central and fundamental significance of the golden bough. Certainly it is this which effects that curious distortion of the language at the moment of the bough's discovery: *Discolor aura:* not the light of revelation but the dubious and shifting colors of the magic forest.

This kind of writing is not useful. Norden with fudge. This is the sort of easy spillage that has brought literary studies into disrepute in recent years. It is such a pleasure to lecture in a centre of Latin studies where cant would not be tolerated.

And there is no excuse for this obfuscation of the golden bough. The problem is already solved and easily explained. Before I divulge the solution, however, I wish to take you into the land of dreams, those of you who are not there already.

III. *The Problem of the Ivory Gate*

> Sunt geminae Somni portae, quarum altera fertur
> cornea, qua ueris facilis datur exitus umbris,
> altera candenti perfecta nitens elephanto,
> sed falsa ad caelum mittunt insomnia Manes.
> his ibi tum natum Anchises unaque Sibyllam
> prosequitur dictis portaque emittit eburna.
> ille uiam secat ad nauis sociosque reuisit.
>   Tum se ad Caietae recto fert limite portum.
> ancora de prora iacitur; stant litore puppes. (6. 893–901)

[10] R. A. Brooks, 'Discolor aura: Reflections on the Golden Bough', *AJPh* 74 (1953), 260–80; repr. in S. Commager, ed., *Virgil: A Collection of Critical Essays* (Englewood Cliffs, 1966), 143–63.

There are two gates of sleep:
one is called the gate of horn
and by it true shades have an easy exit;
the other is made all in gleaming white ivory
but through it the powers of the underworld
send false dreams up towards the heavens.
There on that night did Anchises walk with his son
and with the Sibyl and spake those words to them
sending them on their journey through the gate of ivory.
    Aeneas lost no time in making his way
back to his ships and his comrades.
He then steered a straight course to the harbour of Caieta.
The anchors were thrown from the prows
and the ships stood along the shore.

Why does Virgil send Aeneas out by the ivory gate, the gate of false dreams? Servius, as we have seen, has a simple answer: 'Poetically the sense is clear: for he wants it to be understood that everything he has said is false.' But this is clearly wrong. After all, everything he has said is true. All the prophecies received by Aeneas in the Underworld are *post-eventum*, with one exception, at line 794. They have already been fulfilled before Virgil has written them. Besides, what could have possessed Virgil to utter such an inanity? Let us abandon Servius and our own unsatisfactory century and listen to the robuster voice of eighteenth-century England. 'The final dismissal of our hero,' declares Edward Gibbon in *Memoirs of my Life* (1984), 'through the ivory gate from whence *falsa ad coelum mittunt insomnia Manes*, seems to dissolve the whole enchantment and leaves the reader in a state of cold and anxious scepticism. This most lame and impotent conclusion has been variously imputed to the haste or irreligion of Virgil.'[11] 'The haste or irreligion' of Virgil. It is pleasing to note that the reading 'haste' has been rescued from Gibbon's manuscripts by the Penguin editor Betty Radice. Our printed copies, going back to Lord Sheffield, have the extraordinary reading 'taste'.

In this problem the nations furiously rage together and the people imagine vain things. In Baltimore, E. J. Highbarger (1940)[12] drew a map of Hades with the ivory gate at the *vestibulum Orci* of 273 where vain dreams, the *vana somnia*, are gathered in the great dark elm. This

[11] E. Gibbon, *Memoirs of my Life*, ed. B. Radice (Harmondsworth, 1984), p. 14.
[12] E. J. Highbarger, *The Gates of Dreams: An Archaeological Examination of Virgil, Aeneid VI, 893–899* (Baltimore, 1940).

topographical account gives Aeneas a round trip but does not give us a
satisfying answer to our question. In South Africa, T. J. Haarhoff
(1948)[13] was trying to take *falsa ad caelum* together, false with reference
to the world above, false in the eyes of men, though true in the eyes of the
gods. In Italy, F. M. Brignoli (1954)[14] argued that Aeneas fails to grasp
the truth of his dream. We know it as the truth; to him it was not true.
But even if a reader could grasp this subtle point, why should Virgil
make it? What narrative or dramatic benefit is there in it for him? In
France, L. F. Rolland (1957)[15] explained that Aeneas has left the bough
with Proserpina, and therefore has to evade the shades on guard duty at
the gates. He cannot masquerade as a true shade and emerge by the gate
of horn, so *faute de mieux* he must emerge with the *falsa insomnia* through
the ivory gate. This is unconvincing. The bough was Aeneas' accredi-
tation. He is accredited. It would be unnecessary as well as undignified
for him to try to slip out in a crowd of false dreams. Aeneas has no need
for false moustaches or any other subterfuge to facilitate his departure.

Let us go back in time to a more interesting and more influential
solution proposed by W. Everett in 1900,[16] that false dreams come
before midnight and true dreams after it. Virgil is therefore giving us an
epic time indication. Aeneas left the Underworld before midnight.
Apart from W. V. Clausen's vague feeling (1964), 'I have a sense which I
cannot quite put into words, that Virgil was not merely telling the time of
night',[17] there are some strong arguments against Everett. The very fact
is not incontestable. There is some evidence for it but it is by no means a
common notion that dreams dreamt before midnight are false, and there
are many contrary examples, none more telling than Aeneas' dream of
Hector at 2. 268, which is clearly a true dream: 'Tempus erat quo *prima*
quies mortalibus aegris...' So then 896 is not a clear enough time
indication. It could not convey to Virgil's readers that Aeneas left Hades
before midnight. But even if it could, it is not a convincing explanation of
the line. Why should Virgil here be drawing our attention to the
chronology of the narrative? Aeneas enters the Underworld at dawn
(255); midday has passed by 535–6; 896 would then tell us that he left
the Underworld before midnight, rejoined his colleagues 899, sailed to
Caieta 900, next day presumably, and moored there 901. But in this

[13] T. J. Haarhoff, 'The Gates of Sleep', *G & R* 17 (1948), 88–90.
[14] F. M. Brignoli, 'La porta d'avorio nel libro VI dell' Eneide', *GIF* 7 (1954), 61–7.
[15] L. F. Rolland, 'La Porte d'ivoire (Virgile, Énéide VI 898)', *REL* 35 (1957), 204–23.
[16] W. Everett, 'Upon Aeneid VI, 893–898', *CR* 14 (1900), 153–4.
[17] W. V. Clausen, 'An Interpretation of the Aeneid', *HSCPh* 68 (1964), 139–47, at p.
147.

explanation nothing is made of this detailed time indication. The narrative works equally well if Aeneas emerged at 11 p.m. or 5 a.m. Is it credible that Virgil would have risked the status of this whole great prophecy of Book Six for a time indication that is obscure and entirely unnecessary? Yet Norden believed this. Even T. E. Page is impressed.[18] But it does not stand up for a moment. The success of this theory is yet another indication of the deep unease caused by *falsa insomnia* and the gate of ivory.

The present trend in scholarship is to concentrate on the meaning of *falsa insomnia* and temper the phrase in some fashion so that it does not mean that Aeneas' vision is false. Otis (1964) tries three shifts.[19] 'Aeneas' Hades vision is a dream and a false dream, in the sense that it is not to be taken as literal reality.' Then 'It is not "false", but it is in a dream world.' Then 'From Aeneas' point of view it is not fact but is *within* his own consciousness, not outside it.' Singly each of these three is inadequate. The combination is a muddle. Nicholas Reed (1973) disposes of them:

If one describes an experience as a dream, one means that the experience took place only in the mind of the recipient and is not to be taken as a literal reality.... If an experience is described as a 'false dream', it can only mean that the experience gives a misleading impression of present or future reality.[20]

In other words these explanations based upon the 'imaginative vision' cover *insomnia*. They do nothing for our problem adjective *falsa*.

So Nicholas Reed, having provided a powerful critique of other views, proceeds to erect his own, starting from the contrast in the text between true shades, *ueris ... umbris* (894), and false dreams, *falsa insomnia* (896). They are 'real people', he says, 'and thus false shades. As such they take their departure through the ivory gate.' This view is close to that of E. Christian Kopff and Nanno Marinatos Kopff (1976),[21] who argue that 'the Gate of Horn is for real shades' proceeding to rebirth, whereas 'the Gate of Ivory is more appropriate for Aeneas and the Sibyl who are sent by the Manes into the Upper World to perform a specific task'. They are not true shades, so they do not use the gate of horn. They are, however, not false dreams, but deceiving realities.

[18] T. E. Page, *Virgil, the Aeneid* (London, 1894–1900).
[19] B. Otis, *Virgil: A Study in Civilized Poetry* (Oxford, 1964).
[20] N. Reed, 'The Gates of Sleep in Aeneid 6', *CQ* 23 (1973), 311–15.
[21] E. C. and N. M. Kopff, 'Aeneas: False Dream or Messenger of the Manes? (Aeneid 6, 893 ff.)', *Philol.* 120 (1976), 246–50.

None of this is on the right tack. These refined interpretations of *falsa insomnia* fail to convince because they make Virgil say something which has no poetic or dramatic purpose. Why should Virgil put at hazard his apocalyptic vision of Roman history for either of these frigid scholastic convolutions? There must be a different explanation by which Virgil can be understood as saying something worth saying. There is. But first we return to the golden bough.

IV. *The Reason for the Golden Bough*

Most of the solution is in the text of Virgil. In 6. 138 and 142 we read that Proserpina expected the mystic initiates to present her with a branch. 'The beautiful Proserpina has ordained that this branch should be brought to her as a gift', and Norden confirms the allusion to ritual by suggesting that *pulchra* looks like a Latinization of Proserpina's cult title Κάλλιστη, while *instituit* is a term often used to indicate that a god invents or devises something or imposes or teaches his own cult, as when Pan first taught men to play the panpipes:

> Pan primum calamos cera coniungere plures
> instituit... (*Ec.* 2. 32–3)

So the mystics carry branches, as they do also, for example, in the scholia to Aristophanes' *Frogs* 408. Aeneas, like those mystics, is going down to see the Underworld. Like them, he will present his branch as a gift to Persephone, and like them, he will re-emerge to the upper air. The symbolism is plain and apt, and it is explained to us by Virgil at 142–3 and confirmed at 635–6 where Aeneas lays down the branch on Proserpina's threshold, as instructed.

The Eleusinian mysteries, of course, were familiar to Virgil's contemporaries, and indeed to the man whom the *Aeneid* was designed to praise. Augustus was an initiate of the Eleusinian mysteries. Dio Cassius (51. 4. 1) and Suetonius (*DA* 93) tell us that when the priests of Eleusis came to Rome in a deputation, Augustus, being an initiate, agreed to hear them behind closed doors. So the branch is not only a transparent allusion to the mysteries of Dis and Persephone. It is also an oblique tribute to Augustus. As such it is typical of the *Aeneid*.

We are nearly there. We have explained the branch, but not the gold. This is not a living branch, and therefore not quite apt for the mystical symbolism of life among the dead. It is metal. Nowhere so far in surviving classical literary sources or in surviving art have we met a golden branch. But there is one. Agnes Kirsopp Michels found it as long ago as 1945, hidden amongst flowers.[22] In about 100 BC in his anthology which he called 'The Garland', Meleager of Gadara gave his table of contents in the form of an introductory poem in which he described the separate contributions as different flowers woven into a garland by their different poets, for example, many madonna lilies from Anyte, many narcissi from Moero, from Sappho the flowers were few but roses, βαιὰ μὲν ἀλλὰ ῥόδα (5–6). In 47–8 Meleager refers to the epigrams of a poet called Plato (who also wrote some philosophy):

> ναὶ μὴν καὶ χρύσειον ἀεὶ θείοιο Πλάτωνος
> κλῶνα, τὸν ἐξ ἀρετῆς πάντοθι λαμπόμενον

And also the ever golden branch of divine Plato
Shining all round with virtue.

After long and unavailing search for an *aureus ramus* in classical literature, we have found it at last, a χρύσειος κλών, and it is carried by Plato.

It is impossible to prove that Virgil knew Meleager's *Garland*, but he has at least two other possible exploitations of it. At *Aeneid* 1. 630, at the end of the first words Dido addresses to Aeneas, she tells him that she has known hardship and is learning to help those who suffer. 'Non ignara mali miseris succurrere disco.' A. S. F. Gow and D. L. Page (1965)[23] note that these noble words are very close to a phrase in Meleager 4537 'Having suffered, I know how to pity', οἶδα παθὼν ἐλεεῖν, where F. Dübner said that these three words of Meleager steal the palm from Virgil.[24] 'Tria uerba Meleagri palmam abripiunt Virgiliano "non ignara mali miseris succurrere disco".' A second such resemblance was pointed out by Nicholas Horsfall in 1979 and I thank him for reminding me of it.[25] He refers to the resemblance between the pet stag which had been torn from its mother's udders and was looked after by the maiden Silvia in *Aeneid* 7. 483–9, and the swift-footed pet hare torn from its mother's breast and fed and cherished by sweet-skinned Phanium ἡ γλυκερόχρως Φάνιον in Meleager 4320–4 (Gow–

[22] A. K. Michels, 'The Golden Bough of Plato', *AJPh* 66 (1945), 59–63.
[23] A. S. F. Gow and D. L. Page, *The Greek Anthology: Hellenistic Epigrams* (Cambridge, 1965).
[24] F. Dübner, ed., *Anthologia Graeca* (Paris, 1864–90).
[25] N. Horsfall, review of Fordyce's edn. of *Aen.* 7 and 8, *CR* 29 (1979), 219–23, at p. 223.

Page). But do we need to prove that Virgil knew Meleager? Virgil was
steeped in Greek poetry of all periods, and it is just not credible that he
and his literary friends should not have known and discussed the gems
of Greek lyric poetry collected by Meleager in his *Garland* at the
beginning of Virgil's own century.

Why should Virgil allude to Plato at this point in the *Aeneid*? He
wishes to include in his epic a prophecy of the future heroes of Rome.
He has his usual model to hand. In Homer, when Odysseus slit the
throats of a young ram and a black ewe and let their blood flow into a
trench, the souls of the dead come swarming up from Erebus to flutter
round the trench. But this time the model will not do. Apart from
anything else Homer is producing dead heroes; Virgil wishes to review
heroes yet unborn. Blood for the ghosts would not be appropriate for
that.

But there is another familiar model for Virgil to use at the end of the
sixth book of the *Aeneid*. At the end of the tenth book of Plato's *Republic*,
the myth of Er the Pamphylian tells of a living man who descended into
the Underworld. Er had fallen in battle and when on the tenth day they
came to take up the stinking corpses of the dead, they found Er's body
still fresh. On the twelfth day he came to life as he was lying on the pyre
and told what he had seen in the Underworld. What he had seen closely
resembled what Aeneas was to see: the judges of the dead, the souls
arriving for rebirth and waiting in a meadow for the time of their return
to earth, the fearful punishments meted out to wrong-doers, the shape
and nature of the Universe. Let one passage demonstrate the Platonic
character of Aeneas' vision. Er saw the just dead being sent along the
road to the right which led upward through heaven and the unjust taking
the road to the left which led down to a place of torture. (614 C). In the
Aeneid the Sibyl points out the parting of the ways to Aeneas:

> dextera quae Ditis magni sub moenia tendit,
> hac iter Elysium nobis; at laeua malorum
> exercet poenas et ad impia Tartara mittit. (6. 541–3)

> The right-hand road leads up to the walls of mighty Dis.
> This is the road we take to Elysium.
> On the left is the road of punishment for evil doers,
> leading to Tartarus, the place of the damned.

The descent into the Underworld is a Platonic device. The content of
the vision in the *Aeneid* is also to a large extent Platonic. So the golden
bough, borne by Plato in Meleager's *Garland*, is, first, the mark of the

Eleusinian initiate on his mystic journey to the land of the dead, and, second, a symbol, for those with ears to hear, of the Platonic contribution to Virgil's great vision. And Roman ears would have heard. They would already have been familiar with the similar device in the *Somnium Scipionis*, the dream of Scipio at the end of Cicero's *Republic*.

V. *The Key to the Gate of Ivory*

But Plato is not only the solution to the problem of the golden bough. He is also the key to the ivory gate, and here we are moving on from A. K. Michels. Does Plato believe that his myths are literally true? No. Listen to Socrates in the *Phaedo* (114 D):

It would not be proper for a sensible man to insist that these things are as I have described them. But that this or something like it is the case with regard to our souls and their dwelling-places ... that seems to me not only to be proper but also to be a risk worth taking, for a man who so believes. For the danger is a noble danger.

Or listen to him again in the *Republic* (382 D): 'So too in the myths we have just been talking about, since we do not know the truth about ancient times, when *we make the false as like the truth as possible* are we not doing something useful?' The answer the context demands is 'Yes'.

Virgil is an epic poet, not a philosopher. At the end of his great vision of Rome, he cannot say 'Of course, Aeneas did not really see all those future heroes. What I have been saying is not the truth but a useful lie.' The poet has many ways of distancing himself from assertions he wishes to make but not to be credited with believing. T. C. W. Stinton commented on Virgil's disclaimers in 1976,[26] *si credere dignum est, ut fama est, ut perhibent, auditis si quiequam credimus*, and many others. So then in this climax of the *Aeneid* he uses two different devices. First, he blurs the outlines of the narrative. Aeneas and the Sibyl entered the Sibyl's cave and

> ... furens antro se immisit aperto;
> ille ducem haud timidis uadentem passibus aequat. (6. 262–3)

> ... she moved in a trance into the open mouth of the cave
> and Aeneas strode fearlessly along at her side.

Nothing could be more direct, or sharper in its outline. We believe in

[26] T. C. W. Stinton, 'Si credere dignum est: Some Expressions of Disbelief in Euripides and Others', *PCPhS* 202 (1976), 80–9.

this as a normal narrative. On the other hand, when they come to emerge
at 898, they are sent out by the gate of false dreams. At once the whole
status of the narrative is thrown into doubt. Did they really go down into
the Underworld? Or was it all a dream of Aeneas? To avoid the
incredible, he has blurred the narrative into a dream, exactly as Cicero
had changed the narrative of Er into the dream of Scipio, and, no doubt,
for the same reason. He has a second device for distancing himself from
his myth. Here Virgil has combined Homer's gates of dreams (*Odyssey*
19. 562–7) with Plato's eschatological myth to convey his sublime vision
of the history of Rome. He cannot without ruining the credibility of his
narrative say that this vision is not true, but he devises an utterance
acceptable in epic which conveys allusively to an educated audience that
he holds no brief for the transmigration of souls or the rest of the
Pythagorean dogma in the descent of Aeneas. This he would hold to be a
falsehood which provides an image of the truth (λόγος ψευδὴς
εἰκονίζων τὴν ἀλήθειαν, Aphthonius *Progymnasmata* 1), but the grand
imperial vision is of course true. It has already come true. So his second
device, at the end of this Platonic myth, is to make Aeneas emerge from
the gate of false dreams, thereby hinting in epic terms that the
description he has given of the soul and its mansions is not exactly true.
In Platonic terms it is a falsehood like the truth: in epic terms Aeneas
emerges from the gate of false dreams.

VI. *Conclusion*

So then, the Platonic myth in the sixth book of the *Aeneid* is signalled by a
subtle Platonic allusion at its beginning, and a subtle Platonic disclaimer
in the allusion to the Homeric gates of dreams at the end. The highest
achievements of the Greek literary and philosophical tradition, with a
little help from a poet scholar from Gadara, have been pressed into
service to expound the ideals of the Augustan empire. Within this
brilliant vision there are shadows, reservations, doubts (analysed by
Feeney, 1986),[27] and at the end of it, we now argue, the note of
scepticism subtly struck imparts something of humility and of melancholy as the poet admits man's uncertainty about the ordinances of god.

All this is far from Balder and Loki and Hödur, far from trichoschistic
distinctions between false dreams and unreal shades, but eminently
Virgilian.

[27] D. Feeney, 'History and Revelation in Virgil's Underworld', *PCPhS* 212 (1986),
1–24.

12

Vergil's Second *Iliad*

WILLIAM S. ANDERSON

The exhausting wanderings of Aeneas[1] and Vergil's employment of
motifs from the *Odyssey*[2] come to an end as the Trojans arrive at Cumae.
A new phase opens for Aeneas, and a new pattern of the *Aeneid* is here
announced: Books 7 and 12, according to the commonplace of Vergilian
criticism, constitute the Roman counterpart of the *Iliad*. In 6. 86 ff. the
poet seems to justify Propertius' famous prediction of a new and greater
Iliad as he states, through the mouth of the Sibyl, the pattern of the
coming books:

> bella, horrida bella,
> et Thybrim multo spumantem sanguine cerno.
> non Simois tibi nec Xanthus nec Dorica castra
> defuerint; alius Latio iam partus Achilles,
> natus et ipse dea; nec Teucris addita Iuno
> usquam aberit, cum tu supplex in rebus egenis
> quas gentis Italum aut quas non oraveris urbes!
> causa mali tanti coniunx iterum hospita Teucris
> externique iterum thalami.

The details of the Sibyl's prophecy will concern us more closely later,
but even a cursory glance would not miss the allusions to a new Trojan
War. Aeneas learns that he must fight again the old battles which he has
long struggled to forget.

Conventional critics have tended to ignore Vergil's *Iliad*, as though
Aeneas' struggle to establish himself in Italy did not really parallel
Homer's story very closely. For them, the pattern of events suggested by
6. 86 ff. has never been a problem. In other words, Vergil imitates
Homer, not to enhance the meaning of his poem, but merely to make it

---

[1] Cf. A. W. Allen, 'The Dullest Book of the *Aeneid*', *CJ* 47 (1951–2), 119–23.

[2] Vergil exploits his last allusion to the *Odyssey*, of course, more subtly than any other.
The experiences which Aeneas encounters among the dead, while patterned upon
Odysseus' visit to the shades, serve as a preface to Vergil's *Iliad*: they establish the
principles by which Aeneas will fight, and define in radiant clarity the positive results of his
wars.

more superficially attractive. A lesser poet than Vergil might well have been satisfied with borrowed glory, but we know too much about Vergil's poetic art to accept any such simplification as this.[3] Nor can we be content to say what certainly comes closer to the poet's design, that the Homeric allusions bring out the fact that in Italy Aeneas relives his earlier experiences at Troy. By the beginning of Book 6, Aeneas knows that he must not re-create Troy. When he left Eryx, he abandoned those of his people who clung to a static concept of Ilium, and on his arrival at Cumae, he expresses his feeling of relief at reaching a new world. He has escaped the incubus of Troy (6. 62). If, then, the Sibyl insists on identifying the fate of Aeneas here in Italy with that which he knows— and correctly—is utterly ended, the war to defend his native city, her words raise a problem which involves the whole character of Homeric allusion in 7–12, and in a form not hitherto explored:[4] namely, why Vergil, at this crucial point in the epic, permits the coming conflict to be so specifically equated with the Trojan War as to revive memories dangerous for his hero. It is my hope to show that Vergil created this

---

[3] Cf. the basic principles of research in R. Heinze, *Virgils epische Technik* (Leipzig, 1903), and in V. Pöschl, *Die Dichtkunst Virgils* (Wiesbaden, 1950). Both critics have demonstrated beyond question the complexity of Vergil's vision and the significance with which he treats apparently sterile motifs.

[4] I know of no study which has worked out in detail the purpose, as I see it, of Vergil's allusions to the *Iliad.* Many commentators have applied themselves to identify the source of this or that allusion, a practice which probably goes back far beyond Servius and Macrobius. But Servius and Macrobius illustrate the limited interest of such commentators: they will use such phrases as *sumpti ex Homero* 'taken from Homer' or *Homerica comparatio* 'a Homeric simile', and in some cases they will identify the context to which Vergil refers; but they treat each instance in isolation, tacitly assuming that Homeric allusions serve no purpose in the total thematic pattern. On their general practice, cf. G. Regel, *De Vergilio poetarum imitatore testimonia* (diss. Göttingen, 1907). A.-M. Guillemin, *L'Originalité de Virgile: Étude sur la méthode littéraire antique* (Paris, 1931) has drawn the radical conclusion: 'The influence on the poet of the writings we possess, *Iliad*, *Odyssey*, Greek tragedy, *Argonautica*, the fragments of Ennius and of the Latin annalists, is unfortunately indelibly banal and sterile, since the Latin grammarians have long since exhausted all the interest provided by comparing the *Aeneid* and these works' (p. 11). A recent approach to Vergil's use of Homer has consisted in exploring the particular meaning that he derives from an allusion in a particular passage. This, of course, has been one of the great merits of Pöschl's work, who, among other things, has demonstrated the vital importance of similes in the *Aeneid* in opposition to Heinze. For a brief, but sympathetic, treatment of the same problem, cf. R. S. Conway, 'Vergil as a Student of Homer', *Bull. John Rylands Library* 13 (1929), 272–92. It still remains to disprove Mlle. Guillemin's statements even more conclusively by demonstrating the general plan with which Vergil uses all his Homeric allusions. This certainly can be done for Books 7–12. J. W. Spaeth Jr., 'Hector's Successor in the *Aeneid*', *CJ* 46 (1950–1), 277–80, has treated the question in relation to Aeneas, but his conclusions, I believe, have only partial validity. Aeneas, as I show in this paper, becomes Achilles' successor by the end of the epic.

problem not by mistake, but in order to exploit Homer to the fullest and thereby to reveal more clearly Aeneas' true mission in Italy. In short, the poet constructs a new *Iliad*, much of whose significance depends upon the fact that it gradually alters the role of the Trojans from that of the defeated, as Homer portrayed them, to that of victors, and thus brings them parallel to the Homeric Greeks.

Inspired as she is by Apollo, the Sibyl makes a strong impression; and the comment of Vergil at the end of her prophecy implies that she has correctly, though ambiguously, foretold coming events: *obscuris vera involvens* (6. 100). In the approaching war, she says, circumstances will closely parallel those that Aeneas faced earlier in Troy. The Tiber will replace the Trojan rivers; Greeks will march up and encamp near the settlement of the Trojans; the leader of the Latins will be a formidable enemy, worthy by his own military prowess and his divine mother to be equated with Greece's greatest warrior, *alius Achilles*; Juno will continue her disastrous hostility towards the people of Paris. As if this were not enough, the Sibyl even draws a parallel between the origin of the Trojan War and the cause of the war imminent in Italy. A second marriage between Trojan and foreigner, apparently under circumstances similar to those of Helen's ill-fated union with Paris, will precipitate the bloody conflict. Hearing this, Aeneas might well leap to the conclusion that the whole pattern would repeat itself, that the Trojan settlement would eventually be assaulted, captured, and destroyed by the combined forces of the enemy. Before he plumbs the depths of despair, the prophetess shatters the apparent parallelism (thus affording us an immediate excuse to inspect the whole scheme with some suspicion) and promises Aeneas security by the most paradoxical of ways, that is, from a Greek city (6. 96–7):

> via prima salutis,
> quod minime reris, Graia pandetur ab urbe.

But if this new Trojan War is not to end with the annihilation of Aeneas' people, it may well be that Aeneas' enemy will be less victorious than the Greeks before Troy and the Italian Achilles less decisive in his exploits than the son of Thetis. Indeed, we should be prepared to study the cause of this war with great care, for the Trojans would not ultimately conquer if they were as guilty as the prophecy implies. Divine justice, so important to Vergil, would prevent that.

The remainder of Book 6 takes the Sibyl's grudging promise of security and transforms it gradually into the undeniably glorious pros-

pect of the mighty Roman nation. In Book 7, we revert to the parallelism
with Homer's *Iliad*. At the time that the Trojans land in Italy, Latinus is
deeply concerned over the marriage of his only child and daughter, not
so much because he cannot find a man whom he can like as because a
series of omens have temporarily prevented any decision on his part.
These divine signs all agree in demanding a foreign son-in-law (*externus
gener* 7. 98; cf. 7. 68). Therefore, when Ilioneus announces the peaceful
arrival of the Trojans under Aeneas, Latinus immediately senses the
fulfilment of these portents (256, 270), and offers the hand of his
daughter to the Trojan leader in compliance with the divine will. In all
this, nothing would lead us to draw any parallel with the visit of Paris to
Sparta and the resultant seduction of Helen. Lavinia is unmarried and
freely offered to the Trojan stranger even before he knows of her
existence. Aeneas has indulged his passions at Carthage and long since
brought them under control. Accordingly, as the embassy returns to the
Trojan camp with the good news, nothing in the situation as described
would lead one to anticipate the interpretation placed on these innocent
events by other actors in the drama.

Juno does not like what she sees and immediately exerts her ingenuity
to confound the peaceful intentions of Aeneas and Latinus. Her very
first words revive memories of the destruction of Troy (7. 293 ff.); in
fact, her fury seems to stem from the fact that she was unable to extirpate
the entire Trojan race. Juno realizes clearly that she cannot overcome
the destiny of Aeneas, but, since she can hardly be considered a rational
intellect when enraged,[5] it comes as no surprise that she plans to harry
Aeneas with the evils of Acheron. As she plots it, a destructive war will
arise to divide Trojan and Rutulian, cost many lives on both sides, and
stain the marriage of Aeneas and Lavinia, when it inevitably occurs, with
the memory of needless bloodshed (7. 315 ff.). And in the warped mind
of the goddess, this war assumes the proportions of the Trojan War, so
that she can gloat over her partial success and at the same time excuse
herself. Aeneas, she alleges, will bring disaster on both peoples by
marrying Lavinia, and therefore deserves the same black reputation as
Hecuba's son, *Paris alter* (321). To regard Aeneas as Paris might also
provide an argument for those who instinctively oppose a marriage

---

[5] Cf. Juno's false analogy with Pallas in 1. 39 ff., where she attempts to justify her
violent opposition to destiny by referring to the punishment properly inflicted on Ajax by
Pallas. The propensity to draw false analogies emerges in the passage of Book 7 under
discussion. There again she recalls the just vengeance of Mars and Diana in order to cloak
her own unjust wrath (340 ff.). Thus, this parallel with the Trojan War constitutes but one
more improper comparison.

between their princes and an utter foreigner. Juno, however, alludes to the parallel very briefly; it remains for others to develop its more emotional aspects.

When Allecto begins to stir up war, she selects as her first instrument Amata, who, it soon emerges, entertains the same irrational passions and voices the same inexact analogies as Juno. Amata has opposed Aeneas' marriage from the start, but, after Allecto has inflamed her spirit, she becomes violent in her attempt to thwart her husband's plans. She argues with tears and prejudice. For her, the Trojans are mere exiles, and Latinus has ignored his parental function by permitting this treacherous pirate to steal his innocent daughter: 'perfidus alta petens abducta virgine praedo' (7. 362). Not content with this patent fabrication, Amata continues and expressly compares the present situation with the voyage of the 'Phrygian shepherd' to Sparta and his subsequent departure with Helen of Troy (363–4). She seems to base much of her argument upon the fact that Aeneas is a foreigner and a Trojan. By warping the whole image of this man into another Paris, she expects to direct Latinus' attention to a more liberal interpretation of *externus gener*. With her instinctive preference for her nephew Turnus, she feels bound to show that he qualifies, first, because any city not directly ruled by Latinus should be regarded as foreign, and second, because Turnus can trace his ancestry ultimately to a foreign city, Mycenae (372). Again, we do not need to ponder much to realize the vacuity of her reasoning or the danger of misconstruing the clear warning of repeated omens. No resident of Italy can possibly be accepted as *externus*. Vergil, however, has alluded to Mycenae not merely to illustrate the fantastic efforts of the queen to oppose Aeneas; he also suggests a possible relevance of Turnus to the general pattern of the Rape of Helen. After all, Mycenae, the home of his forebears, was the birthplace of Menelaus, Helen's husband. At this point we have no reason to press the idea, but it will soon become apparent that, in the accelerating illogic of the analogy with the Trojan War, even Turnus will become involved and represent himelf in part as a Menelaus avenging the loss of his bride.

Two major motives rouse Turnus to embark upon this war: that the king spurns his claim to Lavinia and that he must abandon his hope of becoming the successor of Latinus, all because a foreigner is preferred to him (7. 424). He, too, feels a surge of anger at the mention of *externus*, but, unlike Amata, he does not immediately associate the term with the Rape of Helen. Instead, it is racial prejudice that stirs Turnus, and by means of the same prejudice he infuses the spirit of war into his patriotic band of young men (7. 467 ff.). And when the incident occurs which provides the pretext for war, his harangue contains no reference to a private grievance; he prefers to play upon Italian hostility towards the foreigners. On the other hand, Turnus acts from other motives besides patriotism. It seems clear that he had every reason, before the arrival of Aeneas, to regard marriage with Lavinia as a certainty. Moreover, from his excited reaction to the blush on the girl's cheek (12. 70 ff.), we are led to believe that Turnus loved Lavinia. As he thinks of Latinus' plan to give to another woman whom he loves and has expected to marry, he naturally becomes excited. Before long, he imagines himself in the role of Menelaus, and on the first day of battle, at a most ironic point,[6] he attempts to hearten his troops by balancing the special fortunes of Aeneas with his own. It is his destiny, he asserts, to eradicate this hated nation because it has apparently sanctioned the seduction of his wife (*coniuge praerepta* 9. 138). Such an absurd claim quickly evokes an analogy with the sons of Atreus, Menelaus in particular, and their home Mycenae (138–9). Thus, just as Amata imagines Lavinia's marriage, when excited, as the Rape of Helen, so Turnus pictures himself, under emotional stress, as the aggrieved husband Menelaus.

This analogy with the cause of the Trojan War, as Vergil makes entirely clear, is false; it serves to illustrate the irrational basis of all war and the excessive hostility of all Italy to the Trojan settlers. If there were any truth to the pattern, certainly, the poet would have conveyed the parallel not through the unreliable allegations of Juno, Amata, and Turnus, but in a careful description of the events leading up to the marriage of Aeneas and Lavinia, the Paris and Helen of this *Iliad*. As it is, the central figures in this imaginary situation have no dramatic role at all in Book 7. After receiving the happy portent of the eaten tables (7. 120 ff.) and realizing that his voyages are ended, Aeneas moves into the background. He has no other lines to speak, and his one action consists in dispatching the embassy which carries out negotiations in his name. At the outbreak of the war, he has never met his controversial bride-to-be, certainly never dreamed of seduction. The characterization of Lavinia, such as it is, exhibits the same lack of dramatic emphasis. Far from being a beauteous, passionate young wife who yields to the blandishments of a handsome stranger, Lavinia has apparently just reached the age of marriage (7. 52–3) and, in her few actions, seems to be a docile daughter, utterly devoid of romantic personality. Vergil

[6] For discussion of the irony, see below, pp. 246–7.

permits her to speak neither in this book nor in any other, with the result that she remains a fascinating enigma even today, but definitely not a Helen. Finally, Aeneas does not abduct Lavinia, who continues to live with her parents until the end of the war, and the hostilities are ignited by the shooting of the pet deer. From the beginning of the war, then, although Aeneas' enemies furiously stigmatize him as a second Paris and draw an illegitimate parallel with the role of Paris in the *Iliad*, Vergil carefully absolves the Trojan of blame and remains consistent with his dominant theme: nothing in Book 7 suggests that Aeneas intends to build a new Troy.

As there is a factual pattern of events in the origin of the war, which is one thing, and an alleged pattern, which is quite another, so the conduct of the war follows a dual course. There is an actual course in the deeds of the combatants and, on the other hand, a course which the deluded Italians insist on imagining. But whereas in describing the beginning of hostilities Vergil demonstrated the inapplicability of a pattern drawn from the *Iliad*, the poet now exploits Homer with all the complexity of which his genius is capable. As I shall show, he allows the Italians at first to construct a false pattern of hopes based upon the Trojan War; this pattern ultimately becomes symptomatic of their defeat as Vergil reassigns Homeric roles so as to embody in Aeneas the victorious Achilles, Agamemnon, and Menelaus. He does this, however, gradually, fitting the Homeric allusions to the personality already established, never awkwardly borrowing from Homer merely to abbreviate the necessary characterization.

In the opening stages of the war, Vergil lends some verisimilitude to the claims of Aeneas' enemies by allowing them to act in a manner parallel to the Greeks of the *Iliad*; at the same time, he makes no immediate effort to deny that the Trojans are playing the same disastrous part as before and, in fact, seems to offer some confirmation of this idea. At the end of Book 7 the poet embarks upon the catalogue of the Italian forces which, in its general form, closely resembles the catalogue of the Greeks in *Iliad* 2. Moreover, certain details of the list which heretofore have received a rather inadequate interpretation may well serve the same purpose of identifying Italians temporarily with Greeks. The considerable attention devoted to Aventinus and Virbius, for instance, has been explained either as due to an effort for picturesqueness or as quite unimportant.[7] Neither interpretation does

---

[7] Cf. B. Brotherton, 'Vergil's Catalogue of the Latin Forces', *TAPhA* 62 (1931), 199, who attributes the prominence of Aventinus and Virbius to their picturesqueness. In

much credit to Vergil, who might well have used these little stories about sons of Greek heroes, Hercules and Hippolytus, to give some force to the Sibyl's prophecy about the Greek camps. Even more conspicuously relevant is Halaesus, carefully described as *Agamemnonius, Troiani nominis hostis* (7. 723). When the Italians send Venulus south to Diomedes, they assume that any Greek will identify himself with their cause. In the attack upon the Trojan encampment, Turnus and his troops automatically compare themselves with the Greeks who besieged Troy for ten years. Vergil even associates with the grieving mother of Euryalus details borrowed from Homer's picture of Andromache desperately bewailing the dead Hector.[8] Such nuances illustrate the steady development of Vergil's thought, his refusal to hurry towards a simple application of the Homeric parallels.

Homer's broad picture of the Greeks at war distributed the emphasis among three leaders, Agamemnon, Menelaus, and Achilles. These Vergil unites in a single portrait. Similarly, Paris and Hector, the chief Trojans, become one person in this second *Iliad*. The Sibyl foretold an Italian commander who would be another Achilles. It is in accordance with such a prophecy and with his own delusions that Turnus claims identification with Achilles (9. 742). Throughout Book 9, he pictures himself as the greatest warrior of either army as well as the man avenging the seduction of his bride, a combination, that is, of Achilles and Menelaus. His brother-in-law Remulus parrots such feelings, taunts the Trojans with their second siege, and asserts the superiority of the Italian forces to the Greeks who spent ten years capturing Troy (9. 598 ff.). Indeed, the attack on Aeneas' men and the fact that they are Trojans almost establishes the parallel for Turnus and his soldiers. They easily leap to the assumption that they will conquer. Let us look more closely, however, at the context of Turnus' assertion that he plays Menelaus and Achilles. It is immediately after he has fired the Trojan fleet and then watched the miraculous transformation of the ships into naiads that Turnus attempts to counteract the terror of his men with the first claim. But in Homer's epic Greek ships were burned by the Trojan Hector. Furthermore, Hector's achievements depend entirely upon the absence of Achilles; so here, too, the absence of Aeneas encourages

disputing the schematization of Miss Brotherton, *TAPhA* 63 (1932), lxii–lxiii, E. Adelaide Hahn dismissed the two as unimportant.

[8] Cf. J. L. Heller, 'Vergil's Sources in *Aeneid* IX 481–97', *TAPhA* 66 (1935), xxvii–xxviii; he points out that Macrobius' attribution of the passage entirely to a Homeric source must be considerably qualified.

Turnus to battle (9. 8), and Aeneas' return ends the superiority of the Italians. In other words, Turnus fabricates a parallelism which cannot be substantiated by the facts as Vergil presents them. The context of the remarks in 9. 742, where Turnus boasts of being another Achilles, illustrates the same artistic principle. Pandarus, to whom he makes this claim, has been described in terms of the events of *Iliad* 12. He and his brother, who foolishly open the gates and sally forth to their death occupy the same position and receive the same simile (9. 679 ff.) as Polypoites and Leonteus (*Il.* 12. 132 ff.), Greeks who stand by the gates of their camp and ward off the Trojan attack. Again, Turnus deceives himself and plays the role of one of Homer's Trojans.

With the statements of the Italian leader undermined, we can consider more exactly the circumstances of this attack in Book 9. Although the Trojans do suffer the attack, they do not defend a city this time. One city exists in the neighbourhood, that of Latinus. The Trojans do not fight for their native land, inasmuch as they are foreigners. They have arrived by sea and marked out a camp for themselves, but they possess no other land in Italy. These facts, together with the burning of the ships, the absence of Aeneas, and the retention of Lavinia in the Latin city, imply clearly that, if we demand a Homeric parallel, the Trojans represent Homer's Greeks. Still, Vergil leaves it on the level of implication. In depicting the expedition of Nisus and Euryalus (9. 176 ff.), he exploits, as the earliest commentators observed, the scene in *Iliad* 10, where Odysseus and Diomedes venture forth from the Greek camp to wreak havoc among the Trojans.[9] Whereas the two Greeks, however, returned safely to their camp, Nisus and Euryalus suffer the death of Dolon; in other words, it is not at all clear yet that the Trojans will win an automatic victory.

The absence of Aeneas, I suggested, might serve the same function as the withdrawal of Achilles. We must, however, study the portrait of Aeneas in Book 8 more fully, since it so frankly contradicts the blatant assertions of Turnus in Book 9. In the first place, as we have seen, Aeneas is certainly no Paris. He is a highly conscientious leader of his people who has set out to procure the only possible allies in Italy. At Pallanteum, Vergil provides the first significant clue to interpretation. While he has carefully postponed a description of the embassy to Diomedes, leaving it as a latent threat, he does show the ease with which Aeneas secures the support of Evander, whom the Trojan addresses

---

[9] Cf. Servius on 9. 1: 'Sane formatus est iste liber ad illud Homeri, ubi dicit per noctem egressos esse Diomeden et Ulixen...'.

specifically as *optime Graiugenum* (8. 127). Already, then, Aeneas has
fulfilled the most perplexing part of the Sibyl's prophecy and has Greeks
on his side. Moreover, from the events of the end of the book, it appears
that he himself can be compared with the finest of Homer's Greeks,
Achilles.[10] Venus persuades Vulcan to make her son a special set of
armour and expressly compares herself with Thetis (8. 383). When
Vergil describes the armour, he places the greatest emphasis upon
the shield (8. 625 ff.), and, although he utilizes different details, it is
clear throughout that he expects his reader to recall the Homeric
context and the carefully contrived scenes on the shield of Achilles
(*Il.* 18. 490 ff.).

At the end of Book 9 Turnus is driven from the Trojan camp: clearly
he is not to be compared or equated with the irresistible Achilles.[11] On
the following day occurs the decisive battle. In the council of the gods
which opens Book 10, emotional argumentation obscures the issue, but
both Venus and Juno regard the conflict in Italy as another Trojan War:
Venus protesting at the thwarting of destiny (10. 25–30); Juno using the
hypothetical seduction of Lavinia as her excuse (79). Humans, not gods,
determine the issue of the war, so Vergil quickly focuses our attention
upon the desperate plight of the Trojans, then upon the man who will
break the attack of the Italians. Aeneas stands on the deck of his ship, the
object of every gaze, and an ominous flame surrounds his head, in much
the same way as Achilles, making his first appearance after so long an
absence, stood upon the Greek battlements with flames flashing around
his head.[12] To emphasize the menacing presence of the Trojan, Vergil
attaches to him a simile concerning Sirius and its severe effects upon
mortals (10. 272 ff.); Homer had used the same simile to describe the
appearance of Achilles (*Il.* 22. 26 ff.) as he approached Hector for the
final engagement.[13] Within a short time after landing, Aeneas turns the

---

[10] Vergil perhaps prepares the reader to think of Aeneas as a Greek by the consistent
association which he establishes throughout Book 8 between Aeneas and Hercules. Cf.
the general purpose of the story concerning Cacus and the express comparison with
Hercules in 362 ff.

[11] Macrobius, *S.* 6. 3. 1, connects the description of Turnus' fight within the
encampment (9. 806–14) with Homer's description of Ajax when hard pressed by the
Trojans in the battle around the ship (*Il.* 16. 102 ff.). It would seem that Vergil has used his
source in somewhat the same fashion as in 9. 481–97; that is, the poet leaves the exact
position of the Homeric pattern imprecise throughout the early stages of battle, until his
reader has been sufficiently prepared. Thus Book 9 makes many suggestions of the true
interpretation of the war, that Turnus plays the role of Hector and Paris, but it also reflects
the confusion of motives so frequent at the beginning of great events.

[12] Cf. *Aen.* 10.260–2 and *Il.* 18. 205 ff.

[13] Servius refers to this source, but compares the light flashing from the armour to the

course of battle. At first, he fights calmly and efficiently, but, when Pallas is killed and Turnus brutally mocks his fallen enemy, Aeneas becomes transformed. The brutalizing effect of the death of so close a companion resembles the change produced in Achilles by the loss of Patroclus. As Achilles captured twelve Trojans to butcher on the pyre of Patroclus, so Aeneas takes eight prisoners for sacrifice (10. 517–20). As Achilles tauntingly ignored the pleas of his numerous victims, so, in his furious attempt to avenge Pallas, Aeneas contemptuously kills suppliants and boasts over their corpses. His violent progress through the Italians routs them utterly, and simultaneously the Trojans burst from their encampment, free now of any fear of Turnus. When the true Achilles (Aeneas) of this *Iliad* returns to the battle, the man who plays Hector (Turnus) can no longer hold his own.

In refuting the efforts of Juno, Amata, and Turnus to justify the war by inventing a pretext analogous to Paris' Rape of Helen we said that Vergil did not support any such parallel with the *Iliad*. As the war approaches its conclusion, the character of Paris does seem to influence events, Paris in the person of Turnus. The defeat of the Italian forces reverses public feeling towards Turnus, who now becomes the scapegoat. Many of the people who have lost relatives now call it Turnus' war and claim that he has caused the whole vain conflict by his irresponsible desire for marriage (11. 217). It is precisely this feeling of resentment which aroused the Trojans against Paris. Just as Paris caused the war by his abduction of Helen and his stubborn refusal to listen to public protests and return her, so, to the Italians, Turnus' insistence by illegal methods upon his right to Lavinia and his refusal to permit her marriage with Aeneas constitute the unworthy basis of a needlessly ruinous struggle. Therefore, it is Aeneas who should really be regarded as the Menelaus of this *Iliad*, since he has been robbed of the wife promised him and fights for her recovery. In confirmation of our general interpretation, Vergil describes at last the return of Venulus, who reports the refusal of Diomedes to reinforce the Italians, indeed, his condemnation of the entire war. In short, Greeks do not identify themselves with the purpose of Turnus, and Aeneas alone has allies definitely identified as Greeks. It should now be obvious which side in this *Iliad* plays the part of the victorious Greeks of Homer. Vergil has united the personalities of Achilles, Agamemnon, and Menelaus in Aeneas, so that the supreme moral justification motivates the leader and finest warrior of the

context of *Il*. 5. 4, in which Diomedes prepares for his great feats. It would seem to me that *Il*. 18. 205 ff. provides a more exact parallel.

Trojans; and similarly he has made Turnus a poignant combination of Paris and Hector, in order that the defeat and death of Italy's noblest warrior will also remove the need for war.

An important council immediately acts on the bad news from Arpi, to decide whether the Italians should admit their error and accept defeat or whether they should continue to fight. The context closely resembles the situation in Troy when Antenor attempted to have Helen returned, recognizing the inevitable, and Paris utterly refused to bow to popular pressure (*Il.* 7. 344 ff.).[14] Under somewhat unfair attack from Drances, Turnus delivers an impassioned appeal for continuance of the war, using arguments which merely exhibit the relative hopelessness of the Italians. Drances had proposed that Latinus give Lavinia to Aeneas as the pledge of peace (11. 355–6). Turnus does not comment expressly on this proposal, but he declares his intention to fight Aeneas in single combat, if necessary, before he will accede. In his excited mood, he makes a fatal statement: he will defeat his foe even though Aeneas surpass Achilles and wear armour made by Vulcan (11. 438 ff.).[15] What, however, Turnus thinks of as a remote contingency, Vergil has shown actually subsists. The immediate comment on the Italian's confidence comes in the attack of Aeneas, who moves his troops forward against the city of Latinus, now obviously reduced to the same condition as Troy. Turnus seizes his opportunity and once again captures the enthusiasm of his people. While the women supplicate Pallas as the Trojan women did in the *Iliad* (6. 297 ff.), Vergil concentrates our attention on the frenzied actions of their general and depicts him vainly imagining his victory. With the utmost care, he selects a simile to describe the irresponsibility of Turnus (11. 492 ff.), which Homer, with great significance, had assigned first to Paris in *Iliad* 6, then to Hector in *Iliad*

---

[14] In the *Iliad*, the council also considers a truce for the purpose of burying the dead, and this truce constitutes the one concrete result of the Trojan discussions; in the *Aeneid*, Drances and his supporters receive much of their impetus to attack Turnus from the noble reply of Aeneas to their request for a truce. But, although the relative sequence differs, both councils take place in the context of truces to bury the fallen.

[15] Conceivably, too, Turnus had the capacity to inflict wounds through Aeneas' armour, for he possessed a sword specially forged by Vulcan also (cf. 12. 89–91). At the time of the final engagement, he exhibits his characteristic irrationality by leaving this particular sword behind, in his hurry (*praecipitem* 12. 735) to begin battle. Turnus also tries, in his rebuttal of Drances, to overwhelm his opponent with sarcasm, and he sneers: 'Now even the leaders of the Myrmidons tremble at Phrygian arms' (403), as though no Italian would ever fear the contemptible Trojans. Since we know that his troops do fear the enemy after their recent defeat and as we remember how Turnus has arrogated to himself the title of Achilles, we might well feel the irony of his statement.

15.[16] We watch the Italian go forth carrying with him the definite association of both Paris and Hector, and, when Camilla falls, we know that Turnus can delay the end no longer.

That night, the Italians hold another council, and Turnus violently proclaims his resolve to fight Aeneas for the hand of Lavinia (12. 14 ff.). Both Latinus and Amata attempt to dissuade him, afraid for his life, and the context, their arguments, and their almost parental concern[17] suggest once again an analogy with *Iliad* 22, where Priam and Hecuba vainly try to prevent Hector from engaging Achilles. Lavinia's feelings remain tantalizingly ambiguous (12. 64 ff.), although Turnus draws his own conclusions. Eagerly he prepares to battle the man whom he contemptuously and ironically labels 'the Phrygian effeminate'.[18] In the morning, the ratification of the treaty and its immediate violation follow the general organization of *Iliad* 4, as all commentators have observed.[19] No doubt exists but that Turnus here takes the part of Paris, for he is the weaker warrior, and it is from his soldiers that comes the move to upset the ceremonies as well as the arrow which wounds Aeneas. This lawless action unmistakably fixes the identity of Turnus and his troops, and at the same time demands the severe punishment subsequently inflicted by Aeneas. The final combat occurs when Aeneas begins a full-scale attack on the city of Latinus. To save the city, Turnus finally consents to engage Aeneas, and a battle ensues which recalls that between Hector and Achilles and produces the same practical results: with Hector's death the resistance of Troy seems hopeless, and with the fall of Turnus the Italian cause will collapse.

It seems clear, from a relatively close study of allusions in the *Aeneid* to the Trojan War, especially to Homer's version, that Vergil has drawn on his predecessor with precision and economy, consistently subordinating the simple technique of imitation to his thematic purpose. At the outset

---

[16] It is not common for Homer to repeat similes in this fashion, and he clearly interprets the limitations of Hector in *Il.* 15. 263 ff. by re-using in entirety the comparison applied in 6. 506 ff. to the irresponsible Paris.

[17] Both Latinus and Amata address Turnus with great feeling, without, however, signifying any relationship. But in his replies, Turnus calls Latinus *pater* (50) and Amata *mater* (74).

[18] *Aen.* 12. 99. Vergil, of course, interprets this remark by attaching a simile to Turnus, comparing the violence of his mood to that of a wild bull (103 ff.), then contrasting it with the sane behaviour of Aeneas. But there is also calculated irony in the fact that Turnus who now unmistakably plays the part of Paris, still conceives of his enemy as Paris.

[19] Cf. Servius on 12. 116: 'Totus hic de foederibus locus de Homero translatus est, ubi Alexander cum Menelao singulari est certamine dimicaturus.' Cf. Servius also at 170 and 212, and Servius Dan. at 176.

he would realize that the wars of Aeneas could not possibly parallel the course of the conflict at Ilium, for Aeneas is destined to conquer his enemies. Moreover, it would contradict the tendency of the Trojan theme in 1–5 to show Aeneas once again playing the role in which we saw him in 2. On the other hand, Vergil sensed the deep relevance of the Trojan War to Aeneas' experiences in Italy, for Aeneas' whole attitude towards arms has been conditioned by the horror of Ilium's destruction. Therefore, the poet makes the struggle doubly poignant for the Trojan by forcing him to listen to the unjust accusations of Amata and Turnus. He who has slowly learned his mission, who has accepted the necessity of denying his love for a woman, must hear himself compared wtih Paris and try to ignore the slanderous talk which lays the origin of the war upon his shoulders. Aeneas does face these allegations squarely, and through his actions, as they are interpreted by Homeric allusions, he demonstrates not only that he is innocent but also that the pattern of the *Iliad* applied so irrationally by his enemies must be entirely reversed. It is he who has honour and victory on his side in the combined roles of Achilles, Menelaus, and Agamemnon. The Italians, in their guilty retention of Lavinia, in their near-successful attack on the encampment, in their violation of the truce, and finally in the loss of their leader have consistently played the very part which they impute to Aeneas and his men. We can understand why it is, in the symbolic conclusion, that Juno expressly recognizes the total destruction of Troy: 'occidit, occideritque sinas cum nomine Troia' (12. 828).[20] She has attempted to preserve the memory of hateful Troy, but now recognizes the transformation in Aeneas and his purpose: the death of Troy signifies the birth of Rome. And Juno's concessions must work themselves out on earth in the tragic, but seemingly necessary, destruction of Turnus, the man who has done the utmost to keep Ilium alive, both in his misguided words and his actions. Vergil depicts Aeneas as the hero who, having subjected himself and having atoned, in the course of this second *Iliad*, for the guilt of the Trojans in Homer's poem, effaces the only reminder left of the ruinous career of Troy.

[20] This is the last occurrence of the word *Troy* in the *Aeneid*, and, except for the word *Teucri* (836) in Jupiter's reply, the last reference to the Trojans.

13

Some Aspects of the Structure of *Aeneid* 7

EDUARD FRAENKEL

I

On *Aeneid* 7. 37, 'Nunc age', Servius observes: 'hinc est sequentis operis initium; ante dicta enim ex superioribus pendent' ('This is the beginning of the work which follows, for what is said before connects with the previous part'). This is obviously correct. That ll. 37 ff. are to be regarded as the prelude to the whole second part of the *Aeneid* follows from the contents of these lines and also from the fact that the opening words 'nunc age ... Erato' are a quotation from the beginning of the second half of Apollonius' *Argonautica* (3. 1) εἰ δ᾽ ἄγε νῦν, Ἐρατώ. It is with this exordium, then, that 'l'*Odyssée* finit, l'*Iliade* d'Énée commence' (Sainte-Beuve, *Étude sur Virgile*, 2nd edition (Paris, 1870), p. 174). We might expect to see the solemn introduction to Part II coincide with the beginning of the Seventh Book. If ever a poet was sensitive to the effects of symmetry and clearly marked arrangement, it was Virgil.[1] And yet here, at one of the most conspicuous points of the *Aeneid*, he allows himself a glaring asymmetry. An attempt to remove the stumbling-block by means of violent textual criticism has been made, but is now justly

[1] *Eclogue* 8, just because as a work of poetry it is of very modest value, is highly suitable for the purpose of showing that Virgil, even at that early stage, set great store by the perfect balance between the two main parts of his poem and made the fullest possible use of the effects of symmetry accentuated by either parallelism or contrast. To the reader who remembers the Φαρμακεύτρια, the manner in which Virgil spoils his model by twisting it into a happy end is almost revolting; but it is obvious that the Latin poet is anxious at all costs to provide a contrast to the sad finale of Damon's song. In detail, there are striking correspondences between Part I and Part II, e.g. the *coniugis* in 18 is responsible for the (of course un-Theocritean) *coniugis* in 66; to the eulogy of Maenalus in 22–4 the eulogy of the *carmina* in 69–71 is exactly parallel, and it is for the sake of parallelism that the latter piece has been interpolated into the context of the Φαρμακεύτρια (whereby Virgil took advantage of l. 15 of the Theocritean poem). Moreover, the wish to produce exact pendants (and probably also a concern for the uniformity of his book) induced Virgil to turn the Φαρμακεύτρια, a town μῖμος, into a bucolic piece, the action of which takes place in the countryside. This he achieved by introducing the names Daphnis, Amaryllis, and Moeris, and by altering the refrain to *ducite ab urbe domum*. In order to enhance the element of symmetry, Virgil furnished Part I, the song of Damon, with a refrain of indifferent content.

forgotten.[2] The difficulty, however, has still to be faced. Instead of pretending that everything is normal when it is not, we should try to answer the question why Virgil has here avoided what seems to be the most natural arrangement.

When the poet determined to make Aeneas' visit to the Cumaean Sibyl and his descent into the realm of Death the climax and conclusion of the Odyssey-part of the *Aeneid*, it must have been clear to him that the second half of the poem could not follow immediately. The scene of the battles and the final victory was Latium, and therefore the shore of Latium had to be reached by the hero before the Iliad-theme could be announced in a special proem. In theory it might have seemed possible within the frame of Book 6 to carry on the narrative to the point when Aeneas arrived at the mouth of the Tiber. But such a plan would have involved either a completely different conclusion of the Hades-scenes or an improper haste in dealing with the last stage of the voyage.

In the closing section of Book 6 the reader's mind is wholly filled with one of Virgil's most moving pictures: 'tu Marcellus eris. manibus date lilia plenis...' Anything that might impair the impression made on our imagination by the pathetic figure of the much-lamented youth and all the other visions of things beyond the grave is eliminated from the few remaining lines of the book; in quick succession Aeneas is brought back to the upper world to be started forthwith on his voyage towards Gaeta. To go beyond this point and include in the same book Aeneas' landing in Latium without disrupting the unity of the close of the Νέκυια would have been feasible only if the gulf between the departure from Cumae and the arrival at the mouth of the Tiber had been bridged by perhaps two or three short sentences. That would have led to the almost unbearable consequence that the two famous landmarks, Gaeta and Monte Circeo with its atmosphere of fairyland memories, would either have had to be passed over altogether or, at most, be hurriedly mentioned and be done with. Such a heavy price Virgil was not prepared to pay. We may assume that it was no easy decision for him to remove from its natural place at the beginning of Book 7 the invocation of the

---

[2] Hofman Peerlkamp thought that Book 7 ought to begin with the invocation (37) 'nunc age, qui reges, Erato...'. Neither general considerations nor the noble and characteristically Virgilian feeling expressed in l. 4 nor the fact that *tu quoque* at the opening of the second half of the poem reminds us of the *te quoque* with which the second half of the *Georgics* begins deterred that fearless critic from drawing the inevitable consequence of his rearrangement and condemning ll. 1–4 as spurious. The solution which Peerlkamp suggested cannot be taken seriously, but it is to his credit that here, as quite often in his notorious edition of Horace's *Odes* and *Epodes*, he has laid his finger on a real difficulty.

Muse, which was to be the τηλαυγὲς πρόσωπον of the second half of the *Aeneid.* If none the less he did not shrink from so grave an inconvenience, he was probably directed by the conviction that in this case regularity of form, however desirable in itself, was of minor consequence compared with the damage that would have been done to the harmony in the conclusion of Book 6 if he had mingled it with elements alien to its lofty and mysterious contents.

The few lines allotted to the account of the origin of Gaeta (7. 1 ff.) contain a characteristic symbol of the two souls within the poet's breast: while the Italian patriot rejoices at the long and glorious history of his country's towns and monuments ('litoribus nostris ... aeternam ... famam ... dedisti'), the sage, a gentle sage, not a Stoic zealot, strikes a note of mellow resignation: 'si qua est ea gloria', and thus makes us see the glory of earthly things in true perspective. Then there follows, introduced by two lines of incomparable music and suggestive power, 'adspirant aurae in noctem nec candida cursus Luna negat, splendet tremulo sub lumine pontus', one of the loveliest episodes of the *Aeneid.* Here Circe, like her son Telegonus a familiar figure in the lore of Latium, makes a personal appearance, combining with the dangerous charms of the Homeric sorceress some of the domestic virtues of a Roman gentlewoman. At this late hour of the night she is busily engaged in weaving and whiles away the monotony of the ἱστῶν παλίμβαμοι ὁδοί ('the back-walking ways of the loom') with never-ending song, to which the animal orchestra of a whole zoological garden produces the strangest accompaniment. So, before taking his farewell from the sphere of his Odyssey, Virgil once more renews the *speciosa miracula* of the old tale in a scene of delightful freshness.

The deep colours of the dawn that follows the night-voyage and the sudden lull of the winds are described with loving care (25–8); for now at long last the great moment has arrived when the ship of Aeneas enters the Tiber in the shadow of a mighty forest (29–36). No small effort of poetical imagination was required to picture in that manner the scenery near the mouth of the great river; for in the poet's time the area was not, as in the days of Dante[3] and, indeed, within the memory of our own generation, a malaria-stricken desert, but, with Ostia stretching on the left bank of the Tiber towards the sea-coast, part of a flourishing and populous district, resounding with the noisy activities of sailors, fishermen, and tradespeople.

---

[3] In *Purg.* 2. 100 ff., the mouth of the Tiber ('la marina ... dove l'acqua di di Tevero s'insala') is represented as the place where the souls destined for Purgatory collect.

We have now reached the exordium (37–45). Like that of Book 1, it blends the Homeric (*Iliad* and *Odyssey*) invocation of the Muse with the fashion in which a *scriptor cyclicus* opens his epic: Ἴλιον ἀείδω καὶ Δαρδανίην εὔπωλον ('I sing of Ilium and Dardania rich in horses') or 'fortunam Priami cantabo et nobile bellum' and the like.[4] The blending is more subtle in 7 than in 1. For there the beginning shows the pure 'cyclic' type, 'arma virumque cano', and only when the elaborate period has reached its end and the predestined goal of all the long labours has been revealed in the momentous words *altae moenia Romae*, does a fresh start introduce the Homeric pattern: 'Musa mihi causas memora', etc. In Book 7, on the other hand, the Muse is invoked right at the outset (37), but as the prelude goes on it is not the goddess to whom the active part falls, but as in Ἴλιον ἀείδω, the poet himself (40 ff.): 'expediam ... revocabo ... dicam ... dicam'. However, in the midst of the clauses which have the poet as their subject we find the words (41) 'tu vatem tu diva mone' so that the whole invocation comes to the same as the sentence εἰπὲ θεὴ σὺ μὲν ἄμμιν, ἐγὼ δ' ἑτέροισιν ἀείσω ('tell me then, goddess, and I shall sing to others'). This exordium, like that of Book 1, though primarily epic, contains some elements which originally belong to the domain, not of poetry, but of historiography. This applies to the motif (1. 8) 'Musa, mihi causas memora ...'[5] and to the clauses (7. 37 f.) 'quae tempora rerum, quis Latio antiquo fuerit status'.[6] In thus widening the two proems beyond the compass of traditional epic patterns Virgil emphasizes the true character of his work: his theme is in the main mythical, but no sharp line divides it from history; for the ultimate end towards which the whole narrative is moving is signified by the words *Romanam condere gentem*, and features of Roman institutions and the spirit of Rome permeate large portions of the poem.

---

[4] On the 'quite un-Homeric' first person in *B* 493 ἀρχοὺς αὖ νηῶν ἐρέω νῆάς τε προπάσας ('I shall tell of the captains of the ships, and of all the ships') see F. Jacoby, *Sitzgsb. Berl. Akad., Phil.-hist. Klasse* 24 (1932), 576; cf. Leaf on *M* 175 ff.

[5] Cf. M. Pohlenz, 'Causae civilium armorum', *ΕΠΙΤΥΜΒΙΟΝ Heinrich Swoboda dargebracht* (Reichenberg, 1927), pp. 201 ff. In this connection notice also 7. 533, *stant belli causae*.

[6] Cf., e.g., the excerpt from Polybius' description of the Roman State at its height, which begins (6. 11. 2) διὸ καὶ τὸν ὑπὲρ τῆς συστάσεως αὐτοῦ λόγον ἀποδεδωκότες πειρασόμεθα νῦν ἤδη διασαφεῖν ὁποῖόν τι κατ' ἐκείνους ὑπῆρχε τοὺς καιροὺς κτλ. ('accordingly, having given an account of its constitution, we shall now attempt to make clear what the situation was at that time'), and Tac. *Hist.* 1. 4: 'ceterum antequam destinata componam, repetendum videtur qualis status urbis ... fuerit' ('but before I set out my intended narrative, one should go back and ask what the state of the city was').

II

The embassy sent by Aeneas to King Latinus is crowned with complete success. After an exchange of friendly speeches and presents:

> Latini
> sublimes in equis redeunt pacemque reportant. (284–5)

At this moment Juno interferes. Her action sets afoot the mischief from which endless bloodshed and misery is to arise. After the hopeful conclusion *pacemque reportant*, the harsh sequence *ecce autem . . . saeva Iovis coniunx* is full of grim foreboding. This clash, while serving as an effective means of dramatization, also expresses the melancholy truth that often men at the very moment when they fancy that they have at last emerged from their troubles are suddenly plunged into fresh disasters. *Pacem* here becomes the cue for the entry of the Fury of war.

Juno's soliloquy (293 ff.) corresponds exactly to her monologue in the First Book (37 ff.). The circumstances which in either case arouse the anger of the goddess are very similar, and so is the manner in which she expresses her indignation. Both speeches are adorned with a brilliant ἐνθύμημα, and here the parallelism is particularly close as will be seen from a comparison of:

> Pallasne exurere classem .
> Argivom . . . potuit . . . . ?
> ast ego, quae divom incedo regina, Iovisque
> et soror et coniunx, una cum gente tot annos
> bella gero (1. 39 ff.)

with:

> Mars perdere gentem
> immanem Lapithum valuit . . . . . . ?
> ast ego, magna Iovis coniunx, ...
> vincor ab Aenea. (7. 304 ff.)

No doubt this parallelism is intentional. Elsewhere, too, Virgil has taken pains to establish links between the first half of Book 7 and the first half of Book 1. Compare, e.g.,

> externi venient generi, qui sanguine nostrum
> nomen in astra ferant quorumque ab stirpe nepotes
> omnia sub pedibus, qua Sol utrumque recurrens
> adspicit Oceanum, vertique regique videbunt (7. 98 ff.)

with:

> his ego nec metas rerum nec tempora pono,
> imperium sine fine dedi . . . . . .
>
> . . . .
>
> nascetur . . . . Caesar,
> imperium Oceano, famam qui terminet astris. (1. 278 ff.)

There is in Juno's speech a passage which cannot have failed to strike the first readers of the *Aeneid* in a peculiar way:

> hac gener atque socer coeant mercede suorum:
> sanguine Troiano et Rutulo dotabere virgo,
> et Bellona manet te pronuba. (317 ff.)

Many of Virgil's contemporaries were young men at the time when the streets of Rome echoed lampoons such as 'socer generque perdidistis omnia'. It would, of course, be foolish to suggest that Virgil was aiming at an allegory when he wrote those lines and that he used the figures of Latinus and Aeneas as a cloak for Caesar and Pompeius. But he may have thought that a reminiscence of the sinister period before the outbreak of the civil war could, as it flashed through the reader's mind, help him to grasp the full misery of internecine war among kinsmen.

In accordance with her threat 'Acheronta movebo' Juno summons the Tartarean fiend, Allecto. The stirring speech which she addresses to the Fury[7] culminates in the words:

> dissice compositam pacem, sere crimina belli;
> arma velit poscatque simul rapiatque iuventus. (339–40)

Thus the theme of the following narrative is clearly announced.

If we are to appreciate the masterly manner in which Virgil has arranged his account of Allecto's errand, it will be best to begin with a survey of this part of the narrative as a whole. The action of the Fury before she returns to Juno clearly falls into three scenes, each of which is subdivided into two distinct parts, the former representing a first, not

---

[7] At 335 f. Juno says 'tu potes unanimos armare in proelia fratres' etc. It is only proper that a goddess, when addressing another deity and asking him or her to do something, should use the same kind of ceremonious language which is used by mortals in their invocations. For δύνασαι, *tu potes*, etc., as a formula of prayers see, e.g., E. Norden, *Agnostos Theos* (Berlin, 1913), p. 154. In the first book of the *Aeneid* Juno begins her prayer-like speech (64 'supplex his vocibus usa est') to Aeolus with these words: 'Aeole, namque tibi divom pater atque hominum rex . . . dedit . . .'. Here the manner in which the vocative is immediately followed by the explanatory *nam*-clause reproduces a well-known type of prayers; cf., e.g., Pindar, *Ol.* 4. 1 f. Ἐλατὴρ ὑπέρτατε βροιτᾶς . . . Ζεῦ· τεαὶ γὰρ Ὧραι . . . μ' ἔπεμψαν κτλ. ('Highest driver of the thunder . . . Zeus; for your Hours have sent me . . .'; Aristophanes, *Eccl.* 1 ff.

altogether successful, attempt on the part of Allecto, the latter the final achievement of her purpose. Each scene opens with a brief introduction. Summarized in a very schematic manner, the arrangement of the three scenes looks like this: I. Allecto flies to the city of Latinus and there works on Amata and through her on the women of Latium (341–405): introduction (341–5); part (*a*) the venom instilled by the Fury has only a mild effect on the queen, 'necdum animus toto percepit pectore flammam', she speaks gently, 'mollius et solito matrum de more', to Latinus, who remains quite unmoved (346–72); part (*b*) the madness caused by the Fury's serpent reaches its climax and Amata, pretending to be inspired by Bacchus, raves through the city and the neighbouring woods and stirs the other women to frenzy (373–405). II. Allecto flies to Ardea and there incites Turnus and through him his people (406–74): introduction (406–14); part (*a*) the Fury, in the disguise of Juno's old priestess, appears to Turnus in his sleep, but her violent appeal leaves him unruffled and he laughs at her in scorn (415–44); part (*b*) Allecto's renewed assault rouses the passions of the young warrior, 'arma amens fremit, arma toro tectisque requirit', and finally he so stirs the Rutulians that they join him in the preparations for battle (445–74). III. Allecto brings about a conflict between Ascanius and the Trojans, on the one hand, and the family of Latinus' chief herdsman on the other, a conflict which then spreads far (475–539): introduction (475–8); part (*a*) the Fury, after reaching a place on the coast where Ascanius is hunting game, maddens his hounds and kindles a wild ambition in the heart of the young huntsman so that he kills a stag, the favourite of the herdsman's daughter Silvia, and thus causes her brothers and their companions to take up arms against him; the weapons used are of a primitive and rustic kind (479–510); part (*b*) the Fury gives from the roof of a stable the signal with the shepherd's clarion, and the sound spreads all over Latium and beyond; the peasants gather from all sides while the Trojans arm in their turn:

> non iam certamine agresti,
> stipitibus duris agitur sudibusve praeustis,
> sed ferro ancipiti decernunt...

Instantly a number of combatants are killed in battle (511–39).

From this skeleton we now turn to the living substance of the poem. The scenes which we have surveyed are all animated by one basic idea: only through the spread of a particular type of insanity can people who shortly before were leading normal and peaceful lives be brought to the state of mind in which they will resort to something so horrible as war (461 'scelerata insania belli'[8]). To carry them to such an extremity is by no means easy: it is significant that with her first assault the Fury never reaches her ultimate aim. Nor will the same means serve to produce the necessary frenzy in everybody. Virgil, not only a man of high ethical ideals but also an experienced judge of the human heart and its weaknesses, symbolizes in a simple and at the same time very impressive manner the variety of motives which urge a mass of blind mortals towards mutual destruction. It is not through some general incentive that the Fury lures her victims into submission but by gradually persuading each of them that the thing he most wants to obtain or preserve will be lost to him unless he goes to war: βιᾶται δ' ἁ τάλαινα Πειθώ, προβούλου παῖς ἄφερτος "Ατας· ἄκος δὲ πᾶν μάταιον, 'miserable Persuasion forces her way, irresistible child of fore-counselling Destruction; every cure is in vain' (Aeschylus, *Agamemnon* 385–7). In Virgil's opinion the combination of different private egoisms plays an important part in preparing that general confusion which is the breeding-ground of war. Queen Amata is not interested in affairs of State, but as a motherly woman she is afraid of seeing her daughter's match broken off by the interference of a foreigner. This very natural feeling gives the Fury her chance. Turnus, on the other hand, would not wish to be deprived of his bride and the kingdom of Latium: therefore the threat of such a loss is enough to rouse his passion. He easily carries his countrymen with him, when he calls upon them to protect the fatherland from foreign invasion (469 'tutari Italiam, detrudere finibus hostem'). The invention of the last of the three scenes is perhaps the happiest, as Virgil is always at his most perfect and most characteristic when dealing with animals and young people. Here the particular type of egoism brought into play by the Fury is of an innocent and indeed attractive kind. Ascanius does not mean any harm: he yields to a young man's keenness to excel in sport, 'eximiae laudis succensus amore', and thus, by wounding poor Silvia's pet, becomes a tool in the hands of Allecto. The deer itself, the earlier stages of its life, and its present sufferings are represented with the sympathy and precision that might be expected from the author of the *Georgics*. Then there are the hounds, at least as eager as their young master to chase the rare quarry; and so it is their natural instinct which the Fury uses for her own purposes. The second part of the third scene is carefully shaped so as to form not only the

---

[8] Cf. 1. 294 ff.: 'claudentur Belli portae, Furor impius intus ... fremet horridus ore cruento'.

completion of this particular scene but the climax of Allecto's action as a whole. Only now has the moment come when her various preparatory measures have stirred up a sufficient amount of mischief and confusion and everything is ready for the decisive stroke (511 ff.): 'saeva ... tempus dea nacta nocendi ... pastorale canit signum'.

In the second part of each scene Virgil emphasizes the intensification of the action begun in the first. This he has achieved by resuming, and at the same time modifying, motifs and also some expressions which he had employed in his account of the Fury's first attempts. It may suffice to illustrate this point by one example from each scene.

I. Part (*a*):

> dum prima lues udo sublapsa veneno
> pertemptat sensus atque ossibus implicat ignem
> necdum animus toto percepit pectore flammam; (354 ff.)

Part (*b*):

> penitusque in viscera lapsum
> serpentis furiale malum totamque pererrat. (374 f.)

II. Part (*a*), Turnus says:

> sed te victa situ verique effeta senectus,
> o mater—*he believes that he is speaking to the priestess of Juno*—
> curis nequiquam exercet et arma
> regum inter falsa vatem formidine ludit, (440 ff.)

and then he haughtily advises her to mind her own business, πόλεμος δ' ἄνδρεσσι μελήσει, 'and war will be the concern of men', or, in Virgil's words,

> bella viri pacemque gerant, quis bella gerenda.

Part (*b*), the Fury replies:

> en ego victa situ, quam veri effeta senectus
> arma inter regum falsa formidine ludit
> ... adsum dirarum ab sede sororum,
> bella manu letumque gero. (452 ff.)

This is a perfect rejoinder to the speech of the young man, and the vigour of the climax at its end is not impaired by the play on the phrase *bella gerere*, which in Allecto's sentence has a meaning entirely different from that in the words of Turnus.

III. Part (*a*):

olli . . . .
improvisi adsunt, hic torre armatus obusto,
stipitis hic gravidi nodis; quod cuique repertum
rimanti, telum ira facit, (505 ff.)

Part (*b*):

non iam certamine agresti,
stipitibus duris agitur sudibusve praeustis,
sed ferro ancipiti decernunt atraque late
horrescit strictis seges ensibus, etc. (523 ff.)

After the Fury has completed her task, she returns to Juno to tell her that her orders have been fulfilled. She then volunteers a further service:

quandoquidem Ausonio respersi sanguine Teucros,
hoc etiam his addam, tua si mihi certa voluntas:
finitimas in bella feram rumoribus urbes
accendamque animos insani Martis amore,
undique et auxilio veniant; spargam arma per agros. (547 ff.)[9]

But this officiousness is rejected by Juno, who, without a word of thanks, tells the goddess of the nether world rather ungraciously 'that will do'— 'terrorum et fraudis abunde est'—and, after producing an argument which sounds as if it were taken from the chapter *de provinciis* in a handbook on the constitutional law of the gods and their magistracies, 'te super aetherias errare licentius auras haud pater ille velit, summi regnator Olympi', curtly bids her be off, 'cede locis; ego, si qua super fortuna laborum est, ipsa regam'. Exit Allecto (561–71). The transition to the next stage in the narrative is made by the sentence:

---

[9] The last words recall, and mark an advance beyond, the conclusion of Juno's command (339 f.) 'dissice compositam pacem, sere crimina belli: arma velit poscatque simul rapiatque iuventus'. Allecto obeys this injunction not only in general but fulfils to the letter its last clause 'arma velit poscatque ... iuventus'. This is shown by the whole of scenes ii and iii and finds a concentrated expression in Turnus' reaction to the Fury's final assault (460): 'arma amens fremit, arma toto tectisque requirit'. Here, as in 11. 453, 'arma manu trepidi poscunt, fremit arma iuventus', in Aeschylus fr. 140 N.[2] ὅπλων ὅπλων δεῖ, 'there is need for arms, arms', in Horace, *Odes*, 1. 35. 15, 'neu populus frequens ad arma cessantis ad arma concitet', and in Ovid, *Met.* 12. 241, 'certatimque omnes uno ore "arma arma" loquuntur', the duplication of the cry *arma* mirrors a very ancient custom. On this and especially the old German *clamor armisonus*: 'wâfenâ wâfen' see Wilhelm Schulze, *Sitzgsb. Berl. Akad.* 26 (1918), 484 = *Kleine Schriften*, 163 f.

Nec minus interea extremam Saturnia bello
imponit regina manum. (572 f.)

But before we hear anything of Juno's intervention we are given a full
picture of the cumulative effect of the tumults caused by the Fury in the
various sections of the population. The order in which the victims of
Allecto's maddening influence are now mustered is the reverse of the
previous scenes: first come the shepherds (572), then Turnus (577), and
finally the *matres* (580). They swarm round Latinus' palace but do not
succeed in rousing the old king to the mood for war. He replies to the
urgent demand of the crowd with a few sad and resigned sentences
(594–9), 'nec plura locutus saepsit se tectis rerumque reliquit
habenas'.[10] In accordance with his whole conduct Latinus refuses to
unbar the Gates of War:[11]

> tum regina deum caelo delapsa morantis
> impulit ipsa manu portas, et cardine verso
> Belli ferratos rupit Saturnia postes. (620–2)

This act of Juno's instantly sets all 'Ausonia' ablaze, and throughout the
country feverish preparations for war are made: 'omnes arma
requirunt'. The subsequent lines down to the end of the section (626–
40) resound with the ring of trumpets and the clatter of javelins and axes
and swords, helmets and shields, breastplates and greaves. Then (641)
the solemn invocation 'pandite nunc Helicona, deae' marks the beginning of another part of the poem. Before we turn to it, it may be well to
pause and look more closely at a detail which in our brief survey we have
passed over.

The reason given by Juno for ridding herself of Allecto at that
particular moment (552 ff.) is not very convincing. If the Fury could be
allowed so long to roam over the surface of the earth, why has she to be
stopped when she is just about to give the last touch to her performance?
As to the sphere of her activities, no fundamental difference exists
between what she has achieved so far and what she offers to do next.
Moreover, why does the task of throwing open the Gates of War fall to
Juno, who is with great suddenness sped down from the sky (620), for no

---

[10] In 59 BC Caesar 'Bibulum [his colleague in the consulate] ... in eam coegit
desperationem ut, quoad potestate abiret, domo abditus nihil aliud quam per edicta
obnuntiaret' (Suetonius, *Div. Iul.* 20. 1; cf. Cassius Dio 38. 6. 5). There is perhaps in
Virgil an intentional reminiscence, cf. above (p. 258) on *gener atque socer.*

[11] The very fine description of the ritual (607–15) makes it particularly clear that the
city of Latinus is to be considered the πρωτότυπον (prototype) of Rome. This accounts for
the expression *immensam ... per urbem* in 377.

other purpose than to perform a function for which an ideal instrument seemed ready in the person of the demon who could justly boast (545) 'perfecta ... bello discordia tristi'? An attractive answer to these questions was given by Eduard Norden in his book *Ennius and Vergilius* (Leipzig, 1915) and has recommended itself to many scholars. According to Norden the weakness which he finds in Virgil's arrangement is due to the fact that the poet interwove the general plan of his work, in which Juno played a leading part, with a peculiar action of Discordia–Allecto, the gist of which as well as some striking details were derived from the Seventh Book of Ennius' *Annals*. The possibility that this was so need not be excluded, but Norden's hypothesis has not been proved, at any rate so far.[12] Nor is the assumption of Virgil's close adherence to a section in the narrative of Ennius the only possible means of accounting for the somewhat strange turn at the end of the Allecto episode. We have seen how extremely suitable the figure of the infernal monster is for personifying the destructive force of that self-centred madness which in Virgil's opinion is the root of war. No particular model was required to put in the poet's head the idea of making a Fury the instigator of such madness. But since he found in Ennius the figure of Discordia (though perhaps not worked out to the degree which Norden assumed nor playing the part of a leading character in an important episode of the story of the Punic Wars), he enriched his own picture with some features taken over or adapted from Ennius, glad as he always was to pay tribute to his forerunner by quoting from, or alluding to, the older master's work. Virgil may also have welcomed the opportunity of making the dispatch of Allecto at the hands of Juno a pendant to the mission of Aeolus in the First Book. He must, however, have decided from the outset that the crowning act, the loosing of the demon of war, was to be performed, not by a subordinate actor, but by Juno herself, the hero's chief antagonist. The abrupt reappearance of the goddess and the brevity of her action (620–2) need not have struck an ancient reader as odd. Norden (op. cit., p. 9, cf. pp. 33 f.) asks the question: 'what has Juno to do with the opening of the temple of Janus?' If I were a Roman schoolboy I might feel tempted to answer: 'Auspiciis imperioque Iunonis bellum cum Aenea gestum est. Iure igitur, sicut Romae consul, in Latini urbe Iuno Ianum aperuit.' A more special answer could perhaps be given if it were possible to ascertain that the part which in Ovid's account (*Met.* 14. 781 f.; *Fast.* 1. 265 f.) of the capture of the gate

---

[12] See the Appendix (below pp. 271 ff.).

of Janus by the Sabine troops of Titus Tatius[13] is played by Juno belonged to the stock of the older tradition. In the parallel account preserved by Macrobius (1. 9. 17), who says 'porta ... postquam est clausa, mox sponte patefacta est', Juno is not mentioned. So one cannot help suspecting that it was a recollection of Virgil which induced Ovid to bring Juno in. This suspicion is increased when we notice that in *Met.* 14. 782, 'nec strepitum verso Saturnia cardine fecit' the three words 'verso Saturnia cardine' are taken over from *Aen.* 7. 621 f.

III

Virgil's genius for adapting the apparently unadaptable and gaining fresh impulses from certain fixed requirements of a conventional technique, which a minor artist might have resented as a tiresome burden, shows itself triumphantly in his version of the Homeric Catalogue.[14] That the Roman *Iliad* had to contain a Catalogue was a foregone conclusion, but what use the poet was to make of it depended entirely on his own tact and inventiveness. If we needed a foil to set off Virgil's excellence in handling this subject, we could find it in the appalling dryness and monotony of the corresponding section in the poem of Apollonius (1. 23–227).

Virgil planned and executed the *Aeneid* on such a scale as to make it the national epic, not of Rome only but of Italy. If this end was to be achieved, it was highly important that the inhabitants of the whole peninsula, including its half-forgotten rural districts and many *municipia* of little fame, should in the great poem find at least some passage which immediately appealed to the pride they derived from their local traditions and customs. All of them should be made to feel that this was not merely the story of a conflict between a Trojan hero and a young prince of Ardea and his Etruscan ally but something in which they had a share themselves. 'Italians have always been curiously proud of the reputation of their birthplace; even in our own time they have searched Mommsen's "History of Rome" for some allusion to their homes, and

---

[13] See F. C. A. Schwegler, *Röm. Geschichte* (Tübingen, 1853), i. 482, and W. F. Otto in Pauly–Wissowa Suppl. iii. 1180.
[14] It is convenient to use this term although it might be more accurate to speak of the two Catalogues (see F. Jacoby, *Sitzgsb. Berl. Akad.* 24 (1932), 572). Virgil draws not only on the κατάλογος νεῶν ('catalogue of ships', in the introduction, 7. 641 ff., and, e.g., 649 ff., an adaptation of B 671 ff.) but also on the Τρωικὸς διάκοσμος, 'array of Trojans' (so 715 the expression 'qui Tiberim Fabarimque bibunt' comes from B 825 πίνοντες ὕδωρ μέλαν Αἰσήποιο, 'drinking the dark waters of Aisepos', and 753–8 is inspired by B 858 ff.).

treasured up the reference with gratitude. "Ha parlato bene del nostro paese," they would exclaim, as he travelled through their town in later days' (W. Warde Fowler, *Virgil's 'Gathering of the Clans'* (Oxford, 1918), 27 f.). So in many an Italian town, small or large, situated in the fertile plain of Lombardy or perched on a steep hill above the valley of the Sacco, you will see, affixed to the wall of a sombre *palazzo*, a modest marble tablet with a few lines from the *Divina Commedia* referring to the place. In Dante numerous passages, distributed over the whole poem, recall characteristic features of the various landscapes of Italy and immortalize the glories and the crimes, the joys and the disasters of its communities. In Virgil, too, there is a great variety of scattered descriptions and allusions of that kind, but the section in which common patriotism and regional pride find their most concentrated expression is the Catalogue whose principal theme is voiced in the words (643 f.) 'quibus Itala iam tum floruerit terra alma viris'. But besides evoking patriotic recollections and giving many men from many towns a strong feeling of 'tua res agitur', the Virgilian Catalogue fulfils a hardly less important function in singling out for special characterization the most prominent of Aeneas' adversaries and thus, overture-like, preparing the reader's mind for some of the main scenes which he is to expect in the remainder of the poem.

The stately invocation of the Muses at the beginning of the Homeric Catalogue (*B* 484 ff.), ἔσπετε νῦν μοι, Μοῦσαι ᾽Ολύμπια δώματ᾽ ἔχουσαι κτλ., 'tell me now, Muses who dwell in the halls of Olympus', must have been welcome to Virgil since, apart from being in itself a fine and dignified motif, it provided him with a device for marking his Catalogue as a separate unit. Here, if anywhere, Virgil speaks *ore rotundo*:

> pandite nunc Helicona,[15] deae, cantusque movete,
> qui bello exciti reges, quae quemque secutae
> complerint campos acies, quibus Itala iam tum
> floruerit terra alma viris, quibus arserit armis.
> et meministis enim, divae, et memorare potestis:
> ad nos vix tenuis famae perlabitur aura. (641 ff.)

[15] It seems doubtful whether Virgil wanted his readers to visualize in the form of a distinct picture the act of *Helicona pandere*. Virgil may possibly have grafted the name of *Helicon* on simpler images in passages of earlier poets such as those quoted by the commentators, Pindar, *Ol.* 6. 27, χρὴ τοίνυν πύλας ὕμνων ἀναπιτνάμεν, 'now the gates of hymns must be opened', and Bacchyl. fr. 5 (Snell), ἀρρήτων ἐπέων πύλας, 'the gates of sacred words'. On the vagueness with which the Latin poets speak of Helicon see U. von Wilamowitz-Moellendorf, *Reden und Vorträge*, i[4] (Berlin, 1925), pp. 105 f.

In l. 643 we should not disregard the special note in *iam tum*. Unlike Homer, Virgil is not content to tell a tale of bygone events but maintains a historical perspective in that he emphasizes, wherever he has a chance, the continuity of things Roman and points to the threads by which the remote past is linked to his own time. We have just come across a characteristic example in the description of the ceremony of opening the Gates of Janus:

> mos erat Hesperio in Latio, quem protinus urbes
> Albanae coluere sacrum, nunc maxima rerum
> Roma colit ... (601 ff.)

Of other instances I will recall only the famous episode of Aeneas' visit to the site of future Rome.[16] In the lines by which it is introduced much is made of the contrast between 'then' and 'now':

> muros arcemque procul ac rara domorum
> tecta vident, quae nunc Romana potentia caelo
> aequavit, tum res inopes Euandrus habebat. (8. 98 ff.)

The end of the invocation of the Muses deserves special attention. At first sight Virgil seems to follow his Homeric model (*B* 485 f.) pretty closely:

> ὑμεῖς γὰρ θεαί ἐστε πάρεστέ τε ἴστέ τε πάντα,
> ἡμεῖς δὲ κλέος οἶον ἀκούομεν οὐδέ τι ἴδμεν.

> for you are goddesses, and are present, and know all,
> while we hear but a rumour, and know nothing.

But the alterations, though unobtrusive, are significant. In the Greek the contrast is quite sharp between hearsay, which guarantees no true knowledge at all (κλέος οἶον ἀκούομεν οὐδέ τι ἴδμεν), and the possession of complete truth based on autopsy (πάρεστέ τε ἴστέ τε πάντα); it almost looks as if in a rudimentary way the poet were interested in theory of knowledge or at any rate in problems of evidence. In Virgil that particular contrast is blunted or, as might be said more adequately, replaced by an entirely different antithesis. What matters here is the problem of historical tradition, where on the one side there is a solid recollection of facts, 'meministis ... et memorare potestis', and on the other side a thin current of rumours, 'ad nos vix tenuis famae perlabitur aura'. It is the latter alone with which a late generation has to be content

---

[16] Cf. especially 8. 349 f.: 'iam tum religio pavidos terrebat agrestis dira loci, iam tum silvam saxumque timebant'.

unless it is fortified by divine assistance. The melancholy undertone in the last sentence is very noticeable; it is in keeping with Virgil's resigned outlook on human life and his conviction that all our possessions and acquirements are utterly precarious. The words 'vix tenuis famae perlabitur aura' remind us painfully of the long distance that separates us from the sources of genuine information, and every single expression illustrates the flimsiness of such traditions as reach us after their long and weary journey. So it is not only the thought of the prayer to the Muses that has changed its character in passing from Homer to Virgil, but the feeling behind it as well. Of course, Virgil, the *doctus poeta*, devoted as he was to the maxim ἀμάρτυρον οὐδὲν ἀείδω, could, if challenged on the ground of his deviation from Homer, refer his critics to a phrase in that very invocation which introduces the Catalogue (*B* 491 f.):

εἰ μὴ 'Ολυμπιάδες Μοῦσαι, Διὸς αἰγιόχοιο
θυγατέρες, μνησαίαθ' ὅσοι ὑπὸ 'Ίλιον ἦλθον

unless you, the Olympian Muses, daughters of aegis-wielding
Zeus, remember all those who came to Troy,

where μνησαίατο seems to contain the Virgilian thought in a nutshell, and furthermore could defend himself by pointing to the fact that Pindar inserted into the Homeric prayer the well-known conception of the Muses as Μνημοσύνης καὶ Ζηνὸς 'Ολυμπίου ἀγλαὰ τέκνα ('glorious children of Memory and Olympian Zeus') when he addressed them thus (*Paean* 6. 54 f.):

ἀλλὰ παρθένοι γὰρ ἴστε Μοῖσαι
πάντα, κελαινεφεῖ σὺν
πατρὶ Μναμοσύνᾳ τε
τοῦτον ἔσχετε τεθμόν.

but you, maiden Muses, know all, and wield authority with your dark-clouded father and with Memory.

Whatever may be thought of such a plea, a characteristically Roman and Virgilian turn is unmistakable in the lines 'et meministis enim, divae, et memorare potestis', etc.

Surveying the whole of Virgil's Catalogue from the point of view of style, a careful observer[17] cannot fail to notice and admire the adroitness

---

[17] See, e.g., J. Henry, *Aeneidea* (Dublin, 1889), iii. 594; R. Heinze, *Virgils epische Technik*[3] (Leipzig, 1914), p. 366 n. 2, and p. 403; L. Bozzi, *Ideali e correnti letterarie nell' Eneide* (Messina and Milan, 1936), p. 153.

with which he avoids monotony. The subject-matter entailed the necessity of repeating over and over again statements like 'they hailed from such and such a region', 'they brought with them such and such a contingent of armed men', etc. And yet 'not two of the Italian chieftains are, I will not say described in the same manner, but, even so much as introduced in the same form' (J. Henry, loc. cit.). To illustrate the variety of colours which Virgil employs while maintaining a close parallelism in the expression of an almost identical notion it will be enough to select two sets of relative clauses:

> qui Nomentum urbem, qui Rosea rura Velini,
> qui Tetricae horrentis rupes montemque Severum
> Casperiamque colunt Forulosque et flumen Himellae,
> qui Tiberim Fabarimque bibunt, quos frigida misit
> Nursia et Hortinae classes populique Latini,
> quosque secans infaustum interluit Allia nomen (712 ff.)

and

> vertunt felicia Baccho
> Massica qui rastris et quos de collibus altis
> Aurunci misere patres, Sidicinaque iuxta
> aequora quique Cales lincunt. (725 ff.)

The neatness of the variations of thought and phrase is obvious. Nor is the sentence-structure monotonous. I will mention one point only. A possible stiffness in the series of parallel relative clauses is avoided by the device of making the men sometimes the grammatical subject, 'qui ... urbem ... colunt', 'qui Tiberim ... bibunt', 'vertunt ... Massica qui rastris', 'qui ... Cales lincunt', and sometimes the object, 'quos ... misit Nursia', 'quos ... interluit Allia', 'quos ... Aurunci misere patres'. At the same time the deliberate iteration of the pronoun, 'qui ... qui ... qui ... qui ... quos', etc., conveys the idea of an almost endless multitude flocking from all over Italy to the common meeting-place.

Virgil permitted himself a bold deviation from the technique of Homer's (and Apollonius') Catalogue when he interspersed the enumeration of the gathering clans with some elaborate similes (674 ff., 699 ff., 718 ff.). In the Second Book of the *Iliad* similes are not to be found within either the Catalogue of Ships or the Array of Trojans, though they serve as a frame to the former.[18] It seems a fair guess that

---

[18] It is from the introduction (see F. Jacoby, *Sitzgsb. Berl. Akad.* 24 (1932), 580 ff.) to the Catalogue of the Ships (*B* 459 ff.) that Virgil borrowed the swan-simile which he placed inside his Catalogue (699 ff.).

Virgil considered a long unbroken catalogue too prosaic and wanted to
raise it to a higher stylistic level by inserting some fine comparisons. A
similar tendency may be observed in the *Georgics*, where (3. 89 ff.) he
rounds off his rather technical description[19] of the horse of noble breed
with a magnificent pair of mythological similes derived from poetical
sources.

Then there is the element of aetiology which Virgil uses, though
sparingly, to give greater variety and interest to his account of the
gathering of the chieftains. We find it in 706 ff.:

> ecce Sabinorum prisco de sanguine magnum
> agmen agens Clausus ...
> Claudia nunc a quo diffunditur et tribus et gens
> per Latium, postquam in partem data Roma Sabinis.

and again in 778 ff.:

> unde etiam templo Triviae lucisque sacratis
> cornipedes arcentur equi, ...

Here, in the context of the story of Virbius–Hippolytus, the aition marks
the climax of a fairly long mythological digression. The poet seems to
welcome the opportunity to escape for a moment from the task of
enumeration and to dwell on the more congenial theme of a truly
Hellenic myth and the hero of a great tragedy.

The plan that underlies the arrangement of the opening and concluding parts of the Catalogue is easily discerned. 'Virgil places at the head
Mezentius and Lausus, at the end Turnus and Camilla, so that the few
characters who are to play a leading part in the fighting form a frame to
set off the less important ones' (R. Heinze, *Virgils epische Technik*[3], p.
444). In the case of Mezentius it is obvious that he heads the list because
he, the *contemptor divom*,[20] is in every respect the opposite of the *pius
Aeneas*. The manner in which the poet then speaks of Mezentius' son,

---

[19] Its source can be reconstructed with the help of Columella (Varro is quite different).

[20] J. Henry, *Aeneidea*, iii. 361 (who is followed by W. Warde Fowler, *Virgil's 'Gathering
of the Clans'* (Oxford, 1918), p. 43) justly says that *contemptor divom* denotes in the main the
'violator of the divine laws'. He is of course right, too, when he states that the phrase does
not mean 'infidel'; for this word has no place in the vocabulary of Greek and Roman
religion. But how can Henry deny that 'blasphemer' is implied? If Mezentius' boast in 10.
773 f. 'dextra mihi deus et telum, quod missile libro, nunc adsint' is not blasphemy, one
would like to know what is. Servius correctly explains 'ut non alium sibi putet deum esse
sacrilegus quam dextram et fortitudinem'. Nettleship ad loc. compares the similar
arrogance of Parthenopaeus in Aeschylus, *Seven against Thebes* 529 f. (on this and kindred
instances cf. U. von Wilamowitz-Moellendorf, *Aischylos—Interpretationen* (Berlin, 1914),
p. 99 n. 2).

Lausus, forecasts the deeply moving scene of the young hero's death in Book 10. The details of the action in which he sacrifices himself to save his father's life are inspired by a fine episode in the *Aethiopis*.[21] In the first part of that epic the dominating figure was the Amazon Penthesilea, and it was therefore the authority of a venerable poem that justified Virgil in assigning to the fighting virgin Camilla a prominent place among the adversaries of Aeneas and devoting to her as much as half a book of the *Aeneid* (11. 498–867). The appearance of Camilla in the centre of the action is foreshadowed by the ending of the Catalogue. After this delicate and loving introduction of the Volscian maiden no reader could have any doubt that he would hear a great deal more about her at a later stage. So the conclusion of the Catalogue points forward, but it also forms a most harmonious finale for the Seventh Book. Rather than spoil a masterpiece in a vain attempt to paraphrase it we prefer to listen quietly to the poet's own words and, while we do so, enjoy the perfect diminuendo in which the martial rhapsody passes away and feel the intense sadness of so much grace and beauty doomed to death in battle:

> illa vel intactae segetis per summa volaret
> gramina nec teneras cursu laesisset aristas,
> vel mare per medium fluctu suspensa tumenti
> ferret iter, celeris nec tingeret aequore plantas.
> illam omnis tectis agrisque effusa iuventus
> turbaque miratur matrum et prospectat euntem,
> attonitis inhians animis, ut regius ostro
> velet honos levis umeros, ut fibula crinem
> auro internectat, Lyciam ut gerat ipsa pharetram
> et pastoralem praefixa cuspide myrtum. (7. 808–17)

APPENDIX

The Seventh Book of Ennius' Annals *and* Aeneid VII

On the problem to which I have referred above (p. 264) I do not wish to pronounce a final verdict but only to offer a few remarks which may stimulate further investigation. This is perhaps not quite useless, since I know from my own and other scholars' experience how difficult it is not

---

[21] See my article 'Vergil und die Aithiopis', *Philol.* 87 (1932), 242 ff.

to succumb completely to the fascination of Norden's brilliant reconstruction.

Norden begins (pp. 10 ff.) his examination of fragments of Ennius' *Annals* with 521 f. Vahlen:

> corpore Tartarino prognata paluda virago,
> cui par imber et ignis, spiritus et gravis terra.

By combining this fragment on the one hand with Empedocles fr. 17 (Diels), and on the other hand with Virgil's description of Allecto,[22] the *virgo sata Nocte* (331), the *Cocytia virgo* (479), who is one of the *sorores Tartareae* (327 f.), Norden was able to show that the infernal creature, the *paluda virago*, is identical with Νεῖκος, Discordia. This important conclusion was strengthened by E. Bignone, *Riv. di filologia* NS 7 (1929), 10 ff. (reprinted in the author's *Studi sul pensiero greco* (1938), pp. 327 ff.), who improved on Norden's interpretation of the clause *cui par imber*, etc., and made its relation to Empedocles clearer (Hermann Fränkel, *Hermes* 70 (1935), 62 f., without knowing Bignone's article, reached the same result). Unfortunately we know nothing of the context in which Ennius' *paluda virago* appeared. As regards the famous fragment:

> postquam Discordia taetra
> Belli ferratos postes portasque refregit (266–7)

no use can be made of it to elucidate the lines about the *paluda virago*. For, first, it is quite uncertain whether in the text of Ennius the two fragments were found near or fairly near to one another (in fact, I am convinced that they were not, see below), and secondly the sentence *postquam Discordia taetra* ... does not furnish any clue which would enable us to refer it to any particular event in Roman history. Such a clue would indeed exist if the Dutch scholar Paulus Merula, who in 1595 accompanied his edition of the *Annals* of Ennius with a running historical commentary (reprinted by E. Spangenberg in 1825), was right in connecting the Discordia fragment with what our authorities[23] tell us about the closing and subsequent reopening of the *porta Iani* within the one year 235 BC. Merula was followed by, e.g., Lucian Müller, *Quintus Ennius* (1884), 168, and Norden, loc. cit., 56 ff. Norden made this date the cornerstone of his whole edifice. But the underlying interpretation

---

[22] Here Norden had a forerunner in Scaliger, see L. Valmaggi, *Q. Ennio, I frammenti degli Annali* (Turin, 1900), p. 141, and Norden, pp. 20 f.

[23] See F. Münzer in P.–W. xiv. 1207 f.

of the Discordia-fragment is unsound. Vahlen, though he did not produce an argument to support his statement, was right when he protested (p. clxxxvi): 'Quis vero non videt haec quae Ennius scribit *postquam Discordia taetra . . . refregit* non posse ad Iani aperti vel operti tempora astringi.' It is the grammatical form of the sentence which absolutely refutes the conclusion drawn from it by Merula and his followers. We may at once discard the impossible continuation excogitated by Norden (p. 33): 'after Discordia had smashed in the gates of War, she flew away'; for it would not be difficult to think of a more suitable main clause. But, however we continue the passage, the fact remains that the very act in which, according to Norden's reconstruction, the whole errand of Discordia was to culminate, the act which would be the only reason for her appearing on earth, is described, not in an independent sentence, but in a subordinate clause. This I regard as inconceivable in an epic narrative. It would not help us if we tried to get out of the difficulty by making the assumption (improbable though it is in itself) that somewhere before the words *postquam Discordia taetra . . .* the opening of the gate was narrated in a direct manner. For in that case we should be forced to believe that Ennius used for his description of the original act less forcible words than for the sentence which we suppose to be retrospective: otherwise Horace (*Sat.* 1. 4. 60 f.) would not have chosen this very sentence to illustrate the indestructible power of genuine poetical language. It is not, however, considerations of form alone that warn us against following Norden. According to him (p. 146) Ennius in the Seventh Book of his *Annals* related how, after the success in 235 BC of the Carthaginian party which was against war with Rome, peace was restored throughout the territory under Roman control, so that the consul T. Manlius Torquatus closed the gate of Janus: and how Juno disliked this state of affairs, summoned Discordia from Tartarus and ordered her to break the gate open again, which, only a few months after its being closed, Discordia did. 'Whereupon the Fury betook herself back to Hell.' Now while making full allowance for the odd inventions to which a poet may be driven who has taken upon himself the task of mingling Roman history with elements of Homeric mythology, we should not forget that there are limits to what we can believe Ennius to have done. I for one am not prepared to foist on him anything so childish as this. It is tolerable, though perhaps not pleasant, that the description of the Hannibalic War should be interrupted by a scene in Heaven, a *concilium deorum*, in consequence of which Juno at last forsakes her hostility to the Romans (see Vahlen, p. clxxxix, and for a different reconstruction, Norden, p. 147). In this case, and in similar ones, the two actions are set on two separate planes. But that is a very different matter from a narrative in which Discordia steps into the consul's shoes. Are we really to believe that Ennius, after giving an account of T. Manlius closing the gate, shortly afterwards told his readers that for the act of reopening it a mythological monster took the place of the consul? The events which the poet is supposed to have treated in such a fantastic manner occurred during his own lifetime.

The place, then, where the action of *postquam Discordia taetra* ... should be localized is the aether of poetical imagery but not the solid ground on the north side of the Roman forum, near the *infimum Argiletum*, where the *Ianus geminus* stood. Valmaggi appropriately remarks on Ennius, *Ann.* 266 f. (= 149 Valm.)—'it is easy to see that, rather than referring to the physical closing and opening of the temple, the phrase *Belli ... postes portasque refringere* is simply a poetic periphrasis by which the recommencement of war is marked in general terms (cf. Virg. *Aen.* 1. 293 sg. *dirae ferro et compagibus artis claudentur Belli portae)*': cf. also Vahlen[2], p. clxxxvi, and F. Leo, *Geschichte der röm. Literatur* 1 (1913), 176. It seems a hopeless task to try to make out the particular war to the outbreak of which the sentence *postquam Discordia taetra* ... referred. It is conceivable that it was no particular war at all but war in general (e.g. 'once war has broken out, things are like this' or something of that kind). Vahlen, who was followed by Ribbeck, Valmaggi, Leo, and others, placed the Discordia-fragment in the introduction to the account of the Hannibalic War; but this is of course quite arbitrary. Finally, it seems impossible to construct a link between the Discordia-fragment and the *paluda virago* fragment discussed above. Since the sentence *postquam Discordia taetra* ... probably served to symbolize in a concise form the outbreak of war, it is very unlikely that in that context there would have been room for the detailed description *corpore tartarino prognata paluda virago, cui par imber*...

Of three fragments (260–2 Vahlen), viz. (1) 'sulphureas posuit spiramina Naris ad undas', (2) 'russescunt frundes', (3) 'longique cupressis stant rectis foliis at amaro corpore buxum', our authorities tell us that they come from the Seventh Book of Ennius' *Annals*. In a very ingenious section of this book (pp. 25 ff.) Norden endeavours to prove that all three fragments belong to the description of a Πλουτώνιον, or 'entrance to the Underworld', and then goes on to conclude that the Πλουτώνιον in question, a cave in the neighbourhood of Narnia, is the locality through which Ennius' Discordia, after breaking open the Gates of War, made her departure from the earth back to Hades in the same manner in which Virgil's Allecto disappears through the *Ampsancti valles* (7. 561–71). That the fragments *russescunt frundes* and *longique cupressi*, etc., formed part of the description of a *Πλουτώνιον* is possible but quite uncertain, and the similarity with the Virgilian passage 7. 565 f., with which Norden compares them, cannot be said to be particularly close.

As regards the sentence 'sulphureas posuit spiramina Naris ad undas', Norden's idea of making 'Dis' or 'Orcus' its subject, since Virgil (568) terms the cave through which Allecto withdraws *saevi spiracula Ditis*, is certainly attractive and perhaps right. If so, the words *sulphureas posuit* ... would definitely come from the description of a *Πλουτώνιον* in the neighbourhood of Narnia. But does it follow that in Ennius' Seventh Book that place was mentioned as the locality of the disappearance of Discordia? Only if we take for granted what we have to prove, viz. that the main features of Virgil's Allecto episode were borrowed from Ennius. I would, without any undue confidence, suggest that in Priscian, *Gramm.* 2. 223. 4, in the place of *Ennius in vii annalium* we might consider the possibility of reading *in viii*. Supposing this to be correct, the words 'sulphureas posuit spiramina Naris ad undas' could for instance belong to a description of the region in which after the Battle of Cannae important troop movements took place; cf. Polybius 3. 88. 8 συμμίξας δὲ (Fabius) ταῖς ἀπ' Ἀριμίνου βοηθούσαις δυνάμεσι περὶ τὴν Ναρνίαν,[24] Γνάιον μὲν τὸν ὑπάρχοντα στρατηγὸν ... ἐξαπέστειλε κτλ, 'and joining his men with the aiding forces from Ariminium in the region of Narnia, he sent out Gnaeus the then general...'.

The difficulty which Norden (pp. 36 f.) finds in *Aen.* 7. 516 f. 'audiit et Triviae longe lacus, audiit amnis sulphurea Nar albus aqua fontesque Velini' is no real one. Virgil's conception, bold though it is, will be readily appreciated by readers who are familiar with the geography of the country and at the same time willing to use their imagination. The poet describes how the sound of the Fury's horn spreads from somewhere near Pratica di Mare[25] over the plain of the Campagna

---

[24] The MSS have δαυνίαν (cf. the preceding paragraphs), but Seeck's emendation Ναρνίαν has been rightly adopted by, e.g., Büttner-Wobst and G. De Sanctis, *Storia dei Romani*, 3. 2 (Turin, 1917), 47, n. 73.

[25] I do not propose to discuss what town, if any corresponded in reality to Virgil's city of King Latinus, which certainly neither the poet and his contemporaries nor earlier writers ever called 'Laurentum'. In addition to the careful examination of the evidence by Wissowa, *Hermes* 50 (1915), 23 ff., and J. Carcopino, *Virgile et les origines d'Ostie* (Paris, 1919), pp. 171–387, see, e.g., T. Ashby, *The Roman Campagna in Classical Times* (London,

Romana until in the east it breaks against the wall of the Alban Hills, whereas to the north it travels much farther, goes a long way up the valley of the Tiber and finally reaches the mountainous region where the great river is joined by its tributary the Nera. If the idea that the alarm signal of the Fury covered this enormous distance is really 'grotesque' (Norden, p. 38), then it is hard to see how the grotesqueness can be extenuated by Norden's hypothesis. He assumes that Virgil transferred the 'Nar-motif' from its place in Ennius, where it formed part of the description of the cave through which Discordia disappeared, to the different context in which we read it in the *Aeneid*. All I am able to see is that Virgil chose the immense distance from the town of Laurentes to the region of the Nera and the Velino for the sake of its own suggestive grandeur, and then, in order to embellish his description of the locality and also to honour once more the memory of Ennius, added an allusion to the old poet's expression *sulphureas ... Naris ad undas*. Norden himself rightly observes (p. 44) that Virgil often borrows phrases from Ennius without applying them to the same matter or a similar one.

To sum up. When Virgil created his Allecto, he did all he could to make it clear that this monster was to all intents and purposes identical with Discordia. The phrasing of Juno's command (335 ff.) 'tu potes unanimos armare in proelia fratres atque odiis versare domos ... disice compositam pacem, sere crimina belli' and Allecto's own words (545) 'en perfecta tibi bello discordia tristi' are especially characteristic. In working out his picture of the Fury Virgil may perhaps have had in mind Ennius' description of Discordia: *corpore Tartarino prognata paluda virago*, etc., but this is not certain. The famous sentence *postquam Discordia taetra ... refregit* was used by Virgil, not as material for the figure of Allecto, but to give additional force to the scene in which Juno violently throws open the Gates of War. In the preserved fragments of Ennius there is nothing to indicate that anywhere in his narrative Discordia performed an action or a series of actions comparable with the actions begun by Allecto and completed by Juno in the Seventh Book of the *Aeneid*.

1927), pp. 209 f., H. Last, *CAH* 7 (Cambridge), 488, Catharine Saunders, *Vergil's Primitive Italy* (New York, 1930), pp. 53 ff., and especially B. Rehm, *Das geographische Bild des alten Italien in Vergils Aeneis*, Philologus Suppl. 24. 2 (1932), 50 ff.

14

Hercules in the *Aeneid*

G. K. GALINSKY

Vergil's *Aeneid* is one of the most complex works of literature, and, accordingly, the reasons for Herakles' role in the *Aeneid* are many. One of them, however, stands out in particular since it is related to one of the central purposes of the epic. The *Aeneid* was an attempt to make Aeneas the truly popular, national hero of all of Italy, to give him precisely the role that Herakles had held in Greece. The Aeneas legend lacked the popular foundation which the Herakles myth had in Greece and even in Italy. Vergil's contemporary Dionysius relates that

In many other [i.e. outside Rome] places in Italy precincts are dedicated to this god and altars erected to him, both in cities and along highways; and one could scarcely find any place in Italy in which the god is not honoured. (*Rom. Antiq.* 1. 40. 5)

It therefore was by no means impossible that Herakles might have been accepted as the popular ancestor of the Romans and Italians.[1] For even in Rome, Aeneas had been the sole property of a few noble families, among them the Julians, and since Octavian was a member of that family Aeneas was chosen to be the hero of the new epic.

Vergil assimilates Aeneas to Herakles virtually from the very beginning. In its proem, which is a programmatic synopsis of the *Aeneid*, Aeneas is introduced as 'a fugitive by fate' and a man 'persecuted by the relentless wrath of harsh Juno'. The traditional echoes are obvious and intentional. We need only compare what Homer's Achilles, another model of the Vergilian Aeneas, said about Herakles (*Il.* 18. 119): 'But fate subdued him and the troublesome wrath of Hera.' Of all the themes sketched in the seven-line proem, Vergil proceeds to reiterate that of Juno's wrath in the invocation to the Muse. He explicitly impresses upon the reader that of the basic themes in the *Aeneid*, this is the most significant. 'What reason,' asks the poet, 'what hurt drove Juno to make Aeneas undergo so many labours? Is divine wrath so great?' 'Labour'

---

[1] So, e.g., H. Hill in *JRS* 51 (1961), 90. For the lack of the popularity of the Aeneas legend before Vergil see my *Aeneas, Sicily, and Rome* (Princeton, 1969).

and 'wrath' are placed emphatically at the end of lines 10 and 11. Throughout the epic, Juno is the personal enemy of Aeneas and she acts from petty, personal motives. But Juno's prominent role and her characterization are Vergilian innovations which are the result of the poet's desire to portray Aeneas as a second Herakles.[2]

The strongest verbal reminder of Aeneas' Herculean role is the persistent use of *labor* to denote Aeneas' task. Aeneas himself uses it many times to characterize himself and his adventures to those whom he meets on the way. The beginning of his programmatic introduction to Venus, whom he at first fails to recognize, is perhaps the most typical example:

> O dea, si prima repetens ab origine pergam,
> et vacet annalis nostrorum audire laborum,
> ante diem clauso componet Vesper Olympo. (1. 372–4)

O goddess, if I should tell you my story from its beginnings, and you had time to listen to the story of my labours, the Evening Star would close Olympus' gates and end the day before I finished.

Only after Aeneas has stressed his *llabores* does he mention the quality for which he was dear to the Romans and to Augustus in particular, his *pietas* (1. 378).

This conception of Aeneas of himself is confirmed by the many oracular and divine agencies who are guiding him through his trials. Venus pleads with Jupiter to grant Aeneas an end to his *labores* (1. 241), and she uses the term again when she asks Vulcan to provide Aeneas' arms (8. 30). After all the oracles in Book 3 apply the term *labor* to each new trial of Aeneas, Jupiter himself sanctions it in Book 4 when he asks Mercury to tell Aeneas to shoulder his burden (*molitur ... laborem* 4. 233). The expression recalls the exertion of Atlas, but Herakles' shouldering of Atlas' starry burden was well remembered in Augustan Rome. Ovid (*Fasti* 1. 565–8) linked it explicitly to Herakles' fight against Cacus which, as we shall see, plays such a significant part in the *Aeneid*. Aeneas' greatest *labor*, foreshadowed by the Herakles–Cacus episode in Book 8, is his fight against Turnus and the Latins. This is the note on which Anchises ends his prophecy in Book 6:

---

[2] There is nothing in the pre-Vergilian tradition of the Aeneas legend to suggest even remotely a similar role of Juno. For Ennius' view of her see Servius, *Ad Aen.* 1. 281 and 12. 841, and J. Vahlen, *Ennianae Poesis Reliquiae*, 2nd edn. (Leipzig, 1928), CLIX–CLX. It has long been recognized that Allecto is modelled on Euripides' Lyssa, and this is no accident because Vergil deliberately so characterized Juno as to recall the Hera—Tychē of Euripides' *Herakles*.

> exin bella viro memorat quae deinde gerenda,
> Laurentisque docet populos urbemque Latini,
> et quo quemque modo fugiatque feratque laborem. (6. 890–2)

He tells him of the wars which he has to wage and of the Laurentian peoples and the city of Latinus, and how he is to flee and bear each toil.

'The practice of these warning agencies', as one scholar has noted, 'of applying the term *labor* to each fresh trial of Aeneas implies a perception of the similarity of the experience of Aeneas with the labours of Herakles on the part of those who presumably would have a clearer insight into the workings of destiny—Venus and the ghost of Anchises, for example.'[3] Aeneas himself, however, meanwhile expresses far more strikingly that he considers himself Herakles' heir. When he leaves Troy, he lifts his father on his shoulders, a scene which in both art and literature has been considered as the very incarnation of *pietas*. 'This labour will not weigh me down', Aeneas assures Anchises. For, as it turns out, around his shoulders he wears the lion's skin (2. 722). Besides Aeneas' being a saviour, σώτηρ, like Herakles, his immediate task—the pious rescue of his father—and the task for which he is setting out—*Romanam condere gentem*—have both the physical and the spiritual dimension which had characterized Herakles' labours since Pindar. The balance between the two aspects is exquisite; Vergil's Herakles ideal is a world apart from Apollonius'.

Aeneas' Herculean self-awareness is emphasized even more as the epic progresses. When he descends to the Underworld he duplicates a feat of Herakles. It is by reference to Herakles that he tries to dispel the Sibyl's doubts. His justification begins on the note of his *labores*:

> non ulla laborum,
> o virgo, nova mihi facies inopinave surgit:
> omnia praecepi[4] atque animo mecum ante peregi. (6. 103–5)

For me, o prophetess, not one new or unexpected kind of labour rises up: I have foreseen them all and pondered them in my mind.

The analogy is quite precise, for the fetching of Cerberus was Herakles' last and crowning labour. Aeneas then goes on to speak of his first

---

[3] P. McGushin, 'Vergil and the Spirit of Endurance', *AJPh* 85 (1964), 236. James Henry, *Aeneidea* 1 (London, 1873), pp. 187–8, was the first to notice that *labor*, as applied to Aeneas, was meant to correspond to Herakles' ἄεθλος, 'labour'.

[4] *Praecipere* is used here as a technical Stoic term, as is clear from Seneca's comment on this line in *Epist.* 76. 33. Stoicism was another, though not the overriding reason for the association of Aeneas and Herakles in the *Aeneid*; see below.

Herculean labour, the rescue of his father (6. 110–11). All this builds up to the powerful conclusion of his speech:

> quid Thesea magnum,
> quid memorem Alciden?—et mi genus ab Iove summo. (6. 122–3)

Why should I mention Theseus? why the great Herakles? I, too, have descent from Jove most high.

The Sibyl fully understands the force of these arguments by acknowledging that Aeneas is god-born (125) and that he is engaged in a difficult labour: *hic labor est* (129). This labour is not, as Aristophanes' Dionysus believed, the descent to Hades, but the return to the world of reality, to the very *labores* with whose mention Anchises sends Aeneas back from Hades. As in Aeneas' departure from Troy, *labor* here stands for both the immediate—the actual retracing of the steps—and the more comprehensive, future task. One is again reminded of Euripides' Herakles whose real labours only began after he had successfully returned from the Underworld. The terms in which the Sibyl describes the men who prevailed before Aeneas (129–31) clearly shows that she, too, considers Herakles as his chief model. Already Homer had stressed that Herakles was dearest of all to Zeus (*Il.* 18. 118), and in all of Greek and Roman mythology, he was the hero *par excellence* whose *virtus*, ἀρετή, was explicitly said to have raised him to heaven. Aeneas' claim to being Herakles' heir has prevailed, and the Sibyl will help him in his *insanus labor* (6. 135).

The Herculean reminiscences continue. When Aeneas sees various *monstra* (285), he acts like Herakles in Bacchylides' Meleager poem, draws his sword and tries to kill them before he learns that they are only shades.[5] Among the monsters are those against which Herakles fought—the centaurs, the Lernaean hydra, and Geryon. Another is the flame-spouting Chimaera which later appears on the helmet of Turnus. Aeneas' Herculean shadow-fight anticipates the real *labor* he faces after returning from the Underworld.

When the Sibyl and Aeneas reach the river Styx, Charon explicitly refers to the precedent of Herakles and at first refuses to ferry Aeneas over. After the Sibyl reassures him that Aeneas is not a man of force, but *pietas*, Charon permits the 'gigantic Aeneas' (*ingentem Aenean* 413) to step into the boat. The result is almost the same as when Herakles came

---

[5] For the most recent view on a possible epic *katabasis* of Herakles, which was known to Bacchylides, Pindar, Aristophanes, and Vergil, see H. Lloyd-Jones, *Maia* 19 (1967), 221–9.

aboard the *Argo* (413–14): 'The sewn-leather boat groaned under his weight; marshy water seeped in through the rents he had made.' Somewhat later, Aeneas sees Dido as Lynceus in the *Argonautica* saw Herakles for the last time. From then on, Aeneas' way becomes a burden for him (*molitur . . . iter* 477), the kind of burden that Jupiter, implicitly likening Aeneas to Herakles, said Aeneas would have to shoulder (*molitur . . . laborem* 4. 233). Later in Book 6 the shades of the deceased flee before Aeneas (489–93) as they had fled before Herakles in the *Odyssey* (11. 605–6). This Homeric adaptation is all the more remarkable as the literary model for Aeneas' descent into Hades was the Odysseus of the *Nekyia*. But while Vergil was strongly interested— mostly because of the popular *Odissia Latina*, Italy's national epic before the *Aeneid*—that Aeneas should supplant Odysseus, he was just as anxious to stress that Aeneas was Herakles' spiritual heir.

Finally, the Herakles theme in Book 6 recurs in Anchises' ecstatic prophecy about Augustus' future greatness (6. 801–3). 'Not even Herakles', he exclaims, 'traversed so much of the earth, though he shot the bronze-footed deer, or brought peace to the woods of Erymanthus and made the Lernaean hydra tremble at his bow'—

> nec vero Alcides tantum telluris obivit,
> fixerit aeripedem cervam licet, aut Erymanthi
> pacarit nemora et Lernam tremefecerit arcu. (6. 801–3)

The passage is, to be sure, imperial panegyric, and Augustus' association with the Herakles theme needs some additional comment. Before discussing it, however, we should be aware that Vergil never stops at singing the praises of his emperor. The passage—and it is typical of virtually any passage in the *Aeneid*, even the most 'episodic' ones—is carefully integrated into the immediate and larger context. Throughout Book 6 and even earlier Aeneas has been presented as a second Herakles; it is only natural that Augustus, who would bring to fruition the labours begun by Aeneas, should surpass Aeneas and his model, Herakles. The labours are purposely so chosen as to illustrate Augustus' particular achievement.[6] The poet is not really concerned to show that Augustus travelled more widely than Herakles, for of the three labours mentioned, only that of the Ceryneian hind, which Herakles pursued to the Hyperboreans, would have been suitable for that purpose. Rather, Herakles once more is depicted as the *sotēr* who brings peace (*pacarit*) as did Augustus who used the same word, *pacare*, three times in his

6 See E. Norden, *RhM* 54 (1899), 472–3.

autobiography. More specifically, Herakles pacifies Arcadia. Vergil had praised Augustus for this very achievement as early as the First *Eclogue*, and the implication is the same in the *Aeneid*. The fight of Herakles against Cacus also is placed into the bucolic setting of old Italy, which is ruled by Evander, king of the Arcadians.

Anchises follows up the Herakles *exempla* and the prophecy of Augustus' glory with a moral exhortation to Aeneas: he is to add to his *virtus*, the distinctive attribute of both Herakles and the Romans, by doing yet more (806)—

> et dubitamus adhuc virtutem extendere factis ...?

Later in the epic, another father repeats almost the same exhortation to his son. This is in Book 10 when Jupiter consoles Herakles, whom Pallas had invoked to grant him victory over Turnus:

> sed famam extendere factis
> hoc virtutis opus. (10. 468–9)

This intentional echo reinterprets Anchises' admonition to Aeneas. Jupiter's and Anchises' advice is pragmatic in the best Roman tradition. What matters is the *res gestae*, the fulfilment of the task at hand. And, in the spiritual Herculean tradition, outward glory and outward success are minimized, if not eschewed entirely. Pallas fails in his combat with Turnus whereas Aeneas, though ostensibly victorious to the very end, is agonized by the conquests he must constantly make to bring the gods to Latium. The Augustan reign is in the too distant future, and the glories of Homeric carnage are in the too distant past for Aeneas joyfully to partake in either. He is the reluctant hero, somewhat like Jason—*Italiam non sponte sequor*—who is revolted by many things he must do, but accepts the demands of fate and the gods for the sake of a good that is greater than his personal interests. This is Vergil's god-fearing sublimation of Euripides' Herakles ideal. Nor was abhorrence of bloody deeds incompatible with Herakles' character by Vergil's time. The Greek historian Timaeus, who was one of the first to write on Rome and thus exerted a considerable influence over Roman historiography, had further expanded the notion of Herakles' unwillingness to engage in his bloody type of work. According to Timaeus, he did so only because of the orders of others, and when he had his own way, he instituted the Olympic games which featured contests that did not require the shedding of blood.[7] Likewise, Aeneas' ideal and, we might add, Vergil's,

---

[7] *FGH* 566 F 22.

is that of *placida quies*, although the hero can achieve it only through bloody warfare with all its brutalizing effects.

So it is in the spirit of Herakles when, for the third time in the *Aeneid*, a father—Aeneas—addresses his son, Ascanius:

> disce, puer, virtutem ex me verumque laborem,
> fortunam ex aliis. (12. 435–6)

Learn, my son, *virtus* and true labour from me; fortune from others.

Besides echoing the earlier father–son scenes, both of which involved Herakles, Aeneas' admonition recalls two other, earlier exhortations. In Book 3 Andromache, the wife of Troy's greatest warrior, ends her speech by exhorting Aeneas that he and the memory of Ascanius' uncle, Hector, should arouse in Ascanius the old-fashioned (*antiqua*) *virtus* and manly spirit (3. 342–3). It is the Homeric *aretē* of the warrior which Andromache, deprived of her own son, would like to see live on in her nephew. Similarly, in Book 9, where Ascanius has his glorious day in the field, Apollo—Augustus' favourite god—emerges as his divine cheerleader and addresses the victorious Iulus: 'A blessing, boy, on your young *virtus*. That is the way to reach heaven, you offspring and father of gods'—

> macte nova virtute, puer, sic itur ad astra,
> dis genite et geniture deos. (9. 641–2)

But when Aeneas himself, who has just been wounded in battle, finally exhorts Ascanius, he reinterprets the martial *virtus*, to which Andromache and Apollo had appealed, as the Herculean *virtus* of endurance and toil. For a better Fortuna, or Tychē, Ascanius will have to look elsewhere. In the *Aeneid*, Fortuna is as closely associated with Juno as Tychē was with Hera in Euripides' *Herakles*. Herakles endured her bravely, and that is exactly the advice which old Nautes gives Aeneas and which Aeneas will follow in Book 5 after the Trojan women, instigated by Juno and Iris, have burned the ships:

> quidquid erit, superanda omnis fortuna ferendo est. (5. 709)

Whatever will happen, all fortune is to be overcome by bearing.

This is exactly what Aeneas will do, thus establishing himself as the true spiritual and heroic heir of Herakles. But what about Augustus? Or, more precisely, was Vergil motivated by an existing identification of Augustus with Herakles to cast his Aeneas in the image of Herakles also?

Vergil's intent in associating Augustus with Herakles was to hint at Augustus' deification. This is illustrated best by the several passages in which Horace mentions Augustus and Herakles in one breath. In the *Third Roman Ode*, for instance, Horace praises the just and steadfast man, and goes on to say that

> hac arte Pollux ex vagus Hercules
> enisus arces attigit igneas,
>   quos inter Augustus recumbens
>   pupureo bibet ore nectar.

(Odes 3. 2. 9–12)

By these merits Pollux and the far-wandering Herakles reached the citadels of heaven. Augustus will recline in their company and sip nectar with youthful lips.

Because he has the same spiritual qualities as Herakles, Augustus will be deified also. At the beginning of this *Letter to Augustus* Horace established an even more explicit analogy between Herakles and the Roman emperor. The metaphor with which the poem begins, that of Augustus' lonely carrying of many burdens, at once recalls Herakles' endeavours. The three burdens which Horace enumerates in the next lines continue the analogy. They are protection with arms, civilizatory achievement, and correction with laws, the νόμος, as it were.[8] Then follows, as in other poems, the canon of god-born men who were deified, except that Herakles is accorded special mention:

> diram qui contudit hydram
> notaque fatali portenta labore subegit,
> comperit invidiam supremo fine domari.

(Epistles 2. 1. 10–12)

He who crushed the frightful hydra and subdued the fabled monsters through the labour imposed on him by fate, he learned that envy could be overcome only by death that comes at last.

Augustus' fight against the *Invidia*, Envy, of his enemies is a theme to which Vergil had alluded in the proem to the Third *Georgic* (37–9). It is as if Horace in this letter, which was written after the enthusiasm that had greeted the arrival of Augustus' reign had somewhat abated, was trying to console the princeps by reference to Herakles' lifelong frustrations. One is reminded of the furious disappointment of Milton's Samson Agonistes:

---

[8] Compare Jupiter's command, which is defined as *labor* (233), to Aeneas in *Aen.* 4. 231: *ac totum sub leges mitteret orbem.*

Made of my enemies' scorn and gaze
with his heaven-gifted strength.[9]

There is no indication that Augustus promoted his connection with
Herakles. The Hercules cult at Tibur, today's Tivoli, apparently was
linked to Augustus from his own time, but it is uncertain whether the
initiative rested with him as he showed no special favour to the cult of
Hercules in Rome or elsewhere. We need not see the heavy, helping
hand of the emperor behind his association with Herakles in Horace's
and Vergil's poetry because this association suggested itself readily and
was not restricted to poetic allusiveness. When Augustus returned from
warfare in Spain in 24 BC after an absence of almost three years, the
Roman people greeted him joyously, for like Herakles he had risked his
life to protect them from danger.[10] And the notion that a man might be
deified for his service to mankind—and to the Romans in particular—
was familiar in Rome. Cicero cites it repeatedly as the reason for
Herakles' apotheosis; perhaps the passage most typical of both the
sentiment and Cicero's style occurs in the First *Tusculan Disputation*
(33): 'For what better nature is there among the human race than those
men who believed they were born to aid, protect, and preserve mankind?
Herakles went to the gods: he would never have gone unless he had
undertaken that way for himself while he was among men.' Somewhat
too late, Ovid chimed in and wrote from exile that like Herakles,
Augustus had been raised to the stars because of his *virtus* (*Pont.* 4. 8.
63). Long before Cicero's time, the Romans had used the example of
Herakles for deifying the founder of the city, Romulus. Ennius

---

[9] Lines 32–3. *Invidia*, 'Envie', become a topos in the Renaissance; see, e.g., Veen,
Emblemata Horatiana (Antwerp, 1607), pp. 172–3. Thomas Drant, the first translator of
Horace's *Epistles* into English, therefore translated the Horatian passage in a characteristically expansive way (*Horace His Arte of Poetrie, Epistles, and Satyrs Englished* ... [London,
1567], sig. F. viii):

> He that did crowse, and did culpon once
>   *Hydra* of hellish spyte,
> And monsters knowne with fatall toyle
>   to fetters frusshed quyte,
> Perceaved this by experience,
>   the monsters all do fall
> Through manliness; envie is tamed
>   at death, or not at all.

[10] See Horace, *Od.* 3. 14, with the excellent remarks of Kiessling–Heinze. Augustus
came from Spain to Rome, as Herakles had done.—R. Schilling, 'L'Hercule romain en
face de la reforme religieuse d'Auguste', *RPh* 68 (1942), 31–57, offers the most
comprehensive discussion of the Hercules cult under Augustus, but misinterprets
Augustus' indifference to it as Augustus' wish to de-emphasize the cult's significance.

established it in literature 'giving approval to public opinion' (famae adsentiens), as Cicero puts it.[11] That the basis for it was popular rather than poetic can also be seen from some of the earliest Roman coins.[12] Their obverse shows the head of Herakles, their reverse the she-wolf suckling Romulus and Remus. Like Herakles, Romulus was the stronger of a set of twin brothers. With this connection in mind, Livy presents Romulus as adopting, of all foreign religious rites, only the cult of Hercules. 'For', Livy continues (1. 7. 15), 'by so doing he showed himself, even then, a favourer of that immortality which is the reward of virtus. His own destiny was already leading him to the same reward.' Augustus was the second Romulus, and the application of Romulus' Herculean associations to him was therefore entirely apposite.

All this sets Vergil's and Horace's endowment of Augustus with Herakles' aura quite apart from the tawdry servility which romantic prejudice often leads us to associate with court poetry and which in the decades after Augustus indeed came to pass in Rome. Other emperors craved association with Herakles, Caligula and Nero preferring, for good reasons, to play the role of the mad Herakles.[13] Herculean connections were almost forced on any emperor who was receptive as is shown by the example of Vespasian who, however, derided such attempts (Suet., Ves. 12. 2). Whereas Martial's repeated praise of Domitian as 'the greater Herakles'[14] is nothing but the vilest flattery, Horace's and Vergil's comparison of Augustus to Herakles is free from any such cheapness. It is, as is especially evident from Horace's Letter to Augustus, an appeal to that 'moral energy' of which Herakles was the noblest embodiment in antiquity and in Elizabethan and Restoration drama.[15]

By linking Augustus to Herakles the Augustan poets may also have intended to detract from Pompey's and Antony's claims to be the successors of Herakles on earth. Although Antony looks like a good example on the stage of life of the braggart sham-Herakles of comedy, he apparently was quite serious about his presumed Herculean

---

[11] Tusc. 1. 12. 28; cf. Tac. Ann. 4. 38. The identification of famous Romans with Herakles is well discussed by A. R. Anderson, HSCPh 39 (1928), 29–45.

[12] BMC Rep. 2. 145–5 nos. 28–33; E. A. Sydenham, The Coinage of the Roman Republic (London, 1952), 2 no. 6.

[13] Caligula: Dio 59. 26; Nero: Suet., Nero 21 and 53.

[14] Maior Alcides, as opposed to minor Alcides, i.e. Herakles himself: Epigrams 9. 101 and 64; cf. Epigrams 9. 65 and the sneer of Jean Lemaitre de Belges: 'le petit Hercule Grec'.

[15] See E. M. Waith, The Herculean Hero in Marlowe, Chapman, Shakespeare and Dryden (New York, 1962), passim, and esp. pp. 16–18.

ancestry.[16] Appian (*BC* 3. 16) writes that Caesar reluctantly gave up his plan to adopt Antony because Antony was unwilling to exchange kinship with Herakles for the Julian descent from Aeneas. In view of all this it is hardly accidental that Octavian scheduled his great triple triumph, celebrating his victories over Antony and Cleopatra, on the day of the official, annual festival of Hercules at the Ara Maxima, 13 August. It is exactly on this day that Vergil has his Aeneas arrive at the site of Rome and, on that occasion, he develops most extensively the analogies between his own hero and the greatest hero of the Greeks. Aeneas comes to ask for Evander's help (8. 126 ff.). The basis for this proposed alliance, Aeneas says, is his own *virtus* and their ancestral kinship. Consequently, so far from being an unwilling colonizer of Italy—*Italiam non sponte sequor*—Aeneas now willingly accepts the call of fate: *fatis egere volentem* (8. 133). The notion of Aeneas' spirit of endurance is continued by reference to the genealogies of both Aeneas and Evander. Both are ultimately descended from Atlas, and Atlas is therefore singled out twice—'mightiest Atlas, who on his shoulders sustains (*sustinet*) the heavenly spheres' (8. 13–16), and 'the same Atlas who uplifts the starry heavens' (141). In this capacity Vergil had mentioned Atlas in the Augustus panegyric in Book 6, where he was linked to Aeneas, while Horace in his *Letters to Augustus* hailed the princeps for sustaining (*sustineas*) his lonely burden like Herakles.

In his reply, Evander keeps up the Herculean allusions. He met Anchises, he says, when Anchises came to Arcadia during his voyage to the realm of Hesione (8. 157). This recalls Herakles' saving her from the sea monster, just as he would save primitive Rome from the monster Cacus. Evander bids Aeneas participate with him in the ritual and banquet at the Ara Maxima and places Aeneas on the seat of honour, which is cushioned with a lion's skin. After the completion of the meal, Evander tells Aeneas the story of Herakles and Cacus. The way in which this story has been prepared for and its length suggest that it is meant to be an integral part of the epic rather than aetiological appendage.[17]

To understand the poet's intent, it is again best to take as a starting-point the unique features of his version. In contrast to the Cacus of Dionysius and Livy, Vergil's Cacus is not merely a thieving herdsman or

---

[16] Shakespeare's very positive view of Antony's Herculean associations, which is discussed by Waith, pp. 113–21, thus has some historical justification.

[17] I have discussed the Herakles–Cacus episode in more detail and from some other points of view in *AJPh* 87 (1966), 18–51; see also V. Buchheit, *Vergil über die Sendung Roms* (Heidelberg, 1963), pp. 116–33.

a robber but a son of Vulcan and thus of divine origin. He is an infernal creature, a real *monstrum*, who belches forth smoke and fire and lives in a cave that the poet compares to the opening of hell itself:

> The court of Cacus stands revealed to sight;
> the cavern glares with new-admired light.
> So the pent vapors, with a rumbling sound,
> Heave from below, and rend the hollow ground.
> A sounding flaw succeeds; and, from on high,
> The gods with hate behold the nether sky:
> The ghosts repine at violated night,
> And curse the invading sun, and sicken at the sight.
> The graceless monster, caught in open day,
> Enclosed, and in despair to fly away,
> Howls horrible from underneath and fills
> His hollow palace with unmanly yells.

(Dryden's translation)

Accordingly, Vergil does not depict Cacus' theft of the cattle as a clever ruse, but as the act of a man who is possessed by the furies and who acts from sheer impiety and wickedness:

> at furiis Caci mens effera, ne quid inausum
> aut intractatum scelerisve dolive fuisset,
> quattuor a stabulis praestanti corpore tauros
> avertit.... (8. 205–8)

But Cacus, his wits wild with frenzy, lest he leave any crime or craft undared or unattempted, stole four beautiful bulls from their pastures....

Moreover, whereas all other writers—notably Dionysius, Livy, Propertius, and Ovid—describe the actual combat between Herakles and Cacus in a few words or, at most, ten lines, it is Vergil's central concern. Vergil spends almost fifty lines depicting Herakles' hard struggle and his conquest of the Underworld monster. Lastly, Vergil added the hymn on Herakles which the Salian priests sing in commemoration of the event.

The contents of the hymn (8. 287–302) again are so chosen as to underscore the affinity between Aeneas and Herakles. Juno is singled out twice as persecuting Herakles. First, she sent *monstra* and snakes against him. In the epic she has already done the same, through Allecto, in Book 7. Then, more generally, the poet says that Herakles suffered countless, arduous *labores* because of *fatis Iunonis iniquae*. The poet used almost the same phrase when Venus explained to Cupid the reason for Aeneas' suffering: the hatred of unjust Juno (*odiis Iunonis iniquae* 1.

668). The phrase is, of course, reminiscent of the proem also. Herakles is further hailed as the destroyer of Troy, because Laomedon did not keep his promise. Similarly, Aeneas is about to conquer the city of the Latins because Turnus disputes his right to Lavinia, who had been promised to Aeneas. Freely adapting his mythological material, Vergil has Herakles fight against the 'cloud-born' centaurs Hylaeus and Pholus. Two of Aeneas' enemies had been compared, in the catalogue of warriors in Book 7, to such 'cloud-born centaurs' (7. 674–5). Soon after, Vergil frankly identifies Aeneas with Herakles. When Evander bids Aeneas enter his domicile after the festival of Herakles, he tells him: 'Herakles, the victor, walked over this threshold. This house received him. Dare, my guest, to scorn riches; fashion yourself to be worthy also of the god, and come not disdainful of my humble household'—

> haec, inquit, limina victor
> Alcides subiit, haec illum regia cepit.
> aude, hospes, contemnere opes et te quoque dignum
> finge deo, rebusque veni non asper egenis. (8. 362–5)

So Aeneas is the measure of Herakles not only spiritually, but physically also: gigantic, *ingens*,[18] he enters into Evander's house as Herakles had done before him. The parallelism between Herakles and Aeneas is further enhanced as Evander describes them virtually, as contemporaries. The next day, Aeneas turns out to be Herakles' follower indeed. After a sign from Venus confirms to him, beyond all doubt, that his task will be a bloody struggle against Turnus and the Latins, he immediately rises from the throne that, as we saw earlier, was covered with the lion's skin, kindles the fire on Herakles' altar, and joyously brings another sacrifice to Herakles, the household god of Evander (8. 541–4). Anticipating many good Romans, Aeneas himself now sacrifices to Herakles instead of being a mere spectator. And, to cap his association with the Greek hero, Aeneas, accompanied by Pallas, sets out for the war against Turnus on a horse that is caparisoned in a lion's skin (8. 552–3):

> A sprightly courser, fairer than the rest,
> The king himself presents his royal guest.
> A lion's hide his back and limbs infold,
> Precious with studded work, and paws of gold.

> (Dryden's translation)

---

[18] *Ingentem Aenean* (8. 367); cf. *ingentem Aenean*, also at the beginning of the line, in 6. 413 as discussed above on p. 280.

The Herakles–Cacus episode, then, serves as a parable of Aeneas' struggle against Turnus. This is borne out by the many changes made by Vergil which are designed to liken Cacus to Turnus and by the numerous thematic and verbal parallels which underline the similarity of their behaviour.[19] The animal blood-thirstiness of Cacus, for instance, is paralleled by that of Turnus. Cacus' throat is drained of blood (*siccum sanguine guttur* 8. 261), and so are the jaws of the maddened wolf with whom Turnus is compared in Book 9 (*siccae sanguine fauces* 9. 64). The blood-dripping heads that are nailed to the entrance of Cacus' cave (8. 195) anticipate the heads of Turnus' enemies which he attaches to his chariot (12. 511–12) before he does battle with Aeneas. All this indicates that the poet was anxious to impress on the reader the analogy between Herakles and Aeneas, and between Cacus and Turnus even at the risk of seeming tedious.

Great warriors and civilizers as they are, Herakles and Aeneas are not bent on bloodshed. They are goaded into a righteous rage by the deceitfulness and cruelty of their opponents. Vergil deliberately has the Salians hail Herakles as being 'not devoid of reason' (8. 299). Similarly, that heroic paragon of reason, Odysseus, is 'beside himself' with rage in the face of the crimes committed by the *monstrum* Polyphemus (3. 626–9). Polyphemus abides by divinely sanctioned conventions as little as does Cacus. Nor does Turnus, even though he is not a *monstrum*, but he breaks the sacred truce (*foedus*) and keeps the spoils of Pallas instead of giving them to the gods. Both these actions seal his doom. Forced by Turnus' treachery (*insidiisque subactus* 12. 494) as Herakles was by Cacus' crime and deceit (*scelerisve dolive* 8. 205), Aeneas overcomes and kills his opponent, whose tragedy is that he cannot live up to his own ideals, among them *virtus*. These themes reflect traditional concepts. Speaking of warfare, Livy (42. 47. 4) contrasts *dolus* and *insidiae* with *virtus*. To be sanctioned as holy and just, any war the Romans waged had to be defensive, at least in theory, and Herakles and Aeneas are involved in such a *bellum pium et iustum*. It is against this whole background also that the prayer of Pallas in Book 10, who prays to Herakles as any Roman would, takes on its full significance.

Vergil's treatment of the Herakles–Cacus story is a genuine mythopoeic addition to the Herakles myth, and was recognized as such by Renaissance writers and artists. Ronsard, for instance, mentions the 'anger of Herakles killing Cacus' as one of his inspirational sources in

---

[19] For details see the works cited in n. 17 above.

the posthumous preface to the *Franciade*. This brings us to an important point. Whereas in the earlier books of the *Aeneid* Vergil had modelled Aeneas' *labores* on those of Herakles and even adapted Juno's opposition to Aeneas for that purpose, the roles are now reversed as a Herakles legend is adapted and, in large part, created to illustrate the nature of Aeneas' final struggle.[20] It is, above all, Vergil's concept of the heroism of both Aeneas and Herakles that made possible a symbiosis where there had been a seemingly unbridgeable gap in Apollonius. Aeneas' heroism is internal, and it is here that Vergil saw a strong similarity between his hero and Herakles as portrayed, for instance, by Euripides. Yet Vergil did not ignore the tradition of Herakles' warlike heroism especially as Aeneas had traditionally been known as a great warrior,[21] and the Romans, whom Aeneas typifies, had conquered Italy and the Mediterranean basin with arms rather than *pietas*. Like Pindar's Herakles, Aeneas must overcome force with force because Jupiter commands him 'to bring the whole world beneath his laws' (4. 231). This is the *nomos* idea as we know it from the Greek poet. At the same time, as Vergil had Aeneas reinterpret the warlike *virtus* of Ascanius as the Herculean *virtus* of endurance, so he now adapts the madness of Herakles as anticipating the warlike anger of Aeneas. Herakles fights *furens animis* (8. 228), *dentibus infrendens*, and *fervidus ira* (8. 230). So will Aeneas, notwithstanding his compassion especially for his young opponents and his grief about the human sacrifice that is necessary for *Romanam condere gentem*.[22] Like Euripides or Theocritus, Vergil saw in his hero a human being rather than a superman. This is another reason why the emphasis in the Cacus story is not on Herakles' divine reward but on his struggle against the enemy. This also links this episode to Augustus' conquest of the hellish forces of the east at the end of Book 8, and the note of Herakles as a model of the emperor's divinity is sounded

---

[20] This reinforces Aeneas' coming into his own in the second half of the epic. Another function of the Herakles–Cacus episode is that it provides a rejoinder to Lucretius' depreciation of Herakles' fight against *monstra*; yet another is Vergil's utilization of the technique of Greek tragedy to inform the reader in advance of what course the events will take. This allows him to concentrate on their interpretation. Also, it was known in Rome that Herakles was connected with the beginnings of Carthage (Cic. *ND* 3. 42), and thus Vergil emphasized the god's connection with the beginnings of Rome.

[21] For the considerable literary and artistic evidence see the first chapter of my *Aeneas, Sicily, and Rome* (n. 1, above).

[22] To regard *pietas* and martial fervour as mutually exclusive would be to confuse a modern attitude with an ancient one. Compare, in Renaissance literature, the rage of Ariosto's Orlando, comparable to the mad rage of Euripides' or Seneca's Herakles, and the warlike anger of Tasso's Rinaldo, which corresponds to that of Vergil's Herakles.

only very discreetly, far more discreetly than in Horace's poems and incomparably more so than in Martial's and Statius' gross flattery of Domitian.

The important result for the literary tradition of Herakles is that Vergil harmonized what Euripides, for instance, had set off one against another: the internal and outward heroism of Herakles. Like Aeneas, he is still an epic hero whose great deeds are anything but belittled or considered anachronistic. And like Aeneas, he has ample spiritual strength, fortitude, and compassion.

This last quality, among others, indicates that Vergil's portrait of Herakles did not come straight from the Stoic textbook. For when Pallas prays to him, Herakles 'stifles a great sigh deep in his heart, and sheds tears in vain'—

> magnumque sub imo
> corde premit gemitum lacrimasque effundit inanes. (10. 464–5)

This, once more, associates Herakles with Aeneas. When Anna was pleading with him on Dido's behalf, 'he felt anguish through and through in his heart; his mind remained unmoved, and his tears rolled in vain'—

> magno persentit pectore curas;
> mens immota manet, lacrimae volvuntur inanes. (4. 448–9)

Given, however, the varied strands of Vergil's inspiration and the innate Stoicism of the Romans, it is not surprising that Stoic concepts and terminology found their way into the *Aeneid*. This is a well-known phenomenon, although its relevance to Herakles and Aeneas is not that they were portrayed as Stoic sages. Both have pity and compassion, and both, as good Romans, have martial fervour and even fury, which does not agree with the Stoic ideal of imperturbability. But there were other qualities which Herakles exemplified to the Stoics and for which Vergil regarded the hero as a worthy model of Aeneas. The Stoics extolled the principle of *tonos*, 'strain' or 'effort':

This term originally seems to have expressed muscular activity, and was next used by the Cynics to denote that active condition of the soul which is the true end of life; 'no labour', said Diogenes, 'is noble, unless its end is tone of soul.' . . . With Cleanthes the word becomes fairly common, first in the ethical application, in which 'tone' is a shock of fire, which if it be strong enough to stir the soul to fulfil its duties is called strength and force, and then in physics to explain the unceasing activity of the universe.[23]

[23] E. Vernon Arnold, *Roman Stoicism* (London, 1911), p. 160.

In the Stoic allegories, Herakles personified this *élan vital.*[24] Unlike
the Epicurean, the Stoic creed was not passive. Besides enduring
adversity, the ideal Stoic would constantly and actively practise and
exercise virtue, and even would look upon adversity as an opportunity
for such exercise. Epictetus, who lived in the first century AD, gives a
spirited, popular illustration of Herakles' exemplary value in that
respect:

> Or what do you think Herakles would have amounted to if there had not been a
> lion like the one he encountered, and a hydra, and a stag, and a boar, and unjust
> and monstrous men, whom he made his business to drive out and clear away?
> And what would he have been doing had nothing of this sort existed? Is it not
> clear that he would have rolled himself up in a blanket and slept? In the first
> place, then, he would never have become Herakles by slumbering away his
> whole life in such luxury and ease; but even if he had, what good would he have
> been? What would have been the use of those arms of his and of his prowess in
> general, and his steadfastness and nobility, had not such circumstances roused
> and exercised him? What then? Ought he to have prepared these for himself, and
> sought to bring a lion into his own country from somewhere or other, and a boar
> and a hydra? That would have been folly and madness. But since they did exist
> and were found in the world, they were useful as a means of revealing and
> exercising our Herakles. (1. 6. 32–6)

The traditional necessity, *anankē*, of Herakles' labours now is literally
turned into its opposite. The contrast, to which Epictetus returns in
another discourse (2. 16–44), between sitting about at home in luxurious indolence and accepting the call to toil is, to cite only one example,
the basis of Jupiter's appeal to Aeneas in *Aeneid* 4. That the sentiment
voiced by Epictetus was current at Vergil's time is clear from Cicero's
summation of it in a single, albeit Ciceronian, sentence (*Fin.* 2. 118).

Critical analysis, especially of a complex and sophisticated work of art
such as the *Aeneid*, has the inevitable drawback of sorting out and
fragmenting what the poet created as an organic whole. The various
sources of inspiration for Vergil's Herakles—Roman cult and practice,
Greek drama and epic, the Augustan aura of the deified man (θεῖος
ἀνήρ), Stoic concepts, the popularity of the myth in Italy, the reaction
against Apollonius and Lucretius, and some basic, initial similarity
between Herakles and Aeneas which Vergil greatly refined—are not
compartmentalized in the poem but complement one another and form
an inseparable totality. The strongest reason, however, for Vergil's
extensive mythopoeic adaptation of Herakles was, as we saw earlier, his

---

[24] Cornutus, *Theol. Comp.* 31, *Stoicorum Veterum Fragmenta* 1 (von Arnim) fr. 514.

role as the national hero of Greece. Herakles, in many ways, summed up the national experience of that country. His beginnings, like those of primitive Greece, were violent, and there were excesses with the concomitant anxiety to expiate them.[25] Then, at the time of Hesiod, there was growing concern for law; we need only think of lawgivers such as Lycurgus, Dracon, and Solon. Herakles came to personify the rudimentary civilizing efforts—he drains swamps, builds cities, and destroys wild beasts and tyrants. He, the supreme champion of justice and civilizer, precedes Greek colonists wherever they go. Herakles then became the supreme symbol of Greek individualism and humanism in the tragedies of Sophocles and Euripides. The sophists and philosophers finally accentuated his mental powers. Every age in Greece recast Herakles in its own image, and he thus became the incarnation of her history and aspirations. This is precisely the role which Vergil intended for Aeneas in Italy and Rome, and it is primarily for this reason that Herakles became an inspirational model for Aeneas. And, taking his inspiration from the Roman Hercules cult, Vergil doubtless hoped that his Italic readers would regard Aeneas with the same kind of personal intensity with which they worshipped Hercules.

[25] For a summary of the significance of the Greek Herakles in this and the next sentences see already E. Des Essarts, *Du type d'Hercule dans la littérature grecque depuis les origines jusqu'au siècle des Antonins* (Paris, 1871), pp. 229–30.

15

Cernere erat: The Shield of Aeneas

D. A. WEST

In Homer's *Iliad* Achilles needed a new shield because he lost his original armour when Patroclus was killed fighting in it. His new shield carries representations of the sky, a city at peace with a wedding and a lawsuit in progress, a city at war with an ambush in a river bed, scenes from the farm, the vineyard, the hunt, and the dancing-floor, none of them relevant to the plot of the *Iliad*.

In Virgil's epic Aeneas does not need a new shield. His original armour served him adequately throughout the siege of Troy and his subsequent wanderings, and he could still have the use of it. On the other hand, all the illustrations on the new shield are directly relevant to the political purpose of the poem. So, on the face of it, it appears that the shield of Achilles is a necessary and integral part of the *Iliad* while its illustrations are irrelevant to the poem; whereas the illustrations on the shield of Aeneas are relevant to the plot of the poem while the shield itself does not fit very easily. This is a tempting paradox, and a damaging conclusion seems to follow from it. 'Achilles needs to arm, but not Aeneas', argues Becker.[1] 'Here Virgil has imitated a brilliant passage in his Homeric model in a place where it does not belong.' Eden[2] seems to take a similar view.

But this is not the whole truth. The illustrations on the shield of Achilles may be irrelevant to the plot, but this interlude of normal life in town and country, set in a poem of heroic valour, anger, and death, has its own poetic relevance and effect. Similarly it is easy to say that Aeneas does not need a new shield and that his reason for getting one is that Achilles receives one in the *Iliad*, but this does less than justice to Virgil's design. He explicitly provides the motivation:

> ne mox aut Laurentis, nate, superbos
> aut acrem dubites in proelia poscere Turnum. (8. 613–14)

This is perfectly unobtrusive and credible in context, and indeed

---

[1] C. Becker, 'Der Schild des Aeneas', *Wien. Stud.* 77 (1964), 111–27.
[2] P. T. Eden, *A Commentary on Virgil Aeneid viii* (Leiden, 1975), p. xix.

significantly contributes to Virgil's strategy. He is determined that the final part of his epic shall not be an anticlimax, and not simply for literary reasons. Aeneas' wars in Italy are the foundation of the Roman state, the beginning of the *gens Iulia*, and the legendary authentication of the Augustan principate. This is all vital to the purpose of the *Aeneid*, and the acquisition of this new shield to combat this dread new Italian enemy helps Virgil in his attempt to build the poem up towards a climax:

> maior rerum mihi nascitur ordo,
> maius opus moueo. (7. 43–4)

The Homeric imitation is smoothly and successfully welded into the texture of the *Aeneid*.

The illustrations on the shield of Aeneas represent vivid moments in the history of Rome ... But why these particular moments? What is Virgil's criterion of selection? Warde Fowler[3] argues that these are 'scenes of escape from terrible perils both moral and material, ending with the Battle of Actium, the most wonderful escape of all'. But what about Mettus? Rome was not brought into terrible peril by his failure to keep his promise to assist Tullus Hostilius against the Albans. And what about Romulus and Remus? Was that a terrible peril? And what about the Sabine women? Warde Fowler's analysis does not fit the data.

Drew[4] produces a dazzling hypothesis. In 27 BC Augustus received from a grateful Senate a golden shield bearing the inscription CLUPEUS VIRTUTIS CLEMENTIAE IUSTITIAE PIETATIS ERGA DEOS PATRIAMQUE. Drew argues that in the first scene on the shield of Aeneas, Romulus and Remus sucked VIRTUS from the udders of the wolf. In scene 2 CLEMENTIA was shown to the Sabines. In scene 3 the Romans dispensed IUSTITIA to Mettus; and Porsenna in 4 is famous for his IUSTITIA towards the Romans. In scene 5 is displayed the PIETAS of Manlius and the Salii and the Luperci, while scene 6 shows the punishment of IMPIETAS in Tartarus. Ingenious, but not convincing. If Virgil had intended to allude to the four virtues on the shield of Augustus, he would have articulated his allusions in such a way that readers would have perceived them. Virgil could not have expected anyone to taste VIRTUS in the milk of the wolf, or to see CLEMENTIA in the rape of the Sabines and what followed it, or to detect IUSTITIA in the war with Porsenna ... The *Aeneid* is to be heard and understood. It is not a riddle.

---

[3] W. Warde Fowler, *Aeneas at the Site of Rome* (Oxford, 1918), pp. 103–5.
[4] D. L. Drew, *The Allegory of the Aeneid* (Oxford, 1964), pp. 26–30.

Otis[5] is less particular. He sees in these scenes the constant opposition of *uirtus, consilium*, and *pietas* to the forces of violence in all Roman history. This is too general to be helpful. And general as it is it is not even true. Tell it to the Sabine women.

Eicholz[6] believes that Virgil has two criteria. First the incidents have been selected as chronological landmarks. This cannot be taken seriously, since between the war with Porsenna in 508 and the Catilinarian Conspiracy in 63–62 we have only the Gallic invasions of 390. To fill the gaps Eicholz advances a desperate explanation of the Salii as a timeless scene to give the impression of having traversed the whole of Roman history. 'Time is standing still' at the Salii. But Eicholz's second criterion is nearer the truth. These scenes are selected to make sense as plastic art. R. D. Williams' commentary makes the same point.[7]

The main purpose of this paper is to support and develop this proposition in the following form. 'The illustrations on the shield of Aeneas are so presented that they bring vividly before our eyes illustrations which would be conceivable and effective on a metal shield.'

This is not a popular view. 'Menti et animo ea cogitanda, non uidenda proponit' (Heyne–Wagner).[8] 'The never-ending attempts to reconstruct the shield are a complete waste of time: we should just make up our minds here too that we are dealing with a poetic, not a plastic work of art' (Heinze).[9] 'Such attempts lead to no useful results, and are false to the intention of the poet' (Szantyr supporting Heinze).[10] 'The concrete actually recedes, and something ideal and symbolic forces its way in to replace it' (Becker). 'The view that the episodes were chosen because of their visual suitability as pictures ... can also be dismissed: some details simply cannot be "envisaged" ' (Eden, p. 164). The orthodox view is put most succinctly by Warde Fowler: 'It is futile to deal with this description on plastic principles and to look for divisions or compartments on the surface of the shield' (pp. 100–1). On this futility we shall now embark.

This shield is a round *clipeus*, and Virgil suggests the placing of the separate scenes. The Capitol is on top (*in summo*, 652); Tartarus,

[5] B. Otis, *Virgil: A Study in Civilized Poetry* (Oxford, 1964), pp. 341–2.
[6] D. E. Eicholz, *PVS* 6 (1966–7), 45–9.
[7] R. D. Williams, *The Aeneid of Virgil, Books 7–12* (London, 1973), p. 266.
[8] C. G. Heyne, 4th edn. by G. P. Wagner, *Publius Virgilius Maro* vol. iii. 1 (Leipzig, 1830–1), p. 366.
[9] R. Heinze, *Virgils epische Technik* (Stuttgart, 1914; Darmstadt, 1957), p. 401.
[10] A. Szantyr, *Mus. Hel.* 27 (1970), 28–40.

FIG. 1 The Shield

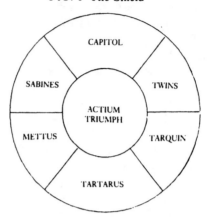

naturally enough, is at the bottom (*hinc procul*, 666); in the middle of the
first half-dozen scenes (that is how Eden takes *haec inter*) is the sea
encircled by dolphins (*et circum*, 673) with the Battle of Actium and the
triple triumph of Octavian depicted in the middle (*in medio*, 675). The
first four scenes are to be arranged somehow or other in the four panels
that remain. The only guidance we receive is that the Sabines are not far
from the Twins, and Mettus is not far from the Sabines (*nec procul hinc*,
635, and *haud procul inde*, 642).

I am not arguing that Virgil is describing a real shield. In fact Virgil
makes it clear that this shield is supernatural, miraculous, impossible:

> illic genus omne futurae
> stirpis ab Ascanio pugnataque in ordine bella.
> fecerat et ... (8. 628–30)

No real shield could contain all the descendants of Ascanius and all the
wars they ever fought. What Virgil describes is only a selection (*fecerat
et*). So the diagram is not a drawing of the shield, but only a representation of what Virgil actually says about these imaginary illustrations
selected from a huge number of imaginary illustrations on this imaginary shield.

The most striking indication that we are meant to think of the shield
in plastic terms is the frequent mention of colour. In the first line, 630,
the cave of Mars is green, *uiridi*. Another is the choice of scenes which
are frequently represented in Roman art. No clearer example could be
asked for than the Twins hanging from the udders of the she-wolf.

Another is the choice of scenes where the line is of artistic interest. The bending back of the wolf's neck is an example. Another indication that we are meant to visualize, and in this case to visualize a work of art in metal, is the repeated reference to texture, to tactile qualities. The wolf's tongue licking the human infants into shape would be a challenge to any smith, despite the fact that Eden chooses this as his example of a detail that 'simply cannot be "envisaged"'.

The Sabine scenes present many of these features. Crowd scenes are common on Roman reliefs. So are sacrifices. The fascination of perspective is suggested in *consessu caueae*, 636.

In the rending of Mettus the four-horse chariots are another favourite subject in Roman art. Our sense of colour and our sense of texture are both stimulated by the brambles sprinkled with a dew of blood. This is a strong argument. The tale of Mettus is not included because of its historical importance or because it fills a gap in the chronological sequence or for any ethical or symbolical reason. Mettus is there for the perspective interest of the four-horse chariot and the blood dripping from the brambles.

The next scene, Horatius holding the bridge and Cloelia swimming the Tiber, are not, it must be admitted, particularly vividly described. This is a weak point in the argument—but they are scenes which would be amenable to artistic representation.

In 654 the pediment of the temple is a familiar artistic feature. The height of the Capitol is another reminder of perspective. The rough thatch of Romulus' cottage is an indication of texture. It is *recens* because the thatch was regularly renewed in the Augustan era.[11] The silver goose fluttering in gilded porticoes is an explicit evocation of the metal-worker's art. The shrubs of 657, like the brambles of Mettus, indicate texture. The darkness well sets off the silver and gold. The Gauls' hair is gold, their clothes are gold. Their cloaks are striped and shining. Their necks are milky white with gold necklaces. *Sagulis*, 660, refers to national dress, a common fascination of Roman art; so the flashing *gaesa* of 661–2, refer to the typical armour of a nation, and in addition exploit the glitter of the metal of the shield. Similarly the Gauls are protecting their bodies with their characteristic long shields. The leaping Salii and the naked Luperci exploit nakedness and line and movement, all of them dear to the eye of the artist. The wool-tufted bonnets of the *flamines*, like the upholstery of the matron's carriages in 666, are another

---

[11] G. Binder, *Aeneas und Augustus* (Meisenheim, 1971), p. 186.

allusion to texture. The fallen figure-of-eight ancilia are a reference to a characteristic piece of armour. The fact that they are fallen must have been indicated on the shield, either by their irregular placing on the ground, or by having some of them *still* falling.

In the scene in the Underworld there is vivid evocation of artistic possibilities in the depth of the mouth of Dis, in Catiline hanging on a cliff, in the faces of the Furies, in the segregation of the pious, and in Cato dispensing the law.

In the seascape 671-4, the swelling of the sea is an appeal to texture, its breadth to perspective. Colour is generously applied in 672 with gold and froth and blue-grey and grey. We can easily visualize the dolphins because we are told their arrangement (*circum*), their colour (*argento clari*), and the effect they have upon the texture of the sea.

The case seems to be made. In almost every line so far there is at least one point which brings vividly before our eyes an illustration which would be conceivable and effective on a metal shield. Instead of labouring through the description of Actium and the triple triumph which followed it, we shall make a selection of the possible observations.

Although it would not be possible to draw the indescribable composi-tion of the shield, *clipei non enarrabile textum*, 625, Virgil does attempt to force us to visualize it by providing continual indications of relative placing. Starting from 675, we read that the fleets were in the middle of the circle of the sea; Augustus was on one side, Agrippa elsewhere on that same side 628, 632; on the other side Antony; behind him, Cleopatra, 685, 688, in the middle of the Antonine forces 696. From 698 onwards we see the Oriental gods and opposite them (*contra*) the Olympians, with Mars in the thick of things; the Dirae are swooping down on the battle from a great height; Discordia and Bellona are arriving in that order; Apollo also is above the fray, either by his temple on the headland of Actium, or high on the cliff at Leucas, or perhaps even aboard Augustus' flagship (*astitit Augusti puppim super*, Prop. 4. 6. 29).

Notable in this passage is the technique of serial narrative familiar in Roman art, whereby the character is displayed in different postures in the same picture to represent phases in a narrative. So Cleopatra is first seen bearing down upon the enemy. In 704 Apollo stretches his bow, the Oriental forces turn and flee. In the next scene, we are approaching the Delta of the Nile. In the next we are in Rome.

Amongst the terms which suggest metalwork are *aeratas* referring to the bronze prows of the ships 675, *feruere* used of the foam, and *flammas* and *sidus* 680–1. In this context we may ask what colour Virgil means us to visualize for the shores of the Red Sea, *litore rubro. Stuppea flamma* is a flash of flame colour set off by the dense black of pitch smoke. *Rubescunt* will have its precise inceptive sense: the furrows of the sea (note the texture in *arua*) begin to grow red with fresh slaughter, that is, the corpses tinge the sea for a moment after they fall into it. Mars in 701 is *caelatus ferro* as befits the god of war. There is blood on Bellona's lash in 703.

Amongst the characteristic scenes of Roman art we notice the lines of ships in 676 which afford the artist the same opportunity for perspective virtuosity as did the four-horse chariot which rent the body of Mettus; the triumph in 714, the sacrifice in the next line; the temples in the line after that; the god at his temple door accepting the abasement of the defeated; the bullocks sacrificed at the altars.

Amongst the perspective effects we shall mention only the emphasis upon height, *celsa in puppi* 680, *arduus* 683, *montis* and *turritis* 692–3 (the ships of Antony were large and had towers, according to Dio 50. 23), *ex aethere* 701, *desuper* 705, *superbis postibus* 721–2.

This whole central panel is a virtuoso evocation of the iconography of foreign peoples, their dress, their arms, and their religions. Against the *Iulium Sidus*, and the *corona naualis* of Agrippa we can set *inter alia* the *sistrum* of Cleopatra from the worship of Isis, the dog-faced Anubis, the Afri with their naked chests, the Euphrates visibly subdued (and *ibat iam mollior undis* is some allusion to texture), the two-horned Rhine, and the God Araxes fretting at the new Roman bridge.

If we 'deal with this description on plastic principles', if we respond to the visual stimuli which Virgil has liberally supplied, our understanding of the poetry is improved at many points. Take Cleopatra. We know that her galleys with their three rams, one on top of another, are rowing into battle because we are told that the sea is churned up by their oars (689–90). The obvious inference is that the sails are tight and side-on to the wind, and we are driven to draw the inference because we have just been told that the enemy, sailing against her enjoys the favouring winds. How else do we know that the *uenti* are *secundi* for Agrippa in 682 if not by his billowing sails set at right angles to his line of advance? The set of the sails is a matter of obvious and necessary inference at this stage, but after Cleopatra turns to flight Virgil provides an explicit description. Cleopatra has been beating into the wind. Now in 707, she prays for the wind to blow. Her sails have been tight. Now she slackens them, and the queen is said to be feeding out the ropes (the sheets in nautical terms),

not because Virgil has any notion that Cleopatra had to double as a
deckhand, but because this is a vivid artistic device for representing her
retreat.

Another advantage of the visual interpretation is in line 697, where we
are told that there are two snakes, the symbol of doom, behind
Cleopatra. She is still advancing. Therefore she is not aware of what
there is coming up behind her. The best way of sensing the drama of this
picture is to read the destruction of it in the Penguin translation by
Jackson Knight. 'She has as yet no thought of the pair of asps which fate
held in store for her.'

Finally, Cleopatra's return to Egypt. 'Virgil's poetry has a whole
dimension that Horace's lacks', write R. G. M. Nisbet and M. Hubbard
on *Odes* 1. 37 (*A Commentary on Horace* Odes *Book 1* (Oxford, 1970)),
quoting *Aeneid* 8. 711 ff. One such dimension is the visualization: the
colours in polar tension which we have met more than half a dozen times
already in this passage, but never so movingly as when we see the pallor
of Cleopatra's skin against the red of her sailor's blood. Opposite her,
that is on the other side of this section of the picture, in the direction in
which the panic-stricken fleet is sailing (we are now told that the wind is
west-north-west, 710), opposite her (*contra autem*) waits the river Nile,
shown as a recumbent deity. There is grief in every line of his huge body
as he opens his voluminous draperies and calls the queen into the refuge
of his blue-green breast and his *latebrosa flumina*, which convey at once
the complex of streams in the delta, and that part of his effigy where
drapery melts into water.

There is a possible objection to this interpretation. Surely, it might be
argued, vivid representation is characteristic of poetry in general and of
Virgil in particular. Is the visualization on the shield different from the
visualization elsewhere in Virgil? We can meet this objection by appealing to a 'control'. The *post-hoc* prophecy on the shield can be compared
with the *post-hoc* vision of Aeneas in the Underworld. This comparison
has already been made by Griffith[12] in order to argue that the incidents
on the shield are selected to avoid chronological overlap with the
episodes of Aeneas' vision in the sixth book. This case does not hold up,
principally because it does not provide a sufficiently positive criterion of
selection; but the comparison vividly demonstrates that the incidents on
the shield are very much more amenable to visual representation than
the episodes in the vision. True there are vivid touches in the vision

---

[12] J. G. Griffith, *PVS* 7 (1967-8), 54-65.

(Virgil is never without vivid touches), notably the headgear of Silvius Aeneas and of Romulus, 769 and 779. But it is enough to read this vision in 6. 756–886 to sense that the drive of the poetry comes much less from what is seen, and much more from emotion (as in the Marcellus passage), from concept (as in the prophecy of the Augustan Empire), and from great roll-calls of evocative proper names

> hi tibi Nomentum et Gabios urbemque Fidenam,
> hi Collatinas imponent montibus arces,
> Pometios Castrumque Inui Bolamque Coramque. (6. 773–5)

This paper has not argued that the shield of Aeneas was a real shield, or that there ever was a shield like this, or that it was 'primarily inspired by particular statue groups which Virgil had seen in Rome' (this a hypothesis rejected by P. T. Eden ad loc.), but rather that its illustrations would be conceivable and effective on a real metal shield.

This is one of the poetic purposes of the passage, and if we forget or deny it we fail to understand the poetry. But another, more important purpose, as emerges clearly from Binder's book, is the praise of Augustus. This is insinuated at many points. On 663 we have to remember that Augustus revived the Lupercalia (Suet. *Aug.* 31); and on the same line that the Salii included the name of Augustus in their hymns when he celebrated his triumph in 27 BC (Drew, pp. 10–15); on 678 it helps to remember the words of the *Res Gestae*, 'iurauit in uerba mea tota Italia sponte sua'. On 679 we note that Augustus was to dedicate a temple to the Penates in 12 BC. On 684 we note that the *corona naualis* was awarded to Agrippa after the defeat of Sextus Pompeius at Naulochos in 36 BC. On 720 we note that Augustus dedicated the great marble temple to Apollo in 28 BC. In general the Augustan panel has pride of place in the centre of the shield and receives an allocation of 54 lines whereas the Republican scenes rate only 41 lines. As Aeneas receives a shield and sets out to do battle on behalf of the Rome that is to be, we may even remember that after Octavian had won a great war on behalf of Rome in 27 BC, he too received a shield, the Clipeus Virtutis.

The shield of Aeneas is of course an imitation of the shield of Achilles in Homer, but like any great *imitatio* in classical literature it is a complete recreation of its model. There is one tiny but crucial difference between Homer and Virgil, and Pluss[13] has explained it. In Homer Hephaistos 'made this'. In Virgil 'had made it' (*fecerat, addiderat, distulerant,*

---

[13] H. T. Pluss, *Vergil und die epische Kunst* (Leipzig, 1884).

extuderat). Homer is presenting the autopsy of the omniscient epic poet. Hephaistos made *x* and *y*, Homer saw him do so. But in Virgil the pluperfects take us into the mind and eyes of Aeneas. It is Aeneas' reaction to the shield which is the heart of the poetry.

> Talia per clipeum, Volcani dona parentis
> miratus rerumque ignarus imagine gaudet
> attollens umero famamque et fata nepotum. (8. 729–31)

Aeneas did not understand his own shield. But he marvelled at it, and took delight in its illustrations as he hoisted up on to his shoulder the fate of his descendants and went to do battle on their behalf. We understand more than Aeneas did, and I hope that we may also marvel and take delight not only in the visual aspect of the illustrations, but also in this mighty metaphor.

16

Numanus Remulus: Ethnography and Propaganda in *Aeneid* 9. 598 ff.

N. M. HORSFALL

Scholarly neglect of Virgil's battle-scenes can be dangerously undiscriminating; thus, for any study of *Aen.* 9. 598–620, a speech of outstanding programmatic importance, we have had to wait for Schweizer's 1967 dissertation.[1] This paper's concern will be with analogies and antecedents, and its aims to clarify a few sources of Augustan propaganda, and to see how much may be said of a Roman's probable response to twenty lines of the *Aeneid*.

During the Latins' attack on the Trojan camp, Numanus Remulus, Turnus' brother-in-law, shouts at the besieged boasts of Italian prowess, and taunts of Trojan weakness. This polarity of form is Homeric in origin; so Diomedes to Paris: τοξότα, λωβήτηϱ, κέϱαϊ ἀγλαε, παϱθενοπῖπα ... κωφὸν γὰϱ βέλος ἀνδϱὸς ἀναλκίδος οὐτιδάνοιο· ἤ τ᾽ ἄλλως ὑπ᾽ἐμεῖο ... ὀξὺ βέλος πέλεται, 'archer, reviler, glorious only with the horn bow, girl-ogler ... ineffective is the spear of a man who is a nobody and a coward ... very differently does the sharp spear come from my hand'. Another correspondence of form is possible: here the Trojans are fighting Italians; 'non hic Atrides, nec fandi fictor Ulixes'. Easy opposition is over for the Trojans, as it would have been for Alexander had he invaded Italy ('non cum Dareo rem esse dixisset'; Liv. 9. 17. 16) after his eastern conquests, with a softened and effeminate Macedonian army (*degenerantem iam in Persarum mores*; ibid. 18. 3). Virgil's debt to this *locus* cannot be proved,[2] but the similarity of the threefold comparisons is tempting.[3] Numanus Remulus' boasts of

---

[1] *Vergil u. Italien* (diss. 1967), pp. 14 f.; as for intellectual antecedents, B. Rehm (*Das geographische Bild des alten Italien in Vergils Aeneis*, Philologus Suppl. 24. 2 (Leipzig, 1932), pp. 67 f.) has made made a useful start; I am indebted to Prof. G. N. Knauer for a reference to Fraccaro's note in *Boll. Filol. Cl.* 17 (1910–11), 160 f.

[2] Liv. 9. 17 f.; cf. too Plut. *Fort. Rom.* 326 c; Callinicus (*Polemonis Declamationes*, ed. H. Hinck (Leipzig, 1873)), p. 43, 10 f.; Jul. *Ep. ad Alex.* 433 c; Wardman in *CQ* NS 5 (1955), 100.

[3] Liv. 9. 19. 10 reports Alexander of Epirus as saying of the Romans *cum feminis sibi*

the national virtues are of a type reaching back to Homer, where, ironically, Alcinoous takes pride in the luxurious habits of the Phacacians (*Od.* 8. 248). For such patriotic self-characterization, the Romans' capacity was boundless and old-established. Servius on 9. 600 sees Cato and Varro behind Virgil at this point.[4] He is clearly right; Numanus Remulus' more laudable claims are arrogated by Cato in the 'de suis uirtutibus': 'ego iam a principio in parsimonia atque in duritia atque in industria omnem adulescentiam meam abstinui agro colendo saxis Sabinis silicibus repastinandis atque conserendis', and proclaimed in the *de agri cultura*.[5] The Rutuli have clearly much in common with the stereotype picture of early Roman or honest countryman,[6] as also with ethnographical notices of barbarian peoples. In the latter, the element of idealization is minimal, for the ethnographers write in terms of conventionalized details, which accumulate in mass and fixity from Hecataeus and Herodotus to Ammianus and beyond.[7] So in this speech, only one item (*uersaque iuuencum...*) could possibly be regarded as an innovation. Virgil also has in mind ideal descriptions of the Cretan and Spartan states.[8] The latter is of particular importance for the description of primitive Italians, for similarities in *mores* had long since suggested a Laconian origin for the Sabines.[9] Finally, Virgil may have been influenced by speculations about the influence of environment on national character. *Rastris terram domat* perhaps implies the great effort involved in cultivating the rugged country of central Italy. Thus, as Cato suggests in the *de suis uirtutibus*, the native Italians are the hard offspring of the hard land.[10]

The *duritia* of the Italians is a dominating theme; they are a *durum*

---

bellum fuisse (cf. Gell. 17. 21. 33; Plut. *vit. Pyrrhi*, 19, *Rhet. ad Hercnn.* 4. 31); so here *o uere Phrygiae neque enim Phryges*. But the insult is of too common a type for the coincidence to signify here.

[4] Cf. P. Fraccaro, *Studi Varroniani* (Padua, 1907), p. 220; behind Varro there may also lie Posidonius (*Hist.* ap. *Athen.* 4. 153 C = fr. I Jac.).

[5] 2 *Praef.* 4; cf. Nep. *Cat. 1* and Plin. *18. 11. 26.*

[6] As, for instance, Sall. *Cat.* 10. 1; Cic. *Leg. Agr.* 2. 84.

[7] Cf. J. G. C. Anderson, Tacitus: *Germania* (Oxford, 1938), pp. ix f., xxvii f.

[8] Crete: Heracl. Pont. *FHG 2. 211.* For Sparta see, e.g., Pl. *Leg.* 7. 823 C; also W. Den Boer, *Laconian Studies* (Amsterdam, 1954), pp. 233 f.

[9] Heinze, *Vergils epische Technik* (Stuttgart, 1965), p. 223 n. 1; cf. A. Schwegler, *Römische Geschichte* (Tübingen, 1853), i. 280; Fraccaro, *Studi Varroniani*, p. 226; Bérard, *Colonisation grecque*, p. 467; Posidonius ap. Athen. 6, p. 273; Cato ap. Serv. Dan. *ad Aen.* 8. 638; Varr. *LL*, 5. 146.

[10] Cf. Lucr. 2. 430. For this type of geographical speculation, cf. Hippocr. *Airs, Waters, Places*, 12; Herod. 1. 143. 2; 9. 122. 3; Cic. *Leg. Agr.* 2. 95; Tac. *Ger.* 4; Liv. 9. 13, 7; Strab. 3. 3. 7; J. O. Thomson, *History of Ancient Geography* (Cambridge, 1948), pp. 106 f.

genus from birth, and they are hardened in icy rivers. The repetition is prominent and deliberate. It is also peculiarly Roman, for there is no Greek word to convey a condition of laudable physical toughness. *Duritia* was the virtue of Cato (*vide supra*), of the Scipios, of the Gauls and Germans, and of the Spartans and Macedonians.[11] Above all, it is the product of hard toil in farm or army.[12] *Durus* and its cognates become almost stock epithets for both farmer and soldier.[13] Anchises warns Aeneas that the people of Latium are a *gens dura atque aspera cultu* (*Aen.* 5. 730). Yet in the poem, the Italians share this virtue with the much-maligned Trojans.[14]

There is a second heavily stressed motif: that of *ferrum. Omne aeuum ferro teritur* stands at the middle of the speech, and the idea of *omne aeuum* is amplified through the sequence of *natos* (603) . . . *pueri* (605) . . . *iuuentus* (607) . . . *senectus* (610); the character of *ferrum* is clearly both agricultural and military: *uersaque iuuencum terga fatigamus hasta* follows directly. *Cedite ferro* (618) is not easy; *TLL* (iii. 725. 13) takes *cedite* as *desistite*. That is possible; but in the context, 'yield to the knife', with an allusion to orgiastic emasculation must be the primary sense. Schweizer (op. cit. 16) suggests that the central reference to *ferrum* places Numanus Remulus and his ideals in the *ferrea saecula* (cf. *Geo.* 1. 145 f.), despite analogies with the ideal rustic life. But here, as in *Geo.* 2, the relationship of Golden and Iron Ages to the historical time-scale would be extremely confusing, and the allusion must remain uncertain.[15] There is a further philosophical concept whose relevance to the interpretation of this speech is doubtful. The *paruo . . . adsueta iuuentus* might seem to recall Cynic or Stoic ideas of frugality. But the ethnographers attributed coarse diet and clothing to innumerable primitive peoples (*vide infra*), and Virgil simply makes a virtue out of the necessity of their hard lives.

The details of the speech must now be considered in order:

Durum a stirpe genus natos ad flumina primum deferimus saeuoque gelu duramus et undis. The process of hardening begins in earliest infancy;

---

[11] Worked into creation stories: *Geo.* 1. 63; Lucr. 5. 926; Ov. *Met.* 1. 414; Scipios, *Geo.* 2. 167 f.; Gauls and Germans, Caes. *BG* 6. 21. 3; 28. 3; Spartans, Cic. *Tusc.* 1. 102; Macedonians, Liv. 42. 52. 10. Used by Col. of the Sabines, 10. 137.

[12] Farm: Lucr. 5. 1360; Sen. *Ep.* 95. 18; army: Tac. *Ann.* 1. 20. 2.

[13] Farmer: *Geo.* 1. 160; Colum. 7. 6. 4; 10. 23; *Aen.* 7. 504; Hor. *S.* 1. 7. 29; Colum. 1. 8. 2; Ov. *Fast.* 4. 691 f., etc. Soldier: Ov. *Ars* 3. 110; Liv. 7. 29. 5; 27. 48. 10; 9. 40. 4, etc.

[14] Trojans: 3. 94; 9. 466; 12. 288; Italians—see too 11. 48, 657.

[15] Cf. W. Richter on *Geo.* 2. 500.

like Thracians, Germans, and Scyths,[16] but, as it happens, unlike the
Spartans,[17] the Italians accustom their infants to cold, developing an
endurance of climate admired and required in soldier and barbarian.[18]
The habit of bathing in icy local rivers[19] will have impressed in a city of
bathhouses, where only the soldier in training ventured into the Tiber.[20]

Venatu inuigilant pueri siluasque fatigant. Virgil makes both Trojans
and Italians keen hunters.[21] This was far more than a characteristic of
rural life[22] and a conventional activity of barbarian peoples.[23] To both
Greeks and Romans, it had a definite moral value, requiring both hard
work (πόνος; cf. *inuigilant, fatigant* here) and courage.[24] Hunting
therefore strengthened the body and was a valuable propaedeutic for
war.[25] Moreover, it was a fit pursuit for a gentleman, whether an
Athenian nobleman, a squire of Xenophon's Laconian shires, or any
Roman from the elder Cato to Horace's Lollius.[26] Sallust's sneer in *Cat.*
4. 1 is the perplexing expression of a minority opinion.[27]

Flectere ludus equos et spicula tendere cornu. Ludus might be thought
slightly ambiguous; however, between *jeu* and *entraînement* it is easy to
decide.[28] For the Italians, riding and archery are far more than boyish
games; like hunting, they were traditional features of the military

---

[16] Galen *De Sanit. Tuenda* 6. 51 (Kühn); Soranus *Gynaec.* 2. 12 (81). 1; Sid. Ap. *C,* 2.
35 f.; Arist. *Pol.* 7. 17. 3 (with Newman's note). Cf. the Celtic practice of immersing babies
in the Rhine; survival proved legitimacy: *AP* 9. 125; Ps. Theoph. Simoc. *Ep.* 10 (R.
Hercher, *Epistolographi Graeci* (Paris, 1873), 766, 20); Jul. *Ep.* 191; *Or.* 2, p. 81 d.; J. A.
Cramer, *Anecdota Oxoniensia* (1835), 3. 158, 20; Tzetz. in Hes. *Erga* Prol., p. 12, 4
(Gaisford); Greg. Naz. *Carm.* 2. 4, 142 f. (*PG,* XXXVII, 1516); Nonn. *Dion.* 23. 94 f.,
Paroem. Gr. 2. p. 569; Claud. *In Ruf.* 2. 112; *CAG,* xviii, 1. p. 125, 30 f.; Georg. Pisid. *Ekstr.
Herakl.,* 1. 41; Lib. *Or in Iul.* 2. p. 26. 10 (Lib.); *Narrat. de Rhen.* 8, p. 56 F.; Theodorus
Hyrtacenus, *Epp.* 25, 37, 52. This note attempts a full statement of the evidence, *exempli
gratia.*
[17] Plut. *Lyc.* 12.
[18] Strab. 3. 3. 7; 15. 3. 18; Caes. *BG* 6. 22. 3; Liv. 5. 48. 3; Veg. *RM* 1. 10; Claud. 7. 39.
[19] Scythians: Valerius Flaccus 6. 335; Lusitani: Strab. 3. 3. 7; Spartans; Sen. *Suas.* 2. 5;
Germans; Caes. *BG* 6. 21. 5.
[20] Hor. *Od.* 3. 7. 25 f.; 3. 12. 8 f.; Tib. 1. 4. 11 f.; Plut. *Cat. Mai.* 20. 4 f.
[21] *Aen.* 1. 315, 336; 4. 158; 9. 771; 11. 777; 7. 651; 9. 245, etc.
[22] *Geo.* 1. 139, 307; 3. 409, etc.
[23] Strab. 7. 4. 8; Amm. 23. 6. 50; Caes. *BG* 4. 1. 8; Herod. 4. 22. 112, 116.
[24] J. Aymard, *Essai sur les chasses romaines* (Paris, 1965), pp. 89 f., 469 f.; Jaeger, *Paideia*
(Eng. tr.), iii. 177 f.
[25] Caes. *BG* 6. 21. 3; 28. 3; Max. Tyr. *diss.* 18 (ed. Hobein, p. 322, 14); Varr. *RR* 2 *praef.*
15 f.; Suet. *Aug.* 43. 4. At Sparta, Plut. *Lyc.* 22; Pl. *Leg.* 1. 633 b; 7. 823 C.
[26] Athens: Xen. *Cyn.* 12 (particularly 13); Laconia; Xen. *Anab.* 5. 3, etc.; Cato: Cic. *Sen.*
56; Lollius: Hor. *Ep.* 1. 18, 49 f. In general, see Aymard, pp. 485 f.
[27] Aymard, pp. 57 f.; Plato's praise is much-hedged (*Leg.* 7. 824).
[28] Marrou, *Historie de l'éducation,* p. 351.

upbringing in Sparta, Crete, and Athens,[29] as also among the Germans and Spaniards.[30] The elder Cato prescribed riding for his son, and it remained one of the sports of the Campus Martius.[31] Neglect of these exercises was a sure sign of decay.[32] *At patiens operum.* This line is first used at *Geo.* 2. 472 in the context of the ideal rural world. There the *opera* need be no more than the continuous work of the farm. Here, they are the twofold labours of war and agriculture, to be borne in addition to the hardships of climate and poverty. The Italians' *patientia* is altogether admirable; it is, after all, a product of their *duritia.*[33] It is not a virtue to be applied lightly or often to peoples other than Romans.[34]

Paruoque adsueta iuuentus. Frugality, a virtue imposed by circumstance, marks the life of the farmer and the solder,[35] as well as of many barbarian peoples.[36] Once more, the coincidence of detail is repeated: Rutulian, barbarian, and idealized peasant-soldier.

Aut rastris terram domat. With this reference to the hard labour of agriculture, Virgil's praise of the Italians comes to an end. Incessant internecine war is the goal of all their physical preparations: *aut quatit oppida bello.* From Aeneas' first sight of the *arx Minervae* (3. 530 f.), there is a strong warlike element in the country's character.[37] This character the Romans admired and fostered;[38] it was, equally, one applied to many of the barbarians.[39]

The deliberate idealization of the type of the Italian farmer-soldier begins apparently with Cicero, above all in his portrait of the elder Cato in the *De Senectute.*[40] Virgil's Rutuli resemble more closely still Horace's Sabines: 'rusticorum mascula militum proles Sabellis docta ligonibus

[29] Sparta: (Xen.). *Resp. Lac.* 2. 2 f.; Plut. *Apoph. Lac.* 227 D; Crete: Pl. *Leg.* 1. 625 D; Athens: K. Pélékidis, *Histoire de l'éphébie attique* (Paris, 1962), p. 108.
[30] Strab. 3. 3. 7; Mela 3. 26.
[31] Plut. *Cat. Mai.* 20. 4 f.; Dio 52. 26. 1; Strab. 5. 3. 8; Ov. *Fast.* 3. 522; Hor. *Od.* 3. 7. 25 f.; 3. 12. 8 f., 3. 24. 54; *Sat.* 2. 2. 9 f.
[32] *Aen.* 4. 86 f., Hor. *Od.* 1. 8. 1 f.
[33] Colum. 7. 6. 9; Veg. *RM*, 1. 3; Sall. *Cat.* 10. 2; to be praised in an enemy, even: Cic. *Cat. 1. 26.*
[34] Caes. *BG* 6. 24. 4; Cic. *Ver.* 2. 7; Amm 17. 13. 27; cf. Polyb. 3. 79. 5; the hardy Libyans and Iberians are contrasted with the Celts.
[35] Hor. *Od.* 3. 21. 1; *Ep.* 2. 1. 39; Cato Cens. *or. fr.* 128.
[36] Amm. 23. 6. 61; Curt. 6. 5. 11; Strab. 15. 1. 53; 3. 3. 7; Caes. *BG* 6. 24. 4; 8. 4. 1; Herod. 1. 136; Hecat. *fr.* 9 (J); Phyl. *fr.* 13 (J).
[37] Similar foreshadowing: *Aen.* 1. 21, 263, 531; 4. 229.
[38] Liv. 9. 9. 11; 7. 6. 3; *Geo.* 3. 346; Prop. 3. 22. 19.
[39] *Aen.* 1. 14; Strab. 14. 2. 27; 4. 4. 2; 4. 4. 5; *TLL* 2, 1810. 27 ff.
[40] Cf. first, apparently *Leg. Agr.* 2. 84.

uersare glaebas...' (*Od.* 3. 6. 37 f.)[41] and the portrait he himself draws of
the Aequi: 'horrida ... gens, adsuetaque multo uenatu nemorum ...
armati terram exercent...' (7. 746 f.).[42] Obviously tough farmers, with
an interest in the land, made the best soldiers, physically and spiritually.[43] Four of Rome's greatest soldiers, Cincinnatus, M' Curius
Dentatus, C. Fabricius Luscinus, and M. Atilius Regulus were
renowned as being also farmers.[44] From the elder Cato to Vegetius, the
textbooks laid down that the army's ranks were best filled from the
Italian peasantry;[45] Marsi and Sabines were particularly renowned.[46]
Thus narratives of recruitment rarely mention Rome, and there is
frequent abuse of the quality of urban troops.[47] To this complex of ideas
we shall have to return.

Omne aeuum ferro teritur. The Italians undertake willingly and with
pride a life of endless toil and strife, though free men might complain
that such burdens were imposed to keep them in subjection.[48] *Versaque
iuuencum terga fatigamus hasta.* This is apparently the only detail in the
speech that is not conventional; de la Cerda provides a remote parallel
from Cassiodorus.[49] The reverse process—that is, the use of rustic
instruments in war, is much better attested.[50]

*Nec tarda senectus debilitat uires animi nutatque uigorem; canitiem galea
premimus.* It was precisely in formal discussions of *senectus* that the
traditional partition of strength to the young and wisdom to the old[51] was
recognized as fallacious. In the *De Senectute*, Cato, though no second
Agesilaus, is full of the virtues of an active old age (32, cf. Plut. *an seni*,
788 A). Again, the benefits of agriculture are prominent: he speaks of
men in Sabinum—soldier-farmers in their prime, of course—as still

---

[41] Cf. also *S.* 2. 7. 23; *Ep.* 2. 1. 139 f.; *Od.* 1. 12. 43 f.; 1. 1. 11 f.; *Epod.* 2. 3; *Od.* 3. 16.
26 f.; A. La Penna, *Orazio e l'ideologia del principato* (Turin, 1963), pp. 59 f.

[42] *Geo.* 2. 513 f.; *Aen.* 11. 318 f.

[43] The ideal had been criticized by Pl. *Rep.* 2. 374 c; Arist. *Pol.* 7. 9. 1 f. Close to the
Roman attitude is Men. *fr.* 63. 408. We may also compare General Dwight D. Eisenhower
(quoted by Louis Heren, *The Times* (1 Apr. 1969), p. 8): 'the pioneers had to learn to
plough a straight furrow with a rifle on their backs. They were not discouraged by constant
dangers. They were a happy people.'

[44] Colum. 1 *praef.* 13 f.; 4, 2, Cic., *Sen.* 56; Liv. 3. 13. 26; DH 19. 15.

[45] Cat. *agr., praef.* 4; Varr. *RR,* 2 *praef.* 2; Colum. 1 *praef.* 17; Veg. *RM* 1. 3.

[46] Sabines: Hor. *Epod.* 2. 41; Liv. 1. 18. 4; Hor. *Od.* 3. 6. 37, etc.; Marsi: *Geo.* 2. 167;
Hor. *Od.* 2. 20. 18., 3. 5. 9; Caes. *BC* 1. 15. 20, etc.

[47] Colum. 1 *praef.* 17; P. A. Brunt in *JRS* 52 (1962), 73 f., 85.

[48] Herod. 3. 134. 2; Liv. 6. 27. 7; etc.

[49] *Var.* 12. 5.

[50] *Aen.* 7. 505; etc.

[51] W. L. Newman, *Aristotle: The Politics,* 4 vols. (Oxford 1887–1902), iii. 379; *Il.* 3.
727 f.; Eur. *fr.* 293, etc.

active in the fields when old (24; cf. 51). There is also a long and noble line of old men actively and successfully engaged in war—from Nestor to Masinissa.[52] Above all, Camillus; Livy stresses the glorious paradox of his victories.[53] *Semperque recentes comportare iuuat praedas et uiuere rapto.* The old men may remain strong, but they are bandits. The obtaining of a livelihood from plunder,[54] like the combination of ability in war with a taste for rapine[55] is a common attribute of barbarian peoples. In *omne aeuum ferro teritur*, there may have been a similar implication: as from Thucydides, the continuous bearing of arms was regarded as the mark of a way of life dependent on banditry.[56] That the Rutuli lived from rapine would strike the Augustans as peculiarly vicious; bandits and pirates constitute an unending threat to peace and order.[57]

At this, Numanus Remulus turns upon the Trojans, to accuse them of luxurious degeneracy. *O uere Phrygiae neque enim Phryges* summarizes his insults: they are not even men. But round the basic form of Ἀχαιΐδες, οὐκέτ' Ἀχαιοί, 'Achaean women, not Achaeans'[58] Virgil has added various more complex ideas. To Romans obsessed by the concept of moral decay and its causes, Trojan *luxuria* represents an obviously later and worse cultural level than Rutulian *duritia*,[59] though the idea of decline could hardly be made explicit in the speech.[60] Nothing but contempt for the Trojans is uttered, and yet it is precisely such τρυφή as theirs that could lead to the decay and collape of Italian virtue.[61] Such was the danger awaiting Aeneas from Carthaginian *luxuria*. There was the temptation was not resisted (4. 215 f., 262).

The disgust felt at the historical Phrygian custom of orgiastic

[52] In general, Cic. *Sen.* 55 f.; *Il.* 14. 86; AR, 1. 44; Cyrus: Cic. *Sen.* 30; Xen. *Cyr.* 8. 7. 6; Agesilaus: Xen. *Ages.* 11. 14 f. (*vires animi*); Cic. *Sen.* 38; Antigonus, Phocion, Masinissa, Cato: Plut. *an seni* 791 E; Masinissa: Cic. *Sen.* 34; the Spartans: Plut. *Apoph. Lac.* 222 A; B. E. Richardson, *Old Age Amongst the Greeks* (Baltimore, 1933), pp. 33 f., 98 f.
[53] 6. 22. 7; 23. 4; 24. 7.
[54] Strab. 4. 3. 3; 7. 5. 12; 3. 4. 4; 3. 4. 8; Pher. 38 (*FHG*).
[55] Newman, Arist. *Pol.*, 3. 523; Mela 3. 3. 27 f.; Strab. 3. 3. 5; Herod. 4. 103. 3.
[56] Thuc. 1. 5 f.; Polyb. 4. 3. 1 f.; Tac. *Ger.* 13. 1; 22. 1.
[57] R. MacMullen, *Enemies of the Roman Order* (Cambridge, Mass., 1967), pp. 192 f., 255 f.; H. A. Ormerod, *Piracy in the Ancient World* (Liverpool, 1924), pp. 190 f.
[58] *Il.* 7. 96 f.; Pease on *Aen.* 4. 215; Herod. 8. 88, 1. 155; Liv. 7. 13. 6; 9. 2. 14; *D.H.*, 9. 7. 2; Herter, 641.
[59] D. C. Earl, *The Political Thought of Sallust* (Cambridge, 1951), pp. 41 f.; P. G. Walsh, *Livy* (Cambridge, 1961), pp. 65 f.; R. Syme, *Sallust* (Berkeley/Los Angeles, 1964), pp. 248 f.; La Penna, op. cit. (n. 41), 59 f.
[60] Sall. *Cat.* 7 f.; Varr. *RR* 2 *praef.* 17; Colum. 1 *praef.* 13 f.
[61] A. Passerini in *SIFC* 11 (1934), 35 f.; J. L. Tondriau in *REA* 1 (1948), 49 f.; F. Egermann, *Die Proömien z.d. Werken des Sallust* (Vienna, 1932), pp. 34 f.

emasculation is here, as often,[62] inflicted upon the Trojans.[63] After Herter's thorough article in *RAC*, a brief examination of Virgil's details will suffice:

Vobis picta croco et fulgenti murice uestis. At 4. 262 Aeneas clad in purple at Carthage could be calculated to arouse Roman indignation: he had adopted an unbecoming foreign garb, which—quite apart from suggestions of rule and wealth—implied luxury and effeminacy.[64] In the debate on the sumptuary Lex Oppia, Livy makes Cato the Censor associate gold and purple with the cult of the Magna Mater.[65] Here the addition of yellow makes the charge all the more pointed—it was the colour of the women[66] and the effeminates.[67]

Desidiae cordi. This is the antithesis of the continuous activity of the Italians. The Trojans are charged not with an honourable σχόλη or *otium*, but with an indolence that was strongly deplored at Rome.[68] 'Luxu atque desidia ciuitas corrupta est', claimed Sallust; to Varro, it was the vice which *maiores nostri* attributed to town-dwellers, while Caesar records the German boast that they practised banditry 'iuuentutis exercendae ac desidiae minuendae causa'.[69]

Iuuat indulgere choreis. That the Trojans should dance is not, in itself, wholly worthy of censure, for not even in early Rome had dancing been altogether deplored,[70] while by the time of Augustus, there were signs of widespread interest and enthusiasm. However, attitudes to dancing had long depended on the type of dance,[71] and the Trojans could be expected to perform the wholly deplorable orgiastic dances of Cybele, to which reference is made in the following lines.[72] A subordinate charge may be their *indulgentia*, an excessive partiality for what may sometimes be a decent activity.

---

[62] H. Graillot, *Le Culte de Cybèle* (Paris, 1912), pp. 21 f.

[63] A. S. Pease on *Aen.* 4. 215; H. Herter, *RAC* col. 630 ff.

[64] Pers. 1. 32; Lucian *Bis Accus.* 17, etc.

[65] Liv. 34. 3. 9; 4. 7.

[66] Athen. 4. 155 c; 12. 519 c; Plut. *an seni* 735 E.

[67] Ov. *Ars* 3. 179; Petron. 68; Juv. 6. 365; Apul. *Met.* 6. 8; Cic. *Har. Resp.* 44.

[68] Herter, p. 632; J. M. André, *L'Otium dans la vie morale et intellectuelle romaine* (Paris, 1966), pp. 61 f.; Rambaud in *REL* 24 (1946), 124 f., and especially V. Pöschl, *Grundwerte römischer Staatsgesinnung in den Geschichtswerken des Sallust* (Berlin, 1940), pp. 27 f. For the Greek attitude, see V. Ehrenberg in *JHS* 67 (1947), 46 f.; C. M. Bowra in *CQ* (1941), 124; A. W. Gomme, *Hist. Comm. Thuc.*, 1. 167 f., 232.

[69] Sall. *Cat.* 53. 5 (cf. Front. *Strat.* 4. 1. 13; Suet. *Tib.* 33); Varr. *RR* 2 *praef.* 1; Caes. *BG* 6. 23. 6.

[70] Macr. 3. 14. 4; Sall. *Cat.* 25; Hor. *S.* 1. 9. 23; Ov. *Ars* 1. 595; Hor. *Od.* 2. 12. 18.

[71] Pl. *Leg.* 2. 656 B; *Rep.* 3. 398 D ff.

[72] Herter, p. 638.

Et tunicae manicas et habent redimicula mitrae. Romans scorned the
sleeve; after all, the toga made for a winter with bare arms. To do
otherwise was a sure mark of effeminacy, and a mode of dress which
associated the wearer with Persians and barbarians at large.[73] The next
insult is more thoroughly barbed. It is bad enough that the Trojans
should wear any headgear at all, and particularly obnoxious that it
should be secured by ribbons.[74] The *mitra* is most appropriate here; its
home is in Asia Minor, as well as further east, and it is often attributed to
the Trojans.[75] Furthermore, it was worn by Attis, by the votaries of
Cybele, and by the archigallus himself.[76] So it was an integral part of the
effeminate's attire from Aristophanes to Juvenal.[77]

Ite per alta Dindyma ... Numanus Remulus uses a formula of
contemptuous dismissal.[78] The Trojans' place is in Dindyma and
Berecynthus, home of the cult of Cybele.[79] There the rites were held to
the wild music of drum and boxwood flute, an association which
contributed largely to the moral censure against the flute.[80] In contrast,
war is for true men only;[81] the Trojans are fit only for emasculation.

Numanus Remulus, after the briefest interval, is shot by Ascanius
with Jupiter's approval and Apollo's congratulations (9. 621–37). Confidence in a marriage-alliance with Turnus is shown to be baseless,
Trojan youth is vindicated, and divine censure of Rutulian ideology
displayed. In *digna atque indigna relatu* (595) Virgil had either proclaimed
his own disapproval of what is reported in advance, or suggested that
what is not reported was even more wild and deplorable. Aeneas and the
Trojans are clearly living down the fall of Troy,[82] and their increasing
success in battle is a standing condemnation of the old association of
Trojan with effeminate and cowardly Phrygian. However, Virgil seems

[73] Suet. *Cal.* 52; L. M. Wilson, *Clothing of the Ancient Romans* (Baltimore, 1938), p. 67;
EAA, s.v. *Barbari*, p. 976.
[74] Cic. *Ver.* 5. 76; Juv. 2. 84; Calp. 6. 38. It is the *tiara* that strictly has the ribbons, not
the *mitra* (H. Brandenburg, *Studien zur Mitra* (Münster, 1966), p. 64).
[75] Pease on *Aen.* 4. 216; C. Roebuck, *Ionian Trade and Colonisation* (New York, 1959),
p. 3.
[76] J. Marquardt, *Römische Staatsverwaltung*, 3 vols. (Leipzig, 1881–5), iii. 369; Pease on
Aen. 4. 216; Prop. 4. 7. 61.
[77] Brandenburg, pp. 58 f.; Ar. *Thesm.* 257, 941; Juv. 3. 115.
[78] *TLL*, v. 2, 632. 67 f.
[79] Roscher *Lexicon*, s.v. Kybele 1643, 5 f.; *TLL*, *Onom.*, C.-Don., 154, 65 f.; Gruppe,
p. 1250 n. 2; Bömer, Ov. *Fast.* 2. 221 f.
[80] Herter, p. 627; Ov. *Fast.* 4. 181 (with Bömer); Gruppe, p. 1539; Graillot, p. 124;
Suet. *Aug.* 68; Newman, Arist. *Pol.* 3. 552; *TLL*, s.v. *buxus*, iii. b.
[81] Hor. *Epod.* 15. 12 *et saep.*
[82] Cf. W. S. Anderson in *TAPhA* 88 (1957), 17 f.

to retain a trace of hesitation and hostility towards the Trojans, for Jupiter promises (12. 834) 'sermonem Ausonii moresque tenebunt'. In practice, the Trojans lack none of the Italians' virtues, but some trace of traditional Graeco-Roman contempt for the East seems ineradicable.

Schweizer (p. 18) has suggested that Aeneas (or Augustus) is to replace the world of Numanus Remulus by a new Golden Age. But the old world is also in part desirable as analogies with *Geo.* 2. 471–2, 531 strongly imply. But the lack of warmth and charm in the picture in this speech make it seem a most unattractive world, far from the happy and simple peasantry of *Geo.* 2. Indeed as propaganda for a united Italy of free peasant cultivators, this speech would be extraordinarily inept. There is in Augustan writing about the return to the soil a scarcely resolved inconsistency between the claims of peace and war.[83]

Within the *pax Augusta* some aptitude for war was necessary, but its application was somewhat limited (cf. 9. 642). Anchises had warned Aeneas 'gens dura atque aspera cultu debellanda tibi Latio est' (5. 730); only the *duritia* is laudable. The taming of Latium falls precisely within the terms of *debellare superbos*, and of *paci ... imponere morem*. The strength which had been developed by simple life, frequent exercise and hard farm labour, was properly employed in the defeat of foreign enemies—Carthage, Pyrrhus, and Antiochus. The Augustans required it for the defeat of Parthia, or for wars in Spain, Germany, North Africa, the Alps, and the Balkans.[84] However, if the farmer fights, who farms? The army might attract countrymen who had failed to make a living, but the effect of a levy was well known (and would of course be the same in the case of *euocati*): 'squalent abductis arua colonis'.[85] The rehabilitation of the *duri agricolae* conflicts with wider economic tendencies in Italian agriculture and with romanticized policies of recruitment. The Rutuli, as over-trained warriors and part-time farmers, emphasize the inconsistency.

There is in this picture very little of the joys of country life, and nothing of rural piety (contrast *Geo.* 2. 473, *Aen.* 12. 835–9). Nor are any elements in it distinctively Augustan or Italian. The developed type of the peasant-soldier, here seen in his most harsh and primitive aspects, derives ultimately from the Greek ethnographers. Of his traditional

---

[83] Not really touched on in the main discussions: F. Klingner in *Hermes* 16 (1931), 159 f.; R. Syme, *RR*, 253 f.; 450 f.; E. de Saint-Denis, *Geo.* (Budé edn.), 8 f.

[84] H. *Od.* 3. 6. 33 f.; 3. 2. 1 f.; 4. 4. 17 f.; 4. 5. 25 f.

[85] *Geo.* 1. 508; cf. *Aen.* 7. 635 f.; Ov. *Fast.* 1. 697 f.; Men. *fr.* 556; P. A. Brunt in *JRS* 52 (1962), 75 n. 64.

material, Virgil has made a stark and original portrait of primitive Italy. There are too many complex and discordant strains for it to constitute adequate propaganda for the type of Italian peasant-soldier that was to be revived.

APPENDIX

Postscript 1988

The passage has been studied intensively of late: see E. Pianezzola in *Studi in onore di Anthos Ardizzoni* (Rome, 1978), 691–9; R. F. Thomas, *Lands and Peoples in Roman Poetry*, Cambr. Phil. Soc., Suppl. vol. 7 (Cambridge, 1982), 98–100 (with Horsfall, *CR* 34 (1984), 134); M. Dickie, *PLLS* 5 (1985), 165–221 (with Horsfall, *CR* 38 (1988), 273–4); N. M. Horsfall, *Enc. Virg.* 3 s.v. *Numano Remulo.* Dickie has added numerous instances of the ethnographic topoi I adduced; the main lines of my 1971 interpretation seem still to stand. See now further Horsfall, *Riv. Fil.* 117 (1989) 57–61.

17

Vergil and the Politics of War

R. O. A. M. LYNE

The Romans had various ways of justifying their imperial aims and methods, some high-minded, some less so.[1] We find in particular that they could give honourable and satisfying explanations of their aims and methods in war. Here, for example, is Cicero:

quare suscipienda quidem bella sunt ob eam causam, ut sine iniuria in pace uiuatur; parta autem uictoria conseruandi ii, qui non crudeles in bello, non immanes fuerunt, ut maiores nostri Tusculanos, Aequos ... in ciuitatem etiam acceperunt, at Carthaginem ... funditus sustulerunt ... mea quidem sententia paci, quae nihil habitura sit insidiarum, semper est consulendum. et cum iis, quos ui deuiceris, consulendum est, tum ii qui armis positis ad imperatorum fidem confugient, quamuis murum aries percusserit, recipiendi.

Therefore wars are to be undertaken for this reason, that life may proceed in peace without injury; but when victory is gained those who were not cruel or monstrous in war should be preserved, just as our ancestors received the Tusculani and Aequi into citizenship, but completely destroyed Carthage. In my view we must always plan for the kind of peace which will provide no surprise attacks, and you must not only make plans for those who you have conquered by force of arms, but also take in those who flee to safety after laying down their arms in obedience to their leaders, even if the battering-ram needs to strike their walls to do it. (*Off.* 1. 35)

Cicero makes basically two points: (1) the aim of Roman war is peace and security; (2) the proper policy towards vanquished peoples is, where possible, magnanimity and mercy. These keynotes are easy to parallel.[2] Here is a passage later in the *De Officiis*:

Much has of course been written on most of the topics dealt with in this paper, and many articles and books are referred to in the notes. A high proportion of the articles are disappointing; one that is not and which I would single out for special mention is R. D. Williams, 'The Purpose of the *Aeneid*', *Antichthon* 1 (1967), 29–41 (repr. in this collection, Ch. 2 above). Messrs P. G. McC. Brown and D. P. Fowler have read and criticized the present paper. My thanks to them. It is not to be assumed they agree with it all.

[1] See the useful paper of P. A. Brunt, 'Laus Imperii', in P. D. A. Garnsey and C. A. Whittaker, eds., *Imperialism in the Ancient World* (Cambridge, 1978).

[2] Cf. too Brunt, loc. cit., especially pp. 178 ff. and E. Norden on *Aen.* 6. 847–53. Be it noted, however, that we find some curious interpretations of what constituted 'mercy', and

sed ea animi elatio, quae cernitur in periculis et laboribus, si iustitia uacat pugnatque non pro salute communi, sed pro suis commodis, in uitio est; non modo enim id uirtutis non est, sed est potius immanitatis omnem humanitatem repellentis. itaque probe definitur a Stoicis fortitudo, cum eam uirtutem esse dicunt propugnantem pro aequitate.

But that kind of rousing of the spirit which is seen in perils and tribulations, if it is void of justice and fights not for the common safety but for its own advantages, is at fault; for this is no part of virtue, but rather of a monstrous nature which repels all humanity. Excellent therefore is the Stoic definition of bravery, when they say that it is virtue fighting for the right. (*Off.* 1. 62)

Note, among other things, *pro salute communi*. Rome's supposed clemency towards her enemies was virtually proverbial—among Romans (Cato *ap*. Gell. 6. 3. 52, Liv. 33. 12. 7, Caes. *BG* 2. 14, etc.); Sallust's reference to Rome's traditional magnanimity in victory also implies that the aim of war was 'peace':

neque uictis quicquam praeter iniuriae licentiam eripiebant [*sc.* maiores]. (*Cat.* 12. 4)

Let us turn now to Augustus. Long before he catalogues his imperial victories and gains in the *Res Gestae* (26–33, 'omnium prouinciarum populi Romani, quibus finitimae fuerunt gentes quae non parerent imperio nostro, fines auxi...'), he records his policy of imperial mercy towards the defeated (3):

externas gentes, quibus tuto ignosci potuit, conseruare quam excidere malui;

just previously to that he celebrates his slightly more ambiguous policy of mercy towards his defeated enemies in the civil wars:[3]

uictorque omnibus ueniam petentibus ciuibus peperci.

And, again long before that catalogue of imperial victories, he focuses on the peace that is to be attributed to those victories: proudly he records the solemn, ritual celebrations of his peace (13):

Ianum Quirinum, quem clausum esse maiores nostri uoluerunt, cum per totum imperium populi Romani terra marique esset parta uictoriis pax ... ter me principe senatus claudendum esse censuit.

of what 'peace and security as the aim of war' involved or allowed. This is amply documented by Brunt.
   [3] Cf. Sen. *Clem.* 2. 3. 1, 'clementia est temperantia animi *in potestate ulciscendi* uel lenitas *superioris aduersus inferiorem* in constituendis poenis'. One can see why an offer of *clementia* might be resented. See the excellent comments of D. C. Earl, *The Moral and Political Tradition of Rome* (London, 1967), p. 60. I return to the question of *clementia* below.

Horace, his poet laureate, hymns that same peace and the same ritual in his final Ode (4. 15. 4 ff.): 'tua, Caesar, aetas ... uacuum duellis / Ianum Quirini clausit', etc.). And lines 49 ff. of Horace's *Carmen Saeculare* are perhaps particularly notable:

> quaeque uos bubus ueneratur albis
> clarus Anchisae Venerisque sanguis,
> impetret, bellante prior, iacentem
>   lenis in hostem.
> iam mari terraque manus potentis
> Medus Albanasque timet securis,
> iam Scythae responsa petunt superbi
>   nuper et Indi.

And may the famed descendant of Anchises and Venus obtain the prayer for which he worships you with white oxen, superior to his enemy in war, gentle to the defeated adversary. Now the Mede fears our bands mighty by land and sea and the Alban axes, now the Scythians, recently so proud, seek our answers, and the Indians.

Military supremacy, magnanimity to defeated foes, peace and security *because* of military supremacy: Horace lyricizes the achievements of his patron. Horace reminds us of Cicero, too, and the others—because Augustus phrased his achievements in traditional, idealizing ways.

The above passages suggest, then, certain ways in which Roman imperialists in idealizing mood liked to present Roman aims and methods in war. The authors in fact (in spite of their idealizing) speak in the main from a political standpoint; indeed, excluding Horace, they are politicians, active or retired.[4] Philosophers offered ways in which the presentation of Roman warfare could be further refined—as *Off.* 1. 62 (and 63) already indicates. It is of particular interest to consider Stoic ideas, because Stoic ethics had so much practical significance in Roman public life[5]—and of course for Vergil.[6] Stoic advocacy of self-denying duty, of subordination, *praebere se fato*, was in tune with traditional Roman and Vergilian ideas and ideals: with *pietas*, with *non sibi sed patriae natus*, and with Vergil's *fatum sequi*.[7] Of course the traditional

---

[4] Cicero speaks (it seems to me) more as a Roman than as a Panaetian in *Off.* 1. 35; though the distinction is perhaps artificial: see below.

[5] See E. V. Arnold, *Roman Stoicism* (London, 1911), esp. pp. 380 ff.

[6] See, e.g., R. Heinze, *Virgils epische Technik*³ (Leipzig, 1914), index *sub* 'Stoa', and see below.

[7] Sen. *Dial.* 1. 5. 8, Verg. *Aen.* 2. 701, 3. 114, etc.; Heinze, op. cit. 301 f. For the attitude *non sibi sed patriae natus* (Cic. *Mur.* 83, etc.) see most usefully J. Griffin, *G & R* 26 (1979), 73–4.

Roman admiration for personal or familial *gloria* was less easily married with Stoicism; but *gloria* was far from beloved by Vergil—and much less in favour in the New Age of Augustus than formerly.[8] *Off.* 1. 62 shows us that the Stoics had views on the proper nature of bravery. But on this topic a discussion in Cic. *Tusc.* is more illuminating:

What of the contention of the Peripatetics that these selfsame disorders (*perturbationes*) which we (Stoics) think need extirpating are not only natural but also bestowed on us by nature for a useful end? . . . In the first place they praise irascibility (*iracundia*, i.e. one of the 'disorders') at great length; they name it the whetstone of bravery (*cotem fortitudinis*) and say that the assaults of angry men upon an enemy or disloyal citizen show greater vehemence (43) . . . The answer to the Peripatetics is given by the Stoics . . . 'disorder is an agitation of the soul alien from reason, contrary to nature' (47) . . . [Examples are then cited where bravery was quite clearly divorced from anger: e.g.] . . . I do not think either that the famous soldier who won the surname of Torquatus was angry when he dragged the torque off the Gaul, or that Marcellus at Clastidium was brave for the reason that he was angry (49). Of Africanus indeed, of whom we have better knowledge, because his memory is fresh in our minds, I can even take my oath that he was not in a blaze of irascibility (*non iracundia . . . inflammatum fuisse*) when on the field of battle he covered M. Allienus Pelignus with his shield and planted his sword in the breast of his enemy . . . Why then do you bring in anger here? Is it that bravery has no impulses of its own unless it begins to lose its wits (*nisi insanire coepit*)? Again, do you think that Hercules, who was raised to heaven by that selfsame bravery you would have to be irascibility, was angry when he struggled with the boar of Erymanthus . . .? . . . See to it that bravery is not the slightest bit frenzied, and that irascibility is wholly part of inconstancy; for there is no bravery that is devoid of reason (*quae rationis est expers*).

(*Tusc.* 4. 43 ff., translated by J. E. King, with some changes)

If we combine this passage with the earlier ones, we can gain an idea of how an idealizing imperialist with Stoic sympathies might view the aims and method of war. The proper *method* of war involves dispassionate, rational bravery and employs judicious, rational mercy; the *aim* of military action is seen solely as peace and security.

We may notice now that when Horace provides a rationale of, and an 'image' for, Augustus' military actions (*Odes* 3. 4) he talks of 'regulated force' (by implication Augustus') and 'irrational force' (the other side's); and clearly this notion of a rational force is allied to the Stoic ideal of a dispassionate, rational bravery. The key lines are 65-7:

[8] See D. C. Earl, op. cit. (n. 3), pp. 65-79. Cf. and contrast section iii of Brunt's paper, op. cit. (n. 1), 'The glory of imperial expansion'.

> uis consili expers mole ruit sua:
> uim temperatam di quoque prouehunt
> in maius.[9]

irrational force collapses under its own weight; regulated force is promoted by the gods, too, to something greater.

We should remember, too, that in the *Aeneid* Vergil suggests the close association, even identity, of a whole range of apparently distinct violent emotions (rage, passionate love, despair), calling them *furor*, 'madness'; and that of course is in the Stoic manner.[10] Further, he represents all *furor* as the inimical polarity to everything that makes for peace, civilized Empire, and justice; in particular *furor* is the inimical polarity to the cardinal virtue of *pietas*. Note in the first place how Vergil phrases the conclusion to Jupiter's grand prophecy of Empire in Book 1:

> aspera tum positis mitescent saecula bellis:
> cana Fides et Vesta, Remo cum fratre Quirinus
> iura dabunt; dirae ferro et compagibus artis
> claudentur Belli portae; Furor impius intus
> saeua sedens super arma et centum uinctus aenis
> post tergum nodis fremet horridus ore cruento. (1. 291 ff.)

Consider, too, the implications of the prominent simile that concludes the great symbolic storm, the first manifestation of Juno's passion, 1. 148–52, esp. 151 f.:[11]

> ... furor arma ministrat;
> tum, pietate grauem ...

---

[9] There is an interesting comparison to be made between these lines and Cic. *Off.* 1. 50.

[10] Cf., e.g., Cic. *Tusc.* 4. 11 ff.: 'This then is Zeno's definition of "passion" (*pertubatio*) ... that it is an agitation of the soul turning its back on right reason, contrary to nature ... (16) ... numerous subdivisions of the same class are brought under the head of each emotion: *ut "aegritudini" inuidentia ... aemulatio, obtrectatio, misericordia, angor, luctus, maeror* (etc.) ... *"libidini" ira, excandescentia, odium, inimicitia, discordia, indigentia, desiderium, et cetera eius modi ... (21) quae autem libidini subiecta sunt ea sic definiunt ut "ira" sit libido poeniendi eius, qui uideatur laesisse iniuria* (cf. 44 *ira ... ulciscendi libido*)...', etc. ('under "distress", envy, rivalry, carping, pity, anguish, grief, sorrow ... under "passion" anger, irritability, hatred, enmity, division, indigence, longing, and others of that kind ... (21) ... those which are placed under "passion" they define in the following way, so that "anger" is the passion for punishing someone who seems to have inflicted hurt unjustly (cf. 44 "anger ... passion for revenge") ...').

[11] The relation between simile and narrative is the reverse of what we expect. We are invited to see the storm as a great symbolic overture: *pietas*, a virtue which involves supreme *subordination* of self to god, duty, and the like and is thus Stoic as well as Roman in colour, is the quality which may prevail in all the passionate struggles which follow, struggles on the road to Rome. Cf. Otis, op. cit. (n. 20), pp. 229–30; *not* that I would subscribe to all Otis says.

This, and much other evidence,[12] suggests that the imperialism of these two poets is coloured by a Stoic idealism. They appear to be imperialists of the type posited above.

Let us concentrate for a while on the *Aeneid*. It is possible to put the case a little more precisely. I do so charily, unwillingly: the application of labels ('Stoic', or whatever) to a poem as elusive as the *Aeneid* is bound to have a distorting effect. Nevertheless: *pius* Aeneas, who follows with difficulty (sometimes in confusion, sometimes in despair) a duty imposed upon him by fate, who finds that his human passions and feelings are in conflict with that duty and must therefore subordinate them ruthlessly to it, clearly bears a resemblance to an aspiring Stoic in a world of Stoic truths.[13] He is also a hero issuing from Homer. He is a hero with a Stoic role thrust upon him—against his nature. Aeneas has much of the traditional heroic impulse to subordinate himself to nothing and no one: remember, for example, Book 2. 314 'arma amens capio; nec sat rationis in armis'—after Hector's solemn instruction. And it is not just a Stoic role that is thrust upon him. The command of fate is to establish a nation and found an empire. He is a hero with a Stoic and imperial role thrust upon him. In obedience to this role he eventually, belatedly, turns his back on love, passion, and Dido—in a very Stoic gesture suppressing that other irrational *perturbatio*, compassion, which to the Stoic is as pernicious a *perturbatio* as say, anger:[14]

> at pius Aeneas, quamquam lenire dolentem
> solando cupit et dictis auertere curas,
> multa gemens magnoque animum labefactus amore
> iussa tamen diuum exsequitur classemque reuisit. (4. 393–6)

In this light, we must have certain clear expectations of Aeneas when he enters upon the war in the second half of the poem. They are quite different from our expectations of a traditional epic hero. Not for him the superb but egotistical ideal of heroic conflict: 'always to excel', in the passionate business of battle; not for him the paramount claim of his own individual glory and honour, or the overriding need to avenge the

[12] For Horace note, e.g., *Odes* 3. 3. 1 ff. *iustum et tenacem*...

[13] Cf. C. M. Bowra, 'Aeneas and the Stoic Ideal', *G & R* 3 (1933–4), 8 ff. (repr. in this collection, Ch. 19 below); but with important parts of Bowra's paper I am in disagreement.

[14] Cic. *Tusc.* 4. 16 (quoted in n. 10), 56 'cur misereare potius quam feras opem ...? ... non enim suscipere ipsi aegritudines propter alios debemus, sed alios, si possumus, leuare aegritudine' ('Why do you pity rather than help? ... for we should not ourselves take on distress for the sake of others, but rather relieve others of distress, if we can.'); Sen. in the *De Clementia* distinguishes *clementia* and *misericordia* (see Motto's index *sub* 'pity'); note esp. *Clem.* 2. 6. 4 'misericordia uicina est miseriae ...'

dishonour of an individual with particular claims on him.[15] His role is Stoic and imperial, Stoically imperial. The end of his war must be peace, the security of all the peoples destined to be his responsibility; he is bound to politic mercy, and his bravery should be cool and rational. These are our expectations; and of course Anchises spells most of it out explicitly to Aeneas himself in his famous summation of the Roman imperial mission:

> tu regere imperio populos, Romane, memento
> (hae tibi erunt artes), pacique imponere morem,
> parcere subiectis et debellare superbos. (6. 851 ff.)

This may be compared with, for example, Cic. *Off.* 1. 35. But Anchises is even more magnanimous: he has no 'exclusion clause' like Cicero's *qui non crudeles*... And we might think that Aeneas should feel more committed to mercy and magnanimity than some generals in some imperial wars, for the Italians are destined, as he knows, to be not a conquered province but part of the unified Roman people: one nation.[16] Another point: we may feel encouraged, perhaps indeed entitled, to believe that Aeneas will uphold Stoically imperial principles in the war in the light of his belated, anguished but finally successful adherence to Stoic imperial principles in other situations in the first half of the poem. Or to put it more specifically and bluntly: it would be curious to precipitate the death of Dido because of principle and duty and then jettison that same principle and duty on an arguably less demanding occasion.

Now Aeneas does on occasion exhibit the attitude we expect of him.[17] Indeed he even surpasses our expectations. Here is his response to a sign that war with the Italians is imminent:

---

[15] Cf., e.g., αἰὲν ἀριστεύειν καὶ ὑπείροχον ἔμμεναι ἄλλων, 'always to be the best and exceed the others' (*Il.* 6. 208, 11. 783) and Hector's words to Andromache at 6. 441–6 (but note J. Griffin, *Homer on Life and Death* (Oxford, 1980), pp. 95–100, on Homer and glory); note the role of θυμός in heroic fighting (e.g. in the formula ὣς εἰπὼν ὤτρυνε μένος καὶ θυμὸν ἑκάστου, 'so saying he encouraged the might and spirit of each', *Il.* 5. 470, etc.), and of χάρμη ('joy of battle', e.g. μνήσαντο δὲ χάρμης, 'they remembered the joy of battle', 4. 222, etc.). Achilles' response to the death of Patroclus in, for example, 18. 91–3 (and following), 19. 199–214, and of course in his actions in Books 21 and 22 (and following), shows how the greatest of heroes viewed his obligations to a dead and dishonoured friend.

[16] Cicero, it might be noted, did not view the Italian wars in this way (*Off.* 1. 35, quoted above).

[17] As well as the passages cited, cf. the beginning of Book 8, which describes Aeneas' concern at the prospect of war and concludes (line 29) *tristi turbatus pectora bello*: this is a far cry from the *Iliad*.

heu quantae miseris caedes Laurentibus instant!
quas poenas mihi, Turne, dabis! quam multa sub undas
scuta uirum galeasque et fortia corpora uolues,
Thybri pater! poscant acies et foedera rumpant. (8. 537 ff.)

heu ... miseris unquestionably suggests *sympathy* with the Italians whom
great slaughter awaits—and, indeed, he might well have sympathy for
those who are to be his people. This feeling of sympathy is highlighted
by a striking echo, by the fact that line 539, *scuta uirum* . . ., virtually
repeats his own words in Book 1 (line 101). Now in Book 1 the river in
question is Simois, in Book 8 it is the Tiber. In Book 1 Aeneas recalls the
devastation at Troy, thinking of Trojan bodies rolled in the river waters;
in Book 8 he looks forward to the destruction that is going to ensue in
Italy, and thinks primarily of Italian bodies, dead at the hand of
victorious Trojans. Now it would have been understandable if Aeneas
had rejoiced in his conviction that the Trojans will reverse the situation
at Troy. Far from it. He has sympathy for the Italians: *heu quantae
miseris*. He grieves (we could say) that history will repeat itself (the
Italians are in a way his people) rather than rejoices in an imminent
reversal of fortunes. Aeneas sympathizes: but he does not allow his
sympathy to degenerate into the compassion that is a disruptive *perturbatio*, fogging reason (see above). Aeneas sees his duty clearly: *poscant
acies* . . . They will get what is coming; he will do the killing that is
necessary. Still, the hero who can thus sympathize with his foe will
surely be able to show mercy at the appropriate moment. He will not be
inflamed with a desire to slaughter the objects of his humane sympathy.

Book 11 also shows the magnanimous Aeneas, true to form. Here
are his words to an embassy of Italians requesting a truce to bury the
dead:

quaenam uos tanto fortuna indigna, Latini,
implicuit bello, qui nos fugiatis amicos?
pacem me exanimis et Martis sorte peremptis
oratis? equidem at uiuis concedere uellem.
nec ueni, nisi fata locum sedemque dedissent,
nec bellum cum gente gero; rex nostra reliquit
hospitia et Turni potius se credidit armis.
aequius huic Turnum fuerat se opponere morti.
si bellum finire manu, si pellere Teucros
apparat, his mecum decuit concurrere telis:
uixet cui uitam deus aut sua dextra dedisset.
nunc ite et miseris supponite ciuibus ignem. (11. 108–19)

Peace is his desire for the *living* Latins. His own role in Italy is imposed upon him by fate. The war, for which he professes no desire or enthusiasm, has occurred only because Latinus and Turnus abandoned the peace that had been agreed, and obstructed his fate-ordained role. He and Turnus (he suggests rationally) should fight it out in a duel—the fairest, most expeditious solution. Again, therefore, we have the Stoic-imperial hero—with that added ingredient, a measured sympathy: *miseris supponite ciuibus ignem.*

Now it cannot be said that Aeneas tells any lies here. But we could forgive the Italian embassy if they felt a little bewildered by these cool, moderate, humane words. In the previous book, as is well known, Aeneas reacted to Turnus' killing of Pallas by bursting into a frenzy of rage (*furor*), callously slaughtering victims who begged for mercy, and taking eight live prisoners with a view to sacrificing them at the funeral of Pallas. It was an orgy of rage, cruelty, and destruction recalling, significantly, the fearful actions of Achilles when he engaged in battle in Book 21 of the *Iliad*. Not until the death of Lausus do things start to change (10. 811–32). When he finds himself impelled to kill that young hero, Aeneas is appalled—to be contrasted at last with Turnus, who reacted so callously to the death of the youthful Pallas.

An immediate thought suggests itself. At times, *in practice*, Aeneas seems to have difficulty in preserving his own and Anchises' high-minded principles. It is noticeable that when he displays qualities of mercy and Stoicism in Books 8 and 11 he is not actually occupied in battle. I return to this point.

What we should now establish is the cause of Aeneas' rage in Book 10. Of course, there are probably many contributory factors. Pallas was the son of a *hospes*; he was sent to learn the art of war under Aeneas as well as to assist him as an ally (8. 514–19; but there is no more suggestion than what is contained in *sub te ... magistro* that Evander expected Aeneas to protect Pallas); the youthful Pallas in death is on any account pathetically affecting, an ἄωρος.[18] But the heart of the matter seems to be the fact that Turnus despoils him, strips him of his baldrick: here seems to be the centre of Turnus' offence. It is accompanied by one of Vergil's most striking interventions in the narrative:

[18] This aspect of Pallas' pathos, that he died 'before his time', is underlined by the myth engraved on his baldrick: so G. B. Conte demonstrates, *I generi e i suoi confini* (Turin, 1980), pp. 96 ff.; his argument is summarized by myself in *JRS* 71 (1981), 222. On Aeneas' motives in Book 10 see too Beare, op. cit. (n. 30), pp. 18 ff., Quinn, op. cit. (n. 20), p. 226.

... et laeuo pressit pede talia fatus
exanimem rapiens immania pondera baltei
impressumque nefas: una sub nocte iugali
caesa manus iuuenum foede thalamique cruenti,
quae Clonus Eurytides multo caelauerat auro;
quo nunc Turnus ouat spolio gaudetque potitus.
nescia mens hominum fati sortisque futurae
et seruare modum rebus sublata secundis!
Turno tempus erit magno cum optauerit emptum
intactum Pallanta, et cum spolia ista diemque
oderit. (10. 495–505)

Pallas is then carted off—and Aeneas' rampage is precipitated. *Pallas, Euander, in ipsis omnia sunt oculis ...* (515 ff.).

All, however, is not simple. It was Roman no less than Homeric custom to despoil a defeated enemy. The action brought nothing but *laus* to the perpetrator, who might hang such *spolia* proudly in his *atrium*. If indeed a Roman general killed and despoiled an opposing commander, the spoils then became the *spolia opima* consecrated in the temple of Jupiter Feretrius: an honour so signal that in the time of Augustus it had to be jealously guarded. Consider too Pallas: it was his stated intention to despoil Turnus in the event of his victory in their duel (10. 449 f.)—a fact that is sometimes curiously overlooked. All indeed is not simple: but the basic issue can be identified. Spoils were the tangible proof and token of triumph, in Rome as in the *Iliad*. As such they enhanced the fame and honour of the despoiler: κλέος, κῦδος, γέρας, *fama, laus, honor*—the same ethic essentially persists. But by the same token, of course, to *be* despoiled was to *be* dishonoured; and friends or family of the dishonoured might think that that necessitated action.[19]

---

[19] On *spolia* see the useful article in *RE*, 2nd series, Sechster Halbband (1929), 1843 ff. I cite a few useful references. For Romans despoiling defeated enemies after individual combat see, e.g., Livy 5. 36. 7, Gell. 2. 11. 3. For the display of *spolia* in houses see Livy 23. 23. 6 (where those 'qui spolia ex hoste fixa domi haberent' are among specially selected categories designated to fill vacant places in the Senate; the principle of selection was 'ita ... ut ordo ordini, non homo homini praelatus uideretur'), 38. 43. 10, Cic. *Phil.* 2. 68. For Roman soldiers trying to prevent the despoliation (dishonour) of their dead consul: Livy 22. 6. 4. Homer of course often describes such attempts to prevent despoliation. The dying Sarpedon's words are worth noting, eloquently appealing to Glaucus not to let the Greeks despoil him (*Il.* 16. 492–501): he clearly thinks Glaucus has a *duty* to him in this respect (σοὶ γὰρ ἐγὼ καὶ ἔπειτα κατηφείη καὶ ὄνειδος / ἔσσομαι ... εἴ κέ μ' 'Αχαιοὶ / τεύχεα συλήσωσι ..., 'for in time to come I will be a shame and reproach to you ... if the Achaeans strip off my weapons'). On the *spolia opima* (and Augustus) see *Cambridge Ancient History* x. 125. Note too Verg. *Aen.* 1. 289 'hunc (Caesar) tu olim caelo spoliis Orientis onustum / accipies secura'. (*spolium* in the *Aeneid* repays study: there are 22 examples; Heinze, op. cit. (n. 6) offers some brief and largely sensible remarks.)

Thus Aeneas. We could say therefore that his motives and conduct in Book 10 are more than defensible. In rage at the death and, most important, the *dishonouring* of Pallas, his noble youthful ally and pupil, Aeneas seeks some sort of revenge, albeit indiscriminate. High motives, large justification for a noble rage. But it is not the highest motive, nor perhaps a sufficient justification. And can rage be noble? Certainly none of it is what we have been led to expect. On three cardinal counts, involving both 'aims' and 'methods', Aeneas fails to uphold the principles of 'Stoic imperialism': he fights in a frenzy (the word *furor* and cognates is attached to him), not with dispassionate bravery; he fails to extend mercy to those who are patently defeated (*subiectus*). And, most important, for a time at least he loses sight of the final purpose of his war. To avenge the dishonour of Pallas is a high aim, but 'peace' is a higher aim, *his* aim, and the former is arguably incompatible with the latter. These issues will concern us in more detail when we discuss Book 12.

Let us here spare a thought for Turnus. He kills Pallas; he is callous in victory, and exultant. But what is his basic *offence* (as I termed it above)? At heart, I suggested, it was the action of despoiling Pallas. Leave aside for the moment the detail that he subsequently chose to *wear* the despoiled baldrick (more on this anon), and leave aside his exultancy: Turnus' 'offence' turns out to be not so very large at all; many commentators mislead us here.[20] Turnus' conduct, like Aeneas', is defensible. His basic actions accords with Roman no less than Homeric codes of honour. But what brings praise to one brings dishonour to another; in the eyes of his friends or family an offence to be avenged, to be furious about. That is how Aeneas sees the despoiling of Pallas. That is why Aeneas acts as he does in Book 10. We understand. But we also understand Turnus. And what we also understand, from another point of view, is that there is something disturbingly inconclusive about this 'morality'. If Pallas had beaten Turnus and, as he promised, despoiled him, Turnus' nearest and dearest might have gone on a rampage of vengeance with nearly as much justification as Aeneas. The 'morality' may be judged yet more harshly: a system of honour like this is relentless and sterile. It may lead to a never-ending cycle of honour and dishonour, vengeance and vengeance in return.

One begins in fact to see why in a heroic world, more particularly in the real Roman world, which maintained heroic ideas of honour, a

---

[20] See, e.g., G. Knauer, *Die Aeneis und Homer* (Göttingen, 1964), pp. 301 ff.; B. Otis, *Virgil* (Oxford, 1963), p. 356; K. Quinn, *Virgil's Aeneid* (London, 1968), pp. 223, 326. Misunderstanding the role of spoils leads to these misinterpretations.

policy of *clementia* might have a specific *practical* function. Towards prospective provincials or client states, the function of *clementia* is easy to discern.[21] But when equals in status were one's enemies (as in civil war) the function is perhaps subtler but no less practical. If lasting peace is to be made one side must (it could be argued) eventually draw a line, swallow an 'offence'. To parade one's *clementia* might have its offensive aspects (above, p. 317), but it was not as offensive as enforcing subjection, nor did it leave dead and dishonoured relations for relations to avenge. *Clementia* could break the cycle of honour and dishonour; it might be the only route to reconciliation and peace. This topic will engage us again.

Before I proceed, I must attend to Vergil's intervention in the narrative accompanying the despoliation (quoted above). Does not Vergil here explicitly condemn Turnus' action? I think not.[22] He remarks that 'a time will come when Turnus would give anything not to have touched Pallas and will hate the spoils'. Of course Turnus will: his actions here eventually bring about his death. Vergil predicts likely facts; he does not pass explicit moral judgment. More significant is *nescia mens … seruare modum …* 'how ignorant are men's hearts to keep within bounds when uplifted by success'. *seruare modum* does have moral overtones. But what does it apply to? It is uttered in response to the previous sentence, presumably therefore to the main action of the previous sentence; and the main action of the previous sentence should be contained in its main verbs, *ouat gaudetque*. So Vergil passes adverse judgment not on Turnus' triumph and the prosecution of his triumph (taking the spoils), but on his *exultation in* that triumph—his exultation 'when uplifted by success'. He passes judgment not on an act but an attitude, adverting in the spirit of Greek tragic poets to Turnus' attitude of foolish, immoderate, premature elation. Much therefore may be criticized in Turnus—callousness, confidence, arrogance even—but we must be quite clear that he commits no absolute offence against morality, divine or human; nor does Vergil say he does.

Of course Vergil's intervention permits the *inference* (so long as we are quite clear about what Vergil actually *says*) that he is *uneasy* about the ethic of spoils—unlike his contemporaries. We may choose to remem-

---

[21] See Brunt, op. cit. (n. 1), p. 184.

[22] Cf. Quinn, op. cit. (n. 20), p. 326 (more non-committal than I am); and there are some very perceptive points—and interesting information—in A. Barchiesi, *Materiali e discussioni per l'analisi dei testi classici* 4 (1980), 45–55; Barchiesi discusses *Aen.* 10. 501–5, but not specifically to make the point I am stressing. Other scholars (e.g. Otis, Williams, Klingner) are curiously silent on this question. Heinze, op. cit. (n. 6), p. 209, gets it wrong.

ber in this connection the fact that was instrumental in the tragic end of Euryalus (9. 373-4, 384)—a suggestive detail. But Vergil has another very obvious reason, besides a desire to express distaste at spoils, for intervening at this moment: simply to mark out the action that will eventually precipitate Turnus' death. Tragic foreshadowing is thereby achieved; and the accompanying tragic irony is enhanced by Turnus' joyful exultation in the action.

Finally, a very significant comparison can be made between Vergil's criticism of Turnus and a passage that must have been in his mind: Zeus' criticism of Hector in *Iliad* 17. Zeus sees Hector arrayed in Achilles' armour and is moved to utter thus:

τοῦ δὴ ἑταῖρον ἔπεφνες ἐνηέα τε κρατερόν τε,
τεύχεα δ' οὐ κατὰ κόσμον ἀπὸ κρατός τε καὶ ὤμων
εἵλευ·

you have slain his good and mighty companion, and have stripped the armour unfittingly from his head and shoulders. (*Il.* 17. 204-6)

This does seem an explicit criticism of an act of despoiling. It is in fact unique in the *Iliad*, out of key with the *Iliad*'s normal ethic—and requires special explanation.[23] But whatever its own explanation it might well have encouraged Vergil to a similar explicit statement, given that his inclinations ran that way. The fact that it does not is indeed remarkable. Vergil's cautious comment is revealed as a deliberate back-pedalling. He is most anxious that Turnus should *not* appear indicted for an absolute or indeed a concrete offence.

We proceed to Book 12. At the beginning of the book, the various obstacles in the way of a duel between Aeneas and Turnus (desired by Aeneas in Book 11) seem to have been cleared away. A truce is

[23] The *scholia* provide their own implausible explanations. Eustathius, ad loc. (backed by S. E. Bassett, 'Hector's Fault in Honor', *TAPhA* 54 (1923), 117-23) ingeniously tries to settle the inconsistency with *Il.* 16. 791 ff. (where Apollo is responsible for Patroclus' loss of his armour) at the same time as interpret Zeus' comment: τὸ δὲ, οὐ κατὰ κόσμον—εἵλευ, ἀντὶ τοῦ οὐκ ἐσκύλευσας ὡς ἔχρην, ἀλλὰ τοῦ Φοίβου τὸν Πάτροκλον ἀφοπλίσαντος, σὺ δῶρον εἵλου αὐτὰ ἢ καὶ ὡς εὕρημα ..., 'and he says "you have stripped unfittingly" instead of "you did not despoil as was right, but when Apollo had disarmed Patroclus, and you took the spoils as a gift or as a mere find"' (and the point is amplified). But clearly one cannot disjoin οὐ from κατὰ κόσμον in the way Eustathius implies; the two books simply are inconsistent. I take it that Zeus' point lies in the excellence *of Achilles*, and in the fact that it was *Achilles*' armour that Hector gained (note σὺ δ' ἄμβροτα τεύχεα δύνεις / ἀνδρὸς ἀριστῆος, 'and you are putting on the armour of a champion warrior'). It would be one thing to strip the defeated Patroclus of Patroclus' arms; it was another to strip him *of the divine arms of Achilles*. This Zeus finds 'inappropriate', 'not quite in order', vel. sim., οὐ κατὰ κόσμον.

established, sanctified by solemn, religious rituals. The two leaders will fight, and the armies abide by the result. A climax along the lines of *Iliad* 22 seems imminent. Actually, the main source at the beginning of the book (where the truce is established and the duel seems set) is the duel between Paris and Menelaus in *Iliad* 3 and 4—a contamination which we shall mention again later.

What are the mood and motives of Aeneas, now and later in Book 12? These are what I want to follow, in the light of our comments above on 'aims' and 'methods'. As he prepares himself at the beginning of the book, on the eve of the contest, Aeneas seems disinclined to eschew anger; it is as if he sees a Peripatetic role for it:

> nec minus interea maternis saeuus in armis
> Aeneas acuit Martem et se suscitat ira ... (12. 107–8)

But this is not the passion that merits the term *furor*—in contradistinction to Turnus who, in spite of much sympathetic treatment hereabouts, is described as being in the grip of monstrous, Homeric frenzy:[24]

> his agitur furiis, totoque ardentis ab ore
> scintillae absistunt, oculis micat acribus ignis ... (12. 101–2)

And Aeneas' mind is on peace:

> oblato gaudens componi foedere bellum. (12. 109)

This is confirmed in his prefatory speech on the actual day of the duel, 176 ff. He solemnly binds the Trojans to accept the consequences if he is defeated; and in the event of his victory, *sin nostrum adnuerit nobis uictoria Martem*:

> non ego nec Teucris Italos parere iubebo
> nec mihi regna peto: paribus se legibus ambae
> inuictae gentes aeterna in foedera mittant. (12. 189–91)

That is to say: he intends his victory to be the route to peace, and a peace in which the 'vanquished' will have equal rights with the 'victors'. In other words, Aeneas sees the *aim* of his fighting as peace, and intends to secure it through a policy of magnanimous *clementia*. The Stoic imperialist presents himself—impeccably, but for that small indulgence in *ira*. We remember, however, that he was nearly as impeccable on two previous occasions when he was similarly disengaged from battle.

---

[24] Cf., e.g., Hom. *Il.* 19. 365 f. τὼ δέ οἱ ὄσσε / λαμπέσθην ὡς εἴ τε πυρὸς σέλας. I choose the word 'monstrous' advisedly: Turnus reminds us of Cacus.

Various factors including the prompting of Juturna, the Italians' own inclinations, an untimely portent, and the Pandarus-like action of the augur Tolumnius (*Iliad* 4 still underlies this section of text), lead eventually to the breaking of the truce by the Italians. Note that the disguised Juturna's inflammatory speech misrepresents, it seems, Aeneas' intentions:

> non pudet, o Rutuli, pro cunctis talibus unam
> obiectare animam? ...
> ille quidem ad superos, quorum se deuouet aris,
> succedet fama uiuusque per ora feretur;
> nos patria amissa dominis parere superbis
> cogemur, qui nunc lenti consedimus aruis. (12. 229–30, 234–7)

Contrast Aeneas' words at 189 ff. (above).

The truce is broken amidst and as a result of an explosion of emotion, Juturna's words 'inflame' the Italians (238). Tolumnius' action 'inflames' the wounded Arcadian's brothers with 'grief' (277), as a result of which they reach for their weapons—and rush headlong 'blindly' (277–9). Battle is joined: a 'love' of war possesses all. Messapus is described as 'greedy' (*auidus*) for the confounding of the truce. Vergil's Stoic sense that all passionate emotions are allied and all destructive and pernicious is evident here in his choice of vocabulary and imagery.[25] How does Aeneas respond to all this? Impeccably. He identifies the cause (or a cause)—passion—and seeks to stem it:

> quo ruitis? quaeue ista repens discordia surgit?
> o cohibete iras! ... (12. 313 ff.)

But then ill luck takes a hand. Even as he speaks, an anonymous arrow wounds him, and he has to retire. Whether his attempt to stem the tide might have succeeded if he had been able to remain, we cannot finally say. Certainly it is over and failed now. Aeneas retires, leaving Turnus to indulge his passion (324 ff.) in a savage *aristeia*.

And now Aeneas' attitude starts to change. The galling frustration of his position—incapacitated while the unwanted, impious battle grows ever fiercely apace (405 ff.)—has its natural effect. We know that Aeneas is susceptible to emotion (see indeed 108), and his emotions now start to be aroused. In his fury he starts to sound distinctly like those very warriors whose passions he has just previously tried to stem: *saeuit* (387), *stabat acerba fremens* (398); and, after he is miraculously healed,

[25] See n. 10 above.

auidus pugnae . . . oditque moras. When he returns to the fray it is with motifs and violence that are designed to recall that superb grim hero of the old heroic order, Ajax.[26] Finally, after Juturna maddeningly keeps Turnus out of his reach and Messapus holds him up and clips his crest, we are given these remarkable lines:

> tum uero adsurgunt irae, insidiisque subactus,
> diuersos ubi sensit equos currumque referri,
> multa Iouem et laesi testatus foederis aras
> iam tandem inuadit medios et Marte secundo
> terribilis saeuam nullo discrimine caedem
> suscitat, irarumque omnis effundit habenas. (12. 494–9)

And frightful slaughter ensues, conducted by both Aeneas and Turnus. *o cohibete iras*: clearly the ideals of Stoic imperialism have been heavily compromised. Aeneas deals out indiscriminate slaughter: this ill coheres with magnanimity and is scarcely the rational *fortitudo* of the sage; *irarumque omnis effundit habenas* is quantitatively if not qualitatively a vast distance even from *se suscitat ira* (108). But two points must be made absolutely clear. First, Vergil has traced with extreme realism how Aeneas has under utmost provocation come to this very comprehensible state of mind. Secondly, and perhaps more importantly, though Aeneas has now lost from view the Stoic ideal of *methods*, he has not fundamentally—perhaps truer to say, not permanently—lost all sight of the ideal *aim*. However deplorably Aeneas is prepared now to counter enraged violence with enraged violence, his high-minded view of the final purpose of all this force is not yet lastingly or wholly abandoned. In this respect the situation is still different from the episodes referred in Book 10 (before the death of Lausus). But the point needs clarifying.

The furious Ajax-like Aeneas returns to war. He has one clearly defined object: 'solum densa in caligine Turnum / uestigat lustrans, solum in certamina poscit' (466–7). Why? It must be:[27] to finish the work that was so rudely interrupted, to remove in a duel with Turnus the obstacle to peace. Vergil, who has so carefully catalogued the 'decline' (if so we must call it) in Aeneas' attitude to the *methods* of warfare, has not yet given us any hint that his *aim*, spelt out so specifically in 176 ff., has fundamentally or lastingly changed. In the present lines (494 ff.) Aeneas recalls the treaty in which he committed himself to a policy of

---

[26] With *Aen.* 12. 435 f. cf. Soph. *Ajax* 550–1 (imitated by Accius (fr. 156) in the form *uirtuti sis par, dispar fortunis patris*). I shall cite more evidence for my assertion at another time.

[27] Cf. William's commentary on 12. 497.

peace as the end of fighting, and justifies his present lack of discrimination by the fact that the Italians have broken that treaty and thus
thwarted the policy. And we have seen that it took time for him to
succumb in this way. It happened only after the final goading provocation of Messapus and because Turnus, whom he still viewed as the key
to peace, was kept out of his way.

And the text reassures us that Aeneas' high-minded aim, peace as the
end of war, is not permanently or wholly abandoned. It is sadly modified
but just about intact. In 554 ff. Aeneas has returned to the single pursuit
of Turnus ('ille ut uestigans diuersa per agmina Turnum / huc atque
huc acies circumtulit...'), when Venus prompts him to attack the Latin
city. He responds to the idea, and speaks thus to his men:

> ne qua meis esto dictis mora, Iuppiter hac stat,
> neu quis ob inceptum subitum mihi segnior ito.
> urbem hodie, causam belli, regna ipsa Latini,
> ni frenum accipere et uicti parere fatentur,
> eruam et aequa solo fumantia culmina ponam.
> scilicet exspectem libeat dum proelia Turno
> nostra pati rursusque uelit concurrere uictus?
> hoc caput, o ciues, haec belli summa nefandi.
> ferte faces propere foedusque reposcite flammis. (12. 565–73)

Fire breeds fire, indiscriminate methods are to be answered by indiscriminate methods. But Aeneas still sees the *aim* of war as peace—of a
sort.[28] That imperial ideal is still there. *foedus reposcite flammis*: the aim of
attacking the city, he says, is to re-establish the treaty, and the treaty is
the route to peace. We must of course lament the methods to which
Aeneas is now prepared to have recourse: *flammis*, more particularly
eruam et aequa solo fumantia culmina ponam, said of a city which contains
innocents; and Aeneas' heated portrayal of the 'city' as *causam belli* is of
course hardly just. We must lament, too, the way in which he now sees
and phrases his necessary victory: *ni frenum accipere et uicti parere fatentur*.
Contrast that with his promise of peace in 189; ironically, he seems to
vindicate Juturna (above p. 330). But in a bloody, ugly way, Aeneas' aim
is intact: *pacique imponere morem; ut sine iniuria in pace uiuatur; foedusque
reposcite flammis*. And much has changed since line 189 and the truce, by
no means all of it to be laid to Aeneas' charge. On this point he himself is
insistent. As in 496, so now:

---

[28] J. P. Poe, 'Success and Failure in the Mission of Aeneas', *TAPhA* 96 (1965), 334,
gets this wrong.

ipse inter primos dextram sub moenia tendit
Aeneas, magnaque incusat uoce Latinum
testaturque deos iterum se ad proelia cogi,
bis iam Italos hostis, haec altera foedera rumpi. (12. 579–82)

Aeneas sees the attack on the Latin city as an alternative to the duel with Turnus he cannot have (*scilicet expectem*..., 570 above). In fact it functions as a tactic to bring Turnus finally into single combat (620 ff., 643 ff., 669 ff.); As soon as that happens Aeneas—significantly, of course—abandons the attack (697 ff.). He has what he wants: the key to peace. The duel is finally to take place. A *de facto* truce is observed. The climax along the lines of *Iliad* 22 is finally to take place.

At this point it is vital for us to have one thing clear. Aeneas and Turnus are indeed embarking on a duel closely recalling and of course based on the climactic duel between Achilles and Hector. But Aeneas does not enter the duel with a motivation and purpose like that of Achilles (desire for vengeance owed to a friend); his *aim* is quite different.[29] Here is the reason (or a reason) why Vergil combined as sources the *Iliad* 3 and 4 duel (Menelaus and Paris) with the *Iliad* 22 duel: it allows him to provide Aeneas with this different initial aim. For Aeneas enters the final duel inspired by rage at the breaking of a treaty, to conclude the original business of that treaty, to establish *pax*: if not the rosy *pax* of 189, *pax* none the less. Turnus perceives the first point (694–5 'me uerius unum / pro uobis foedus luere et decernere ferro'), and Aeneas has recently reaffirmed the second. He attacked the city to force a peace; he attacked the city because he could not corner Turnus. Now he has Turnus.

This question of Aeneas' overriding aim is crucial to bear in mind in the final scene of the poem.[30] When Aeneas wounds Turnus (not mortally), Turnus begs for mercy:

ille humilis supplex oculos dextramque precantem
protendens 'equidem merui nec deprecor' inquit;

---

[29] Quinn, op. cit. (n. 20), p. 273, misunderstands this.

[30] This scene has of course been much discussed. Some scholars are anxious to justify Aeneas' conduct in victory (e.g. Bowra (n. 13), Otis (n. 20), pp. 379–82, Heinze (n. 6), pp. 210–11, G. Binder, *Aeneas und Augustus* (Meisenheim, 1971), p. 146); others are more critical (e.g. Quinn, op. cit. (n. 20), pp. 272 ff., M. C. J. Putnam, *The Poetry of the Aeneid* (Cambridge, Mass., 1965), pp. 193 ff. ('It is Aeneas who loses at the end of Book XII . . .')). More cautious is V. Pöschl, *Die Dichtkunst Virgils*³ (Berlin/New York, 1977), pp. 81–4; cf. too R. Beare, 'Invidious Success: Some Thoughts on the End of the *Aeneid*', *PVS* 4 (1964), 18–30; these two, together with Quinn's discussion, are among the most helpful. None gets to the heart of the matter.

> 'utere sorte tua. miseri te si qua parentis
> tangere cura potest, oro (fuit et tibi talis
> Anchises genitor) Dauni miserere senectae
> et me, seu corpus spoliatum lumine mauis,
> redde meis. uicisti et uictum tendere palmas
> Ausonii uidere; tua est Lauinia coniunx,
> ulterius ne tende odiis.' (12. 930–8)

Turnus supplicates, he is defeated, he is humiliated. His time as a proud
leader of men is finished; he knows it and he knows that everyone else
knows it. There is no question about any of this; it is all quite explicit in
the text. Note particularly *humilis*, *supplex*, and his words *uicisti et uictum
tendere palmas / Ausonii uidere*. Next:

> stetit acer in armis
> Aeneas uoluens oculos dextramque repressit;
> et iam iamque magis cunctantem flectere sermo
> coeperat, ... (12. 938–41)

Turnus begins to persuade Aeneas. Why? Because Aeneas sees that
it is appropriate, perhaps more than appropriate, that he should be
persuaded. The purpose for which he entered the duel with Turnus
is achieved, and nothing—nothing to do with that purpose—can be
lost and perhaps much can be won by sparing Turnus. His aim has
been 'peace'; to establish peace it is necessary to war down the
proud (*pacique imponere morem, debellare superbos*). The proud Turnus
has been warred down and is emphatically no longer proud, unequivo-
cally *subiectus*. He is a foe who should qualify for *clementia, parcere
subiectis*. Perhaps we should put it more strongly. In wars which
involve the honour of equals (like civil wars, or quasi-civil wars)
clementia was not just woolly humanity. Unless (as I said above) a victor
is prepared to extend tactical forgiveness, a sequence of honour,
dishonour, vengeance, and vengeance in return, may never end. Far
from gratuitous largesse, *parcere subiectis* may have as vital a practical
role in the business of establishing peace as *debellare superbos*. Aeneas
has heard the words of Anchises and can see the course demanded
by policy and humanity. And yet he is not in the final count persuaded.
Why?

Because a *new* motive and aim succeeds the former aim, the aim of
pacique imponere morem. He catches sight of the belt of Pallas which
Turnus is wearing, the *spolia*, the token of Pallas' defeat and dishonour;
and Turnus' chance to persuade him is over:

... coeperat, infelix umero cum apparuit alto
balteus et notis fulserunt cingula bullis
Pallantis pueri, uictum quem uulnere Turnus
strauerat atque umeris inimicum insigne gerebat.
ille, oculis postquam saeui monimenta doloris
exuuiasque hausit, furiis accensus et ira
terribilis: 'tune hinc spoliis indute meorum
eripiare mihi? Pallas te hoc uulnere, Pallas
immolat et poenam scelerato ex sanguine sumit.'
hoc dicens ... (12. 941 ff.)

Now, a whole nexus of feelings may be seen working on Aeneas, helping
to change his mind.[31] But one factor is basic and essential: the question
of honour. An honourable impulse to avenge the dishonour of Pallas
succeeds, and overrides, the claims of *pacique imponere morem*. Now, and
only now, Aeneas' motives as well as his actions resemble those of
Achilles in *Iliad* 22.

Before any hasty judgment is passed on Aeneas, some points need
stressing. First, since Aeneas' motive in killing Turnus is basically to
avenge Pallas' dishonour, that motive is not immoderately called
honourable (to talk of 'primitive vendetta' is misleading). It should also
be recalled that Aeneas' own impulse for revenge has the backing of
Evander's compelling and touching plea in Book 11:

quod uitam moror inuisam Pallante perempto
dextera causa tua est, Turnum gnatoque patrique
quam debere uides. meritis uacat hic tibi solus
fortunaeque locus. (11. 177–80)

Evander at any rate feels that Aeneas has a *duty* to him to kill Turnus: cf.
the feelings of Sarpedon (see note 19). And (against Turnus) it is also
right to remind ourselves that while despoiling a defeated enemy was
part of heroic and Roman ethics, the *wearing* of such spoils infringed
what seems to have been some kind of rather hazy taboo.[32] So Aeneas
has honour and an ἄγραπτον νόμιμον ('unwritten ordinance') and piety
on his side. But his new motive replaces a grander one and (I would say)
is in conflict with it (honour and piety conflict with a greater Piety—to
destiny and Rome, as often in the *Aeneid*). An impulsive act of revenge,
however ethically defensible, is not the best way to lay the foundations of
reconciliation and peace. To avenge dishonour is to inflict dishonour;

[31] Good discussion in Quinn and Beare, opp. cit. (nn. 20, 30).
[32] See S. Reinach, *Cultes, Mythes et Religions* (Paris, 1908), iii. 223 ff.; contrast what
happens at *Aen.* 8. 562, 11. 5–11, 83–4, 193–6, and see n. 19 above.

vengeance may provoke vengeance in return (cf. above p. 334). From certain points of view indeed Aeneas' action might be thought rather a mad action. Certainly Aeneas does it in a mad frenzy, *furiis accensus et ira terribilis*, emotions that the ideology of the *Aeneid* condemns. We have by the end of the poem become used to the fact that Aeneas cannot uphold the ideal *methods* of a Stoic imperial warrior. We have seen Aeneas in the grip of *ira*, even of *furor*, many times, and perhaps it is no great surprise to see him thus now. But to see him lose sight of the *aims* enjoined upon the Stoically imperial warrior at the conclusion of the poem, at this moment of climactic political and historical importance—that surely is more surprising. It is obviously more striking and more significant than his temporary inclement abandonment of those aims in Book 10. Aeneas' aim at the end of the poem is human, even in its own way humane (remember Evander), honourable, heroic. But not only is it not the grand aim, it is (I assert once more) arguably in conflict with that aim. If Aeneas achieves his reconciliation and peace, it will *not* surely be due to this last act: rather, in spite of it.[33] And we do not of course hear anything about peace. Unlike the *Iliad*, the *Aeneid* does not proceed after its 'Book 22' into eventual hard-worn harmony. Book 12 ends in an echoing silence.

---

[33] Cf. the very sensible comments of Beare (n. 30), p. 26. Beare, p. 23, also reminds us of Priam's mercy towards Sinon and Anchises' towards Achaemenides, suggesting that mercy is, or should be, a particularly Trojan characteristic. But (it must be said) anyone who recalled Sinon might have felt justified in regarding mercy in a cynical light . . . At this point, I must concede that not all Romans would regard the argument in favour of a practical function to *clementia* as cut and dried. Cic. *ad M. Brutum* 6 (Shackleton Bailey). 2 = 1. 2a 2 (my attention was drawn to this letter by D. P. Fowler) is fascinating: 'scribis enim acrius prohibenda bella ciuilia esse quam in superatos iracundiam exercendam. uehementer a te, Brute, dissentio; nec clementiae tuae concedo, sed salutaris seueritas uincit inanem speciem clementiae. quod si clementes esse uolumus, numquam deerunt bella ciuilia.' ('You write that we should rather be more forceful in preventing civil war than indulge anger against the defeated. I very much disagree with you, Brutus; nor do I give in to your idea of mercy—a salutary severity surpasses an empty show of mercy. If we want to be merciful, there will always be civil wars.') Against this we should recall other Roman and Stoic views: not only the same Cicero's and others cited above, but also Sen. *De ira* 2. 32. 1 ff. 'non enim ut in beneficiis honestum est merita meritis repensare, ita iniuria iniuriis . . .' ('It is not honourable to requite injury with injury, as it is in benefits to requite service with service . . .'), and *Clem.* 1. 21. 1–2 'si quos pares aliquando habuit, infra se uidet, satis uindicatus est . . . perdidit enim uitam qui debet, et quisquis ex alto ad inimici pedes abiectus alienam de capite regnoque sententiam exspectauit, in seruatoris sui gloriam uiuit plusque nomini eius confert incolumis, quam si ex oculis ablatus est'. ('If he sees his sometime rivals below him, he has achieved enough vengeance . . . for he who should have has lost his life, and whoever, cast down from on high to the feet of his enemy, has awaited the judgement of another on his life and his rule, lives on to the glory of his preserver and brings more glory to his name if saved than if removed from men's eyes.')

A thought is worth taking up (see above p. 322–3). On one occasion Aeneas belatedly did not allow a human, humane, honourable impulse to override the great Pietas: in Carthage. The conclusion of the poem imparts further disturbing complexions to that episode.

Now in spite of all I have said I think it is misleading to talk baldly of 'Aeneas' failure' in the poem. Certainly I do not think that Aeneas *progresses* fundamentally as man or hero:[34] I do not think that the passion-prone Aeneas in Books 1–6 becomes a determined and controlled Aeneas in Books 7–12. On the contrary, we see Aeneas displaying the same vulnerability to passionate emotion in the second half as in the first. The theatre of course is different, and the emotions are superficially different. But (as I have said) in the view of the Stoics and, it seems, of Vergil—and indeed of many people—apparently distinct passionate emotions are closely interrelated, even perhaps identifiable. To the Stoic, passion, despair, fear, anger, and hatred are closely allied—and all pernicious; for Vergil they may all be lumped under the condemnatory title of *furor*. Aeneas succumbs at the end as in the beginning. But I should be hesitant about calling it failure.

If Aeneas, the son of a goddess, the hero of the epic, cannot 'succeed', then perhaps no one can. With great realism Vergil shows how an Aeneas who is genuinely in sympathy with Stoic imperial ideas of the appropriate *methods* of warfare cannot, under the relentless pressure of human reality, always uphold them. He shows Aeneas trying to keep in view the high-minded *aims* enjoined by a Stoic imperialism and finding again that sometimes it is simply not humanly feasible. Perhaps that is simply the truth of the matter.

And of course Vergil's Aeneas has great success, as an imperial hero: he reaches Italy, he establishes his people. But he is an honestly depicted imperial hero. Politicians and philosophers may present comforting, self-satisfying descriptions of, or prescriptions for, warfare. Leaders may laud themselves for having adhered to the high principles of such prescriptions. Such a one was Augustus—who also lauded himself for building a temple to Mars the Avenger (*Res Gestae* 21). Poet laureates may then echo the claims of their masters—like Horace, who hymned the *uis temperata* of the *princeps*, his *clementia* and the peace and security that was due to his victories. Horace also hymned Augustus as the avenger of Caesar (*Odes* 1. 2. 41 ff.), and was perhaps less sensitive than

---

[34] But this of course is the common view: see, e.g., Bowra, op. cit. (n. 13), Heinze, op. cit. (n. 6), pp. 275 ff., Otis, op. cit. (n. 20) index *sub* 'Aeneas—development of'.

Augustus to the fact that there might be a clash between the virtue of
vengeance and the virtue of clemency.[35] Vergil was different.

Let us speak bluntly. The notion that force employed on *our* side is
rational and dispassionate, on the *other* side frenzied and irrational is of
course close to nonsense. War is war and violence is violence, and to
distinguish between *our* methods of fighting and *their* methods of
fighting is pleasant and comforting but likely to be cant. What of aims?
Of course one side's aims may be different from another's—but even
here imperial spokesmen often fool themselves or others. Many of
Rome's aggressive wars were designed to procure security for herself,
but they *were* aggressive and 'peace' was hardly their only motivation or
always their motivation—as indeed many Romans were happy enough
to admit.[36]

There is therefore a certain amount of glibness in Horace's lyricizing
of Augustan imperialism. Earlier I associated the two imperial poets,
Horace and Vergil. Now they must be distinguished. For Vergil takes
issue on the politics of war.

Vergil has constructed a hero with whom any founder or refounder of
Rome must be and would no doubt like to be compared. Vergil's hero
understands and espouses the high imperial ideals sung by Horace. But
he finds that in practice *uis temperata* is a chimaera (*uis* is indivisible),
inclementia is often irresistible, and High Motives clash with high
motives; nor is it always possible to keep one's eye on the Highest.
Vergil's hero demonstrates the truth (we might say) of imperial ideals,
what actually happens to them in practice. The hero succeeds in laying
the foundations of a new nation and a great empire; we must not obscure
the measure of his success. But Vergil does not obscure the reality. The
wars that gain empire involve ugly violence, and less than perfect
motivations will sometimes direct even the greatest hero.

[35] Note the careful wording of *Res Gestae* 2–3.
[36] See Brunt, op. cit. (n. 1), pp. 176 ff. (esp. perhaps p. 176).

18

The Reconciliations of Juno

D. C. FEENEY

I

The reconciliation between Juno and Jupiter at the end of the *Aeneid*
(12. 791–842) forms the cap to the divine action of the poem. The scene
is conventionally regarded as the resolution of the heavenly discord that
has prevailed since the first book; in particular, it is normal to see here a
definitive transformation of Juno, as she abandons her enmity once and
for all, committing herself wholeheartedly to the Roman cause. So G.
Lieberg, for example: 'The two hemispheres of Jupiter and Juno meet at
the end of the poem in the totality of the divine universe, guarantee of
the glorious future of Rome';[1] or W. Kühn: 'The divine conversation
ends in a full and brilliant final accord.'[2]

The comments of Servius give rise to second thoughts. As Juno
accedes to Jupiter's requests (841), 'mentem laetata retorsit'), he
observes: 'iste quidem hoc dicit; sed constat bello Punico secundo
exoratam Iunonem, tertio uero bello a Scipione sacris quibusdam etiam
Romam esse translatam', 'he says this; but it is agreed that it was in the
Second Punic War that Juno was won over, and in the Third she was
brought across to Rome with certain sacred objects by Scipio'. The
reconciliation during the Hannibalic war is part of the Ennian tradition,
as Servius informs us on *Aen.* 1. 281, 'consilia in melius referet': 'quia

---

I refer to the following books by author's name only: V. Buchheit, *Vergil über die Sendung
Roms* (Gymnasium Beiheft 3, Heidelberg, 1963); R. Häussler, *Studien zum historischen
Epos der Antike* (Heidelberg, 1. Teil 1976, 2. Teil 1978); W. Kühn, *Götterszenen bei Vergil*
(Heidelberg, 1971); J. Vahlen, *Ennianae Poesis Reliquae*³ (Leipzig, 1928).

[1] p. 165 of 'La Dea Giunone nell' Eneide di Virgilio', *Atene e Roma* 11 (1966), 145–65.
[2] p. 165 (general discussion, pp. 162–7, 169). Cf. P. Boyancé, *La Religion de Virgile*
(Paris, 1963), p. 27, 'L'évolution qui conduit Junon de son hostilité du debout à son
acquiescement de la fin est une des données capitales de la religion de l'*Énéide*'; Buchheit,
pp. 133–50, esp. p. 147; idem, 'Junos Wandel zum Guten', *Gymnasium* 81 (1974), 498–
503; C. H. Wilson, *CQ* NS 29 (1979), 365 ff.; Agathe Thornton, *The Living Universe: Gods
and Men in Virgil's Aeneid* (Mnemosyne Supplement 46, Leiden Brill, 1976), pp. 144 f.,
152 ff.; Gordon Williams, *Technique and Ideas in the Aeneid* (Yale University Press, 1983),
pp. 76 f.

bello Punico secundo, ut ait Ennius, placata Iuno coepit fauere Romanis', 'because in the Second Punic War, according to Ennius, Juno was placated and began to favour the Romans'.[3] If Juno was placated, she had been hostile: Ennius' *Annales* will have shown her ranged against the Romans on the side of Carthage.[4] Now, Ennius was not canonical, and Vergil was not bound to be committed to this Ennian picture of Juno's involvement in the Carthaginian wars; he was free to have his Juno become a supporter of Rome some nine hundred years before Ennius'. At various points in the poem, however, it is plain that Vergil does indeed adhere to this Ennian tradition: by referring back to his predecessor's *Annales* he looks forward to the time when Juno will once again take up arms against the Aeneadae, on behalf of her favoured city Carthage.

The cardinal passage is the *concilium deorum* at the beginning of Book 10.[5] Jupiter chides the gods for causing war between the Trojans and Latins, and for taking sides in that war (6–10). But a proper time for them to fight will come, he tells them: 'adueniet iustum pugnae (ne arcessite) tempus / cum fera Karthago Romanis arcibus olim / exitium magnum atque Alpis immittet apertas: / tum certare odiis, tum res rapuisse licebit' (11–14). This is a promise of a divine conflict to mirror the human one,[6] and it is directed principally at Juno, as Servius observes in his note on *ne arcessite* (11): 'nolite bellorum tempora praeoccupare. et bene satis facit uxori cum prohibitione. significat autem bellum Punicum secundum.' Necessarily, these words of Jupiter will have had far more resonance for their original audience, with school-acquired knowledge of *Annales Quinti Ennii* in their head, than

---

[3] *Ann.* 291 V.

[4] Cf. Buchheit, p. 54: 'Juno was inimically disposed to the Romans until the Second Punic War. Since she gives up her enmity only with the end of the Punic War, she must have been described as the great opponent of Rome on the Carthaginian side.' See, too, Häussler 2, pp. 195 ff. Silius Italicus in the *Punica* is following Ennius as well as Vergil in his use of Juno as Rome's divine antagonist in the Hannibalic war: see L. B. Woodruff, *Reminiscences of Ennius in Silius Italicus* (University of Michigan Studies, Humanistic Series, vol. 4, New York, 1910), pp. 403 ff.

[5] E. Norden, *Ennius und Vergilius: Kriegsbilder aus Roms grosser Zeit* (Leipzig, 1915), pp. 43 ff., contended that the whole setting here was Ennian, based on a putative council in *Annales* 7, at the beginning of the second Punic war. But his case has been undone by W. H. Friedrich, *Hermes* 76 (1941), 113–16; S. Timpanaro, *SIFC* 23 (1948), 37 ff.; M. Wigodsky, *Vergil and Early Latin Poetry* (Hermes Einzelschriften 24, 1972), pp. 65 f.

[6] It is not simply a promise of a future war between men, as interpreted by V. Simpson, p. 26, of 'The Annalistic Tradition in Vergil's *Aeneid*', *Vergilius* 21 (1975), 22–32; See Norden, op. cit. (n. 5), p. 51; Häussler 2, p. 190.

they can for us; Jupiter is foretelling the role Juno will play on the side of Carthage in the *Annales* of Ennius.

If Jupiter prophesies Juno's support of Hannibal, he also prophesies her reconciliation in the *Annales*. He does so in his major speech to Venus in Book 1: 'quin aspera Iuno, / quae mare nunc terrasque metu caelumque fatigat, / consilia in melius referet, mecumque fouebit / Romanos' (279–82). The positioning of these lines causes chronological problems if one takes them to refer explicitly to the scene in Book 12, as is generally done,[7] since they come after the death of Aeneas, after the founding of the city of Rome. As T. Halter puts it:

We may briefly ask the first question which emerges, namely from what point Juno ceases her rage. Since she already abandons her hate in the twelfth book (818), her change of mind should have been mentioned between the fighting and the reign of Aeneas, i.e. between lines 264 and 265. Why does Vergil not follow strict chronology in this important matter?[8]

The answer to Halter's question is that Vergil does follow the chronology here, the Ennian chronology, as Serivus comments (on 281), when he locates Juno's change of heart: 'quia bello Punico secundo, ut ait Ennius, placata Iuno coepit fauere Romanis'. N. Horsfall has drawn the right conclusion, observing that Juno's reconciliation belongs at this point in the prophecy because it was 'a necessary prelude to the defeat of Carthage, the first great obstacle to *imperium sine fine* encountered by Rome overseas and to the great wave of foreign conquests she undertook in the sixty years after the second Punic war— including, of course, *Pthiam clarasque Mycenas*'.[9] After Juno's reconciliation she will acquiesce in the conquest of Greece, seeing her favoured cities of Mycenae and Argos go under, in poetic fulfilment of the pledge she had made to Zeus in the *Iliad*: ἤτοι ἐμοὶ τρεῖς μὲν πολὺ φίλταταί εἰσι πόληες, / ''Ἀργός τε Σπάρτη τε καὶ εὐρυάγυια Μυκήνη· / τὰς διαπέρσαι, ὅτ' ἄν τοι ἀπέχθωνται περὶ κῆρι· / τάων οὔ τοι ἐγὼ πρόσθ' ἵσταμαι οὐδὲ μεγαίρω, 'Three cities there are by far most dear to me, Argos and Sparta and Mycenae of the wide ways; sack them, when they vex you in your heart—I shall not stand before them, or grudge it you.'[10]

---

[7] e.g. by R. G. Austin in his commentary on Book 1 (Oxford, 1971), on 281: 'Juno will amend her design ... For her yielding see 12. 841.'

[8] *Form und Gehalt in Vergils Aeneis* (Munich, 1963), p. 14.

[9] p. 3 of 'Dido in the Light of History', *PVS* 12 (1973–4), 1–13 (repr. in this collection, Ch. 6 above).

[10] *Il.* 4. 51–4. Ovid follows a similar line in *Fast.* 6, where he has Juno boast of the sacrifices she made for the Romans' sake: he is more systematic, including Homer's three

Consider, too, the Homeric paradigm for Jupiter's promise to Venus. In *Odyssey* 1, Zeus comforts Athene over her suffering protégé, promising that Poseidon will eventually lay aside his anger against Odysseus: Ποσειδάων δὲ μεθήσει / ὃν χόλον, 'Poseidon will relax his anger.'[11] Poseidon's relenting is not an action described in the poem itself: Teiresias tells Odysseus how to placate the god (11. 121 ff.), and as the poem ends Odysseus' atonements is still in the future. Similarly, in the *Aeneid*, the final reconciliation of Juno which Jupiter prophesies is not represented in the narrative, but lies beyond the poem's close.

A third and final passage. In the poem's introduction, Vergil describes Juno's love for Carthage (1. 15 ff.), saying 'hoc regnum dea gentibus esse, / si qua fata sinant, iam tum tenditque fouetque' (17 f.). *iam tum* is crucial—'*even then* she was planning for Carthage to rule the peoples of the earth', anticipating the aid she would give Carthage later on, when the issue of who should rule the world was to be decided. It is as good as certain that the motif referred to in 'regnum ... gentibus' is an Ennian one. Lucretius and Livy, in related language, both represent the Punic wars as a contest for world dominion,[12] and E. J. Kenney observes that 'no doubt Ennius was their common model'.[13] Certainly in the case of Lucretius, we may point to clear imitation of an Ennian line, which looks as if it belongs in a description of the final struggle between Scipio and Hannibal: 'Africa terribili *tremit horrida terra tumultu*' (310 V); cf. Lucr.

---

towns plus Samos, mentioned in Vergil's proem as Juno's second favourite city (*Aen.* 1. 16); 'paeniteat Sparten Argosque measque Mycenas / et ueterem Latio supposuisse Samon' (6. 47 f.).

[11] *Od.* 1. 77 f.

[12] Lucr. 3. 833–7, 'ad confligendum uenientibus undique Poenis, / omnia cum belli trepido concussa tumultu / horrida contremuere sub altis aetheris oris, / *in dubioque* fuere utrorum ad regna cadendum / *omnibus humanis* esset terraque marique', 'when the Carthaginians came from all sides to the fray, when all things shook and trembled under the lofty expanses of the sky, shivering with the fearful riot of war, and were in doubt as to whose sway of the two all men should fall by land and sea'; Liv. 29. 17. 6 (quoted by E. J. Kenney in his commentary on Lucr. 3 (Cambridge, 1971), on 832–42), '*In discrimine* est nunc *humanum omne* genus, utrum uos an Carthaginienses principes orbis terrarum uideat', 'the whole human race has now reached the critical point which will decide whether it will see you or the Carthaginians as lords of the world'; idem 30. 32. 2, 'Roma an Carthago iura gentibus daret ante crastinam noctem scituros', 'would know before tomorrow nightfall whether Rome or Carthage would administer laws to the peoples of earth'.

[13] On 832–42. One sees a sign of the same formulation in Polybius, who refers to Carthage and Rome as τὰ πολιτεύματα τὰ περὶ τῆς τῶν ὅλων ἀρχῆς ἀμφισβητήσαντα, 'the states to dispute the supremacy of the whole' (1. 3. 7). But Polybius generally speaks of a solely *Roman* bid for supremacy (see the passages in Walbank's note on 1. 3. 4), while for the Roman literary tradition Ennius will have been the true parent.

3. 834 f., 'omnia cum belli trepido concussa *tumultu / horrida contremuere'.[14] The Vergilian 'regnum … gentibus' employs a word that
appears in Lucretius' use of the motif ('utrorum ad *regna* cadendum',
836), and a word that appears in Livy's ('iura *gentibus* daret', 30. 32. 2).
The rivalry for supremacy posited by the topos is caught by Vergil with
the opposition of *regnum* (17), applied to Carthage, and *regem* (21),
applied to Rome.[15] Vergil, then, in *iam tum* looks forward to Juno's
helping Carthage at a much later date; in 'hoc regnum dea gentibus
esse / … tenditque fouetque' he refers to a commonplace about the
world hegemony of Carthage which is almost certainly Ennian in origin,
applied to the Punic wars; and in 'regnum … gentibus' he may even be
using language from that Ennian context. The likelihood of allusion to
Ennius here is increased if we accord weight to Servius' comment on the
next lines ('progeniem sed enim Troiano a sanguine duci / audierat
Tyrias olim quae uerteret arces', 19 f.): 'et perite "audierat"; in Ennio
enim inducitur Iuppiter promittens Romanis excidium Carthaginis'.
The whole context 'anticipates' the *Annales*.

Ennius had Juno fighting for Carthage against Rome, and so, it
seems, does Vergil. What then to make of the reconciliation between
Juno and Jupiter in Book 12? Some scholars disregard the Vergilian
evidence for Juno's activities in the Punic wars, and will have the
reconciliation in Book 12 as quite complete.[16] Others regard the scene
in Book 12 in the same way, but are aware of the force of the 'Ennian'
passages and conclude, with varying degrees of discomfort, that Vergil
has fallen into self-contradiction. Thus B. C. Fenik, discussing Jupiter's
words in Book 10 ('adueniet iustum pugnae (ne arcessite) tempus' …
etc., 11 ff.); 'This squares poorly with the end of the *Aeneid* where Juno's
reconciliation lapses into an anticlimax if we are to believe that she again
fought against Rome at a later time. We must recognise an inconcinnity
here, which may be the result of Vergil's attempting to combine an
earlier tradition with a version he wished to create himself.'[17]

[14] See Bailey on Lucr. 3. 835, Kenney on 3. 834–5.

[15] Horsfall draws attention to the force of the words, op. cit. (n. 9), p. 3.

[16] e.g. Buchheit, p. 147: 'While Ennius chose for it only the Second Punic War, Horace
the death of Romulus, i.e. the period after the founding of Rome, Vergil shifts the
reconciliation back into the earliest days of Rome [I return to Horace below] Juno is, so to
speak, the friend of Rome from the beginning of Roman history.' See the works cited in
nn. 1 and 2 above.

[17] The influence of Euripides on Vergil's *Aeneid*' (diss. Princeton, 1960), pp. 236 ff.
('discrepancies' and 'contradictions', p. 237); cf. N. Moseley, *Characters and Epithets: A
Study in Vergil's Aeneid* (Yale, 1926), pp. 38 f.; Häussler 2, pp. 189 ff. ('those tell-tale
inconsistencies', p. 189). Häussler sees the references back to the Ennian tradition as an

A few commentators face and accept the implications,[18] but W. R. Johnson is the only writer on the reconciliation scene in 12 to expound at length the case that there is something fundamentally qualified about Juno's acquiescence to Jupiter.[19] His discussion is most valuable and important; my remarks may stand as a supplement.

Exactly what do Juno and Jupiter agree to in Book 12? All the talk is of Troy. Juno pleads that the vile race of Teucer alter nothing of her Latins' *mores*, not name or dress or nationality or language; the hated name which she wishes to be obliterated is the last word we hear from her lips:

> illud te ...
> pro Latio obtestor ...
> ne uetus indigenas nomen mutare Latinos
> neu Troas fieri iubeas Teucrosque uocari
> aut uocem mutare uiros aut uertere uestem.
> sit Latium, sint Albani per saecula reges,
> sit Romana potens Itala uirtute propago:
> occidit, occideritque sinas cum nomine Troia. (12. 819–28).

Jupiter readily concedes: 'commixti corpore tantum / subsident Teucri' (835 f.). This is a great victory for Juno. It settles the point of grievance between her and Venus, as expressed in their speeches in Book 10, where Venus begs Jupiter to allow Troy to be re-established,[20] and Juno will not have it. Above all, it satisfies the vast resentment against the Trojans which the proem of Book 1 had set out as part of Juno's motivation for persecuting Aeneas and his men (1. 23 ff.).

The crucial point is the obvious one, that Juno's hatred of Troy is only half her motivation. As Horsfall points out,[21] she has a 'mythological'

untidy and unwholesome element: 'And immediately it seems to us to have become clear that only an *Aeneid* without this looking back and with an unconditional and definitive reconciliation as its conclusion could have achieved unity of motivation and religious atmosphere' (p.193).

[18] e.g. Büchner, *RE* 2R. 16. 1457: 'The battle and with it the plot only ends when Juno gives up (12. 841). But not for ever: for she is still promised by Fate in the future a great opportunity to fight for Carthage' (10. 11 ff.). Cf. Conway on 1. 281 (see n. 26 below).

[19] *Darkness Visible: A Study of Vergil's Aeneid* (University of California, 1976), pp. 123–7.

[20] *Aen.* 10. 60–2, 'Xanthum et Simoenta / redde, oro, miseris iterumque reuoluere casus / da, pater, Iliacos Teucris'. On the important theme of *Pergama recidiua* in the *Aeneid*, see W. S. Anderson, 'Vergil's Second *Iliad*', *TAPhA* 88 (1957), 17–30; W. Suerbaum, 'Aeneas zwischen Troja und Rom: Zur Funktion der Genealogie und der Ethnographie in Vergils Aeneis', *Poetica* 1 (1967), 176–204; G. N. Knauer, *Die Aeneis und Homer*, Hypomnemata 7 (Göttingen, 1964), pp. 351 ff.

[21] Art. cit. (n. 9) p. 2.

motive for her hatred of the Aeneadae—the judgement of Paris and all
the Homeric matter connected with the name of Troy (1. 23–8)—and
she has an 'historical' motive, her predilection for Carthage and fear of
the fate that awaits the city at the hands of Aeneas' descendants (12–
22).[22] (Bluntly, for the purposes of the first motive she is regarded as
'Argive Hera', while for the purposes of the second she is viewed under
the aspect of the Carthaginian Tanit.)[23] This second, historical motive is
the engine that supplies the momentum of the narrative of Books 1 and
4,[24] which culminates in Dido's curse and the evocation of Hannibal, to
engage Rome and Carthage irrevocably in future warfare.[25] In Book 12
only Juno's 'mythological' grievance is removed;[26] the other remains
potent, its consequences already irresistibly in train. Juno knows it, and
Jupiter knows it: 'es germana Iouis Saturnique altera proles, / irarum
tantos uoluis sub pectore fluctus' (830 f.). I should follow Servius here,[27]
who explains in these words:

'soror Iouis es, id est Saturni filia'. unde non mirum est tantam te iracundiam
retinere sub pectore. nam scimus unumquemque pro generis qualitate in iram
moueri: nobiles enim etsi ad praesens uidentur ignoscere, tamen in posterum
iram reseruant. quod nunc Iunoni uidetur obicere: nam cum se concedere
diceret, petiit tamen quod grauiter posset obesse Troianis.

---

[22] Cf. Büchner, *RE* 2R. 16. 1339.
[23] On this identification, see *RE* 2R. 4. 2184; Pease on *Aen.* 4. 91; Lieberg, op. cit. (n.
1), p. 153 n. 37; G.-Ch. Picard, *Les Religions de l'Afrique antique* (Paris, 1954), pp. 65, 109.
C. Bailey confuses the two faces of Juno here (*Religion in Virgil* (Oxford, 1935), pp. 131 f.):
'out of this hatred of the Trojans arises the special position which Juno holds in the *Aeneid*
of the patron-goddess of the newly founded Carthage'.
[24] See especially Horsfall, art. cit. (n. 9), on the crucial importance of the Carthaginian
theme in the early books; cf. V. Pöschl, *The Art of Vergil: Image and Symbol in the Aeneid* (tr.
G. Seligson, University of Michigan, 1962), pp. 13 ff., esp. p. 15, 'Juno ... is first the
mythical personification of the historical power of Carthage'; W. Warde Fowler, *Virgil's
'Gathering of the Clans'* (Blackwell, 1916), p. 40, 'At the outset of his poem, with all the
emphasis he can use, Virgil associates [Juno] in interest—an interest perverse in the eyes
of all Romans—with the most deadly enemy Rome ever had to meet, and with the mythical
queen of Carthage, the Cleopatra of his poetic fancy.' Wigodsky (op. cit. (n. 5), p. 29) is
quite mistaken to assert that 'Vergil is not interested in the Punic Wars as such'; while
Robert Coleman plays down Juno's association with Carthage, as a result of taking Juno's
reconciliation in 12 as complete (n. 53 to 'The Gods in the *Aeneid*', *G & R* 29 (1982),
143–68).   [25] 4. 622 ff.
[26] As seen by Conway, in his note on Jupiter's promise of Juno's reconciliation (1. 281,
'in melius referet'): 'The time of this final acquiescence of Juno in the greatness of Rome is
left unspecified both here and in 12. 841, where she desists merely from persecuting
Aeneas on condition that the language, religion and government of Rome shall be Italian,
not Asiatic.'
[27] The result is very close to Johnson's, op. cit. (n. 19), p. 126, esp. n. 106. The passage
is much discussed: bibliography in Kühn, p. 164 n. 9; add Wigodsky, op. cit. (n. 5), pp.
67 ff., on 'Saturnia'.

'You are the sister of Jupiter, that is daughter of Saturn.' Hence it is no surprise
that you keep such anger in your heart. For we know that any man is stirred to
anger according to the quality of his birth; nobles, though they may seem to
forgive for the present, nevertheless reserve their anger for a future point. Of
this he now seems to accuse Juno; for though she claims that she is conceding,
she has requested something of serious potential danger to the Trojans.

(he means the loss of their name).[28] My only difference is that Juno is
reserving her anger far longer into the future than Servius suggests—
until she reappears in her old role in the *Annales*. As we read the scene in
Book 12, we must have always in mind the Ennian Juno, of whose
actions Vergil has regularly reminded us.

Does this mean, as Fenik complains, that 'Juno's reconciliation lapses
into an anticlimax if we are to believe that she again fought against Rome
at a later time'?[29] We should rather think of the anticlimax that is
attendant upon the traditional account of the scene, whereby the
daemonic power that has generated the action so far evaporates with an
order, a request, and a smile. It is a question of emphases. Johnson's
eloquent account lays its principal stress on what the scene holds of the
sinister and baleful. While acknowledging the essential accuracy of his
reading, we must recognize that none the less there *is* a resolution of
sorts here, that something *is* accomplished which is not wholly shabby or
a fraud.[30] This much is guaranteed even by the elaborate formal
correspondences between the Jupiter-scene in 12 and the Jupiter-scene
in 1:[31] the relief which Jupiter promises Venus may not be unalloyed
when it comes at the end of the poem, but in some measure it does come.
Another formal sign to mark Juno's acquiescence is seen in the frame of
the scene with Jupiter. At the beginning, Jupiter addresses her as she is
looking down on the fighting from a cloud ('fulua pugnas *de nube*
tuentem', 792). 'de aere, de elemento suo', comments Servius: the
identification is based on the allegorists' equation of "Ηρα (Hera) and
ἀήρ (air).[32] Jupiter chides her: 'aut qua spe *gelidis in nubibus* haeres?'

---

[28] On 12. 830. Servius' interpretation is similar to the comments of the bT scholia on *Il.*
15. 212, where Poseidon stops supporting the Greeks—for the moment: εὐσχήμονα τὴν
ἀπαλλαγὴν ὁρίζεται, ἐπιτείνων τὴν ὀργὴν εἰς ὕστερον, 'he sets out his separation in fair
words, concentrating his anger on a future time'. On such shared themes in the Greek and
Latin commentators see Fraenkel, *JRS* 39 (1949), 151–4.

[29] Loc. cit. (n. 17).

[30] I find some of Johnson's comments of the evil of Jupiter disconcerting (op. cit. (n.
19), p. 126 and n. 110); also his suggested interpretation of *his mentem retorsit* (p. 127).

[31] On these correspondences see Halter, op. cit. (n. 8), pp. 14 ff., 78 ff.; Knauer, op. cit.
(n. 20), pp. 324 ff.; Kühn, pp. 164 f.; Buchheit, art. cit. (n. 2), pp. 499 ff.

[32] See Servius on *Aen.* 7. 300; R. Heinze, *Vergils epische Technik*³ (Leipzig, 1915), p.

(796). At the end of the dialogue, won over by Jupiter, Juno gives a token of her agreement by leaving her element: 'interea excedit caelo *nubemque relinquit*' (842). The device is perhaps rather mechanical, but it signals an accommodation.[33]

What the scene in 12 resolves is the question of Aeneas' settlement in Latium, and the final passing away of Troy; it does not resolve any more of Juno's grudges. The divine reconciliation is qualified to the extent that it reflects only so much of the Roman endeavour as has been accomplished so far: it leaves open what historically remains open. The great anxieties that surround the first beginnings of the Roman state are not dispelled at a stroke; the momentum of empire continues, and the energies of the poem's forward movement are held in suspense, not checked. Ahead lie centuries of strain, with Carthage as the highest crisis, and Juno's hate once more to face.

In a recent paper on 'The Judgement of Paris and *Iliad* xxiv',[34] M. Davies has well described the way in which Homer's final book establishes a contrast between the ability of men to achieve reconciliation with each other, and the relentless nature of the gods' animosities. He goes on to detect a Vergilian reversal of this Homeric pattern:

in *Aen.* xii 791 ff. Jupiter bids [Juno] set aside her resentment and loathing of the Trojans and she consents with surprising speed and readiness. Jupiter smiles, and reconciliation and peace are restored on Olympus. On earth, however, there is no such happy resolution: Turnus begs for mercy but Aeneas is overwhelmed by hatred and anger and kills the suppliant. The whole poem ends not as the *Iliad* does on a note of mortal reconciliation and reintegration, but surprisingly and distressingly on a note of continued hatred, hostility and rage.[35]

This is fine comment on the distinction between the attempts of Homer's men and Vergil's men, but I would suggest that in the *Aeneid* even the immortal sphere is unreconciled within itself at the close, just

---

299; Pease, ed. Cic. *Nat.*, pp. 716 f.; F. Buffière, *Les mythes d'Homère et la Pensée Grecque* (Paris, 1956), pp. 107 f.; Note Juno's '*aeria* ... sede', 12. 810.

[33] 'excedit caelo' is puzzling to me. What does it mean to say that Juno 'left the *caelum*', and what is the relation between this phrase and 'nubemque relinquit'? In the scheme that saw Juno as *aer*, Jupiter was the *caelum* (Pease, ed. Cic. *Nat.*, pp. 715 f.; Buffière, op. cit. (n. 32), p. 106). Hence I have sometimes been tempted to read *cedit* (in the sense of 'deferring' or 'yielding to', *OLD* s.v. 8 and 10); 'she deferred to the Jupiter-element and left her own'. I am by no means confident of this; but note the parallelism between '*cedit* caelo nubemque *relinquit*' and the words spoken earlier in the scene by Juno: 'et nunc *cedo* equidem pugnasque exosa *relinquo*' (818).

[34] *JHS* 101 (1981), 56–62.

[35] p. 61.

as in the *Iliad*. The significant contrast at the end of the poem is that between the deadly weakness of men's efforts and the ease with which the gods can make an arrangement while still unreconciled in full: this is their essential invulnerability, their power—ῥεῖα μάλ᾽ ὥστε θεός ('quite easily, as befits a god').[36] Homer's gods reach a momentary accommodation without their grievances being abnegated;[37] Juno does the same with Jupiter, winning a point, losing a point, and deferring a third.

II

The discussion so far has involved many incidental references to the figure of Juno in Ennius' *Annales*. It is time to turn directly to Ennius, in an attempt to discover what aspects of Ennius' goddess and her activities lie behind the reconciliation scene in *Aeneid* 12. Further evidence will come from Ovid, and above all from Horace, whose third 'Roman Ode' exhibits, like Vergil's closing episode, an angry Juno making an accommodation concerning the incipient Roman power. In Horace, too, the talk is all of the passing away of Troy; if we must try to ascertain what Ennian sanction there may be for the common talk of Troy, we must also express some opinion on the notorious topic of why this subject received such emphasis from these poets at this time.[38]

Even in saying so much I have run ahead of the argument, because it is by no means agreed that the common elements between Vergil and Horace are in fact Ennian, or that the Juno whom we see and hear in Horace's ode bears any relation to the Juno of Ennius' *Annales*. The Ennian episode which is the focus of the problem is the Council of the Gods in the first book.[39] On the agenda of the meeting was the

---

[36] *Il.* 3. 381, 20. 444. Johnson is good here, op. cit. (n. 19), p. 24. J. Griffin, *Homer on Life and Death* (Oxford, 1980), p. 189, has convincing observations on the gods' 'ease' in Homer, and on the Euripidean 'contrast between human misery and the radiant unconcern of the gods'. Vergil's passionately involved deities are, in this regard, rather closer to Homer's than to Euripides'.

[37] Besides Davies, see C. W. Macleod (*Homer Iliad 24* (Cambridge, 1982)) on *Il.* 24. 25–30 ('the judgement of Paris'): 'Homer heightens and extends his tragedy by taking us back to where it started. This reminds us that even if for the moment "the gods" are to unite in allowing the ransom of Hector's body, the gods hostile to Troy still have reason to be as angry as ever; and the city they hate must fall.'

[38] Discussion tends to resolve itself into deciding either for or against the proposition that a real project of moving the capital lies behind the insistence on Troy's total disappearance: Fraenkel has a history of the dispute (a dispute which also involves Liv. 5. 51–4, on transferring the capital to Veii): *Horace* (Oxford, 1957), pp. 267–9. See further n. 80 below.

[39] Frr. 60–5 V; see Vahlen, pp. clix–clxi.

apotheosis of Romulus. We do not rely solely on Horace for this knowledge. Ovid twice tells the story of Mars asking Jupiter for permission to fetch his son Romulus to heaven, reminding Jupiter of an earlier occasion when a promise had been given that this elevation would one day take place (*Fast.* 2. 481 ff.; *Met.* 14. 806 ff.). In the *Metamorphoses* passage, Mars refers explicitly to a *concilium deorum* as the setting for the giving of the promise (*concilio quondam praesente deorum*, 812), and in both passages he quotes an identical line as the exact words of Jupiter's promise: 'unus erit quem tu tolles in caerula caeli' (*Met.* 14. 814 = *Fast.* 2. 487). This line is quoted by Varro as his first example of poetic diction,[40] and is virtually certain to be a line of Ennius.[41] Mars tells Jupiter that he has memorized the words and stored them up in his retentive mind. The verse which conveys this claim refers just as happily to the cultivated poet who has retained from childhood bits of hairy Ennius in his head: 'tu mihi concilio quondam praesente deorum / (nam memoro memorique animo pia uerba notaui) / "unus erit quem tu tolles in caerula caeli" / dixisti', 'you said to me once in the presence of the council of gods (for I recall it, and noted down your holy words in my mindful heart), "One there will be whom you will raise to the blue reaches of heaven"' (*Met.* 14. 812–15).[42]

It is in fact generally reckoned that Horace's poem recalls Ennius' council in *Ann.* 1.[43] The last stanza of Horace's poem declares virtually outright that he has just been 'quoting' epic matter: 'desine peruicax / referre sermones deorum et / magna modis tenuare paruis' (70–2). Ovid refers to Ennius' *concilium* explicitly (*concilio ... deorum*, *Met.* 14.

---

[40] *LL* 7. 5 f., 'Dicam in hoc libro de uerbis quae a poetis sunt posita ... incipiam hinc: "unus erit quem tu tolles in caerula caeli / templa".'

[41] Cf. Vahlen, p. clx, 'That this is a piece of Ennius is not said by Ovid; but Varro *LL* 7. 6, though he does not inform one openly, nevertheless indicates this in a manner not obscure to those who know Varro.'

[42] After the interview with Jupiter, Mars descends and snatches up Romulus in his chariot (*Met.* 14. 818 f.; *Fast.* 2. 496, as befitting the genre, a much more elliptical version). The line from the *Fasti* ('rex patriis astra petebat equis') resembles Horace's reference to Romulus' 'death' ('Martis equis Acheronta fugit', *Carm.* 3. 3. 16): it is natural to assume a common Ennian model (indeed, Horace's *Martis* has been emended to *patris* on analogy with Ovid's line: see Bentley ad loc.).

[43] Cf. Vahlen, p. clix; G. Pasquali, *Orazio Lirico. Studi*[2] (Florence, 1964), p. 687; T. Oksala, *Religion und Mythologie bei Horaz*, Commentationes Humanarum Litterarum 51 (Helsinki, 1973), pp. 102, 156. It seems to be taken for granted that Horace sets the council *after* Romulus has been snatched away by Mars (exceptions include Häussler 2, p. 195 n. 23). But this snatching away is part of what the council is there to decide. Ovid gives us naturally to understand that the gods decided in advance that Mars would be allowed to rescue his son for immortality, and I see nothing in Horace's poem that is at odds with this picture.

812),[44] while Horace's reference characteristically avoids that degree of precision: '*consiliantibus* ... diuis' (17 f.). But although Ennius is not just the formal model (that is, for the basic idea of a *concilium deorum*), but also the model for the *occasion* (to discuss the apotheosis of Romulus), there are few scholars who claim that the content of Juno's speech in Horace is based on anything Juno might have said in Ennius. Some commentators say nothing on the subject.[45] Many deny the notion outright, or express serious doubt,[46] while Heinze, Steuart, Wilkinson, Waszink, and Commager represent the small group who consider that the words of Horace's Juno are drawn originally from the mouth of Ennius.[47] Heinze and Commager point to the strong correspondences between Horace's scene and Vergil's in *Aeneid* 12, with their common insistence on the disappearance of Troy, and conclude that Ennius is the joint source,[48] thus bypassing the argument over whether Horace followed Vergil or Vergil followed Horace.[49]

I think it is fair to say that the *natural* conclusion to draw from Horace's poem and its connection with *Aeneid* 12 is that both go back to Ennius and depend on Juno's voicing of similar sentiments in the council in *Annales* 1.[50] I think it is also fair to say that the *only* reason for declining to draw this conclusion is the belief that Ennius' Juno was not reconciled to Rome until the Hannibalic war, and therefore could not have made any agreement favourable to the Roman state at any earlier stage.[51] The general tendency of my argument will by now be plain.

[44] As does Lucilius, in his parody: 'uellem concilio uestrum, quod dicitis olim, / caelicolae, hic habitum, uellem adfuissemus priore / concilio', frr. 20–2 W.

[45] No comment, for instance, from Gordon Williams, *The Third Book of Horace's 'Odes'* (Oxford, 1969), who rather views the speech as 'a sort of answer to a problem raised by the contemporary epic, the *Aeneid*: how and when did Juno's hostility to Rome cease?' Fraenkel, op. cit. (n. 38), p. 267, and Kiessling–Heinze, on *Carm.* 3. 3. 15, only refer to Horace's taking from Ennius the motif of a 'concilium deorum': in his discussion of the speech itself, Fraenkel does not mention Ennius.

[46] Cf., e.g., Vahlen, p. clix; Oksala, op. cit. (n. 43), p. 156 (both doubting); Pasquali, op. cit. (n. 43), p. 687; Häussler 2, p. 195 n. 23; Buchheit, p. 146 (all denying: 'but above all, there was hardly any talk of Troy in this *concilium deorum*', Buchheit, loc. cit. n. 626).

[47] E. M. Steuart, *The Annals of Quintus Ennius* (Cambridge, 1925), p. 176; R. Heinze, *Vom Geist des Römertums* (Leipzig, 1938), pp. 230 ff.; L. P. Wilkinson, *Horace and his Lyric Poetry* (Cambridge, 1946), pp. 73 f.; J. H. Waszink, *WS* 70 (1957), 325; Steele Commager, *The Odes of Horace: A Critical Study* (New Haven and London, 1962), p. 222 n. 122.

[48] Wigodsky, op. cit. (n. 5), p. 147, draws the same conclusion, but refers to *Ann.* 8, not *Ann.* 1.

[49] Bibliography on the priority question in Wigodsky, loc. cit. previous note; Buchheit, p. 146 n. 626.

[50] Though one may speculate about one poet being 'put on to' the subject by the other.

[51] Cf. Vahlen, p. clix, denying that Juno spoke as Horace says: 'For the goddess, having been hostile to the Romans of old, mitigated her anger at last in the Second Punic War. Cf.

Vergil could depict Juno, at a very early stage of Roman history, making a deal with Jupiter (agreeing to Aeneas' settlement but winning the final annihilation of Troy), while still remaining full of menace until finally placated during the Punic wars. With such a pattern before our eyes, we need not allow the knowledge that Ennius' Juno was likewise not fully reconciled to Rome before Hannibal's time to prevent us from concluding that in *Annales* 1 she may have come to some qualified agreement, the prototype of Vergil's, agreeing to the apotheosis of Romulus on condition that Troy vanish for ever.

The details of the case remain to be worked out, but first it is worth bringing to bear another argument to show that there is likely to have been some sort of reconciliation with Juno involved in Ennius' account of the decision to grant godhead to Romulus. In describing (or inventing)[52] the apotheosis of Romulus, Ennius took over many essential details from the traditional accounts of the apotheosis of Heracles.[53] He is unlikely to have been original in this. As J. K. Newman points out, Theocritus 17 is good evidence for the existence of Hellenistic epics which treated Heracles as paradigm for the deification of Alexander and later monarchs.[54] In that poem we see Alexander and the first Ptolemy enjoying immortality in heaven (16 ff.). They sit opposite Heracles, and escort him to Hebe's chamber after the feast. Their immortality is explicitly said to be a result of their descent from Heracles:

ἔνθα σὺν ἄλλοισιν θαλίας ἔχει Οὐρανίδῃσι,
χαίρων υἱωνῶν περιώσιον υἱωνοῖσιν,
ὅττι σφεων Κρονίδης μελέων ἐξείλετο γῆρας,
ἀθάνατοι δὲ καλεῦνται ἑοὶ νέποδες γεγαῶτες.
ἄμφω γὰρ πρόγονος σφιν ὁ καρτερὸς Ἡρακλείδας,
ἀμφότεροι δ' ἀριθμεῦνται ἐς ἔσχατον Ἡρακλῆα.
(22–7).

Servius on *Aen.* 1. 281 "in the Second Punic War, according to Ennius, Juno was placated and began to favour the Romans" (VIII fr. XVIII). But why should she begin to favour them then, when she had already permitted the Romans to extend the bounds of their dominion far and wide?' Identical reasoning in Buchheit, p. 146.

[52] In favour of Ennius' originality, see, e.g., Wilamowitz, *Der Glaube der Hellenen* (Berlin, 1932), ii. 422 n. 2; A. Elter, *Donarem Pateras ... Horat. Carm. 4, 8* (Bonn, 1907), pp. 40, 31 f.; against, e.g., R. M. Ogilvie, *A Commentary on Livy Books 1–5* (Oxford, 1965), p. 84.

[53] See especially Elter, op. cit. (n. 52); also J. K. Newman, *Augustus and the New Poetry*, Coll. Latomus 88 (Brussels, 1967), pp. 68 ff.

[54] p. 71; cf. n. 2, 'The coincidence of Theocritus and Ennius here (cf. the same phenomenon in Horace, *Odes*, IV, 8) shows that they were both drawing on common Hellenistic material, not that Ennius knew the work of Theocritus.'

There he holds feasts with the other heavenly ones, rejoicing mightily in the sons of his sons, that Zeus has taken old age from their limbs, and that they are called immortal, being his descendants. For to them both the mighty son of Heracles is ancestor, and both are numbered finally back to Heracles. (22–7)

Various items of the Romulus story recall the Heracles legend. Each was the mightier twin;[55] the 'death' of each involves a storm, the disappearance of the body, and the inference amongst those left behind that their leader must have become a god.[56] An Ennian fragment ('Romulus in caelo cum dis genitalibus aeuum / degit', 115 f. V) echoes the conventional phraseology describing Heracles' new life in heaven: cf. *Od.* 11. 602 f., αὐτὸς δὲ μετ᾽ ἀθανάτοισι θεοῖσι / τέρπεται ἐν θαλίης 'and he takes joy in the feast with the immortal gods'; Hes. *Th.* 954 f., ὃς μέγα ἔργον ἐν ἀθανάτοισιν ἀνύσσας / ναίει ἀπήμαντος καὶ ἀγήραος 'who, having achieved a great work amongst men lives free from pain and old age';[57] id. fr. 25. 27 f., ζώει δ᾽ ἔνθά περ ἄλλοι Ὀλύμπια δώματ᾽ ἔχοντες / ἀθάνατος καὶ ἄγηρος 'and he lives where the others live who inhabit the halls of Olympus, deathless and ageless'; Hom. *Hym.* 15. 7 f.; Theoc. 17. 22. Of particular concern for our

---

[55] Cf. A. R. Anderson, *HSCPh* 39 (1928), 31, 'The identification of Romulus as a successor of Hercules was further helped by the fact that each was the mightier twin.' See generally Anderson, pp. 29 ff.

[56] 'subito coorta tempestas cum magno fragore tonitribusque tam denso regem operuit nimbo ut conspectum eius contioni abstulerit; nec deinde in terris Romulus fuit. Romana pubes sedato tandem pauore postquam ex tam turbido die serena et tranquilla lux rediit, ubi uacuam sedem regiam uidit, etsi satis credebat patribus qui proximi steterant sublimem raptum procella, tamen uelut orbitatis metu icta maestum aliquamdiu silentium obtinuit. deinde a paucis initio facto, deum deo natum, regem parentemque urbis Romanae saluere uniuersi Romulum iubent', 'a storm which suddenly arose with great crashing and thunder covered the king with so dense a cloud as to prevent the gathering from seeing him; and after that Romulus was no longer on earth. When the Roman youth, their fear finally calmed once a serene and tranquil light had returned after so disturbed a day, saw that the royal throne was empty, although they were sufficiently convinced by the story of the senators who had stood nearby that Romulus had been snatched up to heaven by a storm-wind, they nevertheless kept sad silence for a whole, as if struck by the fear of being bereft. Then, after a few of them had initiated it, they ordered all together that Romulus should be a god born of a god, the king and father of the city of Rome', Liv. 1. 16. 1–3; cf. D.S. 4. 38. 4 f., εὐθὺς δὲ καὶ κεραυνῶν ἐκ τοῦ περιέχοντος πεσόντων, ἡ πυρὰ πᾶσα κατεφλέχθη. μετὰ δὲ ταῦτα οἱ μὲν περὶ τὸν Ἰόλαον ἐλθόντες ἐπὶ τὴν ὀστολογίαν, καὶ μηδὲν ὅλως εὑρόντες, ὑπέλαβον τὸν Ἡρακλέα τοῖς χρησμοῖς ἀκολούθως ἐξ ἀνθρώπων εἰς θεοὺς μεθεστάσθαι, 'and at once with thunderbolts falling from the surrounding sky, the whole pyre was burnt up. Afterwards when those who accompanied Iolaus to collect the bones found nothing at all, they supposed that Heracles, in accordance with the oracles, had passed from the world of men to that of the gods.' As Ogilvie notes (op. cit. (n. 52), p. 84), this is all typical of the passing of Greek heroes.

[57] West ad loc. says that taking ἐν ἀθανάτοισιν with ναίει produces a very awkward hyperbaton; but the parallel passages incline one to accepting it.

purposes is the fact that a stock element of the Heracles tradition dealt with the problem of how Hera gave over the notorious anger which she had exercised against the hero since his birth.[58] The tradition is unanimous in linking together the enrolment of Heracles amongst the gods, the abandonment by Hera of her anger against him, and the marriage of Heracles to Hebe as a token of the reconciliation. Hesiod gives the details, fr. 25. 26–33:

> νῦν δ᾽ ἤδη θεός ἐστι, κακῶν δ᾽ ἐξήλυθε πάντων,
> ζώει δ᾽ ἔνθά περ ἄλλοι Ὀλύμπια δώματ᾽ ἔχοντες
> ἀθάνατος καὶ ἄγηρος, ἔχων καλλίσφυρον Ἥβην,
> παῖδα Διὸς μεγάλοιο καὶ Ἥρης χρυσοπεδίλου·
> τὸν πρὶν μέν ῥ᾽ ἤχθηρε θεὰ λευκώλενος Ἥρη
> ἔκ τε θεῶν μακάρων ἔκ τε θνητῶν ἀνθρώπων,
> νῦν δ᾽ ἤδη πεφίληκε, τίει δέ μιν ἔξοχον ἄλλων
> ἀθανάτων μετά γ᾽ αὐτὸν ἐρισθενέα Κρονίωνα.

And now already he is a god, and has emerged from all his sufferings, and he lives where the others live who inhabit the halls of Olympus, deathless and ageless, possessing fair-ankled Hebe, daughter of great Zeus and gold-sandalled Hera. Before, the white-armed goddess Hera hated him above all the blessed gods or mortal men; but now she feels love for him, and honours him above all the immortals after the mighty son of Kronos himself.

Apollodorus has a précis: ἐκεῖθεν δὲ τυχὼν ἀθανασίας καὶ διαλλαγεὶς Ἥρᾳ τὴν ἐκεινῆς θυγατέρα Ἥβην ἔγημεν, 'thence winning immortality and being reconciled with Hera, he married her daughter Hebe', 2. 7. 7. For a fuller account, see Diodorus.[59] A late-Etruscan mirror survives, which gives a pictorial representation of the tradition.[60] Jupiter is presiding over the reconciliation between Hercules and Juno;

[58] The rage of Hera is famous since Homer; cf. *Il.* 18. 119, ἀλλά ἑ Μοῖρ᾽ ἐδάμασσε καὶ ἀργαλέος χόλος Ἥρης, 'but Fate subdued him and the violent rage of Hera'; Hes. *Th.* 314 f., [Ὑδρην] Λερναίην, ἣν θρέψε θεὰ λευκώλενος Ἥρη / ἄπλητον κοτέουσα βίῃ Ἡρακληείῃ, 'the Lernean [Hydra], which the white-armed goddess Hera nourished, insatiably wrathful with the might of Heracles'.

[59] 4. 39. 2 f., προσθετέον δ᾽ ἡμῖν τοῖς εἰρημένοις ὅτι μετὰ τὴν ἀποθέωσιν αὐτοῦ Ζεὺς Ἥραν μὲν ἔπεισεν υἱοποιήσασθαι τὸν Ἡρακλέα καὶ τὸ λοιπὸν εἰς τὸν ἅπαντα χρόνον μητρὸς εὔνοιαν παρέχεσθαι ... τὴν δ᾽ Ἥραν μετὰ τὴν τέκνωσιν μυθολογοῦσι συνοικίσαι τὴν Ἥβην τῷ Ἡρακλεῖ, 'and it must be added to what we have said that after his apotheosis Zeus persuaded Hera to make Heracles her son, and in future for the whole of time to show him a mother's consideration ... and they say in myths that after the adoption Hera settled Hebe with Heracles'.

[60] Published *Ann. d.Inst.* 19 (1847), pl. T; a reproduction conveniently in Roscher's *Lexicon*, 1. 2. 2259.

fertility symbols suggest that what we are seeing is Hercules 'being presented as son-in-law'.[61]

It has been claimed that Heracles' marriage to Hebe was reflected by Ennius in Romulus' marriage to 'Hora' (his earthly wife Hersilia, who became, like Hebe, a goddess of youth).[62] This interpretation is based upon a vexed fragment; 'teque Quirine pater ueneror Horamque Quirini' (*Ann.* 117 V). It has been long denied—most recently and vigorously by Skutsch[63]—that Ennius knew of the identification of Romulus and Quirinus, and Skutsch asserts accordingly that fr. 117 V can have nothing to do with the transformation of Hersilia into Hora;[64] the line concerns another god and another consort. Let the verse pass before such disagreement. There is, however, an Ovidian passage which may give some support to the presupposition that Juno's reconciliation in *Ann.* 1 might have involved her playing some part in the marriage of the newly enrolled god. Ovid tells the story of the assumption of Hersilia in *Met.* 14, straight after the heavily Ennian episode of the interview of Mars and Jupiter and the taking up of Romulus into heaven (805–28): note that it is *Juno* who takes the initiative in bringing Hersilia to join her husband: 'flebat ut amissum coniunx, cum *regia Iuno* / Irin ad Hersilien descendere limite curuo / imperat . . .' 'his wife was bewailing him as lost to her, when queen Juno ordered Iris to descend to Hersilie on her curved path . . .' etc. (*Met.* 14. 824–31). Besides the heavenly marriage, the other 'Herculean' elements of Romulus' deification are to be seen condensed in Horace, where Juno says that she will give over her anger, and allow Romulus to be enrolled amongst the gods:

> 'protinus et grauis
> *iras* et inuisum nepotem,
>   Troica quem peperit sacerdos,
> Marti redonabo; illum ego lucidas
> inire sedes, ducere nectaris
>   sucos et *adscribi quietis*
>   *ordinibus patiar deorum*'. (30–6)[65]

---

[61] So J. G. Winter, *The Myth of Hercules at Rome* (Macmillan, New York, 1910), p. 179 n. 2, against the earlier interpretations, as represented by Peter in Roscher. Cf. J. Bayet, *Les Origines de l'Hercule Romain* (Paris, 1926), pp. 380 ff., esp. p. 381, 'The scene is thus strictly analysed as the reconciliation of Hercules and Juno on the threshold of the divine dwelling—it is a variant on the apotheosis of the hero.'

[62] Cf. Elter, op. cit. (n. 52), pp. 40, 33; Anderson, loc. cit. (n. 55); Newman, op. cit. (n. 53), p. 68.

[63] *Enniana* (London, 1968), pp. 132–7 (with introductory bibliography on the discussion, p. 132). Of course, the apotheosis of Romulus and the identification with Quirinus are two separate issues.   [64] p. 133.

[65] Note that Horace has Hercules prominently on display as a paradigm for the

forthwith I will yield to Mars my fierce anger and my grandson that I have hated, the son borne by the Trojan priestess; him I will allow to enter the realms of light, to drink draughts of nectar and to be admitted to the peaceful orders of the gods.

This material is not Horatian. It goes back to Ennius, who had it from Greek epic, nationalistic, encomiastic, mythological.

So far from a reconciliation of Juno being out of place in Ennius' council in *Annales* 1, it appears that the goddess' relenting is an indispensable part of the conception of Romulus' apotheosis.[66] There is no reason to resist this conclusion on the grounds that Juno later fought against Rome for Carthage. It is not a circular argument to bring in the qualified reconciliation of Vergil's *Aen.* 12 as evidence of a qualified reconciliation in *Ann.* 1, because in the first part of the paper the reasons for this interpretation of *Aen.* 12 were self-sufficient and did not depend for their validity on any hypothesis about the content of *Ann.* 1. Further, one may look to Horace's ode, to see there a Juno who is not yet an enthusiastic partisan of the Roman state: 'her promise deals with the deification only, and, so far from indicating the direct protection implied by "fauere" [i.e. in Serv. *Aen.* 1. 281, 'placata Iuno coepit fauere Romanis'], holds out a clear threat of reprisals should there be any attempt to restore Troy'.[67] As Steuart sums up, 'In Bk 1 Juno so far relents as to agree to the deification of Romulus; but active cooperation does not begin till the period of the Second Punic War'.[68]

One paragraph of more speculative matter before returning to Vergil. The congruence between Horace and Vergil in their emphasis on Troy leads one to regard it as likely that when Juno spoke in *Ann.* 1, she stipulated the final end of Troy as a condition of her agreeing to Romulus' apotheosis (Ennius will have had ample room to deploy the

deification of Augustus: 'hac arte Pollux et uagus Hercules / enisus arces attigit igneas, / quos inter Augustus recumbens / purpureo bibet ore nectar', 'by this art Pollux and wandering Hercules strove and reached the fiery citadels; amongst them Augustus will recline and drink nectar with crimson lips', 9–12. On such paradigms in Horace and Vergil, see D. Pietrusiński, 'Apothéose d'Auguste par la comparaison avec les héros grecques chez Horace et Virgile', *Eos* 66 (1978), 246 ff.

[66] The one obvious difference between Ennius' Romulus story and the Greek Heracles legend is that in Ennius the accommodations are made before Romulus' 'death', while with Heracles it seems that it was regular to have them settled after Mt Oeta. See n. 78 below.

[67] Steuart, op. cit. (n. 47), p. 176. Cf. Page on 38 *exules*: 'the word is employed, however, with a certain amount of contempt; with all her magnanimity Juno is not above the feminine weakness of saying something unpleasant (cf. the sneer implied in "perperit sacerdos", l. 32 ...)'. I should not make too much of Juno's 'magnanimity' in this poem.

[68] Loc. cit. (n. 67).

theme of Juno's hatred of Troy in the early part of the book, which dealt with the fall of Troy and the wanderings of Aeneas). She may have demanded that the Troy of Priam remain waste for ever. She may have insisted, like Vergil's Juno, on the matter of the *name*. The *concilium deorum* is usually located by scholars either at the time when the twins are exposed,[69] or else just before the actual foundation of Rome.[70] In either case, but particularly in the latter, the gods may well have wanted to settle the crucial question of what would be the name of the new city and the new people.[71] In Ennius' version, Romulus and Remus were the sons of a woman with the conspicuously Trojan name of Ilia,[72] the very grandsons of Aeneas.[73] Aeneas' first settlement in Latium had been called simply—'Troia':[74] did Juno demand as her price for acquiescence

[69] Vahlen, p. clxi; Skutsch, op. cit. (n. 63), p. 131; E. H. Warmington, *Remains of Old Latin I* (Harvard University Press, Cambridge, Mass., and London, 1935), on fr. 57 W.

[70] Rosenberg, *RE* 'Romulus' 2R. 1. 1097 f.; Waszink, op. cit. (n. 47), 325. This location seems more likely, as being of far greater moment: now is decided the beginning of the state whose achievements are the subject of the whole work. In the *Fasti*, Ovid has Juno tell of how Mars helped placate her, by promising that she would be powerful in the city of her grandson: 'ipse mihi Mauors "commendo moenia" dixit / "haec tibi. tu pollens urbe nepotis eris" ', 'Mars himself said to me, "I entrust these walls to you. You will be mighty in the city of your grandson" ' (6. 53 f.). Mars 'bribes' Juno as Vergil's Jupiter does (12. 838–40); if both scenes go back to Ennius' *concilium deorum*, Mars' words are very apt as spoken to mollify his mother when the city of Rome is on the point of being established: 'commendo moenia haec tibi...'.

[71] In favour of the city's name as a topic of debate in Ennius, I find only L. Mueller, *Q. Enni Carminum Reliquiae* (Petersburg, 1884), p. 178, and L. Valmaggi, *Q. Ennio. I Frammenti degli Annali* (Turin, 1947), pp. 18 f.

[72] 'Ilia' is the original name in the myth, where she was the daughter of Aeneas (see next note). 'R(h)ea Silvia' was invented after Ennius as part of the scheme that devised the Alban king lists: see Rosenberg, 'Rea Silvia', *RE* 2R. 1. 341–5, Bömer on Ov. *Fast.* 2. 383. As Bömer observes on the significance of the name 'Ilia', 'This version emphasizes Trojan origin, and particularly the descent from Aeneas.' This is the version to which Horace alludes, '*Troica* quem peperit sacerdos', 3. 3. 32.

[73] Cf. Serv. Auct. on *Aen.* 1. 273, 'Naeuius et Ennius Aeneae ex filia nepotem Romulum conditorem urbis tradunt'; cf. Serv. *Aen.* 6. 777, 'dicit ... Iliam fuisse filiam Aeneae'.

[74] Cf., e.g., Serv. *Aen.* 1. 5, 'Troiam autem dici, quam primum fecit Aeneas, et Liuius in primo (1. 1. 4) et Cato in Originibus testantur'. Extensive parallel passages, bibliography, and discussion in W. A. Schröder, *M. Porcius Cato: Das erste Buch der Origines. Ausgabe und Erklärung der Fragmente* (Meisenheim am Glan, 1971), pp. 95 ff. As Schröder says, 'Almost all ancient authors concur in calling the first Trojan settlement in Latium "Troy" ' (p. 96). Vergil twice calls Aeneas' first camp *Troia* (10. 214, 378). It must be stressed that there is no *direct* evidence that Ennius utilized this tradition. But the tradition is virtually unanimous in saying that the Trojans arrived at an area called the 'ager Laurens', and *there forthwith founded 'Troia'* (cf. passages listed in Schröder, pp. 95 f.; Paul. p. 504. 11 L; Liv. 1. 1. 4; D.H.*Ant.* 1. 53. 3; Appl *Reg.* fr. 1. 1; Dio fr. 4. 4). A line of Ennius gives the first half of this version: 'quos homines quondam Laurentis terra recepit' (34 V). I do not see it as unlikely that he gave the second.

that the new city of his grandsons *not* receive what might have seemed an obvious name?[75] Ennius was grappling with divergent and incompatible myths: it would not have been out of place for him to explain how the Trojans came and did not leave their name.[76] The question of the city's name was very important to Ennius. As Romulus and Remus take up their posts for the decisive contest in augury at the foundation of the city, the poet tells us: 'certabant urbem Romam Remoramue uocarent' (83 V). In the *concilium deorum* Jupiter had informed Mars that only one of his twin sons would gain immortality.[77] If Juno won her point about the city's not having 'Troy' for title, Jupiter may have told Mars that the city would be named after one of his sons: the winner would receive the prize of godhead.[78]

Hypotheses about 'what must have been in Ennius' become dear to their architects, but to few others. To return to Vergil's last book. The salient elements of his Ennian model which stand out more certainly are the insistence on the passing away of Troy, the limited or qualified nature of the goddess's acquiescence, and the mention of the deification of a god's son. If one has the Ennian archetype in mind, one sees why the dialogue between Jupiter and Juno *starts off* as if it is going to be a discussion on the apotheosis of Aeneas: 'quae iam finis erit, coniunx? quid denique restat? / indigetem Aenean scis ipsa et scire fateris / deberi caelo fatisque ad sidera tolli / quid struis? (793–6).[79] Juno's

---

[75] Cf. Waszink, op. cit. (n. 47), 325, who argues, on the basis of Lucil. fr. 31, that Neptune in Ennius may have objected to the foundation of a 'noua Troia'.

[76] Schröder, op. cit. (n. 74), pp. 102 ff., conveniently collects the various historical and poetic accounts of the name changes and adoptions involved in the Trojan immigrants' losing their proper title.

[77] Cf. Ov. *Fast.* 2. 485–8 (Mars is speaking): 'redde patri natum. quamuis interdicit alter, / pro se proque Remo, qui mihi restat, erit. / "unis erit, quem tu tolles in caerula caeli" / tu mihi dixisti: sint rata dicta Iouis', 'return the son to his father. Though one of the two has perished, the one which remains will serve for himself and for Remus. You said to me "there will be one whom you will raise to the blue expanses of heaven": let Jupiter's words be ratified.' Is there a contrast with Castor and Pollux, twins who were both deified?

[78] Here would be the explanation of Ennius' placing of the reconciliation of Juno *before* Romulus' death, rather than after it, as the strict example of Heracles required: cf. n. 66 above. I realize that in Horace Juno speaks only of Romulus as a candidate for immortality, but it is reasonable to allow ground for Horace's tact in recasting the story of how Augustus' model joined the gods. After all, by any reconstruction of the council, there must have been some mention of the embarrassing Remus, if we follow the evidence of Ovid that Jupiter spoke of both twins, promising immortality for only one of them ('unus erit quem tu tolles' ... etc.; '"unus" is clearly said in contradistinction to "ambo"', Skutsch, op. cit. (n. 63), p. 131). Horace is suppressing *some* talk of Remus: it is only a question of how much.

[79] Cf. N. W. De Witt, *CR* 34 (1920), 66, on the 'similarity of treatment' in *Aen.* 12 and Hor. *Carm.* 3. 3: 'Juno is reminded that Aeneas is to become a deity under the title

harping on the name of Troy may (more tentatively) be seen as an allusion to the words of the same goddess in *Ann.* 1. There she may have demanded that the city should not be called 'Troia' but, if needs be, 'Roma' or 'Remora'; in Vergil, one name crowds in upon another as she ends her speech, pleading that the new race should not be Trojans or Teucri—Latin, Alban, Roman, Italian, anything but Trojan:

> illud te ...
> pro Latio obtestor ...
> ne uetus indigenas nomen mutare Latinos
> neu Troas fieri iubeas Teucrosque uocari
> aut uocem mutare uiros aut uertere uestem.
> sit Latium, sint Albani per saecula reges,
> sit Romana potens Itala uirtute propago:
> occidit, occideritque sinas cum nomine Troia. (12. 819–28)

'cum nomine Troia ...' To Vergil and Horace the lapsing of Troy was a part of their poetic heritage, but one feels compelled to ask what charged the topic with such urgency for them. A tradition of this kind is simply available, and unrigorous: it is up to the inheritors to make something or nothing of it. Fraenkel contests the old idea that the poets are directly disparaging an actual political proposal, as reported in Suetonius, that the capital should be tranferred from Rome to Troy.[80] But Fraenkel is also representative of a reluctance to see anything of more moment in the words of Horace's Juno than 'a matter of ordinary feeling and therefore of poetry, with no political implication whatever'.[81] The implied opposition between poetry and significance is unnatural, while a directly political reference is not the only one which the poems' surfaces may yield.

It seems plain that in both Horace and Vergil Troy represents, at the least, degeneracy and moral shabbiness.[82] The historical setting for each

"Aeneas indiges", and to this she tacitly consents, just as she assented to the assumption of Romulus, but she again makes stipulations.' Cf. Commager, op. cit. (n. 47), p. 222. This is not to say that Aeneas was elevated to heaven in Ennius, a notion argued against by Skutsch, op. cit. (n. 63), p. 131.

[80] The Suetonius passage is *Iul.* 79. 3; see Fraenkel, op. cit. (n. 38), pp. 267 ff. Professor Nisbet suggests to me that the notion of a literal rebuilding of Ilium is perhaps too lightly rejected; there was no question of moving the capital, but the site was of high strategic value, especially for a Parthian campaign, and might have been built up as a base of the type Agrippa maintained in Lesbos. We must await the commentary.

[81] p. 269: cf. the works cited in Commager, op. cit. (n. 47), p. 222 n. 121. Oksala too is cautious about possible 'Allegorie', op. cit. (n. 43), p. 102.

[82] For Horace, note especially the first lines of Juno's speech (3. 3. 18–24). On the degeneracy of Troy in the *Aeneid*, see now Richard F. Thomas (taking the speech of

poet is a remote one, fixed at the time when the nation is being established; while many commentators are content to accept the possibility in Horace of an 'allegorical' reference to the present,[83] it is rare for the same approach to be applied to those portions of the *Aeneid* where Troy and Trojans are the subject. By its nature, the ode can stand in a more direct significative relation to the present than can the overtly 'historical' epic. Horace may generate and exploit a symbolic reference in 'Troy' within his small compass, loading it with the ills of the past and promising *bonus euentus* to the state if that inheritance is forsworn.[84] Vergil, on the other hand, is more tightly bound to his setting, and the significance of Troy is likely to be of a more aetiological character. Such is the approach of Thomas, who sees the dubious moral character and civilized corruption of the Trojans as being 'a flawed element which will be transmitted to the present, and realized in the moral degeneracy which is a part (and only a part) of modern Roman civilization'.[85]

It is important also to bear in mind that the Trojan past dwindles while the epic progresses, as Aeneas and his men escape from the dream of founding simply another Troy, in the manner of Helenus.[86] Especially, the final dialogue between Jupiter and Juno purports to jettison so much of the Trojan background that only their *corpora* are to contribute to the new race ('commixti corpore tantum / subsident Teucri', 835 f.). Alone, these promises are not powerful and unequivocal enough altogether to annul the effect of the earlier fears of Trojan contamination; the Trojans' *corpora* may be sufficient infection. yet Jupiter's words go some way towards dampening these fears, and it is possible that some hope of escape is to be read here. The 'Trojanness' of Rome is not inevitably effective, and may be outgrown.

This is difficult, and uncertain. At least what may be established is the fact that Vergil is using Troy in the same way as he had in the *Georgics* ('satis iam pridem sanguine nostro / Laomedonteae luimus periuria Troiae', 1. 501 f.), and in the same way as Horace had used the murder of Remus in *Epode* 7: the effect is to embody a radical anxiety about the

---

Numanus Remulus as his text, 9. 598–620): *Lands and Peoples in Roman Poetry: The Ethnographical Tradition* (Cambridge Philological Society, Suppl. vol. 7, Cambridge, 1982), pp. 98 ff.

[83] On various allegorical interpretations of Troy in the ode see Commager, op. cit. (n. 47), pp. 215 ff.

[84] Thus Commager, op. cit. (n. 47), pp. 216 ff. My approach owes a great deal to his discussion.

[85] Thomas, op. cit. (n. 82), p. 99.

[86] On this development, see the works cited in n. 20 above.

integrity of the state by pushing far back into the past the original springs of Roman corruption. What is different in the closing stages of the *Aeneid* is the hope expressed of the possibility of rehabilitation: this much is in common with Horace's third Roman ode. The passing of Troy, an 'historical fact' in Ennius, is susceptible to treatment, in the differing textures of ode and epic, as a possible release from 'the weight of all the evil elements in the past'.[87]

Anxiety about the validity of the state may be expressed, in the conventions of epic or lyric, as an apprehension concerning the goodwill of heaven, the divine sanction. This uncertainty is incorporated by the poets in the perennial and potent shape of Juno. As Warde Fowler says of her part in the *Aeneid*,

> this use of Juno ... was perhaps made easier and more natural because, as a goddess, she belonged rather to Rome's early enemies than to Rome herself. She was a familiar figure in many or most of the cities mentioned in the pageant [*Aen*. 7. 647–817]—on the Aventine, at Tibur Praeneste and Falerii, in southern Etruria (as Uni), and in Campania. But at Rome, strange to say, she had no great local name and fame in early times, and thus no feelings could be hurt if a Roman poet made her the deadly enemy of Rome.[88]

One of Juno's towns above all we must add to Warde Fowler's list— Carthage. The identification of Italian Juno with the chief goddess of the Carthaginians was no fiction of the poets.[89] The Pyrgi inscription appears to show the grouping as early as *c.* 500 BC.[90] Hannibal himself, in honouring Juno Lacinia, linked the goddesses togther,[91] as did the Roman goverment, by some mode of thought of other, when they strenuously honoured Juno during the war to which Hannibal gave his name:

> During the Second Punic War, the Juno Regina of the Aventine and the Juno of Lanuvium received numerous and important signs of devotion and respect [Liv. 21. 62. 8, 22. 1. 17], this betrayed the worry of the Romans, who felt that their

---

[87] Commager's phrase, op. cit. (n. 47), p. 221.

[88] Loc. cit. (n. 24). On this disparity between Juno's cult in Rome and the other local towns, see G. Wissowa, *Religion und Kultus der Römer*[2] (Munich, 1912), pp. 187 ff. She was, of course, part of the Capitoline triad from Etruscan times, but dramatically inferior to Jupiter in cult.

[89] On the identification, see n. 23 above.

[90] Cf. G. Dumézil, *La Religion romaine archaïque* (Paris, 1974), pp. 665–7.

[91] Liv. 28. 46. 16 (cf. Cic. *Div.* 1. 48); cf. Dumézil, p. 465; R. Bloch, p. 388 of 'Héra, Uni, Junon en Italie centrale', *Comptes Rendus de l'Académie des Inscriptions et Belles Lettres* (1972), 384–95; V. Basanoff, *Evocatio: Étude d'un rituel militaire romain* (Paris, 1947), pp. 63 ff.

Punic enemies were protected by a goddess eminently dangerous to Rome, just as Hera had been for Aeneas and his Trojans.[92]

From both an historical and literary point of view, the most significant supplication to Juno was that of 207.[93] Here was sung a *carmen* by Livius Andronicus, and it may have been this ceremony which Ennius selected as the occasion for the long-awaited final reconciliation of Juno.[94] Juno's position as Rome's most respected divine antagonist is reflected in the disproportionate number of *euocationes* which the tradition accords to her. Four cases of *euocatio* are reported, and in three of them Juno is the deity concerned.[95] One of these (at Carthage) is very problematical as an historical event,[96] and Ogilvie is certainly right to say that there 'were many other "euocationes" now unknown to us (Pliny, *N.H.* 28. 18), and the ratio of three Junos to one (Vertumnus) may be perfectly coincidental'.[97] What is probably not coincidental is the evidence, implied in the sample, that the *euocationes* involving Juno were the ones dwelt upon and retained.

Buchheit would trace the origin of Juno's role in Latin poetry back to Naevius.[98] However that may be, she embodies antipathy to Rome in Ennius, Vergil, Horace, Ovid, and Silius. Each of these poets shows her being reconciled, and on different occasions. 'Consistency is not necessary with these legends', observe Nisbet and Hubbard, remarking on the various dates.[99] The dates vary, but the paradigms of vindictiveness and conditional tolerance are remarkably consistent, a tribute to the power of the goddess. For poets writing even about their own times, it is natural to treat her as unmanageable and disquieting. In a major key, there is Horace's picture of Carthaginian Juno still active in the civil wars, avenging her people's defeats: 'Iuno et deorum quisquis amicior / Afris inulta cesserat inpotens / tellure, uictorum nepotes / rettulit inferias Iugurthae', 'Juno, and whichever of the gods is more friendly to

---

[92] Bloch, p. 394. What most Romans of this era knew about Aeneas and the Trojans is a controversy best left untouched here.

[93] Liv. 27. 37. 7; cf. Horsfall, Ch. 6 p. ooo above.

[94] As suggested by Steuart, op. cit. (n. 47), pp. 175 ff., and Buchheit, pp. 144 f., esp. n. 620. Other suggestions include a 'concilium deorum' after Cannae (Vahlen, p. clxxxix); a dialogue between Jupiter and Juno at the same date (Norden, op. cit. (n. 5), pp. 168 f.); a divine discussion upon Hannibal's appearance before the walls of Rome (on the basis of Sil. *Pun.* 12; G. Fürstenau, 'De Silii Italici imitatione quae fertur Enniana' (diss. Berlin, 1916), pp. 61, 63).

[95] At Veii, Falerii Veteres, Carthage (the fourth is Vertumnus at Volsinii); see Ogilvie, op. cit. (n. 52), p. 674.

[96] A comprehensive discussion by E. Rawson, in *JRS* 63 (1973), 168 ff.

[97] Loc. cit. (n. 95).   [98] pp. 54 ff.   [99] On 2. 1. 25.

Africans, had left in powerlessness that unavenged land, brought the victors' grandsons as funeral offerings to Jugurtha' (*Carm.* 2. 1. 25–8). In a minor key, there is Ovid's Juno in the *Fasti*, asserting her claim in queenly fashion to be the bestower of the name for the month of June (6. 21–64). Strife supervenes when her claim is contested by Iuventas (67–88), and even Concord's arrival fails of a resolution, as that goddess too joins in the bickering (91–6). The poet bows his way out, with a bland allusion to the issue of an earlier quarrel of Juno's: 'perierunt iudice formae / Pergama' (99 f.).

In the *Aeneid* Juno moves some considerable distance from her original stance of total opposition to Rome. At the end of the epic the forces represented by Juno nudge closer to those of Jupiter, and rest there for the while, in tension. One thinks perhaps of Plutarch's good and evil divine principles, which hold the universe in shifting balance;[100] the lines of Euripides which he quotes as his leitmotif[101] are in harmony with the poem's close:

> οὐκ ἂν γένοιτο χωρὶς ἐσθλὰ καὶ κακά,
> ἀλλ᾽ ἔστι τις σύγκρασις ὥστ᾽ ἔχειν καλῶς.

Good and evil may not occur together, but there is some kind of satisfactory mixture.

---

[100] *De Is. et Os.* 369A f.
[101] 369B (fr. 21 Nauck).

19

Aeneas and the Stoic Ideal

C. M. BOWRA

In an age like the present which is sceptical of untutored inspiration and sets a high value on style, it is not surprising that the *Aeneid* should have regained some of the prestige it held in the sixteenth and seventeenth centuries. The hostility which the nineteenth century felt for its deliberate and self-conscious progress has abated, and Virgil is again regarded as the poet of unfaltering taste in emotions as in words. But the reviving admiration for the *Aeneid* has no word of praise for Aeneas. He is either neglected or dismissed with a few disparaging sentences. Even so generous a critic as Professor Garrod calls him 'the wrong man in the wrong place', and the hero of the *Aeneid* seems relegated to that undistinguished limbo which contains so many heroes of great epics. It seems that he is no better and no worse than Tennyson's King Arthur or Milton's Jehovah or the indistinguishable heroes of the different books of *The Faerie Queene*. He is as lifeless as they are, and for the same reason. His appeal is not to the imagination, but to the conscience, and the conscience has changed its ideals and left him and them behind. Perhaps to the Romans he was a symbol of much inspiring morality, but he means nothing to us. So far as he has any personality, he is a prig and a bore.

Such seems to be the force of most modern views about him, and it is undeniable that it is hard to controvert them. It is quite true that Aeneas never appeals to us with the same thrill as Dido or Turnus or even Mezentius, that he is so burdened with morality that he loses his individual lineaments and becomes too often a mass of disparate ideals. Yet it is just this difference between him and the other characters of the *Aeneid* which makes him a fit study for enquiry. Virgil had considerable insight into human nature, and his lesser characters, whether in heaven or earth, are as alive as those in any epic not written by Homer. He was not a decorator like Tennyson nor an allegorist like Spenser. They could not or would not put human beings into their poetry. With Virgil it is different. He could, and often did, create living characters: so if he failed with Aeneas, it must have been because he was more deeply concerned with some end outside the delineation of character. What this end was, criticism claims to know, and it answers, 'Morality! Aeneas was the ideal Roman.' So then the perfect man was created and set in the discordant company of real persons that his superior excellence might be more apparent. If this was Virgil's aim, he failed. The good Aeneas is no longer good, and we find more real heroism in the murderous Mezentius. In other words what is really wrong with Aeneas is not that he is too good, but that he is not good enough. The exemplar of manly virtue is a coward, a muddler, and a seducer, who tries to justify his behaviour by attributing it to divine ordinance. Yet this view must prompt uneasy feelings in us. We cannot readily believe that weaknesses so apparent to us were invisible to Virgil's moral sensibility, and yet, if we hold such to be the truth, we must admit that, in creating his ideal Roman, Virgil showed an obtuseness of conscience such as we should not find among any of his more enlightened contemporaries. Surely Virgil cannot have thought Aeneas perfect. He was aiming at something else in creating him, and it is important to find out what this was. It is clear that he was not concerned merely with the creation of character. He was aiming at something which may well be moral, but it was not the cheap morality of a patently unsuccessful hero.

It is true indeed that orthodox Romans believed in Aeneas as an ideal man. Virgil's contemporaries and successors reiterated with wearisome devotion praises of Aeneas. Even to Horace he is 'pius Aeneas', and the long series of poets, on whom the magic of Virgil's style laid its paralysing influence, from Tibullus and Ovid to Statius and Juvenal and even to Sidonius Apollinaris, regarded Aeneas as the pattern of piety and courage. Seneca singles him out as an example of filial devotion,[1] and emperors like Pertinax found pride in claiming descent from him.[2] The *Aeneid* became a stock part of educational curriculum, and the pages of Donatus are full of dull panegyric of Aeneas' excellences in peace and war. To quote his example was to justify behaviour, and no doubt Diocletian felt some such sense of justification when in killing Aper he used the words which Aeneas spoke when he killed Lausus, 'Gloriare, Aper; Aeneae magni dextra cadis.'[3] Relics of his travels were shown. There was the altar at Eryx and the temple at Segesta which he had built, and Procopius saw, with much scepticism, his galley in the sixth century.[4] No doubt much of this hero-worship was meant not for the hero of the *Aeneid* but for the ancestor of the Roman race, and we

---

[1] *Ben.* 3. 37. 1.   [2] Herodian, 2. 3. 3.
[3] *Hist. Aug.* 30. 13. 3.   [4] 8. 22. 7.

must not attribute too much to Virgil's influence. But it is also beyond question that the *Aeneid* was so vital a part of Roman education that its character was accepted beyond cavil or criticism by the orthodox, and represented for four centuries an ideal which had long ceased to be a reality, if indeed it had ever been one. But all this hero-worship proves nothing about Virgil's intentions. One of the disadvantages of posthumous glory is an excess of uncritical admiration. When we quote what we consider the sublimest lines of *Paradise Lost*, we forget that often its author himself put them on the lips of the Prince of Darkness and would have felt nothing but disapprobation for their sentiments. So, too, where Roman posterity praised, Virgil may have meant to blame, and its generous admiration cannot be taken as evidence for the poet's own intimate intentions.

There is, moreover, in Roman literature a little trickle of hostility to Aeneas, of which traces have survived, and this shows that even in antiquity there were those who did not find it easy to accept him as the ideal man. No doubt this hostile criticism began with the *Aeneomastix* of Carvilius Pictor,[5] whose title shows it to have been the scourge not of the *Aeneid* but Aeneas. Unfortunately we know nothing of its contents, but in the conscientious pages of Donatus we find many answers to hostile criticisms of Aeneas, which must have been found in works like the *Aeneomastix*. Thus he was accused of having deserved the hostility of Juno, of having deserted, if not betrayed, his country of Troy, of sleeping when the attack was made, of not carrying the Penates himself, of losing Creusa, of not restoring Troy, and of deserting his comrades in Sicily. In the matter of the loss of Creusa even Donatus himself finds it hard to excuse him and says that he might have sat and waited for her or helped her if she was tired. There are traces, too, of criticism of his unfortunate settlement in Crete in defiance of Creusa's prophecy. Even the orthodox Macrobius blames him here,[6] saying that he had had ample and abundant warning. Much of these points seem trifling enough, but they are important because they show that criticism existed quite different from the deferential applause of the poets. The culmination of this criticism is to be found in the Christian fathers. One of the greatest obstacles the Church had to overcome was the influence of literature. It was the stronghold of pagan culture and morality, and the venom of the fathers was often expended in exposing or vilifying the ideals which it expressed. Tertullian sneers at Aeneas for escaping from Troy only to

[5] Suet. *Vit. Verg.* 44.   [6] *Comm.* 1. 7. 7.

fall into the arms of 'the Carthaginian woman'.[7] Augustine takes him as
typical of Stoic hardness of heart in his treatment of Dido;[8] Lactantius
bitterly compares his promises of goodwill and peace to the Latin
ambassadors with his actual behaviour after the death of Pallas, when he
takes prisoners for sacrifice and at the death of Turnus;[9] Tertullian is
even flippant and makes fun of the hero whose weapon is a stone—'what
a vulgar and dog-like weapon'.[10] In all this hostility we can notice the
stirrings of the Roman conscience against the deification of a hero
whose behaviour in some ways revolted them. In attacking his character
the fathers doubtless knew that they were appealing to moral convictions
which were deep in their hearers, even if overlaid by education. They
probably did not know that these convictions were largely shared by
Virgil himself.

When Augustine condemns Aeneas as a Stoic, he gives us a clue to
the solution. Aeneas is a Stoic, but like all Stoics he has to go through a
period of probation, and during this his temptations and difficulties are
often too much for him, and he fails. The Stoics, like the Christians,
believed that virtue was impossible without trial, and Virgil, adapting
himself to the current Stoicism of his age, set himself to describe the
development of such a man. He was not so bad an artist as to make him
triumph over all his temptations, nor so precise a Stoic as to confine
himself to the letter of the doctrine. But unquestionably in the first six
books the clue to Virgil's treatment of Aeneas is that he is using not only
the doctrine but in some cases the terminology of Stoicism. He takes his
hero through a course of tests and trials, which are the indispensable
condition of his moral development, and it is only after he has passed
through them and found in them his moral weaknesses that he is allowed
the vision of the destined glories of Rome.

The Stoics made a fourfold division of goodness, into justice,
moderation, courage, and wisdom. To these divisions they attached
highly specialized meanings, which we shall have to consider in turn.
Justice is the one compartment in which Aeneas never fails. His
relations with the gods, with his family, with his followers, indeed all that
Virgil meant by *pietas*, are beyond question, and all this is pointed out in
its due place by Donatus. But *pietas* was this and no more, and when
Virgil calls his hero 'pius Aeneas' he must not be thought to be crediting
him with virtues which plainly he does not possess. Especially we must
not confuse his *pietas* with courage, moderation, or wisdom. It was the

---

[7] *ad Nat.* 2. 9.   [8] *Civ. Dei*, 9. 4.
[9] *Inst.* 5. 10. 5.   [10] *ad Nat.* 2. 9.

indispensable preliminary to them, but they were not any of them identical with it or with a part of it. It is in these three qualities that Aeneas most conspicuously fails, and his failure must have aroused the condemnation of any perceptive and consistent Stoic of the Augustan Age.

The Stoics had a clear view of 'wisdom', or, as the Romans called it, *prudentia*. It was a practical quality, the knowledge of what end was desirable and of what means were necessary to attain that end. Cicero, both in his public and private utterances, leaves no doubt that so he understands the word. In his *De Officiis*[11] he defines it as 'the knowledge of what should be sought and of what should be avoided', and again as 'the knowledge of the occasion for suitable actions'.[12] In it Aeneas fails lamentably, and admits as much in his own account of the capture of Troy. He believes the tale of Sinon and helps to bring in the Wooden Horse, an action in which on his own admission he and his friends are *immemores caecique furore*.[13] In this he lacks that form of wisdom which Cicero, in Stoic language, describes as 'memory of the past and foresight for the future':[14] despite his long experience of Greek wiliness he allowed the Wooden Horse to be taken into Troy. To the same weakness must be ascribed his loss of Creusa. He knew that he wanted her to escape, but he failed to take the right precautions to see that she did. Even the faithful Donatus has to admit his fault here. In Book 3 he settles in Crete, and plague and disaster follow, all because he has not listened to Creusa's prophecy that he will settle in Italy. On all these occasions he was guilty of *imprudentia*. He knew what the end was, and did not take the right means to secure it. But the climax of his lack of wisdom is to be found in the Dido episode. In this the Stoics would probably not have blamed him, as the fathers blamed him, for being the victim of passion. The passion was nearly all on Dido's side, and the most Aeneas seems to have felt for her was a kindly sympathy. For him the business was only a love-affair. Such an affair was allowed to epic heroes: there were the precedents of Jason and Medea, of Odysseus and Calypso. So far as passion was concerned Dido was more to blame than Aeneas. She had abandoned her vow of faithfulness to her dead husband Sychaeus and violated the deep and ancient belief that a woman should only be married once. But Aeneas was much to blame too, if for a different reason. He had forgotten his duty, and it is with this forgetfulness that he is taxed by Mercury. The essence of the rebuke is

---

[11] 1. 153. [12] *Off.* 1. 142.
[13] *Aen.* 2. 244. [14] *de Sen.* 78.

the reference to his having forgotten his fated kingdom and his duty to
Ascanius. He was guilty this time of even a worse aberration. He was
guilty of *insipientia*; he had the wrong notion of what was right,
preferring to stay in Carthage when it was his duty to go to Italy.
His failure in moderation is equally noticeable and equally admitted.
The Stoic conception of moderation was simply control of the passions,
even of passions which are occasionally reputable like anger or more
generally approved like pity. In the good Stoic the passions were always
subordinated to the reason, and any failure so to subordinate them was a
failure in moderation. In other words, moderation meant self-control.
In the capture of Troy, Aeneas admits that more than once he acted
from fury and madness, from blind impulse instead of from deliberate
choice. When he took up his arms, 'arma amens capio'[15] he says of
himself, and a little later 'furor iraque mentem praecipitat'. His thought
is not of a battle which can lead to victory, but of a desperate struggle in
which consequences are not to be considered. In this mood of frantic
desperation he calls on his companions to rush into the battle and die,
and tells them that the only safety for the conquered is to hope for no
safety.[16] The climax of this unreasoning fury is reached when he finds
Helen and wishes to wreak vengeance on her. His own words would
condemn him before any tribunal of Roman moralists,

> exarsere ignes animo: subit ira cadentem
> ulcisci patriam et sceleratas sumere poenas. (*Aen.* 2. 575–6)

He was the victim of anger and a desire for vengeance. He had utterly
lost control of himself, and he was only saved by the appearance of his
divine mother. At the end of the same book, when he loses Creusa, his
'madness' (his own word again) is so great that he is not only wild but
blasphemous, and frantically accuses men and gods of her loss. No
reader of Virgil's description of the sack of Troy can fail to feel that
Aeneas' behaviour is typical of the wild carelessness which led to the
destruction of the city on that night of horror. A little more prudence
before, a little more concerted and deliberate action during the siege,
might have saved the city. Instead, we see him acting from passion, and
failing to do anything which might have stopped the disaster.

To accuse Aeneas of a failure in courage must at first sight seem
hazardous and unsubstantiated. He is not a coward in the ordinary sense
and the Romans regarded him always as a courageous and gallant
soldier. As such Homer had described him, and such he remains in the

[15] *Aen.* 2. 314.   [16] *Aen.* 2. 354.

Aeneid. But he lacks courage precisely as the Stoics defined it. Cicero as usual gives their definition of it. It is, he says, the business of a brave heart not to be disturbed in times of trouble and to be prepared for any emergency.[17] Aeneas did not mind danger, but he is often taken unawares and his lack of confidence in himself often obstructs his capacity for action. The Stoics, with their ideal of the omnicompetent man prepared for anything, would have found him futile in his behaviour after the storm in the first book. There, though he has had signs from heaven to help him, he is uncertain what to do and what his destiny is. He has even forgotten that he is destined to settle in Italy. He tries to hide his grief from his companions but in his own mind it recurs and keeps him worrying over the fate of his lost men, whom with characteristic defeatism he assumes to be dead. In this mood he meets his mother and tells her his tale of woe, and perhaps Virgil here too, as in the Helen episode, implicitly censures Aeneas' lack of confidence by making Venus interrupt his story and tell him not to worry any more. Yet even this does not finally cheer him, and it is only when he sees the sculptured scenes of the Trojan War in the new Carthage that he allows his attention to be diverted and begins to hope for better things. In this case his anxiety is rather of detail than of his ultimate destiny. It does not worry him whether he will achieve his destiny or not: he is concerned with the present difficulties which overwhelm him. But in Book 5 his confidence fails in a much more notable way. There in his despair over the burning of the ships he falters in his central and unquestioned purpose of going to Italy. Not even the comforting words of Nautes, the inspired interpreter of Pallas, can really help him, and it is only when the dead Anchises appears to him in sleep, commanding him to visit the Underworld and assuring him that Italy is his fated and final destination that he makes up his mind to sail.

It seems then that, judged by Stoic standards, Aeneas fails, but it might well be claimed that Virgil wrote for an audience larger than the circle of Stoic moralists in Rome, and that to the majority of his hearers or readers this doctrine was unknown and its implications unintelligible. But to claim this is both to over-emphasize the number of literary people in Rome and to under-estimate the influence of Augustus and his ideas. The Augustan circle had a certain set of ideas in common, and among these was a firm belief in Stoic morality, if not in Stoic physics, and their conviction of its value was strengthened by a happy identification of

---

[17] *Off.* 1. 80.

Stoic precepts with the precepts of Catonian Rome. To them at least Aeneas' failure by Stoic standards would have been as obvious as the moral failure of Lancelot was to the Victorians. The circle of Maecenas and Augustus was busy with thoughts for the regeneration of the Roman character, and found the solution in a popularization of the Stoic type. The ideal Roman must be self-controlled, he must know how to achieve his end, he must be prepared for any emergency. The type of *iustum et tenacem propositi virum* which Horace exalted in his laureate odes was this type: Aeneas in the first five books of the *Aeneid* was not. He was *pius*, he was brave in the old-fashioned way, but morally perfect he was not, and none of the Augustan circle can have thought him so. Nor can it be objected that Virgil did not know the thought or the language of Stoicism. In two significant and vital passages he uses its technical terminology to describe the moral testing of Aeneas by adversity and gives us the clue to his design. The first occasion is in Crete when Aeneas is in despair, having found plague and famine, and the second in Sicily when he has just seen four ships burned and has thought of abandoning his quest altogether. Both occasions show him at his least confident and least decided, and on both he is saved by Anchises, first in the flesh and later as a ghost in dream, who addresses him with the words: 'nate Iliacis exercite fatis' (3. 182, 5. 725). The word *exercite* is the clue. In Stoic language it meant 'tested', almost 'tested by ordeal'. In all Stoic writing we find this notion, and Seneca says expressly and emphatically: 'deus quos probat, quos amat, indurat, recognoscit, *exercet*'.[18] Whom the gods loved, they tested. They loved Aeneas, there was no question, and therefore they tested him. Without such testing virtue was impossible. Aeneas might be *pius* but he could not ever attain to the real heights of virtue, he could not, in Stoic language, become the wise man like Hercules, unless he learned to endure and to overcome adversity. This notion is essential to Stoic morality. It lies behind the teaching of Cicero with his belief in *exercitatio*, behind Seneca, and behind Marcus Aurelius, who said that 'The man who makes a right use of adversity becomes stronger and more praiseworthy.'[19] Such then is the plan of the earlier books of the *Aeneid*. In them Aeneas is severely tested, and often he fails. To the Stoics it was ultimately unimportant that in the course of his moral development he should fail. The past would count for nothing provided that in the end he found virtue. What mattered was his final disposition.

[18] *Dial.* 1. 4.   [19] *Meditations* 10. 33. 4.

When we compare the Aeneas of the later books with the Aeneas of the earlier, we see that the testing has largely been successful. In Book 6 he is a changed man. Confident of his destiny, he does not relapse again into his old weakness. He is never again assailed by doubt, and, though he is worried at the outbreak of war with the Latins, his worry is then not despair but anxious thought over the details of action. Once in Italy nothing gets between him and his goal but the hostility of circumstance. He is no longer his own worst enemy. The change comes suddenly at the beginning of Book 6 where Virgil marks it in a way that his audience could not miss. In his address to the Sibyl Aeneas says, 'omnia *praecepi* atque animo mecum ante peregi' (6. 105). Here again a technical Stoic word is used. The duty of the truly brave man was to foresee all emergencies and to be prepared for them. The word for this foreseeing was *praecipere*. Cicero uses it when he says that the duty of a great nature is to foresee what can happen, whether good or bad,[20] and Seneca quotes these very words spoken by Aeneas to illustrate his view of a good man, 'whatever happens, he says "I knew it" '.[21] The moment he arrives on Italian soil, the change has taken place in Aeneas. There are no more mistakes, no more panic. He is by Stoic notions both wise and brave. Once the prophecies begin to be accomplished, his confidence is assured, and the great vision of future Rome confirms with overwhelming evidence what he has already begun to take for granted.

So far then Virgil works out his hero's development on a consistent plan. So far as it provided a system for the testing and building of character, Stoicism was much to Virgil's taste and to the taste of his age. But there was in Stoicism, as any reader of Marcus Aurelius must have noticed, an almost inhuman detachment from some common and reputable characteristics. In particular it held the emotions in small esteem and indicated that they should be subordinated to the reason. So far as the less generous emotions were concerned, Virgil would, in theory at least, have agreed with this. But the Stoics were entirely consistent, and meted out the same treatment to anger and pity that they meted out to passion and cowardice. In this the Augustan adaptation of the Stoic ideal differed from the strict doctrine, and Virgil, following his own emotional nature, readily agreed. The correct Stoic view of anger is abundantly stated in ancient literature. They defined anger as the desire for revenge and found it horrible, because in anger deliberate and considered action was impossible. Seneca says that it is the result not of

---

[20] *Off.* 1. 80. [21] *Ep.* 76. 33.

goodness but of weakness, often frivolous or flippant, and that any good
it may do in the way of punishment or correction can be done better from
a sense of duty. Marcus Aurelius condemns it with majestic austerity: in
anger, he says, the soul wrongs itself: anger against wrongdoers is
senseless because they act unwillingly through ignorance of the right,
and it is not a proper function of man.[22] This severe and splendid view
was not to the taste of the Augustan circle. Augustus himself boasted
that he had revenged himself on the murderers of Julius, and where
there was revenge there was anger. So we find anger treated as a
legitimate passion by the poets and historians of Rome. Horace, when
he affects Stoic principles, adopts the Stoic view of anger, calling it a
brevis furor (Ep. 1. 2. 62), and perhaps that was his own personal view.
But in his more public and official utterances he gives a different
opinion. In the *Odes* he compares the Roman soldier to the lion driven by
anger through the middle of the slaughter (3. 2. 12), and he praises the
anger which is not afraid of the Norican sword (1. 16. 10). So, too, the
historians were not afraid of attributing anger to the gods, and Livy (9. 1)
sees the gods as angry over the breach of a treaty. Tacitus, who held in so
many ways to Augustan ideals of manhood and morality, noted that the
gods cared more for our punishment than for our peace of mind (*Hist.* 1.
3). This view of anger as a legitimate passion was part of the Augustan
ideal, and Virgil, perhaps against his own better judgement, included it
in his conception of the strong and capable Aeneas in the later books,
where it is the mainspring of his martial activity. It arises from the death
of Pallas and takes the form of a violent desire to punish Turnus, though
for a time it is exercised at the expense of opponents so inoffensive as
Magus, Tarquitus, and Lucagus. In the early stages of the war Aeneas
shows no passionate anger against Turnus for destroying his hopes of a
peaceful settlement. Even when he first sees his divine armour and
knows that he will punish Turnus, his emotion is comparatively free
from passion and he does not exceed the limits imposed by Stoic rules,
which allowed punishment to be justifiable if a sense of safety was
assured by the removal of the guilty.[23] But after the death of Pallas his
behaviour cannot be excused on these grounds. He is uncontrollably
angry with Turnus and clamours for his death in revenge. Nor is mere
revenge enough for him: his fury makes him unreasonably cruel to the
innocent. In the second half of Book 10 his desire for revenge leads him
into a passion of fury against all his opponents. When he first looks for

[22] *Meditations* 2. 16; 11. 18. 3; 11. 18. 10.   [23] Sen. *Clem.* 1. 22. 1.

Turnus, remembering the ties of hospitality which bind him to Evander and to the dead Pallas, he carves his way through slaughter and his cruelty increases as he tastes blood. He takes the four sons of Sulmo to be a human sacrifice at Pallas' funeral pyre, and not all the admiration of Donatus—'quanta Aeneae virtus ostenditur, quantum obsequium propter honorandam memoriam mortui'—can make us feel that he is acting coolly and deliberately. When Magus makes a pitiful appeal for mercy and ransom, Aeneas refuses with heartless irony, asserting that his death is due to the ghosts of Anchises and to the boy Iulus.[24] He throws Tarquitus to the fishes and denies him the recognized decencies of burial, crying derisively that his mother will not bury him nor lay his limbs to rest in his ancestral tomb.[25] When Lucagus appeals to him in the name of Anchises and a father's love for his son, Aeneas kills him without a qualm. He goes over the plain raging like a torrent or a whirlwind in his anger. Its fierceness drives him to pursue Lausus and take his life, and though it abates in the interval for burial, and he is full of peaceful sentiments in his reply to the Latin ambassadors, he does not omit to sacrifice prisoners at Pallas' funeral and, when the battle starts again, hatred and wrath drive him to kill Turnus. At the end, when Turnus lies helpless before him, the sight of the belt which Turnus had looted from Pallas inflames him again and he kills Turnus without quarter.

This continual display of anger as a martial quality was quite alien to Stoic principles, but it was not, as we have seen, alien to the Augustan adaptation of those principles to their own needs. In particular, it seems that in these angry scenes Virgil must have had Augustus himself in mind, not the statesman of the later years but the merciless avenger of Julius' death. After Philippi Augustus was said to have behaved much as Aeneas behaved after the death of Pallas. Both had deaths to avenge and both were merciless in exacting vengeance. Aeneas refuses burial to Tarquitus, telling him that he would be left to the birds and the fishes would lick his wounds. It was told of Augustus that in answer to a man who begged humbly for burial, he said that the birds would soon settle that question.[26] Aeneas is so angry that no appeal to the names of Anchises and Ascanius move him to spare Magus or Lucagus: it was told of Augustus that he made sons play 'mora' with their fathers to decide which should live, and then looked on while both died.[27] Aeneas sacrificed the sons of Sulmo at Pallas' pyre: Augustus was said to have

---

[24] *Aen.* 10. 522–35.   [25] *Aen.* 10. 550–6.
[26] Suet. *Vit. Aug.* 13.   [27] Ibid.   [28] Ibid. 15.

sacrificed three hundred prisoners of war after Perusia on the Ides of March at the altar of Julius.[28] In these remarkable parallels perhaps we find the clue to the anger which Virgil attributes to Aeneas. It must have been alien to his own gentle and senstive disposition, but he had to create a warrior, and in this one respect at least he modelled him on the one great general he knew. This involved indeed an inconsistency with his earlier treatment of Aeneas as a Stoic type, but this inconsistency was precisely one which all the writers of the Augustan Age had to admit when they brought down the good man of Stoic theory to the level of the Roman world. As with anger, so with pity the Augustans disagreed with the Stoics. The Stoics condemned it unconditionally, in the words of their founder, Zeno, as a disease of the soul. They considered it was due to the mistaken notion that a man's sufferings were really evils, and claimed that more could be done by a reasonable act of clemency than by the emotion of pity. With this view on the whole many of the Augustans agreed in theory, but they adapted it to suit their own purposes. When Augustus in the *Monumentum Ancyranum* claimed with pride that he has pardoned those of his enemies who could be safely pardoned, he would not be guilty of what Seneca calls 'the vice of a feeble mind which succumbs at the sight of the sufferings of others':[29] he is only exercising the princely virtue of clemency. But the Romans had other views than this and tended to accept the Peripatetic idea that pity was useful for giving assistance and helping others to endure calamity, and that liberality was impossible without it. We find traces of this view even in Cicero and no doubt it was in Horace's mind when he praises Augustus in the *Carmen Saeculare* for his gentleness to his enemies. Aeneas is much more prone to pity than ever Augustus was, and his pity is of an overwhelming kind. Yet it never really interferes with his action or his performance of his duty. There is no more moving passage in the *Aeneid* than that in which Aeneas stands over the dying Lausus and pities him, thinking of a father's love for his son.[30] There is also great beauty in the lines where he pities the unburied dead who are condemned to wander for a hundred years,[31] or where he sheds tears over the body of Pallas, whom death has prevented from driving back as a conqueror to his father.[32] Yet in none of these cases does his pity affect his action, and perhaps this was the compromise which the Augustans made between Stoic theory and their own practice. It was right to feel pity, no matter what the Stoics said, but it must not be allowed too free a rein in action.

[29] *Clem.* 2. 5. 1.
[30] *Aen.* 10. 823-4.
[31] *Aen.* 6. 332-3.
[32] *Aen.* 11. 42-4.

Such certainly was the view of Augustus, whose clemency was always controlled, and though Virgil was less cold-blooded than his patron, such seems to have been the measure which he allotted to Aeneas. These two divagations from the Stoic ideal, the one considerable, the other slight, were due ultimately to the martial traditions of Rome. Rome had always been an implacable enemy, but when occasion demanded she could be kind. The attempts to identify Romans such as Cato and Regulus with the wise man of Stoic philosophy had never really aimed at dismissing these traditional qualities of the Romans, and Virgil, when he kept them in Aeneas, was conforming to the standard ideas of his time. For the rest in these later books his Aeneas is a good man by Stoic standards. This is not only apparent in his perfected self-control outside battle and his careful anticipation of every emergency. It comes out markedly in his attitude towards the conduct of war. The Stoics laid down that war was only justifiable when peace was the desired end. This is precisely Aeneas' attitude towards it. Even after the events of the tenth book, in his speech to the Latin envoys he disclaims his desire for war and says that he would rather grant peace to the living than to the dead.[33] When the treaty is broken, his chief thought is how it can be resumed. He is not anxious that the war should become general and is still quite willing to settle the issue by a single combat with Turnus. He calls to the excited armies to restrain their fury and reminds them of their pledged obligations. Once the war is over, he presumably follows the dictates of Jupiter's decision and gave the conquered equal rights with the conquerors and liberty to keep their own language and customs. Where Aeneas keeps the rules of war, the Latins break them. Their actions are inspired by the fiend Allecto, the traditional companion of Tisiphone and the Virgilian counterpart to the Strife of Hesiod and the Lyssa of Euripides. Her interference is the result of Juno's boast that she will stir up Hell, and her infernal character is soon revealed. She likes wars and plots and harmful crimes: she arms brothers against brothers and ruins homes with hatred, and her most congenial task is to destroy peace and to bring contempt or ruin on friendship or promises. The motives of her victim, Turnus, are the antithesis of the Stoic ideal. He fights not for his country's wrongs nor even for her safety, but for his own glory. His is a case of that elation of mind described by Cicero (*Off.* 1. 19) which fights for its own advantage and is therefore a vice. His motive is at first mere desire for war—*amor*

---

[33] *Aen.* 11. 110–11.

ferri et scelerata insania belli[34]—and later this is reinforced by his feelings of injured pride at the loss of Lavinia and the taunts of Drances. His standards are those of the heroic, rather than of the Augustan Age, and, splendid as he is, he is still a barbarian. The climax of the Latins' guilt comes when they break the treaty in Book 12. Without qualification the Romans condemned any breach of a promise. Their horror comes out in their treatment of Carthage, whose destruction was justified as the proper punishment for its treachery. It was this feeling which prevented them from admiring Hannibal, whom Cicero expressly excepts from his list of the gallant enemies of Rome[35] and for whose dishonesty and perfidy Livy has hard words indeed.[36]

If then we examine Aeneas by the standards of his time he becomes a more interesting and consistent character, even if he fails to excite that interest which falls always to passionate, rather than to moral, characters in literature. But at least he is seen to be a symbol of a respectable code of thought, and not an incompetent and inconsequent mixture of conflicting notions. This was the sort of man that the age of Augustus admired, and they thought with some reason that it was only by trial and temptation that he could be produced. In this belief they have much subsequent moral theory on their side, and even from the literary standpoint Aeneas gains in appreciation, when we think of him not as a perfect character, but as a good man who is hardly tested and sometimes fails. The competent Aeneas of the later books may still revolt us when he is in his battle fury in a way that the noble barbarian, Achilles, never does. His savagery has a cold and unpleasant quality which suits ill with him, because he is nearer to us than Achilles, and we therefore expect more from him. This strain of savagery was deep in the Roman character and is perhaps a bar to our final understanding of it. To later Romans, as to the men of the Renaissance, it was a princely quality expected in a great fighter, and it is hard to see how Virgil in writing an epic of war and conquest could have dispensed with it altogether. We find it in the most peerless knights of the Elizabethan Age, even in the sensitive soul of Spenser, who urged a callous policy of extermination for Irish rebels. And yet their brutality is not quite the same as that of Aeneas. His seems more at discordance with his pitying and philosophic character than ever theirs can. It is a trifle too unexpected, and perhaps too successful, in a man who expects so little of life. And here no doubt Virgil himself is to blame. His gentleness was never at home with the

---

[34] *Aen.* 7. 461.   [35] *Off.* 1. 38.   [36] 21. 4. 9.

martial qualities. We cannot question that he had an honest admiration for the character and performances of Augustus, and that he tried to give a hint of them in his character of Aeneas. His mind acquiesced in the necessity of the Augustan régime, but his imagination was never fully touched by it. He has none of Ennius' sense of the glory of marching armies and the qualities by which battles are won. He tried to have it, he studied his models studiously, and he produced what his time considered, what he himself often considered, the type of warrior prince in Aeneas. He could write well about Italy and Rome and he had a great sense of Roman rule in the world, but somehow his fancy never quite warmed to the task, and Aeneas, consistent and honest creation as he is, never in his martial moments strikes us to heroic transports.

Perhaps this was just a failure in the end, and there is no more to be said about it. Or perhaps the poet in Virgil knew what he was doing, and by making us feel some qualms about Aeneas he gave us his own inmost feelings about this heroic type. It is remarkable that it is always the enemies of Rome with whom he makes us sympathize. We can weep, as Augustine did, for Dido, and feel a deep sympathy for the soul of Turnus when it flies complaining beneath the shades. And no doubt, wherever his head was, Virgil's heart was with them. He saw perhaps the necessity for Roman domination and saw too that it was qualities like those of Aeneas which made it possible. The uniform Roman world had no place for the high confidence of Turnus or the absorbing passion of Dido. They had to go. Only at such a price was the empire of Augustus possible. Virgil with his reason saw this, but he was sorry that the price had to be paid and in his verse he paid a last tribute to the passing of such greatness from the earth.

20

Aeneas Imperator: Roman Generalship in an Epic Context

R. G. M. NISBET

Aeneas is a man of many facets. He is a second Ulysses, *immersabilis* if not *versutus*, with intermittent hints of Achilles, Hercules, and other heroes. He is a Stoic exemplar, willingly obedient to the fates, and painfully growing in authority on his pilgrimage. He is a proto-Augustus, carrying the destiny of his nation on his shoulders, and prefiguring the political ideology of Virgil's own patrons. In this paper I shall consider him as he undertakes one of the most important functions of Roman government, republican or imperial, the command of an army. The *Aeneid* is like a great novel of war and politics, and the poet can help the historian not so much by describing institutions as by making attitudes come alive. As the relevant material is scattered, I shall proceed book by book in the chronological order of the events described, that is to say beginning with Book 2.

At the fall of Troy Virgil must establish three things about Aeneas. In the first place it must be made clear that the disaster was not his fault. In Homer he appears as a prudent soldier and a wise statesman,[1] apparently second in esteem only to Hector himself, and after Hector's death his position in the hierarchy ought to have been improved. But in Virgil he is consulted neither on the horse nor the serpents, when the enemy attacks he does not know what is happening, and Panthus has to tell him that the war is lost (324 ff.). There was a very literal lack of *vigilantia*, one of the suspicious Romans' most prized virtues, but though Aeneas uses first person plurals to describe what the Trojans did, he does not seem to admit any individual responsibility. There is an implicit moral on the dangers of oligarchy and plutocracy, where a leaderless nation listens to uninformed voices, and nobody is in overall charge. Such a lesson would seem a natural one in Augustan Rome, and

---

[1] G. K. Galinsky, *Aeneas, Sicily, and Rome* (Princeton, 1969), pp. 20 ff., 36 ff.; N. Horsfall, *CQ* 29 (1979), 372 f.

it is worth remembering that in Horace's third Roman Ode, Troy has been thought to suggest the fallen Republic.

Secondly, Virgil must emphasize Aeneas' courage. It could be held against him that he had survived his city, and Turnus touched a sore point when he called him *desertorem Asiae* (12. 15). That is why Virgil makes him organize resistance, though only at a local and subordinate level: he takes up arms without regard for consequences (314 'arma amens capio, nec sat rationis in armis'), if he had been fated to fall he deserved it by his actions (433 f. 'si fata fuissent ut caderem meruisse manu'), he emphasizes several times his own *furor* or loss of control (316, 588, 595). He even takes a leaf out of his enemies' book and stoops to disguise (390 'dolus an virtus quis in hoste requirat?'), but it is made clear by what happens that such subterfuges did no good in the long run: like other successful imperialists the Romans were under the illusion that they themselves fought according to the rules (Liv. 1. 53. 4 *minime arte Romana, fraude ac dolo*). The climax comes in the disputed passage where he considers killing Helen at the altar, a scene that is Virgilian[2] not only in style but in imaginative power and psychological appropriateness (extending beyond the immediate context to the epic as a whole). There is a conflict here between the passionate and the reasoning parts of the soul, and it suits the Augustan ideal that rationality prevails.

Thirdly, Virgil must confirm the legitimacy of Aeneas' *imperium*; he cannot like de Gaulle appoint himself. In the *Iliad* Achilles had taunted Aeneas with wishing to succeed Priam, an ambition that seemed absurd as long as the king was in good health and had living sons (20. 180 ff.). Now the changed situation must be formally recognized. Aeneas is entrusted with the Penates by Hector's ghost (293 ff.), and they are brought by Panthus to the house of Anchises (320 f.), who carries them from the fallen city (717). The party does not leave without explicit instructions from Venus Genetrix (619 f.). Above all, when the flame plays round the head of Iulus (682 ff.), the spontaneous phenomenon provides an excellent instance of *auspicia oblativa*, and when Anchises with Roman prudence insists on a double-check, they are promptly converted by celestial phenomena into *auspicia impetrativa*.[3] All this

---

[2] R. G. Austin, *CQ* 11 (1961), 185 ff.; otherwise G. P. Goold, *HSCPh* 74 (1970), 101 f. (repr. in this collection, Ch. 5 above), C. E. Murgia, *CSCA* 4 (1971), 203 ff. Opponents of authenticity may stress too much the difficulties of the transmission; the lines are far too good to have been written later than the first century AD, and though we cannot show how they survived, any view of their authorship presents some problems.

[3] C. Bailey, *Religion in Virgil* (Oxford, 1935), pp. 19 ff.

corresponds to the taking of the omens when a Republican general sets out to war.

At this point we are faced by a constitutional puzzle: who has *imperium maius*? The taking of the omens by Anchises might suggest that the expedition was begun under his own *ductu auspiciisque*, but such a conclusion is belied by his words 'nec, nate, tibi comes ire recuso' (2. 704), as well as by the traditional form of the legend. Aeneas reports prodigies to his father (3. 58 f., 179), as M. Caedicius did to the magistrates in Livy (5. 32. 6, cf. 2. 36. 7), but Anchises may be acting rather as a priest; by the Roman system religious authority was vested in suitable statesmen (cf. Laocoon and Panthus), who interpreted the divine will more sensibly than whole-time professionals like Calchas or Tolumnius (12. 258 ff.). Anchises is supported by *delecti proceres* (58) not a council of war on the Homeric model (it is only the Latins who give scope to a politician like Drances), but an advisory *consilium*; as the institution was found in many spheres of Roman life, the old man may be represented as *pontifex maximus* rather than *imperator*. Apart from his interpretation of religious phenomena, Anchises determines the successive stages on the journey;[4] Aeneas is thus absolved from responsibility for the wanderings, and in particular for the abortive settlement in Crete (100 f.). On the other hand, it is Aeneas who organizes the details of administration (137 'iura domosque dabam') and commands in the battle against the Harpies (234 ff.), from which his father is excluded by age and infirmity. The allocation of *provinciae* between father and son corresponds to nothing in historical Roman practice; elderly rulers presented no problem under the Republic, when middle-aged consuls were annually replaced, and in the Principate the issue first becomes important with the declining years of Tiberius. Rather the situation reflects a vision of primitive society: Anchises occupies a position somewhere between Laertes,[5] who seems to have abdicated, and Priam, who remains in nominal control even though Hector commands in battle. With the death of Anchises at the end of the third book (709 ff.) the anomaly is removed, and Aeneas assumes the undivided authority that *pietas* had kept him from usurping.

When we first meet Aeneas off Carthage, he is shivering in the storm (1. 92 'extemplo Aeneae solvuntur frigore membra'). His sufferings are modelled on those of Odysseus (Hom. *Od.* 5. 297, 5. 472) but such

---

[4] R. B. Lloyd, *TAPhA* 88 (1957), 44 ff.
[5] M. I. Finley, *The World of Odysseus*, 2nd edn. (London, 1977), pp. 86 f.

weakness is much more conspicuous[6] at the beginnning of the epic. Conventional panegyrics of generals emphasized their endurance as much as their courage,[7] and particularly their indifference to the elements, but Virgil is more interested in the Aristotelian distinction between fortitude and insensibility (*Eth. Nic.* 1115^b 24 ff.). Augustus himself was surprisingly susceptible to cold, and wore four tunics in the winter (Suet. *Aug.* 81-2), and though the poet is unlikely to have intended so specific a reference, he would at least have been aware that the great man's dominance was more psychological than physical.

The storm is stilled by Neptune with a calm but firm exercise of authority (1. 132 ff.), that symbolically suggests Roman *imperium*. The drill of the Trojans on landing is more systematic than anything in Homer: the lighting of fire and baking of bread (174 ff.) follow the prosaic priorities of the Roman army (cf. 6. 8 for *aquatio*), even if the stag-hunt and roast venison belong to traditional epic. The allocution of Aeneas to his men, though formally modelled on Homeric rodomontade (199 *o passi graviora*, cf. *Od.* 12. 208 ff.) shows a topical awareness of the anxieties of leadership (209 'spem vultu simulat, premit altum corde dolorem'). After a typically restless night (305), the cautious commander sends out *speculatores* (more professional than the 'looking in all directions' at *Od.* 10. 146), and camouflages his fleet under a wooded cliff (310 ff.). In spite of all the Odyssean disappearing-tricks, the meeting with Dido is conducted with realistic circumspection, and Aeneas stays in the background like a Roman *imperator* till he sees how his legate gets on. There follows top-level diplomacy of the sort that a distinguished personality still could influence in the ancient world: the negotiation is supported by appeals to traditional ties (619 ff.), military and political alliance is treated in terms of private *amicitia* (whose moral component can too easily be underestimated[8]), and though mutual advantage is implicit in the understanding (548 ff., cf. 563 f.), the emphasis is placed on magnanimity and obligation. The spontaneous gifts that conclude the conversations have more binding force than the interchanges at modern State Visits; the Homeric pattern[9] would still be valid with foreign potentates, as it surely was in the world of Lawrence of Arabia.

---

[6] Serv. Auct. ad loc. 'reprehenditur sane hoc loco Vergilius...' Virgil is defended by A.J. Gossage, *Phoenix* 17 (1963), 131 ff.

[7] Xen. *Hell.* 5. 1. 15, Sall. *Cat.* 5. 3, Liv. 21. 4. 6, K.J. Dover, *Greek Popular Morality* (Oxford, 1974), p. 163.

[8] P.A. Brunt, *PCPhS* 11 (1965), 1 ff.

[9] Finley, op. cit. 120 ff.

But *amicitia* ought not to have included emotional entanglements; the hint of Cleopatra is unavoidable in a poem written in the decade after her death. Antony might claim precedent in Alexander, who had to deal with the queens of the East, but a Roman *imperator* should have been less cosmopolitan. When the gods give Aeneas new sailing-directions, the *foedus* by which he bound others is superseded for himself; Virgil writes without cynicism, but he has the imaginative sympathy to see how Roman *fides* must have looked to the losers (4. 376 ff.), as to the Samnites after the Caudine Forks. A realistic general knew how to cut his losses (as is shown in Book 3), even if it meant a voyage in winter (4. 313), and the evacuation is planned with the two essentials of secrecy and speed. When Dido looks down from her acropolis she sees no longer productive bees (1. 430 ff.) but ants on the move:

> it nigrum campis agmen praedamque per herbas
> convectant calle angusto; pars grandia trudunt
> obnixae frumenta umeris, pars agmina cogunt
> castigantque moras, opere omnis semita fervet. (4. 404 ff.)

There could be no better description of the legalized destructiveness of the Roman army with its requisitioning of corn (*frumentum imperatum*), organized supply-columns, and discipline on the march; when a centurion said 'go', you went.

The celebrations in Book 5 suggest national Roman *ludi* rather than regimental sports, but though Aeneas presides from a mount of turf (290) with the affability of a civilian Princeps, military lessons are implicit. The boat-race teaches that opportunities should be seized without running unreasonable risks; these were the methods of Pompey and Augustus (rather than of an *aleator* like Julius Caesar), and it is significant that the reckless Sergestus is the ancestor of the Sergii (121), that is to say of Catiline. The boyish loyalties of Nisus and Euryalus foreshadow their tragic sortie in story-book manner (even if their notion of playing the game was different from Sir Henry Newbolt's); the moral education of the young in ideals appropriate to a military society must have seemed a natural function of the new epic. In the same way the boxing-match idealizes the controlled courage of experience as opposed to the mindless brutality of the prize-fighter: 'vis consili expers mole ruit sua' (Hor. *Carm.* 3. 4. 65). The flame that ends the archery contest teaches the validity of omens (as well as suggesting Caesar's Comet), while the *lusus Troiae* describes the equestrian exercises of Virgil's own day.

The military lessons of the games are brought out in practice at the burning of the boats. Ascanius shows his initiative and discipline by quelling the riot and summoning assistance, where a less responsible officer would have attempted too little or too much; with an aristocratic belief in heredity the Roman governing class gave its favoured young men rapid promotion, and the first signs of leadership must have been eagerly welcomed, as in the case of Marcellus. Aeneas' actions in turn show *pietas* and *consilium*, both desirable qualities in a Roman commander. After a prayer to Jupiter, which is providentially heard (cf. 235 ff. in the boat-race), he listens to the experienced Nautes (709 ff.); a good *imperator* founded cities as well as destroying them, and those who did not wish to sail further were left behind without recriminations (contrast the Phocaeans at Herodotus 1. 165. 3). This readiness to cut knots and not batter heads against brick walls illustrates the sense of the possible that made the Roman empire last longer than some others.

The fifth book must have suggested Roman campaiging in another way; anybody who had read about the first Punic War and experienced the campaigns against Sextus Pompeius would have been moved in Sicilian waters to patriotic 'home-thoughts from the sea'. When Aeneas in the storm accepts the advice of Palinurus (26 ff.), we may recognize the respect for the expert that Octavian must have shown in his naval wars. It seems significant that both the serene regatta and the sinister burning of the boats (which was assigned to various places by the tradition) are set by Virgil at Drepanum (Trapani), the scene of a famous naval disaster in the First Punic War (Polyb. 1. 49–51); the Roman commander had thrown the sacred chickens into the sea ('if they will not eat, let them drink'), and his ill-fated impiety[10] is implicitly contrasted with the faith and hope of Virgil's heroes. When Aeneas sacrifices a lamb to the Tempestates (772), we may compare Octavian's dedications from the same period (App. *Civ.* 5. 98. 406, *ILS* 3279 'Ara Ventorum'); for a topical parody of the rite cf. Hor. *Epod.* 10. 23 f., where a goat is promised to the Storm-Winds for the drowning of Mevius. When Palinurus is washed ashore on the Lucanian coast, Virgil is likely to have remembered the setback of 36 BC, when many of Octavian's men, including perhaps Maecenas and Horace, met a similar experience in the same area.[11] And when a pyre is built for Misenus (6. 179 ff.), who

---

[10] Pease on Cic. *Nat.* 2. 7, T. P. Wiseman, *Clio's Cosmetics* (Leicester, 1979), pp. 90 f., 110 f. The battle is mentioned by F. Della Corte, *La Mappa dell' Eneide* (Florence, 1972), pp. 96 f., but he sees a moral simply in the need for fast ships.

[11] Vell. 2. 79. 3, App. *Civ.* 5. 98. 410, Dio 49. 1. 3, E. Wistrand, *Horace's Ninth Epode* (1958), pp. 16 f. = *Opera Selecta* (1972), 304 f.

gave his name to Rome's naval base, Aeneas' timber-felling (more mechanized than in Homer or Ennius) suggests the deforestation (Strab. 5. 4. 5.), familiar to Virgil in Naples, at the construction of the Portus Iulus.

The Aeneas of the sixth book must make his *katabasis* alone, but in the second half of the epic he resumes his position as an *imperator*. The invasion comes ashore not at the traditional landing-place *in agrum Laurentinum* (Liv. 1. 1. 7), but farther north at the mouth of the Tiber; Virgil is not trying to protect Aeneas' left flank, but rather to associate him with the Roman river. A settlement is fortified with *agger* and *fossa* on the formidable lines of a Roman camp (159);[12] an allusion to the Ostian *castrum* has been suspected but is difficult to prove. Legates are despatched to King Latinus with a blend of bluff and appeasement (as was wise in the Trojans' plight). Odysseus may boast 'I captured the city and killed the men' (*Od.* 9. 40), but like a good Roman *imperator* Aeneas conserves his outnumbered forces and tries to use *socii* on the spot.[13] With an instinct for the workings of Roman conquest Virgil envisages an immediate *foedus* that would include the all-important right of *conubium* (as shown by the betrothal of Aeneas and Lavinia), and lead to an ultimate merging of political and religious institutions.

The Trojans showed a Roman assurance in the sanctity of their *foedus*, but not surprisingly it proved acceptable only to a section of the Latins. Historians know that wars originate from deep-seated causes and trivial occasions, and so it was with the shooting of Silvia's stag. Allecto plays on natural resentments with the fiendish insight of a political manipulator, and the crisis escalates[14] in clearly defined stages to a general mobilization. Aeneas can do nothing for most of the book: though in all but a technical sense he is the aggressor, as the historical tradition recognized (Liv. 1. 1. 5., Dion. Hal. *Rom. Ant.* 1. 57. 1, 1. 58. 1), Roman legalism about the *iustum bellum*[15] required that his posture should be defensive.

In Book 8 the two sides seek to extend their network of alliances (a side of warfare more emphasized in Livy than in Homer). The Latins send a mission to Diomede in Apulia (9 ff.) with a realistic appeal to self-interest (note the historian's *oratio obliqua* at 15 ff.); Aeneas, after

---

[12] J. Carcopino, *Virgile et les origines d'Ostie*, 2nd edn. (Paris, 1968), pp. 358 ff.

[13] E. N. Luttwak, *The Grand Strategy of the Roman Empire* (1979), pp. 30 ff.

[14] E. Fraenkel, *JRS* 35 (1945), 4 ff. = *Kleine Beiträge zur klassischen Philologie* 2 (Rome, 1964), 151 ff. (reprinted in this collection, Ch. 13).

[15] W. V. Harris, *War and Imperialism in Republican Rome* (Oxford, 1979), pp. 166 ff.

agonizing in the night, sees that he can do more by diplomacy than fighting (18 ff.), and resolves to negotiate with Evander in person. His voyage up the Tiber shows Virgil's imaginative awareness of how to penetrate a forested interior. The conversations at the site of Rome begin as usual with expressions of respect and claims to shared antecedents (134 ff., 157 ff.); with a disdain for explicit bargaining characteristic of gentlemanly societies (think of Augustan poets and their patrons), Aeneas suggests the common danger, mentioning his own contribution only as an afterthought (150 f. 'sunt nobis fortia bello pectora'). The next day Evander points out the advantages of an alliance with the anti-Mezentian faction at Agylla (the Caere that was to be so important in the Latin Wars); such interference in the stasis of neighbours was characteristic of Rome as of more recent imperialisms (cf. the Parthian rebellion of 26), but justification is naturally found in the misgovernment of Mezentius. Evander proves his *fides* by sending his son Pallas, and the party ride in splendour from the North Gate like a Roman commander and his *comites* setting out to war: 'stant pavidae in muris matres oculisque sequuntur pulveream nubem et fulgentis aere catervas' (592 f.).

The removal of Aeneas from the battlefield produces a critical change in the balance of forces (9. 6 ff.) without impugning the martial or other virtues of the hero: Achilles had sulked in his tent out of personal pique, but for a responsible and rational leader diplomacy was an indivisible element of war. Ascanius is left in charge, though Aletes plays the experienced *legatus* (246); the arrangement (derided by Juno at 10. 70) suggests in exaggerated form the aspirations of Marcellus, whose role may have been extended during Augustus' illnesses (he would have been preferred by Maecenas to Agrippa). When the attack comes, the Trojans retreat to their base (9. 38 ff.) as Aeneas had instructed, secure in the knowledge that his commands would be obeyed; the Roman army was to prosper by a combination of threatening attitudes and defensive tactics,[16] which were resolutely maintained in spite of provocation (54 ff.) till the moment for counter-attack. The lesson could be learned from a contemporary prose work, the Hannibalic books of Livy, as well as from Augustus' own policies.

In the middle of the crisis Nisus and Euryalus try to summon help from Aeneas (192 ff.) by breaking out on the unexpected seaward side (238). Unauthorized combat in the Nelson manner played no part in

---

[16] Luttwak, op. cit. 1 ff.

Roman heroics, as the story of Torquatus shows (Liv. 8. 7), so they correctly ask permission from Ascanius. Nisus is mature enough to understand that inner promptings may be delusive (185 'an sua cuique deus fit dira cupido?'), but he is diverted from his mission by a wish for the more obvious forms of military glory. Euryalus, who has been set to guard the rear, is brought down by his own battle-lust (354 *cupidine ferri*) and greed for loot (384), and Nisus is also killed in a futile attempt to save him. In the circumstances anything but eulogy would be ungracious, but like a good novelist, Virgil does not always make his moral explicit;[17] older heads would have seen that though magnificent, the escapade was not war.[18] Aeneas is as far away as ever (10. 25 *Aeneas ignarus abest*), and when the light flashes on Euryalus' captured helmet (373 f.), he is betrayed by the childish love of prizes that the pair has already shown in the foot-race (5. 343 ff.).

After the success of his diplomatic initiatives, Aeneas returns in the tenth book to the rescue of the Trojan encampment. The enchanted Odyssean atmosphere is piquantly combined with more realistic elements: the newly acquired *socii* provide the cavalry and the fleet (as was inevitable in Rome's foreign wars), the combined military and naval operations foreshadow the sort of thing that happened at Actium, the Etruscan order of battle (included against the tradition perhaps in deference to Maecenas) is a proper reminder of Etruria's part in the development of Roman power. Turnus naturally tries to repel the invasion before it gets ashore (277 *litora praecipere et venientis pellere terra*); ships smash on sandbanks and soldiers slither down poles. But the dispositions of Aeneas' D-Day are far from obvious. If the Trojan settlement stretched to the Tiber, why was the disembarkation made on the open beaches against an opposing army? On the other hand, if the Trojan landing-place was not included in the main fortifications, that goes against the principles both of Homeric and Roman warfare. There is also some obscurity about the movements of Evander's cavalry, which is fighting on foot near the Tiber's mouth (10. 362 ff.) and cut off between the settlement and the sea (378 *pelagus Troiamne petemus?*). But we should not read the *Aeneid* any more than the *Iliad* for precise topographical detail; Virgil would be less zealous in exploring the Campagna than some of his interpreters.

The interest of the book is not strategic but psychological, and centres

[17] K. Quinn, *Virgil's Aeneid* (London, 1968), 339 f.

[18] G. E. Duckworth, *AJPh* 88 (1967), 129 ff. On the other hand, P. G. Lennox defends Nisus, though not Euryalus (*Hermes* 105 (1977), 331 ff.).

round Aeneas' response to the death of Pallas. To understand his agony we must remember the sacred responsibilities of *contubernium*, by which a general took a young man under his wing;[19] *haec mea magna fides?* says Aeneas (11. 55) and though his self-reproaches are less justified than those of Achilles over Patroclus they make him lash out in the same way. When he promises human sacrifices to Pallas (10. 517 ff., 11. 81 f.), there is an obvious parallel to the destructive deeds devised by Achilles (*Il.* 21. 27 ff., 23. 175 ff.), and in a Roman context the idea is a particular abomination (*RE* 15. 955).[20] Though it is true that the slaughter of prisoners was permitted in ancient warfare,[21] Aeneas kills suppliants with barbaric insults (10. 560, 592 ff.) that remind us again of Achilles in his rage. The same blind fury is directed against Lausus, though Virgil goes out of his way to emphasize that *pietas* operated on both sides (cf. 10. 822 *Anchisiades*, 824, 826). Some scholars invoke the conventions of heroic and Roman war to suggest that our distaste is a modern anachronism, but this view goes against the whole tenor of the poem, ignores philosophical disquisitions on *ira* and political panegyrics of clemency, and is more objectively refuted by the Homeric parallels. Virgil would read the *Iliad* in a moralizing spirit, which in spite of its unhistorical formulations has more essential truth than is sometimes supposed. Whatever the original form of the saga, in the epic as we have it the wrath of Achilles extended from his feud with Agamemnon to his revenge on Hector, until he redeems himself by receiving Priam at the end of the poem.

In the eleventh book Aeneas shows a more Roman fortitude at the fate of Pallas (which seems to reflect the death of Marcellus in 23), and does not allow his emotions to interfere with his responsibilities. He gives commands to his army with the menacing understatement of a successful soldier (17 'nunc iter ad regem nobis murosque Latinos'); in the manner of the later Roman army, which avoided unconsidered offensives, he aims at careful material and psychological preparation (18

---

[19] Cic. *Sull.* 34, *Planc.* 27, *Cael.* 73, *Brut.* 105, Serv. *Aen.* 5. 546 '(custodem) secundum Tullium qui dicit ad militiam euntibus dari solitos esse custodes, a quibus primo anno regantur; unde ait de Pallante [8. 515] *sub te tolerare magistro militiam et grave Martis opus*' ('(guardian) following Cicero who says that those who go on military service are usually given guardians, by whom they are to be ruled in their first year; thus he says of Pallas . . .').

[20] There can hardly be a conscious reference to Octavian's massacre at Perusia (Sen. *Clem.* 1. 11. 1 *Perusinas aras*, Suet. *Aug.* 15, Dio 48. 14. 4); *mactare* is a natural metaphor in Roman political invective, and though something very ugly happened, a solemn sacrifice of three hundred senators and *equites* is not to be believed (R. Syme, *The Roman Revolution* (Oxford, 1939), p. 212).

[21] Harris, op. cit. 50 ff.

'arma parate, animis et spe praesumite bellum'). When the Latins ask
for recovery of their dead, he receives them with brief but conciliatory
words (113 'nec bellum cum gente gero') that are carefully designed to
detach them from Turnus (in which they have their effect); unlike
modern ideologists the more rational ancient imperialists knew that the
aim of war is peace (Ar. *Eth. Nic.* 1177^{b} 5 f.), that is to say an
advantageous political settlement. Having thus asserted his dominance,
Aeneas marches while the enemy is still in disarray (446). While his
cavalry fights Camilla in the plain, he makes a sudden swoop through the
hills (what hills?); the manœuvre is unconvincing, as the Romans
captured cities *sedendo* rather than by surprise thrusts. Turnus lies in
wait in a defile, the usual terrain in Livy for Roman disasters, but in his
madness abandons the ambush even before he hears of Camilla's
defeat. The strange manœuvres on both sides are determined not by
military necessity but by the strategy of the poem: Virgil wishes to keep
the protagonists apart as long as possible.

The framework of the last book is Homeric, but Roman attitudes
sometimes intrude. When Turnus takes up the idea of a single combat
the tactics are epic (or Livian), but the tone becomes more realistic when
Aeneas promises an *aequum foedus* (189 ff.); and when he is wounded in
trying to preserve the truce, the adaptation of the Homeric episode in
the *Iliad* (*Il.* 4. 127 ff.) gives him the moral excuse that meant so much to
Roman empire-builders. He shows more fortitude over his injury than
Menelaus; and when he is treated by Iapyx with his *dictamnum* a
contemporary might think not just of the Homeric leech but of Antonius
Musa, who had saved Augustus from more than one illness (for his
experti· · ·harmacology cf. Galen 13. 463 K). As his resolution grows,
Aenea.   ses the destruction of the Latin capital in the bleak,
authoritative tones of a real *imperator*, which show a Roman confidence
in the righteousness of his cause: 'urbem hodie, causam belli, regna ipsa
Latini ... eruam et aequa solo fumantia culmina ponam' (567 ff.). Yet he
is talking here not of Mezentius or even Turnus but of kind, bumbling
Latinus: there is a disconcerting parallel with Priam and the fires of
Troy. With his feeling for Rome's mission and his sense of loyalty to his
patrons, Virgil is not making an outright rejection of imperialism. But in
Greek tragedy the sack of Troy, however justified, is nothing to boast
about (cf. Aesch. *Ag.* 472 'may I not be a sacker of cities'), and in the only
comparable Latin work the loss of humanity cannot be unintended.

The plot required that Turnus should die, but he did not have to
plead 'ulterius ne tende odiis' (939), and his killing is no more endorsed

by the poet than the slaughter in the tenth book. It cannot be justified by appeals to the epic tradition and the Roman laws of war: Aeneas has been built up as a philosophic hero, and no philosopher could commend revenge on impulse. He is actuated not by a sense of honour, as he himself imagines (cf. 11. 178 f. for Evander's plea), nor even by a higher necessity (as in his corresponding destruction of Dido), but by a loss of control that reduces him to the level of his enemy:[22] nothing could be more explicit than Virgil's words *furiis accensus* (12. 946). The climax is disturbing because it denies us the expected moral ending (as if Virgil were as smug as Livy), not because it is false to human nature or the facts of Roman or more recent history. Though he had so little experience of the world, the poet intuitively understood what it costs to build a city, and at this stage of the epic he had to write what he felt, without regard for the only Man of Destiny on view. In spite of his solid exterior, Aeneas is an unfulfilled hero, clutching at phantoms, pursuing receding shores, issuing from the Gate of Illusions (6. 898), fated to wander but not quite to arrive, not to found his city (*dum conderet*, not *condidit*), but to fall before his time on the barren sand (4. 620), in Stoic terminology sometimes *proficiens* but never *perfectus*. The *imperator* wins his *spoila opima* from Turnus, but the supreme command has eluded him: 'imperare sibi maximum imperium est' (Sen. *Ep.* 113. 30).

[22] C. M. Bowra, *G & R* 3 (1933), 17 f., K. Quinn, op. cit. 272 f. Aeneas is criticized too much by M. Putnam, *The Poetry of the Aeneid* (Cambridge, Mass., 1965), pp. 193 ff., too little by B. Otis, *Virgil: A Study in Civilized Poetry* (Oxford, 1963), p. 381.

The greatest power is power over oneself.

21

Vergil's *Aeneid* and Homer

G. N. KNAUER

Often since Vergil's *Aeneid* was edited by Varius and Plotius Tucca immediately after the poet's death (18/17 BC) and Propertius wrote his (2. 34. 65 f.)

> cedite Romani scriptores, cedite Grai,
> nescio quid maius nascitur Iliade

> Make way, ye Roman authors, clear the street, O ye Greeks,
> For a much larger Iliad is in the course of construction

(Ezra Pound, 1917)

scholars, literary critics, and poets have tried to define the relation between the *Aeneid* and the *Iliad* and *Odyssey*.

As one knows, the problem was not only the recovery of details and smaller or larger Homeric passages which Vergil had used as the poetical background of his poem. Men have also tried from the very beginning, as Propertius proves, to evaluate the literary qualities of the three respective poems: had Vergil merely stolen from Homer and all his other predecessors (unfortunately the *furta* of Perellius Faustus have not come down to us), is Vergil's opus a mere imitation of his greater forerunner, an imitation in the modern pejorative sense, or has Vergil's poetic, philosophical, even 'theological' strength surpassed Homer's? Was he—not Homer—the *maximus poetarum, divinissimus Maro* (Cerda)? For a long time Vergil's *ars* was preferred to Homer's *natura*, which following Julius Caesar Scaliger one took to be chaotic, a *moles rudis et indigesta* (Cerda, following Ovid *Met.* 1. 6 f.).

In Germany Vergil fell behind when the discovery of the originality of the Greek mind, the *Originalgenie*, led to an all too high esteem of Greek literature, a development started by men like Robert Wood (1717–71) or Johann Joachim Winckelmann (1717–68). It seems to me that throughout the nineteenth and part of the twentieth century Latinists took to the pecularities and characteristic qualities of Latin literature only *ex officio*, by a sense of duty, rarely by real inclination or genuine understanding. A distinguished Latin scholar has told me recently that he considered Vergil's greatest work to be Dante's *Divina Comedia*.

Yet Richard Heinze's (1867–1929) *Vergils epische Technik* and Eduard Norden's (1868–1941) commentary on the sixth book of the *Aeneid*, both published in 1903, proved a turning-point. Though when it comes to Vergil's relation to Homer they contented themselves mainly with the investigation of comparable passages, similes, and groups of typical scenes.

It is odd to say, but this was the consequence of the analytical approach to Homer, because at least since Friedrich August Wolf (1759–1824) German Greek scholars—to mention only Ulrich von Wilamowitz-Moellendorf (1848–1931)—could look at the Homeric epics only analytically, that is as the work of several poets. But a new generation of scholars could look afresh at these poems and could try to see them as a unity. In this context one has to mention Wolfgang Schadewaldt's (born 1900) *Iliasstudien* (1938) and Karl Reinhardt's (1886–1958) *Die Abenteuer der Odyssee* (1948).

After this change of perspective the question became still more urgent. Had Vergil taken over Homeric structures and if so, in which way and why? That means: can one compare the *Aeneid* as a whole with both of Homer's poems as a whole? Karl Büchner in his Pauly–Wissowa article on Vergil (1955–8) has at least sought for an answer to this question and he boldly states that the amounts of Homeric 'material' in the *Aeneid* could by now, after centuries of search, be looked at as firmly established (col. 1449).

We must now test this statement and ask where one can find that material, who has collected it, and, most important of all, what is the actual value of the Homeric quotations in the Vergilian commentaries. One will agree that we can compare the three epics only if we can be certain of the quantity and quality of that material in detail.

When, a few years ago, I first asked these questions and started to compare some commentaries, I soon saw that in them one finds at a random passage of the *Aeneid* either a great many, very few, or no Homeric passages at all (e.g. in J. W. Mackail's (1859–1945) edition of 1930). No commentator ever makes it clear what principles he follows when he annotates a given Vergilian verse. The commentators normally don't distinguish between genuine quotations of Homer by Vergil, transformed paraphrases, or notes meant merely to help the modern reader in understanding Vergil's text. This means that the vital question, whether Vergil has really thought of a certain Homeric verse—and if he has, why—is asked only in very rare cases.

The prevalent chaos one can judge best by the number of parallels with which editors have annotated Vergilian similes. One will find six, seven, or eight parallel Homeric similes, never all of them together, never the question: which simile is really the relevant one, and if one is, is it only that one, or others too? The same applies to Homeric repetitions as quoted in commentaries on the *Aeneid*. Another annoying habit is it to annotate e.g. '*Aeneid* 12. 56 ff.' only with '*Iliad* 22. 82 ff.' The casual reader will never be able to find out that Vergil has here, in 12. 56–63, imitated not so much the content of Hecabe's speech to Hector, *Iliad* 22. 82–9, as the exact number of these Homeric verses. Amata's speech to Turnus is eight verses long, as is Hecabe's. Moreover, in the *Aeneid* Amata's speech occupies the same position as Hecabe's within this scene, which as a whole is shaped after the moving attempt of Hector's parents to save their son's life.

That these inconsistencies and this want of clarity in annotating have led to an intolerable situation is apparent from the fact that there are on the one hand many papers on Dido as a tragic character, the image of *pius* Aeneas, or the *Aeneid* as a symbol and so on, whereas on the other hand there are no means of establishing to what extent Vergil has really made use of Lucretius, Apollonius of Rhodes, or Homer, to mention only his preserved 'sources'.

In other words, there is not a single Vergil edition with an *index fontium*, long since a matter of course for the Biblical quotations in Christian authors. If one considers, in addition to all that, the innumerable erroneous or tendentious parallels which—often for centuries—have been taken over unverified from one commentary to another, Büchner's statement about the definitive collection of the Homeric material proves utterly wrong.

In collecting Homeric quotations cited by earlier scholars I have collated some twenty commentaries on the entire *Aeneid*, commentaries on single books, and relevant monographs, from Servius and Macrobius down to the twentieth century. Every reference regardless of its real value was recorded. The commentary of John Conington (1825–69) and Henry Nettleship (1839–93) provided a useful basis. A study of this collection of several thousand alleged Homeric parallels leads to surprising conclusions.

1. The major part of all quotations observed hitherto has been contributed by Vergil commentators of the sixteenth century, more precisely between 1550 and 1620. Of these I mention only a few names, now almost wholly forgotten. The first study containing more material

than the commentaries of Servius and Macrobius is the *Annotationes* of Johannes Hartung (1505–79), a Greek scholar at Freiburg/Breisgau University. They are printed as a supplement to the fine Vergil edition of Georg Fabricius of Chemnitz (1516–71), first published at Basle in 1551. Hartung's discoveries have been used and augmented by all his successors, namely J. C. Scaliger (1484–1558) in his *Poetics* (1561), the Vatican librarian Fulvius Ursinus (1529–1600) in his *Collatio* of 1568, and Germanus, who is Germain Vaillant de Guélis (1517–87), bishop of Orleans, a friend of Ronsard and Jean Dorat, in his *Commentationes* of 1575. His is the first Vergil commentary which can be called a modern one. This first period ended with the monumental commentary in three volumes by the learned Spanish Jesuit Joannes Ludovicus de la Cerda (1558–1643), written between 1608 and 1617. Only with the commentary of Christian Gottlob Heyne (1729–1812), published between 1767 and 1775, have these early achievements been surpassed. Today the basis for our work on Vergil is the commentary by Conington, first published between 1858 and 1871.

2. The survey of the whole material and the checking of each reference showed at once that many valuable discoveries of Renaissance scholars have been forgotten long ago. On the other hand it eventually became clear that large sections of the *Iliad*, and still more important, of the *Odyssey*, have so far never been recognized as being imitated in the *Aeneid*, even when the imitations are extended over hundred of verses.

In this study I shall try to indicate how Vergil has in fact incorporated the whole *Iliad* and the whole *Odyssey* into the *Aeneid*, incomparably transforming the Homeric epics. I must start with a few methodological considerations. I shall then seek to explain the relation of some of the most important passages of the *Aeneid* to their Homeric counterparts. Finally I shall try to suggest how we ought to understand this grand poetical *agōn*.

I

If, without requiring the reasons, we assume that Vergil really wanted from the very beginning to incorporate both Greek epics in his poem, it is obvious that he had to shorten them drastically. There are 27,803 verses in the *Iliad* and *Odyssey*; in the *Aeneid*, as it has come down to us, only 9,896, i.e. little more than one-third of Homer's poems. Such compression can be achieved by cutting down the extensive Homeric battle-scenes, *aristeiai*, assemblies of gods and men, etc., that is the so-called typical scenes. Very often Vergil has composed only a single one of such scenes, in which he condensed elements of all the relevant Homeric prototypes. Recall the sole *consilium deorum* at the beginning of the tenth book. In Homer we have ἀγοραὶ θεῶν (divine assemblies) at the beginnings of Books 4, 8, 20, etc.

Homer's chronology could also be abridged. So the one day in the *Aeneid*, starting 1. 305 ('ut primum lux alma data est', 306) with Aeneas *en route* to Carthage and ending 4. 5 '(Dido) nec placidam membris dat cura quietem' after his narrative, corresponds to those two days of the *Odyssey* which Odysseus passes with the Phaeacians. At *Odyssey* 6. 48 Nausikaa awakes, at the end of *Odyssey* 7 Odysseus' bed is prepared for the first night, in the evening of the second day (it's morning at 8. 1) follows his narrative and not until *Odyssey* 13. 17 does everyone go to sleep.

Again, the four books of Odysseus' narrative, Books 9–12, 2,233 verses long, are cut down to two books in the *Aeneid*, the second and third, 1,500 verses long. But in doing so Vergil has still preserved the proportion of his narrative to the whole of the poem: four books are one-sixth of the twenty-four books of the *Odyssey* as two are the sixth part of the twelve books of the *Aeneid*.

Again, Vergil has mingled or contaminated large Homeric passages which contain parallel events. Thus the visits Telemachus pays to Nestor at Pylos as related in *Odyssey* 3 and to Menelaus at Sparta, the first part of which is related in Book 4, the second part not until Book 15—these the Roman poet has combined into Aeneas' single visit to Evander's Pallanteum in *Aeneid* 8. In spite of such necessary constrictions Vergil has retained almost the original length of some Homeric passages. Thus the games for Anchises in *Aeneid* 5 (42–603) are spread over 562 verses, those for Patroclus in *Iliad* 23 (226–897) over 672, or more obviously, the 666 verses of Aeneas' *katabasis* (6. 236–901) even surpass the number of verses in the *nekyia*: *Odyssey* 11 has only 640 verses. Short scenes sometimes have the same length as their Homeric prototypes. Thus the Dido scene in *Aeneid* 6 equals with its 27 verses the corresponding Aias scene in the *nekyia* (6. 450–76: *Od.* 11. 541–67).

Moreover Vergil has sometimes combined several Homeric characters into one. Three examples suffice: in Aeneas Odysseus, Telemachus, and Achilles are united; in Dido more—Arete, Alcinous, Circe, Calypso (and of course Medea); Lavinia must fulfil the functions of Helen and of Penelope. But the reverse too may occur. One Homeric character is split up into three: Elpenor falls drunken to his death at the end of *Odyssey* 10, he asks for his funeral in 11, and receives it from Odysseus at the beginning of 12. Even so, at the end of *Aeneid* 5, the sleepy Palinurus falls to his death, he asks Aeneas for his funeral in Book 6, but at the beginning of 7 the latter buries his nurse Caieta instead of Palinurus, whereas Vergil has already imitated, in the funeral of Misenus in Book 6, details of that of Elpenor. Elpenor thus has become Palinurus, Misenus, and Caieta.

One wonders further. What does Vergil do when he wants to transform a larger Homeric passage? I shall describe two procedures.

1. Vergil very often translates, that is, quotes one or several Homeric verses with such a degree of exactitude that his listeners would at once recognize the passage in the poet's mind. Such *Leitzitate* were meant to tell the listener that he was now in this or that larger Homeric context. It thus becomes clear, for example, not only that the verses which describe Apollo of Soracte as partly consenting, partly disapproving Arruns' prayer in Book 11 (794–8) are an exact and immediately recognizable quotation of the similar partly consenting, partly disapproving reaction of Zeus of Dodona to Achilles' prayer in *Iliad* 16 (249–52), but also that the whole description of Camilla's death is shaped after that of the death of Patroclus. Vergil has in *Aeneid* 11. 778–885 transformed *Iliad* 16. 783–867.[1]

---

[1] The literal quotation of Zeus' reaction proves that one has to compare the preceding prayers too. Achilles prays to the Pelasgian Zeus of Dodona who is worshipped by the *Selloi*, *with unwashed feet* (*Il. 16. 233–5*); *Apollo of Soracte is worshipped by the Hirpi*, who in his honour walk *with bare feet over* burning coal (*Aen.* 11. 785–8). This is a typical Vergilian variation. Arruns will be content to return even as an *inglorius*, if only the god concedes him to kill Camilla (11. 792 f.). Achilles prays for Patroclus' return to the camp (*Il.* 16. 241, 246–8): Vergil has reversed the content of the prayer to its opposite. Camilla is blinded by her desire to kill the richly dressed priest of Cybele, Chloreus (11. 774–82), because Patroclus was blinded by his success over the Trojans (*Il.* 16. 784–9). This blindness makes it possible for Apollo, who approaches Patroclus unnoticed (*Il.* 16. 789, οὐx ἐνόησεν), to render him defenceless. Then Euphorbos wounds him badly and flees immediately (*Il.* 16. 813, ὁ μὲν αὖτις ἀνέδραμε, μίxτο δ' ὁμίλῳ). Finally Hector kills Patroclus. Vergil has united these three, Apollo, Euphorbos, and Hector, in the one Arruns, who just like Euphorbos is mentioned only here in the whole epic. When Arruns kills Camilla *ex insidiis* (11. 783), Camilla doesn't notice the sound of the weapon at all (11. 801–4). Arruns flees immediately (11. 806 'fugit ante omnis exterritus Arruns' and 815 'contentusque fuga mediis se immiscuit armis'). Camilla dies as Patroclus died; 11. 831 'vitaque cum gemitu fugit indignata sub umbras' will be repeated when Vergil describes Turnus' death (12. 952, closing line of the *Aeneid*); this line, the second literal quotation in this context, is a translation of the two lines describing Patroclus' death, which are repeated in the description of Hector's death (*Il.* 16. 856 f. = 22. 362 f.). The reason for this well-considered Vergilian repetition will be found again in Turnus' blind obsession that is comparable to Camilla's. Overwhelmed by his *violentia* (cf. 12. 9 and 45) he is not able to see that victory is destined to Aeneas. So only in his last forlorn monologue do his

2. But not only quoted details make the listener understand which larger Homeric passage Vergil had in mind. When, let us say, Aeneas and his followers sail from Sicily as *laeti* (1. 34), Juno delivers her first angry monologue, and the storm drives the shipwrecked men to the Libyan shore, it is not by literal quotation but by the similarity of the situation that the listener thinks of Odysseus, who leaves Ogygie as γηθόσυνος (*Od.* 5. 269) and sails unhindered for many days, till Poseidon sees him and, after an angry monologue, releases the storm in which Odysseus loses his raft and is swept to the Phaeacian shore. Here the structural correspondence provides the clue to the Homeric proto-type, already adduced in antiquity. This correspondence was so obvious that it deterred readers from seeing that Vergil contaminated *Odyssey* 5 and 10 in *Aeneid* 1. I shall return later to this point.

In other words, we have to check in each case whether an obvious quotation of a detail is a *Leitmotiv*, the complete context of which Vergil has incorporated into the *Aeneid*, or whether, vice versa, the scenic imitation is so evident that detailed literal imitations could be neglected. Whether it is literal quotations or only faint reminiscences which hint at particular Homeric passages, or whether it is the number of verses of a speech, a simile, a scene or its structure, even its position in the course of the book—we shall have to consider all these phenomena, because they can possibly be traced to Homer. Their meaning and their function become clear only when one recognizes why Vergil transformed his model.

II

We must now attempt to outline these structural relationships, begin-ning with the first half of the *Aeneid*. Books 1–6 have rightly been called the 'Vergilian Odyssey'. But on closer inspection one will have to restrict this statement because, if action in the *Aeneid* (I leave the proem apart) starts at 1. 34 with the departure of the Trojans from Sicily, this beginning corresponds not to *Odyssey* 1, but only to the middle of *Odyssey* 5. At 5. 263 Odysseus on his raft leaves Ogygie, an island like Sicily. At the end of *Aeneid* 1 we have reached the same point as at the end of

---

ἀτασθαλίαι (*Il.* 22. 104) dawn upon Hector, i.e. that he was blinded like Patroclus. The poetical *motivation* of Patroclus' death is the same as that of Hector's. Therefore Vergil connected Camilla's and Turnus' deaths in the way in which Homer indicates parallel events, namely by repeating verses. Hector's death as a result of that of Patroclus, and its *meaning* for the structure of both epics, will be discussed below (see pp. 409–10).

Odyssey 8. There Alcinous asks his still unknown guest his name and wants to hear his adventures. Odysseus' narrative follows in the four books 9–12. It starts with the departure from Troy and ends with the arrival at Calypso's island Ogygie. Dido on the other hand asks the already beloved guest to narrate the fall of Troy and the wanderings of the Trojans. Aeneas does so in Books 2 (Iliupersis) and 3. In this second book of his narrative he, like Odysseus, relates the events from his departure from Troy until the departure from Sicily and his arrival in Libya which has led to the encounter with Dido.

Thus in *Aeneid* 1 are condensed the events from the middle of *Odyssey* 5 to the end of Book 8, three and one-half books (5. 263–8. 586). The first-person narrative in *Aeneid* 2 and 3 as a whole corresponds to that of Odysseus from *Odyssey* 9 and 12. More exactly Vergil's third starts like Homer's ninth and ends like his twelfth; because we see at once that the end of Aeneas' narrative *hinc* (i.e. from Sicily) 'me digressum vestris deus appulit oris' (3. 715) looks back literally not only to the end of Odysseus' narrative (*Od.* 12. 447 f.)

> … δεκάτῃ δέ με νυκτὶ
> νῆσον ἐς Ὠγυγίην πέλασαν θεοί, ἔνθα Καλυψὼ
> ναίει

'and on the tenth night the gods brought me to the island of Ogygie, where Calypso lives'

but also to the beginning of the action of the *Aeneid*:

> vix e conspectu Siculae telluris in altum
> vela dabant laeti … (1. 34 f.)

In exactly the same way the end of Odysseus' narrative looks back to the proper beginning of the action of the *Odyssey*, his departure from Ogygie (5. 263 ff.):

> 263 τῷ δ᾽ ἄρα πέμπτῳ [*sc.* ἤματι] πέμπ᾽ ἀπὸ νήσου δῖα Καλυψώ …

'then on the fifth day the divine Calypso sent him from the island'

> 269 γηθόσυνος δ᾽ οὔρῳ πέτασ᾽ ἱστία δῖος Ὀδυσσεύς.

'joyfully god-like Odysseus spread his sails before the favouring breeze'.

Book 1–3 of the *Aeneid* thus follow the construction of *Odyssey* 5. 263 to the end of *Odyssey* 12.

Moreover it is obvious that Vergil has removed Book 11, the *nekyia*, from Odysseus' narrative and tranformed it into a book of action, Book 6 of the *Aeneid*. We are not concerned here with Vergil's reasons for doing so. But I have already mentioned that the figure of Elpenor has been split into that of Palinurus at the end of *Aeneid* 5 and that of Caieta at the beginning of *Aeneid* 7. If, in addition, one now considers that Anchises appears to his dreaming son, one year after his death, and asks him to undertake the *katabasis*, the trip to the *Ditis . . . domūs* (5. 731 f.), just as Circe at night reveals to Odysseus, who has stayed with her for one year, that he must go εἰς Ἀίδαο δόμους (*Od.* 10. 491), the following becomes evident: Vergil has not only imitated *Odyssey* 11 in his sixth book but has transformed the end of *Odyssey* 10 (469–574) into the end of his fifth (700–871). Moreover he has transformed the beginning of *Odyssey* 12 which follows the *nekyia* into the beginning of his seventh book (cf. 7. 1–20: *Od.* 12. 1–15).

I cannot here attempt to demonstrate that Vergil has not only condensed the beginning of Odysseus' narrative in *Odyssey* 9 and its end in 12 but has in fact by a very clever reshaping condensed the whole content of these two books into *Aeneid* 3. In these Aeneas is represented throughout as a hero surpassing his Greek counterpart, Odysseus, who had passed through the same or similar situations shortly before him (in epic time). Odysseus, the victor, destroys Ismaros in Thrace; Aeneas, the exile (3. 11), founds Ainos in the same region. On his way home to the πατρίς, Ithaca, west of the Peloponnesus, Odysseus is shipwrecked by a storm at Cape Maleia; Aeneas, in spite of a storm, successfully passes this cape (cf. 5. 193) on his way to the west, where in the end he will find the promised *patria*, Hesperia. Here for the first time one begins to sense Vergil's purpose in following Homer.

At any rate we may say that Vergil has united *Odyssey* 9 and 12, i.e. the first and the last books of Odysseus' first-person narrative, into the second, the last book of Aeneas' first-person narrative. Furthermore he placed *Odyssey* 11, i.e. the third book of the narrative, together with the closing part of the tenth and the beginning of the twelfth as its natural components, as his sixth book at the end of the first half of the *Aeneid*. He connected the sixth book with the end of the fifth and the beginning of the seventh after the Homeric analogy. Finally he made the first book of action in the *Aeneid* correspond to the action in the *Odyssey* from the middle of the fifth to the end of the eighth book. Having these structural alterations in mind, one must eventually ask where he may have used the two major remaining passages of this part of the *Odyssey*. First, there is the beginning of Book 5 (1–262), the second conversation between Athene and Zeus, which leads to Hermes' mission to Calypso. She is asked to release Odysseus, and she actually does so after a vain attempt to keep him with her. Next we must ask where he has put the greater part of Book 10 (1–468), the beginning of the second book of narrative, in which are related Odysseus' adventures from the encounter with Aiolos to his love affair with Circe. Both these passages Vergil has, for good reasons, placed elsewhere.

The beginning of *Odyssey* 5 he has shifted to his fourth book. Here it is Iarbas, the son of Jupiter Ammon, who asks his father to provide for the separation of Aeneas and Dido. Mercury communicates the god's order not to Dido but to Aeneas, who obeys, while Dido, exactly like Calypso, vainly implores him to marry her. For Calypso too, unlike Circe, had tried to win Odysseus as her husband. She had compared herself to Penelope, and only because of Penelope Odysseus had not yielded (*Od.* 5. 203–24). Just the same thing happens in the *Aeneid*: Aeneas, and through him Dido, knows that another wife is destined for him in Hesperia. That is why, although ruefully, he can withstand the temptation (cf. 4. 198–407 with *Od.* 5. 1–262, and especially the speeches *Od.* 5. 203–13 and *Aen.* 4. 305–30).

In the *Odyssey* it is the episode with Calypso which by its relation to Penelope points to the second half of the epic, to the death of the suitors. This relation to Penelope is completely missing in the episode with Circe. Vergil must have recognized—and this seems to me very important—the difference in the relationship of Circe and Calypso to Odysseus; otherwise he would scarcely have made of Dido another Calypso only in Book 4. Aeneas' renunciation makes the second half of the *Aeneid* possible. This means at the same time that the second half of the *Aeneid* must have been determined also from the *Odyssey* and that to Lavinia has been assigned the same function as to Penelope.

And the beginning of *Odyssey* 10? Aiolos, the loss of the whole fleet, the stag hunt, and the consolation of the despairing companions in Circe's Aiaie lost and recovered companions, Circe's kind reception of Odysseus? To enumerate these elements already helps us to recognize the place where Vergil has intended them to stand: Juno hurries to king Aeolus, in a storm Aeneas loses for the first time a major part of his fleet, after the landing in Libya follows the hunt in which seven stags are killed, he consoles his despairing companions who have survived, he finds the lost ones with Dido, who receives him kindly. In other words, in *Aeneid* 1 Vergil has contaminated two large portions of the Odyssey without changing the sequence of their single parts, 5. 263–8. 586 and 10. 1–468.

Let us examine just one passage, the relation of which to the *Odyssey* has been as little recognized as the whole of this contamination. In *Odyssey* 10 when Circe vainly attempts to transform Odysseus, who has not told her his name, into a pig (310 ff., esp. 320), she finally breaks out in utter astonishment:

> τίς πόθεν εἰς ἀνδρῶν; ...
> θαῦμά μ' ἔχει ὡς οὔ τι πιὼν τάδε φάρμακ' ἐθέλχθης,
> nobody had ever achieved that (327–9),
> ἦ σύ γ' 'Οδυσσεύς ἐσσι πολύτροπος, ὅν τέ μοι αἰεὶ
> φάσκεν ἐλεύσεσθαι χρυσόρραπις ἀργεϊφόντης,
> ἐκ Τροίης ἀνιόντα θοῇ σὺν νηὶ μελαίνῃ.
> ἀλλ' ἄγε δή, κολεῷ μὲν ἄορ θέο, νῶϊ δ' ἔπειτα
> εὐνῆς ἡμετέρης ἐπιβήομεν, ὄφρα μιγέντε
> εὐνῇ καὶ φιλότητι πεποίθομεν ἀλλήλοισιν.

Who are you amongst men and where from? ... I am seized by wonder that you were not at all enchanted after drinking the potion, ... surely you are the versatile Odysseus, who the slayer of Argos of the golden rod always used to say would come to me, returning from Troy with his swift dark ship. But come now, put your sword in its sheath, and let us two mount upon our bed, that mingling in union and love we may trust one another (325–35).

'Or art thou he? the man to come foretold / By Hermes ...,/ The man from Troy .../ The man for wisdom's various arts renown'd / Ulisses?' in Pope's translation. Then follows the deliverance of the companions.

In the *Aeneid* Venus dissolves the protective cloud round Aeneas and Achates when it becomes clear that Dido is willing to give shelter to the shipwrecked Trojans (1. 579 ff.). This finds its counterpart in *Odyssey* 7, where the protective cloud round Odysseus vanishes at the moment when he kneels before Arete, who alone can save him. But it is a trait not of the Phaiakes but of the Circe story, when the reunited Trojans greet each other most heartily. Then Vergil proceeds:

> **obstipuit** primo aspectu Sidonia Dido,
> casu deinde viri tanto, et sic ore locuta est:
> **quis te, nata dea, per tanta pericula casus**
>   **insequitur?** ...
> **tune ille Aeneas, quem** Dardanio Anchisae
> Alma Venus Phrygii genuit Simoentis ad undam? (*Aen.* 1. 613–18)

And Dido continues:

> atque equidem Teucrum memini Sidona venire ...
> **tempore iam ex illo casus mihi** cognitus urbis

Troianae nomenque tuum regesque Pelasgi ...
quare **agite** o tectis, iuvenes, succedite nostris. (619-27)

'At her first sight of Aeneas Sidonian Dido was awestruck, thinking of the horrible fate which had been his. Then she spoke: Son of the Goddess, what is this fortune which has been pursuing you through such fearful perils? ... Can you truly be that Aeneas whom Venus, the kind love-giver, bore to Dardan Anchises by the waters of Phrygian Simois? Now I myself remember Teucer coming to Sidon ... Ever since that time I have known of the calamity which befell Troy, and known you, and the Greek princes, by name ... Therefore, come, gallant friends, and proceed to my home.' (Translation of W. F. J. Knight (Penguin, 1958).)

Dido had heard long ago from Telamonian Teucer of Aeneas and the fall of Troy; she already knew his name before Ilioneus' report. Just so Circe had long known through the god Hermes of the man Odysseus, who would come one day from Troy. Certainly the love of the Vergilian Dido had to be of a different nature from that of Homer's Circe. It is all the more astonishing that Vergil has left unchanged the inner core of Homer's narration, out of which he could let the passion of this noble couple grow.

To form the Dido of *Aeneid* 1, Arete, Alcinous, and Circe are in fact combined. In Book 4 she becomes Calypso. I cannot deal here with the Medea of Apollonius and the Dido of Naevius, nor can I prove why Vergil has switched the places of the first part of *Odyssey* 5 and that of *Odyssey* 10. The reasons must be sought in the complicated structure of the *Odyssey*, which Vergil has simplified by transposing its various parts. For the moment we must be content to acknowledge that Vergil split *Odyssey* 5 and 10 into two parts.

Summarizing our first results, we now can say that it is possible to state with a greater degree of exactitude than hitherto that in his first six books Vergil has not transformed the whole of the *Odyssey* but only the eight books 5-12—only one-third, but the essential third of the epic. Of this core no vital part has been left out.[2] On the other hand, Books 1-4, the Telemacheia, have not been incorporated into *Aeneid* 1-6, nor has the whole of the second half of the *Odyssey*, the twelve books 13-24.

Furthermore we can assume that Vergil clearly realized how Homer conceived the structure of the *Odyssey* and that Vergil therefore did not

---

[2] The games for Patroclus in *Iliad* 23 together with the Phaeacian games in honour of Odysseus (*Od.* 8) serve as the basis of the games for Anchises in Vergil's fifth book.

simply imitate sporadic Homeric verses or scenes. On the contrary he
first analysed the plan of the *Odyssey*, then transformed it and made it the
base of his own poem.

III

We now come to the difficult task of discovering the relations of the
second half of the *Aeneid*, Books 7–12, to the *Iliad* and to those parts of
the *Odyssey* which had not been adapted earlier. The *Iliad* is not only
longer than the *Odyssey* but of an infinitely more complicated structure.
This has made Vergil's task more difficult, and ours as well.

Let us look first at the end. Richard Heinze (p. 180) rightly pointed
out that, if Vergil wanted to close the *Aeneid* with Turnus' death, it was
obvious to model it upon Hector's death in *Iliad* 22. We must ask
ourselves now whether Vergil has not rather chosen this prototype for
other more weighty reasons, reasons resulting from a penetrating
analysis of the *Iliad*.

The memorable closing verse of the *Aeneid* runs (12. 952 = 11. 831):

> vitaque cum gemitu fugit indignata sub umbras.

This is a shortened translation of the two verses describing Hector's
death (*Il.* 22. 362 f. = 16. 856 f.):

> ψυχὴ δ' ἐκ ῥεθέων πταμένη 'Αϊδόσδε βεβήκει,
> ὃν πότμον γοόωσα, λιποῦσ' ἀνδροτῆτα καὶ ἥβην.

and his soul flitting from his limbs went down to Hades, lamenting its fate,
leaving its manliness and youth.

For the present we may say that the end of the *Aeneid* is just as little in
keeping with the end of the *Iliad* as its beginning with the beginning of
the *Odyssey*. Since the end of the *Iliad* from Hector's death onward (*Il.*
22. 364) could not be used for the closing of the *Aeneid*, Vergil was at
liberty to use its various sections at other places in his poem. The
description of the violation of Hector's body and the laments of the
Trojans (to the end of *Il.* 22) has been used for the description of the
violation of the bodies of Nisus and Euryalus and the laments of the
latter's mother in *Aeneid* 9. The funeral of Patroclus in *Iliad* 23 supplied
elements for that of Misenus in Book 6. The games he transferred to
Book 5. The ransom and the return of Hector's corpse in *Iliad* 24
furnished parts of the return of Pallas' body in *Aeneid* 11.

Still, a comparison of the end of the *Aeneid* with the end of the *Iliad* is possible. The hearer knows at the end of the *Iliad* that Troy is doomed by Hector's death. Just so the hearer knows at the end of the *Aeneid* that Rome will rise by Turnus' death. Now Jupiter's prophecies in Books 1 and 12, those of Anchises in Elysium in Book 6 can come true. Just so the pernicious prophecies of Troy's fall direct the action of the *Iliad*. The beginning of the second half of the *Aeneid*, i.e. Book 7, is more difficult to understand than its end. In order to visualize the situation more clearly, we must turn back to the prophecy of the Sibyl at the beginning of *Aeneid* 6. The Cumaean Sibyl promises Aeneas, who has just survived many a danger on the sea, even greater ones on land (6. 83 f.). She announces *bella, horrida bella* (6. 86) and she sees a bloody Tiber which she identifies witht the Trojan rivers Simois and Xanthus (6. 87–9). Another Achilles, also son of a Goddess, has already arisen. Juno will pursue the *Teucri*, the Trojans, with her rage. Finally the cause of such evils will again be 'a wife' (93 f.; 6. 83–97):

> causa mali tanti coniunx iterum hospita Teucris
> externique iterum thalami.

The words of the Sibyl leave us in no doubt that Aeneas, who has already re-enacted the adventures of Odysseus, will have to endure a second Trojan War, and for the same reasons. Lavinia, whose name is of course not mentioned here, will be the *causa mali tanti* exactly like Helen. ἥ τ' ἔπλετο νείκεος ἀρχή, 'and she was the beginning of the strife', said Hector in his final monologue (*Il.* 22. 116). In addition to fulfilling the function of Penelope which resulted from her relation to Dido as a second Calypso, Lavinia takes up the part of Helen. Vergil seems to have regarded the functions of Helen and Penelope in the Homeric epics as comparable and parallel. He thus was able to weld them into one person.

The parallelism goes even further. Since Norden's investigations in Ennius and Vergil (1915), it has been well known that the great scene between Juno and Allecto in Book 7 has been shaped after the scene between Juno and Aeolus in Book 1 (*Aen.* 7. 286–340). Now, after Latinus has promised the newcomers peace and the hand of his daughter Lavinia, Allecto is charged with stirring up war. Bellona will be *pronuba* for Lavinia (7. 319). The wedding will be delayed by the war, and here also a hint of Troy is not lacking. Aeneas, the son of Venus, will be a torch to set afire the new Troy, *iterum*, as Paris, the son of Hecabe, had once enkindled the old:

> quin idem Veneri partus suus et Paris alter
> funestaeque iterum recidiva in Pergama taedae. (7. 321 f.)

One knows how successful Allecto was. Forced by circumstance, Latinus declares war (7. 601–22). The deployment of the Latin forces, the so-called catalogue of the Itali, follows, preceded by an invocation to the Muse (7. 641–817), which of course corresponds to the catalogue of ships of the *Iliad* (2. 484–779). Such is often said. But is it parallel only as a catalogue? Because a heroic epic is not complete without a catalogue?

We must therefore ask where in the action of the *Iliad* the catalogue of ships has its place. This consideration will help us to find the clue for the Vergilian reshaping of the structure of the *Iliad*. The commencement of the *Iliad*, the quarrel between Agamemnon and Achilles, Vergil could not use. *Iliad* 1 is absent from the *Aeneid*, but in the *Iliad* the quarrel prompts Zeus to restore Achilles' τιμή (honour), because Thetis has asked him to do so. Zeus' intention is realized through the dream which he sends Agamemnon, advising him to lead the army towards Troy at once. This dream scene has in fact served as pattern for the dream scene with Allecto and Turnus. It also motivates in both epics the gathering of the armies. But Vergil has nevertheless taken another motif far more important, which in the *Iliad* is only a consequence of Agamemnon's order. Agamemnon first wants to test the army (*Il.* 2. 73). Following his orders but against his expectations, the army joyfully retreats to the ships to embark for home (*Il.* 2. 142–54). Now Hera acts. She asks Athene if all has been in vain. Will Helen, for whose sake so many Greeks and Trojans have lost their lives, be left to Priam and the Trojans (*Il.* 2. 160–7)? Athene succeeds in stopping the army. After the resumed assembly, the deployment of the army and the catalogue of ships follow.

In other words, Zeus achieves his aims only by a detour, for the intervention of Hera, who dispatches Athene, makes her unwittingly a tool of the father of gods. This is quite the same in the *Aeneid*. We can now understand not only that the Juno–Allecto scene of Book 7 is a parallel to the Juno–Aeolus scene in Book 1—and indeed both stem from the Poseidon scene in *Odyssey* 5—but also that their structural pattern is that of the Hera–Athene scene in *Iliad* 2. 155–68. None of the goddesses—neither Hera in the *Iliad* nor Juno in the *Aeneid*—can alter the course of events (*Aen.* 7. 314 *immota manet fatis Lavinia coniunx*). They are as ineffectual as Poseidon in *Odyssey* 5. At a point like this Vergil's genius for perceiving parallel developments in both Homeric epics and making use of them becomes most clear. Furthermore, both goddesses refer to the respective causes of war, Helen and Lavinia. Both send their aides, be it Athene or Allecto. In both cases the gathering of the respective forces follows. Thus for his seventh book Vergil has clearly chosen as a pattern the starting-point of the Trojan War as it becomes evident in *Iliad* 2. He clearly has imitated the second book of the *Iliad* as a whole instead of merely picking out the catalogue as a conventional epic ingredient.

The hostile forces are now readied, but not Aeneas, the newcomer. That means that Vergil from now on could not follow the next events in the *Iliad*. Only in Book 12 was he able to do so again, where *Iliad* 3 and 4, the ὅϱϰια and the archery of Pandarus, are indeed united with the closing section of the Patrocleia, the first part of *Iliad* 22. In Book 8 Aeneas is—and this was a surprising discovery—in rather the same situation as the unarmed Odysseus in *Odyssey* 13, after the Phaeacians have dropped the sleeping hero in his homeland, Ithaca. Vergil has taken Odysseus' encounter with Athene and her taking counsel with him as to how they could subdue the suitors, as model for the dream-vision of the river god Tiber, who reveals to Aeneas his arrival in his predestined *patria* (cf. 8. 39) and advises him to seek support at Pallanteum, the city of the Arcadians, for the forthcoming struggle with the Italic forces of his rival suitor Turnus. That the transformation of the *Odyssey* continues here in Book 8, a fact which has passed unnoticed hitherto, becomes easily understandable if we realize that Turnus in Book 7 has taken over the part of the suitors in the *Odyssey*. As the struggle for Lavinia corresponds to that for Penelope, Aeneas' situation, his lack of means compared to the mighty suitor Turnus, corresponds to that of Odysseus in *Odyssey* 13, but there is no comparable situation in the *Iliad*.

Thus Evander as an ally is not only a new Eumaios—for *Odyssey* 14 has also been laid under contribution to Book 8—he is, most important of all, a new Nestor in Pylos, contaminated with the Spartan Menelaus of *Odyssey* 4 and 15, both of whom Telemachus visits when he sets out to look for his father. A great many of Vergil's literal, detailed quotations from this part of the *Odyssey* have been recognized long ago, but it has not yet been noted that Vergil follows in Book 7 and especially in Book 8, *Odyssey* 13 and 14, thus continuing in the second part of his epic the imitation of the second part of the *Odyssey*. He then passes over to his transformation of the Telemacheia (from the end of *Odyssey* 2 to that of 4).

If one considers that in Book 8 Aeneas' relation to his rival Turnus can be compared to that of Odysseus to the suitors, it becomes easier to understand why Vergil could also submit the Telemacheia to transform-

ation. The so-called *signum Veneris* (*Aen.* 8. 520–40) gives us the clue for
this. For, when early in the morning Venus flies through the air with the
clashing arms Vulcan had made the night before, nobody but Aeneas,
her son, is able to explain this as a sign promising victory: 'ego poscor
Olympo 8. 533) ... quas poenas mihi, Turne, dabis' (8. 538). This
famous scene Vergil has developed from the parting scene in Sparta
when Telemachus takes leave of Menelaus and Helen and the eagle
portent occurs (*Od.* 15. 160–81). There only Helen, the daughter of
Zeus, is able to interpret the portent: Odysseus will return home and
take his revenge, οἴκαδε νοστήσει καὶ τίσεται. The purpose of
Telemachus' journey has been achieved. He now can return, full of new
hope. Father and son will unite their efforts (*Od.* 16). The last act of the
Odyssey begins.

Vergil has made one character out of the two here. Another Odysseus,
Aeneas is also Telemachus, in that he obtains from his mother the
hopeful portent that prepares the way for the last act of the *Aeneid*.

But the last books of the *Odyssey*, 16–24, defied transformation.
Instead Vergil turns completely to the *Iliad*. Let us see what he has done.
From 8. 370 'at Venus ... exterrita mater (Volcanum adloquitur)'
onwards, he relates what happens while Aeneas is asleep at Evander's.
At 369 'nox ruit et fuscis tellurem amplectitur alis', Vergil's imitation of
the Telemacheia had reached the point which corresponds to *Odyssey* 3.
403 and 4. 305 respectively, when Nestor or Menelaus and their guest
lie down to sleep. But in the *Odyssey* these nights are not described at
either place, for already in the next verse, in 3. 404 as well as in 4. 306,
the dawn, Eos, of the respective next morning appears. This corresponds perfectly to Vergil's 'Euandrum ex humili tecto lux suscitat
alma' (8. 454). The following events also have their counterpart in this
part of the *Odyssey*. But in the *Aeneid* Vergil inserts into these *Odyssey*-
nights the important events of one night in the *Iliad*. Exactly as Homer's
Hephaistos fulfils the request of Achilles' mother Thetis for weapons
for her son, so does Vergil's Vulcan fulfil Venus' request for her son
(these scenes start *Iliad* 18. 369 and *Aeneid* 8. 370 respectively). The
signum Veneris—the clatter of weapons in the air—thus represents a
contamination of the τέρας Διός (portent of Zeus) of the *Odyssey* and
Thetis' delivery of the weapons at the beginning of *Iliad* 19. Now after
the description of the shield (till the end of *Aeneid* 8) Aeneas is fortified
by divine weapons and allies as Achilles is in *Iliad* 19 and Odysseus in
Odyssey 16.

This amalgamation of both Homer's epics in *Aeneid* 8 and the transition from the imitation of the *Odyssey* into that of the *Iliad* at precisely *this* point may be explained by the fact that Vergil has obviously compared the situation of Achilles after Patroclus' death with that of Odysseus after his landing in Ithaca (that means, in the *Aeneid*, after Aeneas' landing in Latium). For Achilles, bereft of his divine weapons now in the hands of Hector (*Il.* 17), on whom Patroclus must be avenged, is therefore as defenceless as Odysseus after his disembarkation in *Ithaca*. Thetis' aid makes it possible for Achilles (as Athene's for Odysseus) to face his enemy fully armed. When Vergil makes Venus help Aeneas, he thus repeats once again the basic situation which had been prefigured in *both* Homeric epics.

Before entering upon Book 10, one should perhaps recall the fact that in the *Iliad* two actions are intertwined. First there is the action round Helen for whom the war is fought. This at first glance has nothing to do with Achilles. Next the Patroclus-action: Achilles fights again only after his ἕταιρος (companion) Patroclus has been slain and stripped by Hector in an unfair duel. This in its turn has little to do with Helen. We are not concerned here about the way in which these two strands have been entwined and eventually made to lead the action in the *Iliad* towards the ultimate aim, the fall of Troy. But we are now in a position to explain why Vergil has made *Iliad* 2 the foundation of Book 7, but *Iliad* 18 and the beginning of 19 the basis of Book 8. In *Iliad* 2 the Helen-action begins. In 18 Achilles is allowed to start his revenge, which will lead finally to the fall of Troy. We have reached the same situation at the end of *Aeneid* 8.

Book 9 may be left aside. Heinze has rightly said that it contains those parts of the *Iliad* in which battles without Achilles' participation are described, roughly Books 8 and 12. Of *Aeneid* 10 we shall deal only with the death of Pallas, who is killed by Turnus. I suggest, only briefly, that Pallas' death is a contamination of the death of Sarpedon with that of Patroclus in *Iliad* 16. This book has served as the basis for *Aeneid* 10 in structure as well as in details. Moreover Vergil has contaminated it with parts of the assembly of gods in *Iliad* 20 and the Scamander battle in 21. Special attention may be called to only one of the many so far unnoted relations between *Iliad* 16 and *Aeneid* 10. It is a passage which has always been wrongly interpreted. For the catalogue of the Etruscans is not an imitation of the catalogue of the Trojans in *Iliad* 2 (816–77) but an exact and structurally determined transformation of the catalogue of the Myrmidons in *Iliad* 16, a section situated in *Aeneid* 10 at almost the same spot as in *Iliad* 16 (16. 168–97: *Aen.* 10. 163–214).

Vergil had good reasons to shape *Aeneid* 10 after *Iliad* 16, because he understood that here was the turning-point of the Trojan war as Homer saw it: the death of Patroclus will cause Achilles' decisive intervention. In the same way by Aeneas' arrival when the battle for the camp is raging and by Pallas' death the battle for Latium is brought to a crisis in *Aeneid* 10. That is why Vergil made only this book start with an assembly of gods (*Il.* 4 and 20), where Jupiter solemnly states that *hodie*, today (*Aen.* 10. 107, cf. *Il.* 20. 127 σήμερον, 'today'), both parties would have the same chance—*rex Iuppiter omnibus idem* (10. 112).

How does Turnus forfeit his chance? The Sibyl had predicted in Book 6 that Aeneas would meet as opponent another Achilles, also the son of a goddess. Turnus by descent and excellence is Aeneas' equal. Both too, after the events of Books 7 and 8, are equals in allies and weapons. But when Turnus has slain Pallas, the very young son of Evander, and insolently stripped him of his *balteus*, Vergil reflects upon the naïve shortsightedness of men that does not know how to restrain itself—'nescia mens hominum fati sortisque futurae et servare modum' (10. 501 f.). Soon Turnus would curse the day on which he had slain and stripped Pallas:

> Turno tempus erit, magno cum optaverit emptum
> intactum Pallanta et cum spolia ista diemque
> oderit. (10. 503–5)

For Pallas, as Vergil expressly describes, was not Turnus' equal, either in age or strength. The encounter begins *viribus imparibus (10. 459)*. Aeneas bewails the *miserandus puer* (11. 42). Evander the father deplores the *immatura mors* (11. 166 f.).

Through his excess Turnus forfeits the chance Jupiter had granted him. This guilt, the result of a victory without honour over young Pallas, who had been entrusted to Aeneas by Evander, is the reason for his own defeat at Aeneas' hand. When the Trojan sees Turnus wearing Pallas' *balteus*, he is enraged and kills Turnus as a sacrifice for Pallas. Turnus pays with his 'criminal blood' the debt for Pallas' death:

> ... Pallas, te hoc volnere Pallas
> immolat et poenam scelerato ex sanguine sumit. (12. 948 f.)

These are Aeneas' last words before he slays Turnus. They follow after Turnus had acknowledged Aeneas' victory and his claim for Lavinia: 'vicisti ...; tua est Lavinia coniunx' (12. 936 f.). Now it becomes clear that Vergil has in fact concluded the two elements of action in the *Aeneid*.

Aeneas, suitor of Lavinia, has defeated his rival. This theme sets the tone for the whole second half of the epic and it refers back to Penelope of the *Odyssey* as well as to Helen of the *Iliad*. Further, Aeneas has taken revenge for Pallas' death. This second theme determines the structural patterns between Books 10 and 12.

Vergil again has developed the Pallas theme from his analysis of the Patroclus-action in the *Iliad*. Hector, in slaying Patroclus exactly as Turnus slays Pallas, does not kill an opponent who is his equal, but only the ἕταρος, 'companion' (*Il.* 16. 240), the θεράπων, 'servant' (16. 244) of Achilles. Hector's victory is also inglorious because he kills a rival already rendered defenceless by Apollo, and even worse: he strips him of the weapons, which in reality belong to Achilles (*Il.* 17. 188–97). When Vergil, the poet, deplores the *nescia mens hominum* after Pallas' death, his reflection is modelled upon Zeus' sorrowful reaction to Hector's errors. Zeus reflects and observes (17. 201 f.) that Hector's death is imminent because he did not act according to moral order, οὐ κατὰ κόσμον (205), when he stripped Patroclus of his armour.

When Vergil in Book 10 makes Turnus a villain by his murder of Pallas and at the end of Book 12 makes Aeneas kill Turnus as punishment for his guilt, it becomes evident that the poet here wanted to imitate the structure of the *Iliad*, i.e. the relation in composition which exists between *Iliad* 16 and 22. Because Hector has violated the code of honour of the Homeric heroes[3] and because Achilles must therefore take revenge for the death of Patroclus, on another level the same must occur once more in the *Aeneid*.

The plan of Vergil's structural imitations of Homer may now have become at least partly clear: the four great units of action in Homer, the Helen-action and the Patroclus-action in the *Iliad* (not Book 1, the Menis), the Telemacheia and the wanderings of Odysseus in the *Odyssey*, must after a thorough study have seemed to him to be not only comparable but actual parallels beteen the Homeric epics. Remember only the wrath of the gods or the women as cause of war. Such apparent parallelism induced him to unite the two in a single poem, the *Aeneid*— to put it daringly, to treat the same matter a third time.

The complete structure of the Homeric epics, not simply occasional quotations, was no doubt the basis for Vergil's poem. I cannot explain these findings otherwise than by the suggestion that Vergil must have intensively studied the structure of the Homeric epics before he drafted

---

[3] Cf. Samuel E. Bassett, 'Hector's Fault in Honor', *TAPhA* 54 (1923), 117–27.

in prose his famous first plan for the whole *Aeneid*. Propertius' 'nescio quid maius nascitur Iliade' in about 26 BC is not against this view.

IV

What can we say of the significance of Vergil's transformation of Homer? At our present state of knowledge we can merely ask the questions which necessarily arise from these findings.

The simplest first. It seems clear that Aeneas, who excelled Odysseus in the first part of the *Aeneid*, now surpasses the Greeks who had been victorious in Troy. Diomedes in Arpi expressly confronts the *pietas* of Aeneas with the *scelus* of the Greeks (*Aen.* 11. 258). The moral strength and piety of the 'new Achilles', and indeed of the whole line of the *Aeneadae*, has its beginnings in the *Iliad* (20. 307 f., translated at *Aen.* 3. 97 f.). The way in which he completes the divine mission to found a new Troy, that is Rome, elevates him morally far above the Greek heroes.

One next would have to ask to what extent Vergil made use of the various ancient interpretations of Homer. To what extent did they influence and enhance his own? There are indications in the *Aeneid* that Vergil was well acquainted with the current expositions of Homer, especially the allegorical explanation of the Stoics.[4]

It is much more difficult to answer a third question. Had any of his Latin forerunners earlier imitated Homeric structure, if only in parts, or is this sort of analysis of Homer original with Vergil? The discussion about Naevius' *Bellum Punicum* is still in flux. I think it not impossible that Vergil could have found in Naevius a tendency towards it, in Ennius scarcely.

Next comes the question of the position of the *Aeneid* within the development of the Latin epic. Vergil's *Aeneid* is in fact a Latin epic in the tradition of the annalistic-historical epics of Naevius and Ennius. 'Historical' in this sense means to take as the actual beginning of Roman

---

[4] One example only. In *Aen.* 1. 740–6 the Carthaginian bard Iopas sings about nature, i.e. *de rerum natura*. In *Aen.* 1 he sings at a point that corresponds in a way to the situation of Demodokos' (second) song about Ares and Aphrodite (*Od.* 8. 266–366). Both sing for the pleasure of the distinguished guests and in both epics follow the narrations of the Iliupersis (*Od.* 8. 499–520 and *Aen.* 2) and the wanderings of the heroes (*Od.* 9–12 and *Aen.* 3). The song of Ares and Aphrodite had long been interpreted not only as an amusing story about love affairs on Olympus but as an allegorical poem about nature, περὶ φύσεως. The proem of Lucretius' *De Rerum Natura* proves that he too interpreted Venus and Ares allegorically. Vergil, who in the *Georgics* (4. 346) let the nymph Clymeme in Cyrene's palace sing *Vulcani Martisque dolos et dulcia furta*, in the *Aeneid* replaced the old story by its allegorical interpretation, namely a poem with a philosophical explanation of nature.

history the end of the Trojan War, the flight of Aeneas, his wanderings, and his landing in Latium.

But all this does not satisfy us entirely, indispensable as it may be for the understanding of the *Aeneid*. It does not explain why the *Aeneid* should have had such an astonishing impact through the centuries. Rather it is the decisive step Vergil has made towards an epic much nearer to Homer than the traditional Latin epic with its rough attempts at Homeric imitation.

It seems to me as if Vergil had understood the relation of his poem to Homer's epics in a way which can be compared to that of Christian exegesis in understanding the relation between the Old and the New Testament, namely by 'typology'. The Old Testament was understood as an account of real historic events which represent in an earlier stage the expectations of salvation which are fulfilled in the New Testament. The same event is repeated in the New Testament, only on another level, even by way of reversal.[5]

This analogy may suggest the reason why Vergil made the Sibyl and Juno declare that the events of the Trojan war would be re-enacted, *iterum*, that a new Troy, Rome, would rise—and also the reason why Vergil could found his own characters upon the Homeric. This is *not* an aesthetic or literary interpretation—rather an 'historical' one.

This view is confirmed by the observation that Vergil's *Aeneid* is marked by an eschatological interpretation of history, apparently a *sine qua non* of the typological method. Compare the relation between Old and New Testament. Contrary to usual Roman practice, the deeds of the ancestor of the *gens Iulia* do not just represent the beginning of Roman history, deeds to which simply are added those of all his successors. Aeneas instead unites in his person, in the epic acting in the *present*, the awful Trojan *past*—represented for instance in the reliefs of the temple of Juno in Carthage—as well as the glorious Roman *future* reaching to Augustus. Of course eschatology for a Roman of this period could not mean the same thing as for a Christian; but it could mean the hope that now, at this very moment, in Augustus' and Vergil's lifetime, the Golden Age of Saturnus might return. Here, too, history is understood as a repetition of things past. The Neo-Pythagorean flavour of this conception is, by the way, a distinctive element of the Roman epic.

This Vergilian yearning, already eloquently articulated in the *Fourth*

---

[5] Within the last ten years several scholars in Germany have tentatively ventured in this direction. For further information see my book (below, n. 6), pp. 354 ff.

Eclogue, is nowhere stated more grandly than in Anchises' prediction in
Elysium:

> hic vir, hic est, tibi quem promitti saepius audis,
> Augustus Caesar, Divi genus, aurea condet
> saecula, qui **rursus** Latio regnata per arva
> Saturno quondam ... (6. 791–4)

'And there in very truth is he whom you have often heard prophesied,
Augustus Ceasar, son of the Deified, and founder of golden centuries
once more in Latium, in those same lands where once Saturn reigned'
(trans. Knight).

The *imperium sine fine* that Jupiter promises Venus will now be
realized in the *aurea saecula* of Augustus' reign—all of that is but the
repetition of what has come before. Is this mere fancy? No, for Vergil has
enlarged this prophecy of Anchises from an Homeric original. It is the
prophecy of Teiresias in the underworld that Odysseus eventually will
die as a very old man amidst prosperous people—ἀμφὶ δὲ λαοὶ ὄλβιοι
ἔσσονται, 'and about him there will be prosperous peoples' (*Od.* 11.
136 f.). The simple, natural death of the aged Odysseus, whose rule has
made the tribes of Ithaca blessed, becomes in Vergil a grand vision, the
vision of the return of the Golden Age under the rule of Augustus, of the
pax Romana, which embraces the *orbis terrarum*, an *imperium* unlimited
by time and space.

It was left for a Roman to achieve such a transfiguration of Homer, for
a Roman whose historical insight had been sharpened by the blood and
pain of civil war, who knew that the ancient, revered *res publica* was no
longer enough. It was this Roman who tranformed the 'historicity' of the
Iliad and the *Odyssey* into that of the *Aeneid* and linked his poem to the
hopes of Augustus' reign. In such a context, one would do well to
understand the epigram—perhaps even said by Vergil: 'facilius est
Herculi clavam quam Homero versum subripere'.[6]

---

[6] The interested reader may turn for more information to my book, *Die Aeneis und
Homer: Studien zur poetischen Technik Vergils mit Listen der Homerzitate in der Aeneis*
(Göttingen, 1964).

22

The Language of Virgil and Horace

L. P. WILKINSON

As in literature poetry precedes prose, so in poetry a special and 'heightened' diction seems to precede everyday language.[1] Mr T. S. Eliot has put it thus: 'Every revolution in poetry is apt to be, and sometimes to announce itself as, a return to common speech.'[2] How does this apply to Greek and Latin? There are objections to considering words in isolation from this point of view, since neutral ones are apt to go now grey, now purple, according to their company; but if we do not do so, we deny ourselves the only considerable method of investigation (unsatisfactory though it is) that is still open to us. Again, we must recognize that most poems are composed largely of ordinary words, though these are often used in a way that is not ordinary. It is a matter of degree. Pindar, and indeed Aeschylus, used a comparatively high proportion of poetical words. But when Euripides revolutionized Greek tragedy by introducing 'homely things such as we use and live among', he also made concomitant innovations in style which are harder for us to detect. As Aristotle remarked in his *Rhetoric*, 'A poet can beguile us successfully (κλέπτεται εὖ) by picking and combining words from the language of daily life. This is what Euripides does, and he was the first to indicate the way.'[3]

There is a certain hesitancy, or even confusion, in Aristotle's remarks on poetic diction. In the *Poetics* he insists that it must be clear, but not mean: a style consisting wholly of ordinary words would be the clearest, but it would also be mean. The poet must therefore give it distinction by the introduction of unusual words or forms, without overdoing this. He concedes, however, that in the iambic verse of tragedy, which reproduces natural speech as nearly as may be, the most suitable diction is such

---

[1] See O. Jespersen, *Language* (London, 1922), p. 432.
[2] *The Music of Poetry* (London, 1942), p. 16.
[3] 1404^b5 κλέπτεται δ᾽ εὖ ἐάν τις ἐκ τῆς εἰωθυίας διαλέκτου ἐκλέγων συντιθῇ· ὅ περ Εὐριπίδης ποιεῖ καὶ ὑπέδειξε πρῶτος. Cf. Aristophanes, fr. 471, on Euripides and himself: χρῶμαι γὰρ αὐτοῦ τοῦ στόματος τῷ στρογγύλῳ, τοὺς νοῦς δ᾽ ἀγοραίους ἧττον ἢ κεῖνος ποιῶ, 'for I make use of the neatness of his mouth, but present common minds less often than he does'. στρογγύλος seems to mean neat, terse, compact.

as one might find in prose, namely ordinary words, with metaphor and ornament.[4] Likewise in the *Rhetoric* he recommends an unusual diction for poetry, but he immediately subjects this to the overriding rule of propriety (τὸ πρέπον), saying that language must be convincing (πίθ-ανον), and sound natural in the mouth of the character concerned.[5] In fact Aristotle's general view, that poetic diction should be enriched by rare words, is tempered by his Euripidean feeling that in dramatic or quasi-dramatic verse the diction should be more naturalistic.

A further source of confusion lurks in the word σύνθεσις (putting together), and, I think, in its Latin descendant *iunctura*, as we shall see.[6] When Aristotle used συντιθῇ (put together) in the passage quoted just now, he was no doubt thinking merely of the way in which Euripides composed his verse of ordinary words. But Longinus (if I may so call the author περὶ ὕψους, 'On Sublimity') introduces into a chapter on the structure of periods,[7] dealing with the effect of τὸ συνθεῖναι καὶ ἁρμόσαι (which Hamilton Fyfe translates as 'composition and verbal carpentry') an illustration which seems really more appropriate to Aristotle's point.[8] After mentioning Euripides as a poet who for the most part employs ordinary language, he continues: 'Thus Heracles, when he has killed his children, uses the words

"I am truly laden with troubles, and there's no room left for more":

γέμω κακῶν δὴ κοὐκέτ' ἐσθ' ὅποι τεθῇ.

The expression is extremely commonplace, but is heightened by the aptness of the structure of the line. If you put it together in any other way this will become clear, the fact being that Euripides is a poet in virtue of his handling of words rather than his thoughts.' (σφόδρα δημῶδες τὸ λεγόμενον, ἀλλὰ γέγονεν ὑψηλὸν τῇ πλάσει ἀναλογοῦν· εἰ δ' ἄλλως αὐτὸ συναρμόσεις, φανήσεταί σοι, διότι τῆς συνθέσεως ποιητὴς ὁ

---

[4] 1458ᵃ–1459ᵃ 'mean'—ταπεινός, 'ordinary'—κύριος, 'unusual'—ξενικός. Oddly enough, the first example he gives of the virtue of unusual diction is a line of Aeschylus, φαγέδαινα δ' ἥ μου σάρκας ἐσθίει ποδός, 'a sore is eating up the flesh of my foot', which was redeemed from the banal (εὐτέλες) to the noble (καλόν) by Euripides, who heightened ἐσθίει (is eating up) to θοινᾶται (feasts upon). For other instances of far from ordinary language in Euripides see F. R. Earp, *The Style of Aeschylus* (Cambridge, 1944), p. 72.
[5] 1404ᵇ1–5.
[6] The literal Latin for σύνθεσις is *collocatio*, and this is also ambivalent, since it can refer either to arrangement of topics, or to fitting together of words, usually with a view to ἁρμονία, *concinnitas*. The word is also rendered by *compositio*, as in the title of Dionysius' περὶ συνθέσεως ὀνομάτων.
[7] XL.
[8] The inappropriateness was remarked by O. Immisch, *Horazens' Epistel über die Dichtkunst*, Philologus Suppl. 24. 3 (Leipzig, 1932), p. 83 n.

Εὐριπίδης μᾶλλόν ἐστιν ἢ τοῦ νοῦ.) *γέμω* is not an unpoetic word, being found indeed three times in Aeschylus and three in Sophocles.[9] It seems likely, therefore, that the impression of common speech was given by the phrase *κοὐκέτ' ἐσθ' ὅποι τεθῇ*. This introduction of a colloquial phrase to give poignant reality to a moment of tragedy is comparable with Dido's

> si quis mihi *paruulus* aula
> luderet Aeneas

—almost 'some tiny Aeneas'—or Othello's

> the pity of it, Iago,

or Lear's

> pray you, undo this button.

It is hard to see how the line could have been *put together* in any other way so as to destroy the *ὕψος*, and one cannot help suspecting that two wires of traditional Peripatetic criticism have got crossed here, one concerning the effect of *σύνθεσις* in the sense of the harmonious arrangement of words—*ἁρμονία, concinnitas*—and the other concerning the effect of it from the semantic point of view, the telling combination of ordinary words and phrases. But it remains noteworthy that so sensitive a critic should throw out as an *obiter dictum*, as if it were a commonplace of criticism, that Euripides was a poet in virtue of his handling of words rather than his thought.

Cicero, who was praised by Caesar for being the first Latin orator to apply selection to vocabulary,[10] recommended that orators choose words as euphonious as possible, but taken from the common stock, not sought out for sound, *as by the poets*.[11] Clearly it was orthodox to assume that poetry employed recherché words, as the *cantores Euphorionis* did. Nevertheless, it was recognized, as by Aristotle, that drama at least might effectively employ ordinary language; for, when discussing tragedy in the *Orator*, Cicero imagined someone as interposing, 'I love Ennius, because he does not depart from ordinary usage in his diction.'[12] But the distinction between dramatic and other forms of poetry in this respect does not seem to have been always kept in view. We have

---

[9] Of course, for all we know, *γέμω κακῶν* may be an unpoetic phrase.
[10] Cic. *Brut.* 253. Cf. Tac. *Dial.* 22.
[11] *Orat.* 163: 'Verba ... legenda sunt potissimum bene sonantia; sed ea non ut poetae exquisita ad sonum, sed sumpta de medio.' Cf. *de Orat.* 1. 12.
[12] *Orat.* 36: 'Ennio delector quod non discedit a communi more uerborum.'

thus the first known phase in European literature of the recurrent interaction between two styles of poetry.[13] What Euripides had done Wordsworth was to advocate, with his 'selection of the language really spoken by men'. There is a fragment in the second book of Philodemus περὶ ποιημάτων ('On Poems') to the effect that poems characterized by recherché diction are often worthless, whereas poems made of words that are colloquial and ordinary, but well combined, are often good: ἐξ ἰδιωτικῶν τε καὶ εὐτελῶν, συγκειμένων δὲ καλῶς, χρηστόν.[14] The point is elaborated by Dionysius of Halicarnassus in Chapter III, of his *De Compositione Verborum*: 'Many poets, as well as oratorical and philosophical prose-writers, who have picked out words which are definitely beautiful and appropriate to the subject, but have fitted them together in a random and inartistic way, have reaped no benefit from their pains: whereas others have taken words that are humble and unregarded, and by combining them in a pleasing and uncommon way, have invested their style with great charm.' And again he says in Chapter XII: 'No part of speech that signifies any person or thing will prove so mean or squalid or otherwise offensive as to have no possible fitting place in literature'; and he goes on to point out that Homer had used τὰ εὐτελέστατα τῶν ὀνομάτων, 'the most ordinary of words', as had Herodotus and Demosthenes.

This brings us to the Roman poets I wish to discuss; for Philodemus is inseparable from Siro, the mentor of Virgil and the Epicurean poets of the circle that frequented the area of Naples;[15] and Horace, who refers to an epigram of his which has not come down to us,[16] can hardly have failed to know his prose works also; while Dionysius came to Rome in 30 BC, just when Virgil was embarking on the *Aeneid* and Horace on the *Odes*, and remained there, teaching young Romans, at least until 8 BC, the year of Horace's death.[17] There is thus every reason for supposing

---

[13] For the modern situation see G. S. Fraser, 'Writing', in *A New Outline of Modern Knowledge*, ed. A. Pryce Jones (London, 1956), p. 329.

[14] ii. 275. 9 Hausrath.

[15] *Catalepton* V. Servius on *Aen.* 6. 264; *Ecl.* 6. 13. Probus, *Vita Verg.* p. 73. 10 Br. Cic. *Fin.* 2. 119. Philodemus, *Pap. Herc.* 312; W. Crönert, *Kolotes und Menedemos* (Leipzig, 1906), p. 126. Rostagni, *L'Arte Poetica di Orazio* (Turin, 1930), p. xiii, says that Philodemus probably addressed one of his works to Horace, along with Virgil, Varius, and Quintilius Varus. But it is more than likely that the corrupt name in περὶ φιλαργυρίας should be restored as Πλώ]τιε rather than 'Ορά]τιε (as he admits elsewhere, p. xxix n.). 'Plotius et Varius Sinuessae Vergiliusque / occurrere', says Horace on his journey to Brundisium (*S.* 1. 5. 40); and Plotius Tucca is inseparable from Varius, while Horace is hardly likely to have known the circle in the period when it seems to have centred round Siro (*c.* 50–40 BC).

[16] *S.* 1. 2. 121.   [17] *Ant. Rom.* 1. 7.

that the Augustan poets were familiar with what Greek critics had said, and were saying, about poetic diction.

Now there is a curious sentence in the part of the Suetonian Life of Virgil which deals with his detractors (ch. 44): 'M. Vipsanius called Virgil a puppet of Maecenas, inventor of a new kind of affected style, neither inflated nor jejune but composed of ordinary words and therefore unobtrusive.' ('M. Vipsanius a Maecenate eum suppositum appellabat nouae cacozeliae repertorem, nec tumidae nec exilis sed ex communibus uerbis atque ideo latentis.') The manuscript reading Vipsarius is an obvious blunder, and M. Vipsanius *tout court* can only be the great Agrippa. *Cacozelia* was a tasteless excess of any sort; and *atque ideo latentis* is a distant reminder of Aristotle's κλέπτεται δ' εὖ in the passage on the same subject from the *Rhetoric* which I have already cited (1404^{b}5).[18] Beside this dictum we may set a remark of Maecenas himself, quoted by the elder Seneca, though it refers to treatment of ideas rather than to diction, to judge from the illustration attached. He said that Virgil managed to be sublime without being tumid, so that his lines were *et magna et tamen sana*.[19]

Suetonius' probable source was a work he mentions two sentences later, the book 'against the detractors of Virgil' by Asconius Pedianus, who flourished under Tiberius. The story can be taken as authentic, for who would have been likely to father on Agrippa a spurious piece of literary criticism? Not that he was indifferent to culture: he seems to have aspired to be sung by Horace,[20] and the elder Pliny tells us that he made a speech recommending that works of art should be taken out of the seclusion of private houses and made accessible to the public. But Pliny adds that he was *uir rusticitati propior quam deliciis*.[21] We are not here considering his relations with Maecenas (after all, he *may* only have been teasing), nor his view of Maecenas' relations with the poets of his circle, but the basis and validity of his criticism of Virgil's style. Arresting though it is, the passage has often been surprisingly neglected. It was the subject of an article by Friedrich Marx in the *Rheinisches Museum* for 1925, to which I am indebted.[22] Marx set out clearly the Greek precedents, but when he came to consider its validity for Virgil he was extremely sceptical about our ability to judge, because of our ignorance of the nuances of Roman speech. The point I want to make is, that he may have been unduly sceptical, in the light of subsequent research.

[18] F. Marx, *RhM* 74 (1925), 185–8; Immisch, op. cit. 86–90.
[19] *Suas.* 1. 12.   [20] *Odes* 1. 6.   [21] *Nat.* 34. 62; 35. 26.
[22] 'M. Agrippa und die zeitgenössische römische Dichtkunst', pp. 174–94.

The same year, 1925, saw the publication of W. Baehrens's *Skizze der lateinischen Umgangsprache*, and in 1936 J. B. Hofmann produced his important *Lateinische Umgangsprache*. The publication of our most useful tool, the *Thesaurus Linguae Latinae*, will be complete in the foreseeable future. Meanwhile some relevant work has been done on Horace. I have not been able to see Giuseppina Brunori's extensive analysis of his language, dated 1930, and in any case it has been rather severely criticized.[23] But in the bimillenary year, 1935, J. Smereka contributed an article to the Polish Academy's *Commentationes Horatianae* which began with useful lists for the *Odes* of archaisms, colloquialisms, grecisms, neologisms, and barbarisms.[24] Finally, B. Axelson included a most interesting chapter (4) on the diction of the *Odes* in his *Unpoetische Wörter*, published in 1945. It has long been recognized that the *sermones* are largely colloquial, and Horace expressly abjured any claim that they were poetical.[25] We shall not be concerned with these. The *Odes* present a more difficult problem, for they are *sui generis*; there is no Latin work with which they can be compared. They are mostly far from the colloquial style of Catullus' *nugae*, and many of them are clearly high poetry in the grand manner; but they vary considerably in this respect, unlike epic, which rarely allowed itself to sink below a certain level.

For the *Aeneid* we now have a massive and thorough analysis by A. Cordier, which appeared in 1939. Cordier's work is not impeccable, and must be used with reservations.[26] Thus he has chosen to take no account in his statistics of repeated instances; and we must remind ourselves, for example, that the word *aequor* in the poetic sense of 'sea' occurs a hundred times in the *Aeneid*.[27] However, that is scarcely more significant than if we found that Wordsworth used 'deep' for 'sea' a hundred times in the *Prelude*; and Cordier's figures do seem to permit of rough generalizations. Let us take his three headings of archaisms, rare words (γλῶτται), and compounds, and see what emerges about Virgil's practice in the *Aeneid*.

Not only the example of the Homeric poems, but also his devotion to

[23] *La Lingua di Orazio* (Florence, 1930). K. Büchner, *Report on Horace* in Bursian Jahresberichte (1939), pp. 53–6.
[24] pp. 65–91. Büchner, op. cit. 58. There are also some valuable observations in M. Leumann, *Die lateinische Dichtersprache* (Mus. Hel. 1947), pp. 116 ff.
[25] See, e.g., F. Leo, 'Römische Literaturgeschichte', in *Kultur der Gegenwart*, i. 8³ (Leipzig, 1912), p. 445. Hor. S. 1. 4. 39–44; *Ep.* 2. 1. 250–1.
[26] See F. H. Sandbach in *CR* 54 (1940), 196–7.
[27] p. 151.

Ennius, might have led Virgil to overload the *Aeneid* with words (or meanings of words), forms, and constructions that were archaisms in his day, the more so as he was by nature *amantissimus uetustatis*[28] and Augustus was anxious to encourage reverence for the past. Now Cordier finds that, if we take account not only of archaic words, but of words by that time reserved to certain spheres such as religion, words used in an archaic sense, and archaic constructions, the *Aeneid* displays about 250 different examples, or one in every 40 lines.[29] It is true that some of these recur; on the other hand, constellations of examples are crowded into a few lines where the context calls for them, there being, for instance, no fewer than 22 in the 20 solemn lines where Aeneas comes to the Styx (6. 317–36).[30] All things considered, an average of 2·52 different archaisms per hundred lines seems too low a percentage to diffuse a markedly archaic flavour throughout. This impression is strengthened by comparison with Cicero's translations from Homer, for which the figure is 11 per cent.[31] Quintilian remarked that too frequent or obtrusive archaisms constituted the most odious of all affectations, and elsewhere praised Virgil for the unique discrimination he showed in this respect.[32]

Turning to γλῶτται, which comprise poetic, technical, rare, and foreign words, we find an average of 3·65 per 100 lines of the *Aeneid*. It is true that Lucretius' average is no higher than Virgil's, but that is understandable, since he was largely bent on explaining his subject in language his contemporaries would understand. The percentage in Catullus' *Epyllion*, however, is as high as 8·32, which suggests what we should here expect, a purposeful search for unusual words in the Alexandrian manner. Even in Cicero's verse the percentage is 8·0, so that Virgil's 3·65 indicates a marked reaction against the practice of his immediate predecessors.[33]

For compound words the story is much the same. Leaving aside words like *carnifex*, which were part of everyday speech, we find that Cicero used 3·60 per 100 lines in his translations, and as many as 7·88 in his other poems, and Catullus 4·16 in his *Epyllion*; whereas the percentage for the *Aeneid* is only about 1·00.[34]

Cordier nowhere mentions Agrippa's remark,[35] but it does seem

---

[28] Quint. 1. 7. 18   [29] p. 29.   [30] pp. 67–8.   [31] p. 29.
[32] 1. 6. 40; 8. 3. 24: 'eoque ornamento acerrimi iudicii P. Vergilius unice usus est'.
[33] Cordier, p. 150.
[34] pp. 222–3, 230, 234, 270. The figure for Lucretius is 1·3 (p. 232).
[35] Nor does A. Meillet in his *Esquisse d'une histoire de la langue latine* (Paris, 1953), nor J. Marouzeau in his *Traité de stylistique latine* (Paris, 1945), though the meagre indexing of even the most important French works makes it hard to verify a negative statement. W. F.

relevant to his conclusion, that Virgil was concerned to keep contact between epic vocabulary and contemporary speech; that he was in reaction against both the Ennian archaizers and the Neoteric experimenters with γλῶτται.[36] He may be right in thinking that Virgil's primary motive was to make sure that his national epic was not esoteric. But that does not exclude the possibility that he was also cultivating for its own sake a style which had had its advocates since the time of Euripides. (Incidentally, it is more likely that Agrippa was thinking of the *Aeneid* than of the way in which the *Georgics* ennobled humble things which were conventionally felt to be beneath the dignity of poetry, the process to which Virgil referred as 'angustis hunc addere rebus honorem'.)[37]

But before investigating Virgil's practice further, let us turn to his friend Horace. There are two crucial, but unfortunately disputed, passages in the *Epistle to the Pisones* which bear on our subject. The first is ll. 46–9 (accepting Bentley's transposition):

> in uerbis etiam tenuis cautusque serendis
> hoc amet hoc spernat promissi carminis auctor.
> dixeris egregie notum si callida uerbum
> reddiderit iunctura nouum.

This I take to mean: 'In disposing words also the aspiring author of a poem should be subtle and cautious, fancying one word and rejecting another. Your language will have distinction if cunning combination makes a familiar word fresh.'[38] It is tiresome that the Roman critical vocabulary was even less clearly defined than ours. *Iunctura* is

---

Jackson Knight, in his suggestive ch. 5, says briefly: 'It was partially at least a mixed style out of countless spoken and written idioms of different places and ages. The Romans of the time liked it immediately. Agrippa, who thought it rather a grotesque and dishonest style, was very much in the minority.' *Roman Vergil* (1944), p. 261.

[36] pp. 314–16.

[37] *Geo.* 3. 290. Immisch (op. cit. 88) connects Agrippa's remark with Porphyrion's note on Horace, *AP* 47 (*callida iunctura*), which gives as an example *Geo.* 1. 185: 'Nam licet aliqua uulgaria sint, ait tamen illa cum aliqua compositione splendescere. Verbi gratia "curculio" sordida uox est, ornatu antecedente uulgaritas eius absconditur hoc modo: "populatque ingentem farris aceruum curculio" ', 'For though some things are vulgar, he nevertheless claims that they can shine in some kind of combination. To pick a word, "weevil" is a low term, but its vulgarity can be concealed by a preceding ornament as follows: "and the weevil lays waste the mighty pile of flour".'

[38] Rostagni rightly stresses that Horace is here dealing with ἐκλογή (not σύνθεσις) ὀνομάτων; but it seems gratuitous to follow him in driving *serendis* from *sere* 'to sow' rather than *serere* 'to weave'. The latter was a common metaphor for literary composition, and its use with *iunctura* here is echoed by *series iuncturaque* in the same sense in ll. 242–3.

sometimes used for the collocation of words that produces euphony.[39] But here it refers to semantic collocation, as Heinze, Rostagni, and Steidle have seen. For how else could it be said to make a word fresh? (Wickham's translation, 'setting', is as good as any.) It includes metaphor-making, and a passage in the *Rhetorica ad Herennium* (4. 42) is apposite. The author quotes a sentence; 'Postquam iste in rem publicam impetum fecit, fragor ciuitatis imprimis.' The last word seems corrupt, but it is clear that he considers that *fragor* becomes a metaphor in combination with *ciuitatis*, and he actually refers to this in the next sentence as *nouum uerbum*.[40]

The other passage in the *Epistle to the Pisones* is ll. 240–3:

> ex noto fictum carmen sequar, ut sibi quiuis
> speret idem, sudet multum frustraque laboret
> ausus idem: tantum series iuncturaque pollet,
> tantum de medio sumptis accedit honoris!

'I will aim at a poem created out of the familiar, such that anyone might hope to emulate it, but sweat much and labour in vain if he ventured to emulate it; such is the power of texture and combination, such the dignity that can accrue to words taken from the common stock.' Horace is here speaking of propriety (τὸ πρέπον) in relation to the diction of Satyric Drama,[41] which must differ from Comedy, not employing only *inornata et dominantia* (κύρια) nouns and verbs (l. 234), because supernatural characters, for instance, must not talk the language of slaves,[42] but on the other hand avoiding exoticism. It was characteristic of this style that it looked deceptively easy, but was in fact very hard to use well. Such was the art of Euripides, as we saw; and as an epigram in the Anthology emphasized: 'Tread not the path of Euripides, singer, nor aspire to it, for it is a hard way for men to go. It looks smooth, but those who set foot on it will find it rougher than a bed of cruel stakes. Try scratching but the surface of the *Medea*, and you will be doomed to lie below in oblivion. Hands off his garlands.'[43] Such also was the plain style of oratory, as Cicero says in the *Orator*: 'The audience, even though

---

[39] Quint. 9. 4. 32 ff. Immisch (op. cit. 80) takes it so here.

[40] Of course *uerba nouare* can mean to create new words as by compounding— *expectorare, uersutiloquus*—or otherwise, '*senius desertus, dii genitales*, bacarum ubertate incuruescere', Cic. *de Orat.* 3. 154.

[41] I agree with Rostagni that he is still treating of diction.

[42] Compare this application of the doctrine of τὸ πρέπον to ἦθος (Arist. *Rhet.* 3. 7) with the observation at ll. 95–8 that Euripides' Telephus, when poor and in exile, rightly uses *sermo pedestris*, not tragic grandiloquence, in his complaints.

[43] *AP* 7. 50, by Archimedes, or Archimelus (third cent. BC).

they are not orators, are confident that they can speak like that: for that
plainness of style (*subtilitas*) looks easy, but nothing is less so when you
try.'[44]

We must first consider, however, whether these precepts of Horace
are likely to reflect his own practice. The fragment of Philodemus to the
same effect which I quoted just now may, as is often the case with him,
be a quotation from someone he is castigating; if so, it may be from
Neoptolemus of Parium, whom Horace is known to have used for his
Epistle to the Pisones, so that Horace may have been guided by his source
rather than his experience. Again, we have little reason to suppose that
Horace or the Pisones were really writing Satyric Drama, so that the
second passage may be particularly academic. And finally, we have in the
Epistle to Florus Horace's advice on diction to the man who would create
a poem on true artistic principles. He will boldly cut out words that have
too little lustre (*parum splendoris*), revive forgotten words, unearth
splendid names that have grown rusty in recent years, admit new ones
sanctioned by usage, and flow like a strong, pure stream enriching the
Latin tongue. He will prune and refine his language.[45] There is no
suggestion here that there is any virtue in using ordinary words, though
the two Epistles must have been written at no great interval of time from
one another. Commentators have pointed out a certain similarity
between the views given here and those given by Cicero with regard to
propria uerba in *De Oratore* 3,[46] and dependence on Cicero or a common
source, apparent elsewhere, cannot be ruled out here. Everything warns
us to hesitate before we take Horace's critical utterances as relevant to
his own practice in the poetry of the Odes. Let us therefore examine this
independently.

Marx, who dealt with Horace incidentally when discussing Agrippa's
dictum on Virgil, mentions only one instance of what might exemplify
callida iunctura, the application of *diuites* to *insulae* (instead of the normal
fortunatae) at *Epode* 16. 42 and *Odes* 4. 8. 27. But we now have the help of
Professor Axelson's study. His most important conclusion is that
Horace, while in some respects more fastidious over *delectus uerborum*

[44] Ch. 76. Cf. Hor. *Ep.* 2. 124: 'ludentis speciem dabit et torquebitur'.
[45] *Epp.* 2. 2. 109–25.
[46] Ch. 150: 'in propriis igitur est illa laus orationis, ut abiecta atque obsoleta fugiat,
lectis atque illustribus utatur, in quibus plenum quiddam et sonans inesse uideatur', 'for
this is what commends style of speaking in the matter or proper terms, namely to avoid the
commonplace and obsolete and to use the choice and brilliant, in which there seems to be
something full and resonant'.

than any of his contemporaries,[47] showed a far stronger tendency to admit rather prosaic words, such as *obire, ordinare, praesidium, pecunia,* or *negotium,* than one would expect of a high lyric poet.[48] An astonishing example is *recte, rectius,* found four times in the *Odes* and some thirty times elsewhere in Horace, but never in Catullus, Propertius, Tibullus, Virgil, Seneca (tragedies), Lucan, Valerius, or Silius.[49]

Can we perhaps suppose that these prosaic words were given distinction or freshness by *series* and *iunctura?* It is hard for us to judge, for how can we recapture the sense of novelty that may have excited a Roman? What did Quintilian mean when he said that Horace was *uerbis felicissime audax?*[50] If the metaphorical use of *fragor* for a political crash or uproar was a *nouum uerbum* to the author *ad Herennium,* with what a shock of excitement may Horace's audience have first heard the words

> auditumque Medis
> Hesperiae sonitum ruinae!

and the sound of Hesperia's ruin, heard by the Mede!

A casual perusal of the *Odes* reveals at least a hundred examples of what *may* have been such innovations, for all we know. Most of them fall within recognizable categories.

Some of the metaphors, such as 'to bridle licence' or 'sunny flowers' have become commonplace to us.[51] Some were extensions of already familiar ones, as *tepebunt* in

> quo *calet* iuuentus
> nunc omnis et mox uirgines *tepebunt,*

for whom now all the young men are heated and soon maidens will be warm,

and *commissi calores fidibus.*[52] Some involved witty play on words

---

[47] *Unpoetische Wörter,* ch. 4, pp. 98–113. Axelson does not mention Agrippa's remark in this connection, but he refers to Marx's article in his Introduction, p. 15.

[48] pp. 108–10.

[49] p. 63.

[50] 10. 1. 96.

[51] *Frena licentiae iniecit* (4. 15. 10), *apricos flores* (1. 26. 7). Here are some more metaphors. Verbs: *spem resecare* (1. 11. 7); *mero caluisse uirtus* (3. 21. 12); *sacrare plectro* (1. 26. 11); *merces defluat* (1. 28. 27); *te bearis nota Falerni* (2. 3. 8); *uoltus adfulsit* (4. 5. 6); *diem mero fregi* (2. 7. 6); *transiliat munera Liberi* (1. 18. 7); *carpere obliuiones* (4. 9. 33). *Laudes deterere* (1. 6. 12) and *Notus deterget nubila* (1. 7. 15) are instanced by Heinze *ad AP* 47. Nouns: *Carminis alite* (1. 6. 2: Heinze); *copia narium* (2. 15. 6); *inimice lamnae* (2. 2. 2); *plenum opus aleae* (2. 1. 6). Adjectives: *auream mediocritatem* (2. 10. 5); *uultus lubricus adspici* (1. 19. 8); *sepultae inertiae* (4. 9. 29); *pigris campis* (1. 22. 17).

[52] 1. 4. 20; 4. 9. 11.

(*paronomasia*): thus *non erubescendis adurit ignibus* means 'she does not fire you with a flame at which you need blush', with a play on the similar effect on the face of literal and metaphorical flame.[53] *Opacam porticus excipiebat arcton* means 'a colonnade caught the northern shade', but it also means 'trapped the Bear'.[54] Messalla is fond of wine, though he is *steeped* in Socratic dialogues; Lydia must bring out wine to lay siege to embattled philosophy; Jupiter turns himself into a bribe for Danaë's warder.[55] Horace often uses anthropomorphic language of natural subjects, animate or inanimate, in a charming way reminiscent of the *Georgics*. A farm lets its owner down, the trees blaming now the rains, now the parching heat, now the cruel winters.[56] The plane-tree is unwed, the ashes are bereaved of their leaves, ivy clings wantonly, and oaks have ears to hear Orpheus.[57] A wind may be Bacchic, or commit crime; it may be companion of winter or governor of a sea.[58] The sea may be too over-mastering; a river may be uxorious, or gnaw its water-meadows.[59] A jar can be taught to imbibe smoke, or enticed out by a little box of nard.[60] There are, indeed, passages in which there is a sustained treatment of natural phenomena in terms which suggest human experience.[61] Personification also plays its part: Love keeps vigil on young cheeks, as in a chorus of Sophocles; Confidence pours out secrets and is more transparent than glass; Care rides pillion behind the horseman.[62] Sometimes a subtler thought is involved: like the Stoic wise man who is always king the spirit of Lollius has been consul not for his one year only, but all the time he has been winning his moral victories; on the other hand, a consul's lictors have no power to remove the wretched tumults of the mind and the cares that flit round coffered ceilings; and Death, whether summoned or not, hears the poor man's plea for relief[63] (see further M. Andrewes, *Greece and Rome* (1950), 106–15).

---

[53] 1. 27. 15.

[54] 2. 15. 16; cf. *excipere aprum* (3. 12, *fin.*) and our phrase 'a sun-trap'.

[55] *Socraticis madet sermonibus* (3. 21. 9); *munitaeque adhibe uim sapientiae* (3. 28. 4); *conuerso in pretium deo* (3. 16. 8).

[56] 3. 1. 30, *fundusque mendax, arbore nunc aquas culpante* ...

[57] 2. 15. 4, *caelebs*; 2. 9. 8, *uiduantur*; 1. 36. 20, *lasciuis hederis ambitiosior*, 1. 12. 11, *auritas*.

[58] 1. 25. 11, *bacchante*; 3. 27. 20, *peccet*; 1. 25. 20, *sodali*; 1. 3. 15, *arbiter*.

[59] 1. 14. 8, *imperiosius*; 1. 2. 20, *uxorius*; 1. 31. 8, *mordet*.

[60] 3. 8. 11, *institutae*; 4. 12. 17, *eliciet*. Other examples: 1. 25. 3, *amat ianua limen*; 4. 11. 7, *ara auet spargier*; 4. 11. 6, *ridet argento domus*; 1. 14. 5, *malus saucius*.

[61] 2. 9. 1–10; 2. 3. 9–16; 1. 9 throughout; ?cf. *Epode* 13. 1–5. L. P. Wilkinson, *Horace and his Lyric Poetry* (Cambridge, 1945), pp. 126–31.

[62] 4. 13. 8, *Cupido excubat in genis*, cf. *Antig.* 782; 1. 18. 16; 3. 1. 40.

[63] 4. 9. 39; 2. 16. 9; 2. 18. 40, *uocatus atque non uocatus audit*.

Besides metaphor and quasi-metaphor there are bold uses of transferred epithet—*adulteros crines, sublimi anhelitu, uices superbae*[64]—and of
oxymoron—*splendide mendax, insanientis sapientiae consultus, sollicitum
taedium*,[65] and all the variations on the theme of γλυχύπιχρος 'Ερως,
'Love the bitter-sweet',[66] not to mention unusual constructions, many of
them borrowed from Greek.

Enough has been said to substantiate what is indeed a commonplace,
that clever use of words in an unfamiliar setting was a characteristic of
Horace's *Odes*. But were these also peculiar in being markedly everyday
words? Axelson could find little ground for thinking them specially
prosaic in the instances he considered.[67] Are we then to suppose that in
his predilection for prosaic words, Horace was simply insensitive to their
associations, or consciously aiming at propriety and adequacy as an ideal
of expression, in accordance with his temperamental 'matter-of-fact-
ness', his 'formidable realism'[68] (*furchtbare Realität*), as Goethe called it?
Axelson quotes, without division into verses, six lines of what he takes to
be prosaic diction and everyday word-order from *Odes* 4. 9: 'non
possidentem multa uocaueris recte beatum; rectius occupat nomen
beati, qui deorum muneribus sapienter uti duramque callet pauperiem
pati, peiusque leto flagitium timet.'[69] I wonder if we are in a position to
judge the effect of that in Roman ears. Here, treated in the same way, is a
stanza from Tennyson's *In Memoriam*, equally commonplace in vocabulary and word-order, which does not, however, strike me at least as
unpoetical in its context: 'I sometimes hold it half a sin to put in words
the grief I feel; for words, like nature, half reveal and half conceal the
soul within.'

Smereka found 62 different colloquialisms in the 3,134 lines of the
Odes: quite a high proportion. On the other hand, he found 52
archaisms, which would militate against any naturalistic effect.[70] Such

---

[64] 1. 15. 19, 31; 1. 28. 32. Also 3. 2. 16 *timido tergo*; 3. 5. 22 *tergo libero*; 1. 17. 28
immeritam uestem.
[65] 3. 11. 35; 1. 34. 2; 1. 14. 17. Also 1. 22. 16, *arida nutrix*; 3. 21. 13, *lene tormentum*.
[66] 1. 27. 11, *beatus uolnere*; 1. 33. 14 and 4. 11. 23, *grata compede*; 2. 12. 26, *facili saeuitia*;
cf. 1. 8. 2, *amando perdere*.
[67] Op. cit. 110.
[68] *Goethes Gespräche*, Biedermann², 1. 458. E. Castle has suggested that *furchtbare* is a
misprint for *fruchtbare. Mitteil d. Verein d. Freunde d. human. Gymnasiums*, 33. Heft (Vienna,
1936), p. 14. 'Formidable' is Prof. Fraenkel's word (*Horace*, p. 276); otherwise an English
reader might assume from the context that Goethe meant 'frightful'.
[69] 45–50, iii. One may doubt, however, whether *occupat nomen* or *callet uti* are phrases of
ordinary prose.
[70] Op. cit. 67.

statistics cannot help us much here, because the *Odes* vary so greatly in tone; nor could we in any case use them satisfactorily for comparisons with epic poetry, since the length of Horace's lines varies so that it is hard to compare his verse with hexameters.

Let us now return to Virgil, and consider his diction in the light of what we have deduced about *noua uerba* with reference to Horace. In Virgil's case we are fortunate in having some corroborative evidence, in the *Saturnalia* of Macrobius. Nettleship, in his excursus on *Virgil and his Ancient Critics*,[71] showed that the observations on Virgil's use of language in Macrobius 6. 6, though put into the mouth of Seruius, are independent of the extant Servian Commentary; and that both appear to be drawing on a common source; and further, that this source seems to be a defence against hostile and inept critics. We know from Suetonius[72] that Asconius Pedianus, who lived under Tiberius, had written a book *Contra Obtrectatores Vergilii*, his opponents including one Herennius, who had made a collection of Virgil's *uitia*, and this book may well be the common source. If so, then the usages quoted were selected for blame or praise not long after Virgil's death, and when we are told that they are novelties, we can accept the evidence as contemporary.

The Macrobian Seruius is asked to say what instances he has noted in Virgil of figurative usage invented by himself, not borrowed from predecessors, or applied by him in a new but fitting way.[73] He obliges with some examples. *Recens caede locus*, for instance, is *noue dictus*,[74] and in *frontem rugis arat* the verb is *non nimie sed pulchre dictum*; and *aquae mons, telorum seges*, and *ferreus imber* are applauded.[75] Of especial interest, in view of Horace's *uerbum reddiderit iunctura nouum*, are the paragraphs (17–19) on *excogitatio nouorum sensuum*. Here we are told that Virgil was the first person to speak of harnessing waters, with his *glacie cursus frenaret aquarum*, or to say that a flower smiles, with his

> mixtaque *ridenti* colocasia fundet acantho;[76]

and there are ten other instances, most of which would never have struck

---

[71] Conington–Nettleship–Haverfield, i[5], pp. xxix–liii.

[72] *Vita Verg.* 43–6.

[73] 6. 6. 1: 'quae in Vergilio notauerit ab ipso figurata, non a ueteribus accepta, uel ausu poetico noue quidem sed decenter usurpata'. *Ausu* recalls Quintilian's characterization of Horace as 'uerbis felicissime *audax*'.

[74] 3; *Aen.* 9. 455.

[75] 6–7; *Aen.* 7. 417.

[76] 18; *Geo.* 4. 136; *E.* 4. 20. But in Greek we have γελῶντα κρίνα, 'laughing lilies' in Meleager, *AP* 5. 147 (ἀναγελῶντα, Giangrande, *RhM* (1958), 54); cf. *AP* 5. 144. 5.

us as novelties.[77] Mr John Sparrow, in an article published in 1930, illustrated our predicament with some good examples.[78] 'When English is a dead language', he wrote, 'the novelty will have gone from such a phrase as [Tennyson's]

> all her dress
> *Wept* from her sides as water flowing away.

Now that Latin is a dead language, can we recapture the thrill given to its first readers by

> tota cohors ... relictis
> ad terram *defluxit* equis?'

The whole unit, leaving its horses, *flowed* down to the ground.

Macrobius also provides evidence of Virgil's use of natural language. He defends by analogy with Homer his lines which are 'as it were plucked and shorn and indistinguishable from colloquial speech',[79] instancing

> omnia uincit Amor: et nos cedamus Amori

and

> nudus in ignota, Palinure, iacebis harena.

And a critic named Cornutus, who blamed Virgil for meiosis in calling Busiris merely *inlaudatus* and saying that Scylla merely *uexasse* ships, also blamed him for homely diction in the phrase *dixerat ille aliquid magnum*.[80] At *Aen.* 12. 296 Messapius gives Aulestes his death-blow with the cry which (as we are reminded by the comic poets) the crowd used to raise when a gladiator was laid low: 'Hoc habet!'—'He's had it!' Of *callida iunctura*, in the sense I have assumed for it in discussing Horace, Mr Jackson Knight has drawn attention to many and diverse examples from Virgil, concluding that his art lay in combining his few words so as to elicit a great variety of meanings.[81]

---

[77] *Aen.* 2. 422, *mentitaque tela*; 9. 773, *ferrumque armare ueneno*; *Geo.* 2. 36, *cultusque feros mollire colendo*; ibid. 51, *exuerint siluestrem animum*; *Aen.* 11. 804, *uirgineumque alte bibit acta cruorem* (cf. *Il.* 21. 168); *Geo.* 2. 59, *pomaque degenerant sucos oblita priores*; *Aen.* 4. 67, *tacitum uiuit sub pectore uulnus*; *Aen.* 5. 681, *duro sub robore uiuit stuppa uomens tardum fumum*; ibid. 257, *saeuitque canum latratus in auras*; 7. 792, *caelataque amnem fundens pater Inachus urna*; *Geo.* 4. 239, *animasque in uulnera ponunt*.

[78] 'Thoughts on Virgil's Bimillenary', in the *Nineteenth Century* (Oct. 1930), 512–13.

[79] 5. 14. 5: 'uolsis ac rasis similes et nihil differentes ab usu loquendi'. Nettleship remarks (ibid., p. xxx) that *uolsis ac rasis* has all the air of a quotation from a hostile critic.

[80] *Geo.* 3. 4; *E.* 6. 75; Gellius 2. 6 = Macrobius 6. 7. 4–5; *Serv. on Aen.* 10. 547; Cornutus ut sordidum improbat.   [81] Op. cit. 263.

Let us now sum up. There was a long critical tradition that good poetry could be composed of everyday words. Horace on occasion paid lip-service at least to this tradition. Agrippa thought that Virgil had introduced the idea, apparently unaware that it was as old as Euripides in practice and as Aristotle in criticism. Examination of the vocabulary of Horace's *Odes* and Virgil's *Aeneid* has established the fact that both poets do use ordinary words to a marked degree, even if we make allowance for the strong random element that must affect such statistics. To some extent it seems likely that the ordinariness of the words in themselves was offset by bold and clever combinations that imparted freshness and overtones, and by poetical or abnormal constructions; but in many cases there seems to be no question of this. The practice of these two closely associated poets seems therefore to represent a reaction, sufficiently marked to be considered conscious, against the tendency of their immediate predecessors, particularly the νεώτεροι, 'New Poets', to enrich their language with words unfamiliar to the plain man.[82] It was no doubt in part a literary reaction of a kind we now recognize. But it was also in harmony with the Augustan idea that the poet had a right and a duty to address the citizens at large.

[82] In the time of the elder Seneca there were still those who ἐπὶ τὸ λεξικὸν μαίνονται, 'mad on the dictionary' (*Contr.* 9. 26).

23

Multiple-Correspondence Similes in the
Aeneid

D. A. WEST

Similes in the *Aeneid*, like Homeric similes, have commonly been thought of as similes *à queue longue*, as similes which have *one* point of comparison with the narrative and a large ornamental development. The purpose of this paper is to show that almost all the similes in the *Aeneid* contain *many* details which correspond to details in the surrounding narrative. Correspondences involving explicit details in both simile and narrative I call *bilateral* correspondences. Sometimes there occurs in a simile a detail for which we should clearly supply in our imagination a corresponding detail for the narrative; similarly we should sometimes imagine a detail for the simile to correspond with some detail in the narrative: these I call *unilateral* correspondences. Sometimes there occurs a correspondence which does not fit the main comparison: this I call an *irrational* correspondence. To establish and study these three types of correspondence, we shall take as our sample the second book of the *Aeneid* and look at every simile in it. Then we shall take some similes from other books and see if this approach helps us to understand the text of the *Aeneid*.

I. *Bilateral Correspondences in* Aeneid 2

clarescunt sonitus armorumque ingruit horror.
excutior somno et summi fastigia tecti
ascensu supero atque arrectis auribus asto:
in segetem ueluti cum flamma furentibus Austris
incidit, aut rapidus montano flumine torrens
sternit agros, sternit sata laeta boumque labores
praecipitisque trahit siluas: stupet inscius alto
accipiens sonitum saxi de uertice pastor.
tum uero manifesta fides, Danaumque patescunt
insidiae. iam Deiphobi dedit ampla ruinam
Volcano superante domus, iam proximus ardet
Vcalegon; Sigea igni freta lata relucent. (2. 301–12)

Aeneas watching the burning of Troy is compared to a shepherd watching a fire or flood. For Aeneas *clarescunt sonitus*, so the shepherd is *accipiens sonitum*; for Aeneas *ingruit horror*, so for the shepherd *flamma* ... *incidit*, both verbs being frequently used in military contexts; Aeneas climbs *summi fastigia tecti*, so the shepherd listens *alto* ... *saxi de uertice*; Aeneas stands there with his ears pricked up, *arrectis auribus asto*, so the shepherd *stupet*. In lines 306–7 of the simile the flood damage is expressed in a tricolon of which the first two cola are linked by the anaphora of *sternit*, so the burning of Troy is expressed in a tricolon of which the first two cola are linked by the anaphora of *iam*. Further these tricola are both somewhat unusual in that they are not ascending.

> tum Danai gemitu atque ereptae uirginis ira
> undique collecti inuadunt, acerrimus Aiax
> et gemini Atridae Dolopumque exercitus omnis;
> aduersi rupto ceu quondam turbine uenti
> confligunt, Zephyrusque Notusque et laetus Eois
> Eurus equis; stridunt siluae saeuitque tridenti
> spumeus atque imo Nereus ciet aequora fundo. (2. 413–19)

The Greeks under Ajax have abducted Cassandra. The Trojans with Coroebus and Aeneas have rescued her. The Greeks rallying to the spot are compared to the winds clashing when a whirlwind bursts. There is *gemitus atque* ... *ira* at the rescue of Cassandra, so *siluae stridunt* and *saeuit Nereus*; the Greeks *undique collecti inuadunt*, so the winds *aduersi confligunt*; the Greeks are divided into three groups in an ascending tricolon; so there are three winds in an ascending tricolon.[1]

> instat ui patria Pyrrhus; nec claustra nec ipsi
> custodes sufferre ualent; labat ariete crebro
> ianua, et emoti procumbunt cardine postes.
> fit uia ui; rumpunt aditus primosque trucidant
> immissi Danai et late loca milite complent.
> non sic, aggeribus ruptis cum spumeus amnis
> exiit oppositasque euicit gurgite moles,
> fertur in arua furens cumulo camposque per omnis
> cum stabulis armenta trahit. uidi ipse furentem
> caede Neoptolemum ... (2. 491–500)

The Greeks *rumpunt aditus*, so the river bursts its banks *aggeribus ruptis*; *immissi Danai*, so *amnis exiit*; *nec claustra nec ipsi custodes sufferre*

---

[1] For other responsive tricola see 8. 241–5 *specus et ingens regia et penitus cauernae* answered by *sedes et regna superque immane barathrum*.

ualent, so the river *cum stabulis armenta trahit*; the doors are dislodged from their sockets and collapse, *emoti procumbunt cardine postes*, so the river *oppositas euicit gurgite moles*; *et late loca*, so *camposque per omnes*; *milite complent*, so *fertur cumulo*; the river is *furens*, so in the reprise of the narrative in 500, Neoptolemus is *furentem*.

II. *Unilateral Correspondences in* Aeneid 2

tum uero omne mihi uisum considere in ignis
Ilium et ex imo uerti Neptunia Troia;
ac ueluti summis antiquam in montibus ornum
cum ferro accisam crebrisque bipennibus instant
eruere agricolae certatim; illa usque minatur
et tremefacta comam concusso uertice nutat,
uulneribus donec paulatim euicta supremum
congemuit traxitque iugis auulsa ruinam. (2. 624–31)

A straightforward example of what I mean by a unilateral correspondence lies in the word *antiquam* 626. Troy is compared to an ashtree. The tree is said to be old. We all know that Troy is old. So this term in the simile corresponds to the narrative although there is no corresponding term in the text of the narrative (so R. G. Austin ad loc). This is a simple and unimportant example but the main force of the simile must be explained on such a procedure.

Troy is ablaze and Neptune is tearing the whole city up from its foundations, *totamque a sedibus urbem eruit* 611–12. In 624 Aeneas sees it settling down into its fires and turning over from the bottom, and this is compared to the felling of a wild ash-tree. There is no close verbal correspondence here between simile and narrative, but it is easy to see the main point of the comparison. Troy was a city of tall buildings, and when the fire brings them down, they turn over from the bottom, *ex imo uerti*, and settle into the flames. This is exactly what happens when a tree is felled. It turns in a quarter-circle and comes to rest on the ground. But in the simile the visual details are highly elaborated. The mountain ash threatens to fall, its foliage trembles, its top is shaken and sways until at last it is gradually overwhelmed by its wounds, it gives the final creak as it breaks, and it spreads destruction along its ridge. All these details apply *mutandis mutatis* to the fall of a high building and enrich our visual reaction to Virgil's description of the destruction of the buildings of Troy. Similarly the personification of the tree, its trembling hair, its shuddering and nodding head, its wounds, its gradual

weakening, and its death cry, heighten our emotional reaction to the
Trojan narrative.

> uestibulum ante ipsum primoque in limine Pyrrhus
> exsultat telis et luce coruscus aena;
> qualis ubi in lucem coluber mala gramina pastus,
> frigida sub terra tumidum quem bruma tegebat,
> nunc, positis nouus exuuiis nitidusque iuuenta,
> lubrica conuoluit sublato pectore terga
> arduus ad solem, et linguis micat ore trisulcis. (2. 469–75)

In this comparison of Pyrrhus to a snake there are many bilateral
correspndences. Pyrrhus is *uestibulum ante ipsum primoque in limine*, so
the snake is coiling *in lucem* and is therefore presumably just emerging
from its *hibernaculum*; Pyrrhus *exsultat telis*, so the snake is *sublato pectore
arduus* and *linguis micat*; Pyrrhus is *coruscus*, so the snake *linguis micat ore
trisulcis*, and *coruscus*, *micat*, and *trisulcis* are all lightning words; in line
470 Pyrrhus is *luce coruscus*, so the simile has *in lucem* 471, *nitidus iuuenta*
473, and *ad solem* 475. But more important than these is the unilateral
correspondence in line 473 *nunc positis nouus exuuiis nitidusque iuuenta*.
The sanke has cast its slough, it is renewed and resplendent in its youth.
How does this correspond with Pyrrhus? The salient fact about Pyrrhus
is that he is the son of Achilles (cf. 2. 491, 540, 549). The snake has cast
its old slough and is resplendent in its new skin, so Achilles is dead and
the young Neoptolemus is gleaming with youth. There is nothing
abstruse about this (see B. M. W. Knox, *AJPh* 71 (1950), 394). The
reader who does not tranfer this simile detail to the narrative is
comatose.

A third and last example of unilateral correspondence occurs at the
description of the Trojan women taking refuge at the altar.

> aedibus in mediis nudoque sub aetheris axe
> ingens ara fuit iuxtaque ueterrima laurus
> incumbens arae atque umbra complexa penatis.
> hic Hecuba et natae nequiquam altaria circum,
> praecipites atra ceu tempestate columbae,
> condensae et diuum amplexae simulacra sedebant. (2. 512–17)

Line 516 appears to form the simile, 'like doves swooping down in a dark
storm'. *Praecipites* has some sort of analogue in *sedebant* but it is a
unilateral correspondence in the sense that it is clearly meant to apply
not only to the doves but also to Hecuba and her daughters. Conversely
condensae is used of the women but it is such a natural word to use of

birds that it would be perverse to read this passage without imagining the pigeons flocking together.

These unilateral correspondences are to be distinguished from the correspondences for which the text offers no explicit authority. For example, Austin argues that this 'simile is carefully chosen, not only for the innocence of the doves and their affection for one another, but because they are preyed upon by hawks or eagles'. Such associations arising in the imagination of the critic, may in certain cases be perfectly valid and helpful to the reader. But they are different from the unilateral correspondences I am talking about. They are not in the text at all. They are nullilateral correspondences.

III. *Irrational Correspondences in* Aeneid 2

The third and last category to be exemplified from this second book of the *Aeneid* covers those details in a simile which resemble details in the narrative but do not fit the main corresponsion between simile and narrative. For example, the first simile discussed in this paper compares Aeneas standing on the top of the palace watching the destruction of Troy to a shepherd standing on a rock watching a fire or flood, and the details mentioned in my analysis fit this general picture. But the narrative immediately continues in lines 316–17, *ardent animi: furor iraque mentem praecipitat*, where *ardent*, *furor*, and *praecipitat* closely resemble *flamma*, *furentibus*, and *praecipitis* in the simile. The main pattern of correspondence is that the destruction of Troy is likened to the fury of a crop fire, and to the headlong destruction of a flood. But by this irrational correspondence the crop fire and the flood now seem to be set against the blazing fury and headlong impetus of the despairing Trojans.

Similarly in 370–82 where Androgeos stumbles upon a party of Trojans disguised as Greeks, greets them as friends and then suddenly realizes his mistake, he is compared to a man who steps on a snake. This is again a multiple-correspondence simile where *inscius*, *tremefactus abibat*, *extemplo*, and perhaps *medios ... in hostes* of Androgeos, correspond to *improuisum*, *trepidus refugit*, *repente*, and *aspris sentibus* of the simile; similarly *retro pedem ... repressit* in 378 echoed in sound by *repente refugit* in 380. But the simile contains also a responsion which does not fit the main comparison; Androgeos in 378 *pedem cum uoce repressit*, so in 380 the traveller *anguem pressit humi nitens*. This simile compares a man falling amongst enemies with a man treading on a snake and the other details fit these two pictures. But the responsion between a man 'repressing his foot' and 'a man pressing a snake as he puts his weight on the ground' is a verbal play which cuts across the main comparison.

James Henry (*Aeneidea* (London, 1873), i. 725) cites the comparison between the warriors and the wolves in 2. 355–60 amongst those which 'are not the less but the more striking ... on account of the utter dissimilarity in all respects between the objects compared except alone in the precise particular with respect to which they are compared'. But this simile too has several points of correspondence: *furor* is added to the warriors by Aeneas' harangue, so *rabies exegit* the wolves; the wolves are *atra in nebula*; for the warriors *nox atra caua circumuolat umbra*. These are bilateral. *Per tela per hostes* of the warriors is unilateral, suggesting the ring of steel round a hunted animal as in 9. 552–5 and 793–6. There is no irrational link between simile and context here but there is a verbal echo or irrational link between the narrative and its reprise. Aeneas adjures his men in 352–3, *succurritis urbi incensae: moriamur et in media arma ruamus*. They respond like ravening wolves and in the reprise of the narrative in 359–60 *uodimus haud dubiam in mortem mediaeque tenemus urbis iter*. This multiple verbal responsion binds the whole passage together, even if the substance of the two lines is not identical.

For a similar link between the narrative and its continuation after a simile, where the responsion is entirely verbal, compare the dove simile we have already examined for its unilateral correspondences. Here in line 514 there is an ancient bay tree *incumbens arae atque umbra complexa Penatis*. Here in 516–17 Hecuba and her daughters take refuge like doves in a dark storm and *diuum amplexae simulacra sedebant*. It is a strict fact that learning, shade, embracing, and household gods are followed by a dark storm, gods, embracing, and sitting. This fact may be inadvertent and insignificant. The only criterion is to establish whether such facts frequently occur in Virgil.

This will emerge in the second half of this paper. So far we have looked at every simile in the second book of the *Aeneid* and attempted to classify some correspondences. Almost all the similes in the *Aeneid* are multiple-correspondence similes in this sense. Straightforward examples from the second half of the *Aeneid* are the boiling pot of 7. 456–66 (see D. A. West, *Reading Horace* (Edinburgh, 1967), 69), the earth fissure in 8. 241–9, the animals at bay in 9. 549–55 and 788–800, the lion and the bull in 10. 451–5, the hawk and the dove 11. 718–24, and any of the half-dozen similes listed by W. S. Maguiness in the introduction to his edition of the twelfth book as similes where 'the poet acts for a moment as if he forgot that the function of the simile is that of comparison, and treats the picture it contains as one to be developed because of its own interest'.

We shall now try to show the validity and utility of these classifications by looking at some similes selected from other books of the *Aeneid*.

IV. *Some Other Examples*

In the first book (487–506) Dido is compared to Diana. Dido has an escort of warriors crowding around her *magna iuuenum stipante caterua*, so a thousand attendant Oreads are gathered about Diana *mille secutae hinc atque hinc glomerantur Oreades*, and so Dido in the reprise walked proudly in the middle of her men *se ferebat per medios*; Dido *incessit* and in the reprise *se ferebat*, so Diana is *gradiens*; *exercet Diana choros*, a detail which according to Servius 'non ad comparationem pertinet sed est poeticae descriptionis euagatio', but so Dido is *instans operi*. So much for some of the bilateral correspondences. In 502 joy tempts the secret heart of Diana's mother, so by an irrational correspondence, in 503 Dido *se laeta ferebat*; similarly Diana wears a quiver on her shoulder and Dido is *saepta armis*. Most bizarre of all, the goddess Diana in 501 is very properly taller than her nymphs; it would be unbecoming if Dido were taller than her warriors, but an irrational correspondence is achieved in 506 by setting her high on a throne *solioque alte subnixa resedit*. There is no need to follow G. N. Knauer, *Die Aeneis und Homer* (Göttingen, 1964), 155, in thinking of the couch of Odysseus (*Odyssey* 4. 136).

These correspondences could theoretically be coincidences. To refute this theory it is enough to look at the Homeric prototype of this simile. 'After Nausikaa and her servants had enjoyed their meal, the girls threw off their veils and played at ball, while Nausikaa struck up a song. Just as the arrow-showering goddess who delights in boars and swift hinds comes down from Mount Taygetus or Erymantus and with her play the country nymphs, the maidens of aegis-bearing Zeus, and Leto rejoices in her heart. Artemis is easily picked out amongst them, head and forehead above them all, and they are all beautiful. So the maiden Nausikaa stood out amongst her servants' (*Odyssey* 6. 99–109). Here the bilateral correspondences are few and simple, in fact—the retinue and their playing, and the conspicuousness of Nausikaa/ Artemis. Of the Virgilian correspondences we see that some have been added to both narrative and simile (these include the numbers of the retinue, their crowding around the central figure, the moving and the active leadership, as listed above). More revealing are the three details which Virgil has supplied to the narrative to make it fit the simile (*saepta armis, Latonae gaudia,* and *solio alte*). This establishes my case. Three of the details of the Homeric simile which have no responsion in the Homeric narrative, are fitted out with irrational responsions in the *Aeneid.* This is not coincidence. This is engineering.

In passing it is interesting to notice that the two geographical details in the Homeric simile are purely ornamental, with no analogue in the narrative. These ornaments survive in Virgil *in Eurotae ripis aut per iuga Cynthi,* and they are all that does survive of the *queue longue* of the Homeric simile.

After this analysis it is interesting to look across to two points in Probus' attack upon this simile as preserved by Aulus Gellius (9. 14–17). 'Dido pressing on the work of her rising kingdom can have no points of similarity corresponding with the sports and hunts of Diana.' But Virgil has provided one in *exercet.* 'Secondly, Homer mentions plainly and directly Diana's interest and pleasure in the chase, while Virgil not having said a word about the goddess's hunting, merely pictures her as carrying a quiver on her shoulder, as if it were a burden or a pack.' Quite, Virgil has played down the chase, in which Dido cannot here be compared to Diana, and referred to Diana's armoury, for which he then provides the correspondence in *saepta armis.*

Viktor Pöschl (*Die Dichtkunst Virgils* (Innsbruck, 1950), 100–15) has already noticed some of the correspondences in the Dido/Diana simile; he also shows, with Servius, that the simile of the wounded hind in 4. 66–73 is a multiple-correspondence simile (ibid. 131–5). More complex is the simile of the oak in the wind.

talibus orabat, talisque miserrima fletus[1]
fertque[2] refertque soror. sed nullis ille mouetur[3]
fletibus[1] aut uoces[4] ullas tractabilis audit;
fata obstant placidasque uiri deus obstruit auris.
ac uelut annoso ualidam[9] cum robore quercum
Alpini Boreae nunc hinc[2] nunc flatibus[1] illinc
eruere[3] inter se certant; it stridor,[4] et altae
consternunt[8] terram concusso[5] stipite[6] frondes;[7]
ipsa haeret[3] scopulis et quantum uertice ad auras
aetherias, tantum radice in Tartara tendit:[9]
haud secus adsiduis hinc atque hinc[2] uocibus[14] heros
tunditur,[5] et magno[9] persentit pectore[6] curas;
mens[6] immota[3] manet, lacrimae[7] uoluontur[8] inanes. (4. 437–9)

The figures indicate the main correspondences, but three of them are particularly noteworthy: first, *fletibus* in line 439 corresponding to *flatibus* in line 442,[2] second, the trunk is shaken and the lofty leaves strew the ground in 443 but the tree itself holds fast, so the hero feels in his breast, but his mind remains unmoved and the empty tears roll down. The trunk corresponds to the *pectus*, the *mens* within it corresponds to the tree itself, *ipsa*, the leaves strewing the ground are (as Pöschl sees, op. cit. 76–9) the falling tears. 'Frondes sicut lacrimae Aeneae' is Servius' note on line 444, and the whole architecture of the passage bears him out, although commentators and translators commonly attribute the tears to Dido or hedge their bets, as Servius himself does in line 449, 'quidam tamen lacrimas inanes uel Aeneae uel Didonis uel Annae uel omnium accipiunt'. So Austin, 'These tears could not be denied to Aeneas: but in the changing moods that repeated reading of Virgil always brings, few could withhold them for ever from Dido.' The third point to comment upon in this passage is *magno . . . pectore*. '*Magno* would be banal', writes Austin, 'if the context did not emphasize its importance.' To look at this question more closely, *magno* not only presents Aeneas as a great-hearted hero and 'magnifies the picture of his struggle' but it also brings the narrative into closer correspondence with the simile. His breast is the tree trunk and it is a large breast because it is a large tree (441 and 445–6).

> saeuo e scopulo multa uix arte reuulsus
> amissis remis atque ordine debilis uno
> inrisam sine honore ratem Sergestus agebat.
> qualis saepe uiae deprensus in aggere serpens,
> aerea quem obliquum rota transiit aut grauis ictu
> seminecem liquit saxo lacerumque uiator;
> nequiquam longos fugiens dat corpore tortus
> parte ferox ardensque oculis et sibila colla
> arduus attollens; pars uulnere clauda retentat
> nexantem nodis seque in sua membra plicantem:
> tali remigio nauis se tarda mouebat;
> uela facit tamen et uelis subit ostia plenis. (5. 270–81)

The main point of comparison here is the two modes of locomotion, the *pars ferox* is the makeshift sails, the *pars clauda* what remains of the oars. In line 280 the boat moved itself by rowing which was like the movements of the back half of a wounded snake, *pars uolnere clauda retentat nexantem nodis seque plicantem* corresponding to *tali remigio se*

---

[2] There are striking puns between narrative and simile at 8. 703, 704, *aeratas aeriam*, and on *rostris* 9. 119.

tarda mouebat. But they put up sails and came up to the harbour under
full sail 281, and this corresponds to the front half of the wounded
serpent *parte ferox ... arduus attollens.* *Saxo* in 275 has this note in R. D.
Williams's edition: 'Mackail comments on the awkwardness of the two
ablatives *ictu* and *saxo.* Henry, followed by Page, suggests that *saxo* is a
local ablative ("half-dead on the road"), but this greatly strains the
meaning of *saxum.* We must take it as instrumental with *seminecem,*
helped a little by *lacerum.*' But the meaning of *saxum* is not greatly
strained if it refers to the rock of the road (compare, for example,
Lucretius 1. 316; Statius, *Siluae* 4. 3.3, 46, and 52). This interpretation
is borne out by the clear responsion between *seminecem liquit saxo* in the
simile and *infelix saxis ... haesit* in the narrative at line 204.

In the sixth book most of the important correspondences between
simile and narrative have been noted in E. Norden's great commentary,
but it may still be useful to look at three famous similes from this point of
view.

> discolor unde auri per ramos aura refulsit,
> quale solet siluis brumali frigore uiscum
> fronde uirere noua, quod non sua seminat arbos,
> et croceo fetu teretis circumdare truncos
> talis erat species auri frondentis opaca
> ilice, sic leni crepitabat brattea uento. (6. 204–9)

Here *discolor* is picked up by *quod non sua seminat arbos,* and *noua* carries
a similar implication (cf. *nouas frondes et non sua poma* of a graft in *Geo.* 2.
82); *auri* is picked up by *croceo; per ramos* by *circumdare truncos;* so, in the
reprise of the narrative *talis* corresponds to *quale; frondentis* to *fronde;* and
it would be cowardice not to point out that the inexplicable poetry of *auri
aura,* the breath of gold, in the narrative has some sort of reprise and
perhaps explanation in *brattea uento,* in the gentle breeze which rattles
the gold foil in 209 (so Norden ad loc.)

In 6. 268–73 there are many bilateral correspondences.

> ibant obscuri sola sub nocte per umbram
> perque domos Ditis uacuas et inania regna:
> quale per incertam lunam sub luce maligna
> est iter in siluis, ubi caelum condidit umbra
> Iuppiter, et rebus nox abstulit atra colorem. (6. 268–72)

Ibant is answered by *est iter; obscuri* by *incertam; sub nocte* by *sub luce
maligna; per umbram* by *condidit umbra;* the *domos Ditis* by *caelum Iuppiter;*
and less rationally *uacuas et inania regna* by *abstulit.* In a narrative in

which every detail has some sort of explicit responsion in the simile, it would be over-rigorous to keep *sola* in 268 out of the simile. This is a unilateral correspondence. The night walk in the woods is also a lonely walk.

But these correspondences are very simple. More striking and more typical are the responsions in the comparison between Rome and Cybele.

> en huius, nate, auspiciis illa incluta Roma
> imperium terris, animos aequabit Olympo,
> septemque una sibi muro circumdabit arces,
> felix prole uirum: qualis Berecyntia mater
> inuehitur curru Phrygias turrita per urbes
> laeta deum partu, centum complexa nepotes,
> omnis caelicolas, omnis supera alta tenentis. (6. 781–7)

Here in the prospect of heroes offered to Aeneas, after Romulus son of Ilia of the [Trojan] stock of Assaracus, *Romulus Assaraci quem sanguinis Ilia mater educet*, we find Rome herself compared to the great mother goddess of Asia, *Berecyntia mater*. So Virgil repeatedly places the Rome of his own day in the long perspective of the legendary past, supplying here an historical justification for her contemporary hegemony; and so here the closeness of the correspondences is important to the main purpose of the *Aeneid*. Cybele is *turrita*, so Rome *muro circumdabit arces*; Cybele is carried in procession *Phrygias per urbes*, so Rome's dominion will be co-extensive with the earth, *imperium terris*; Cybele is *laeta deum partu*, so Rome is *felix prole uirum*; Cybele is *centum complexa nepotes* whereas Rome *septem circumdabit arces*; all of Cybele's grandchildren are divine, *omnis caelicolas omnis supera alta tenentis* whereas Rome *animos aequabit Olympo*.

> uoluitur Euryalus leto, pulchrosque per artus
> it cruor inque umeros ceruix conlapsa recumbit:
> purpureus ueluti cum flos succisus aratro
> languescit moriens, lassoue papauera collo
> demisere caput pluuia cum forte grauantur. (9. 433–7)

Here the sword which breaks the breast of Euryalus corresponds to the plough by which the flower is cut; *leto* is picked up by *moriens*; the blood has an irrational responsion in *purpureus* and *papauera*;[3] the *ceruix*

---

[3] Cf. *purpureum, cruer,* and *cruentat* in 10. 722, 728, and 731; *sanguine* and *cruor* 11. 720 and 724; *rubor, sanguineo,* and *rubent* in 12. 66, 67, and 68; *sanguineus* and *sanguineos* in 12. 332 and 340.

conlapsa is the *lasso collo*; *uoluitur Euryalus*, and so the purple flower *languescit*; his neck *recumbit* and so the poppies *demisere caput*.

> cingitur ipse furens certatim in proelia Turnus;
> iamque adeo rutilum thoraca indutus aenis
> horrebat squamis surasque incluserat auro,
> tempora nudus adhuc, laterique accinxerat ensem,
> fulgebatque alta decurrens aureus arce
> exsultatque animis et spe iam praecipit hostem:
> qualis ubi abruptis fugit praesaepia uinclis
> tandem liber equus campoque potitus aperto
> aut ille in pastus armentaque tendit equarum
> aut adsuetus aquae perfundi flumine noto
> emicat arrectisque fremit ceruicibus alte
> luxurians, luduntque iubae per colla, per armos. (11. 486–97)

Turnus is now armed *iamque adeo* (see J. W. Mackail, *The Aeneid of Virgil* (Oxford, 1930), ad loc.), so the stallion is at last free *tandem*; his chest, ankles, and side receive their proper equipment, so we hear about the stallion's *ceruicibus colla* and *armos*; he *fulgebat*, so the stallion *emicat*; he is *alta decurrens arce*, so the stallion *campo potitus aperto*; he is *decurrens*, so the stallion *fugit*; he *spe iam praecipit hostem* so the stallion *in pastus armentaque tendit equarum*; he *exsultat animis*, so the stallion is *arrectis ceruicibus alte luxurians*; Turnus *horrebat* and so does the stallion have *arrectis ceruicibus*.

But a question arises. Why in 489 does Turnus not put his helmet on? Servius answers that this is *pro economia*. He is just about to speak to Camilla, and he must in the succeeding scenes be easily recognizable. Werner Kühn in *Gymnasium* 64 (1957), 32, adds that Virgil by this device also makes sure that the features of Turnus do not altogether disappear behind the gleaming of the hero's armour. There is another reason: Turnus keeps his head bare; so the stallion's mane in 497 is playing over his neck and flanks.

As with the first simile considered in this section, the Homeric model provides some control of the argument and some insight into Virgil's intentions. In Homer *Iliad* 6. 503–13 Paris leaving the lofty palace (the high citadel of Troy in the reprise 512), donning his shining armour, speeding through the city trusting in his swift feet, is compared with a stallion breaking away from the manger, running across the plain trusting in its shining beauty, his knees carrying him swiftly to the places where the horses are pasturing. So much for the correspondences. The ornamental development includes the participial phrase qualifying the stallion, 'being accustomed to bathe in the broad river'[4] and his physical description 'he held his head high and the mane fell about his shoulders'. Virgil tries to remove this *queue longue* by making the bathe in the river one of the two possible destinations of the stallion, and by providing some sort of correspondence in the narrative to the description of the flowing mane, *tempora nudus adhuc* to correspond to *luduntque iubae per colla*. Other Virgilian additions which produce a more detailed fit between narrative and simile are the three pairs of references to parts of the body, and the allusion to Turnus' destination.

V. Transfusion of Terms, Metaphorical and Literal

Sometimes in the second half of the *Aeneid* the narrative is expressed in terms of a metaphor closely related to an adjacent simile. So too a simile will sometimes contain a metaphor closely related to the adjacent narrative. These phenomena I call transfusions of metaphor.

For example in 10. 356–9 a battle is compared to warring winds, *discordes uenti proelia ceu tollunt animis*,[5] *anceps pugna diu*, that is to say in the simile the activity of the winds is described in a metaphor closely related to the adjacent military narrative. In a passage very like this in the second book (415–21, discussed above), Virgil keeps specifically military terms out of the wind simile. Another simple example of transfusion of metaphor occurs where Aeneas taking cover is compared to a man sheltering from a storm; so *Aeneas nubem belli dum detonet omnis sustinet* (10. 809–10). Similarly when the coalescence of separate battles is compared to the coalescence of separate flames, a military metaphor dominates the fire simile.

> ac uelut optato uentis aestate coortis
> dispersa immittit siluis incendia pastor,
> correptis subito mediis extenditur una
> horrida per latos acies Volcania campos,
> ille sedens uictor flammas despectat ouantis:
> non aliter socium uirtus coit omnis in unum
> teque iuuat, Palla. (10. 405–11)

In this simile the bilateral correspondences are *extenditur* and *coit, mediis*

---

[4] On this line see D.J.N. Lee, *The Similes of the* Iliad *and the* Odyssey *Compared* (Melbourne, 1964), p. 39. On the relationship between these two similes see further R. Heinze, *Virgils epische Technik* (Darmstadt, 1957), p. 259. On the simile in the *Aeneid* see G.N. Knauer, *Die Aeneis und Homer*, p. 286.

[5] *Animis* could be a pun in this context (cf. Servius on *Aeneid* 1. 57).

una and *omnis in unum, pastor* and *Pallas*, and there is a notable irrational correspondence between *ouantis* and *iuuat*. But what concerns us now is the transfusion of metaphor whereby the simile is expressed in terms closely related to the adjacent narrative: *acies, uictor,* and *ouantis* are all obviously applicable to the battle scene, but so too are *horrida, campus, sedens,* and *despectat.* In 11. 621–35 the swaying battle is compared to the waves on a beach, but after the third Tuscan attack *sanguine in alto uoluontur equi, pugna aspera surgit.* Here the bodies rolling in deep blood and the rough battle rising are both the metaphorical application of the world of the simile to the world of the narrative, again different from the earlier treatment in 7. 523–30, where there is no transfusion of terms between the military narrative and the sea simile. The reverse phenomenon occurs at the beginning of the twelfth book where Turnus is compared to a lion and a metaphor closely related to the narrative occurs in the simile when the lion *mouet arma.*

So much for transfusion of metaphor. Sometimes the term which crosses the fence cannot be explained as a metaphor. It is simply a detail which would fit the narrative but occurs instead in the simile which it does not fit, or conversely a detail which would be appropriate in the simile but which occurs instead in the narrative. So perhaps *sanguine in alto uoluontur equi* and *mouet arma leo* in the last two examples cited above. So at 10. 718 where, if the text is right, Mezentius is *dentibus infrendens et tergo decutit hastas.* Why is he grinding his teeth? Why have these spears in the back not been mentioned?[6] Why have they not impaired his movements? Where have they come from? Surely the grinding and the spears both come from the multiple-correspondence simile in which Mezentius has just been compared to a boar caught in the nets.

> postquam inter retia uentum est,
> substitit infremuitque ferox et inhorruit armos,
> nec cuiquam irasci propiusque accedere uirtus,
> sed iaculis tutisque procul clamoribus instant;
> haud aliter, iustae quibus est Mezentius irae,
> non ulli est animus stricto concurrere ferro,
> missilibus longe et uasto clamore lacessunt.
> ille autem impauidus partis cunctatur in omnis
> dentibus infrendens et tergo decutit hastas. (10. 710–18)

The first simile of the seventh book, in which Amata driven berserk by

---

[6] But La Cerda, quoted by Henry ad loc., takes *tergo* as 'shield'.

Allecto is compared to a spinning top, exemplifies most of the categories of correspondence treated in this article. Bilateral correspondences leap to the eye: the top is *actus* 380, so Amata *agitur* 384 and *matres idem simul omnes ardor agit* 392–3, and *reginam Allecto stimulis agit undique Bacchi* 405 (cf. *agit ueluti agitatus* 4. 465, 469, 470); the top goes *in gyro, atria circum*, curuatis spatiis, so Amata calls out to Bacchus *te lustrare choro*; the top is flying under the whip, as tops do if properly struck, *torto uolitans sub uerbere* 378, so Amata flies off to the woods *euolat* 387. But this is not the end of the twisting or the flying: irrational correspondences occur in 399 where Amata is *torquens aciem* and in 382 where, if the pun be allowed, the top is *uolubile buxum*. But most conspicuous here are the transfusions of literal terms: why is Laurentum so large, *immensam per urbem* 377? Because the boys are whipping the top *magno in gyro* 379. Why does Allecto use the goads of Bacchus, *stimulis agit undique Bacchi* 405? Because the top is *uolitans sub uerbere* 378, *actus habena* 380, and *dant animos plagae* 383. Why does Allecto drive her from all sides? Because several boys with whips would gather round one top. Perhaps we have even solved the problem of the *empty* halls. Why are the boys playing *uacua atria circum*? Where is everybody? The answer comes in the resumptive couplet

talem inter siluas inter deserta ferarum
reginam Allecto stimulis agit undique Bacchi. (7. 404–5)

The boys are playing in empty rooms because Amata is running wild through the *desolate* haunts of wild beasts. Similarly we may also explain why Virgil 'disfigured' the *Aeneid* with line 384, 'one of those exaggerations which are unhappily of but too frequent occurrence in Virgil', according to Henry. Amata *per medias agitur urbes populosque feroces*, so later she flies to the woods 385, and Allecto drives her *inter siluas inter deserta ferarum*; we have already seen Virgil resorting to verbal jugglery to procure correspondence between simile and narrative and even different parts of the same narrative.

VI. *Conclusion*

The main weakness in the contention of this paper is that we have been so eager to find correspondences that we were bound to succeed, the mesh of our net was so narrow that we were bound to catch something. In the last few examples for instance it might be argued that in any thirty lines of Virgil there would be totally separate references to such concepts as twisting, flying, and rolling, hugeness, whips, surrounding, and desolation.

This argument we resist by experimenting with random sets of thirty lines, by reference to the Homeric prototypes where we have been able to see that Virgil manipulated his models to produce more correspondences between narrative and simile,[7] and by the sheer weight of incontestable correspondences as in the similes studied in Section III or those cited at the end of that section. Some of the detailed resemblances which the argument has led me to adduce may well be far-fetched or coincidental, but the general conclusion seems to be secure, that Virgil took pains to develop correspondences verbal and substantive between his narrative and his similes.

If this contention were to be accepted, that would naturally not impugn other levels of interpretation of the similes. Virgil is interested in large structural effects, in emotional colouring, he is also a symbolist: but he is apart from all this a miniaturist, he worked with words singly, polishing them for their immediate settings.

---

[7] This test could often be repeated, for instance in almost all the similes of the second book.

24

Cleverness in Virgilian Imitation

E. L. HARRISON

In the Sixth Book of the *Aeneid*, when Aeneas meets Dido's ghost in the Underworld, the hero declares: 'invitus, regina, tuo de litore cessi' (460). This is an echo of Catullus 66. 39, where Berenice's deified lock of hair tells the Egyptian queen: 'invita, o regina, tuo de vertice cessi'. The clash that this involves between the trivial Catullan context and the deep emotion of the Virgilian scene has produced different reactions. Most commonly it is assumed that the reminiscence must be unconscious,[1] but this can scarcely be correct. The reference is too specific—Virgil would surely not recall another poet's queen without remembering who she was and how she figured in his predecessor's lines. On the other hand a recent writer has denied the existence of any clash, maintaining that the quotation is entirely apt.[2] But Virgil's account of the last meeting between Dido and Aeneas is a world apart from the playful Alexandrian conceit; and to follow out the parallelism between the already deified lock of hair and Aeneas, destined for deification in the future, only serves to emphasize the incongruity. Finally, the line has been accepted as a conscious reminiscence in which Virgil takes the Catullan line and deliberately alters the character of its role: 'Virgil took this comic line for an intensely tragic moment'.[3] Now if we accept this view, as I believe we should, then the clash that so concerns the modern reader[4] was obviously of no importance to Virgil. His aim was simply to display cleverness and originality in the way he employed his model; and judged in terms of this aim, the result must be considered a success.

[1] e.g., W. B. Anderson, *PCA* 40 (1943), 11; F. Fletcher, *Aeneid VI* (Oxford, 1941), ad loc.; L. J. D. Richardson, *CQ* 36 (1942), 40; C. J. Fordyce, *Catullus* (Oxford, 1961), ad loc.

[2] A. H. F. Thornton, *AUMLA* 17 (1962), 77–9.

[3] W. F. Jackson Knight, *Roman Vergil* (London, 1944), p. 90. Cf. A. Cartault, *L'Art de Virgile dans l'Énéide* (Paris, 1926), p. 510; R. E. H. Westendorp Boerma, *Acta classica* 1 (1958), 59. There is a remarkable parallel to this in Virgil's description of blazing Troy (*Aen.* 2. 310 ff.), which clearly recalls Horace's comic description of the kitchen fire in his Brundisium satire (1. 5). See R. G. Austin, *Aeneidos liber secundus* (Oxford, 1964), p. 141.

[4] e.g., T. R. Glover, *Studies in Virgil* (London, 1904), p. 60, 'This is the very last thing of which we should wish to be reminded in the situation.'

In fact we have here, I would suggest, an example of a special type of reminiscence in the *Aeneid*: one in which the poet's primary concern is indeed to employ the work of a predecessor cleverly, whether by drastically changing the role of a quoted phrase or line, or by some other piece of studied subtlety. An example comparable to the first occurs in Virgil's citation of Ennius' 'it nigrum campis agmen'.[5] In Ennius the words referred to the ponderous progress of Hannibal's elephants: in Virgil's passage the creatures in question are—ants. Had some other animal been involved, perhaps in this case we *could* have accepted the possibility of unconscious reminiscence, since there is nothing very specific about the line. But when such massive creatures suddenly dwindle to such minute ones, that surely must be intentional. And here again it is worth noting that this fresh employment of the phrase (which Norden concedes is 'fast lustig zu lesen')[6] occurs in the highly emotional context of the break between Aeneas and Dido (cf. esp. 4. 393 ff. and 408 ff.). Once more it is clear that the clever manipulation of his original is Virgil's chief concern, irrespective of whether the artifice is appropriate to the general context or not.

A comparable example, involving cleverness of a rather different sort, is to be found towards the end of *Aeneid* 6, when Anchises shows Aeneas the future heroes of Roman history in the Elysian Fields. Prior to this, Aeneas has himself been on the move through the Underworld, but now he is static (as Odysseus was in the Homeric analogue) and it is the souls that pass by in review. The form of Anchises' commentary is skilfully varied to avoid monotony, and among the final group of heroes he addresses directly as they pass are the Fabii: 'quo fessum rapitis, Fabii? tu Maximus ille es, / unus qui nobis cunctando restituis rem' (845–6). Few Ennian quotations can have been discussed more frequently or more fully than this one; but commentators concentrate, with dreary unanimity, on the conventional aspect of the rhetorical question that introduces it, on the metrical contrast between *rapitis Fabii* and the four heavy spondees of the Ennian quotation, and on 'the noble close to the catalogue of heroes' thus produced?[7] And invariably, it seems to me, the real point is missed, or at least fails to emerge with any clarity. For her Virgil was faced with the problem of employing a line from Ennius

---

[5] *Ann.* 474 V; *Aen.* 4. 404.

[6] E. Norden, *Ennius und Vergilius* (Leipzig, 1915), p. 44 n.

[7] e.g., E. Norden, *P. Vergilius Maro Aeneis VI*⁴ (Darmstadt, 1957), ad loc.; F. Fletcher, op. cit., n. 1 ad loc.; T. E. Page, *The Aeneid of Virgil, I–VI* (London, 1894), ad loc.; Knight, op. cit. 87–8 n. 3; Thornton, op. cit. 77 n. 2. The quotation is from Fletcher's commentary.

which, by his day, had become almost proverbial.[8] How then was he to introduce it without running the risk of banality? His solution, quite simply, was to use the line to bring a sudden smile to his readers' lips. The parade is almost at an end, and Anchises is weary (*fessum*); but at this point a group of heroes make his task as reviewer more difficult by scurrying past him (*rapitis*) instead of proceeding at the stately pace of the rest of the parade. And they prove in fact to be members of the *gens Fabia*. How better, then, to chide them, than by picking out from their number the one man in Roman history one would least expect to be in such a hurry, Quintus Fabius Maximus Cunctator? Once more, then, we have clever manipulation of the original: and once more the context stands in strong contrast with the effect thereby achieved. (The grave *excudent alii* passage immediately follows, 847 ff.)[9]

Finally, there are two interesting examples of studied cleverness in the employment of a predecessor's work, both of which occur in Book 8, and both of which take us back to Apollonius, whose influence on that book is especially pronounced.[10] In the *Argonautica* there are two celebrated similes used by the poet to illustrate Medea's emotional state. In one, her passion for Jason as it blazes up for the first time is compared to the blazing up of a heap of dry twigs, kindled by a poor woman who rises early in the morning to spin wool.[11] In the second, the restless anxiety of Medea's mind as she ponders the dangers facing Jason is compared to sunbeams whose rays, reflected from a cauldron of water, dance round the walls of a room.[12] Now since Dido is Medea's equivalent in Virgil's poem, one would naturally expect him to recall these similes (if at all) in his treatment of the Carthaginian queen; but in fact in both cases he studiedly avoids such an obvious move. Thus the simile of the reflected light is now used to describe the anxieties not of a woman in love, but of Aeneas himself as he ponders the growing opposition of the people of Italy.[13] Moreover, instead of serving merely

---

[8] See J. Vahlen, *Ennianae Poesis Reliquiae²* (Leipzig, 1903), ad loc. (*Ann.* 370) for refs.

[9] The cleverness here works in the opposite direction to that displayed in the first example: here a noble line in the original is treated with a sudden playfulness. For Virgil's comparable treatment at the hands of Ovid, cf. *Ars* 1. 453, where *hoc opus, hic labor est* is transferred from a hero's return from the Underworld (*Aen.* 6. 129) to a seduction that will cost the seducer nothing.

[10] For parallels, cf. esp. the importance of Hercules in *Argon.* 1 and *Aen.* 8. Besides the similes to be discussed there are also clear parallels, e.g., between Virgil's description of the Cyclops' forge (*Aen.* 8. 424 ff.) and that of Apollonius (*Argon.* 1. 730 ff.) and between Virgil's Evander, who tells his guest of Hercules' exploits and entrusts to him his son (8. 185 ff. and 514 ff.) and Apollonius' Lycus, who does the same (2. 774 ff. and 802 ff.).

[11] *Argon.* 3. 291 ff.   [12] Ibid. 3. 756 ff.

[13] *Aen.* 8. 22 ff. It is interesting to contrast the conflicting views of scholars on the

to describe a mental state, the simile also anticipates symbolically the help that will come from a river-god,[14] as well as forming a bridge from the oppressive world of struggle in which Aeneas now finds himself, to the ideal pastoral world through which he will move in the rest of Book 8.[15] But it is in his employment of the image of the blazing twigs that Virgil's *calliditas* is perhaps most in evidence.[16] For if he was not to use this simile to describe Dido's passion, then Book 8 could indeed supply the most obvious alternative, since it contains the only truly erotic scene in the whole epic—the seduction of Vulcan by Venus. But in the actual employment of the motif Virgil seems deliberately to tease the reader who is familiar with the Alexandrian model. For Vulcan's passion as it blazes up is in fact compared, not to blazing twigs, but to lightning in the heavens.[17] And Apollonius' simile of the industrious woman who kindles an early-morning fire is now transformed from an image of blazing passion to a time-fixing device[18] relating to the coldly sober aftermath: 'haud secus Ignipotens nec tempore segnior illo / mollibus e stratis opera ad fabrilia surgit'. Once again, moreover, the Virgilian simile explores possibilities that were lacking in the original. For (as in the last example) it forms a bridge, this time from the palace of Vulcan to the Cyclops' forge, where the god, like the Roman matron, will give instructions to subordinates, as they too work by a fire.[19] And the picture of the chaste Roman matron industriously striving to preserve the home and family she cherishes makes an effective contribution to the ethos of the book as a whole.[20]

relative merits of the two passages. Cf., e.g., R. Y. Tyrrell, *Latin Poetry* (London, 1904), p. 141; Cartault, op. cit. 638 n. 3; W. W. Fowler, *Aeneas at the Site of Rome* (Oxford, 1918), pp. 35–6; M. Hügi, *Vergils 'Aeneis' und die Hellenistische Dichtung* (Berne, 1951), p. 36; M. C. J. Putnam, *The Poetry of the Aeneid* (Cambridge, Mass., 1965), pp. 107–8.

[14] Cf. K. Büchner in *RE* 8 A (1958), 1402.

[15] Cf. Putnam, op. cit. 108–9; V. Pöschl, *Die Dichtkunst Virgils* (Innsbruck, 1950), pp. 239–40.

[16] *Aen.* 8. 407 ff.   [17] Ibid. 8. 388 ff.

[18] Cf. H. Fränkel, *Noten zu den 'Argonautika' des Apollonios* (Munich, 1968), p. 141, on 'Stundenbilder' and their relation to similes. This particular example does actually become a simile as well in the course of its development, *cum* (408) leading on to *haud secus* as well as to *nec tempore segnior illo* (414).

[19] Cf. Putnam, op. cit. 130–40, where he points out also that the children the housewife seeks to support are matched by the *Aeneadae* Venus wishes to protect.

[20] Cf. Pöschl, op. cit. 277. Hügi, op. cit. 47, rightly subordinates the Homeric model used by Apollonius (*Il.* 12. 433 ff.) since it lacks the essential ingredients of the early rising and the fire lighting. It is, however, worth noting that Virgil's 'castum ut servare cubile / coniugis et possit parvos educere natos' (412–13) has no parellel in Apollonius, but recalls the Homeric ἵνα παισὶν ἀεικέα μισθὸν ἄρηται, 'to make shameful pay for her children' (*Il.* 12. 435).

25

Anti-Antiquarianism in the *Aeneid*

F. H. SANDBACH

The subject that lies concealed under my somewhat catch-penny title, is that deliberate anachronism as regards the material background which stands out in many places in the *Aeneid*. In writing a story of the heroic age, Virgil was of course less well-informed archaeologically than, say, Mary Renault is today, but he was by no means ignorant. Positively he had the evidence of Homer, then considered a more reliable authority than now; negatively there was the record of inventions, which ascribed many innovations to dates long after the Trojan War. With all this a man of his learning must have been familiar, yet he chose largely to disregard it, and to depict a world materially closer to his own. I shall put in the forefront what might be called primary anachronism, that which contradicts the evidence that was available to Virgil; but it is hard to draw a line between this and a secondary type, which imparts to the heroic age features of contemporary life for which no warrant could be adduced and perhaps no verisimilitude claimed, but which did not explicitly conflict with the historical evidence that he knew.

I begin with ships, for they are introduced in the first lines of the story, 'uix e conspectu Siculae telluris in altum / uela dabant laeti et spumas salis aere ruebant' (1. 34), 'sent flying with their bronze the salty spray'. There was no bronze on the prow of the Homeric ship. This is the ram of the later ship-of-war, and sure enough when Aeneas after the storm looks for his missing fleet, he hopes to see *Phrygias biremes* (1. 182). Biremes occur again in the eighth book, when he chooses two to take him up the Tiber, 'geminasque legit de classe biremis' (8. 79). Not only the Trojans, but also the Etruscans possess at least one bireme, the ship that is described at 10. 207 in the words 'centenaque arbore fluctum / uerberat'; for the ship with a *hundred* oars is not the old penteconter, which had approached the maximum feasible length for a wooden boat,[1] but must be a double-banked vessel. But Aeneas could do better than this; he had among his fleet a trireme, named *Chimaera*, one of the four ships that took part in the race in Book 5.

---

[1] A. Koster, *Das Antike Seewesen* (Berlin, 1923), p. 97.

> ingentemque Gyas ingenti mole Chimaeram,
> urbis opus, triplici pubes quam Dardana uersu
> impellunt, terno consurgunt ordine remi. (5. 118)

One might suppose that the other three competitors, who are not so circumstantially described, were *not* triremes. We know from Servius that some in antiquity drew this conclusion. But I think that scholars who take all four to be triremes are right. Not because the contest would otherwise have been unfair; just as in boxing and the pancration there were no classes divided by weight—boys, youths, and men being the only divisions—so the ship-race might have been open to all types. Nor because the four ships are called *pares*, since *Chimaera*'s larger manpower might have been offset by her greater bulk; but because each crew is rewarded by a prize of three bullocks—clearly one bullock to each bank of oars (5. 247).

These triremes and biremes cannot be anything but a deliberate anachronism. Thucydides is the authority for the tradition that the Corinthians were the first Greeks to build triremes, and that the Corinthian Ameinocles built four of them for the Samians about 700 BC. Many generations after the Trojan War, he observes, the Massiliots and Carthaginians were clashing with fleets consisting mainly of pentecontrs, having only a few triremes (1. 13. 2; 1. 14. 1). More than this, there was preserved at Rome a ship which traditionally was the one in which Aeneas had come to Italy, and she was a penteconter.[2] There does not seem to be any literary tradition giving a firm date for the introduction of biremes, but the archaeological evidence favours the view that they were a Phoenician invention, quickly improved on by the Greeks, who found room for a third row of oars. And Servius informs us that Varro took biremes to be much more recent than the Trojan War.[3]

In the race itself the water is torn into by prows armed with three teeth: 'conuulsum remis rostrisque tridentibus aequor' (5. 143). Here again we meet the bronze ram of the later warship, with its three teeth arranged vertically.

Another feature of the ships of the *Aeneid* which is not Homeric is that they are adorned with figure-heads. This is most explicit in the case of some Etruscan ships (10. 156 ff.) That which carries Aeneas has yoked Phrygian lions at her bow, with Mt Ida towering above them; another, the huge *Centaur*, as she is called, has a representation of that monster rearing up and threatening to hurl a rock—'saxumque undis immane

---

[2] Procopius, *De Bello Gothico*, 4. 42. 9.   [3] Servius Danielis on 1. 182.

minatur / arduus'; a third is the vast *Triton*, and her figure-head is fully described: the god blows a blast on his horn, from his belly downwards he takes the form of a shark, and the water foams and gurgles round his chest. Without doubt this is a carved figure-head, and all three (together with the ship from Mantua that bears a representation of the river Mincius) are to be understood as decorated in the same way, even though Servius suggests that the ship that carries Aeneas had *painted* lions: his reason is the prosaic and pedantic one that there would have been no time to carve this appropriate emblem: some old picture must have been overpainted! The descriptions of Book 10 make it plausible that the ships of Book 5, named *Shark, Chimaera, Centaur*, and *Scylla*, are all to be thought of as similarly adorned with figure-heads: and possible (I say no more) that the blueness of *Scylla* is that of her figure-head rather than of her hull. (5. 123).

Figure-heads of the above sort were not, so far as is known, used in the navies of classical Greece, although there are vase-paintings that show the ram given the form of an animal head. But the Romans so decorated their ships; there is a well-known example of a bireme on a relief from Praeneste, up the bow of which there clambers a carved crocodile: this dates from the earlier half of the first century BC.[4]

Lastly, it may be added that whereas Homeric ships moored themselves by large stones (εὐναί), Aeneas' have anchors, *unco ... ancora morsu* (1. 169, cf. 6. 3).

In an interesting article, entitled 'Sails and Oars in the Aeneid' (*TAPhA* (1948), 46), S. L. Mohler maintains that Virgil displays considerable technical knowledge about the handling of ships and their performance; that Aeneas' ships in their courses relative to the winds and in their speeds come up to the standards of the *naves longae* of the Augustan age; he even claims that the account of how Aeneas left Carthage shows Virgil to have been familiar with the changes in wind-direction usual there in the early morning. This may be taken with a grain of salt, but it is true that there does not seem to be any place in the *Aeneid* where there is anything obviously primitive about either the ships or their manœuvres, so that where the language used about the sails is imprecise and equally applicable to that of the Roman war-ships and the much simpler arrangements of the old penteconter, the reader's imagination will supply that with which he is familiar. Occasionally he *must* think in modern terms, as when the ships leave Drepanum tacking

---

[4] A. Baumeister *et al.*, *Denkmäler des klassischen Altertums* (Munich/Leipzig, 1885–8), iii. 1634; C. Torr, *Ancient Ships* (Cambridge, 1894), plate V and often elsewhere.

this way and that in unison, following the lead of Palinurus, 'una omnes fecere pedem pariterque sinistros nunc dextros soluere sinus: una ardua torquent cornua detorquentque' (5. 830). This is the disciplined manœuvring of a Roman fleet; and in Virgil's time the backbone of the Roman navy was provided by the fast 'Liburnian', which is generally thought to have been two-banked, a bireme like the bulk of Aeneas' ships.[5]

Turning now to architecture, we are on the threshold of what I have termed secondary anachronism. The Homeric poems give no very clear picture of the palaces, still less of the temples, of the heroic age. Menelaus' palace is large, brilliant, and high-roofed: that of Alcinous is a fairy-tale affair, where even the dogs at the gate are made of gold and silver; something can be made of the plan of Odysseus' home, but it was that of a minor provincial prince, and need not serve as a paradigm. A later poet was, therefore, not encumbered by precedent, and if he liked to describe buildings that recalled those of his own time, he could not certainly be convicted of anachronism. Yet there were traditions about the development of architecture through the ages, and anyone who had the mind of an antiquarian would have found it plausible to introduce *some* primitive features into any reconstruction of an early town. This must apply to the original Carthage, whether it belongs in our imagination to its historical date or whether we allow Virgil to carry it back to the times of the Trojan War.

In fact, among the first sights to meet Aeneas' eyes as he looks down upon the new city, is one that brings it right into Virgil's times. The foundations are being laid for a great theatre, and other colonists are quarrying huge monolithic columns to adorn the wall that will stand behind the stage.

> hic lata theatris
> fundamenta locant alii, immanisque columnas
> rupibus excidunt, scaenis decora alta futuris. (1. 427)

Virgil's contemporaries must have known as well as we do that the great wall behind the stage, the *scaenae frons* treated as an elaborate architectural façade, was a recent invention then being developed in the Roman West. Drama itself, for which theatres were built, had its origins, according to Horace, with Thespis' rude productions staged upon a cart, and Thespis was supposed to have been young when Solon was old. The first stone theatre at Rome (Pompey's) was not built until 55 BC,

[5] *RE* 13. 144.

and the splendid Theatre of Marcellus was probably begun in the 30s.

No doubt early towns have paved streets, but *strata uiarum* will suggest to the Roman a familiar kind of thoroughfare; and the excavation of a harbour—'hic portus alii effodiunt'—is only necessary for a town that will be visited by the great merchant-ships of deep draught, such as plied between Egypt and Italy in Virgil's time. The excavation of a harbour at Ostia, although perhaps planned by Julius Caesar and Augustus, had to wait for the Emperor Claudius for execution.

When Aeneas reaches the temple in the centre of the city, it faces him at the head of a flight of steps, with doorway and doors of bronze.

> aerea ... gradibus surgebant limina nixaeque
> aere trabes, foribus cardo stridebut aenis. (1. 448)

Nixaeque, given by Servius as the reading of *multi* and accepted by Probus, is more attractive than *nexaeque* of our MSS. The picture is of the long architrave resting upon capitals—Corinthian capitals I imagine—of bronze, not necessarily solid bronze. Such, Pliny tells us (*Nat.* 23. 13), were a feature of Agrippa's Pantheon, completed in 26 BC. and thus erected while Virgil was beginning his poem.[6]

Virgil does not specifically say where Aeneas found the pictures of the Trojan War which brought him comfort, but they seem to be *in luco* and *sub ingenti templo* (1. 450, 453). A Roman could hardly help applying his own experiences and imagining them as adorning a colonnade enclosing the sanctuary; this was pointed out already by G. G. Heyne. By a strange chance paintings (now lost) of Trojan scenes were found at Pompeii on the walls of the colonnade of Apollo's temple there.[7]

Let us enter Dido's palace. The purple stuffs, the gold and silver plate, have their Homeric counterparts, even though in view of what has preceded there is a temptation to imagine them to possess the refinement of Hellenistic workmanship. Yet the gilded coffered ceilings and the lamps that hang from them belong to the Roman nobleman's house.[8] The servants hand round not only bread in baskets, as in Homer (*Od.* 1. 147), but also un-Homeric table-napkins—'Cereremque canistris expediunt, tonsisique ferunt mantelia uittis' (1. 701): just so Statius describes a Roman banquet in less euphuistic terms—'panaria can-

---

[6] See A. Boethius, *Eranos* (1952), 147. The sculptured parts of the capitals of the temple of Baal at Palmyra (1st cent. AD) were of bronze gilt: D. S. Robertson, *History of Greek and Roman Architecture*[2] (Cambridge, 1943), p. 222.

[7] A. Mau, *Pompeii*[2] (Leipzig, 1903–13), p. 84.

[8] Pliny, *Nat.* 33. 57, says that such ceilings were first used in temples in the late 2nd cent. BC, and subsequently spread to private houses.

didasque mappas subuectant' (*Silv.* 1. 6. 31). The waiters and waitresses, too, are matched not only in numbers—a hundred of each sex—but also in age, *pares aetate*. Presumably Vestinus, who in the time of Nero kept *seruitia pari aetate*, had his Augustan predecessors (Tac. *Ann.* 15. 69).

Here we are firmly in the realm of secondary anachronism. None of these domestic arrangements positively conflicts with what was known of early times; yet they go to reinforce the primary anachronisms.

The palace of Priam in Book 2 has been the subject of much study and in particular of two papers by Professor Erik Wistrand.[9] He has argued that it inconsistently combines the plan of a classical Greek house divided into men's and women's quarters, with that of a Roman house where atrium, tablinum, and peristyle lie on an axis, so that when the front door is broken down, 'apparet domus intus et longa patescunt' (2. 483). I think that if there is any inconsistency it is due to Virgil's methods of piecemeal composition. The *peruius usus tectorum* (2. 453), the passage-way that is held to suggest that which separated men's and women's quarters, comes in what may be called the roof-sequence, whereas the series of rooms belong to another in which the view point is at ground-level. But I doubt whether Priam's palace has much to offer that is to my purpose: it hints at the great houses of Virgil's time, but the main impression is of a great complex of rooms, such as might have been found in a palace of any date.[10] Nor is there anything very striking about the look-out tower on the roof, which the Trojans topple over upon the besiegers (2. 460); the Romans were doubtless familiar with such erections on their villas; they can be seen on paintings and the younger Pliny describes the one on his house at Ostia (*Ep.* 2. 17), but a wooden tower on a flat roof is a construction that would cause no surprise even in a comparatively primitive milieu.

The temple in which Latinus gives audience also lacks striking features; it is tall with a hundred columns, but the round number merely lends it dignity without recalling any particular modern building; that the ancestral statues are made of cedar-wood, not marble or bronze, is an archaizing touch; conceivably there is another in the fact that the first weapons among the trophies at the door are battle-axes, which had become obsolete in Italy centuries before Virgil's time; the only item to

---

[9] *Eranos* (1939), 1. *Klio* (1960), 141. Cf. C. van Essen, *Mnemos.* 3rd series 7 (1939), 225.

[10] 'It is possible that Virgil had no very formal picture in mind, only a vista of linked apartments', R. G. Austin ad loc.

which an antiquarian could object are the beaks of captured warships—
ereptaque rostra carinis (7. 186).

The third sphere in which we may look for anachronism is that of war.
Now although Homer was, as R. Heinze says,[11] the authority on the
warfare of the heroic age, he was no authority on the weapons and tactics
of ancient Italy. If Greeks and Trojans, for all the latters' repute as
'breakers of horses', knew nothing of fighting on horseback, it cannot be
called anachronism that Latins and Etruscans should engage in a cavalry
battle. But Virgil had no hesitation about letting the Trojans also fight on
horseback.

Must we expect modernity on the battlefield as on the sea? The
answer is that there is a mixture of old and new that is not without
interest. The most striking peculiarity of Homeric weapons and armour
is that they are made of bronze, although Homer indicates that iron was
known to his heroes, for a great lump of pig-iron serves both as discus
and as prize in the funeral games. To account for this, it was later
conjectured that the early smiths had possessed some secret by which
bronze could be tempered to have the hardness of steel and that iron was
adopted when this secret was lost (Plut. *Mor.* 395 B). For Virgil, there is
a sharp distinction between weapons and defensive armour. Swords,
spear-heads, and the heads of missiles, arrows, javelins, etc. are of iron,
never of bronze, except for the inhabitants of Bella, whose bronze
swords are as unusual and as primitive as their cork helmets (7. 743). I
was surprised to find how frequently the metal is specified. The use of
iron for these purposes accords, as is obvious, with the practice of his
own times, and must be seen as a conscious anachronism.[12]

For defensive armour bronze remained in use alongside iron up to
and long after Virgil's time. He was therefore able, by giving his heroes
bronze armour, to respect history without making them old-fashioned.
Bronze is in fact almost universal as the metal of armour; the only
exception is Pallas' shield (10. 482), which has layers of bronze and
iron—*tot ferri terga tot aeris*—as well as of leather. It would not, however,
be true to say that Virgil's soldiers are armed as they might have been in a

---

[11] *Vergils epische Technik*, p. 194. Heinze's invaluable pp. 194–205 depict Virgil as
joining the Homeric with the *old* Roman. A view nearer to mine is taken by L. Wickert,
'Homerisches und römisches im Kriegswesen der Aeneis', *Philologus* NS 39 (1930), 285,
where detail is systematically given.

[12] Swords: 2. 510, 4. 580, 6. 294, 9. 331, 850, 10. 546, 12. 666, 737, 950. Spears and
javelins: 1. 313, 5. 306, 9. 701, 11. 637, 747, 12. 165, 278, 488, 578, 774. Arrows: 11. 682.
The material of the obsolete battle-axe is never given. I use 'iron' to include the iron-alloy
steel; *ferrum* covers both.

Roman legion. To discover how he did imagine them, we must look at some pieces of armour in turn.

Shields

Homer did not always understand what he was describing, but his tradition knew, besides round shields, great shields that reach from neck to ankles. We can envisage their shape from Mycenean monuments, but Virgil would have no such aid. He dropped them entirely as quite unfamiliar. The round shield, which in Latin is called *clipeus*, he accepted, and several times describes it as being made of bronze, once 'of hollow bronze': this is the shield of the classical Greek hoplite, and it will probably have been carried by the heroes of the Trojan war in all Greek painting, as it is in vase-painting, and as it is in the famous picture (from the House of the Dioscuri in Pompeii) of the discovery of Achilles among the maidens of Scyros.

But it was not the shield of the Roman army, in which (except for some auxiliaries) the round *clipeus* was replaced by the long *scutum* at an early date. Tradition associated the change with Camillus at the beginning of the fourth century.[13] The *scutum* was made of wood covered with linen or leather, and strengthened by a metal boss and a metal rim. Now although the *clipeus* predominates in the *Aeneid*, there is a considerable minority of *scuta*, about one case in four, almost evenly divided between Trojans and Italians. Being made of wood, light wood like willow and agnus castus, they are whirled along by the river Simois; or they are imagined as borne upon the waves of the Tiber; Evander can make a bonfire of them (1. 101; 8. 539; 8. 562). In spite of this, I expected to find that Virgil often used *clipeus* and *scutum* interchangeably for metrical convenience, as Homer does σάκος and ἀσπίς. But this is not so. No *individual* warrior ever carries a *scutum*, and with one exception they never appear in actual use in battle: that is when, as the beleaguered Trojans pour missiles upon the Rutulians who are attacking their camp, 'their *scuta* and hollow helmets resound' (9. 666). Conversely, when the scene is not one of fighting, both sides are found to be armed with *scuta*, even (as an extreme instance) at a pause in the battle: when Aeneas withdraws his troops to address them on his new strategy, they do not ground their *scuta*, even (as an extreme instance) at a pause in the battle: when Aeneas withdraws his troops to address them on his new strategy, they do not ground their *scuta* (12. 563). Similarly

---

[13] My information about Roman armour is drawn from Coussin's standard work, *Les armes romaines*.

the night council of Trojan leaders hold their *scuta* as they lean upon their spears (9. 229), and the crews of the ships that row up the Tiber hang their *scuta* over the side (8. 93). *Clipei*, on the other hand, hardly occur outside battle-scenes, except as the possession of a named person: twice they appear as battle-trophies, (3. 286, 7. 186), and Turnus' contingent is described as *clipeata agmina*, but the first company named is *Argiua pubes*, who might reasonably be expected to carry the hoplite shield, and the rear is brought up by *scuta Labici* (7. 793–6).

What emerges from this is that, when Virgil describes the feats and fates of individual warriors in battle, he thinks in Homeric terms, and gives them the round shield—ἀσπὶς πάντόσ' ἐίση, 'shield equal in all directions'. But when he conceives of men in the mass, particularly in un-Homeric situations, he prefers to imagine them armed with the familiar shield of the first century.[14]

Cuirass

'As to the exact form of the Homeric cuirass,' says Dr Stubbings, 'the poems cannot be said to help us much.'[15] Virgil was therefore able to describe his heroes' cuirasses more or less as he pleased. What he pleased to do was to take the types best known to the Romans. The most usual legionaries' wear in the first century seems to have been a jerkin on which metal chains were sewn. Another type, apparently new in the first century, was made of small plates of bronze or iron threaded together with wire. One or other of these is intended wherever Virgil is specific: *aerea suta* 'bronze things that have been sewn' (10. 313), *loricam consertam hamis*, 'a cuirass put together with hooks' (3. 467), *duplici squama lorica fidelis* (9. 707), *thoraca aenis squamis* (11. 487). The last phrase suggests that *thoracas aenos* (7. 634) need not be the obsolete Greek hoplite solid breastplate; even Aeneas' *loricam ex aere rigentem* (8. 621) is not necessarily such (cf. 11. 72).

When a metal is mentioned, apart from decorative gold or silver,[16] it is always bronze, in spite of the fact that iron seems to have been more

---

[14] But Virgil does not go so far as to show knowledge of the semi-cylindrical shield that had recently been adopted by the army from the gladiators. On the *parma* carried by Lausus and Helenor see Heinze, p. 204.

[15] F. Wace and A. Stubbings, *A Companion to Homer* (London, 1962), p. 507.

[16] In our practical days we are tempted to think of Virgil's frequent mention of precious metals in connection with armour as due to a romantic view of the heroic age. But Plutarch says of Brutus' army at Philippi, χρυσὸς γὰρ ἦν αὐτοῖς τὰ πλεῖστα τῶν ὅπλων καὶ ἄργυρος ἀφειδῶς καταχορηγηθείς, 'for most of their weapons were gold and silver, unsparingly lavished' (*Brutus*, 38. 3). I do not know to what Virgil's phrase *auroque trilicem* refers (3. 467, 5. 259, 7. 639 cf. *bilicem* 12. 375).

frequently used by the Romans. Iron was of course cheaper, but one cannot assume that grandees always wore bronze cuirasses, for Lucullus is described as going into battle glittering with a *thorex* of iron (or steel) scales (Plut. *Luc.* 28).

Virgil sticks to bronze because he is thus both modern and traditional. He does the same with helmets (*galeae*), which are of bronze on the few occasions when the material is mentioned (5. 491, 10. 836). (The *aurea galea* of 9. 50 will be gilt (cf. 12. 536 *aurata tempora*) like some examples in our museums.) Yet iron was quite as commonly used in the first century.

Spears

Once again Homer spoke with an uncertain voice, obscuring what must have been an original distinction between the heavy thrusting spear, the ὄβριμον ἔγχος, 'mighty spear', and the throwing spear δόρυ, which went in pairs, so that it is familiar in the dual δοῦρε. Virgil regards the spear as primarily a missile weapon, and obscures any distinction between different kinds. The same weapon may be *hasta* and *iaculum* (10. 585–8); the usual pattern is that the warrior throws his single spear and then resorts to the sword: thus, e.g., Pallas at 10. 380 and 474.

Yet before the battle in Book 12 Turnus has a pair of spears, as does Aeneas when he goes out scouting on the coast of Carthage, and Nisus actually uses two successively in his attempt to rescue Euryalus (12. 165, 1. 313, 9. 410–17). Mezentius, too, once drops his 'spears', in the plural, to take up a sling (9. 586), although in his *aristeia* (10. 689 ff.) he has only one; and the Italian Messapus hurls one of a pair at Aeneas, but earlier, when he stabs with a spear from horseback, he too will be conceived of as having but one (12. 488, 12. 294). Except for this last incident, un-Homeric because Homer does not know cavalry, Virgil seems to base himself on tradition not experience. It is noteworthy that he makes no use of the typically Roman weapon, the *pilum*, discharged before the legionary engaged with the sword. But we may perhaps see a parallel with his treatment of bronze and iron armour. Archaeological evidence suggests that only some of the legionaries used *pila*; the points of ordinary spears are much more frequently found.[17] By sticking to the *hasta*, Virgil again gets the best of both worlds.

---

[17] So Couissin. *Pila* are carried by some of Aventinus' men (7. 664) in the catalogue, where many weapons are mentioned that are not used in the battles. Most of them, unlike the *pila*, are archaic, for Virgil here wished to suggest comparatively primitive peoples.

Siege-craft

Ancient tradition was well aware that siege-craft, as opposed to block-ade, was a late development. The invention of the battering-ram (which looks obvious enough) was ascribed by Vitruvius to the Carthaginians in Spain, by Servius (on 9. 503) to one Artemon of Clazomenae of unknown date, but that town was founded 93 years after Rome. Artemon was also supposed to have invented the *testudo*, a movable shed to protect men who tried to undermine the fortress wall. Yet certainly the battering-ram appears in the *Aeneid*, used against Priam's palace and Latinus' town (2. 492, 12. 706). Possibly the *testudo*, too, for the palace door is *obsessum acta testudine*; and similarly the Volsci attack the Trojan camp *acta testudine* (2. 441, 9. 505). But both passages may refer to the Roman tactic of approaching a fortification under cover of linked shields (*scuta*) held overhead; although *agere* is the proper word for pushing forward the armoured shed, which Vitruvius says was used when filling in ditches (10. 20) and in Virgil we have *fossas implere parant*, yet the great stone that falls upon the attackers *armorum resoluit uincula*. Even more striking in their modernity are the great wooden towers[18] associated with defensive walls. The odd thing about these is that they do not seem to make much military sense. One could understand that the Trojans might have profitably built such a tower *inside* their camp, to provide an eminence from which to pour their missiles (cf. Caesar, *BG* 5. 40); but what is it doing outside, where it is easily set on fire, and why is it so insecure that, when the garrison moves to one side to avoid the flames, it falls over (9. 503 ff.)? Equally puzzling is the great tower at Latinus' town, which Turnus had built and which Aeneas sets on fire: it is on wheels (12. 675). One could imagine that, if there were a clear space inside the walls, it could (as Servius suggests) be rolled to any point that was attacked, but such a device seems to be unheard of in military history. What is known is the use of such towers by an *attacking* force who could pass from them by gangways on to the walls from which their missiles drove the defenders. Such was Turnus' tower, for *pontis instrauerat altos* (12. 675), i.e. he had given a protective roofing to the gangways that led from its upper storey. (Servius, not unnaturally embarrassed by *pontis*, thinks the word is used for *tabulata*, 'storeys'.) A movable tower of this sort would not be excessively stable, and if the tower of the Trojans was so conceived, one can understand the fatal

---

[18] They were invented by Diades, who served with Alexander the Great and wrote a monograph on their construction, Vitruvius 10. 13. 3.

accident that overtook it, although not their motive in constructing it.

No one supposes that Virgil made any attempt to reconstruct and reproduce the modes of thought and feeling that were current in the heroic age. We have found that in the material background to his story also there is a pervading modernity, achieved in part by selection of what was both old and new, in part by deliberate anachronism. The antiquarianism so often ascribed to him is confined to a few passages in Book 7, where it is his concern to depict a primitive Italy that needs a new element if it is to develop the Roman civilization, and in Book 8, where he wishes to contrast the humble beginnings of Rome with her present grandeur. Elsewhere his characters inhabit a world of remarkably modern aspect.

Was this feature of the Virgilian treatment of the heroic past something peculiar to him, or one adopted by other writers of epic? The answer is easy so far as the Greeks are concerned. The procedure is foreign to Apollonius Rhodius. His *Argo* uses no anchor, but ties up to rocks. To be sure, she has an un-Homeric ὑπόζωμα (undergirdle) to hold her timbers together (1. 368), but this device might well have been used in primitive ships. Amycus enters the ring (2. 63) with no horrific *caestus*, but binds his hands with the plain thongs that are used by contestants in the *Iliad*.[19] Jason's shield is large enough for him to hide under it. I must confess that I have not read Quintus Smyrnaeus *in toto*, but enough to feel pretty sure that he, too, attempts to follow Homeric precedent.[20] There is no reason, then, for supposing that Virgil took a hint from the Greeks, although it is of course possible that if more Greek epic were restored to us, we should find that he had predecessors there.

Turning to the Romans, neither Valerius Flaccus nor Statius did as much as Virgil to depict the material background of their stories, Valerius perhaps less than Statius. As a result the material is scantier, but shows that neither was concerned with antiquarian correctness. It would, of course, have been absurd for Valerius to represent the *Argo*, for him the first wooden ship to be built, as a bireme. Indeed he makes it

[19] *Il.* 23. 684. In Theocritus 22 the boxers use up-to-date ring-craft but old-fashioned thongs. Virgil draws a vivid word-picture of heavily loaded *caestus*, for which others less damaging, but not specifically described, are substituted in the contest itself—a clever way of suggesting the new world without committing himself.

[20] e.g. his weapons are regularly of bronze. A *testudo* of shields is formed at 11. 358, a passage reminiscent of *Aen.* 9. 505 ff.; but it is implied that this was not a standard practice, but an *ad hoc* device of the wily Odysseus.

light enough to be carried down to the sea by its crew at a run (1. 185). But it has its anchor (2. 428, cf. 4. 72)—and what is more surprising it has the ram of the later warship—*spumas uomit aere tridenti* (1. 688, cf. 339). Of other elements that do not belong to the heroic age there are a few, but only a few: *ferrum* is occasionally used of a sword or other weapon (e.g. 2. 2380, trumpets sound for battle (2. 129, 3. 43), there is a marble statue or pair of statues (5. 187). These are all small points, and I have the impression that Valerius had little interest in the material setting of his story.[21]

Statius has more to offer that is to my purpose. His *Argo* is so large that she is a floating mountain; she has the warship's bronze prow, and a Triton as her figure-head (5. 335 ff.). So far she recalls Aeneas' ships; but she is an open boat without a deck, like that which carries the Greeks to Troy on the François vase, for Jason has to tread on the rowers' backs as he passes up and down the ship (5. 404). Statius thus seems to waver in his view of her. His battle scenes, unlike those of Virgil, show no sign of generalship or strategy; infantry, cavalry, and war-chariots are committed pell-mell; the fighting is neither Homeric nor anything else. When the Thebans have retreated behind their walls one of the besiegers careers about in a scythed chariot (10. 544), an act more likely to cause alarm to his friends than to the enemy. Details about armour are less common than in Virgil, but *ferrum* is often used collectively of weapons. Thebes has modern defences: the walls are equipped with armoured loopholes which spit out whistling missiles, and when the defenders find javelins and arrows are of little use, they are able to fall back on *tormenta* (10. 859). The attackers, too, do not lack corresponding equipment (10. 527–30): they have their rams and *testudo*: 'scrutanturque cauas caeca testudine turres'—this is clearly the movable shed used to cover a search for weak spots in the defences, a device as anachronistic as the Theban artillery.

But the most striking instance of modernity in the *Thebaid* is in the funeral games for Archemorus (6. 238 ff.). They follow the construction in a mere nine days of an enormous stone temple with marble reliefs, showing the whole story; the athletic events themselves are preceded by a parade of statues of the child's ancestors: the first is explicitly of bronze and all that follow may be presumed to be of the same material, since

---

[21] The cataphract Sarmatian met in Phasis (6. 231) is of a type only recently known to the Romans (Mr H. McL. Currie reminds me of the article by Sir Ronald Syme, *CQ* (1929)), but he might at a pinch be supposed to have existed for a thousand years in the unexplored East.

they have lifelike expressions, which that medium was universally supposed to be capable of reflecting. The chariot-race with which the programme begins is no mere out-to-a-tree-and-back-again affair, as in the *Iliad*, but is round and round, lap after lap, as in a Roman circus, and Oeclides comes in to the finish, 'ceu modo carceribus dimissus in arua solutis', as if he had only just left the starting box. For the foot-race the sprinters limber up, a precaution unknown to Homer or to Virgil; they have starting-gates, and they are naked, although Thucydides remarks that loin-cloths were *de rigeur*, even in the Olympic games, until not so long before his own days.[22] The discus is of bronze, not the shapeless lump of metal that was the best the Achaeans had at Troy, nor a round stone such as was used by the Phaeacians. Finally the boxing-match sees the use of the lead-weighted boxing-gloves of later professionalism—*nigrantia plumbo tegmina cruda boum.*

Such modernity is less frequent in Statius than in Virgil, but all the more striking when it occurs, standing out by contrast and by its thoroughness. There can be no doubt that it is deliberate, and it would hardly be rash to suppose that he was deliberately following Virgil's example, when he remembered it.

In the Fitzwilliam Museum at Cambridge there is a pair of lively pictures representing the death of Hector and the Trojan Horse, painted by Biagio di Antonio, a Florentine of the later fifteenth century. Off the shore is a round-bellied medieval ship with prow and poop towering above the low waist; the Greek knights on horseback are plated in suits of armour from crown to toe; and inside the walls of Troy there rise buildings of extraordinary likeness to the cathedral at Florence (completed 1462), to the Loggia della Signoria, and to the leaning tower of Pisa. This happens neatly to exemplify anachronism in the three spheres with which I have dealt, but the pictures are typical of the way in which painters, not only the early and naïve, but also sophisticated ones like Titian and Veronese, long dealt with scenes from worlds that had disappeared, attempting no antiquarian reconstruction but depicting the costumes, furnishings, and architecture of their own day. The painters of the ancient world do not seem to have acted otherwise.[23] Some well-known wall-paintings of the first century BC found on the

---

[22] Thuc. 1. 6. 5. Contrast Quintus Smyrnaeus 4. 188, who emphasizes the loin-cloths of his runners. Virgil wisely says nothing one way or the other.

[23] Margaret R. Scherer, *The Legends of Troy* (New York, 1963), provides a convenient and well-reproduced collection of their representation in art through the ages.

Esquiline show scens from the *Odyssey*. A contemporary Roman might well have copied the façade of Circe's house for his own residence—a round-headed front-door, surmounted by a pediment, set back behind a curving *vestibulum*, in front of which runs an arcade in the Tuscan order. In other scenes ships are represented on which the oars are so close-set that I think they must be biremes: but the pictures have now been cleaned, and it may be possible to see the details more clearly than in present reproductions. In the famous relief, the Tabula Iliaca of the first century AD, it *looks* like a bireme on which Aeneas escapes. The warriors' shields there are probably all intended to be round, but Hellenistic models doubtless lie behind these representations.

I would not say that in considering Virgil's material anachronisms the anachronisms of contemporary painting should be disregarded. They must have done something to prejudice the reader to accept or even to expect such things. But the situation of the painter is not that of the poet. Before the days of excavations, museums, and archaeological reconstructions, the painter does not, perhaps *cannot*, paint the vanished age that he cannot see. The poet, on the other hand, works within a literary tradition, which provides him with information about the past, not only in the writings of his poetic predecessors, but also underlined in the commentaries upon them, and preserved in the records of historians. He does not lie under the same necessity to be modern as does the visual artist. Apollonius, Quintus, and to some extent Valerius Flaccus, show this to be true. To account for Virgil's practice better reasons are needed than the influence of contemporary art. Nor is it sufficient to say that he followed literary practice, for we do not know of any previous poet who provided a precedent.[24]

Any attempt to arrive at Virgil's motives must be speculative, and they may have been multiple, reinforcing one another. One can only hope to make suggestions that are not plainly inadequate to account for his practice. Some comments that have been made clearly are inadequate. Warde Fowler, noting the anachronism of Turnus' tower in Book 12, calls it 'amusing'.[25] That, certainly, was not the effect that Virgil intended here, whatever may have been Ovid's intention over the anachronisms of the *Metamorphoses*. To do Warde Fowler justice, he was probably recording his own reactions rather than explaining the poet's wishes, but he would hardly have made the comment had he been

---

[24] We cannot affirm that Ennius, as Professor Skutsch reminded me, or even Naevius did *not* provide a model.

[25] *The Death of Turnus* (Oxford, 1919), p. 120.

aware how characteristic the passage is. A. Cartault explains that ships are moored by fluked anchors, not by stones, because although Virgil 'certainly gives his poem a certain heroic colour, he does not wish to disconcert his contemporaries by things that had become obsolete long ago'.[26] It is possible that he was affected by this consideration, which might be enough to explain the anchors if they were an isolated phenomenon; but it will not explain the whole complex of gratuitous modernity. Even W. Kroll, who added to his rightly praised *Studien zum Verständnis der römischen Literatur* (Stuttgart, 1924) an appendix on anachronisms (p. 178), mainly in the *Aeneid*, hardly gets beyond stating a fact: 'Virgil felt justified in projecting backwards upon the old Italians such circumstances of the present-day as seemed good to him.' He then speaks of an effort to lift the heroic age into a fairy-tale atmosphere— this because of the greater frequency of gold in the *Aeneid* as compared with Homer, a frequency which he admits suggests later luxury—and concludes by saying that learned poets of antiquity were untouched by antiquarian pedantry.

My own belief, for what it is worth, is that the material modernity met in the *Aeneid* is to be seen as the counterpart of another characteristic that has often been noted. I mean the way in which Virgil ascribes to his Trojans and to his Italians customs familiar among the Romans of his own times. To take familiar examples, Anchises on seeing the harmless flame that plays around Iulus' head prays to Jupiter *haec omina firma*, and is rewarded by a shooting-star, whereupon he rises to his feet (2. 687 ff.). Here is the Roman distinction between the *auspicium oblatiuum* that comes without being asked, and the *auspicium impetratiuum*, which is a reply to a prayer; and if Servius is to be believed, it was the Roman custom so to require a confirmatory augury, and to rise from the sitting position in which auspices were awaited so soon as they had been received. Or Turnus acts like the Roman *pater patratus* when he declares war on the Trojans by hurling his spear, not at them but into the air:

> iaculum adtorquens emittit in auras
> principium pugnae, et campo sese arduus infert. (9. 52)

Virgil's concern was to underline the continuity between the men about whom he wrote and those for whom he wrote, and he does it by showing them as sharing customs; the *mos maiorum* acts as a link. There is no

---

[26] *L'Art de Virgile dans l'Énéide* (Paris, 1926), i. 148. I cite Warde Fowler and Cartault as writers who have illuminated so much in Virgil that one might hope for illumination here too.

question here of anachronism, since no one in his time could have argued that the ancient Trojans and the ancient Latins would *not* have possessed these customs: on the contrary it would appear plausible that they should have done so.

The desire to achieve continuity and likeness worked also, I believe, to encourage the anachronisms which have been the subject of this paper, whether they ascribed without warrant to the heroic age things that were familiar to the poet's audience, or whether they took what seems to the modern reader the strange and exaggerated form exemplified by biremes and the *turris ambulatoria*. Another consideration may also have played a part. It is undeniable that Aeneas, although he does not 'stand for' Augustus, although he is no allegorical figure, not infrequently recalls Augustus: he performs acts and finds himself in situations that anticipate and foreshadow those of his descendant. This role may be an easier and more credible one because he moves in surroundings that are not primitive, but assimilated to those of the Augustan age.

Virgil invented a new kind of epic in which the apparent mythological subject carried within itself the story of a nation right down to its living present. It suited his conception that the unity of early and late, of beginning and achievement, should extend—if it were not so fashionable a word I might say *symbolically* extend—to the material setting and background. The taste of his time did not forbid anachronism, and he used it with a more serious purpose than any poet who followed him.

26

Virgil and the Conquest of Chaos

N. M. HORSFALL

The hunt for Virgil's sources has been, by unspoken agreement among Latinists, largely abandoned. This regrettable development may in part have been a by-product of the justifiable revulsion against the excesses of *Quellenforschung* as practised *c.* 1880–*c.* 1930 (everyone read Posidonius and Varro: no one else was read), in part of the opening of alluring new vistas in Virgilian studies, where apparent progress might be made without the need of painstaking consultation of *HRR, GRF, FGH, FHG,* and similar collections. It has therefore escaped notice that just as the detailed examination of Virgil's use of Homer (G. N. Knauer, *Die Aeneis und Homer*) or even of the Homer scholia (R. R. Schlunk, *Virgil and the Homeric Scholia*) can lead to immensely valuable advances in our understanding of the poet's compositional techniques, so the survey of Virgil's prose sources and the analysis of how he handles the material available to him can be employed to precisely comparable ends. It is the purpose of this paper to indicate some ways in which such a survey may be put into effect.

Chaos[1] was indeed what confronted Virgil whenever he turned to consider a story in the mythology of Italy. In his brilliant paper, *Origines Gentium*, Elias Bickerman writes: 'One could write on the subject in an original manner, disentangling the difficulties [i.e. any problem of religion, topography or antiquities] in most satisfactory fashion, yet without coming into conflict with accepted mythology' (*CP* 47 (1952), 67). We should not forget that Virgil was the pupil of Parthenius (Macr. 5. 17. 18), whose collection of arcane and curious tales of love survives (cf. Horsfall, *Échos du monde classique* 23 (1979), 80).[2]

After I had completed and revised this paper, I became aware that some of the same ground had been lightly covered in A. M. Guillemin, *L'Originalité de Virgile* (Paris, 1931); some cross-references to that uneven but stimulating book are included.

[1] Cf. Guillemin, p. 47, who speaks specifically of the 'chaos' of contradictory legends.

[2] Of rare Greek stories in Virgil, I give four examples: elements in the tale of Laocoon (R. G. Austin on 2. 95); on Orpheus, see C. M. Bowra, *CQ* (1952), 113 ff., L. P. Wilkinson, *Georgics of Virgil* (Cambridge, 1969), pp. 116 ff.; on 7.304, see Horsfall, *CR* 29

To begin with a modest range of examples of the sort of fluidity which confronted Virgil in his sources:

(i) First, an instance where there was no settled Greek version and Roman writers only increased the range of possibilities: in the texts, the Trojans' homeland is given variously as the Troad itself (*Il.* 20. 216 ff.), Arcadia (*RE* s.v. Dardanos, 2168. 55 ff. on Hellanicus), Crete—probably on account of association between the two Idas (*Aen.* 3. 94 ff.; from Callinus on), Samothrace—as the product of speculation about the origin of the mysteries (cf. *Aen.* 7. 207 f.), and Etruria (*Aen.* 3. 168 f.), though it is not certain that Virgil is not innovating here (cf. Horsfall, *JRS* 63 (1973), 74 ff.).

(ii) Just as diverse and confusing is the range of explanations given for the origin of the name of the Palatine hill: according to Virgil (*Aen.* 8. 54), Evander named it after his ancestor Pallas. But Varro (*LL* 5. 53) offers five other possibilities (e.g., following Naevius, *a balatu ovium*).

(iii) The length of the era from Aeneas' arrival in Italy to the foundation of Rome.[3] Virgil records idiosyncratically an era of 333 years (*Aen.* 1. 257 ff.); Naevius and Ennius, on the other hand, make Romulus a grandson of Aeneas (Serv. Dan. *ad Aen.* 1. 273), while (e.g.) Cato counts 432 years between the fall of Troy and the foundation of Rome (*Orig.* fr. 17P).

(iv) (v) The site of Anchises' death and the places visited by Aeneas on the Campanian coast will shortly emerge as comparable.

It should not be thought that the legend of Aeneas is a special case. Nor, for that matter, is the story of Romulus. It might not appear at first sight that the story of Tarpeia was so important (and therefore so liable to variation). That is far from the case.[4] Livy 1. 11 may give to the casual reader, as does the *Aeneid*, an altogether misleading impression of the classical and definitive statement of a long, settled and normalized tradition.

However, we should not suppose that Virgil regularly confronted directly a mass of conflicting prose and verse texts. Prolonged study of Virgil's sources confirms me in the view already argued most lucidly by B. Rehm (*Philol. Supplbd.* 24. 2 (1932), 92 ff.) that for many of the more minute details of Italian legend—and one might wonder whether Virgil

---

(1979), 222; Troilus: see Austin on 1. 474. A certain delight in lesser-known versions emerges.

   [3] H. A. Sanders, *CP* 3 (1908), 317 ff.; Horsfall, *CQ* 24 (1974), 111 ff.

   [4] H. A. Sanders in *Roman History, Sources and Institutions* (New York, 1904), pp. 1 ff.; Horsfall in *CJ* 76 (1981), forthcoming = *BICS* Suppl. 52 (1987), 68–70.

was really as interested in them as he was in Greek stories—he confronted the range of discrepant texts at one remove, as they stood arrayed in Varro's surveys, cited by name, sometimes quoted, sometimes arrayed in partial order of credibility. One should, of course, think of a considerable range of texts: *res humanae* 2, 8, and 11, the *de vita* and *de gente populi romani*, the *de familiis troianis*, and the *imagines*.[5] But Varro is characteristically descriptive, not prescriptive; the impact of his normative date of 753 BC for the foundation of the city is not typical of his effect on the state of scholarship at Rome. That the poet also read (e.g.) Cato's *Origines* is of course highly likely, but his extensive reading in Roman antiquarian prose cannot be demonstrated and is indeed not a necessary deduction from the poem or from general probabilities.[6]

I turn first to the simplest *modus operandi* under discussion: instances where the poet simply selects and omits from a clearly far more substantial register of people or places:

(i) It was observed in a notably valuable discussion by R. B. Lloyd (*AJPh* 77 (1957), 382 ff.) that Virgil had nine episodes on Aeneas' voyage from Troy to Sicily, of which four (Crete, Strophades, Scylla and Charybdis, Cyclops) seem not to have been associated with Aeneas previously. In contrast, seventeen stopping-places for Aeneas are attested, of which fourteen appear in Dionysius' narrative. Virgil clearly selects to avoid sameness and repetition; mere economy of number is less important as is evident from the readiness with which he exploits the mythical connections between Troy and Crete, the Argonautic Harpies, and the Odyssean episodes of Scylla and Charybdis and of the Cyclops in order to enrich and diversify the aridities of the antiquarian tradition.

(ii) Closely comparable is Aeneas' passage along the coast of Campania: connections are attested[7] with Cape Palinurus, Leucosia (Isola Piana), Inarime (Ischia), Prochyta (Procida), Baiae, Cape Misenus, Cumae, Capua, Formiae, and Caieta. Virgil merely alludes in passing in a simile (9. 710 ff.) to Baiae, Prochyta, and Inarime; no connection with Aeneas is drawn. The *aetia* of the two capes are of course given (6. 234, 281), but Aeneas only in fact lands at (i) Cumae and (ii) Caieta, before reaching the Tiber mouth; to the north, he sails

---

[5] For *Imagines*, see Horsfall, *Anc. Soc.* (Macquarie) 10 (1980), 20 ff.; for *de gente*, id., *C et M* 30 (1969), 299 and *CR* 28 (1978), 365 f.; *de fam. tro.*, see G. J. M. Bartelink, *Etymologisering bij Vergilius* (Amsterdam, 1965), p. 63 n. 1. Use of the *de vita* and of *res hum.* 2 and 8 is not, so far as I know, provable, just highly likely.

[6] Horsfall, *Prudentia* 8 (1976), 77 f.

[7] H. Boas, *Aeneas' Arrival in Latium* (Amsterdam, 1938), pp. 27 ff.

past Circeii, in the interests of narrative economy and the avoidance of retardation.

(iii) It is very clear indeed, even from a simple comparison of *Aen.* 7. 647 ff. with Sil. 8. 349 ff. that Virgil is vastly more self-denying in his selection of material from a common geographical source, i.e. Varro, *res humanae* 11 (Rehm, pp. 84 ff.);[8] his intention, after all, is, in the footsteps of Homer, impressionistically to evoke the diversity of country and people, not to versify a gazetteer. But again, he does have ingenious techniques for alluding to people and places which he does not include in the catalogues, for example, by the topographical associations of such names as Umbro, Messapus, and Asilas.[9]

(iv) We can see elsewhere in very different contexts how far Virgil is concerned to eliminate a superfluity of detail that could raise only satiety in a reader and to achieve a simplicity in his outlines of place and time:

Thus in *Aen.* 5 there are only four contests in the games, as against the Homeric eight: wrestling is too like boxing and field events are the narrator's despair: hence, only archery as against discus–archery–javelin;[10] the Homeric spear-fight is unattractively and inappropriately menacing. So too an increased economy of narrative is achieved by the elimination of retardatory up-country episodes in Book 3;[11] we might compare the omission of Capua, later. In Book 6, the juxtaposition of Avernus, Cumae, and Misenum is apparently unreal and 'inaccurate'; on 6. 13 Austin aptly cites an admirably perceptive comment by Bertha Tilly on 'Virgil's habit of telescoping, or even ignoring, distances. For him the epic must move more quickly, against a shadowed background of omissions.'[12] Time, just as much as place, demanded straight and rapid outlines: the foremost example is, of course, the well-known acceleration of the action in Books 7–12, from the three or four campaigning seasons of the annalistic tradition, to a matter of days.[13]

[8] Fordyce (ad loc.) is right to insist that Virgil's source for the Italian *leaders* was not alphabetical, against L. W. Daly, *AJPh* 84 (1963), 68 f.; *res hum.* 11, moreover, was not a list of people, nor was the book's arrangement geographical (R. Reitzenstein, *Hermes* 20 (1885), 534).

[9] Asilas: cf. Sil. 8. 445; in Picene country. Cf. L. A. Holland, *AJPh* 56 (1935), 202 ff. C. Saunders, *TAPhA* 71 (1940), 544 ff. Names familiar from legends other than that of Aeneas are an extreme case: for Acro 'the Greek' at 10. 719, see Horsfall, *JRS* 63 (1973), 69 n. 11.

[10] Cf. H. A. Harris, *PVS* 8 (1968–9), 14 ff.

[11] e.g. that at Dodoma; cf. Horsfall, *CQ* 29 (1979), 378; likewise, Lloyd 384 on Arcadia.

[12] *Gnomon* 47 (1975), 363. Through Miss Tilly's recent death, we have lost a passionate and perceptive student of Virgil, a real lover of Italy, and a true friend; this article should be taken as a tribute to her memory.

[13] R. Heinze, *Vergils epische Technik*³ (Leipzig, 1928), pp. 172 ff., cf. 340 ff.

I have pointed already to Virgil's technique of geographical allusion through his choice of personal names.[14] Allusive poetry requires erudite readers and the *Aeneid* is an extreme case: the poet borrowed and alluded *hoc animo ut vellet agnosci* (Sen. *Suas.* 3. 7): his most careful readers were expected to recognize not only poetic but scholarly allusions. So just as the poet borrowed isolated lines at times with conscious glee from bizarre and apparently inappropriate contexts,[15] straining his readers' memories, or even altered an Homeric original in the expectation that the scholiastic comment on that original which prompted the alteration would itself be recalled (Schlunk, pp. 7, 110), so his erudite public will have been expected to recognize the most fleeting allusions to stories which are not narrated, or which are narrated, but in an entirely different form:

(i) 4. 427 *nec patris Anchisae cineres manesve revelli*: Dido alludes to the (Varronian) story that Diomedes dug up and carried off the bones of Anchises and later restored them to Aeneas (Serv. ad loc.). In *Aen.* 3–5, Anchises is, of course, buried at Drepanum in Sicily. Other sites are also attested: Trojan Ida, the peninsula of Pallene, Aeneia (in NW Chalcidice), Arcadia, Anchisos in Epiros, and Latium.[16]

(ii) 5. 298: Salius and Patron, one an Acarnanian, one a native of Tegea; this Salius, according to Varro (Serv. Dan *ad Aen.* 8. 285, Isid. *Orig.* 18. 50) was an Arcadian and founded the Salii: to the alert reader, this familiar and important name is the only hint in the poem of Aeneas' traditional visit to Arcadia.

(iii) *ultra virum poenas inimico a fratre recepi* says Dido (4. 656). But is it enough that Pygmalion's treasure was carried away (1. 340 ff.)? The possibility exists (cf. Sil. 8. 143) that Virgil is hinting at some story of altogether more drastic punishment (so A. S. Pease ad loc., most attractively).

(iv) 4. 421 f. (Dido to Anna): *solam nam perfidus ille / te colere . . .* may hint at the (Varronian) story (Serv. *ad Aen.* 5. 4, Serv. Dan. *ad Aen.* 4. 682) that Aeneas was in love with Anna not Dido (cf. Horsfall, *PVS* 13 (1973–4), 11; Ch. 6 above).

It is also worthy of note that Virgil is evidently concerned to hint at, in polemic allusion, and to reject, certain versions of the legends of Aeneas hostile to his hero:

[14] One might refer also to the technique of hinting at a name by means of etymological play: for 7. 182, cf. Bartelink (n. 6 above), pp. 61 f.

[15] Cf. E. L. Harrison, *CP* 65 (1970), 241 ff. (repr. in this collection, Ch. 24 above).

[16] Cf. Guillemin, pp. 60 ff.; see Horsfall, *CQ* 29 (1979), 381 f. for the widespread story of the burning of the ships, located by Virgil in Sicily.

(v) *qui primus ... Italiam ... Lavinaque venit / litora* (1. 1 f.) is as G. K. Galinsky (*Lat.* 28 (1969), 3 ff.; cf. Guillemin, pp. 43 ff.) recognized, polemic against the claims and achievements of both Odysseus and Antenor (cf. Horsfall, *CQ* 29 (1979), 379 ff., 387).

(vi) 1. 599 describes the Trojans as *omnium egenos*, in sharp and arguably deliberate conflict with versions in which the Trojans left their city by negotiation, well loaded with riches—like Dido, indeed.[17]

(vii) Ilioneus is at pains to assure Latinus (7. 231 ff.) that the Trojans will be respectable immigrants in Latium: contrast Cato, *Orig.* fr. 10P *cum Aeneae socii praedam agerent* (the banditry alleged at *Aen.* 7. 362 is of another kind). When Ilioneus asks for *litus ... innocuum* (230 f.), an active sense, *non nocens*, is required for the adjective by the argument of the passage—notably *non erimus regno indecores*.[18]

Allusions to rejected stories are one thing, extended references to conflicting accounts, another. 'Inconsistencies in the *Aeneid*' have fortunately ceased to attract much learned attention. But it may not be inappropriate to suggest a novel mode of explanation (hinted at by Guillemin, p. 59): that is, that Virgil, confronted by a multiplicity of accounts in his sources, simply set down different accounts in different places, with no thought of a single 'authorized version'. This, after all, is far and away the simplest explanation of confusions and inconsistencies in the eschatology of *Aen.* 6 (cf. Austin on 724, for example): Homeric, Pythagorean/Orphic, and Stoic theories simply coexist and it is as misguided to attempt a coherent synthesis (something of the sort recently in both A. Thornton, *The Living Universe* (Leiden, 1976) and R. J. Clark, *Catabasis*) as it is to reprove the poet for incoherence (low marks awarded by H. E. Butler in his commentary on Book 6, p. 18). If we turn to the 'classic' inconsistencies, it is striking how often both versions are established and traditional: I would point to the following:

(i) In *Aen.* 3, the Trojans are sometimes presented as unaware of their goal (7 f.), sometimes, as following oracular prescriptions. Both conceptions are attested earlier: we may contrast Sallust's *Troiani, qui Aenea duce profugi sedibus incertis vagabantur* (*Cat.* 6. 1), with Naevius' account of Venus having given *libros futura continentes* to Aeneas (fr. 13 Marm.: cf. H. T. Rowell, *AJPh* 78 (1957), 1 ff.).

(ii) The kings of Alba are variously presented as descendants of

---

[17] Cf. G. K. Galinsky, *Aeneas, Sicily and Rome* (Princeton, 1969), p. 49; but see Horsfall, *CQ* 29 (1979), 384, 386.

[18] Cf. *TLL* 7. 1. 1708. 73; Fordyce characteristically misses the antiquarian point. This whole area of Virgilian allusion has been, up till now, barely explored. I have given, therefore, a rather wider range of instances.

Aeneas and Creusa (1. 267 ff.: cf. Liv. 1. 3. 2) and descendants of
Aeneas and Lavinia (6. 760 ff.; cf. Liv. 1. 1. 11). Both genealogies are
well attested and have a long history: that in Book 1 clearly does more
honour to the Julii and the persistence of conflicting versions in this case
is best explained by the annalists' political involvement (cf. R. M. Ogilvie
on Liv. 1. 3. 2).

(iii) The prophecy of the tables is given by the harpy Celaeno (3. 255)
or by Anchises (7. 127). In the antiquarian tradition, it was given
variously by Zeus at Dodona, the Erythraean Sibyl, Delphic Apollo, and
Venus. Virgil does not therefore appear at first sight to have a source for
either version, but we have just seen that Naevius granted Anchises
oracular associations and they recur at Enn. *Ann.* 18–9: thus when *OGR*
11. 1 refers to Anchises as having remembered a prediction of Venus to
him that when they ate their tables, *illum condendae sedis fatalem locum
fore*, it is not unlikely that the author has some respectable, if garbled,
warrant for his story.

Celaeno's role, on the other hand, is the product of an eminently
Virgilian proceeding, the enrichment of Roman and antiquarian
material by a reminiscence Greek, poetical, and mythological *(vide
infra)*; structurally, the warning of famine corresponds to Circe's
warning about the cattle of the sun (*Od.* 12. 127–41; Knauer, p. 187 n.
1), while the attribution of an impeding and alarming role to an Harpy is
in turn a recollection of AR 2. 178 ff. (Jason, Phineus, Harpies).

(iv) In *Aen.* 3. 389 ff. the sow, found with her thirty piglets, indicates
the site of Aeneas' future city (*is locus urbis erit, requies ea certa laborum*);
in 8. 42 ff. Tiberinus refers the prodigy to the ultimate foundation of
Alba, *ex quo ter denis urbem redeuntibus annis / Ascanius clari condet
cognominis Albam*... The fine distinction in formulation (obscured,
Williams, *Aen.* 3. 138) is real and traditional: for the correspondence of
the piglets to the thirty years which will elapse until the foundation of
Alba, we may compare Varro, *LL* 5. 144 and *RR* 2. 4. 18 (cf. Schol. Lyc.
1232 = DC 1, fr. 4–5 and Schol. Lyc. 1255); for the sow as indicating
the site of a nameless city, the end of Aeneas' wanderings, we turn, on
the other hand, to Fabius Pictor, fr. 4P (where the litter pressages a
foundation date in 30 years), Caesar, and Lutatius ap. *OGR* 11. 2 and
DH 1. 55. 4.

I would end with a minor and curious example:

(v) At 6. 825, Camillus is described as *referentem signa*; the gold of the
annalistic tradition has, as Austin persuasively suggests, been replaced
by a reminiscence of the contemporary preoccupation with the recovery

of Crassus' standards from the Parthians: at all events, the story is the conventional one of Camillus as Rome's saviour; not so at 8. 656 *arcemque tenebant*, where O. Skutsch sensed problems in the Latin (*JRS* 43 (1953), 77) and K. W. Gransden (*Virgil: Aeneid 8* (Cambridge, 1976), p. 171) rightly suggests that the plain meaning is a reference to the original version of the story, in which the Gauls seized and held the Capitol (cf. further Horsfall in *CJ* (1981), forthcoming) = *BICS* Suppl. 52. 1987, 63–75.

Virgil's large-scale recasting of his Italian source-material is necessarily an isolated phenomenon: the structure of Books 7–12 remains Iliadic and from his antiquarian sources what Virgil has to extract is a coherent and essentially familiar account of the situation at Aeneas' arrival, a credible narrative of how the war began (the criticism preserved by Macrobius 5. 17. 1 is deservedly well known, though in many ways unfair) and a vision of the war in Latium capable of narration in Homeric terms, in six books. How Virgil reduced the three or four campaigns of the antiquarian tradition to a few clear and tumultuous weeks of war was brilliantly outlined by Richard Heinze (*Vergils epische Technik³*, pp. 171 ff.). Far less familiar is the formidable and suggestive economy with which he outlines the situation in Latium at the time of the outbreak of Aeneas' arrival. All further developments in the plot arise out of the reworking of traditional material in 7. 45–58:

> rex arva Latinus et urbes
> iam senior longa placidas in pace regebat. (45–6)

Latinus is regularly described as a warrior who died in battle (Cato, *Orig.* fr. 9, 10P; Liv. 1. 2. 2; DH 1. 64. 3); Dionysius of Halicarnassus specified his age (1. 44. 3)—about 55. Virgil on the other hand alters the tradition; his Latinus is conveniently too old to fight against his fellow-ancestors of Rome. In the *Aeneid*, his old age is emphasized: the weakness of his resistance (7. 591 ff.) to Latin war-fever and the guilt-stricken perfidy of his opposition to the Trojans (11. 113 f., 304 f., 471 f.; 12. 27 ff.) provide Aeneas with a rightful claim to Lavinia (one absent in the tradition), yet do not alienate our sympathy, for Latinus' faults are exculpated by his senility (cf. 7. 597 f.; 12. 611; Heinze, pp. 174 f.). Latinus' failings are seen most clearly in the matter of Lavinia's betrothal: he thinks he is still free to decide on a son-in-law (7. 58 ff.); Turnus does not, nor, clearly enough, does Amata. In many accounts, Lavinia is formally betrothed to Turnus before Aeneas' arrival and Latinus' sudden preference for a stranger was variously explained

(Strab. 5. p. 229; Liv. 1. 1. 8; DH 1. 57. 4; DC 1. fr. 2; *OGR* 13. 2; Justin 43. 1. 10). In Virgil, Lavinia's betrothal to Turnus is only alleged by him and Amata (7. 366; 10. 79, etc.); it is never objectively confirmed in the poet's narrative. Aeneas must hold right on his side; that he is another Paris is merely alleged against him (7. 36. 3 f.) and Turnus' fight for the bride and kingdom supposedly owed him (cf. 7. 421 ff., 469, 478 f.; 9. 737; 11. 369 ff., etc.) is thus misconceived and in consequence his motives can be represented as personal and selfish, not patriotic and national.

Secondly,

> arva ... et urbes
> ... longa placidas in pace regebat.

Certainly, Virgil exhibits two opposed conceptions of the condition of primitive Italy; it seems likely that he found antecedents for both conceptions in his sources.

Appropriately, it is the peaceful condition of Latium which is stressed at 7. 45 ff., in keeping with (49) Latinus' descent from Saturn, and in contrast both with the Sibyl's prophecy of war (6. 85 ff.) and with the invocation of Erato's aid in singing *horrida bella*, immediately before the passage under discussion. More important, there are thematic consequences here for Virgil's preference for the peaceful image of Latium[19]—it is evidently in keeping with king Latinus' old age; unreadiness reinforces vacillation and serves further to exculpate the old king. Above all, this unreadiness and the warm welcome he naïvely offers the Trojans amid the ancient martial glories of his race (7. 170 ff.)[20] greatly heighten the chaotic drama with which rural Latium plunges into war (475 ff.) and takes up arms (623 ff.).

In the *Aeneid*, Latinus is regularly presented (7. 151, 160, e.g.) as ruler over Latins:[21] hitherto *Latini* had designated the joint Trojan-native stock, and Aborigines, Latinus' people before the settlement with Aeneas, dwelling in the *ager Laurens*. Aborigines are colourless, remote, and unmetrical (but cf. 7. 181 *cunctique ab origine reges*, where the etymological reference is unmistakable), in sharp contrast to the

---

[19] There is no certainty, though, that Naev. *Bell. Pun.* fr. 23 *silvicolae homines bellique inertes* refers to Latium (see, e.g., *Bell. Pun.* ed. Strzelecki (1959), 63 f.).

[20] So elsewhere too Virgil alludes to the warlike condition of early Latium (cf. 8. 146 ff., 492 ff.; 9. 603 ff.); this latter conception seems to have been widely attested: Liv. 1. 1. 5; DH 1. 57. 2; *OGR* 13. 1.

[21] Laurentes too, 11. 909; 12. 240; see J. Carcopino, *Virgile et les origines d'Ostie*[2] (Paris, 1968), pp. 245 f.; they are irrelevant to this discussion.

familiar and historical Latini and Latium. Virgil builds up the land as Saturn's own (7. 322 ff.) and the people as direct ancestors, under a proudly unchanged name (12. 819 ff.), of Rome, her customs and her greatness (1. 6 ff.; 6. 876 ff.; 7. 601 ff.; 12. 826 ff.). Now Latinus' role as the embodiment of the old Italy is greatly helped by his evocative genealogy; Circe, Odysseus, and Heracles are attested in the Greek historiographical tradition,[22] but Virgil dispenses with alien origins in favour of a well-attested (second-century BC annalistic)[23] family tree which involves the local and Italian Faunus, Marica, and Picus (7. 47 ff.).

At the same time that Virgil simplified, clarified, and abbreviated the main lines of the narrative of Aeneas' progress which he had inherited from the antiquarian tradition, he was under a strikingly contrasted obligation: not only did he have to create order out of chaos, but Eden out of the desert, for not only were the narratives in his sources sorely confused, but also, so far as we can judge from much in Dionysius, they were trite, jejune, and mechanical, a mere chronicle of events in episodic sequence, intermittently enriched by pedantic digressions. Virgil's fundamental recasting of this material[24] is not, of course, the matter of this paper. But Virgil's erudite readers will have relished some of the exquisitely elaborate combinations of sources and textures in *Aen.* 7–12.

This re-elaboration is of the texture of individual episodes; I give a pair of examples, both quite complex, from *Aeneid* 7, whose sources constitute an extraordinarily entangled and largely unexplored maze, to show just how Virgil simultaneously simplifies and elaborates:

761 ff. Virgil's first catalogue is a direct inheritance from *Iliad* 2, but also reveals details which suggest powerfully a Varronian origin (*res hum.* 11).[25] Yet these double foundations may be subject to further elaboration, as at 7. 761 ff., from Callimachus' *Aetia*;[26] detailed and extended borrowing is likely, as features such as *namque ferunt fama, verso nomine,* and *unde etiam* . . . suggest. An interesting parallel (note 7. 781 :: 10. 194)

22 DH 1. 43, etc.; see A. Schwegler, *Römische Geschichte* (Tübingen, 1867), 1. 405, 216 n. 21, etc.

23 Schwegler, 1. 214 ff.; G. Wissowa, *Religion und Kultus*[2] (Munich, 1912), p. 66.

24 Of which the most striking and familiar aspect is Virgil's entirely original vision of events in Latium in Homeric terms, G. N. Knauer, *GRBS* 5 (1964), 61 ff.; for example, the familiar Lavinia of the antiquarian tradition acquired the roles—in part—both of Helen and Penelope; Knauer, *Aeneis und Homer,* pp. 327 ff., 343.

25 Aug. *CD* 6. 3; Macr. 3. 16. 12. R. Ritter, *Diss. Phil. Halenses* 14. 4 (Halle, 1901); Rehm, op. cit. 84 ff. (a brilliant discussion).

26 *Aetia* fr. 190; cf. Horsfall, *JRS* 65 (1975), 228 f. and *CR* 29 (1979), 223.

may be drawn with a detail in the catalogue of Aeneas' Etruscan allies: the story of Cycnus' love for Phaethon;[27] the catalogue itself recalls that of the Trojans' allies in *Iliad* 2, but Virgil is under compulsion to include it, for the Aeneas of his recast narrative has no allies at the outset of the war against Turnus and must do on the grounds of narrative credibility. Cycnus' son Cupavo fights for Aeneas. The connection of Cycnus with the Ligurians is traditional (Plat. *Phaedr.* 237 A) and it is again likely that much of Virgil's geographical detail in his second catalogue at large is Varronian,[28] but the erotic vignette *namque ferunt* . . . (189 ff.) is Alexandrian and elegiac in tone and Phanocles' *Ἔρωτες ἢ Καλοί* ('Loves or Beautiful Boys') has been suggested as a likely source.[29]

Secondly, 7. 475 ff. On the trenchant criticism preserved by Macr. 5. 17. 1 we have touched already: 'quid Vergilio contulerit Homerus hinc maxime liquet quod, ubi rerum necessitas exegit a Marone dispositionem inchoandi belli, quam non habuit Homerus . . . laboravit ad rei novae partum', 'What Homer contributed to Vergil is particularly clear from this fact, namely that when the necessities of plot required from Virgil the ordering of the beginning of a war, something which Homer had not . . . he struggled in bringing forth this novelty'. The critic's analysis of detail is often peculiarly silly and trivial. But the absence of an Homeric model is of course true and Virgil's answer is elegant, ingenious, and effective. He starts the third section of his narrative, I have suggested, from a hint in Cato (*Orig.* fr. 10P) and develops it with borrowings from at least six quarters: the name of the bailiff, Tyrrhus (485), is traditional (Schol. Ver. *nomen . . . ab historicis traxit*) and traces of his presence in the antiquarian writers survive.[30] The deer, beloved pet of his daughter, Silvia, is described in terms which are, I have suggested elsewhere,[31] clearly modelled upon the description of a pet hare in an epigram of Meleager (*AP* 7. 207); Virgil's best-educated readers will have recalled with delight that the hare died of overeating. Allecto maddens Ascanius' hounds in pursuit of the deer in a manner surely reminiscent of the scene in Aeschylus' lost *Toxotides* in which Lyssa, bearing a torch, maddens the hounds of Actaeon (fr. 422M). When the deer returns to its home, Silvia *auxilium clamat* and to

[27] Cf. S. Timpanaro, *Contributi di Filologia* (Rome, 1978), p. 317.

[28] R. Ritter, *de Timaei fabulis* (diss. Halle, 1901), pp. 40 ff.

[29] J. Knaack in Roscher 3. 2187. 15 ff., Eur. *Phaethon*, ed. J. Diggle, 8.

[30] Serv. on *Aen.* 1. 270; 6. 270 (falsely attributed to Cato; see R. M. Ogilvie, *CR* 24 (1974), 64 f.; the parallel with Livy is decisive against Catonian authorship) and DH 1. 70. 2, where Tyrrhenus is called superintendent of the royal swineherds.

[31] *CR* 29 (1979), 223.

reinforce the effect, Allecto *pastorale canit signum*: *auxilium* was the traditional term for a formal appeal, publicly, for aid to one's fellow-citizens[32] and the trumpet-signal likewise belongs to the world of antiquarian traditions: according to Cic. *Ver.* 2. 4. 96, it was still in use in central Sicily as an emergency signal and it had been used (Prop. 4. 1. 13; Varr. *LL* 6. 92) to summon the primitive assemblies of Rome. The effect of the trumpet is described—as has long been recognized—in terms borrowed from the language used by Apollonius to portray the effect of the Colchian dragon's hiss (4. 131 f.). The range is startling: the Latin antiquarian writers, Greek tragedy, and epigram; in small details, more echoes will be found.

It would not be true to say that Virgil's narrative is wholly clear and coherent in all details; careful analysis of the subject-matter reveals, at times, I believe, that Virgil was *not* passionately interested in antiquarian or technical minutiae, and we have already seen that consistency mattered much less than effect. The disorder that survives is the diversity or disdain of great art, not the quibbling of antiquarians and pedants.

APPENDIX

Postscript 1988

Source-criticism as an instrument of literary criticism remains unsurprisingly unpopular. But W. Suerbaum in *Et scholae et vitae* (*Beitr. . . . K. Bayer*) (Munich, 1985), 22–32, has developed some of my ideas. Cf. too G. D'Anna in *Atti del Convegno virgiliano di Brindisi* (Perugia, 1983), 323–43. Some elements in my argument I have developed further in *Vergilius* 32 (1986), 8–17, and *Athen.* 56 (1988), 31–51. The topic is, for me, very much 'work in hand'.

[32] W. Schulze, *Kl. Schr.* (Göttingen, 1934), p. 176.

Printed in the United States
124086LV00001B/300/A